A Historical Introduction to the Philosophy of Mind

A Historical Introduction to the Philosophy of Mind

Readings With Commentary

Peter A. Morton

broadview press

Canadian Cataloguing in Publication Data

Main entry under title:
A historical introduction to the philosophy of mind: readings with commentary

Includes index.
ISBN 1-55111-087-3

1. Philosophy of mind. I. Morton, Peter Alan.

BD418.3.H57 1997   128'.2   C96-932366-2

Broadview Press is an independent, international publishing house, incorporated in 1985.

North America:
P.O. Box 1243, Peterborough, Ontario, Canada K9H 7H5
3576 California Road, Orchard Park, NY, USA 14127
TEL: (705) 743-8990; FAX: (705) 743-8353; E-MAIL: 75322.44@compuserve.com

United Kingdom:
Turpin Distribution Services Ltd., Blackhorse Rd., Letchworth, Hertfordshire SG6 3HN
TEL: (1462) 672555; FAX: (1462) 480947; E-MAIL: turpin@rsc.org

Australia:
St. Clair Press, P.O. Box 287, Rozelle, NSW 2039
TEL: (02) 818 1942; FAX: (02) 418 1923

www.broadviewpress.com

Broadview Press gratefully acknowledges the support of the Ontario Arts Council and the Ministry of Canadian Heritage. We acknowledge the financial support of the Government of Canada through the Book Publishing Industry Development Program for our publishing activities.

printed in Canada

For Barbara

CONTENTS

Preface

This book has come about through a process of trial and error in the class-room. A difficulty I have often encountered there is the unfamiliar and some-times counterintuitive nature of philosophical theories of mind. I have tried various techniques to make these theories accessible to students in a way that does not gloss over or water down the difficult issues involved. As I explain in the Introduction, the approach I came to adopt is to try to show students how the contemporary set of theories and issues arises out of an ongoing proc-ess of revising and rethinking previous theories. I also began accompanying primary readings with my own lecture notes that explained the central argu-ments in each text. The idea of putting this material together into a book came up one day when I was chatting with Don LePan of Broadview Press.

I am grateful to many people for their contributions to the book. My first note of thanks is to my students. They have contributed to the book not only through their enthusiasm and dialogue when my ways of approaching the subject worked, but also through their honest skepticism when things didn't work out as I had hoped. An equally important note of gratitude is to my wife, Barbara, and my son, Paul, for their encouragement and too fre-quently their patience and generosity.

Anyone who teaches is also a student, and I have been fortunate in hav-ing had superb teachers. I wish to thank especially my doctoral supervisor, William Demopoulos, and my first teacher of philosophy, Terrance Tomkow. I would also like to acknowledge the contributions to my understanding of the issues in this book from Robert Butts, Ausonio Marras, Keith Humphrey, Thomas Vinci, Robert Martin, Margaret Osler, and Richmond Campbell.

Ausonio Marras read the first complete draft and made many helpful sug-gestions, most of which I was able to incorporate. My colleague Mark Gardiner had the idea of using the chapter from Hilary Putnam's *Reason, Truth and History* in chapter 14. Don LePan has been unfailing in his support for the project, even when deadlines were unmet. Eileen Eckert did the work of designing and editing with both a sharp eye and sound judgement. Nicole Shukin-Simpson arranged the copyright permissions, and Andrew Bailey proofread the book. To all of these people I extend my sincere thanks.

Typographic conventions

I have followed a particular set of conventions for the use of quotation marks, and italicized and bold font. Single quotes are used only to refer to words, phrases or sentences, as in the following example:

'Light' is a word with five letters.

Double quotes are used to indicate either a quotation from a text or a word used in an unusual sense. I have used italicized font for book titles, for foreign words, and frequently also for emphasis. Bold font indicates that the word or phrase occurs in the Glossary at the back of the book. I have put words and phrases in bold at the place where the definition occurs in the commentary, which is not always the first occurrence of the word.

The use of angle brackets (< and >) in the readings from Descartes (chapters 3, 4, and 5) indicates phrases that were not in the first editions of his works, but were added in subsequent translations approved by Descartes. This convention was established by the translators of the Descartes writings that are reproduced in this book.

Peter Morton

Introduction

The mind-body problem

The issues introduced in this book are today referred to collectively as "the mind-body problem." The simplest way to describe this problem is to say that it is a search for an answer to the question, 'What is the relationship between the mind and the physical body?' This search raises such issues as whether the mind and body are one thing or two, and whether artificial machines could have minds.

According to a standard textbook explanation, the mind-body problem arises in something like the following way. We have a reasonable understanding of our own physical body. That is, we are confident that we have identified the functions of most of the major systems of the body, and we have a pretty good idea of how they work. The mind, however, is more mysterious. We have a rough idea of what we *mean* when we talk about the mind: It is that part of us that contains our thoughts, experiences, and feelings. But we aren't entirely sure what thoughts, experiences, and feelings really *are*. Are they the activities of an immaterial substance — a soul? Are they activities of the brain? Do thoughts, experiences and feelings even exist as we understand them?

The changing nature of the problem

The standard characterization of the problem is reasonably accurate as far as it goes. But it also glosses over some of the most interesting aspects of the issue. In the first place, we don't entirely know what we mean when we talk about the mind. The meanings of the terms 'thought,' 'experience,' and 'feeling' are very obscure and are a matter of debate. And, second, our understanding of the physical body and how it works is constantly evolving. New ideas and discoveries are always altering our conception of how the body works, especially those parts of the body most closely connected with thought and experience. The discoveries of such things as the mechanical function of the heart, the structure of the cell, and the processes of evolution have changed how we think of the body and subsequently of how it might be related to the mind. Most recently, new advances in neuroscience are changing our theories of how the processes of the brain operate. What we have, then, is not a fixed and static problem. As Noam Chomsky puts it, there is no single mind-body problem; there have been as many mind-body problems as there have been ways of thinking about the body and the mind.

The historical development

Although the character of the mind-body problem is constantly changing, the changes haven't been random and unconnected. There is a historical continuity to the succession of theories about the mind that make up the Western tradition beginning in ancient Greece. Each change in thinking about the mind has been the result of an attempt to solve a puzzle that previous theories were unable to resolve. The range of theories that are currently defended have grown out of this process.

Whether these changes have formed a progressive evolution — providing a better and better understanding of the mind — or whether earlier insights have been lost in the process is an interesting question. Certainly each stage in the development was perceived at the time as an advance over earlier views. And if you defend one of the current theories as the correct view, then you will almost certainly see the process within which it was devised as a progressive one. But there have been frequent occasions when older views have been resurrected and restored to prominence, albeit in a different form from when they were first put forward. So the resolution of this question is best left as part of the general argument over which theory is most likely to give us a true understanding of the mind.

The approach taken in this book

I have chosen to introduce the mind-body problem in this book by outlining some major trends in its history. There are two reasons for this. One reason is to make clear the points I mentioned in the preceding two sections. One gains a false impression of the mind-body problem if it is introduced as a static issue with the range of current options fixing the terms of the debate. The best way to perceive the flexibility of the framework within which the debate is conducted is to see how it evolved and notice the difference between earlier frameworks and current ones.

The second reason for taking a historical approach is pedogogical. The theories that are presently at the front of debate, and that new students of the discipline must learn, are not self-evident options for most people. A natural reaction when first shown the theories surveyed in Part Two of this book is one of puzzlement: Why *these* theories? Why not think about the issues in some completely different way? And some theories — logical behaviourism, for example — seem just bizarre upon first encounter. Over the years I have come to use the historical development to help explain why philosophers think that the contemporary theories offer the best hope of arriving at the right answers, or, more accurately, why philosophers think we are now asking the right questions.

One side benefit of the historical approach is to dispel the tendency to treat older theories and arguments simply as crude versions of the current ones. This tendency is a mistake because to some extent the issues themselves have changed. Let me offer one example of this. A central theory in the mind-body debate is the one constructed by René Descartes in the seventeenth century. According to Descartes, the mind and the body are two distinct and utterly different entities that are somehow linked together. Descartes' most famous argument that the mind and the body are distinct is sometimes presented in introductory texts as if Descartes' argument is flawed because of some errors of reasoning that he was simply unaware of. But Descartes' reasoning is built upon a very old idea, the idea of *substance*, that Descartes inherited from his predecessors. This idea formed part of the manner in which Descartes framed the issue, and his argument is only understood if it is seen in this way. Because the concept of substance has been abandoned, it is natural to ignore this aspect of his argument, and so to see it as simply a mistaken piece of logic. There is little doubt that Descartes' argument is unsuccessful, but it is so for much more interesting reasons than the ones usually given. And the real reasons show us by example that arriving at the right theory of the mind depends on more than just brushing up on our logic.

The readings

A second feature of this book is the relationship between the readings and my own commentary. This aspect is a product of my own experiences as a teacher. It seems absolutely essential that students approaching the mind-body problem do so by way of *primary texts*, that is, by reading the original writings of the people who proposed the theories and arguments in the first place. The only way to get a good grasp of the ideas proposed by Aristotle, Descartes, or the logical positivists is to read Aristotle, Descartes, and the logical positivists. Without this, you miss the force of the arguments and the subtleties of the theories. More importantly, it is wrong to foist a single interpretation of these works onto students without letting them read them for themselves and examine the interpretation critically.

On the other hand, the primary texts are often hard to read. One reason for this is that they are sometimes very old, and so are written in archaic language using concepts that have long lost their currency. Another reason is that these works were not primarily written for students new to the discipline, but for other professional philosophers who know a lot of the jargon and the background. So it doesn't work to simply hand out primary texts and ask students to read them.

The solution I have adopted in this book is to accompany the primary texts — the readings — with commentaries that explain their content, or at least some of the central ideas they contain. Sometimes the commentary follows the reading paragraph by paragraph, but often it is only possible to focus in on certain central passages that contain the main arguments or theories. But the commentary is always aimed directly at the readings with the goal of making the readings clear to someone who does not have the background knowledge to read it on their own. In each case the commentary also attempts to provide a general historical background to the text, outlining some of the major historical developments that influenced them and the connections that exist between the different readings.

One consequence of such an emphasis on primary texts is that only certain figures in the debate can be examined closely, to the exclusion of other important writers. There are many versions of the main theories, and arguments for them, that are not addressed in the book. This is revealed in the amount of emphasis on Descartes, who was certainly not the only mind-body dualist of his time. Similarly, the theory of functionalism, which I outline in chapter 11, is a much more complex theory than I have covered here, with more versions than the ones I have presented. The focus on primary readings also forces huge jumps between historical periods. The readings leap directly from Aristotle to the seventeenth century, ignoring more than a whole millennium. Medieval scholars are right to protest the tendency to ignore their period as if nothing of consequence happened in all that time. But, as choices have to be made, I prefer to sacrifice comprehensiveness in favour of a close, ground-level familiarity with the ideas in their original form.

An overview of the book

The book is divided into three major parts. Part One sketches some of the major developments in the mind-body problem before the twentieth century. The first person within the Western tradition to construct a reasonably detailed and full theory of the mind is Plato. Every aspect of thinking about the mind since his day has been influenced by the ideas that he put forward. Chapter 1 looks at Plato's contention that the soul, which includes what we now think of as the mind, is separate from, and even stands in opposition to, the natural world. His student, Aristotle, whom we read in chapter 2, had an equally large impact on the ways in which we have formed our views of the mind. In certain ways Aristotle's theory contrasts directly with Plato's, for he argued that the soul is an integral part of the natural order and inseparable from it.

After Aristotle we jump fifteen hundred years to the scientific revolution. The mechanical view of nature developed by modern scientists forced a re-thinking of the mind and its relation to the body. In the remaining chapters of Part One we look at the ideas proposed in response to this change. By far the greatest emphasis in these chapters is on René Descartes. This is because Descartes has had the profoundest influence on the mind-body problem since the seventeenth century, even though his theory of mind-body dualism is no longer a strong contender today.

Part Two of the book examines the central theories that have been defended in this century and that still have proponents among contemporary philosophers working in the Anglo-North American tradition. This tradition has its roots partially in a philosophical movement called logical positivism, which rejects metaphysics as a meaningless activity. The theory of the mind that logical positivism generated, called logical behaviourism, is the subject of chapter 7. In many ways logical behaviourism set the agenda for the debates of this century, although (like Descartes' dualism) it is no longer widely defended. Chapter 8 looks at two positions closely related to logical behaviourism, which rose to prominence around the middle of the century, and retain a strong influence on debates today. One is defended by Gilbert Ryle and the other by Ludwig Wittgenstein. Ryle and Wittgenstein both attack an idea that forms the basis of Descartes' theory of the mind; namely, that what goes on in a person's mind is immediately known to that person but hidden from other people.

Three broad views of the mind have been at the centre of most debate in the past twenty-five years: mind-brain identity theory, functionalism, and eliminativism. Each of these theories has been defended in several forms and is under constant revision. Mind-brain identity theory is the idea that states of mind are states of the central nervous system, particularly the brain. The second theory, functionalism, is an outgrowth of both the mind-brain identity theory and behaviourism, together with ideas taken from the study of computers. The versions of functionalism that I present here contend that the activities of the mind are something like the functions of a computer program realized in the brain, which can be realized in physical structures very different from the brain. Finally, eliminativists argue that many of the traditional ideas of the mind, upon which other philosophical theories are based, are entirely mistaken. Modern neuroscience, they claim, will eliminate most of the categories and concepts that we use to describe the mind and replace them with concepts formed from an improved understanding of the brain.

Part Three looks at two of the most difficult issues surrounding the mind-body problem in recent years. The first such problem is that of consciousness and subjective experience. After you read Thomas Nagel's article, "What Is It Like To Be a Bat?", think of how our perception of the world around us — our experiences of colour, sound, and so on — differs from the experiences of creatures like bats that have very different perceptual organs. According to some philosophers, these differences reveal a subjective element of conscious experience that is necessarily hidden from the objective methods of neuroscience and cognitive psychology. Because of this, they argue, conscious experience forms an element of the mind that cannot be explained by any of the theories outlined in Part Two. Other philosophers attempt to show how such explanations are possible, or else deny that conscious experience has any of the problematic features cited.

The second issue addressed in Part Three is what philosophers call "the problem of intentionality." The problem here is how to account for the fact that states of mind are *about* things, that our thoughts have *meaning*. A central aspect of this puzzle is to work out how the contents of our thoughts and beliefs are related to the objective features of the world around us. Can you determine the contents of someone's thoughts just from what is going inside their head? Or do you also need to know certain facts about their environment? If the answers to these questions is 'yes' to the first and 'no' to the second, then it turns out to be hard to explain how our thoughts are connected to the world at all. If you give the opposite answers, then it seems that we cannot know the contents of our own thoughts. The puzzle, then, is how to avoid both horns of this dilemma.

These two problems certainly do not exhaust the issues that occupy the attention of contemporary philosophers. The space devoted to carefully explaining the arguments in the readings restricts the range of issues that can be included. For example, I have not included an introduction to the recent debates over how states of mind, such as beliefs and desires, can be *causes* of our behaviour, which have come to centre around the technical concept of "supervenience." My hope is that the issues I have chosen provide sufficient background to enable a student to move on to the other problems without difficulty.

1

Historical Background

CHAPTER ONE

Plato: The Soul and the Forms

Introduction

The origin of the Western view of the mind lies in ancient Greece. The world view developed by the Greeks in the fourth and fifth centuries B.C. has provided much of the philosophical framework of European civilization. When medieval and early modern philosophers and scientists constructed their explanations of the natural world, they developed their ideas directly from classical Greek philosophers. These ideas have been greatly modified over time, but their influence is still felt in our modern scientific theories. To a large extent our modern conception of the mind has its roots in the ancient Greek idea of the soul. To understand the current issues and debates surrounding the nature of the mind, it is illuminating to begin by looking at their origins in the ancient world.

Plato and Socrates

Plato (c. 428–347 B.C.) is one of the most influential philosophers of European civilization. Plato formulated many questions that have remained central to philosophical enquiry throughout the centuries, and proposed answers to them that still have their influence today. Plato was a student of Socrates (470–399 B.C.), who was put to death by the Athenians on the official charge of corrupting the youth of Athens. Socrates himself put nothing in writing but instead spent his time conversing with people and forcing them to critically examine their beliefs, often to their discomfort. Plato's writings take the form of dialogues between his teacher Socrates and various interlocutors. How reflective the dialogues are of the historical Socrates is difficult to decide accurately; often it is clear that the Socrates in the dialogues is serving as a spokesman for views that Plato developed after Socrates' death.

In this chapter, we will read sections of a dialogue entitled *The Phaedo*, named after the person who narrates the story. *The Phaedo* is an account of the death of Socrates. In it Socrates explains to his friends, Simmias and Cebes, why he is unafraid of his impending execution and why death is something to be looked forward to by anyone who leads a truly philosophical life. The defence of the philosophical life that Plato presents in the dialogue hinges on two theories that are central to Plato's work. One is a theory about the world and our knowledge of it that we can call "the theory of the Forms." The other is a belief in the immortality of the soul. In this chapter I will emphasize the importance of the relationship between these ideas.

Dualism

Plato was perhaps the first to articulate a detailed theory of the mind and its relation to the physical body. Several central elements of what we think of today as the mind are aspects of what Plato called the soul. In *The Phaedo* Plato defends a position that today we call **mind-body dualism**. Roughly, dualism is the belief that the mind is in some way *nonphysical* or *immaterial.* Over the centuries there have been many different theories that can be labelled as dualist theories. But all of them agree in the basic claim that mind and matter are distinct from one another. Plato's theory of the soul is one of the earliest formulations of this idea. According to Plato, the soul is immortal, existing both before birth and after death. The human body and all other material objects are impermanent, existing only for a certain period of time. Thus the soul and the physical body are, in Plato's view, two distinct entities. Plato argues in *The Phaedo* and elsewhere that the best life for a person to lead is the cultivation of the soul while turning one's attention away from the influence of the physical body.

Plato's conception of the soul

What does Plato mean when he talks about "the soul," a term that conjures up many different images? Probably a good part of the portrait of the soul in *The Phaedo* represents the views of his teacher, Socrates. *The Phaedo* presents a first sketch of a theory of the soul. This theory is more fully developed in later dialogues, particularly in a dialogue called *The Republic*. In *The Republic* Plato is clearly moving beyond what Socrates provided him and offers a detailed account of the soul and its different parts. We will restrict ourselves to the sketch given in *The Phaedo* as it covers the essential elements of Plato's theory without bringing in too many difficult details.

Plato inherited from Socrates the idea that sensual pleasures and the cultivation of the body hinder a person's well-being. This asceticism sets up an opposition between the body and senses on the one hand and the "true self" on the other. So we can think of the soul as the "real person," which can be distinguished from the body and the senses. The opposition between soul and body is a central component in the picture of the soul developed in *The Phaedo*. As we will see, it plays a major role in Plato's argument that soul and body are two distinct entities.

Another element of the soul that Plato refers to in *The Phaedo* is derived from early Greek tradition. This element is closest to the meaning of the original Greek word *psychē*: the idea that the soul is what brings life to the body. The difference between a living thing and a dead body is the presence of a soul. At one point in *The Phaedo* Plato claims that the soul by its very nature is "that which brings life."

Besides these traditional meanings attached to the word 'soul,' Plato adds two additional ideas. First, Plato identifies the soul as the seat of reason and knowledge. According to Plato, the soul is the rational part of us while our irrational nature comes from the influence of the body. Plato believes that it is through the activity of the rational soul that we have knowledge. Second, the soul experiences different states of consciousness stemming from the influence of the senses and the condition of the body. For example, the eyes and ears produce experiences of colour and sound in the soul, while injury to the body produces sensations of pain. According to Plato, these experiences are states of the immaterial soul produced by the changes in the body.

These last two elements in Plato's conception of the soul are important to Plato's reasons for believing in dualism. As we will see in this chapter, Plato believes that the soul can be a source of reason and knowledge only if it is a distinct entity from the physical body. To follow Plato's arguments for dualism, we will have to understand a certain amount about his theory of knowledge.

Plato's idea that the soul is the seat of both reason and consciousness is also essential in forming an understanding of our current psychological theories. For this idea is the historical antecedent to the concept of the mind in modern psychology and philosophy. In the final section of this book we will look at how recent thinkers have attempted to explain the characteristics of thought and consciousness in terms of modern neuroscience.

Socrates' defence

We can now begin reading *The Phaedo*. The entire dialogue is fairly lengthy, so we'll read some central sections, beginning about eight pages into the text with a section we'll call "Socrates' defence." A group of friends has gathered with Socrates in prison where he is awaiting his execution. To ease their grief Socrates has said that a philosopher does not fear death because he can look forward to a better existence in the next world. In this first section of *The Phaedo* Socrates defends this claim on the grounds that the philosophical life is nothing more than the art of dying. (Simmias points out the joke in this: Most people would agree that death is precisely what philosophers should undergo.)

Socrates begins his argument with a description of death as "nothing but the separation of the soul from the body" (64c5).[1] He claims that a genuine philosopher will ignore the pleasures of the body and seek instead to release the soul from the influence of the body. The body, he says, is a hindrance in the gaining of wisdom because sight and hearing, which rely on the sensory organs of the body, do not "afford men any truth" (65b2). This is a striking claim. According to Plato, our eyes and ears are not sources of information about the world around us, but actually form an obstruction to knowledge. This idea, which identifies the soul with knowledge and denies the reliability of the senses, forms an essential part of the portrayal of the soul in *The Phaedo*. To see what basis he has for making this claim we need to look at Plato's theory of knowledge.

What is revealed to the soul

At 65c2 Socrates says,

> "So isn't it in reasoning, if anywhere at all, that any of the things that *are* become manifest to [the soul]?"

A few lines later is the following exchange.

> "Well, now, what about things of this sort, Simmias [i.e., things that are revealed to the soul]? Do we say that there is something *just* or nothing?"
> "Yes, we most certainly do!"
> "And again, something *beautiful* and *good*?"
> "Of course."
> "Now did you ever yet see any such things with your eyes?"
> "Certainly not."
> "Well, did you grasp them with any other bodily sense-perception? And I'm talking about them all — about largeness, health, and strength, for example — and, in short, about the Being of all other such things, what each one actually is; is it through the body that their truest element is viewed, or isn't it rather thus: whoever of us is prepared to think most fully and minutely of each object of his inquiry, in itself, will come closest to the knowledge of each?"
> "Yes, certainly."

This is a difficult passage, but it is important. Notice first that Socrates is claiming that there are certain things that are manifest (or revealed) to the soul, but not to the bodily senses such as sight. The idea is that there is a certain kind of knowledge or awareness that the soul possesses, which is not obtained through the senses.

He also says that the things revealed to the soul are "the things that *are.*" He means that the things revealed to the soul are the things that are lasting and unchanging, while the things perceived by the senses are impermanent and constantly changing. So what are the things "that *are*"? What significance does Plato see in this claim? To answer these questions we need to understand something that philosophers nowadays call **universals**. This will take us away from our main topic of the soul for a page or two. But the diversion will help us understand Plato's ideas about soul and body more properly.

Universals

Let's look, then, at universals. A universal is a characteristic or property that may be possessed by more than one object. Consider a simple example: if two objects are both red, there is something they have in common, namely the redness. So Plato distinguishes between individual things and the universal, redness, that they have in common. Plato was interested in the sorts of universals that arise in ethics, politics, and mathematics. In ethics there are such properties as virtue and justice, and in mathematics there are such properties as equality and circularity.

Another way to describe universals is to say that they are the means by which we classify objects into kinds. When we say that two objects are red, we are assigning a certain label to them. This label is given to all objects that are similar to one another in a particular way. In ethics and mathematics we classify a certain kind of person as virtuous and certain shapes as circular.

Plato's teacher, Socrates, was the first person to draw attention to universals and to recognize their importance. Many of Plato's dialogues emphasize the significance of universals in obtaining knowledge. For example, suppose we ask the question, "What is virtue?" This question cannot be answered simply by giving a list of examples of particular people or actions, for this still leaves the important question, "What do all these things have in common that makes them virtuous?" Without knowing the answer to this question, we cannot claim to know what virtue is. Plato points out that the answer to this last question consists of a description of a universal, which he would call "virtue itself." Using examples such as this, Plato argues that real knowledge requires an understanding of universals. Such an understanding, he maintains, is more than just a familiarity with individual things. A fundamental question for Plato, then, is the question of how knowledge of universals is obtained.

Knowledge of universals

Plato believes that we grasp universals through the **intellect** and not through the senses. According to him, when I see that two objects are beautiful, my eyes are involved in the perception, but it is the intellect or the mind that grasps what they have in common. That is, I might see two beautiful objects, but to see *that* they are beautiful I must have an understanding of the universal, beauty, which both possess. Similarly, when we see that someone is virtuous, this perception is achieved by the mind's understanding of the universal, "virtue itself."

In Plato's view, the senses give a certain kind of information, which we may think of as "raw data." But it is the soul that interprets and understands these data by identifying what objects have in common. Moreover, he maintains that the data provided by the senses are misleading in certain ways, and so we cannot classify objects just by analyzing what the senses bring in. The soul must provide additional knowledge that it brings from within itself.

But what basis does Plato have for believing that only the intellect can grasp universals? Why can't our eyes perceive the beauty of something directly without the aid of the intellect? The answer to this lies in his account of what universals are. This takes us to Plato's famous theory of "the Forms."

The Forms

Plato believes that universals must exist independently of individual objects. For example, even if there were no virtuous people, the universal, "virtue itself," would exist on its own. He had many reasons for this belief. Partly his conclusion came from his study of mathematics. Consider the following example from geometry. Once we understand the rule that the angles of a triangle are equal to two right angles, this knowledge can be applied to any and all triangles. In Plato's view, this means that our knowledge is not of any *particular* triangle. It is knowledge of the *property* of triangularity. This is especially evident when we realize that no physical object is *exactly* triangular, but only approximately so. Plato argues that the universal, triangularity, must be a separate thing from any particular object, because knowledge of one is distinct from knowledge of the other. We can apply the same reasoning to the other universals that Plato was concerned with, such as beauty and virtue. According to Plato, then, universals are objects in their own right, existing independently of the things we perceive with the senses.

Plato gives universals the name *eidos*, usually translated as **Forms** or **Ideas**. In the passage we just read, the "things that *are*," to which Socrates refers, are the Forms. When Socrates asks Simmias whether "there is something just" or "beautiful, and good," he is asking about the Forms of Justice, Beauty, and Goodness.

Material objects and the Forms

According to Plato, the Forms as a whole make up a distinct realm from the natural world. The Forms are changeless, eternal entities. By contrast, the material objects that we perceive with the senses are always changing, taking on new characteristics, and existing at one time but not at others. For example, a painting might be beautiful for a time and then lose its beauty through decay or damage. But the universal, Beauty itself, never changes and never ceases to exist; it is timeless and immutable. This is what is meant in the quotation above, when Socrates says that the Forms are the things that *are*. Material things are impermanent and constantly changing. To use Plato's description, they are in a perpetual state of *becoming*. The Forms, on the other hand, never change and never cease to be — they don't become anything; they just *are*.

If universals are entities separate from material objects, how can we say that material objects possess them? If Beauty is an entity separate from all material objects, how can paintings and other material objects *be* beautiful? Plato's answer to this is that material objects have properties in common by *resembling* the same Forms. Thus paintings or sculptures can all be beautiful to the extent that they resemble the Form of Beauty.

I used the word 'extent' in the last sentence to point out that, as resemblance is never perfect, objects in the material world never possess properties perfectly. There are no perfectly beautiful paintings, perfectly virtuous people, or perfectly triangular objects. This adds another interpretation to Socrates' claim that the Forms are the only things that *are*. For in Plato's view, no material thing is ever really beautiful, or virtuous, or triangular.

Knowledge of universals again

Because the senses inform us of the material world around us, Plato maintains that they provide us only with fleeting glimpses of the imperfect images of the Forms. Only the intellect or the soul can acquire genuine knowledge of what is eternal and unchanging by coming to know the Forms directly. This knowledge is obtained through reason and reflection, as in mathematics and philosophical debate. This is why Plato claims that the things that really exist — the timeless, eternal Forms — are known only through the intellect. What is given to us through the senses is imperfect and constantly changing as objects take on and lose their resemblance to the Forms. The distractions of sensory stimulation get in the way of our coming to know the true nature of universals, which are the sources of all the features of the world.

This is the end of our excursion into Plato's theory of universals and our knowledge of them. We can now return to Socrates' defence, picking up the dialogue where we left it at 65c2.

The problem of immortality

With Simmias' acceptance of the theory of the Forms, Socrates argues that as long as we possess a physical body our soul will be confused by the distractions of the senses and drawn away from genuine knowledge. At 66b3 he claims that "as long as we possess the body, and our soul is contaminated with such an evil, we'll surely never adequately gain what we desire — and that, we say, is truth." The idea is that the bodily senses reveal only shadows and images of the Forms, but direct knowledge of the Forms by the intellect gives us genuine knowledge. Thus a true "lover of knowledge" will welcome death as a release from the body (67a1–68b5), and the practice of philosophy is nothing but the "cultivation of dying" (67e5).

But in the next section at 70a1, Cebes points out that not everyone believes that the soul exists after death. Some people, he says, "fear that when it's been separated from the body, it may no longer exist anywhere" (70a1). So to defend the philosophical life and his attitude toward death, Socrates must also demonstrate the truth of dualism. He must show that the soul is not a part of the physical body, or dependent upon it, but that it exists as an independent entity after death. In *The Phaedo* Plato has Socrates offer four different arguments for this theory of the soul. The first is called "the cyclical argument."

The cyclical argument

In the cyclical argument Plato's intent is to show that when we die our souls exist in another world and are reborn. Plato bases his argument on a general principle, with which the others agree. The principle is that "opposites come to be only from their opposite." For example, what comes to be larger comes to be from something smaller, and what comes to be colder comes to be from something hotter. Socrates then has Cebes agree that being dead is the opposite of being alive (71c5). So from the general principle, Socrates argues, it follows that life and death come from each other (71d8). Socrates compares this to sleeping and being awake: going to sleep is the process of going from wakefulness to sleep, and waking up is the process of going from sleep to wakefulness (71d1). In the same way, he argues, in birth "living people are born from the dead no less than dead people from the living" (72a5). If this comparison is accurate, it must follow that the souls of the dead exist somewhere until they are born again.

From 72a11 to 72d3 Socrates supports the general principle on which the argument is based by claiming that if it were not true, everything would eventually have the same form. If people went to sleep, but there were no waking up from sleep, eventually everyone would be asleep. In the same way, he argues, if things died but did not return to life, ultimately everything would be dead.

Notice, by the way, that at this point Socrates extends the argument from people to "all things that partake in life" (72c6). It is not only the souls of people to which his argument applies, but all living things. Here Plato is clearly referring to the soul as the source of animation, that which brings life to the body. This raises the question of how this element of the soul can be combined with its role as intellect or seat of consciousness. He represents the intellect as resembling the immaterial Forms. How, then, can the soul be the source of life in material things? What is the connection between matter and the Forms? This is a problem that Plato's successor, Aristotle, resolves by rejecting both Plato's dualism and his theory of universals.

The recollection argument

At 72e4 Cebes reminds the others of a theory that Socrates has used before to justify the belief that the soul is immortal. This is the theory that "learning is nothing but recollection." According to the theory, what we take to be the acquisition of new knowledge is actually a matter of being reminded of what we have learned in a previous life. Cebes points out that if the recollection theory is true, then our souls must have existed before this life. This provides Socrates with another argument for dualism, as the recollection theory entails the possibility of the soul existing independently of the body.

The question, then, is what reason there is to believe the theory, and Simmias asks Cebes to remind him of the arguments for it. (The pun here is intentional.) What follows is a lengthy discussion of the recollection theory, and of one of the arguments for it based on the theory of the Forms.

Defending the recollection theory

Cebes first raises very briefly an argument that is given extended treatment in another dialogue, *The Meno*. This is the idea that if we are questioned in the right way, we will arrive at the correct answers to problems on our own, without the answers being supplied to us. The conclusion drawn is that the answers must have been in us before our birth, and the questioning merely reminds us of them. In *The Meno* Socrates leads a slave-boy in this way to solve the problem of determining the length of the sides of a square that is double in area to a given square. The slave-boy arrives at the correct answer by providing Socrates with answers to a series of questions, without Socrates actually supplying him with the correct answers.

At 73c1 Socrates begins a different argument for the recollection theory, based on the theory of the Forms. At 73d1 he presents a definition of recollection, which serves as the first premise in his argument. According to this definition, recollection is defined as "perceiving one thing and as a result coming to think of something else." The example Socrates offers is that of a lover who is reminded of his beloved by recognizing an object that belongs to the loved one. He adds that sometimes a recollection is occasioned by something similar to the object itself, as with a picture, and sometimes by something dissimilar, as with a piece of clothing owned by the loved one. At 74a5 he says that when we are reminded of something from a similar thing, we must be aware of the fact that the object that prompts the recollection is "lacking … in its similarity, in relation to what one is reminded of." His point is that even in the case of similar objects, what prompts a recollection does not possess all the qualities of what it brings to mind. A picture, for example, is a two-dimensional image of a person, not a perfect duplicate.

At this point the theory of the Forms is brought into the argument, using for illustration the universal Equality. Socrates first has Simmias agree that there is a Form of Equality (which he calls here "the equal itself") (74a11). Then he adds the following two premises:

1. Things that we perceive to be equal are distinct from the equal itself. That is, the material objects we perceive and the Forms are distinct from one another (74c5).
2. Our knowledge of equality is produced by the perception of equal things (74c7).

The basis for premise 1 is that material objects are always in some ways unequal while this cannot be true of "the equal itself." This reflects the differences between material things and the Forms that I described earlier. Premise 2 is drawn from the fact that we are first taught the *concept* of equality by perceiving particular material objects. When we first learn the meaning of the term 'equality,' it is usually by being shown examples of equal things. So although sensory perception by itself cannot provide us with the concept of equality, it is only in the act of perceiving equal things that the concept is first brought to mind.

Given the definition of recollection as the act of perceiving one thing and thinking of something different as a result, Socrates concludes from premises 1 and 2 that our knowledge of equality must be a case of recollection. Because certain pairs of material things *resemble* the Form of Equality, our perception of them can bring the idea of that Form to mind. We perceive one thing with our senses (namely, the material objects) and are thereby prompted to think of something else (namely, the Form).

So it is agreed that knowledge of universals like Equality is a matter of being reminded of the Forms when we observe things that resemble them. But because perception begins at birth, the conclusion is that our knowledge of universals was obtained prior to our birth. It follows from this theory that our souls must have existed before our birth, during which time we gained our acquaintance with the Forms. At 76e4 Socrates reminds the others that this argument depends on the theory of the Forms, and without the theory it "will have gone for nothing."

Two additional arguments for immortality

The remaining portions of *The Phaedo* are too long to reproduce in the readings.[2] At 77d5 Socrates says that despite the two arguments given already, Cebes and Simmias are still afraid that at death "as the soul goes out of the body, the wind may literally blow it apart and disperse it." So Socrates offers two additional arguments to allay their fears.

The first argument is called "the affinity argument," because in it Plato contends that the soul is most similar to the Forms, which are eternal and unchanging. The argument has two premises:

1. The things that are most liable to destruction are the things we perceive with our bodily senses like sight and touch, and the things that are not susceptible to destruction are the Forms.
2. The soul is most similar to the unchanging, invisible Forms and not to the realm of ever-changing objects that we perceive with the senses.

The fourth argument in *The Phaedo* is called "the argument from opposites." In this final argument, Socrates points out that the existence of each kind of object depends upon its possessing certain qualities essential for its existence. For example, the existence of snow depends on coldness — in the presence of warmth, snow disappears. He argues that when an object possesses a particular property in this way, it cannot possess the opposite of that property. Because coldness is essential to snow, snow cannot possess warmth. Cebes and the others agree that the soul is the source of life by its very nature. It follows, then, that the soul cannot also admit of death. Hence the soul is immortal.

Plato's influence

We have seen how Plato developed a theory of the soul to explain our knowledge of universals. This knowledge, Plato believed, could not be acquired through the senses but only through the activity of the intellect. As the intellect is associated with the Forms, which are eternal and indestructible, the soul too must be immortal.

From the beginning there was an awareness of various problems in Plato's theory of the Forms, and Plato himself looked on his theories as hypotheses to be amended and worked over. The largest problem was in explaining how material objects could resemble and be influenced by the immaterial Forms. Eventually the problems in reworking his ideas became so difficult that Plato began to rethink his commitment to the theory of the Forms. Once the theory of the Forms was given up, it became possible for his student, Aristotle, to reject the theory of the soul that came with it.

As we will see in the next chapter, Aristotle abandons the contrast Plato draws between the senses and the intellect. Aristotle maintains that the senses are a reliable (though incomplete) source of knowledge. This difference between Plato and Aristotle is part of what led to Aristotle's rejection of Plato's theory of the soul. Interestingly, however, the developments that created the modern mathematical sciences in the seventeenth century A.D. brought back doubts about the veracity of sensory perception. Even though Plato's theory of the Forms was never resurrected, we will see that two aspects of Plato's views returned with the rise of modern science: the idea that the senses are not entirely reliable as a guide to knowledge of the world, and the idea that mind and body are two distinct entities. In a different guise again, these ideas continue to have an influence in present-day psychology and neuroscience.

NOTES

1 These numbers occur in the margin of the reading. They refer to a standard page numbering system, used with all translations of Plato and based on the pagination of a standard edition of the original Greek text. The first number refers to the page number, the letter refers to the column, and the second number refers to the line.

2 For the complete dialogue, see *Plato: The Phaedo*, translated with notes by David Gallop (Oxford: Oxford University Press, 1975).

Plato
Selections from *The Phaedo*

Socrates' Defence
• • •

'Let him be,' he said. 'Now then, with you for my jury I want to give my defence, and show with what good reason, as it
10 seems to me, a man who has truly spent
64 his life in philosophy feels confident when about to die, and is hopeful that, when he has died, he will win very great benefits in the other world. So I'll try, Simmias and Cebes, to explain how this could be.

'Other people may well be unaware
5 that all who actually engage in philosophy aright are practising nothing other than dying and being dead. Now if this is true, it would be odd indeed for them to be eager in their whole life for nothing but this, and yet to be resentful when it comes, the very thing they'd long been eager for and practised.'

Simmias laughed at this and said:
'Goodness, Socrates, you've made me
b laugh, even though I wasn't much inclined to laugh just now. I imagine that most people, on hearing that, would think it very well said of philosophers—and our own countrymen would quite agree—that they are, indeed, verging on death, and that
5 they, at any rate, are well aware that this is what philosophers deserve to undergo.'

'Yes, and what they say would be true, Simmias, except for their claim to be aware of it themselves; because they aren't aware in what sense genuine philosophers are
c verging on death and deserving of it, and what kind of death they deserve. Anyway, let's discuss it among ourselves, disregarding them: do we suppose that death *is* something?'

'Certainly,' rejoined Simmias.

'And that it is nothing but the separa-
5 tion of the soul from the body? And that being dead is this: the body's having come to be apart, separated from the soul, alone by itself, and the soul's being apart, alone by itself, separated from the body? Death can't be anything else but that, can it?'

'No, it's just that.'

'Now look, my friend, and see if 10 maybe you agree with me on these points; because through them I think we'll d improve our knowledge of what we're examining. Do you think it befits a philosophical man to be keen about the so-called pleasures of, for example, food and drink?'

'Not in the least, Socrates,' said Sim-
5 mias.

'And what about those of sex?'

'Not at all.'

'And what about the other services to the body? Do you think such a man regards them as of any value? For instance, the possession of smart clothes and shoes, 10 and the other bodily adornments—do you think he values them highly, or does he disdain them, except in so far as he's absolutely compelled to share in them?'   e

'I think the genuine philosopher disdains them.'

'Do you think in general, then, that such a man's concern is not for the body, 5 but so far as he can stand aside from it, is directed towards the soul?'

'I do.'

'Then is it clear that, first, in such matters as these the philosopher differs from 65 other men in releasing his soul, as far as possible, from its communion with the body?'

'It appears so.'

'And presumably, Simmias, it does seem to most men that someone who finds
5   nothing of that sort pleasant, and takes no part in those things, doesn't deserve to live; rather, one who cares nothing for the pleasures that come by way of the body runs pretty close to being dead.'

'Yes, what you say is quite true.'

10   'And now, what about the actual gaining of wisdom? Is the body a hindrance or
b   not, if one enlists it as a partner in the quest? This is the sort of thing I mean: do sight and hearing afford men any truth, or aren't even the poets always harping on such themes, telling us that we neither hear nor see anything accurately? And yet if
5   these of all the bodily senses are neither accurate nor clear, the others will hardly be so; because they are, surely, all inferior to these. Don't you think so?'

'Certainly.'

'So when does the soul attain the
10   truth? Because plainly, whenever it sets about examining anything in company with the body, it is completely taken in by it.'

c   'That's true.'

'So isn't it in reasoning, if anywhere at all, that any of the things that *are* become manifest to it?'

'Yes.'

5   'And it reasons best, presumably, whenever none of these things bothers it, neither hearing nor sight nor pain, nor any pleasure either, but whenever it comes to be alone by itself as far as possible, disregarding the body, and whenever, having the least possible communion and contact with it, it strives for that which is.'

10   'That is so.'

'So there again the soul of the philoso-
d   pher utterly disdains the body and flees

from it, seeking rather to come to be alone by itself?'

'It seems so.'

'Well now, what about things of this sort, Simmias? Do we say that there is   5
something *just*, or nothing?'

'Yes, we most certainly do!'

'And again, something *beautiful*, and *good*?'

'Of course.'

'Now did you ever yet see any such things with your eyes?'

'Certainly not.'   10

'Well did you grasp them with any other bodily sense-perception? And I'm talking about them all—about largeness, health, and strength, for example—and, in short, about the Being of all other such things, what each one actually is; is it   e
through the body that their truest element is viewed, or isn't it rather thus: whoever of us is prepared to think most fully and minutely of each object of his inquiry, in itself, will come closest to the knowledge of each?'

'Yes, certainly.'   5

'Then would that be achieved most purely by the man who approached each object with his intellect alone as far as possible, neither adducing sight in his thinking, nor dragging in any other sense to   **66**
accompany his reasoning; rather, using his intellect alone by itself and unsullied, he would undertake the hunt for each of the things that are, each alone by itself and unsullied; he would be separated as far as possible from his eyes and ears, and virtually from his whole body, on the ground   5
that it confuses the soul, and doesn't allow it to gain truth and wisdom when in partnership with it: isn't it this man, Simmias, who will attain that which is, if anyone will?'

'What you say is abundantly true, Soc-   10
rates,' said Simmias.

b   'For all these reasons, then, some such view as this must present itself to genuine philosophers, so that they say such things to one another as these: "There now, it looks as if some sort of track is leading us, together with our reason, astray in our in-
5 quiry: as long as we possess the body, and our soul is contaminated by such an evil, we'll surely never adequately gain what we desire—and that, we say, is truth. Because the body affords us countless distractions,
c owing to the nurture it must have; and again, if any illnesses befall it, they hamper our pursuit of that which is. Besides, it fills us up with lusts and desires, with fears and fantasies of every kind, and with any amount of trash, so that really and truly we are, as the saying goes, never able
5 to think of anything at all because of it. Thus, it's nothing but the body and its desires that brings wars and factions and fighting; because it's over the gaining of wealth that all wars take place, and we're
d compelled to gain wealth because of the body, enslaved as we are to its service; so for all these reasons it leaves us no leisure for philosophy. And the worst of it all is
5 that if we do get any leisure from it, and turn to some inquiry, once again it intrudes everywhere in our researches, setting up a clamour and disturbance, and striking terror, so that the truth can't be discerned because of it. Well now, it really has been shown us that if we're ever going to
e know anything purely, we must be rid of it, and must view the objects themselves with the soul by itself; it's then, apparently, that the thing we desire and whose lovers we claim to be, wisdom, will be ours— when we have died, as the argument indicates, though not while we live. Because,
5 if we can know nothing purely in the body's company, then one of two things must be true: either knowledge is nowhere
67 to be gained, or else it is for the dead; since

then, but no sooner, will the soul be alone by itself apart from the body. And therefore while we live, it would seem that we shall be closest to knowledge in this way— if we consort with the body as little as pos-
5 sible, and do not commune with it, except in so far as we must, and do not infect ourselves with its nature, but remain pure from it, until God himself shall release us; and being thus pure, through separation from the body's folly, we shall probably be in like company, and shall know through our own selves all that is unsullied—and
b that, I dare say, is what the truth is; because never will it be permissible for impure to touch pure." Such are the things, I think, Simmias, that all who are rightly called lovers of knowledge must say to one
5 another, and must believe. Don't you agree?'

   'Emphatically, Socrates.'

   'Well then, if that's true, my friend,' said Socrates, 'there's plenty of hope for one who arrives where I'm going, that there, if anywhere, he will adequately pos-
10 sess the object that's been our great concern in life gone by; and thus the journey now appointed for me may also be made
c with good hope by any other man who regards his intellect as prepared, by having been, in a manner, purified.'

   'Yes indeed,' said Simmias.

   'Then doesn't purification turn out to
5 be just what's been mentioned for some while in our discussion—the parting of the soul from the body as far as possible, and the habituating of it to assemble and gather itself together, away from every part of the body, alone by itself, and to live, so far as it can, both in the present and in the hereaf-
d ter, released from the body, as from fetters?'

   'Yes indeed.'

   'And is it just this that is named "death"—a release and parting of soul from
5 body?'

'Indeed it is.'

'And it's especially those who practise philosophy aright, or rather they alone, who are always eager to release it, as we say, and the occupation of philosophers is just 10 this, isn't it—a release and parting of soul from body?'

'It seems so.'

'Then wouldn't it be absurd, as I said e at the start, for a man to prepare himself in his life to live as close as he can to being dead, and then to be resentful when this comes to him?'

'It would be absurd, of course.'

'Truly then, Simmias, those who prac- 5 tise philosophy aright are cultivating dying, and for them least of all men does being dead hold any terror. Look at it like this: if they've set themselves at odds with the body at every point, and desire to possess their soul alone by itself, wouldn't it be quite illogical if they were afraid and re- 68 sentful when this came about—if, that is, they didn't go gladly to the place where, on arrival, they may hope to attain what they longed for throughout life, namely wisdom—and to be rid of the company of that with which they'd set themselves at 5 odds? Or again, many have been willing to enter Hades of their own accord, in quest of human loves, of wives and sons who have died, led by this hope, that there they would see and be united with those they desired; will anyone, then, who truly longs for wisdom, and who firmly holds this b same hope, that nowhere but in Hades will he attain it in any way worth mentioning, be resentful at dying; and will he not go there gladly? One must suppose so, my friend, if he's truly a lover of wisdom; since this will be his firm belief, that nowhere 5 else but there will he attain wisdom purely. Yet if that is so, wouldn't it, as I said just now, be quite illogical if such a man were afraid of death?'

'Yes, quite illogical!'

'Then if you see a man resentful that he is going to die, isn't this proof enough c for you that he's no lover of wisdom after all, but what we may call a lover of the body? And this same man turns out, in some sense, to be a lover of riches and of prestige, either one of these or both.'

'It's just as you say.'

'Well now, Simmias, isn't it also true 5 that what is named "bravery" belongs especially to people of the disposition we have described?'

'Most certainly.'

'And then temperance too, even what most people name "temperance"—not being excited over one's desires, but being scornful of them and well-ordered—be- 10 longs, doesn't it, only to those who utterly scorn the body and live in love of wisdom?'

'It must.' d

'Yes, because if you care to consider the bravery and temperance of other men, you'll find it strange.'

'How so, Socrates?'

'You know, don't you, that all other 5 men count death among great evils?'

'Very much so.'

'Is it, then, through being afraid of greater evils that the brave among them abide death, whenever they do so?'

'It is.' 10

'Then, it's through fearing and fear that all men except philosophers are brave; and yet it's surely illogical that anyone should be brave through fear and cowardice.'

'It certainly is.' e

'And what about those of them who are well-ordered? Aren't they in this same state, temperate through a kind of intemperance? True, we say that's impossible; but still that state of simple-minded temperance does turn out in their case to be like 5 this: it's because they're afraid of being deprived of further pleasures, and desire

69 them, that they abstain from some because they're overcome by others. True, they call it "intemperance" to be ruled by pleasures, but still that's what happens to them: they overcome some pleasures because they're overcome by others. And this is the sort of thing that was just mentioned: after a fashion, they achieve temperance because of intemperance.'

5 'Yes, so it seems.'

'Yes, Simmias, my good friend; since this may not be the right exchange with a view to goodness, the exchanging of pleasures for pleasures, pains for pains, and fear
10 for fear, greater for lesser ones, like coins; it may be, rather, that this alone is the right
b coin, for which one should exchange all these things—wisdom; and the buying and selling of all things for that, or rather with that, may be real bravery, temperance, justice, and, in short, true goodness in company with wisdom, whether pleasures and
5 fears and all else of that sort be added or taken away; but as for their being parted from wisdom and exchanged for one another, goodness of that sort may be a kind of illusory facade, and fit for slaves indeed, and may have nothing healthy or true about it; whereas, truth to tell, temperance,
c justice, and bravery may in fact be a kind of purification of all such things, and wisdom itself a kind of purifying rite. So it really looks as if those who established our
5 initiations are no mean people, but have in fact long been saying in riddles that whoever arrives in Hades unadmitted to the rites, and uninitiated, shall lie in the slough, while he who arrives there purified and initiated shall dwell with gods. For truly there are, so say those concerned with
d the initiations, "many who bear the wand, but few who are devotees". Now these latter, in my view, are none other than those who have practised philosophy aright. And it's to be among them that I myself have

striven, in every way I could, neglecting nothing during my life within my power. Whether I have striven aright and we have 5 achieved anything, we shall, I think, know for certain, God willing, in a little while, on arrival yonder.

'There's my defence, then, Simmias and Cebes, to show how reasonable it is for e me not to take it hard or be resentful at leaving you and my masters here, since I believe that there also, no less than here, I shall find good masters and companions; so if I'm any more convincing in my defence to you than to the Athenian jury, it would be well.'   5

The Cyclical Argument

When Socrates had said this, Cebes rejoined: 'The other things you say, Socrates, I find excellent; but what you say about the soul is the subject of much dis- 70 belief: men fear that when it's been separated from the body, it may no longer exist anywhere, but that on the very day a man dies, it may be destroyed and perish, as soon as it's separated from the body; and that as it goes out, it may be dispersed like breath or smoke, go flying 5 off, and exist no longer anywhere at all. True, if it did exist somewhere, gathered together alone by itself, and separated from those evils you were recounting just now, there'd be plenty of hope, Socrates, and a fine hope it would be, that what you say is true; but on just this point, b perhaps, one needs no little reassuring and convincing, that when the man has died, his soul exists, and that it possesses some power and wisdom.'

'That's true, Cebes,' said Socrates; 'but 5 then what are we to do? Would you like us to speculate on these very questions, and see whether this is likely to be the case or not?'

'For my part anyway,' said Cebes, 'I'd gladly hear whatever opinion you have about them.'

10 c   'Well,' said Socrates, 'I really don't think anyone listening now, even if he were a comic poet, would say that I'm talking idly, and arguing about things that don't concern me. If you agree, then, we should look into the matter.

5   'Let's consider it, perhaps, in this way: do the souls of men exist in Hades when they have died, or do they not? Now there's an ancient doctrine, which we've recalled, that they do exist in that world, entering it from this one, and that they re-enter this world and are born again from the dead; yet if this is so, if living people are born again from those who have died, surely our souls would have to exist in that world? Because they could hardly be born again, if they didn't exist; so it would be sufficient evidence for the truth of these claims, if it really became plain that living people are born from the dead and from nowhere else; but if that isn't so, some other argument would be needed.'

5   'Certainly,' said Cebes.

'Well now, consider the matter, if you want to understand more readily, in connection not only with mankind, but with all animals and plants; and, in general, for all things subject to coming-to-be, let's see whether everything comes to be in this way: opposites come to be only from their opposites—in the case of all things that actually have an opposite—as, for example, the beautiful is opposite, of course, to the ugly, just to unjust, and so on in countless other cases. So let's consider this: is it necessary that whatever has an opposite comes to be only from its opposite? For example, when a thing comes to be larger, it must, surely, come to be larger from being smaller before?'

'Yes.'

'And again, if it comes to be smaller, it will come to be smaller later from being larger before?'

'That's so.'

'And that which is weaker comes to be, presumably, from a stronger, and that which is faster from a slower?'

'Certainly.'

'And again, if a thing comes to be worse, it's from a better, and if more just, from a more unjust?'

'Of course.'

'Are we satisfied, then, that all things come to be in this way, opposite things from opposites?'

'Certainly.'

'Now again, do these things have a further feature of this sort: between the members of every pair of opposites, since they are two, aren't there two processes of coming-to-be, from one to the other, and back again from the latter to the former? Thus, between a larger thing and a smaller, isn't there increase and decrease, so that in the one case we speak of "increasing" and in the other of "decreasing"?'

'Yes.'

'And similarly with separating and combining, cooling and heating, and all such; even if in some cases we don't use the names, still in actual fact mustn't the same principle everywhere hold good: they come to be from each other, and there's a process of coming-to-be of each into the other?'

'Certainly.'

'Well then, is there an opposite to living, as sleeping is opposite to being awake?'

'Certainly.'

'What is it?'

'Being dead.'

'Then these come to be from each other, if they are opposites; and between the pair of them, since they are two, the processes of coming-to-be are two?'

'Of course.'

'Now then,' said Socrates, 'I'll tell you
10 one of the couples I was just mentioning,
the couple itself and its processes; and you
tell me the other. My couple is sleeping
and being awake: being awake comes to be
d from sleeping, and sleeping from being
awake, and their processes are going to
sleep and waking up. Is that sufficient for
you or not?'

'Certainly.'

5   'Now it's for you to tell me in the same
way about life and death. You say, don't
you, that being dead is opposite to living?'

'I do.'

'And that they come to be from each
other?'

'Yes.'

10   'Then what is it that comes to be from
that which is living?'

'That which is dead.'

'And what comes to be from that
which is dead?'

'I must admit that it's that which is living.'

'Then it's from those that are dead,
15 Cebes, that living things and living people
are born?'

e   'Apparently.'

'Then our souls do exist in Hades.'

'So it seems.'

'Now *one* of the relevant processes here
5 is obvious, isn't it? For dying is obvious
enough, surely?'

'It certainly is.'

'What shall we do then? Shan't we assign the opposite process to balance it? Will
nature be lame in this respect? Or must we
10 supply some process opposite to dying?'

'We surely must.'

'What will this be?'

'Coming to life again.'

'Then if there is such a thing as com-
72 ing to life again, wouldn't this, coming to
life again, be a process from dead to living
people?'

'Certainly.'

'In that way too, then, we're agreed
that living people are born from the dead   5
no less than dead people from the living;
and we thought that, if this were the case,
it would be sufficient evidence that the
souls of the dead must exist somewhere,
whence they are born again.'

'I think, Socrates, that that must fol-   10
low from our admissions.'

'Then look at it this way, Cebes, and
you'll see, I think, that our admissions were
not mistaken. If there were not perpetual
reciprocity in coming to be, between one   b
set of things and another, revolving in a
circle, as it were—if, instead, coming-to-
be were a linear process from one thing
into its opposite only, without any bend-
ing back in the other direction or reversal,
do you realize that all things would ulti-   5
mately have the same form: the same fate
would overtake them, and they would
cease from coming to be?'

'What do you mean?'

'It's not at all hard to understand what
I mean. If, for example, there were such a
thing as going to sleep, but from sleeping
there were no reverse process of waking up;
you realize that everything would ulti-   c
mately make Endymion seem a mere trifle: he'd be nowhere, because the same fate
as his, sleeping, would have overtaken everything else. Again, if everything were
combined, but not separated, then
Anaxagoras' notion of "all things together"
would soon be realized. And similarly, my   5
dear Cebes, if all things that partake in life
were to die, but when they'd died, the dead
remained in that form, and didn't come
back to life, wouldn't it be quite inevitable
that everything would ultimately be dead,
and nothing would live? Because if the liv-   d
ing things came to be from the other
things, but the living things were to die,
what could possibly prevent everything

from being completely spent in being dead?'

5   'Nothing whatever, in my view, Socrates,' said Cebes; 'what you say seems to be perfectly true.'

'Yes, it certainly is true, Cebes, as I see it; and we're not deceived in making just those admissions: there really is such a thing as coming to life again, living peo-

e   ple *are* born from the dead, and the souls of the dead exist.'

• • •

The Recollection Argument

'Yes, and besides, Socrates,' Cebes replied,
5   'there's also that theory you're always putting forward, that our learning is actually nothing but recollection; according to that too, if it's true, what we are now reminded of we must have learned at some
73   former time. But that would be impossible, unless our souls existed somewhere before being born in this human form; so in this way too, it appears that the soul is something immortal.'

'Yes, what are the proofs of those
5   points, Cebes?' put in Simmias. 'Remind me, as I don't recall them very well at the moment.'

'One excellent argument,' said Cebes, 'is that when people are questioned, and if the questions are well put, they state the truth about everything for themselves—
10   and yet unless knowledge and a correct account were present within them, they'd be
b   unable to do this; thus, if one takes them to diagrams or anything else of that sort, one has there the plainest evidence that this is so.'

'But if that doesn't convince you, Simmias,' said Socrates, 'then see whether maybe you agree if you look at it this way.
5   Apparently you doubt whether what is called "learning" is recollection?'

'I don't *doubt* it,' said Simmias; 'but I do need to undergo just what the argument is about, to be "reminded". Actually, from the way Cebes set about stating it, I do almost recall it and am nearly convinced; but I'd like, none the less, to hear now how you set about stating it yourself.'   10

'I'll put it this way. We agree, I take it,   c that if anyone is to be reminded of a thing, he must have known that thing at some time previously.'

'Certainly.'

'Then do we also agree on this point: that whenever knowledge comes to be   5 present in this sort of way, it is recollection? I mean in some such way as this: if someone, on seeing a thing, or hearing it, or getting any other sense-perception of it, not only recognizes that thing, but also thinks of something else, which is the object not of the same knowledge but of another, don't we then rightly say that he's been "reminded" of the object of which he   d has got the thought?'

'What do you mean?'

'Take the following examples: knowledge of a man, surely, is other than that of a lyre?'

'Of course.'

'Well now, you know what happens to   5 lovers, whenever they see a lyre or cloak or anything else their loves are accustomed to use: they recognize the lyre, and they get in their mind, don't they, the form of the boy whose lyre it is? And that is recollection. Likewise, someone seeing Simmias is often reminded of Cebes, and there'd surely be countless other such cases.'   10

'Countless indeed!' said Simmias.

'Then is something of that sort a kind   e of recollection? More especially, though, whenever it happens to someone in connection with things he's since forgotten, through lapse of time or inattention?'

'Certainly.'

5   'Again now, is it possible, on seeing a horse depicted or a lyre depicted, to be reminded of a man; and on seeing Simmias depicted, to be reminded of Cebes?'

'Certainly.'

'And also, on seeing Simmias depicted,
10 to be reminded of Simmias himself?'

74   'Yes, that's possible.'

'In all these cases, then, doesn't it turn out that there is recollection from similar things, but also from dissimilar things?'

'It does.'

5   'But whenever one is reminded of something from similar things, mustn't one experience something further: mustn't one think whether or not the thing is lacking at all, in its similarity, in relation to what one is reminded of?'

'One must.'

'Then consider whether this is the case.
10 We say, don't we, that there is something *equal*—I don't mean a log to a log, or a stone to a stone, or anything else of that sort, but some further thing beyond all those, the equal itself: are we to say that there *is* something or nothing?'

b   'We most certainly are to say that there *is*,' said Simmias; 'unquestionably!'

'And do we know *what it is?*'

'Certainly.'

'Where did we get the knowledge of it?
5   Wasn't it from the things we were just mentioning: on seeing logs or stones or other equal things, wasn't it from these that we thought of that object, it being different from them? Or doesn't it seem different to you? Look at it this way: don't equal stones and logs, the very same ones, sometimes seem equal to one, but not to another?'

10 'Yes, certainly.'

c   'But now, did the equals themselves ever seem to you unequal, or equality inequality?'

'Never yet, Socrates.'

'Then those equals, and the equal it-   5
self, are not the same.'

'By no means, Socrates, in my view.'

'But still, it is from *those* equals, different as they are from *that* equal, that you have thought of and got the knowledge of it?'

'That's perfectly true.'   10

'It being either similar to them or dissimilar?'

'Certainly.'

'Anyway, it makes no difference; so long as on seeing one thing, one does, from this   d
sight, think of another, whether it be similar or dissimilar, this must be recollection.'

'Certainly.'

'Well now, with regard to the instances in the logs, and, in general, the equals we   5
mentioned just now, are we affected in some way as this: do they seem to us to be equal in the same way as *what it is* itself? Do they fall short of it at all in being like the equal, or not?'

'Very far short of it.'

'Then whenever anyone, on seeing a thing, thinks to himself, "this thing that I   10
now see seeks to be like another of the things that are, but falls short, and cannot   e
be like that object: it is inferior", do we agree that the man who thinks this must previously have known the object he says it resembles but falls short of?'

'He must.'   5

'Now then, have we ourselves been affected in just this way, or not, with regard to the equals and the equal itself?'

'Indeed we have.'

'Then we must previously have known the equal, before that time when we first,   **75**
on seeing the equals, thought that all of them were striving to be like the equal but fell short of it.'

'That is so.'

'Yet we also agree on this: we haven't   5
derived the thought of it, nor could we do

so, from anywhere but seeing or touching or some other of the senses—I'm counting all these as the same.'

'Yes, they are the same, Socrates, for
10 what the argument seeks to show.'

'But of course it is *from* one's sense-per-
b   ceptions that one must think that all the things in the sense-perceptions are striving for *what equal is,* yet are inferior to it; or how shall we put it?'

'Like that.'

'Then it must, surely, have been before
5   we began to see and hear and use the other senses that we got knowledge of the equal itself, of *what it is,* if we were going to re-fer the equals from our sense-perceptions to it, supposing that all things are doing their best to be like it, but are inferior to it.'

'That must follow from what's been said before, Socrates.'

10 'Now we were seeing and hearing, and were possessed of our other senses, weren't we, just as soon as we were born?'

'Certainly.'

c   'But we must, we're saying, have got our knowledge of the equal *before* these?'

'Yes.'

5   'Then it seems that we must have got it before we were born.'

'It seems so.'

'Now if, having got it before birth, we were born in possession of it, did we know, both before birth and as soon as we were
10 born, not only the equal, the larger and the smaller, but everything of that sort? Be-cause our present argument concerns the
d   beautiful itself, and the good itself, and just and holy, no less than the equal; in fact, as I say, it concerns everything on which we set this seal, *"what it is",* in the questions we ask and in the answers we give. And so
5   we must have got pieces of knowledge of all those things before birth.'

'That is so.'

'Moreover, if having got them, we did not on each occasion forget them, we must always be born knowing, and must con-tinue to know throughout life: because this
10 is knowing—to possess knowledge one has got of something, and not to have lost it; or isn't loss of knowledge what we mean by "forgetting", Simmias?'

'Certainly it is, Socrates.'   e

'But on the other hand, I suppose that if, having got them before birth, we lost them on being born, and later on, using the senses about the things in question, we regain those pieces of knowledge that we possessed at some former time, in that case
5   wouldn't what we call "learning" be the re-gaining of knowledge belonging to us? And in saying that this was being reminded, shouldn't we be speaking correctly?'

'Certainly.'

'Yes, because it did seem possible, on **76**
sensing an object, whether by seeing or hearing or getting some other sense-per-ception of it, to think from this of some other thing one had forgotten—either a thing to which the object, though dissimi-lar to it, was related, or else something to which it was similar; so, as I say, one of
5   two things is true: *either* all of us were born knowing those objects, and we know them throughout life; *or* those we speak of as "learning" are simply being reminded later on, and learning would be recollection.'

'That's quite true, Socrates.'

'Then which do you choose, Simmias?
That we are born knowing, or that we are b
later reminded of the things we'd gained knowledge of before?'

'At the moment, Socrates, I can't make a choice.'

'Well, can you make one on the fol-lowing point, and what do you think 5
about it? If a man knows things, can he give an account of what he knows or not?'

'Of course he can, Socrates.'

'And do you think everyone can give an account of those objects we were discussing just now?'

10   'I only wish they could,' said Simmias; 'but I'm afraid that, on the contrary, this time tomorrow there may no longer be any man who can do so properly.'

c   'You don't then, Simmias, think that everyone knows those objects?'

'By no means.'

'Are they, then, reminded of what they once learned?'

5   'They must be.'

'When did our souls get the knowledge of those objects? Not, at any rate, since we were born as human beings.'

'Indeed not.'

'Earlier, then.'

10   'Yes.'

'Then our souls did exist earlier, Simmias, before entering human form, apart from bodies; and they possessed wisdom.'

'Unless maybe, Socrates, we get those
15   pieces of knowledge at the very moment of birth; that time still remains.'

d   'Very well, my friend; but then at what other time, may I ask, do we lose them? We aren't born with them, as we agreed just now. Do we then lose them at the very time at which we get them? Or have you any other time to suggest?'

5   'None at all, Socrates. I didn't realize I was talking nonsense.'

'Then is our position as follows, Simmias? If the objects we are always harping on exist, a beautiful, and a good and all such Being, and if we refer all the things

e   from our sense-perceptions to that Being, finding again what was formerly ours, and if we compare these things with that, then just as surely as those objects exist, so also must our soul exist before we are born. On the other hand, if they don't exist, this argument will have gone for nothing. Is this

the position? Is it equally necessary that   5
those objects exist, and that our souls existed before birth, and if the former don't exist, then neither did the latter?'

'It's abundantly clear to me, Socrates,' said Simmias, 'that there's the same necessity in either case, and the argument takes opportune refuge in the view that our soul   **77** exists before birth, just as surely as the Being of which you're now speaking. Because I myself find nothing so plain to me as that all such objects, beautiful and good and all the others you were speaking of just now, *are* in the fullest possible way, so in my   5 view it's been adequately proved.'

• • •

CHAPTER TWO

Aristotle: Naturalizing the Soul

Introduction

According to Plato, the universe is divided into two distinct realms: the material realm of objects perceived by the senses and the realm of the eternal, immutable Forms. The body belongs to the first of these and the soul to the second. Only in this way, Plato believed, can we explain our knowledge of universals. Plato's interest in universals arose in large part from his studies of mathematics and politics, and so his theory of the soul was shaped by these concerns. But his student Aristotle (384–322 B.C.) was most interested in the place of human beings in the natural world. Aristotle was as much a natural scientist as a philosopher, conducting careful studies of plant and animal life and devising detailed theories to explain change and motion in the physical world. Although he inherited the problem of universals from Plato, Aristotle believed universals to be part of the natural world itself rather than a distinct realm of immaterial Forms.

The largest single difficulty with Plato's theory of the Forms is to explain the relationship between material objects and the Forms. As Plato's student, Aristotle was aware of this difficulty and of the attempts to solve it. Moreover, as a botanist Aristotle believed that change and growth in the natural world come from a force in material things themselves, and this made it difficult to believe that material things are simply shadowy images of the Forms. His solution was to replace the idea of two distinct realms with the idea that material things have two distinct aspects: their matter and their form. The former played the role of Plato's material realm, while the latter played the role of Plato's realm of Forms. This means that universals are aspects of material things, and not independent entities as Plato argues in *The Phaedo.*

Aristotle on the soul

Given his rejection of the theory of Forms, Aristotle was led to a different conception of the soul. For Aristotle, the soul is not a separate entity from the body, but rather an aspect of a person's biological makeup. Aristotle argued that, as living creatures, we are more than just a mass of tissue and bone. The explanation of why we grow and reproduce and move about must involve more than just the matter that makes up our bodies, for that matter is common to both living and dead things. Adopting from Plato and others the idea that the soul is what brings life to the body, Aristotle sought to explain the nature of the soul by defining it as the source of all the activities that constitute life.

In a text called *On the Soul,* Aristotle presents a detailed description of the soul in terms of the way in which its various elements produce the different aspects of living things. In Book I of *On the Soul* he criticizes earlier theories, and in Book II he presents his own views, beginning with a general definition of the soul and its relation to the body, and moving to descriptions of its specific functions. We will start with chapter 1 of Book II, where he presents and defends his general definition. Then we will look at his descriptions of two important functions of the soul: visual perception and thought.

The soul as "substance"

At the outset of chapter 1, Book II, of *On the Soul* Aristotle asks, "What is soul?" In asking this question Aristotle is adopting the definition of the soul as that which brings life. In these terms his question can be interpreted as meaning, "What is the origin of life?"

In the second paragraph he begins his answer by talking about what he calls **substance**. Exactly what this word means for him is a deep and complex question. But in simplest terms 'substance' is a word for the basic elements of the world. The things we see around us are constantly moving and changing: the stars revolve in the sky, the seasons change, and plants and animals are born and grow. What accounts for these changes? What is it that remains throughout the changes? For Aristotle, these are questions about the nature of substance. To understand Aristotle's conception of the soul, we have to form some understanding of his notion of substance.

Substance as matter and form

Aristotle's opening remark on the concept of substance is as follows.

> We say that substance is one kind of what is, and that in several senses: in the sense of *matter* or that which in itself is not a this, and

in the sense of *form* or *essence*, which is that precisely in virtue of which a thing is called a this, and thirdly in the sense of that which is compounded of both.

Notice that in this sentence Aristotle identifies three different concepts that fall under the general term 'substance.' They are labelled as

(a)   substance as **matter**
(b)   substance as **form** or **essence**
(c)   substance as the combination of (a) and (b).

The distinction between the concepts of matter and form is a central feature of Aristotle's theory of the soul.

Roughly, the difference between matter and form is that between what something is made of and what makes it the kind of thing it is. Here's an example. Think of two statues of Socrates, one of marble and one of bronze. Insofar as they are both statues of Socrates they are the same *kind* of thing. But they are composed of different material. In this case, what makes these the same kind of thing is that they both portray the actual person Socrates, and this is a result of their shape. So, in this example, the form is the shape. The matter of each statue is the marble or bronze out of which it is composed.

Now think of another two statues of Socrates, this time both of marble. Again, they are the same kind of thing, both statues of Socrates, but of different *pieces* of marble. Here again they have the same form but different matter. For even though the matter in each case is of the same kind, there are still two distinct lumps of marble. One way to look at it is that form is what any two objects of the same kind have in common, and matter is what differentiates one from another.

Aristotle applies the same distinction to the natural world. Plants and animals of the same species share the same form or essence. The form of a particular plant or animal is what it has in common with other members of the same species. The matter is what differentiates it from those other members.

We need to be a bit careful about what the previous sentence means. Consider the two marble statues again. The fact that there are two pieces of marble explains why there are two statues and not one. But the interesting differences between the two statues, their sculptural features, are not just reflections of different matter, but are features of the shape the form takes in each individual. The same is true of living things. The differences in character and personality among people and animals is a result of differences in the way in which the species is realized in the individual. So your form or essence is what makes you a human being, but it is also what makes you the person you are.[1]

There are some points about matter and form that are worth noting:

1. What is matter and what is form depend on the object we are talking about. For example, a lump of clay is the matter of a brick, but a brick can be part of the matter of a house. Similarly, an eye is part of the matter of a person, yet the eye itself has its own form and matter. So there is no absolute distinction between matter and form.

2. Only certain kinds of material can be the matter for a particular kind of object. Marble and bronze can both form the matter of a statue, but water cannot. Similarly, only certain kinds of natural material, tissue and bone for example, can form the matter of living things.

3. The previous point explains why, in the second paragraph, Aristotle says that matter is "potentiality" while form is "actuality." Certain kinds of material (lumps of marble, for example) are potentially statues. Other kinds of material (such as matter in the womb at conception) are potentially living things. Marble becomes a statue, and flesh becomes a living thing by possessing a certain form, that is, by passing from potentiality to actuality. This is also why in the passage quoted above, Aristotle refers to matter as "that which is not a *this*," and to form as "that precisely in virtue of which a thing is a *this*." It is only in virtue of possessing a form that matter can be identified as a particular kind of thing — a *this*. In the case of artificial things, like the statue, the transition from potential to actuality happens by human action. But in living things it happens by a principle of change within the thing itself, as when a seed or egg becomes a fully formed plant or animal.

The definition of soul

In the third and fourth paragraphs, Aristotle presents a line of reasoning to yield a general definition of the soul, according to which the soul is the form or essence of living things. The third paragraph presents the following two premises:

1. Natural bodies are substances in the sense of composites of form and matter.
2. Some natural bodies are living things, and some are not.

By "natural bodies" Aristotle means things like rocks, trees, water and animals; that is, objects that are of natural origin. So according to these two premises, natural things comprise both matter and form, and some are alive and others not.

The first sentence of the fourth paragraph gives us another premise:

3.   Because a living body is a body of a particular kind (one that lives), the body cannot be soul.

Think here of the difference between a living animal and a dead body. They are different in that one possesses a soul and one does not. Hence, the collection of tissues, bones, and organs that make up the physical body cannot be the soul. The body is not what brings life into being but what makes life *possible*. In this sense, the body is to a living thing what the bronze is to a statue.

Putting together all of the points established so far, we get the following argument. The soul is substance; that is, it is a *fundamental* element of the world. Hence it must be either matter, form, or the combination. All natural bodies, living or not, are combinations of matter and form, and so the soul must be one or the other. But it can't be matter because matter is only *potentially* a living thing. Thus Aristotle arrives at the following conclusion.

Hence, the soul must be a substance in the sense of the form of a natural body having life potentially within it.

The difference between a natural body that is only *potentially* alive and one that is *actually* alive is the presence of a soul. The soul is thus the form or essence of living things.

Soul as the form of living things

The form of something is what makes it the kind of thing it is. Among living things the form is what makes a plant or animal a member of one species rather than another. It is a principle of life that makes something, say, a rabbit rather than a person or a tree. An acorn grows into an oak rather than an elm because it possesses the form or soul of an oak. Accordingly, living things of the same species have the same kind of soul. Because a soul can only enliven matter that is organized in a particular way, with all of the parts necessary for the processes of life, Aristotle describes the soul in the fifth paragraph as the actuality of a "natural organized body."

In the natural world, what makes something the kind of thing it is — its form — is a principle of growth and movement within the thing itself. With respect to living things, the activities of growth and movement that constitute life spring from something within the plant or animal itself. According to Aristotle, it is the specific nature of this power that determines the species to which something belongs. We might say that a thing belongs to a species in virtue of what it *does* rather than how it looks. For example, there are certain kinds of activity that are natural to horses, and it is the capacity for this activity that makes an animal a horse. The physical characteristics of a species (such as the hooves and skeletal structure of a horse) make this activity possible. But it is the *soul* of the animal that makes this possibility actual.

In the sixth paragraph, Aristotle illustrates his idea by saying that if an axe were a natural thing, its soul would be what makes it an axe. This would be its ability to cut wood. But an axe is not a natural thing because, if it were, it would have the power *in itself* to cut wood. Living things, plants and animals, have the power in themselves to do the kinds of things that make them the things they are: growth, reproduction, perception, movement, and so on. This is their soul.

He then asks us to think of the parts of animals. He says that if an eye were a living thing, sight would be its soul, since sight is what makes an eye what it is. The difference between an eye of a living creature and that of a statue is that one sees and the other doesn't, no matter how "life-like" the statue. Similarly, he says, the general faculty or power of sense — what we might call **sensibility** — is what gives form to the sensitive organs of the body as a whole. In these terms we can think of the soul of a living thing as composed of a hierarchy of forms, each contributing to the powers and abilities that constitute life for that particular species.

Body and soul

At the end of the chapter Aristotle concludes that the soul is inseparable from the body. This is because form cannot exist except as realized in some matter. There cannot be form without matter, any more than there can be matter without form. In a similar vein, he had said in the fifth paragraph that the question whether the body and soul are one is "unnecessary." He explains this point by saying

> It is as though we were to ask whether the wax and its shape are one, or generally the matter of a thing and that of which it is the matter. Unity has many senses (as many as 'is' has), but the proper one is that of actuality.

In the second sentence he means that things exist as separate individuals — as "units" — only insofar as they possess both matter and form.

So, unlike Plato, Aristotle does not believe that the soul can exist independently of the body. The soul is one aspect of a single indivisible whole that is the living creature. And it cannot exist except in the context of the whole. For Aristotle, then, the soul is an essential and integral part of the natural order rather than something that exists as a separate entity from things in the natural world.

However, near the very end of the chapter he qualifies this belief. He says

Yet some [souls] may be separable because they are not the actualities of any body at all.

This seems to allow that in certain instances there may be such a thing as form without matter, and hence pure soul. As we will see later on in this chapter, Aristotle appears to have in mind something like the possibility of "pure intellect."

The faculties of the soul

So far, Aristotle has established the general point that the soul of living things is their form or essence, by which he means that which makes them the kind of thing they are. We have seen that the form of a living thing is that which gives it its ability to perform the activities of life such as growth, reproduction, movement, and perception. According to Aristotle, the various species form a hierarchy according to the nature of their activities. For example, while all species grow and reproduce, not all forms of life possess sensory organs to perceive the world around them. This hierarchy leads Aristotle to distinguish between different divisions or faculties of the soul whereby species can be categorized in accordance with the specific faculties they possess.

All living things have the power to feed themselves, and to reproduce. Hence, all living things have what Aristotle calls a **nutritive** soul, or a nutritive faculty of the soul. In addition to a nutritive faculty, some species have powers of locomotion and perception, which he calls the **sensitive** soul, or the faculty of sensibility. Finally, human beings have what Aristotle terms a **rational** soul, which is the faculty of reason and reflection.

In the remaining chapters of *On the Soul* Aristotle explains how these various faculties operate in nature. This part of the text should be looked upon as a scientific treatise or a textbook on biology. (In fact, it probably served as a textbook for Aristotle's students.) Book II, chapter 7 is devoted to the faculty of visual perception. We will begin there because Aristotle's theory of vision forms a good contrast with later views on the mind.

Colour and the transparent

He starts chapter 7 with a definition. The **visible**, he says, is the object of sight. That is, the visible is what we perceive through sight. He claims that there are two kinds of things that are visible:

1. colour
2. something else to be explained later.

In the second sentence he says that colour "lies upon what is in itself visible." (You can ignore the rest of the sentence.) By this he means colour is what lies on the surface of visible objects.

Read the next sentence carefully. Aristotle says that the nature of colour is "to set in movement what is actually transparent." By 'movement,' he means something broader than change of location. His actual meaning is something more like what we would call change. Understood in this way, the nature of colour is to change what is **transparent**. In the next paragraph he begins to explain what he means by "what is transparent." In English, of course, something is "transparent" when we can see other things through it, and that's what Aristotle means as well. He expresses this by saying that what is transparent is not visible "in itself, but rather owing its visibility to the colour of something else." We don't actually see what is transparent — we see other things through what is transparent. In the next sentence he says that there is a transparent substance in air, water, and other things.

Putting these ideas together we get the following. There is a certain substance in the air or water between the surface of coloured objects and the eye. Colour is by definition something on the surfaces of objects that changes this substance. As a result of this change, colour is made visible to the eye.

Light and vision

Aristotle now explains what light is. It is "the activity of what is transparent *qua* transparent." This is difficult wording, but his point is the following. The transparent substance found in air is either active or inactive. To say that the transparent substance is active means that colour is visible through it, and to say it is inactive is to say that colour is not visible through it. Light is the active state of the substance, and darkness is the inactive state.

He also says that fire excites this substance to activity — in our terms, fire produces light. The reason we can see in the presence of fire in the sun or in a candle is that the fire renders the transparent substance active. We should not think here of light from the fire *travelling through the air* as in our modern theory. Think instead of the transparent medium becoming active in the presence of fire and transmitting colour as a result of this activity.

We can pass over the next few paragraphs to the one beginning, "The following makes the necessity ..." Here he argues for the necessity of a medium (the transparent) between the eye and the object. He says,

> Colour sets in movement what is transparent, e.g. the air, and that, extending continuously from the object of the organ, sets the latter in movement.

In the passage copied from *Sense and Sensibilia* that follows, Aristotle explains that there must be a transparent substance in the eye as well, and this he thinks is water. So the idea is that when the transparent substance in the air and in the eye is active, colour is transmitted to the soul. It is when this substance in the eye becomes active that we experience the colour that is on the object.

Putting all the pieces together, we get the following picture. In the presence of fire, colour on the surface of objects is communicated to the soul as a result of the activity of the transparent substance in air or water and the water in the eye. So according to Aristotle, visual perception is a matter of the soul literally taking on the colours of the things around us. Our visual experience of colour is an event whereby the soul receives the colours of the surrounding environment.

The passive intellect

In chapters 4 and 5 of Book III Aristotle turns his attention to the activity of thinking, which is the product of the faculty of mind or intellect. In chapter 4, he considers what we can call the "passive" mind, and in chapter 5 he considers the "active" mind.

In the second paragraph of chapter 4, he assumes that thinking must be like sense perception. The difference between thinking and sense perception, he believes, lies simply in what is perceived. Each of the senses is responsible for our awareness of a particular quality of objects. Vision is responsible for our awareness of colour, and hearing is responsible for our perception of sound. In each case the quality of the object acts on the sense organ in a way that reproduces the same quality in the soul. The eye transmits colour to the soul, and sound is reproduced in the soul through the ear. In a similar manner, Aristotle says, in thinking, the soul "is acted upon by what is capable of being thought." What he means is that, in the act of thinking, the soul takes on the nature of what it thinks about.

In the next sentence he indicates what it is that is capable of being thought. He says,

> The thinking part of the soul must therefore be, while impassable, capable of receiving the *form* of an object; that is, must be potentially identical in *character* with its object without being the object.

According to Aristotle, then, the mind perceives the form or essence of things in the world. Let's look at this idea carefully.

Forms and the intellect

Recall the difference between form and matter. The form of an object is what makes it the kind of thing it is. Now think about perceiving something, say, a galloping horse. We feel the rush of wind, we see the white colour, and we hear the thundering hooves. Each of these sensations is the perception of a sensible quality: colour, sound, coolness on the skin. But how do we know that it is a *horse* that we perceive? We are not very much aware of perceiving the individual sensible qualities at all — we perceive a horse. How is that possible? That is, how is it that we perceive not just the colour and sound, but also the quality of "horseness" in the object? Aristotle's answer is that there must be a special faculty by which we perceive the *essences* of things, and this he calls the mind. So to think about something is to receive its form or essence in the faculty of mind.

We can see vestiges of Aristotle's theory in modern English. We often talk of being "informed" about something, and of things "impressing" themselves on our mind. The metaphor here is that of the form of something impressing itself on the mind just as a seal is impressed on a blob of warm wax. Along these same lines, Aristotle argues that the mind "can have no nature of its own." His reasoning is that the mind is capable of thinking about any essence whatsoever, and so it cannot have an essence of its own. Just as a piece of warm wax can receive any impression, the mind can take on the form of any object. Compare this with the faculty of vision. The soul is capable of seeing because the eyes have the potential to take on the colour of their object. So the eyes have their own nature, namely, to become coloured. But this also means that in vision we can only perceive colours. As the mind, on the other hand, can think of any form at all, it cannot have any form of its own except a "certain capacity" to take on forms.

Aristotle expresses this another way by saying that before it thinks, the mind "is not actually any real thing." For this reason, he argues, the mind is not "blended" with the body (as the senses are), because that would give it a physical nature like the organs of sense. How this fits with his earlier claim that mind and body are inseparable is unclear. Here we are reminded of the intriguing comment at the end of chapter 1 that some souls "are not the actualities of any body at all."

The active intellect

In chapter 5, Aristotle argues that there must be more to the mind than an ability to take on forms. In the first sentence Aristotle says that for every kind of thing there must be both a "matter" and a "cause." Think again of our statue example from the beginning of the chapter. In order for a statue to exist there must be material (the matter) that is capable of becoming a statue, and there must also be something that causes the material to take on the appropriate form. In this case, the matter might be the marble, and the cause the sculptor.

In the case of vision, we have as matter the faculty of sight in the soul, which is potentially coloured. And what causes the act of vision, whereby the soul takes on the colour of the object, is fire.

The mind as we have described it so far is merely passive in its potential for taking on the forms of its objects. As such it constitutes the matter of thought. So Aristotle's point in chapter 5 of *On the Soul* is that there must be an *active* cause that brings thought about, that plays the role that fire plays in vision. But in this case there is no *external* cause — the mind is, in effect, the cause of its own thinking. So in addition to the passive mind, there must be an active mind that is the cause of thought.

In the second paragraph, then, he says that in addition to mind that becomes all things, there is mind that makes all things. The former is the passive intellect, and the latter is the active intellect.

The next two paragraphs are among the strangest and most controversial in all of Aristotle's writings. Of the active mind he says,

> When separated it is alone just what it is, and this above all is immortal and eternal ... and without this nothing thinks.

It seems that Aristotle is claiming here that the active mind is independent of the body and is immortal. How this is to be understood is not clear. It appears to be an echo of the view expressed at the end of chapter 1 of Book I: that there can be such a thing as pure soul that exists without being realized in matter. But these are murky waters, and I'll leave it to you to puzzle over.

Naturalizing the soul

Aristotle clearly continues certain lines of thought begun by Socrates and Plato. For example, Aristotle's view of the mind is deeply affected by the problem of universals and by the conception of the soul as both the source of life and the seat of the intellect. But Aristotle's theory differs sharply from that of Plato. According to Plato, the soul is part of the realm of the Forms, which are perfect, eternal objects — a realm altogether separate from the natural world that we perceive through the senses. Aristotle, on the other hand, creates a theory wherein the soul is part and parcel of the natural world of material objects and living things. According to his theory, the principles by which the soul operates are the same in general character as the principles that govern rocks, trees, and stars. Even though he speaks of the active intellect as eternal and separate from the body, the operation of the intellect follows the same pattern as the operations of sensory perception and organic activity generally. This forms a sharp contrast with Plato's view, according to which reason and reflection require the mind's removal from the world of ordinary objects.

We can give a label to the changes that Aristotle introduces to thinking about the mind by describing it as a **naturalist** theory. That is, he constructs a theory wherein the soul is an integral part of the natural order of material objects, plants and animals.

One advantage that Aristotle's theory possesses over Plato's is that it resolves the difficulties in combining the conceptions of the soul as both the source of life and the seat of the intellect. Plato understood rational thought to be an activity distinct from, and even in conflict with, the activities of the physical body. But this view makes it hard to understand how the soul can *also* be that which brings life to the body. Within Aristotle's theory there is no such difficulty. According to Aristotle, a creature is alive by virtue of the fact that it is capable of the activities belonging to a particular species. The life of a plant consists of the activities of growth and nutrition as they are realized in the species to which it belongs; and the life of an animal (such as, say, a mollusk or a turtle) consists of these activities plus locomotion and perception. In each case, the soul is the cause of these various activities. Aristotle then conceives of rational thought as the kind of activity that is natural and peculiar to the human species. In this way he considers the human soul to be the cause of reason and reflection in exactly the same way that the soul is the cause of nutrition and locomotion in other species. For Aristotle, then, the activity of the intellect is just one aspect of life as a human being.

The reliability of perception

Another important aspect of Aristotle's theory of the soul is his idea that sensory perception is a direct and reliable link with the world. According to Aristotle, there is a similarity between sensory perception and the action of the intellect in that, in each case, the forms and qualities in the world are reproduced in the soul. Thus in both cases our perceptions reflect the world as it really is. Contrast this with Plato's view. According to Plato, the senses can trigger our recollection of the Forms, but they are not themselves a reliable or direct source of knowledge. The senses provide us with only fleeting and imperfect glimpses of what can really only be understood through the exercise of pure thought.

In the next few chapters, we will see how the invention of modern mathematical physics led one important scientist of the early modern era — René Descartes — to "de-naturalize" the mind. In resolving the difficulties that Aristotle's scientific program encounters, Descartes severed the connection between the mind and the natural world that is found in Aristotle's theories. To see how this development occurred we have to examine the basic ideas behind the rise of modern science in the seventeenth century.

NOTES

1. This point is made by Abraham Edel, *Aristotle and his Philosophy* (Chapel Hill, NC: University of North Carolina Press, 1982), p. 127.

Aristotle
Selections from *On the Soul* and *Sense and Sensibilia*

ON THE SOUL

Book II

1 · Let the foregoing suffice as our account of
the views concerning the soul which have been
handed on by our predecessors; let us now
make as it were a completely fresh start, endeav-
ouring to answer the question, What is soul?
i.e. to formulate the most general possible account of it.

We say that substance is one kind of what
is, and that in several senses: in the sense of
matter or that which in itself is not a this, and
in the sense of form or essence, which is that
precisely in virtue of which a thing is called a
this, and thirdly in the sense of that which is
compounded of both. Now matter is potentiality, form actuality; and actuality is of two
kinds, one as e.g. knowledge, the other as e.g.
reflecting.

Among substances are by general consent
reckoned bodies and especially natural bodies;
for they are the principles of all other bodies.
Of natural bodies some have life in them, others not; by life we mean self-nutrition and
growth and decay. It follows that every natural
body which has life in it is a substance in the
sense of a composite.

Now given that there are bodies of such and
such a kind, viz. having life, the soul cannot be
a body; for the body is the subject or matter,
not what is attributed to it. Hence the soul
must be a substance in the sense of the form of
a natural body having life potentially within it.
But substance is actuality, and thus soul is the
actuality of a body as above characterized. Now
there are two kinds of actuality corresponding
to knowledge and to reflecting. It is obvious

that the soul is an actuality like knowledge; for
both sleeping and waking presuppose the existence of soul, and of these waking corresponds
to reflecting, sleeping to knowledge possessed
but not employed, and knowledge of something
is temporally prior.

That is why the soul is an actuality of the
first kind of a natural body having life potentially in it. The body so described is a body
which is organized. The parts of plants in spite
of their extreme simplicity are organs; e.g. the
leaf serves to shelter the pericarp, the pericarp
to shelter the fruit, while the roots of plants are
analogous to the mouth of animals, both serving for the absorption of food. If, then, we have
to give a general formula applicable to all kinds
of soul, we must describe it as an actuality of
the first kind of a natural organized body. That
is why we can dismiss as unnecessary the question whether the soul and the body are one: it
is as though we were to ask whether the wax
and its shape are one, or generally the matter
of a thing and that of which it is the matter.
Unity has many senses (as many as 'is' has), but
the proper one is that of actuality.

We have now given a general answer to the
question, What is soul? It is substance in the
sense which corresponds to the account of a
thing. That means that it is what it is to be for
a body of the character just assigned. Suppose
that a tool, e.g. an axe, were a *natural* body,
then being an axe would have been its essence,
and so its soul; if this disappeared from it, it
would have ceased to be an axe, except in name.
As it is, it is an axe; for it is not of a body of
that sort that what it is to be, i.e. its account,
is a soul, but of a natural body of a particular
kind, viz. one having in itself the power of set-

ting itself in movement and arresting itself. Next, apply this doctrine in the case of the parts of the living body. Suppose that the eye were an animal—sight would have been its soul, for sight is the substance of the eye which corresponds to the account, the eye being merely the matter of seeing; when seeing is removed the eye is no longer an eye, except in name—no more than the eye of a statue or of a painted figure. We must now extend our consideration from the parts to the whole living body; for what the part is to the part, that the whole faculty of sense is to the whole sensitive body as such.

We must not understand by that which is potentially capable of living what has lost the soul it had, but only what still retains it; but seeds and fruits are bodies which are potentially of that sort. Consequently, while waking is actuality in a sense corresponding to the cutting and the seeing, the soul is actuality in the sense corresponding to sight and the power in the tool; the body corresponds to what is in potentiality; as the pupil *plus* the power of sight constitutes the eye, so the soul *plus* the body constitutes the animal.

From this it is clear that the soul is inseparable from its body, or at any rate that certain parts of it are (if it has parts)—for the actuality of some of them is the actuality of the parts themselves. Yet some may be separable because they are not the actualities of any body at all. Further, we have no light on the problem whether the soul may not be the actuality of its body in the sense in which the sailor is the actuality of the ship.

This must suffice as our sketch or outline of the nature of soul.

• • •

7 · The object of sight is the visible, and what is visible is colour and a certain kind of object which can be described in words but which has no single name; what we mean by the second will be abundantly clear as we proceed. Whatever is visible is colour and colour is what lies upon what is in itself visible; 'in itself' here means not that visibility is involved in the definition of what thus underlies colour, but that that substratum contains in itself the cause of visibility. Every colour has in it the power to set in movement what is actually transparent; that power constitutes its very nature. That is why it is not visible except with the help of light; it is only in light that the colour of a thing is seen. Hence our first task is to explain what light is.

Now there clearly is something which is transparent, and by 'transparent' I mean what is visible, and yet not visible in itself, but rather owing its visibility to the colour *of something else;* of this character are air, water, and many solid bodies. Neither air nor water is transparent because it is air or water; they are transparent because each of them has contained in it a certain substance which is the same in both and is also found in the eternal upper body. Of this substance light is the activity—the activity of what is transparent *qua* transparent; where this power is present, there is also the potentiality of the contrary, viz. darkness. Light is as it were the proper colour of what is transparent, and exists whenever the potentially transparent is excited to actuality by the influence of fire or something resembling 'the uppermost body'; for fire too contains something which is one and the same with the substance in question.

We have now explained what the transparent is and what light is; light is neither fire nor any kind whatsoever of body nor an efflux from any kind of body (if it were, it would again itself be a kind of body)—it is the presence of fire or something resembling fire in what is transparent. It is certainly not a body, for two bodies cannot be present in the same place. The opposite of light is darkness; darkness is the absence from what is transparent of the corresponding positive state above characterized; clearly therefore, light is just the presence of that.

Empedocles (and with him all others who used the same forms of expression) was wrong in speaking of light as 'travelling' or being at a given moment between the earth and its envelope, its movement being unobservable by us; that view is contrary both to the clear evidence of argument and to the observed facts; if the distance traversed were short, the movement might have been unobservable, but where the distance is from extreme East to extreme West, the strain upon our powers of belief is too great.

What is capable of taking on colour is what in itself is colourless, as what can take on sound is what is soundless; what is colourless includes what is transparent and what is invisible or scarcely visible, i.e. what is dark. The latter is the same as what is transparent, when it is potentially, not of course when it is actually transparent; it is the same substance which is now darkness, now light.

Not everything that is visible depends upon light for its visibility. This is only true of the 'proper' colour of things. Some objects of sight which in light are invisible, in darkness stimulate the sense; that is, things that appear fiery or shining. This class of objects has no simple common name, but instances of it are fungi, horns, heads, scales, and eyes of fish. In none of these is what is seen their own proper colour. Why we see these at all is another question. At present what is light colour remains invisible. Its being colour at all means precisely its having in it the power to set in movement what is actually transparent, and the actuality of what is transparent is just light.

The following makes the necessity of a medium clear. If what has colour is placed in immediate contact with the eye, it cannot be seen. Colour sets in movement what is transparent, e.g. the air, and that, extending continuously from the object of the organ, sets the latter in movement. Democritus misrepresents the facts when he expresses the opinion that if the interspace were empty one could distinctly see an ant on the vault of the sky; that is an impossibility. Seeing is due to an affection or change of what has the perceptive faculty, and it cannot be affected by the seen colour itself; it remains that it must be affected by what comes between. Hence it is indispensable that there be *something* in between—if there were nothing, so far from seeing with greater distinctness, we should see nothing at all.

We have now explained the cause why colour cannot be seen otherwise than in light. Fire on the other hand is seen both in darkness and in light; this double possibility follows necessarily from our theory, for it is just fire that makes what is potentially transparent actually transparent.

The same account holds also of sound and smell; if the object of either of these senses is in immediate contact with the organ no sensation is produced. In both cases the object sets in movement only what lies between, and this in turn sets the organ in movement: if what sounds or smells is brought into immediate contact with the organ, no sensation will be produced. The same, in spite of all appearances, applies also to touch and taste; why there is this apparent difference will be clear later. What comes between in the case of sounds is air; the corresponding medium in the case of smell has no name. But, corresponding to what is transparent in the case of colour, there is a quality found both in air and water, which serves as a medium for what has smell; for animals that live in water seem to possess the sense of smell. Men and all other land animals that breathe. perceive smells only when they breathe air in. The explanation of this too will be given later.

• • •

SENSE AND SENSIBILIA

• • •

That without light vision is impossible has been stated elsewhere; but, whether the medium between the eye and its objects is air or light, vision is caused by a process through this medium.

Accordingly, that the inner part of the eye consists of water is easily intelligible, water being transparent.

Now, as vision outwardly is impossible without light, so also it is impossible inwardly. There must, therefore, be some transparent medium within the eye, and, as this is not air, it must be water. The soul or its perceptive part is not situated at the external surface of the eye, but obviously somewhere within: whence the necessity of the interior of the eye being transparent, i.e. capable of admitting light. And that it is so is plain from actual occurrences. It is matter of experience that soldiers wounded in battle by a sword slash on the temple, so inflicted as to sever the passages of the eye, feel a sudden onset of darkness, as if a lamp had gone out; because what is called the pupil, i.e. the transparent, which is a sort of lamp, is then cut off.

• • •

ON THE SOUL

Book III

4 · Turning now to the part of the soul with which the soul knows and (whether this is separable from the others in definition only, or spatially as well) we have to inquire what differentiates this part, and how thinking can take place.

If thinking is like perceiving, it must be either a process in which the soul is acted upon by what is capable of being thought, or a process different from but analogous to that. The thinking part of the soul must therefore be, while impassible, capable of receiving the form of an object; that is, must be potentially identical in character with its object without being the object. Thought must be related to what is thinkable, as sense is to what is sensible.

Therefore, since everything is a possible object of thought, mind in order, as Anaxagoras says, to dominate, that is, to know, must be pure from all admixture; for the co-presence of

what is alien to its nature is a hindrance and a block: it follows that it can have no nature of its own, other than that of having a certain capacity. Thus that in the soul which is called thought (by thought I mean that whereby the soul thinks and judges) is, before it thinks, not actually any real thing. For this reason it cannot reasonably be regarded as blended with the body: if so, it would acquire some quality, e.g. warmth or cold, or even have an organ like the sensitive faculty: as it is, it has none. It was a good idea to call the soul 'the place of forms', though this description holds only of the thinking soul, and even this is the forms only potentially, not actually.

• • •

5 · Since in every class of things, as in nature as a whole, we find two factors involved, a matter which is potentially all the particulars included in the class, a cause which is productive in the sense that it makes them all (the latter standing to the former, as e.g. an art to its material), these distinct elements must likewise be found within the soul.

And in fact thought, as we have described it, is what it is by virtue of becoming all things, while there is another which is what it is by virtue of making all things: this is a sort of positive state like light; for in a sense light makes potential colours into actual colours.

Thought in this sense of it is separable, impassible, unmixed, since it is in its essential nature activity (for always the active is superior to the passive factor, the originating force to the matter).

Actual knowledge is identical with its object: in the individual, potential knowledge is in time prior to actual knowledge, but absolutely it is not prior even in time. It does not sometimes think and sometimes not think. When separated it is alone just what it is, and this above is immortal and eternal (we do not remember because, while this is impossible, passive thought is perishable); and without this nothing thinks.

CHAPTER THREE

The Scientific Revolution

Introduction

In this chapter we introduce a major shift in thinking about the mind, which reached its greatest momentum in the seventeenth century. There were many origins of this change, but I have chosen to focus on one of the central factors: the rise of the modern mathematical sciences. It is in the seventeenth century, through the work of such people as Galileo Galilei, René Descartes, and Isaac Newton, that the mathematical sciences burst into full bloom and in the process replaced many of the earlier ways of thinking about the world — including the ways people thought about the mind. In order to see how modern views of the mind developed, we need to look at the deep changes brought about by the new sciences.

Although it is a common error to oversimplify the philosophy and science of medieval Europe, it is safe to claim that Aristotle was the predominant intellectual influence on the European continent in the middle ages. When Aristotle's work became widely available in Latin, medieval scholars set to work to reconcile Aristotle's theories with the Holy Scriptures and with the doctrines laid down by the Church Fathers. The result of this effort was an extensive science and philosophy based equally on common sense, Aristotelian principles, and Christian faith.

But by the sixteenth century serious problems had become apparent in the Aristotelian system. The reasons for this are numerous and complex, and it is not possible for us to look at them in detail. But to give you an idea, here are a few sketches.

Problems with Aristotle's theories

In the sixteenth century Galileo Galilei challenged the Aristotelian theory of motion with detailed studies of the times and motions of falling bodies. Galileo's careful studies of pendulums and rolling balls demonstrated that Aristotelian theories of motion were inconsistent with the observable facts. Another blow to the Aristotelian worldview was Copernicus' discovery that the earth is in motion around the sun. In Aristotle's system the Earth is at the centre of the cosmos, with the moon, sun, planets and distant stars all revolving around the Earth in concentric circles; his explanations of change and motion in the natural world were built around this cosmological scheme. Once the heliocentric system was adopted, central portions of Aristotle's scientific system fell apart.

Perhaps the most damaging criticism of Aristotle's schema of matter and form was the charge that Aristotle's theories become vacuous when they are applied to complex problems. Critics of the Aristotelian method illustrated this point with the following rhetorical example. Followers of Aristotelian method might explain how a sleeping powder achieves its result by claiming that it possesses "dormative" qualities: that which is potentially asleep becomes actually asleep in the presence of these qualities. This claim is obviously true, but it doesn't help us understand how sleeping powders work. In the same way, an unsympathetic reader could argue that Aristotle's definition of the soul contains a circularity. Aristotle explains the nature of the soul by saying that it is the form of living things. But given the definition of form as that which makes something the kind of thing it is, and the definition of the soul as that which brings life, it seems that Aristotle explains the soul — the source of life — by saying that it is that which brings life to living things. Once again, true but not very helpful.

Teleological explanations

The decline of the Aristotelian system was due not only to problems within that system itself, but also to the increasing success of a new approach to science. The most significant element of this new science was the rejection of Aristotle's explanations of cause and effect.

Aristotle's explanations of change are always given in terms of things taking on forms and qualities. An important feature of these explanations is that they involve things moving *toward* the full realization of the respective forms and qualities. For example, an acorn grows into an oak by moving toward the form of a fully developed tree, and this form is latent in it from the moment it is created. You might compare the process to the building of a house, in which the builders are guided by the blueprint. The idea of the house is present from the outset, and the building of the house is a development toward the physical realization of the plan. The same idea is used in Aristotle's explanation of natural motion. The Earth is "heavy" because its proper place is at the centre of the cosmos, and so without interference it will naturally move toward that location. For the same sort of reason, fire always moves upward toward its natural place in the outer regions.

These kinds of explanations are called **teleological** from the Greek word *telos*, which means "end," "goal," or "purpose." Teleological explanations appeal to an end or final purpose toward which things are directed.

Mechanical explanations

Compare Aristotle's conception of change and motion with our modern ideas. The modern law of inertia tells us that in the absence of any external force an object will maintain a constant state of rest or uniform motion. In this picture, matter is entirely *inert* — it has no natural direction of motion and it doesn't move toward anything from any kind of internal drive. Explanations of motion in our modern physics are in terms of external forces acting on objects that otherwise will remain in their current state. We can call explanations of this sort **mechanical** explanations.

A distinctive feature of the scientific revolution of the seventeenth century is that all forms of teleological explanation were rejected in favour of a search for mechanical explanations. Part of the motivation behind this change was the alleged vacuity of Aristotelian explanations. It is of no value to explain change in terms of goals and purposes, critics of Aristotle maintained, if the goal itself is simply a redescription of the change. For instance, it doesn't help in understanding why an object falls to the ground to be told that it's the kind of thing that naturally moves in that direction. The solution, the critics argued, was to explain all motion and change by appeal to mechanical causes.

Mathematical laws

The other distinctive feature of the new science is an emphasis on mathematics as a tool for describing natural laws. By contrast, Aristotle's system is entirely **qualitative**. The basic elements of Aristotle's science are earth, fire, air, and water. These elements are described in terms of four basic qualities (hot, cold, dry, and wet) and in terms of their natural motion. Nowhere in this system do mathematical relations play any part. Medieval scientists took mathematics to be a curiosity, an interesting pastime, but not of any real value in understanding the world.

A distinctive aspect of the new science, however, is the formulation of mathematical laws. Scientists like Galileo and Newton replaced the qualitative descriptions of the world with measurements of time, distance, weight, and so on. The measurements were used to formulate and test mathematical laws. It is this use of mathematical laws relating measurable quantities that distinguishes the new science from medieval theories.

Platonism

Part of the move towards mathematical descriptions of nature involved a revival of interest in Plato. The text of Plato most familiar to medieval scholars was a book called *The Timaeus*. In this book Plato is heavily influenced by the followers of the mathematician, Pythagoras. Following ideas developed by the Pythagoreans, Plato explained the observable characteristics of matter in terms of hidden geometrical properties, a view now called "geometrical atomism." In *The Timaeus* each of the four elements of Greek science — earth, water, air, and fire — is associated with one of the five regular solids: the tetrahedron, octahedron, icosahedron, cube, and dodecahedron. (The fifth solid Plato associated with the cosmos as a whole.) The properties of these figures could then be used to explain facts about the observable behaviour of matter, such as the fact that water evaporates while earth does not. According to *The Timaeus*, the divine creator of the world used mathematical principles to construct a cosmos of ultimate beauty and rational harmony.

As Aristotelian science became more rigid and unworkable in the late middle ages, many scholars returned to the Platonic notion that the world can only be understood by discovering its hidden mathematical and divine nature. A perfect example of this development is the construction of the heliocentric theory of the planetary system. Copernicus wrote of his heliocentric theory, "We find then in this arrangement an admirable harmony of the world, and a dependable, harmonious interconnection of the motion and size of the paths, such as otherwise cannot be discovered." Kepler's subsequent discoveries of the elliptical shape of the planetary orbits and the laws of planetary motion were driven by a mystical search for divine order and mathematical harmony.

Splitting perception from reality

The new mathematical sciences dealt a direct blow to the Aristotelian confidence in the reliability of perception. Mathematical laws are *idealizations* of what we actually observe.[1] The acceptance of the new mathematical laws did not arise from the fact that they can be directly observed, but from the fact that they yielded more accurate predictions than any other laws.

Moreover, within the new science all of nature was to be explained in terms of the mathematical relations between inert particles of matter. Hence the only qualities of matter that made their way into the new physics were those that could be assigned numerical values: size, shape, motion, and mass. Other qualities, such as colour, warmth, and wetness, were either explained in terms of the size, shape, motion, and mass of inert particles or were rejected as not really belonging to nature at all.

The new scientists concluded from this that the real qualities of objects are not necessarily the ones we perceive them to have. The appearances of things, they argued, are not a direct, straightforward guide to the nature of the real world. We need to distinguish carefully between our perceptions and the real nature of the world around us — between how things look and how they really are. Accordingly, the new scientists set about unravelling Aristotle's account of the relation between the perceiving mind and the physical world to show that the real qualities of objects are not like the sensations of colour, warmth, and taste that we receive from them.

Galileo's *Assayer*

We begin with a selection from a book by Galileo called *The Assayer*. Galileo Galilei was born in 1564 at Pisa and died in 1642, the year of Newton's birth. He was a teacher of mathematics and physics at the universities of Pisa and Padua. At the end of his life he served in Florence as chief mathematician of the Duke of Tuscany. In his early career he was a respected teacher of Aristotle, but at Padua he began work on his new mathematical physics. He came under increasing criticism by the Aristotelians, and in 1633 he was imprisoned by the Inquisition for teaching Copernicus' heliocentric theory. The Aristotelians said that as he became a better mathematician he became a worse physicist, because he moved away from descriptions of the world as it appears in simple observations, and focussed instead on abstract and ideal mathematical descriptions of times and motions.

In our first selection from *The Assayer* Galileo is defending his claim that "motion is the cause of heat." Galileo argues that in order to defend his claim, he needs to correct the mistaken view that the sensation of heat, *as we experience it*, is a real quality residing in the objects that warm us.

The argument from conceivability

Galileo's first argument is based on the claim that only certain qualities are recognized as being essential to the existence of physical objects. He argues that we cannot conceive of material objects existing at all without thinking of them as having a shape, a size, a position, and a state of motion or rest.

> Now I say whenever I conceive any material or corporeal substance, I immediately feel the need to think of it as bounded, as having this or that shape; as being large or small ... as being in motion or at rest; as touching or not touching some other body; and as being one in number, or few, or many.

From this he concludes that these are essential qualities of matter that are part of its real nature and not merely reflections of our perceptions. The same is not true, he maintains, of tastes, odours, and colours. We can conceive of material objects lacking any one of these. He concludes from this that the latter qualities "are no more than mere names," and that they exist "only in the consciousness," not in the objects themselves. If there were no living creatures possessing such consciousness, he claims, these qualities would not exist at all.

According to Aristotle, the qualities of matter are those it appears to have in our immediate perception of it. A physical object does not appear to have merely a size, shape, and location. We are also aware of qualities such as warmth, colour, and odour, and these appear to be real qualities of physical things. Galileo's claim is that we should not trust this perception. In a move reminiscent of Plato, Galileo seems to be asking us to turn our attention away from the immediate appearances of things and focus instead on what we can *conceive in our minds* as essential to the existence of matter.

The argument from analogy

Galileo then offers a second argument, this time drawing an analogy between qualities that we mistakenly attribute to matter and a quality that we know exists only in our own minds. He compares the sensations of taste, odour, and colour with the sensation of tickling. When a hand or feather is run lightly over our body we feel a tickling sensation, but everyone agrees that the tickling "belongs to us, and not the hand." If we run our hand over a statue, no one believes that this motion produces the same tickling. Hence, the tickling is not a quality of the hand or the feather. It exists solely in the consciousness of the person tickled. He argues that the sensations of touch, taste, smell, and sound have the same nature as tickling: each is a sensation produced in us by the action of external objects, but not existing as a real quality in the objects themselves.

In the next page or two he suggests ways in which the motion of particles of matter might produce the sensations of tastes, odours, and sounds. Particles that possess a certain kind of motion may be able to enter into the tiny passages of the tongue and nostrils, and in so doing stimulate in the mind the sensations of taste and fragrance. Sensations of sound are produced, he suggests, by the motion of air particles causing a vibration of the eardrum. Differences in the vibration of the eardrum cause differences in the sensation of sound in the mind. In each case, all that exists in the physical environment is the motion of minute particles.

From these explanations Galileo draws the conclusion that the only qualities that really exist in material objects are the sizes, shapes, and motions of the particles that cause the sensations. The tastes, odours, and sounds that we experience are merely sensations in our mind, and so do not exist outside our consciousness. You might be thinking at this moment of the old saw, "If a tree falls in the forest, and no one is there to hear it, is there a sound?" Galileo's answer would be "No." There would be a motion of air particles produced by the tree falling but no quality of sound such as exists in our experience.

He concludes that the same can be said of heat as can be said of sound and taste. Heat, he claims, is a sensation in the mind produced by the rapid motion of tiny particles on our skin. Just as the motion of air particles vibrating the eardrum produces a sensation of sound, the rapid motion of particles on the skin produces in us a sensation of warmth. Remove the person experiencing that sensation and there is no quality of warmth.

René Descartes

Galileo's way of expressing this conclusion gives the appearance that in his view there is no such thing as colour, taste, heat, or odour in physical objects. But this is not the best way of understanding the point. A better description is found in arguments offered by another important figure in the new science, René Descartes.

Descartes was born in France in 1596. He was equal parts scientist, mathematician, and philosopher, and had a profound influence in all three disciplines. As a young man, Descartes' interest in physics and mathematics was stimulated by his friendship with the scientist Isaac Beekman. The first problem he worked on was the law of falling bodies, the same problem that exercised Galileo. After Galileo's condemnation by the Inquisition in 1633 Descartes suppressed his own scientific work, *The World*, and turned his attention to philosophical issues. In 1649 he accepted an invitation to serve as tutor to Queen Christina of Sweden, and he died there the next year of pneumonia.

Our first reading from Descartes is chapter 1 of *The World*. Here Descartes defends a view similar to the one advanced by Galileo in the previous reading, applied in this case to the nature of light. His objective is to show that "there may be a difference between the sensation we have of light ... and what it is in the objects that produces this sensation within us."

Qualities and sensations

Descartes first prepares the ground by distinguishing between two different things, both of which we associate with the word 'light.' The first is "the sensation we have of light" and the second is "what it is in the objects that produces this sensation within us." This distinction is straightforward, and in a sense Aristotle would accept it. There is something in the physical environment that we call light. In order for us to perceive this light, it must produce some effect in our mind. Descartes calls this effect a **sensation**.[2] So there are two distinct items: (1) the quality of light in the physical environment, and (2) the sensation in our mind.[3]

Aristotle would have no objection to the existence of both the sensation in the mind (although he wouldn't have called it that) and the quality of the object that causes that sensation. But beyond this Descartes and Aristotle part company. The position Descartes says he wants to oppose is the assumption that

> the ideas [or sensations] we have in our minds are wholly *similar* to the objects from which they proceed.

This is the very assumption upon which Aristotle's link between mind and nature is based. According to Aristotle, the qualities in the mind by which we perceive the world are identical to the qualities of the things around us. As we saw in the last chapter, Aristotle explains our perception of colour by postulating that the action of light produces the same colour in the eye as that in the object. Descartes' point in distinguishing between sensations and qualities of objects is to argue that there need not be any such identity. Sensations in the mind need not be the same as what produces them.

Descartes' arguments from analogy

Descartes bases his conclusion on a series of analogies. The first analogy is between the sensation of light and words in a language. Words, he says, make us think of their objects, even though they do not resemble them. Think, for example, of the word 'dog.' When someone utters this word, the sound brings to mind a certain kind of animal. Yet the sound bears no resemblance to that animal in any way. Descartes claims that there is no reason to reject the possibility that light is like words in this way. That is, it is something in nature that produces an idea or sensation in our minds, although it has no resemblance to that sensation at all.

His next comparison is with the nature of sound. He points out that, as sounds are produced by motions in the air, if sounds produced sensations that resembled their causes, we would have sensations of air motions rather than the sounds that we hear. But there is no similarity between our sensation of sound and the action of air motions. Different motions produce different sensations, but beyond this correlation there is no resemblance between the two. In the same way, Descartes claims, we should expect no similarity between the sensation of light and whatever it is that produces it.

He follows this argument with a version of Galileo's tickling analogy. The sensation of tickling, Descartes claims, shows that there is no similarity between actions that occur on our skin and the events in the mind that they produce. He supports this point with another example. He tells the story of a soldier who believes he is wounded in battle although the actual cause of his sensation is a buckle under his armour. If the sense of touch produced sensations that are identical to their causes, such confusion couldn't occur.

He concludes that there is nothing in the perception of light that would lead us to suppose it is different in nature from sounds or sensations of touch: the sensation of light produced in our minds may have no resemblance to the light in the external world that causes it. Thus the real nature of light is open to question and cannot be directly determined from the qualities of our sensations.

Resemblance

Notice the difference between Descartes' conclusion and Galileo's. According to Galileo, qualities such as taste, odour, and heat do not exist in the object. (To that list we can add colour, sound, and light.) But this isn't a very perspicuous way of making the point. For there is something in the physical environment that produces our sensations, which Galileo and Descartes claim is the different motions of particles; and we do use the words 'taste,' 'colour,' and so on to refer to them. Descartes' conclusion is a bit clearer than Galileo's. He does not deny that there are some qualities in the physical world that we call taste, colour, and light. Descartes' position is simply that there need be no *similarity* between the real qualities in the physical world and our sensations of them. Another way he makes the point is by the observation that there is nothing in the real quality that *resembles* the sensation that it produces.

Seen in terms of resemblance or similarity, the idea that Descartes and Galileo are advancing can be put in the following way: there is nothing in physical objects similar to the sensations of colour, taste, odour, and warmth. On the other hand, there is something in physical objects that resembles our sensations or ideas of shape, size, and motion. We want to distinguish, then, between two kinds of qualities that we attribute to objects: those that resemble our sensations of them and those that don't.

Qualities in the world and sensations in the mind

Galileo and Descartes take the view that the physical world is composed entirely of particles that possess no qualities except size, shape, solidity and motion. All other qualities of objects — warmth, light, colour, taste, odour, and sound — are merely certain shapes and motions of these minute particles, which strike our sense organs and produce particular effects in the mind.

This position is expressed in a comment in the second selection from Descartes, drawn from a book entitled *Principles of Philosophy*. At the end of Part Four, Section 198, Descartes makes the following remark:

In view of all this we have every reason to conclude that the properties in external objects to which we apply the terms light, colour,
smell, taste, sound, heat and cold ... are, so far as we can see, simply
various dispositions in those objects which make them able to set up
various kinds of motions in our nerves which are required to produce the various sensations in our soul.

What we call colour or sound in the physical world, then, is nothing more
than the motion of various minute particles. The characteristics of colours,
odours, and tastes with which we are familiar — what colours *look like* to us,
and what sounds *sound like* to us — are merely products of our own consciousness, bearing no resemblance to anything in the physical world.[4]

Descartes' theory of colour perception

In order to get a clearer grasp of just how the ideas advanced by the new
scientists differ from those of Aristotle, let's look briefly at Descartes' explanation of colour perception. According to Descartes, all matter is composed
solely of minute particles, variously shaped and in constant motion. The particles of air are smooth and spherical, and it is the pressure exerted on the
retina of the eye by these particles that causes our sensations of light. Experiments with prisms show us that colour is an attribute of light. As the only
qualities that the particles of light possess are their size, shape, and motion,
the different colours in light must be produced by some differences in one of
these three qualities. Descartes had reason to believe that all air particles are
the same size and spherical shape, so colour must be a product of their motion. His suggestion is as follows.

Given their spherical shape, air particles will spin, and because they are
in contact with one another, the rotation of one particle will affect the rotation of its neighbours. When light particles reflect from opaque surfaces or
pass through the surface of water or glass, their spin is affected by the angle
at which they strike the surface. It follows that light particles reflecting off
the surfaces of objects and striking the retina will have different rates of rotation. These differences in rotation rates are communicated through the particles of the nerves to the brain, where each different rate of rotation produces
a different sensation of colour.

According to Descartes, then, colour as it exists in the physical world consists entirely of differences in the rotations of minute air particles. These particles themselves have no colour; their only qualities are their shape, size, and
motion. But colour *as it exists in the mind* is a sensation that appears to us in
the various hues of red, blue, green, and so on. These two — colour in the
world and colour in the mind — are completely different.

Notice the contrast between Descartes' theory of colour perception and Aristotle's theory sketched in the last chapter. According to Aristotle, the colour that is produced in the soul is the same quality as the colour in the object that produces it. Colour perception is thus made possible by the affinity between us and the things that surround us. This affinity between the soul and the world is abandoned by Descartes.

While Descartes' theory of light has been superseded by more sophisticated theories, the gap between the qualities of our sensations and the qualities we attribute to the world has not altered. We now explain light and colour in terms of photons and the biochemistry of retinal cells. But it is still possible to argue in the manner of Descartes and Galileo that there is no resemblance between the properties of photons and retinal cells and our conscious experience of colour.

Explaining the facts about perception

The central idea in Descartes' explanation of colour is that each difference in the colour of objects corresponds to a difference in the motion of particles. From this general idea Descartes draws the conclusion that the shapes and motions of minute particles are all that is needed to explain the facts of perception. As long as each sensation is correlated with a specific motion in the nerve fibres and we can show how such a motion is produced by motions generated in the sensory organs by physical objects, we can explain all we need to in understanding sense perception.

This point is made by Galileo in *The Assayer*. After giving his descriptions of how taste, odour, and sound can be produced by the shapes and motions of particles, Galileo makes the following remark:

> To excite in us tastes, odours, and sounds I believe that *nothing is required* in external bodies except shapes, numbers, and slow or rapid movements.

Similarly, in the selection from *Principles of Philosophy* quoted earlier, Descartes says,

> ... we know that the nature of our soul is such that different local motions *are quite sufficient* to produce all the sensations in the soul.

By contrast, Descartes argues, the Aristotelian theory cannot explain the facts of perception. Just before the passage quoted above, he points out that different kinds of motions can cause sensations of light, sound, and heat. For example, pushing the eyeball from the side with your finger will produce a sensation of colour. This is easy to explain, he says, if the sensations are caused by motions in the nerves, for we know that motions can cause other motions. Then he says,

> But there is no way of understanding how [size, shape and motion] can produce something else whose nature is quite different from their own — like the substantial forms and real qualities which many philosophers suppose to inhere in things; and we cannot understand how these qualities or forms could have the power subsequently to produce local motions in other bodies.

The idea here is that Aristotelian science cannot explain how sensations of colour and sound can be caused by motion. This is reminiscent of the criticism of Aristotelian science described at the beginning of the chapter: the Aristotelian system of forms and qualities often fails to provide the explanations we seek. Explaining our perception of the world in terms of the soul's potential to take on the forms and qualities of things around us still leaves the question of *how* this takes place.

The scientific worldview

We have been led to the following conclusion. The basis for the claim that our sensations of colour, warmth, taste, and so on have no resemblance to real qualities in the world is the assertion that the qualities of size, shape, and motion are sufficient by themselves to explain perception. That is, the only qualities we *need* to suppose exist in the real world are the mathematical qualities. Given these qualities, we can explain all of the facts of perception. The rejection of the Aristotelian affinity between the perceptions of the soul and the nature of the world is thus a result of the confidence in mechanical explanations of perception.

This view is part of the general belief that the mechanical sciences are sufficient for explaining all natural phenomena. For instance, we find in *The Assayer* the following statement from Galileo that without mathematics there can be no understanding of the natural world:

> Philosophy is written in this grand book, the universe, which stands continually open to our gaze. But the book cannot be understood unless one first learns to comprehend the language and read the letters in which it is composed. It is written in the language of mathematics, and its characters are triangles, circles, and other geometrical figures without which it is humanly impossible to understand a single word of it; without these, one wanders about in a dark labyrinth.

The successes of the new science in discovering mathematical laws led to the confident expectation that in time everything would be explained in these terms. This confidence is expressed in the beginning of the third selection from Descartes, *Principles of Philosophy*, Part Two, section 64.

> The only principles which I accept, or require, in physics are those of geometry and pure mathematics; these principles explain all natural phenomena, and enable us to provide quite certain demonstrations regarding them.

The problem of perception

The successes of the mechanical sciences have done much to vindicate the confidence of Galileo and Descartes. But in the specific case of perception, there is also something misleading in the claim that mechanical explanations are sufficient to explain all of the facts.

When Descartes and the others say that the motion of particles is sufficient to explain the facts about perception, what they mean is something like the following. For each distinct sensation produced in the mind, it is possible to identify a particle motion that can produce that sensation. Look, however, at Descartes' criticism of the Aristotelian theory. As we saw earlier, his complaint is that we cannot understand how motion can produce anything but other motions. Yet this same criticism can be made of the mechanical explanation. According to Descartes and the others, there is no similarity between our sensations and the motions in the physical world that produce them. They must claim this in order to maintain that the only real qualities of objects are size, shape, and motion. But, in that case, the motions produce sensations that are completely different in nature from their causes. And this is precisely what Descartes rejects in the Aristotelian theory. The question that remains unanswered in the mechanical explanation is how particle motions can cause sensations, given that the two are completely unlike.

The problem is this. There are certain aspects of perception that are not explained by Aristotle's claim that qualities in the world and sensations in the soul are identical. Descartes provides a number of examples in Part Four, Section 198, of *Principles of Philosophy*. He says, for instance,

> If someone is struck in the eye, so that the vibration of the blow reaches the retina, this will cause him to see many sparks of flashing light, yet the light is not outside his eye. And if someone puts a finger in his ear he will hear a throbbing hum which comes simply from the movement of air trapped in the ear.

But, at the same time, Aristotle's theory does render the connection between the soul and the natural world comprehensible: if the qualities of each are the same, it is easy to see how one causes the other. The mechanical view solves the problem of locating a distinct cause for each sensation. What it doesn't do is explain the connection between the sensations and their putative causes.

The larger question

The advantage enjoyed by Aristotle's theory is that soul and nature have a natural affinity. This makes the connection between our thoughts and sensations and the external world easy to explain. By eliminating all but the mechanical qualities from the physical world, the new science is able to construct explanations of many natural phenomena that Aristotle's theory cannot account for. However, one phenomenon it does not provide an explanation for is the connection between mind and body. How are things in the world related as cause and effect to the states and activities of the mind?

The bigger question that begs an answer in the mechanical philosophy is to explain what the mind is in general terms. We are told that particle motions cause sensations, and that sensations are not like their causes. But what *are* sensations? The attributes of matter are the mechanical qualities of size, shape and motion, mass, and so on. But what are the attributes of mind? What definition of the soul (or, in modern terms, the mind) can be provided by the new sciences? Descartes and others of the new philosophy were aware of these questions and debated them at length. In the next three chapters we look at Descartes' answers to these questions, and the reception they received.

NOTES

1 For example, in order to obtain measurements consistent with Newton's law of motion, $F = ma$, we have to discount the effects of friction.

2 Descartes sometimes uses the word 'sensation' and sometimes the word 'idea' in this paragraph and elsewhere. We can safely ignore any difference between these two in reading this passage.

3 Notice that if we apply the same distinction to the question about the tree in the forest, we can see what's wrong with the question. When we hear a tree fall in the forest, there are two things that we designate by the word 'sound.' One is the movement of the air caused by the tree falling. The other is the sensation in the mind that this movement produces. If no one is in the forest there is no sensation of sound, but there are nonetheless the air motions that would produce that sensation in a sentient creature. The question is silly because it is ambiguous — you don't know which of the two items you're being asked about.

4 The person who developed this view most carefully and fully is John Locke. Locke distinguished between what he called *primary qualities*, such as size, shape and motion, which resemble the sensations we have of them, and *secondary qualities*, like colour and sound, which consist of nothing more than motions of tiny particles that produce sensations in the mind.

Galileo Galilei
Selections from *The Assayer*

On the Senses

• • •

It now remains for me to tell Your Excellency, as I promised, some thoughts of mine about the proposition "motion is the cause of heat," and to show in what sense this may be true. But first I must consider what it is that we call heat, as I suspect that people in general have a concept of this which is very remote from the truth. For they believe that heat is a real phenomenon, or property, or quality, which actually resides in the material by which we feel ourselves warmed. Now I say that whenever I conceive any material or corporeal substance, I immediately feel the need to think of it as bounded, and as having this or that shape; as being large or small in relation to other things, and in some specific place at any given time; as being in motion or at rest; as touching or not touching some other body; and as being one in number, or few, or many. From these conditions I cannot separate such a substance by any stretch of my imagination. But that it must be white or red, bitter or sweet, noisy or silent, and of sweet or foul odor, my mind does not feel compelled to bring in as necessary accompaniments. Without the senses as our guides, reason or imagination unaided would probably never arrive at qualities like these. I think that tastes, odors, colors, and so on are no more than mere names so far as the object in which we place them is concerned, and that they reside only in the consciousness. Hence if the living creature were removed, all these qualities would be wiped away and annihilated. But since we have imposed upon them special names, distinct from those of the other and real qualities mentioned previously, we wish to believe that they really exist as actually different from those.

I may be able to make my notion clearer by means of some examples. I move my hand first over a marble statue and then over a living man. As to the effect flowing from my hand, this is the same with regard to both objects and my hand; it consists of the primary phenomena of motion and touch, for which we have no further names. But the live body which receives these operations feels different sensations according to the various places touched. When touched upon the soles of the feet, for example, or under the knee or armpit, it feels in addition to the common sensation of touch a sensation on which we have imposed a special name, "tickling." This sensation belongs to us and not to the hand. Anyone would make a serious error if he said that the hand, in addition to the properties of moving and touching, possessed another faculty of "tickling," as if tickling were a phenomenon that resided in the hand that tickled. A piece of paper or a feather drawn lightly over any part of our bodies performs intrinsically the same operations of moving and touching, but by touching the eye, the nose, or the upper lip it excites in us an almost intolerable titillation, even though elsewhere it is scarcely felt. This titillation belongs entirely to us and not to the feather; if the live and sensitive body were removed it would remain no more than a mere word. I believe that no more solid an existence belongs to many qualities which we have come to attribute to physical bodies—tastes, odors, colors, and many more.

A body which is solid and, so to speak, quite material, when moved in contact with any part of my person produces in me the sensation we call touch. This, though it exists over my entire body, seems to reside principally in the palms of the hands and in the finger tips, by whose means we sense the most minute differences in texture that are not easily distinguished by other parts of our bodies. Some of these sensations are more pleasant to us than others.... The sense of touch is more material than the other senses; and, as it arises from the solidity of matter, it seems to be related to the earthly element.

Perhaps the origin of two other senses lies in the fact that there are bodies which constantly dissolve into minute particles, some of which are heavier than air and descend, while others are lighter and rise up. The former may strike upon a certain part of our bodies that is much more sensitive than the skin, which does not feel the invasion of such subtle matter. This is the upper surface of the tongue; here the tiny particles are received, and mixing with and penetrating its moisture, they give rise to tastes, which are sweet or unsavory according to the various shapes, numbers, and speeds of the particles. And those minute particles which rise up may enter by our nostrils and strike upon some small protuberances which are the instrument of smelling; here likewise their touch and passage is received to our like or dislike according as they have this or that shape, are fast or slow, and are numerous or few. The tongue and nasal passages are providently arranged for these things, as the one extends from below to receive descending particles, and the other is adapted to those which ascend. Perhaps the excitation of tastes may be given a certain analogy to fluids, which descend through air, and odors to fires, which ascend.

Then there remains the air itself, an element available for sounds, which come to us indifferently from below, above, and all sides—for we reside in the air and its movements displace it equally in all directions. The location of the ear is most fittingly accommodated to all positions in space. Sounds are made and heard by us when the air—without any special property of "sonority" or "transonority"—is ruffled by a rapid tremor into very minute waves and moves certain cartilages of a tympanum in our ear. External means capable of thus ruffling the air are very numerous, but for the most part they may be reduced to the trembling of some body which pushes the air and disturbs it. Waves are propagated very rapidly in this way, and high tones are produced by frequent waves and low tones by sparse ones.

To excite in us tastes, odors, and sounds I believe that nothing is required in external bodies except shapes, numbers, and slow or rapid movements. I think that if ears, tongues, and noses were removed, shapes and numbers and motions would remain, but not odors or tastes or sounds. The latter, I believe, are nothing more than names when separated from living beings, just as tickling and titillation are nothing but names in the absence of such things as noses and armpits. And, as these four senses are related to the four elements, so I believe that vision, the sense eminent above all others in the proportion of the finite to the infinite, the temporal to the instantaneous, the quantitative to the indivisible, the illuminated to the obscure— that vision, I say, is related to light itself. But of this sensation and the things pertaining to it I pretend to understand but little; and since even a long time would not suffice to explain that trifle, or even to hint at an explanation, I pass this over in silence.

Having shown that many sensations which are supposed to be qualities residing in external objects have no real existence save in us, and outside ourselves are mere names, I now say that I am inclined to believe heat to be of this character. Those materials which produce heat in us and make us feel warmth, which are known by the general name of "fire," would then be a multitude of minute particles having certain shapes and moving with certain velocities. Meeting with our bodies, they penetrate by means of their extreme subtlety, and their touch as felt by us when they pass through our substance is the sensation we call "heat." This is pleasant or unpleasant according to the greater or smaller speed of these particles as they go pricking and penetrating; pleasant when this assists our necessary transpiration, and obnoxious when it causes too great a separation and dissolution of our substance. The operation of fire by means of its particles is merely that in moving it penetrates all bodies, causing their speedy or slow dissolution in proportion to the number and velocity of the fire-corpuscles and the density or tenuity of the bodies. Many materials are such that in their decomposition the greater part of them passes over into additional tiny corpuscles, and this dissolution continues so long as these continue to meet with further matter capable of being so resolved. I do not believe that in addition to shape, number, motion, penetration, and touch there is any other quality in fire corresponding to "heat"; this belongs so intimately to us that when the live body is taken away, heat becomes no more than a simple name....

Since the presence of fire-corpuscles alone does not suffice to excite heat, but their motion is needed also, it seems to me that one may very reasonably say that motion is the cause of heat.... But I hold it to be silly to accept that proposition in the ordinary way, as a stone or piece of iron or a stick must heat up when moved. The rubbing together and friction of two hard bodies, either by resolving their parts into very subtle flying particles or by opening an exit for the tiny fire-corpuscles within, ultimately sets these in motion; and when they meet our bodies and penetrate them, our conscious mind feels those pleasant or unpleasant sensations which we have named heat, burning, and scalding. And perhaps when such attrition stops at or is confined to the smallest quanta, their motion is temporal and their action calorific only; but when their ultimate and highest resolution into truly indivisible atoms is arrived at, light is created. This may have an instantaneous motion, or rather an instantaneous expansion and diffusion, rendering it capable of

occupying immense spaces by its—I know not whether to say its subtlety, its rarity, its immateriality, or some other property which differs from all these and is nameless.

• • •

On mathematics and nature

• • •

In Sarsi I seem to discern the firm belief that in philosophizing one must support oneself upon the opinion of some celebrated author, as if our minds ought to remain completely sterile and barren unless wedded to the reasoning of some other person. Possibly he thinks that philosophy is a book of fiction by some writer, like the *Iliad* or *Orlando Furioso*, productions in which the least important thing is whether what is written there is true. Well, Sarsi, that is not how matters stand. Philosophy is written in this grand book, the universe, which stands continually open to our gaze. But the book cannot be understood unless one first learns to comprehend the language and read the letters in which it is composed. It is written in the language of mathematics, and its characters are triangles, circles, and other geometric figures without which it is humanly impossible to understand a single word of it; without these, one wanders about in a dark labyrinth.

• • •

René Descartes
Selections from *The World or Treatise on Light*

Chapter I. The difference between our sensations and the things that produce them

The subject I propose to deal with in this treatise is light, and the first point I want to draw to your attention is that there may be a difference between the sensation we have of light (i.e. the idea of light which is formed in our imagination by the mediation of our eyes) and what it is in the objects that produces this sensation within us (i.e. what it is in a flame or the sun that we call by the name 'light'). For although everyone is commonly convinced that the ideas we have in our mind are wholly similar to the objects from which they proceed, nevertheless I cannot see any reason which assures us that this is so. On the contrary, I note many observations which should make us doubt it.

Words, as you well know, bear no resemblance to the things they signify, and yet they make us think of these things, frequently even without our paying attention to the sound of the words or to their syllables. Thus it may happen that we hear an utterance whose meaning we understand perfectly well, but afterwards we cannot say in what language it was spoken. Now if words, which signify nothing except by human convention, suffice to make us think of things to which they bear no resemblance, then why could nature not also have established some sign which would make us have the sensation of light, even if the sign contained nothing in itself which is similar to this sensation? Is it not thus that nature has established laughter and tears, to make us read joy and sadness on the faces of men?

But perhaps you will say that our ears really cause us to perceive only the sound of the words, and our eyes only the countenance of the person who is laughing or weeping, and that it is our mind which, recollecting what the words and the countenance signify, represents their meaning to us at the same time. I could reply that by the same token it is our mind which represents to us the idea of light each time our eye is affected by the action which signifies it. But rather than waste time debating the question, I prefer to bring forward another example.

Suppose we hear only the sound of some words, without attending to their meaning. Do you think the idea of this sound, as it is formed in our mind, is anything like the object which is its cause? A man opens his mouth, moves his tongue, and breathes out: I do not see anything in these actions which is not very different from the idea of the sound which they make us imagine. Most philosophers maintain that sound is nothing but a certain vibration of air which strikes our ears. Thus, if the sense of hearing transmitted to our mind the true image of its object then, instead of making us conceive the sound, it would have to make us conceive the motion of the parts of the air which is then vibrating against our ears. But not everyone will wish to believe what the philosophers say, and so I shall bring forward yet another example.

Of all our senses, touch is the one considered the least deceptive and most certain. Thus, if I show you that even touch makes us conceive many ideas which bear no resemblance to the objects which produce them, I do not think you should find it strange if I say that sight can do likewise. Now, everyone knows that the ideas of tickling and of pain, which are formed in our mind on the occasion of our being touched by external bodies, bear no resemblance to these bodies. Suppose we pass a feather gently over the lips of a child who is falling asleep, and he feels himself being tickled. Do you think the idea of tickling which he conceives resembles anything present in this feather? A soldier returns from battle; in the heat of combat he might have been wounded without being aware of it. But now, as he begins to cool off, he feels pain and believes himself wounded. We call a surgeon, who examines the soldier after we remove his armour, and we find in the end that what he was feeling was nothing but a buckle or strap caught under his armour, which was pressing on him and causing his discomfort. If his sense of touch, in making him feel this strap, had imprinted an image of it in his mind, there would have been no need for a surgeon to inform him of what he was feeling.

Now, I see no reason which compels us to believe that what it is in objects that gives rise to the sensation of light is any more like this sensation than the actions of a feather and a strap are like a tickling sensation and pain. And yet I have not brought up these examples to make you believe categorically that the light in the objects is something different from what it is in our eyes. I merely wanted you to suspect that there might be a difference, so as to keep you from assuming the opposite, and to make you better able to help me in examining the matter further.

• • •

René Descartes
Selections from *Principles of Philosophy*

Part Four

198. *By means of our senses we apprehend nothing in external objects beyond their shapes, sizes and motions.*

Moreover, we observe no differences between the various nerves which would support the view that different nerves allow different things to be transmitted to the brain from the external sense organs; indeed, we are not entitled to say that anything reaches the brain except for the local motion of the nerves themselves. And we see that this local motion produces not only sensations of pain and pleasure but also those of light and sound. If someone is struck in the eye, so that the vibration of the blow reaches the retina, this will cause him to see many sparks of flashing light, yet the light is not outside his eye. And if someone puts a finger in his ear he will hear a throbbing hum which comes simply from the movement of air trapped in the ear. Finally, let us consider heat and other qualities perceived by the senses, in so far as those qualities are in objects, as well as the forms of purely material things, for example the form of fire: we often see these arising from the local motion of certain bodies and producing in turn other local motions in other bodies. Now we understand very well how the different size, shape and motion of the particles of one body can produce various local motions in another body. But there is no way of understanding how these same attributes (size, shape and motion) can produce something else whose nature is quite different from their own — like the substantial forms and real qualities which many <philosophers> suppose to inhere in things; and we cannot understand how these qualities or forms could have the power subsequently to produce local motions in other bodies. Not only is all this unintelligible, but we know that the nature of our soul is such that different local motions are quite sufficient to produce all the sensations in the soul. What is more, we actually experience the various sensations as they are produced in the soul, and we do not find that anything reaches the brain from the external sense organs except for motions of this kind. In view of all this we have every reason to conclude that the properties in external objects to which we apply the terms light, colour, smell, taste, sound, heat and cold—as well as the other tactile qualities and even what are called 'substantial forms'—are, so far as we can see, simply various dispositions in those objects which make them able to set up various kinds of motions in our nerves <which are required to produce all the various sensations in our soul>.

• • •

Part Two

64. *The only principles which I accept, or require, in physics are those of geometry and pure mathematics; these principles explain all natural phenomena, and enable us to provide quite certain demonstrations regarding them.*

I will not here add anything about shapes or about the countless different kinds of motions that can be derived from the infinite variety of different shapes. These matters will be quite clear in themselves when the time comes for me to deal with them. I am assuming that my readers know the basic elements of geometry already, or have sufficient mental aptitude to understand mathematical demonstrations. For I freely acknowledge that I recognize no matter in corporeal things apart from that which the geometers call quantity, and take as the object of their demonstrations, i.e. that to which every kind of division, shape and motion is applicable. Moreover, my consideration of such matter involves absolutely nothing apart from these divisions, shapes and motions; and even with regard to these, I will admit as true only what has been deduced from indubitable common notions so evidently that it is fit to be considered as a mathematical demonstration. And since all natural phenomena can be explained in this way, as will become clear in what follows, I do not think that any other principles are either admissible or desirable in physics.

• • •

CHAPTER FOUR

Descartes: Knowledge of Mind and Matter

Introduction

As we saw in the last chapter, Descartes' goal was to develop and defend the new mathematical sciences. In pursuing this goal, Descartes was especially aware of the religious and philosophical implications it carried. Where Galileo defended the new science on the grounds of its experimental success, Descartes wished to demonstrate once and for all the correctness of its methods using principles drawn from "the light of reason." His intent was not merely to develop the science itself, but to create a complete philosophical system of which the physical sciences would form an integral part. The result of this effort produced a theory of knowledge, a theory of mind, and a theology, as well as a foundation for the physical sciences.

Descartes' dualism

The theory of mind that Descartes constructed is a version of dualism, and is thus reminiscent in some ways of Plato's view. According to Descartes, the mind is an immaterial entity, entirely distinct from the physical body. Like Plato, Descartes argued that the characteristics of the mind are altogether different from those of material objects. According to Descartes, the nature of the physical world is described in entirely mathematical terms; its only real properties are those of shape, size, position, motion, and number. None of these characteristics belongs to the mind, which has only one attribute: conscious intelligence. The mind *thinks*, where thinking includes conscious experience, reason, and will. And just as the mind lacks any of the attributes of size, shape, and location, objects in the material world are utterly devoid of any thought or consciousness.

Although one of his primary goals was to create an account of mind that left room for the methods of the new science, Descartes did not determine the nature of the mind from scientific principles. Instead he developed an ingenious theory of knowledge wherein both the nature of the mind *and* the mathematical character of the physical world could be deduced. According to Descartes, once we establish the real sources of knowledge and determine from that what can be known with absolute certainty, we will recognize that the only real properties of matter are those of pure mathematics, and we will see that the mind is entirely distinct from the physical body.

The *Meditations*

Our readings for this chapter and the next are from a small book entitled *Meditations on First Philosophy* that Descartes wrote in both Latin and French between 1638 and 1640. Descartes intended the *Meditations on First Philosophy* to provide a short and accessible presentation of his philosophy; in this little book all of the central tenets of his philosophical system are laid out and defended. It is written in the first person because his theory of knowledge begins with our reflective knowledge of our own mind, and it proceeds from there to deduce the difference between mind and body and the nature of each. The book is divided into six chapters, which he calls Meditations. The most important parts of the *Meditations* for our purposes, and hence those included in the readings, are the Second and Sixth Meditations and the first two paragraphs of the Third. We need to begin, however, with an outline of the First Meditation where the groundwork of his position is established.

The search for certainty

In the first paragraph Descartes says that many of the principles upon which his beliefs have been based have turned out to be mistaken. He is thinking here largely of his early education in Aristotelian philosophy and science. He concludes from this that if secure knowledge of the world is possible, he must first reject all of his beliefs and start again from the very foundations. To this end he makes the following important assertion.

> Reason now leads me to think that I should hold back my assent from opinions which are not completely certain and indubitable just as carefully as I do from those which are patently false. So, for the purpose of rejecting all my opinions, it will be enough if I find in each of them at least some reason for doubt.[1]

The position he is taking here is that he cannot accept any of his opinions as genuine knowledge unless it is *impossible* for him to doubt their truth. This principle serves as the basis of his system, and, as we will see, it is the origin of his theory of mind and body. It is usually referred to as Descartes' "Method of Doubt."

Doubts about the senses and the intellect

The Method of Doubt provides Descartes with a way of undermining the Aristotelian system. For that system is based on the assumption that our thoughts and sensory perceptions are direct copies of the world around us. By showing that this confidence in the senses and the intellect does not survive the Method of Doubt, Descartes is free to establish his own system. Accordingly, Descartes spends most of the First Meditation casting doubt on the idea that things are necessarily the way they appear.

Clearly the sensory appearances of things are sometimes possible to doubt, for things are often not exactly as they appear. On the other hand he points out that some of what we perceive by the senses would seem to be *absurd* to doubt.

> For example, that I am here, sitting by the fire, wearing a winter dressing-gown, holding this piece of paper in my hands, and so on. Again, how could it be denied that these hands or this whole body are mine?[2]

Yet even what appears to be most evident is sometimes false. If I am dreaming, even the clearest of my perceptions are illusory, so we need a test to distinguish dreams from reality. But Descartes points out that there is no test that would make it *impossible* to doubt that we are dreaming. For any test we can use could in principle be part of the dream itself.

Nor can we have a simple, unreflective confidence in the use of reason. For even the simplest truths of the intellect (say, the belief that 2+3=5) are drawn from certain basic operations of the mind: counting, calculating, drawing inferences, and so on. This means that the truths of reason are safe from doubt only if we cannot doubt the reliability of our powers of reasoning. How can we be absolutely sure of our powers of reason? Suppose, for example, that you made the *same* mistake every time you calculated something. No matter how many times you checked your conclusion, you would still miss your error.

Thought experiments

Descartes ends the First Meditation with what we call nowadays a **thought experiment**. Because thought experiments will play a central role in our readings beyond this chapter, it is worthwhile to look at what they are intended to do.

In simplest terms a thought experiment is simply a fictional story that is used to test and challenge the ways we think about the world. The idea of using fiction in this way is familiar from the science fiction genre. People in science fiction stories are constantly forced into situations that violate our expectations, and this forces us to reexamine our ways of thinking about things.[3]

Exactly what thought experiments can prove is a matter of debate. Some argue that, unlike real experiments, thought experiments do not reveal anything about the world. They only show us more vividly the implications of our own ways of thinking. (Daniel Dennett, whom we will read in chapter 13, calls them "intuition pumps.") Others contend that they show us what *could* be true, even if what they describe isn't actually true. And facts about what could be true, they argue, can form the basis for substantial conclusions about the nature of the world.

The evil demon

Descartes' thought experiment involves the possibility that all of our perceptions and thoughts about the world might be false. He does this by asking us to consider the possibility of an evil demon who has complete control of our mind. Let's follow Descartes' reasoning here. Imagine an evil demon, infinitely cunning and powerful, and imagine that the demon is wholly bent on deceiving you into false beliefs. If it is possible for you to be mistaken about anything at all then the demon will manage it. The demon has control of your memory, your sensory perceptions, and your faculty of reasoning, so that everything you see, remember, or deduce is simply an illusion the demon creates.

Such a description gives an ideal way to identify those beliefs that it is impossible to doubt: any belief you would continue to hold *while imagining that you are being deceived by an evil demon* is one of which you must be absolutely certain. Accordingly, Descartes ends the First Meditation with the conclusion that he will accept as a foundation for knowledge *only* those beliefs that he would continue to hold even while under the power of such an evil demon.

"I think, therefore I am"

The Second Meditation begins with a reiteration of the evil demon scenario, and Descartes asks what beliefs could possibly survive such an all-encompassing doubt. It seems that the only beliefs that would meet this requirement are those that must necessarily be true simply because we believe them to be true.

In the third paragraph of the Second Meditation Descartes points out that the statement 'I exist' is just such a belief. As long as I believe it, it cannot be false. For in order to have any belief, I must exist. This gives him his first principle and foundation for knowledge:

I am, I exist, is necessarily true whenever it is put forward by me
and conceived in my mind.

In a different book, he expresses the same idea with his famous line, "I think,
therefore I am." Notice, however, that only the *first-person* belief '*I* exist' is
impossible to doubt. It is possible to doubt that *other* people exist. This is
the reason the Meditations are written in the first person: all knowledge begins with knowledge of oneself.

"I exist as a thinking thing"

The next step in Descartes' argument is the claim that knowledge of one's
own existence, when understood properly, leads directly to other knowledge.
In order to recognize myself as existing I must know something about what I
am. Accordingly Descartes turns next to the question what the word '*I*' refers
to in the quotation above.

Keep in mind that Descartes is still searching for beliefs that are absolutely
certain. The inference from his own existence to any further knowledge must
pass the evil demon test — he can only draw the inference if he would be willing to do so in the presence of an evil demon. Accordingly, Descartes spends
a few paragraphs rejecting many of the beliefs about himself he usually accepts:
he believes himself to have a certain physical body, and there are many events
he remembers as part of his life history. All of these things could be the illusions of an evil demon. So knowledge of his own existence does not come from
knowledge of any of these things, even if they are all true.

In light of this, Descartes argues that his knowledge of his own existence
is based only on his awareness of his own *thinking*. The statement, 'I exist,'
must be true as long as I *think* that it is. He says,

Thinking? At last I have discovered it — thought; this alone is inseparable from me. I am, I exist — that is certain. But for how long?
For as long as I am thinking.

This is true, he maintains, even if all his sensory perceptions and memories
are entirely false. Hence, knowledge of our own individual existence is derived from nothing more than the awareness of our own thought.

In paragraphs nine and ten he adds that in order to know that he thinks,
he must also have some conception of what thinking is. So this adds another
small piece of knowledge. He asks the question, "What is a thing that thinks?"
The answer is that a thing that thinks is a thing that doubts, understands,
affirms, denies, wills, refuses, and also imagines and senses. The existence of
each of these various states of mind, he claims, is directly evident whenever
we reflect on our own conscious experience.

Thought as consciousness

In the next paragraph Descartes reflects on the list of states of mind that he recognizes as belonging to himself. At the end of this paragraph is the following important comment:

> Lastly, it is the same 'I' who has sensory perceptions, or is aware of bodily things as it were through the senses. For example, I am now seeing light, hearing a noise, feeling heat. But I am asleep, so all this is false. Yet I certainly *seem* to see, to hear, and to be warmed. This cannot be false; what is called 'having a sensory perception' is strictly just this, and in this restricted sense of the term it is simply thinking.

In the first sentence of this quotation Descartes is pointing out that he has included sense perception on the list of different kinds of thinking. In the third sentence he admits that these perceptions may be illusions. But, he says, he is nonetheless aware of the perception itself; that is, of his conscious experience of seeming to perceive something. Even if his perceptions are illusory, he is still aware that he has them. In the last sentence of the passage, he adds that this experience of perception is a form of thinking.

In this paragraph Descartes is constructing an altogether new understanding of **thought** or thinking.[4] Normally, sensing is thought of as an activity that necessarily involves the bodily organs — you can't perceive without organs to perceive with. But here Descartes has *redefined* sensing as an activity that one cannot doubt even while doubting the existence of the physical body. So this conception of sensing carries no assumption that the physical body exists. And understood in this new way, sensing is described as an aspect of **thinking**.

In these two steps Descartes has introduced a new conception of thinking as whatever we *cannot doubt* when we reflect on our own internal experience. The implication of this is that the mind itself is here given an entirely new definition. The mind is understood to be that part of us that thinks, and thinking is defined in terms of the contents of our conscious experience. In this way Descartes introduces a new idea of the mind as a centre of consciousness.

Taking advantage of this new definition of the mind, Descartes concludes that our awareness of our own mind forms the foundation for all of our knowledge. Even if all of our thoughts and perceptions are false, and the world is not as we perceive it or remember it, the fact that we are having those thoughts and those perceptions is impossible to doubt. According to Descartes, the nature and content of the mind is directly evident to us. We cannot be mistaken about the immediate contents of our own thoughts.

Knowledge of physical objects

Descartes' arguments so far have given him the material he needs to draw striking conclusions about the nature of the mind. But in order to complete his argument for dualism, Descartes also has to establish certain claims about the physical world. In the tenth paragraph, beginning with the line "From all this I am beginning to have a better understanding of what I am ...," Descartes re-examines the basis for our beliefs about the physical world. Aristotle's system is based on the idea that the nature of the physical world is revealed to us directly by the senses. Accordingly, Descartes' first project is to undermine this belief.

Descartes begins by admitting that the conclusion he has reached about the mind conflicts with our ordinary view of things. Common sense suggests that our knowledge of ordinary physical objects is more immediate and more certain than our knowledge of this mysterious thing, the mind. So he attempts to confirm his conclusion by answering the question, 'How *do* we have knowledge of ordinary physical objects?'

In his answer to the question Descartes implicitly assumes that there are three distinct faculties of the mind by which we might have knowledge of physical objects: the senses, the imagination, and the intellect. He offers an argument that has the following form.

1. Knowledge of physical objects is not obtained through the senses.
2. Nor is it obtained through the imagination.

Hence it is obtained through the intellect.

Let's look first at his argument for the two premises, and then at what he intends in his conclusion.

The "piece of wax" argument

The argument for the first premise occurs in paragraph eleven. Descartes argues here that a physical object is distinct from any of the sensible qualities (colour, shape, odour, and so on) that it has at any particular time. But our senses perceive only those qualities. Therefore, what we perceive through the senses is not the object itself but only certain qualities it happens to have.

The reasoning here is illustrated by an example of an ordinary physical object: a piece of wax. As the wax is heated, every quality perceived by the senses changes — its colour, its taste, its fragrance, and its size and shape. Nothing sensible remains of the piece of wax before it was heated. *Yet it remains the same object.* The piece of wax didn't vanish while a new object appeared in its place. The same object simply changed in its appearance. Hence the object that we recognize as the piece of wax cannot be anything perceived by the senses.

The argument for the second premise is presented in the next paragraph. Descartes here considers the possibility that our idea of the piece of wax is formed through our ability to *imagine* all the particular sensible qualities it may have over time. On this hypothesis, the reason we recognize the changed object as the same piece of wax is because our idea of it includes all of the changes it might undergo. So our recognition of the object would be a function of the imagination, not the senses. But this Descartes rejects on the grounds that an object may have an infinite number of particular sensible qualities. Think, for example, of how many shapes a piece of wax can have. He can only imagine a finite number of these qualities, and so he cannot possibly have formed his idea of the object through the imagination.

Perception involves judgement

Because it is not through either the senses or the imagination, our knowledge of physical objects can only be through the intellect. This is similar to an idea that we have already encountered in Aristotle. Recall the question raised in chapter 2 of how we are capable of perceiving a horse from our awareness of a collection of sensible qualities. The answer Aristotle gives is that our mind is capable of taking on the forms or essences of things. In his piece-of-wax argument Descartes is making the related point (applied to a piece of wax rather than a horse) that perception cannot consist merely of the perception of sensible qualities. What answer does Descartes give, then, to Aristotle's question?

Near the end of the paragraph Descartes says our perception of the piece of wax is a case of "purely mental scrutiny." But what does he mean by that? The answer is found in the next paragraph. There he describes the intellect as the "faculty of judgement." When we perceive an object like the piece of wax, there is an act of judgement involved in our perception. I don't *see* the piece of wax — I *infer* that it is there from appearances provided by my senses.

He begins that paragraph by admitting that his claim that perception involves the intellect conflicts with how we *seem* to have knowledge of physical objects. We are not aware of any acts of judgement or inference in our ordinary perception of the world. But Descartes points out that we often make judgements without noticing them, and he gives the following example. He looks out the window, and it seems that he sees men in the street; but on closer inspection he notices that he does not actually see any men but only hats and coats, from which he *judges* that it is men that he sees. There was an act of judgement in this perception, but it went unnoticed. So he concludes that:

... something which I thought I was seeing with my eyes is in fact grasped solely by the faculty of judgement which is in my mind.

The idea of matter

But this isn't the whole story. Judgement always involves some kind of conclusion. What exactly is it that I infer when I perceive something like the piece of wax? The answer to this puzzle lies in a comment that Descartes makes in the middle of the piece-of-wax argument. In asking what his idea of the piece of wax is, he says,

> Perhaps the answer lies in the thought which now comes to my mind; namely, the wax was not after all the sweetness of the honey, or the fragrance of the flowers, or the whiteness, or the shape, or the sound, but was rather a body which presented itself to me in these various forms a little while ago, but which now exhibits different ones. But what exactly is it that I am now imagining? Let us concentrate, *take away everything which does not belong to the wax*, and see what is left: merely something extended, flexible, and changeable. [emphasis mine]

In the highlighted phrase we have a version of Galileo's argument from conceivability whereby Galileo concludes that **matter** has no other qualities than shape, size, and motion. Descartes is asserting the same idea. By "something extended," he means something extended in space, that is, something that has a size, shape, and location.

So the idea of the piece of wax that we have in our mind is just the idea of something that possesses a certain size and shape, and that is perceptible by the organs of sense. When we perceive an object like the wax, we form a judgement to the effect that there is before us something extended in space that produces certain sensations in our mind.

It is important to see just how it is that this idea is involved in the act of perception. According to Descartes, the common opinion that our ideas and experiences of the world come directly from the senses is mistaken. Without the activity of the intellect, he believes, our sensations would not provide us with a coherent, structured perception of an enduring physical world. The idea of matter as extended in space does not come to us *from* our sensory experience; rather it is an idea supplied by the mind that we *read into* the sensations supplied by our sensory organs. This, I believe, is what Descartes means when he says that the perception of the wax is an act of "purely mental scrutiny." In a manner reminiscent of Plato, Descartes' view is that, although the senses provide us with a certain amount of confused information, the conceptual framework needed to make sense of that information is provided by the intellect alone.

Descartes' rule

The idea that perception of the physical world involves an act of "mental scrutiny" raises a problem: if our conception of physical objects is supplied by the mind, how can we assure ourselves that this conception is correct? Descartes turns to this problem in the Third Meditation.

In the second paragraph of the Third Meditation, Descartes says that in the previous Meditation he has already discovered a rule that he can use to acquire knowledge about the physical world. He goes back to the first belief established in the Second Meditation: "I am, I exist — that is certain. But for how long? For as long as I am thinking." Given that this statement is beyond doubt, he asks what *reason* he had for accepting it as such. His answer is that, "In this first item of knowledge there is simply a clear and distinct perception of what I am asserting..." This thought suggests to him the following rule:

Whatever I perceive very clearly and distinctly is true.

What does he mean by this? Recall that in the Second Meditation, when he first establishes the belief 'I exist,' he discovers that this knowledge is based solely on the existence of his own conscious thought. It is only after he has clearly and distinctly perceived the *precise content* of the belief that he sees that it must be true. So the idea he draws from this is as follows. There are certain ideas and thoughts that occur in the conscious mind. Some of these thoughts and ideas are clear and distinct; others are confused and vague. Our beliefs are often false when they are based on confused and vague ideas and impressions. But our beliefs are always true when they are based on clear and distinct ideas and impressions. Because he has relied on this rule in establishing the certainty of his own existence, he now maintains that the rule *must* be acceptable as a means of acquiring knowledge, or else he must give up his claim to know that he exists, which would be absurd.

The existence of God

In the remainder of the Third Meditation Descartes argues that we can demonstrate the truth of this rule by proving the existence of a benevolent and powerful God. Once this has been proven, we can see that such a God would not create us in such a way that our clearest beliefs can be mistaken.

This argument gives us a further clue to what Descartes means by "clear and distinct ideas." In the Sixth Meditation, while discussing what can be known of physical objects, he makes the following claim:

Despite the very high degree of doubt and uncertainty involved here, the very fact that God is not a deceiver, and the consequent impossi-

bility of there being any falsity in my opinions which cannot be corrected by some other faculty supplied by God, offers me a sure hope
that I can attain the truth even in these matters.

The idea expressed here is that we will not fall into errors that we are incapable of correcting. It follows that as long as we do everything that is within
our power to avoid error, our beliefs will always be true. A clear and distinct
idea, understood in this light, is one that appears to be true even after it has
been examined critically with every faculty of reason and analysis we possess.

Descartes' critics have maintained that proving the existence of God in
order to support his rule is circular. For one of the premises in his argument
that God exists, they maintain, is the rule itself, so that a person will only
accept the premises as true if they already accept the conclusion. To pursue
this problem is beyond our scope here, so I will pass it by and look instead at
what Descartes does with his rule once it is established.

Using the rule

The Sixth Meditation is the culmination of the book, and Descartes declares
two objectives here: to establish the existence and nature of physical objects,
and to demonstrate that the mind and the physical body are two distinct entities. In the Second Meditation he introduced the idea of matter as something extended in space. Descartes now argues that the spatial properties of
size, shape, and motion are the properties of matter of which we can form a
clear and distinct idea. He says,

> It remains for me to examine whether material things exist. At least
> I now know they are capable of existing, in so far as they are the
> subject matter of pure mathematics, *since I perceive them clearly and
> distinctly.* [emphasis mine]

The claim here is that the only clear and distinct, and hence truly accurate,
conception he has of physical objects is that of something extended in space,
and thus possessing size, shape, position, and motion. This is because the idea
of spatial extension is based on the sciences of arithmetic and geometry, and
the principles of these sciences are all clear and distinct.

In paragraph four Descartes admits that there are other qualities commonly attached to the idea we have of material objects: colours, sounds, scents,
and so on. And all of these are derived from our sensory perceptions. How
are these sensory perceptions related to the world of material objects? To answer this question Descartes turns to the relationship between mind and matter. This topic is the subject of the next chapter.

NOTES

1 *The Philosophical Writings of Descartes, Volume Two*, translated by John Cottingham, Robert Stoothoff and Dugald Murdoch (Cambridge: Cambridge University Press, 1984), p. 12.

2 *The Philosophical Writings of Descartes, Volume Two*, p. 13.

3 For example, in an episode of *Star Trek: The Next Generation*, the robot, Data, creates a replica of himself that he represents to others as his daughter. The fleet commander insists that the replica is simply a machine that should be dismantled and tested, but Data refuses to cooperate. The subsequent events in the story force us to reconsider the distinction between machines and people.

4 This point is made very effectively by Gareth Matthews in "Consciousness and Life," reprinted in *The Nature of Mind*, David M. Rosenthal (ed.) (Oxford: Oxford University Press, 1991).

René Descartes
Selections from *Meditations on First Philosophy*

SECOND MEDITATION

The nature of the human mind, and how it is better known than the body

So serious are the doubts into which I have been thrown as a result of yesterday's meditation that I can neither put them out of my mind nor see any way of resolving them. It feels as if I have fallen unexpectedly into a deep whirlpool which tumbles me around so that I can neither stand on the bottom nor swim up to the top. Nevertheless I will make an effort and once more attempt the same path which I started on yesterday. Anything which admits of the slightest doubt I will set aside just as if I had found it to be wholly false; and I will proceed in this way until I recognize something certain, or, if nothing else, until I at least recognize for certain that there is no certainty. Archimedes used to demand just one firm and immovable point in order to shift the entire earth; so I too can hope for great things if I manage to find just one thing, however slight, that is certain and unshakeable.

I will suppose then, that everything I see is spurious. I will believe that my memory tells me lies, and that none of the things that it reports ever happened. I have no senses. Body, shape, extension, movement and place are chimeras. So what remains true? Perhaps just the one fact that nothing is certain.

Yet apart from everything I have just listed, how do I know that there is not something else which does not allow even the slightest occasion for doubt? Is there not a God, or whatever I may call him, who puts into me the thoughts I am now having? But why do I think this, since I myself may perhaps be the author

of these thoughts? In that case am not I, at least, something? But I have just said that I have no senses and no body. This is the sticking point: what follows from this? Am I not so bound up with a body and with senses that I cannot exist without them? But I have convinced myself that there is absolutely nothing in the world, no sky, no earth, no minds, no bodies. Does it now follow that I too do not exist? No: if I convinced myself of something then I certainly existed. But there is a deceiver of supreme power and cunning who is deliberately and constantly deceiving me. In that case I too undoubtedly exist, if he is deceiving me; and let him deceive me as much as he can, he will never bring it about that I am nothing so long as I think that I am something. So after considering everything very thoroughly, I must finally conclude that this proposition, *I am, I exist,* is necessarily true whenever it is put forward by me or conceived in my mind.

But I do not yet have a sufficient understanding of what this 'I' is, that now necessarily exists. So I must be on my guard against carelessly taking something else to be this 'I', and so making a mistake in the very item of knowledge that I maintain is the most certain and evident of all. I will therefore go back and meditate on what I originally believed myself to be, before I embarked on this present train of thought. I will then subtract anything capable of being weakened, even minimally, by the arguments now introduced, so that what is left at the end may be exactly and only what is certain and unshakeable.

What then did I formerly think I was? A man. But what is a man? Shall I say 'a rational animal'? No; for then I should have to inquire what an animal is, what rationality is, and in this way one question would lead me down the slope to other harder ones, and I do not now have the time to waste on subtleties of this kind. Instead I propose to concentrate on what came into my thoughts spontaneously and quite naturally whenever I used to consider what I was. Well, the first thought to come to mind was that I had a face, hands, arms and the whole mechanical structure of limbs which can be seen in a corpse, and which I called the body. The next thought was that I was nourished, that I moved about, and that I engaged in sense-perception and thinking; and these actions I attributed to the soul. But as to the nature of this soul, either I did not think about this or else I imagined it to be something tenuous, like a wind or fire or ether, which permeated my more solid parts. As to the body, however, I had no doubts about it, but thought I knew its nature distinctly. If I had tried to describe the mental conception I had of it, I would have expressed it as follows: by a body I understand whatever has a determinable shape and a definable location and can occupy a space in such a way as to exclude any other body; it can be perceived by touch, sight, hearing, taste or smell, and can be moved in various ways, not by itself but by whatever else comes into contact with it. For, according to my judgement, the power of self-movement, like the power of sensation or of thought, was quite foreign to the nature of a body; indeed, it was a source of wonder to me that certain bodies were found to contain faculties of this kind.

But what shall I now say that I am, when I am supposing that there is some supremely powerful and, if it is permissible to say so, malicious deceiver, who is deliberately trying to trick me in every way he can? Can I now assert that I possess even the most insignificant of all the attributes which I have just said belong to the nature of a body? I scrutinize them, think about them, go over them again, but nothing suggests itself; it is tiresome and pointless to go

through the list once more. But what about the attributes I assigned to the soul? Nutrition or movement? Since now I do not have a body, these are mere fabrications. Sense-perception? This surely does not occur without a body, and besides, when asleep I have appeared to perceive through the senses many things which I afterwards realized I did not perceive through the senses at all. Thinking? At last I have discovered it—thought; this alone is inseparable from me. I am, I exist—that is certain. But for how long? For as long as I am thinking. For it could be that were I totally to cease from thinking, I should totally cease to exist. At present I am not admitting anything except what is necessarily true. I am, then, in the strict sense only a thing that thinks; that is, I am a mind, or intelligence, or intellect, or reason—words whose meaning I have been ignorant of until now. But for all that I am a thing which is real and which truly exists. But what kind of a thing? As I have just said—a thinking thing.

What else am I? I will use my imagination. I am not that structure of limbs which is called a human body. I am not even some thin vapour which permeates the limbs—a wind, fire, air, breath, or whatever I depict in my imagination; for these are things which I have supposed to be nothing. Let this supposition stand; for all that I am still something. And yet may it not perhaps be the case that these very things which I am supposing to be nothing, because they are unknown to me, are in reality identical with the 'I' of which I am aware? I do not know, and for the moment I shall not argue the point, since I can make judgements only about things which are known to me. I know that I exist; the question is, what is this 'I' that I know? If the 'I' is understood strictly as we have been taking it, then it is quite certain that knowledge of it does not depend on things of whose existence I am as yet unaware; so it cannot depend on any of the things which I invent in my imagination. And this very word 'invent' shows me my mistake. It would indeed be a case of fictitious invention if I used my imagination to establish that I was something or other; for imagining is simply contemplating the shape or image of a corporeal thing. Yet now I know for certain both that I exist and at the same time that all such images and, in general, everything relating to the nature of body, could be mere dreams <and chimeras>. Once this point has been grasped, to say 'I will use my imagination to get to know more distinctly what I am' would seem to be as silly as saying 'I am now awake, and see some truth; but since my vision is not yet clear enough, I will deliberately fall asleep so that my dreams may provide a truer and clearer representation.' I thus realize that none of the things that the imagination enables me to grasp is at all relevant to this knowledge of myself which I possess, and that the mind must therefore be most carefully diverted from such things if it is to perceive its own nature as distinctly as possible.

But what then am I? A thing that thinks. What is that? A thing that doubts, understands, affirms, denies, is willing, is unwilling, and also imagines and has sensory perceptions.

This is a considerable list, if everything on it belongs to me. But does it? Is it not one and the same 'I' who is now doubting almost everything, who nonetheless understands some things, who affirms that this one thing is true, denies everything else, desires to know more, is unwilling to be deceived, imagines many things even involuntarily, and is aware of many things which apparently come from the senses? Are not all these things just as true as the fact that I exist, even if I am asleep all the time, and even if he who created me is doing all he can to deceive me? Which of all these activities is distinct from my thinking? Which of them can be said to be separate from myself? The fact that it is I who am doubting and understanding and willing is so evident that I see no way of making it any clearer. But it is also the case that the 'I' who imagines is the same 'I'. For even if, as I have supposed, none of the objects of imagina-

tion are real, the power of imagination is something which really exists and is part of my thinking. Lastly, it is also the same 'I' who has sensory perceptions, or is aware of bodily things as it were through the senses. For example, I am now seeing light, hearing a noise, feeling heat. But I am asleep, so all this is false. Yet I certainly *seem* to see, to hear, and to be warmed. This cannot be false; what is called 'having a sensory perception' is strictly just this, and in this restricted sense of the term it is simply thinking.

From all this I am beginning to have a rather better understanding of what I am. But it still appears—and I cannot stop thinking this—that the corporeal things of which images are formed in my thought, and which the senses investigate, are known with much more distinctness than this puzzling 'I' which cannot be pictured in the imagination. And yet it is surely surprising that I should have a more distinct grasp of things which I realize are doubtful, unknown and foreign to me, than I have of that which is true and known—my own self. But I see what it is: my mind enjoys wandering off and will not yet submit to being restrained within the bounds of truth. Very well then; just this once let us give it a completely free rein, so that after a while, when it is time to tighten the reins, it may more readily submit to being curbed.

Let us consider the things which people commonly think they understand most distinctly of all; that is, the bodies which we touch and see. I do not mean bodies in general—for general perceptions are apt to be somewhat more confused—but one particular body. Let us take, for example, this piece of wax. It has just been taken from the honeycomb; it has not yet quite lost the taste of the honey; it retains some of the scent of the flowers from which it was gathered; its colour, shape and size are plain to see; it is hard, cold and can be handled without difficulty; if you rap it with your knuckle it makes a sound. In short, it has everything which appears necessary to enable a body to be known as distinctly as possible. But even as I speak, I put the wax by the fire, and look: the residual taste is eliminated, the smell goes away, the colour changes, the shape is lost, the size increases; it becomes liquid and hot; you can hardly touch it, and if you strike it, it no longer makes a sound. But does the same wax remain? It must be admitted that it does; no one denies it, no one thinks otherwise. So what was it in the wax that I understood with such distinctness? Evidently none of the features which I arrived at by means of the senses; for whatever came under taste, smell, sight, touch or hearing has now altered—yet the wax remains.

Perhaps the answer lies in the thought which now comes to my mind; namely, the wax was not after all the sweetness of the honey, or the fragrance of the flowers, or the whiteness, or the shape, or the sound, but was rather a body which presented itself to me in these various forms a little while ago, but which now exhibits different ones. But what exactly is it that I am now imagining? Let us concentrate, take away everything which does not belong to the wax, and see what is left: merely something extended, flexible and changeable. But what is meant here by 'flexible' and 'changeable'? Is it what I picture in my imagination: that this piece of wax is capable of changing from a round shape to a square shape, or from a square shape to a triangular shape? Not at all; for I can grasp that the wax is capable of countless changes of this kind, yet I am unable to run through this immeasurable number of changes in my imagination, from which it follows that it is not the faculty of imagination that gives me my grasp of the wax as flexible and changeable. And what is meant by 'extended'? Is the extension of the wax also unknown? For it increases if the wax melts, increases again if it boils, and is greater still if the heat is increased. I would not be making a correct judgement about the nature of wax unless I believed it capable of being extended in many more differ-

ent ways than I will ever encompass in my imagination. I must therefore admit that the nature of this piece of wax is in no way revealed by my imagination, but is perceived by the mind alone. (I am speaking of this particular piece of wax; the point is even clearer with regard to wax in general.) But what is this wax which is perceived by the mind alone? It is of course the same wax which I see, which I touch, which I picture in my imagination, in short the same wax which I thought it to be from the start. And yet, and here is the point, the perception I have of it is a case not of vision or touch or imagination—nor has it ever been, despite previous appearances—*but of purely mental scrutiny;* and this can be imperfect and confused, as it was before, or clear and distinct as it is now, depending on how carefully I concentrate on what the wax consists in.

But as I reach this conclusion I am amazed at how <weak and> prone to error my mind is. For although I am thinking about these matters within myself, silently and without speaking, nonetheless the actual words bring me up short, and I am almost tricked by ordinary ways of talking. We say that we see the wax itself, if it is there before us, not that we judge it to be there from its colour or shape; and this might lead me to conclude without more ado that knowledge of the wax comes from what the eye sees, and not from the scrutiny of the mind alone. But then if I look out of the window and see men crossing the square, as I just happen to have done, I normally say that I see the men themselves, just as I say that I see the wax. Yet do I see any more than hats and coats which could conceal automatons? I *judge* that they are men. And so something which I thought I was seeing with my eyes is in fact grasped solely by the faculty of judgement which is in my mind.

However, one who wants to achieve knowledge above the ordinary level should feel ashamed at having taken ordinary ways of talking as a basis for doubt. So let us proceed, and consider on which occasion my perception of the nature of the wax was more perfect and evident. Was it when I first looked at it, and believed I knew it by my external senses, or at least by what they call the 'common' sense—that is, the power of imagination? Or is my knowledge more perfect now, after a more careful investigation of the nature of the wax and of the means by which it is known? Any doubt on this issue would clearly be foolish; for what distinctness was there in my earlier perception? Was there anything in it which an animal could not possess? But when I distinguish the wax from its outward forms—take the clothes off, as it were, and consider it naked—then although my judgement may still contain errors, at least my perception now requires a human mind.

But what am I to say about this mind, or about myself? (So far, remember, I am not admitting that there is anything else in me except a mind.) What, I ask, is this 'I' which seems to perceive the wax so distinctly? Surely my awareness of my own self is not merely much truer and more certain than my awareness of the wax, but also much more distinct and evident. For if I judge that the wax exists from the fact that I see it, clearly this same fact entails much more evidently that I myself also exist. It is possible that what I see is not really the wax; it is possible that I do not even have eyes with which to see anything. But when I see, or think I see (I am not here distinguishing the two), it is simply not possible that I who am now thinking am not something. By the same token, if I judge that the wax exists from the fact that I touch it, the same result follows, namely that I exist. If I judge that it exists from the fact that I imagine it, or for any other reason, exactly the same thing follows. And the result that I have grasped in the case of the wax may be applied to everything else located outside me. Moreover, if my perception of the wax seemed more distinct after it was established not just by sight or touch but by many other considerations, it must be admitted that I now know myself even more distinctly. This is because every considera-

tion whatsoever which contributes to my perception of the wax, or of any other body, cannot but establish even more effectively the nature of my own mind. But besides this, there is so much else in the mind itself which can serve to make my knowledge of it more distinct, that it scarcely seems worth going through the contributions made by considering bodily things.

I see that without any effort I have now finally got back to where I wanted. I now know that even bodies are not strictly perceived by the senses or the faculty of imagination but by the intellect alone, and that this perception derives not from their being touched or seen but from their being understood; and in view of this I know plainly that I can achieve an easier and more evident perception of my own mind than of anything else. But since the habit of holding on to old opinions cannot be set aside so quickly, I should like to stop here and meditate for some time on this new knowledge I have gained, so as to fix it more deeply in my memory.

THIRD MEDITATION
The existence of God

I will now shut my eyes, stop my ears, and withdraw all my senses. I will eliminate from my thoughts all images of bodily things, or rather, since this is hardly possible, I will regard all such images as vacuous, false and worthless. I will converse with myself and scrutinize myself more deeply; and in this way I will attempt to achieve, little by little, a more intimate knowledge of myself. I am a thing that thinks: that is, a thing that doubts, affirms, denies, understands a few things, is ignorant of many things, is willing, is unwilling, and also which imagines and has sensory perceptions; for as I have noted before, even though the objects of my sensory experience and imagination may have no existence outside me, nonetheless the modes of thinking which I refer to as cases of sensory perception and imagination, in so far as they are simply modes of thinking, do exist within me—of that I am certain.

In this brief list I have gone through everything I truly know, or at least everything I have so far discovered that I know. Now I will cast around more carefully to see whether there may be other things within me which I have not yet noticed. I am certain that I am a thinking thing. Do I not therefore also know what is required for my being certain about anything? In this first item of knowledge there is simply a clear and distinct perception of what I am asserting; this would not be enough to make me certain of the truth of the matter if it could ever turn out that something which I perceived with such clarity and distinctness was false. So I now seem to be able to lay it down as a general rule that whatever I perceive very clearly and distinctly is true.

. . .

SIXTH MEDITATION

The existence of material things, and the real distinction between mind and body

It remains for me to examine whether material things exist. And at least I now know they are capable of existing, in so far as they are the subject-matter of pure mathematics, since I perceive them clearly and distinctly. For there is no doubt that God is capable of creating everything that I am capable of perceiving in this manner; and I have never judged that something could not be made by him except on the grounds that there would be a contradiction in my perceiving it distinctly. The conclusion that material things exist is also suggested by the faculty of imagination, which I am aware of using when I turn my mind to material things. For when I give more attentive consideration to what imagination is, it seems to be nothing else but an application of the cognitive faculty to a body which is intimately present to it, and which therefore exists.

To make this clear, I will first examine the difference between imagination and pure understanding. When I imagine a triangle, for example, I do not merely understand that it is a figure bounded by three lines, but at the same time I also see the three lines with my mind's eye as if they were present before me; and this is what I call imagining. But if I want to think of a chiliagon, although I understand that it is a figure consisting of a thousand sides just as well as I understand the triangle to be a three-sided figure, I do not in the same way imagine the thousand sides or see them as if they were present before me. It is true that since I am in the habit of imagining something whenever I think of a corporeal thing, I may construct in my mind a confused representation of some figure; but it is clear that this is not a chiliagon. For it differs in no way from the representation I should form if I were thinking of a myriagon, or any figure with very many sides. Moreover, such a representation is useless for recognizing the properties which distinguish a chiliagon from other polygons. But suppose I am dealing with a pentagon: I can of course understand the figure of a pentagon, just as I can the figure of a chiliagon, without the help of the imagination; but I can also imagine a pentagon, by applying my mind's eye to its five sides and the area contained within them. And in doing this I notice quite clearly that imagination requires a peculiar effort of mind which is not required for understanding; this additional effort of mind clearly shows the difference between imagination and pure understanding.

Besides this, I consider that this power of imagining which is in me, differing as it does from the power of understanding, is not a necessary constituent of my own essence, that is, of the essence of my mind. For if I lacked it, I should undoubtedly remain the same individual as I now am; from which it seems to follow that it depends on something distinct from myself.

And I can easily understand that, if there does exist some body to which the mind is so joined that it can apply itself to contemplate it, as it were, whenever it pleases, then it may possibly be this very body that enables me to imagine corporeal things. So the difference between this mode of thinking and pure understanding may simply be this: when the mind understands, it in some way turns towards itself and inspects one of the ideas which are within it; but when it imagines, it turns towards the body and looks at something in the body which conforms to an idea understood by the mind or perceived by the senses. I can, as I say, easily understand that this is how imagination comes about, if the body exists; and since there is no other equally suitable way of explaining imagination that comes to mind, I can make a probable conjecture that the body exists. But this is only a probability; and despite a careful and comprehensive investigation, I do not yet see how the distinct idea of corporeal nature which I find in my imagination can provide any basis for a necessary inference that some body exists.

But besides that corporeal nature which is the subject-matter of pure mathematics, there is much else that I habitually imagine, such as colours, sounds, tastes, pain and so on—though not so distinctly. Now I perceive these things much better by means of the senses, which is how, with the assistance of memory, they appear to have reached the imagination. So in order to deal with them more fully, I must pay equal attention to the senses, and see whether the things which are perceived by means of that mode of thinking which I call 'sensory perception' provide me with any sure argument for the existence of corporeal things.

To begin with, I will go back over all the things which I previously took to be perceived by the senses, and reckoned to be true; and I will go over my reasons for thinking this. Next, I will set out my reasons for subsequently calling these things into doubt. And finally I will consider what I should now believe about them.

First of all then, I perceived by my senses that I had a head, hands, feet and other limbs making up the body which I regarded as part of myself, or perhaps even as my whole self. I also perceived by my senses that this body was situated among many other bodies which could affect it in various favourable or unfavourable ways; and I gauged the favourable effects by a sensation of pleasure, and the unfavourable ones by a sensation of pain. In addition to pain and pleasure, I also had sensations within me of hunger, thirst, and other such appetites, and also of physical propensities towards cheerfulness, sadness, anger and similar emotions. And outside me, besides the extension, shapes and movements of bodies, I also had sensations of their hardness and heat, and of the other tactile qualities. In addition, I had sensations of light, colours, smells, tastes and sounds, the variety of which enabled me to distinguish the sky, the earth, the seas, and all other bodies, one from another. Considering the ideas of all these qualities which presented themselves to my thought, although the ideas were, strictly speaking, the only immediate objects of my sensory awareness, it was not unreasonable for me to think that the items which I was perceiving through the senses were things quite distinct from my thought, namely bodies which produced the ideas. For my experience was that these ideas came to me quite without my consent, so that I could not have sensory awareness of any object, even if I wanted to, unless it was present to my sense organs; and I could not avoid having sensory awareness of it when it was present. And since the ideas perceived by the senses were much more lively and vivid and even, in their own way, more distinct than any of those which I deliberately formed through meditating or which I found impressed on my memory, it seemed impossible that they should have come from within me; so the only alternative was that they came from other things. Since the sole source of my knowledge of these things was the ideas themselves, the supposition that the things resembled the ideas was bound to occur to me. In addition, I remembered that the use of my senses had come first, while the use of my reason came only later; and I saw that the ideas which I formed myself were less vivid than those which I perceived with the senses and were, for the most part, made up of elements of sensory ideas. In this way I easily convinced myself that I had nothing at all in the intellect which I had not previously had in sensation. As for the body which by some special right I called 'mine', my belief that this body, more than any other, belonged to me had some justification. For I could never be separated from it, as I could from other bodies; and I felt all my appetites and emotions in, and on account of, this body; and finally, I was aware of pain and pleasurable ticklings in parts of this body, but not in other bodies external to it. But why should that curious sensation of pain give rise to a particular distress of mind; or why should a certain kind of delight follow on a tickling sensation? Again, why should that curious tugging in the stomach which I call hunger tell me that I should eat, or a dryness of the throat tell me to drink, and so on? I was not able to give any explanation of all this, except that nature taught me so. For there is absolutely no connection (at least that I can understand) between the tugging sensation and the decision to take food, or between the sensation of something causing pain and the mental apprehension of distress that arises from that sensation. These and other judgements that I made concerning sensory objects, I was apparently taught to make by nature; for I had already made up my mind that this was how things were, before working out any arguments to prove it.

Later on, however, I had many experiences which gradually undermined all the faith I had had in the senses. Sometimes towers which had looked round from a distance appeared square from close up; and enormous statues standing on their pediments did not seem large when observed from the ground. In these and count-less other such cases, I found that the judgements of the external senses were mistaken. And this applied not just to the external senses but to the internal senses as well. For what can be more internal than pain? And yet I had heard that those who had had a leg or an arm amputated sometimes still seemed to feel pain intermittently in the missing part of the body. So even in my own case it was apparently not quite certain that a particular limb was hurting, even if I felt pain in it. To these reasons for doubting, I recently added two very general ones. The first was that every sensory experience I have ever thought I was having while awake I can also think of myself as sometimes having while asleep; and since I do not believe that what I seem to perceive in sleep comes from things located outside me, I did not see why I should be any more inclined to believe this of what I think I perceive while awake. The second reason for doubt was that since I did not know the author of my being (or at least was pretending not to), I saw nothing to rule out the possibility that my natural constitution made me prone to error even in matters which seemed to me most true. As for the reasons for my previous confident belief in the truth of the things perceived by the senses, I had no trouble in refuting them. For since I apparently had natural impulses towards many things which reason told me to avoid, I reckoned that a great deal of confidence should not be placed in what I was taught by nature. And despite the fact that the perceptions of the senses were not dependent on my will, I did not think that I should on that account infer that they proceeded from things distinct from myself, since I might perhaps have a faculty not yet known to me which produced them.

But now, when I am beginning to achieve a better knowledge of myself and the author of my being, although I do not think I should heedlessly accept everything I seem to have acquired from the senses, neither do I think that everything should be called into doubt.

First, I know that everything which I clearly and distinctly understand is capable of being created by God so as to correspond exactly with my understanding of it. Hence the fact that I can clearly and distinctly understand one thing apart from another is enough to make me certain that the two things are distinct, since they are capable of being separated, at least by God. The question of what kind of power is required to bring about such a separation does not affect the judgement that the two things are distinct. Thus, simply by knowing that I exist and seeing at the same time that absolutely nothing else belongs to my nature or essence except that I am a thinking thing, I can infer correctly that my essence consists solely in the fact that I am a thinking thing. It is true that I may have (or, to anticipate, that I certainly have) a body that is very closely joined to me. But nevertheless, on the one hand I have a clear and distinct idea of myself, in so far as I am simply a thinking, non-extended thing; and on the other hand I have a distinct idea of body, in so far as this is simply an extended, non-thinking thing. And accordingly, it is certain that I am really distinct from my body, and can exist without it.

Besides this, I find in myself faculties for certain special modes of thinking, namely imagination and sensory perception. Now I can clearly and distinctly understand myself as a whole without these faculties; but I cannot, conversely, understand these faculties without me, that is, without an intellectual substance to inhere in. This is because there is an intellectual act included in their essential definition; and hence I perceive that the distinction between them and myself corresponds to the distinction between the modes of a thing and the thing itself. Of course I also recognize that there are other faculties (like those of changing position, of taking on various shapes, and so on) which, like sensory perception and imagination, cannot be understood apart from some substance for them to inhere in, and hence cannot exist without it. But it is clear that these other

faculties, if they exist, must be in a corporeal or extended substance and not an intellectual one; for the clear and distinct conception of them includes extension, but does not include any intellectual act whatsoever. Now there is in me a passive faculty of sensory perception, that is, a faculty for receiving and recognizing the ideas of sensible objects; but I could not make use of it unless there was also an active faculty, either in me or in something else, which produced or brought about these ideas. But this faculty cannot be in me, since clearly it presupposes no intellectual act on my part, and the ideas in question are produced without my co-operation and often even against my will. So the only alternative is that it is in another substance distinct from me—a substance which contains either formally or eminently all the reality which exists objectively in the ideas produced by this faculty (as I have just noted). This substance is either a body, that is, a corporeal nature, in which case it will contain formally <and in fact> everything which is to be found objectively <or representatively> in the ideas; or else it is God, or some creature more noble than a body, in which case it will contain eminently whatever is to be found in the ideas. But since God is not a deceiver, it is quite clear that he does not transmit the ideas to me either directly from himself, or indirectly, via some creature which contains the objective reality of the ideas not formally but only eminently. For God has given me no faculty at all for recognizing any such source for these ideas; on the contrary, he has given me a great propensity to believe that they are produced by corporeal things. So I do not see how God could be understood to be anything but a deceiver if the ideas were transmitted from a source other than corporeal things. It follows that corporeal things exist. They may not all exist in a way that exactly corresponds with my sensory grasp of them, for in many cases the grasp of the senses is very obscure and confused. But at least they possess all the properties which I clearly and distinctly understand, that is, all those which, viewed in general terms, are comprised within the subject-matter of pure mathematics.

What of the other aspects of corporeal things which are either particular (for example that the sun is of such and such a size or shape), or less clearly understood, such as light or sound or pain, and so on? Despite the high degree of doubt and uncertainty involved here, the very fact that God is not a deceiver, and the consequent impossibility of there being any falsity in my opinions which cannot be corrected by some other faculty supplied by God, offers me a sure hope that I can attain the truth even in these matters. Indeed, there is no doubt that everything that I am taught by nature contains some truth. For if nature is considered in its general aspect, then I understand by the term nothing other than God himself, or the ordered system of created things established by God. And by my own nature in particular I understand nothing other than the totality of things bestowed on me by God.

There is nothing that my own nature teaches me more vividly than that I have a body, and that when I feel pain there is something wrong with the body, and that when I am hungry or thirsty the body needs food and drink, and so on. So I should not doubt that there is some truth in this.

Nature also teaches me, by these sensations of pain, hunger, thirst and so on that I am not merely present in my body as a sailor is present in a ship, but that I am very closely joined and, as it were, intermingled with it, so that I and the body form a unit. If this were not so, I, who am nothing but a thinking thing, would not feel pain when the body was hurt, but would perceive the damage purely by the intellect, just as a sailor perceives by sight if anything in his ship is broken. Similarly, when the body needed food or drink, I should have an explicit understanding of the fact, instead of having confused sensations of hunger and thirst. For these sensations of hunger, thirst, pain and so on are

nothing but confused modes of thinking which arise from the union and, as it were, intermingling of the mind with the body.

I am also taught by nature that various other bodies exist in the vicinity of my body, and that some of these are to be sought out and others avoided. And from the fact that I perceive by my senses a great variety of colours, sounds, smells and tastes, as well as differences in heat, hardness and the like, I am correct in inferring that the bodies which are the source of these various sensory perceptions possess differences corresponding to them, though perhaps not resembling them. Also, the fact that some of the perceptions are agreeable to me while others are disagreeable makes it quite certain that my body, or rather my whole self, in so far as I am a combination of body and mind, can be affected by the various beneficial or harmful bodies which surround it.

There are, however, many other things which I may appear to have been taught by nature, but which in reality I acquired not from nature but from a habit of making ill-considered judgements; and it is therefore quite possible that these are false. Cases in point are the belief that any space in which nothing is occurring to stimulate my senses must be empty; or that the heat in a body is something exactly resembling the idea of heat which is in me; or that when a body is white or green, the selfsame whiteness or greenness which I perceive through my senses is present in the body; or that in a body which is bitter or sweet there is the selfsame taste which I experience, and so on; or, finally, that stars and towers and other distant bodies have the same size and shape which they present to my senses, and other examples of this kind. But to make sure that my perceptions in this matter are sufficiently distinct, I must more accurately define exactly what I mean when I say that I am taught something by nature. In this context I am taking nature to be something more limited than the totality of things bestowed on me by God. For this includes many things that belong to the mind alone—for example my perception that what is done cannot be undone, and all other things that are known by the natural light; but at this stage I am not speaking of these matters. It also includes much that relates to the body alone, like the tendency to move in a downward direction, and so on; but I am not speaking of these matters either. My sole concern here is with what God has bestowed on me as a combination of mind and body. My nature, then, in this limited sense, does indeed teach me to avoid what induces a feeling of pain and to seek out what induces feelings of pleasure, and so on. But it does not appear to teach us to draw any conclusions from these sensory perceptions about things located outside us without waiting until the intellect has examined the matter. For knowledge of the truth about such things seems to belong to the mind alone, not to the combination of mind and body. Hence, although a star has no greater effect on my eye than the flame of a small light, that does not mean that there is any real or positive inclination in me to believe that the star is no bigger than the light; I have simply made this judgement from childhood onwards without any rational basis. Similarly, although I feel heat when I go near a fire and feel pain when I go too near, there is no convincing argument for supposing that there is something in the fire which resembles the heat, any more than for supposing that there is something which resembles the pain. There is simply reason to suppose that there is something in the fire, whatever it may eventually turn out to be, which produces in us the feelings of heat or pain. And likewise, even though there is nothing in any given space that stimulates the senses, it does not follow that there is no body there. In these cases and many others I see that I have been in the habit of misusing the order of nature. For the proper purpose of the sensory perceptions given me by nature is simply to inform the mind of what is beneficial or harmful for the composite of which the mind is a part;

and to this extent they are sufficiently clear and distinct. But I misuse them by treating them as reliable touchstones for immediate judgements about the essential nature of the bodies located outside us; yet this is an area where they provide only very obscure information.

I have already looked in sufficient detail at how, notwithstanding the goodness of God, it may happen that my judgements are false. But a further problem now comes to mind regarding those very things which nature presents to me as objects which I should seek out or avoid, and also regarding the internal sensations, where I seem to have detected errors—e.g. when someone is tricked by the pleasant taste of some food into eating the poison concealed inside it. Yet in this case, what the man's nature urges him to go for is simply what is responsible for the pleasant taste, and not the poison, which his nature knows nothing about. The only inference that can be drawn from this is that his nature is not omniscient. And this is not surprising, since man is a limited thing, and so it is only fitting that his perfection should be limited.

And yet it is not unusual for us to go wrong even in cases where nature does urge us towards something. Those who are ill, for example, may desire food or drink that will shortly afterwards turn out to be bad for them. Perhaps it may be said that they go wrong because their nature is disordered, but this does not remove the difficulty. A sick man is no less one of God's creatures than a healthy one, and it seems no less a contradiction to suppose that he has received from God a nature which deceives him. Yet a clock constructed with wheels and weights observes all the laws of its nature just as closely when it is badly made and tells the wrong time as when it completely fulfils the wishes of the clockmaker. In the same way, I might consider the body of a man as a kind of machine equipped with and made up of bones, nerves, muscles, veins, blood and skin in such a way that, even if there were no mind in it, it would still perform all the same movements as it now does in those cases where movement is not under the control of the will or, consequently, of the mind. I can easily see that if such a body suffers from dropsy, for example, and is affected by the dryness of the throat which normally produces in the mind the sensation of thirst, the resulting condition of the nerves and other parts will dispose the body to take a drink, with the result that the disease will be aggravated. Yet this is just as natural as the body's being stimulated by a similar dryness of the throat to take a drink when there is no such illness and the drink is beneficial. Admittedly, when I consider the purpose of the clock, I may say that it is departing from its nature when it does not tell the right time; and similarly when I consider the mechanism of the human body, I may think that, in relation to the movements which normally occur in it, it too is deviating from its nature if the throat is dry at a time when drinking is not beneficial to its continued health. But I am well aware that 'nature' as I have just used it has a very different significance from 'nature' in the other sense. As I have just used it, 'nature' is simply a label which depends on my thought; it is quite extraneous to the things to which it is applied, and depends simply on my comparison between the idea of a sick man and a badly-made clock, and the idea of a healthy man and a well-made clock. But by 'nature' in the other sense I understand something which is really to be found in the things themselves; in this sense, therefore, the term contains something of the truth.

When we say, then, with respect to the body suffering from dropsy, that it has a disordered nature because it has a dry throat and yet does not need drink, the term 'nature' is here used merely as an extraneous label. However, with respect to the composite, that is, the mind united with this body, what is involved is not a mere label, but a true error of nature, namely that it is thirsty at a time when drink is going to cause it harm. It thus remains to inquire how

it is that the goodness of God does not prevent nature, in this sense, from deceiving us.

The first observation I make at this point is that there is a great difference between the mind and the body, inasmuch as the body is by its very nature always divisible, while the mind is utterly indivisible. For when I consider the mind, or myself in so far as I am merely a thinking thing, I am unable to distinguish any parts within myself; I understand myself to be something quite single and complete. Although the whole mind seems to be united to the whole body, I recognize that if a foot or arm or any other part of the body is cut off, nothing has thereby been taken away from the mind. As for the faculties of willing, of understanding, of sensory perception and so on, these cannot be termed parts of the mind, since it is one and the same mind that wills, and understands and has sensory perceptions. By contrast, there is no corporeal or extended thing that I can think of which in my thought I cannot easily divide into parts; and this very fact makes me understand that it is divisible. This one argument would be enough to show me that the mind is completely different from the body, even if I did not already know as much from other considerations.

My next observation is that the mind is not immediately affected by all parts of the body, but only by the brain, or perhaps just by one small part of the brain, namely the part which is said to contain the 'common' sense. Every time this part of the brain is in a given state, it presents the same signals to the mind, even though the other parts of the body may be in a different condition at the time. This is established by countless observations, which there is no need to review here.

I observe, in addition, that the nature of the body is such that whenever any part of it is moved by another part which is some distance away, it can always be moved in the same fashion by any of the parts which lie in between, even if the more distant part does nothing. For example, in a cord ABCD, if one end D is pulled so that the other end A moves, the exact same movement could have been brought about if one of the intermediate points B or C had been pulled, and D had not moved at all. In similar fashion, when I feel a pain in my foot, physiology tells me that this happens by means of nerves distributed throughout the foot, and that these nerves are like cords which go from the foot right up to the brain. When the nerves are pulled in the foot, they in turn pull on inner parts of the brain to which they are attached, and produce a certain motion in them; and nature has laid it down that this motion should produce in the mind a sensation of pain, as occurring in the foot. But since these nerves, in passing from the foot to the brain, must pass through the calf, the thigh, the lumbar region, the back and the neck, it can happen that, even if it is not the part in the foot but one of the intermediate parts which is being pulled, the same motion will occur in the brain as occurs when the foot is hurt, and so it will necessarily come about that the mind feels the same sensation of pain. And we must suppose the same thing happens with regard to any other sensation.

My final observation is that any given movement occurring in the part of the brain that immediately affects the mind produces just one corresponding sensation; and hence the best system that could be devised is that it should produce the one sensation which, of all possible sensations, is most especially and most frequently conducive to the preservation of the healthy man. And experience shows that the sensations which nature has given us are all of this kind; and so there is absolutely nothing to be found in them that does not bear witness to the power and goodness of God. For example, when the nerves in the foot are set in motion in a violent and unusual manner, this motion, by way of the spinal cord, reaches the inner parts of the brain, and there gives the mind its signal for having a certain sensation, namely the sensation of a pain as occurring in the foot.

This stimulates the mind to do its best to get rid of the cause of the pain, which it takes to be harmful to the foot. It is true that God could have made the nature of man such that this particular motion in the brain indicated something else to the mind; it might, for example, have made the mind aware of the actual motion occurring in the brain, or in the foot, or in any of the intermediate regions; or it might have indicated something else entirely. But there is nothing else which would have been so conducive to the continued well-being of the body. In the same way, when we need drink, there arises a certain dryness in the throat; this sets in motion the nerves of the throat, which in turn move the inner parts of the brain. This motion produces in the mind a sensation of thirst, because the most useful thing for us to know about the whole business is that we need drink in order to stay healthy. And so it is in the other cases.

It is quite clear from all this that, notwithstanding the immense goodness of God, the nature of man as a combination of mind and body is such that it is bound to mislead him from time to time. For there may be some occurrence, not in the foot but in one of the other areas through which the nerves travel in their route from the foot to the brain, or even in the brain itself; and if this cause produces the same motion which is generally produced by injury to the foot, then pain will be felt as if it were in the foot. This deception of the senses is natural, because a given motion in the brain must always produce the same sensation in the mind; and the origin of the motion in question is much more often going to be something which is hurting the foot, rather than something existing elsewhere. So it is reasonable that this motion should always indicate to the mind a pain in the foot rather than in any other part of the body. Again, dryness of the throat may sometimes arise not, as it normally does, from the fact that a drink is necessary to the health of the body, but from some quite opposite cause, as happens in the case of the man with dropsy. Yet it is much better that it should mislead on this occasion than that it should always mislead when the body is in good health. And the same goes for the other cases.

This consideration is the greatest help to me, not only for noticing all the errors to which my nature is liable, but also for enabling me to correct or avoid them without difficulty. For I know that in matters regarding the well-being of the body, all my senses report the truth much more frequently than not. Also, I can almost always make use of more than one sense to investigate the same thing; and in addition, I can use both my memory, which connects present experiences with preceding ones, and my intellect, which has by now examined all the causes of error. Accordingly, I should not have any further fears about the falsity of what my senses tell me every day; on the contrary, the exaggerated doubts of the last few days should be dismissed as laughable. This applies especially to the principal reason for doubt, namely my inability to distinguish between being asleep and being awake. For I now notice that there is a vast difference between the two, in that dreams are never linked by memory with all the other actions of life as waking experiences are. If, while I am awake, anyone were suddenly to appear to me and then disappear immediately, as happens in sleep, so that I could not see where he had come from or where he had gone to, it would not be unreasonable for me to judge that he was a ghost, or a vision created in my brain, rather than a real man. But when I distinctly see where things come from and where and when they come to me, and when I can connect my perceptions of them with the whole of the rest of my life without a break, then I am quite certain that when I encounter these things I am not asleep but awake. And I ought not to have even the slightest doubt of their reality if, after calling upon all the senses as well as my memory and my intellect in order to check them, I receive no conflicting reports from any of these sources. For from the fact that God is not a deceiver it follows that in cases like these I am completely free from error. But since the pressure of things to be done does not always allow us to stop and make such a meticulous check, it must be admitted that in this human life we are often liable to make mistakes about particular things, and we must acknowledge the weakness of our nature.

CHAPTER FIVE

Descartes' Dualism

Introduction

Descartes' aim in the final part of the *Meditations on First Philosophy* is to establish the real qualities of mind and matter, and to show how the two interact. To this end Descartes has established three points. In the Second Meditation he introduces a conception of the mind as defined by the contents of conscious thought. In the Third Meditation he presents the general rule that whatever is clearly and distinctly perceived is always true. And the opening of the Sixth Meditation makes the claim that the idea of physical objects as extended in space is clear and distinct as it is understood through the sciences of geometry and arithmetic. In the ninth paragraph of the Sixth Meditation Descartes puts these assertions together in an ingenious argument to prove the independent existence of mind and body.

Descartes' argument for dualism

The argument has three premises, which we can paraphrase as follows.

1. Anything that I can clearly and distinctly understand can be created by God exactly as I understand it. So if I can clearly and distinctly understand one thing apart from another, this is enough to make me certain that the two things are distinct.
2. I can form a clear and distinct understanding of my own existence as depending on nothing more than the fact that I think, and hence (from Premise 1) it follows that nothing belongs to my essence except thought.
3. I also have a clear and distinct understanding of physical bodies (including my own) simply as extended matter, without possessing any thought.

Hence, I (or my soul) am distinct from my physical body, and can exist without it.

The first premise is an application of the rule introduced in the Third Meditation. If we can form a clear and distinct idea of a certain state of affairs, then such a state of affairs must at least be possible. In essence, the claim is that there can be no contradiction in any idea we can form clearly and distinctly in our minds.

The particular state of affairs Descartes has in mind is the independent existence of mind and body. By definition two things are distinct (that is, they are *two* things, not one) if each one can exist when the other doesn't. So Descartes' idea is this: if he can conceive clearly and distinctly of the mind existing without the body, and the body without the mind, then these must be real possibilities, and hence they must be two distinct things.

The clear and distinct ideas of mind and body

The basis of the second premise goes back to the Second Meditation. There Descartes redefined thinking in terms of the contents of conscious thought and experience. In this premise he maintains that this conception of the mind is clear and distinct. The longer and more critically we reflect on what is necessary for the soul to exist, the more we are convinced that it will exist just as long as it is engaged in conscious thought. According to Descartes, the new understanding of the mind that he formed in the Second Meditation is not merely an interesting new hypothesis. It is the understanding we arrive at when we reflect as sharply as possible on what is absolutely necessary for the mind to exist.

Another way of understanding Descartes' point in the second premise is to see that solipsism is a real possibility. **Solipsism** is the idea that nothing exists but your own mind, that is, your current thoughts and sensations. To imagine that solipsism is true, imagine that the contents of your current conscious experience are all that exist. There is no physical world — no planets, trees, houses, or mountains — and no other people; only your own internal thoughts. Although no one actually believes this to be true, Descartes' point here is that it is not an incoherent idea.

The third premise asserts what he has established in the first part of the Sixth Meditation: our understanding of pure mathematics gives us a clear and distinct idea of material objects as things that occupy space but have no other attributes. In the study of geometry we can form a conception of physical objects possessing only the properties of size, shape, and motion. Because the principles of geometry are clear and distinct, it follows from Premise 1 that these are the only properties that material things require in order to exist.

As the only attribute that the soul needs to exist is conscious thought, and the only attribute that the physical body (including the brain and the organs of sense) needs to exist is spatial extension, Descartes concludes that each can exist independently of the other. Destruction of the body will not destroy the mind, for the mind exists just as long as there is consciousness, which is not an attribute of matter. Similarly, the body can exist as a material object even in the absence of the mind because it is nothing more than a spatially extended object. Because each can exist without the other, mind and body are two different objects. Moreover, each possesses completely different properties from the other.

The existence of the physical world

Notice, however, that this argument does not actually demonstrate that there are any material objects. So far Descartes has shown only that the *idea* of material objects extended in space is clear and distinct, and that the mind is not a material object. But the conclusions he has established so far do not rule out the possibility that nothing exists at all except his own consciousness, which simply forms the idea of material objects within itself. In the next paragraph Descartes argues that these objects do exist, and that his mind is conjoined to a physical body just as he perceives it to be.

The argument depends again on the rule of the Third Meditation. This rule implies that we are always capable in principle of correcting any error into which we might fall. For otherwise we could fall into error even with our clearest and most distinct perceptions. But we have no ability (or faculty as he calls it) to distinguish whether material objects exist or whether the entire material world as it is perceived is an illusion. There is no noticeable difference between reality as we think of it and a perfect illusion created by an evil demon. Because the absence of any noticeable difference contradicts what was established in the Third Meditation, it follows that the illusion is impossible.

Material objects must therefore exist, at least insofar as we have a clear and distinct comprehension of them. This last qualification is important. For all that has been assured is that material objects exist as spatially extended objects that possess a size, shape, location, and motion, but not that they exist exactly as they appear to the senses.

Mind-body interaction

In paragraph twelve Descartes turns to the precise nature of the relationship between mind and body. He points out that nature has taught him that he has a body to which he is "closely joined."[1] The mind feels sensations of pain, hunger, and thirst when the body is injured or has need of food and drink.

In similar ways the mind receives other sensations that inform it of the condition of the body. Our sensory impressions instruct us of the existence of bodies other than our own; from the fact that the mind receives sensations of colour, sounds, tastes, and so on, it is certain that there are features of surrounding objects that correspond to these different sensations.

But Descartes reminds us that it is not necessarily the case that there are qualities in the objects that *resemble* these sensations. All that is certain is that there is something in the object corresponding to each different sensation. Moreover, nothing can be ascertained of the world from the sensations produced by external objects without careful attention by the mind. For example, from the fact that the sensation produced by a candle flame is larger than that produced by a star, it does not follow that this difference reflects their actual relative sizes. This supports the point made in the Second Meditation that conclusions about the world from sensations require acts of judgement of the intellect. We can't simply *see* what the world is like; we have to infer what it is like from our sensations.

The connection between mind and body

In paragraph fifteen Descartes admits that his theory so far does not explain how some sensations are actually misleading, as when poisons have a pleasant taste. His long consideration of this problem leads him in paragraph nineteen to re-examine the relationship between mind and body more closely. He argues that although the body is divisible into spatial parts, the mind is not. His point here is that the mind is not spatially distributed around the body, having neither spatial extension nor parts in any other real sense.[2] It is also clear, he argues in the next paragraph, that the mind receives impressions only from the brain and not from other regions of the body. His reasoning here is that the mind receives the same sensations no matter where a nerve is stimulated, as long as the signal reaching the brain is the same. From these points Descartes gives the following explanation of the source of sensations in the mind.

Stimulation of the nerves, by external objects or by changes in the body, is communicated through the nerve fibres to produce motions in the brain. These motions are finally gathered in a region of the brain Descartes calls the "common sense," which he identified as the pineal gland. Each distinct motion in the pineal gland produces a distinct sensation in the mind. On the basis of these changing sensations, the mind can determine the state of the surrounding physical environment. Similarly, but in the opposite direction, certain actions of the mind produce motions in the brain, which in turn generate muscle contractions. For example, if the mind wills the arm to raise, a certain motion is produced in the brain that indirectly causes the necessary muscles in the arm to contract.

The argument from mechanics

Descartes' argument for dualism in the *Meditations*, which we have just surveyed, is deduced from the "clear and distinct ideas" of mind and matter. In a different work, Descartes uses his theory of the mechanical nature of the body to argue that certain aspects of human behaviour cannot be the product merely of the physical body but must involve an immaterial soul. This argument occurs in Book V of an earlier work known as *Discourse on the Method*. Descartes' argument in the *Discourse* relies on what he takes to be observable differences between the abilities of humans and physical machines.

In the first paragraph of this reading, Descartes reviews a set of (unpublished) theories about the structure and function of the human body based on mechanical principles. These theories were intended to show how all of the biological functions of the body could be explained on the supposition that the body is a machine operating on the same principles as mechanical clocks and hydraulic pumps. In the next paragraph he contends that, although an artificial machine of this sort could be constructed to perfectly resemble a nonhuman animal, it is impossible to build one that duplicates human behaviour. He appeals to two aspects of human behaviour: language use and what we can call **behavioural plasticity**.

Language and behavioural plasticity

The first difference that Descartes describes between human actions and what a machine is capable of performing is that:

> [Machines] could never use words, or put together other signs, as we
> do in order to declare our thoughts to others.

He agrees that we can construct a machine that will produce language-like sounds in response to certain stimuli. But even "the dullest of men" are capable of putting words together into an *endless* number of *different* sentences, and to use these sentences in an unending number of different circumstances. This, Descartes contends, a machine would never be able to do. His reasoning here is that machines can only be constructed to utter a finite number of different utterances, each one in response to a single particular stimulus. In this way, machine language-ability would resemble something like what we now call **reflex** actions: a set of fixed responses to a limited set of stimuli. He concludes that the human ability to speak and understand language cannot be the product of the physical body, which operates on purely mechanical principles.

The reflex nature of machine response reveals a second difference between humans and mechanical devices, Descartes contends. Because a machine can only be built to respond in a single way to a particular given situation, it can respond to a variety of different situations only by combining a number of different such reflex actions, which he calls "dispositions." By contrast, human reason is a single "universal" instrument designed to respond appropriately to any given situation. We can say that the "organ" that controls human behaviour is unendingly flexible, adapting itself to any of an indefinite variety of circumstances. This ability is now referred to as **behavioural plasticity**. According to Descartes, machines, constructed on a reflex-action principle, are incapable of this kind of plasticity.

In the next paragraph Descartes claims that human behaviour differs in the same manner from animal behaviour. Like artificial machines, animals can only respond in fixed ways to a finite number of circumstances. This shows that nonhuman animals lack intelligence, even though their behaviour at times appears to resemble or surpass our own.[3] Animals, he claims, are nothing more than complex living machines, no different in kind from clocks.[4]

Minds and machines

In the final paragraph Descartes argues that, given these differences between humans and machines (including living machines), it follows that the human soul is not the product of matter and hence is "entirely independent" of the body. As the variety and plasticity of human behaviours transcends what matter can produce, only an immaterial soul can be the cause of our actions.

An interesting feature of Descartes' argument here is its reliance on the assumption that machines can only respond to situations in a reflex manner. Although we can combine series of reflex actions into enormously complex behaviours, Descartes believed that there is always an upper limit on the flexibility of behaviour that machines can exhibit. The same is not true, he contends, of human actions produced by the intellect. In this contention Descartes identifies a problem in machine construction that is a major topic in computer construction today. As we will see in chapter 10, programmable computers are machines that can perform in ways that Descartes did not envision. However, there are still serious problems facing the design of machines capable of the flexibility of human behaviour.

Antoine Arnauld and the criticisms of the *Meditations*

When Descartes' *Meditations on First Philosophy* was complete, it was circulated in manuscript form to a number of prominent intellectuals, who were invited to submit their comments and objections to the arguments in the

Meditations. These were then published in the first edition of the *Meditations,* as were Descartes' replies. The fourth of these Objections was written by Antoine Arnauld (1612–1694), a theologian and philosopher at the Sorbonne in Paris. Arnauld's criticism of the argument for dualism in the Sixth Meditation is very useful in understanding Descartes' reasoning. In addition to this criticism, Arnauld is known for raising the most powerful objection to the *Meditations*: that the argument for the rule, "Whatever I perceive very clearly and distinctly is true," is circular.

Arnauld's analysis of Descartes' argument

We start with the section Arnauld entitles "The Nature of the Human Mind." His first point here is that much of Descartes' reasoning in the Second Meditation is similar to what Saint Augustine had written centuries earlier. He follows this with a concise description of Descartes' argument for mind-body dualism. According to Arnauld, Descartes argues as follows:

> I can doubt whether I have a body, and even whether there are any bodies at all in the world. Yet for all that, I may not doubt that I am or that I exist, so long as I am doubting or thinking. Therefore I who am doubting and thinking am not a body. For, in that case, in having doubts about my body I should be having doubts about myself.

Arnauld begins his criticism of this argument by raising an earlier version of Descartes' argument in *Discourse on the Method.* In response to criticisms of his argument in the *Discourse,* Descartes admits that

> the proof excluding anything corporeal from the nature of the mind was not put forward "in an order corresponding to the actual truth of the matter" but merely in an order corresponding to his "own perception."[5]

Arnauld's point is that Descartes' argument appears to derive the conclusion that the mind can exist without the body solely from the fact that he can *imagine* his body not existing. But where do we get the assurance that whatever we can imagine must be possible? So Arnauld asks the following question.

> How does it follow, from the fact that he is aware of nothing else belonging to his essence, that nothing else does in fact belong to it?

Why should we conclude that the body is not a part of the mind simply from the fact that we can doubt the former but not the latter?[6]

Questioning the first premise

In the Second Meditation Descartes redefines thinking as conscious thought: that which is impossible to doubt when we reflect on our own internal experience. Arnauld's point here is that there are in fact *two* components to this redefinition. For Descartes concludes not only (1) that he knows that he exists as a thinking thing, but also (2) that thinking, including only the contents of conscious experience, is *all* that truly belongs to the mind. As we cannot doubt the existence of our own conscious thoughts, Descartes contends, it is *only* the latter that truly belong to the mind.

Arnauld claims that there is no justification for this conclusion in the Second Meditation. That is, the new conception of the mind does not *by itself* show that the mind can exist without the body. The argument relies crucially on the first premise of the argument, which Arnauld refers to as the "major premise":

> hence the fact that I can clearly and distinctly understand one thing apart from another is enough to make me certain that the two things are distinct, since they are capable of being separated by God.

Arnauld raises two questions about this premise: (1) Under what conditions could this principle be true? (2) Are those conditions met in our comprehension of mind and body?

Adequate knowledge

Arnauld's answer to the first question is that the principle would only be true if one's knowledge were what Descartes elsewhere calls "adequate knowledge." By this Descartes means knowledge that includes an understanding of every aspect of the things in question. So the principle is only true if there is nothing at all one does not know about the things to which it is applied. If we know *everything* about the mind, then we know whether or not it depends on the body for its existence. Arnauld takes this answer from Descartes himself, who says that inadequate knowledge is sufficient to establish a "formal" distinction between two things, but not to establish a "real" distinction, and that there is a "real" distinction between mind and body.[7]

So the question is, what evidence is there that our knowledge of mind and body is adequate in this sense? Arnauld points out that Descartes' justification here is simply that he can clearly and distinctly conceive of the mind as existing without the body, and vice versa. In response Arnauld presents an example intended to show that this is not sufficient to achieve the desired conclusion. Consider someone who clearly understands the concept of a right-angled triangle, but who has not yet grasped the rule of the hypotenuse. Then, says Arnauld, he might then reason as follows.

I clearly and distinctly perceive that the triangle is right-angled; but I doubt that the square on the hypotenuse is equal to the squares on the other two sides; therefore it does not belong to the essence of the triangle that the square on its hypotenuse is equal to the squares on the other sides.

Obviously it does not follow from the fact that someone can *imagine* triangles violating the rule of the hypotenuse that there could actually be triangles that do violate the rule. The person merely has a less than "adequate" grasp of the nature of right triangles. Arnauld's question, then, is how our understanding of the mind is any clearer than the understanding of the triangle in this story. He maintains that Descartes offers no proper answer to this question, and hence the argument is unsound.

Descartes' reply

We should begin at the sixth paragraph of Descartes' reply. Descartes argues that, contrary to Arnauld's claim, he never asserted that "adequate" knowledge was required to establish a real distinction between things. Only God, he argues, can know that His knowledge is adequate in this sense. Given our limited abilities, humans are not capable of an adequate knowledge of anything. Rather, he says five paragraphs further on, one's knowledge must be "complete." This point seems at first to be a purely semantic quibble. But it is the crux of Descartes' reply and, in fact, of his argument that mind and body are distinct.

He says that "a complete understanding of something" is the same as "understanding something to be a complete thing." So it seems that Descartes' point is that the first premise of his argument is true only when the things to which it is applied are "complete things." And a **complete thing**, he says, is a "substance." The heart of the issue, then, is what Descartes understands as "substance."

We have seen this word used in Aristotle's *On the Soul*, and Descartes' use of it has some similarity. In the *Principles of Philosophy*, Part One, Section 1, Descartes says that a **substance** is "a thing which exists in such a way as to depend on no other thing for its existence." This implies that substances are the *fundamental* or basic constituents of the world. This much Aristotle would perhaps agree to. But Descartes puts it to use in his own way. For Descartes has argued that he can conceive of his mind existing, as a thinking thing, by itself without any body. Mind conceived in this way is a substance. So Descartes holds that his major premise is true of our clear and distinct ideas of substances — complete things that can exist on their own.

The argument for dualism revisited

Accordingly Descartes restates the major premise this way:

> The mere fact that I can clearly and distinctly understand one *substance* apart from another is enough to make me certain that one excludes the other.

So his point is, then, that if I conceive of two things as substances, *and* I can conceive of each existing without the other, then they are two distinct things. This permits him to reject Arnauld's triangle example as irrelevant. For the question in that example is whether a right triangle can exist without a certain *property* (namely, having the square of the hypotenuse equal to those on the other sides). That property is not a complete thing in itself, able to exist without figures to which it belongs. As the principle stated in the major premise of Descartes' argument applies only to substances, it does not apply to the example.

Descartes claims that, stated in this way, the major premise follows directly from the definition of substance. For if we can conceive of two things existing as complete things — as substances — and each is conceived of as having different properties from the other, then it follows from the idea of substance that each can exist without the other. We can see here the important use that Descartes makes of the argument (found also in Galileo) that matter cannot exist without shape, size, and location, although the same is not true of colour, taste, sound, and fragrance. In Descartes' hands this becomes the basis for a view of matter extended in space as a complete thing, able to exist without any other properties. In the same way, he conceives of mind as a complete thing, existing with no other attribute than thought and not dependent on anything else for its existence.

Descartes' two substances

In Section 53 of Part One of the *Principles of Philosophy*, Descartes claims that mind and matter are each substances with only one principal attribute. In the case of mind that attribute is thought, and in the case of matter the principal attribute is extension in space. All other attributes of mind and matter are simply modes (or modifications) of thought and extension. Hence, on Descartes' view, there are in the natural world only two kinds of things, minds and bodies, and each has only one attribute. All other things are to be explained in terms of these two attributes. For example, sense perception is just a particular mode of thought, as is reason and judgement. Colour, taste, fragrance, and sound *as we perceive them* are all qualities of our subjective experience. In objects these qualities are simply shapes and sizes of the particles on surfaces that produce sensations in us by changing the motions of light and air.

Locke's rejection of innate ideas

In this chapter and the last we have seen how Descartes' arguments rest to a large extent on the clarity and distinctness rule introduced in the Third Meditation. According to Descartes, there are certain "clear and distinct" ideas of mind and matter that are found in the intellect. Because they are not derived from our sensory experiences, these are "innate ideas" that reside in the mind independently of experience or observation. The Method of Doubt becomes Descartes' way of isolating the content of these ideas, and thus they form the basis for all of our knowledge.

Our last reading for this chapter is from a book by John Locke (1632–1704) entitled *An Essay Concerning Human Understanding*. Locke was born to a Puritan family in Somerset, England. He studied and taught logic, moral philosophy, and medicine at Oxford, and then in 1666 entered the service of the Earl of Shaftesbury. There he met the chemist, Robert Boyle, who stimulated his interest in the new science. Following Shaftesbury's trial for treason Locke was forced to flee to Holland, but he returned to England and entered public service after the accession of the Protestant William of Orange. Locke's avowed philosophical goal was to ascertain the limits and nature of human knowledge in order to avert extreme skepticism. In this endeavour he became a primary exponent of the philosophical view known as "empiricism," which holds that all knowledge of the world is derived only from our sensory experiences.

Although Locke was in essential agreement with Descartes in defending the new science, on other issues they were in sharp disagreement. The core of Locke's theory of knowledge is that there are no innate ideas. All ideas and all knowledge, according to Locke, are obtained from experience. In this reading we look at Locke's argument that our knowledge does not extend to an understanding of the relation between mind and body, as Descartes maintains.

Locke's skepticism about knowledge of mind

The first few sections of the chapter lay out some general points concerning knowledge. Our interest begins at Section 6. Locke maintains that not only does our knowledge not extend to all of reality, but that it falls short even of a full understanding our own ideas. This is illustrated by the fact that, although the ideas of a circle and a square are well enough known, we might never be able to construct a circle equal in area to a square. He applies this point to the ideas of mind and body: while the concepts of matter and of thinking are familiar, it is impossible just by contemplation of these ideas to determine whether matter is capable of thought. As far as we know, he claims, God could add a faculty of thinking to matter just as easily as he could create a distinct substance that has the power of thought.

Locke's argument amounts to a denial that we have anything like a "clear and distinct idea" of mind and body such as Descartes claims. The method of doubt may well reveal that thought is an attribute that belongs to us, but it does not reveal to us anything about the *nature* of thought or where it resides. In particular, there is nothing in the idea of thought that rules out thinking as a faculty of the material body. The fact that we can doubt the existence of the body even though it is impossible to doubt the existence of the mind reveals only the limitations of our ideas of mind and matter. He says:

> We have the Ideas of Matter and Thinking, but possibly shall never be able to know, whether any mere material Being thinks, or no; it being impossible for us, by the contemplation of our own Ideas, without revelation, to discover, whether Omnipotency has not given to some Systems of Matter fitly disposed, a power to perceive and think.

Mind-body interaction

Locke adds another point that raises a difficult question for dualists like Descartes. Dualists maintain that God has connected mind and body in such a way that motions in the nerves produce sensations in the mind. But, according to Locke, this is just as mysterious as the idea that matter itself is capable of thinking. Many critics of dualism have pointed out that the connection between mind and body is asserted by dualists but never *explained*. If mind and body are utterly different as Plato and Descartes claim, how is it possible for motions in the body to produce sensations in the mind, or acts of will to produce changes in the body? The interaction of mind and body is thus left a mystery. Locke says:

> Motion, according to the utmost reach of our Ideas, being able to produce nothing but Motion, so that when we allow it to produce pleasure or pain, or the Idea of a Colour, or Sound, we are fain to quit our Reason, go beyond our Ideas, and attribute it wholly to the good Pleasure of our Maker.

In conclusion, he claims that those who find it impossible to see how such a property as thought can belong to bodies ought to recognize thereby just how weak our understanding of the soul is.

The point that Locke raises here is one that we have seen is an abiding problem for dualism. Both Descartes and Plato maintain that mind and body are completely different. Yet each maintains that there is an interaction between the two. How this is possible is never completely explained. In Chapter 3 we saw this problem arise in Descartes' theory of perception. Although he berates the Aristotelians for failing to explain how forms and qualities are received in the mind, he himself offers no account of how motion in the pineal gland produces sensations in the immaterial mind. According to Descartes, this connection is an act of God beyond our comprehension. Locke replies by arguing that if this is beyond comprehension, it is no more of a mystery than how matter in the brain might have the ability to think.

NOTES

1 The expression 'that my own nature teaches me,' which occurs in this sentence and elsewhere, refers to the irresistible beliefs that arise as the result of our union with the body.

2 This paragraph serves to some extent as a second argument that mind and body are distinct, as Descartes indicates in the last sentence. But it is widely seen as a weak argument, and I will focus here on its more important role in explaining the connection between mind and body.

3 An example of the kind of thing Descartes has in mind is the behaviour of certain varieties of spiders. Many spiders have elaborate procedures for burying their eggs and camouflaging the hole. This activity looks for all the world like the product of genuine intelligence. But if the spider is interrupted in its task, it will repeat its previous step, and it will do so over and over again without ever noticing the interruption. This, Descartes would say, is because its behaviour just a complex series of reflex actions, not an intelligent understanding of what it is doing.

4 There is a debate about what Descartes' views on nonhuman animals were with regard to questions such as whether they experience sensations like pain or colour. His writings are open to a number of different interpretations.

5 The passage that Arnauld is quoting here occurs in the Preface to the *Meditations*.

6 This last question suggests an interpretation of Descartes' argument as follows. "If mind and body are one thing, then whatever is true of the body must be true of the mind. But I can doubt the existence of the body without doubting the existence of the mind. Therefore, they cannot be one thing." But this argument is clearly fallacious, and Descartes' reply to Arnauld suggests that he is not relying on this line of reasoning.

7 A "formal distinction," according to Descartes, is that between two properties or characteristics of a thing, like size and shape. A "real distinction," he says, is that between two *substances*. The meaning of Descartes' notion of substance will come up when we read Descartes' reply to Arnauld.

René Descartes
Selections from *Discourse on the Method of rightly conducting one's reason and seeking the truth in the sciences*

Part V

•••

I explained all these matters in sufficient detail in the treatise I previously intended to publish. And then I showed what structure the nerves and muscles of the human body must have in order to make the animal spirits inside them strong enough to move its limbs—as when we see severed heads continue to move about and bite the earth although they are no longer alive. I also indicated what changes must occur in the brain in order to cause waking, sleep and dreams; how light, sounds, smells, tastes, heat and the other qualities of external objects can imprint various ideas on the brain through the mediation of the senses; and how hunger, thirst, and the other internal passions can also send their ideas there. And I explained which part of the brain must be taken to be the 'common' sense, where these ideas are received; the memory, which preserves them; and the corporeal imagination, which can change them in various ways, form them into new ideas, and, by distributing the animal spirits to the muscles, make the parts of this body move in as many different ways as the parts of our bodies can move without being guided by the will, and in a manner which is just as appropriate to the objects of the senses and the internal passions. This will not seem at all strange to those who know how many kinds of automatons, or moving machines, the skill of man can construct with the use of very few parts, in comparison with the great multitude of bones, muscles, nerves, arteries, veins and all the other parts that are in the body of any animal. For they will regard this body as a machine which, having

been made by the hands of God, is incomparably better ordered than any machine that can be devised by man, and contains in itself movements more wonderful than those in any such machine.

I made special efforts to show that if any such machines had the organs and outward shape of a monkey or of some other animal that lacks reason, we should have no means of knowing that they did not possess entirely the same nature as these animals; whereas if any such machines bore a resemblance to our bodies and imitated our actions as closely as possible for all practical purposes, we should still have two very certain means of recognizing that they were not real men. The first is that they could never use words, or put together other signs, as we do in order to declare our thoughts to others. For we can certainly conceive of a machine so constructed that it utters words, and even utters words which correspond to bodily actions causing a change in its organs (e.g. if you touch it in one spot it asks what you want of it, if you touch it in another it cries out that you are hurting it, and so on). But it is not conceivable that such a machine should produce different arrangements of words so as to give an appropriately meaningful answer to whatever is said in its presence, as the dullest of men can do. Secondly, even though such machines might do some things as well as we do them, or perhaps even better, they would inevitably fail in others, which would reveal that they were acting not through understanding but only from the disposition of their organs. For whereas reason is a universal instrument which can be used in all kinds of situations, these organs need some particular disposition for each particular action; hence it is for all practical purposes impossible for a machine to have enough different organs to make it act in all the contingencies of life in the way in which our reason makes us act.

Now in just these two ways we can also know the difference between man and beast. For it is quite remarkable that there are no men so dull-witted or stupid—and this includes even mad-men—that they are incapable of arranging various words together and forming an utterance from them in order to make their thoughts understood; whereas there is no other animal, however perfect and well-endowed it may be, that can do the like. This does not happen because they lack the necessary organs, for we see that magpies and parrots can utter words as we do, and yet they cannot speak as we do: that is, they cannot show that they are thinking what they are saying. On the other hand, men born deaf and dumb, and thus deprived of speech-organs as much as the beasts or even more so, normally invent their own signs to make themselves understood by those who, being regularly in their company, have the time to learn their language. This shows not merely that the beasts have less reason than men, but that they have no reason at all. For it patently requires very little reason to be able to speak; and since as much inequality can be observed among the animals of a given species as among human beings, and some animals are more easily trained than others, it would be incredible that a superior specimen of the monkey or parrot species should not be able to speak as well as the stupidest child—or at least as well as a child with a defective brain—if their souls were not completely different in nature from ours. And we must not confuse speech with the natural movements which express passions and which can be imitated by machines as well as by animals. Nor should we think, like some of the ancients, that the beasts speak, although we do not understand their language. For if that were true, then since they have many organs that correspond to ours, they could make themselves understood by us as well as by their fellows. It is also a very remarkable fact that although many animals show more skill than we do in some of their actions, yet the same animals show none at all in many others; so what they do better does not prove that they have any intelligence, for if it did then they would have more intelligence than any of us and would excel us in everything. It proves rather that they have no intelligence at all, and that it is nature which acts in them according to the disposition of their organs. In the same way a clock, consisting only of wheels and springs, can count the hours and measure time more accurately than we can with all our wisdom.

After that, I described the rational soul, and showed that, unlike the other things of which I had spoken, it cannot be derived in any way from the potentiality of matter, but must be specially created. And I showed how it is not sufficient for it to be lodged in the human body like a helmsman in his ship, except perhaps to move its limbs, but that it must be more closely joined and united with the body in order to have, besides this power of movement, feelings and appetites like ours and so constitute a real man. Here I dwelt a little upon the subject of the soul, because it is of the greatest importance. For after the error of those who deny God, which I believe I have already adequately refuted, there is none that leads weak minds further from the straight path of virtue than that of imagining that the souls of the beasts are of the same nature as ours, and hence that after this present life we have nothing to fear or to hope for, any more than flies and ants. But when we know how much the beasts differ from us, we understand much better the arguments which prove that our soul is of a nature entirely independent of the body, and consequently that it is not bound to die with it. And since we cannot see any other causes which destroy the soul, we are naturally led to conclude that it is immortal.

• • •

Antoine Arnauld
Objections to Descartes' Meditations

THE NATURE OF THE HUMAN MIND

The first thing that I find remarkable is that our distinguished author has laid down as the basis for his entire philosophy exactly the same principle as that laid down by St Augustine—a man of the sharpest intellect and a remarkable thinker, not only on theological topics but also on philosophical ones. In Book II chapter 3 of *De Libero Arbitrio*, Alipius, when he is disputing with Euodius and is about to prove the existence of God, says the following: 'First, if we are to take as our starting point what is most evident, I ask you to tell me whether you yourself exist. Or are you perhaps afraid of making a mistake in your answer, given that, if you did not exist, it would be quite impossible for you to make a mistake?' This is like what M. Descartes says: 'But there is a deceiver of supreme power and cunning who is deliberately and constantly deceiving me. In that case I too undoubtedly exist, if he is deceiving me.' But let us go on from here and, more to the point, see how this principle can be used to derive the result that our mind is separate from our body.

I can doubt whether I have a body, and even whether there are any bodies at all in the world. Yet for all that, I may not doubt that I am or exist, so long as I am doubting or thinking.

Therefore I who am doubting and thinking am not a body. For, in that case, in having doubts about my body I should be having doubts about myself.

Indeed, even if I obstinately maintain that there are no bodies whatsoever, the proposition still stands, namely that I am something, and hence I am not a body.

This is certainly very acute. But someone is going to bring up the objection which the author raises against himself: the fact that I have doubts about the body, or deny that it exists, does not bring it about that no body exists. 'Yet may it not perhaps be the case that these very things which I am supposing to be nothing, because they are unknown to me, are in reality identical with the "I" of which I am aware? I do not know,' he says 'and for the moment I shall not argue the point. I know that I exist; the question is, what is this "I" that I know? If the "I" is understood strictly as we have been taking it, then it is quite certain that knowledge of it does not depend on things of whose existence I am as yet unaware.'

But the author admits that in the argument set out in the *Discourse on the Method* the proof excluding anything corporeal from the nature of the mind was not put forward 'in an order corresponding to the actual truth of the matter' but merely in an order corresponding to his 'own perception'. So the sense of the passage was that he was aware of nothing at all which he knew belonged to his essence except that he was a thinking thing. From this answer it is clear that the objection still stands in precisely the same form as it did before, and that the question he promised to answer still remains outstanding: How does it follow, from the fact that he is aware of nothing else belonging to his essence, that nothing else does in fact belong to it? I must confess that I am somewhat slow, but I have been unable to find anywhere in the Second Meditation an answer to this question. As far as I can gather, however, the author does attempt a proof of this claim in the Sixth Meditation, since he takes it to depend on his having clear knowledge of God, which he had not yet arrived at in the Second Meditation. This is how the proof goes:

I know that everything which I clearly and distinctly understand is capable of being created by God so as to correspond exactly with my understanding of it. Hence the fact that I can clearly and distinctly understand one thing apart from another is enough to make me certain that the two things are distinct, since they are capable of being separated, at least by God. The question of what kind of power is required to bring about such a separation does not affect the judgement that the two things are distinct ... Now on the one hand I have a clear and distinct idea of myself, in so far as I am simply a thinking, non-extended thing; and on the other hand I have a distinct idea of body, in so far as this is simply an extended, non-thinking thing. And accordingly, it is certain that I am really distinct from my body, and can exist without it.

We must pause a little here, for it seems to me that in these few words lies the crux of the whole difficulty.

First of all, if the major premiss of this syllogism is to be true, it must be taken to apply not to any kind of knowledge of a thing, nor even to clear and distinct knowledge; it must apply solely to knowledge which is adequate. For our distinguished author admits in his reply to the theologian, that if one thing can be conceived distinctly and separately from another 'by an abstraction of the intellect which conceives the thing inadequately', then this is sufficient for there to be a formal distinction between the two, but it does not require that there be a real distinction. And in the same passage he draws the following conclusion:

By contrast, I have a complete understanding of what a body is when I think that it is merely something having extension, shape and motion, and I deny that it has anything which belongs to

the nature of a mind. Conversely, I understand the mind to be a complete thing, which doubts, understands, wills, and so on, even though I deny that it has any of the attributes which are contained in the idea of a body. Hence there is a real distinction between the body and the mind.

But someone may call this minor premiss into doubt and maintain that the conception you have of yourself when you conceive of yourself as a thinking, non-extended thing is an inadequate one; and the same may be true of your conception of yourself as an extended, non-thinking thing. Hence we must look at how this is proved in the earlier part of the argument. For I do not think that this matter is so clear that it should be assumed without proof as a first principle that is not susceptible of demonstration.

As to the first part of your claim, namely that you have a complete understanding of what a body is when you think that it is merely something having extension, shape, motion etc., and you deny that it has anything which belongs to the nature of a mind, this proves little. For those who maintain that our mind is corporeal do not on that account suppose that every body is a mind. On their view, body would be related to mind as a genus is related to a species. Now a genus can be understood apart from a species, even if we deny of the genus what is proper and peculiar to the species— hence the common maxim of logicians, 'The negation of the species does not negate the genus.' Thus I can understand the genus 'figure' apart from my understanding of any of the properties which are peculiar to a circle. It therefore remains to be proved that the mind can be completely and adequately understood apart from the body.

I cannot see anywhere in the entire work an argument which could serve to prove this claim, apart from what is suggested at the beginning:

'I can deny that any body exists, or that there is any extended thing at all, yet it remains certain to me that I exist, so long as I am making this denial or thinking it. Hence I am a thinking thing, not a body, and the body does not belong to the knowledge I have of myself.'

But so far as I can see, the only result that follows from this is that I can obtain some knowledge of myself without knowledge of the body. But it is not yet transparently clear to me that this knowledge is complete and adequate, so as to enable me to be certain that I am not mistaken in excluding body from my essence. I shall explain the point by means of an example.

Suppose someone knows for certain that the angle in a semi-circle is a right angle, and hence that the triangle formed by this angle and the diameter of the circle is right-angled. In spite of this, he may doubt, or not yet have grasped for certain, that the square on the hypotenuse is equal to the squares on the other two sides; indeed he may even deny this if he is misled by some fallacy. But now, if he uses the same argument as that proposed by our illustrious author, he may appear to have confirmation of his false belief, as follows: 'I clearly and distinctly perceive', he may say, 'that the triangle is right-angled; but I doubt that the square on the hypotenuse is equal to the squares on the other two sides; therefore it does not belong to the essence of the triangle that the square on its hypotenuse is equal to the squares on the other sides.'

Again, even if I deny that the square on the hypotenuse is equal to the square on the other two sides, I still remain sure that the triangle is right-angled, and my mind retains the clear and distinct knowledge that one of its angles is a right angle. And given that this is so, not even God could bring it about that the triangle is not right-angled.

I might argue from this that the property which I doubt, or which can be removed while leaving my idea intact, does not belong to the essence of the triangle.

Moreover, 'I know', says M. Descartes, 'that everything which I clearly and distinctly understand is capable of being created by God so as to correspond exactly with my understanding of it. And hence the fact that I can clearly and distinctly understand one thing apart from another is enough to make me certain that the two things are distinct, since they are capable of being separated by God.' Yet I clearly and distinctly understand that this triangle is right-angled, without understanding that the square on the hypotenuse is equal to the squares on the other sides. It follows on this reasoning that God, at least, could create a right-angled triangle with the square on its hypotenuse not equal to the squares on the other sides.

I do not see any possible reply here, except that the person in this example does not clearly and distinctly perceive that the triangle is right-angled. But how is my perception of the nature of my mind any clearer than his perception of the nature of the triangle? He is just as certain that the triangle in the semi-circle has one right angle (which is the criterion of a right-angled triangle) as I am certain that I exist because I am thinking.

Now although the man in the example clearly and distinctly knows that the triangle is right-angled, he is wrong in thinking that the aforesaid relationship between the squares on the sides does not belong to the nature of the triangle. Similarly, although I clearly and distinctly know my nature to be something that thinks, may I, too, not perhaps be wrong in thinking that nothing else belongs to my nature apart from the fact that I am a thinking thing? Perhaps the fact that I am an extended thing may also belong to my nature.

Someone may also make the point that since I infer my existence from the fact that I am thinking, it is certainly no surprise if the idea that I form by thinking of myself in this way represents to my mind nothing other than myself as a thinking thing. For the idea was derived entirely from my thought. Hence it seems that this idea cannot provide any evidence that nothing belongs to my essence beyond what is contained in the idea.

It seems, moreover, that the argument proves too much, and takes us back to the Platonic view (which M. Descartes nonetheless rejects) that nothing corporeal belongs to our essence, so that man is merely a rational soul and the body merely a vehicle for the soul—a view which gives rise to the definition of man as 'a soul which makes use of a body'.

If you reply that body is not straightforwardly excluded from my essence, but is ruled out only and precisely in so far as I am a thinking thing, it seems that there is a danger that someone will suspect that my knowledge of myself as a thinking thing does not qualify as knowledge of a being of which I have a complete and adequate conception; it seems instead that I conceive of it only inadequately, and by a certain intellectual abstraction.

Geometers conceive of a line as a length without breadth, and they conceive of a surface as length and breadth without depth, despite the fact that no length exists without breadth and no breadth without depth. In the same way, someone may perhaps suspect that every thinking thing is also an extended thing—an extended thing which, besides the attributes it has in common with other extended things, such as shape, motion, etc., also possesses the peculiar power of thought. This would mean that although, simply in virtue of this power, it can by an intellectual abstraction be apprehended as a thinking thing, in reality bodily attributes may belong to this thinking thing. In the same way, although quantity can be conceived in terms of length alone, in reality breadth and depth belong to every quantity, along with length.

The difficulty is increased by the fact that the power of thought appears to be attached to bodily organs, since it can be regarded as dormant in infants and extinguished in the case of madmen. And this is an objection strongly pressed by those impious people who try to do away with the soul.

So far I have dealt with the real distinction between our mind and the body. But since our distinguished author has undertaken to demonstrate the immortality of the soul, it may rightly be asked whether this evidently follows from the fact that the soul is distinct from the body. According to the principles of commonly accepted philosophy this by no means follows, since people ordinarily take it that the souls of brute animals are distinct from their bodies, but nevertheless perish along with them.

I had got as far as this in my comments, and was intending to show how the author's principles, which I thought I had managed to gather from his method of philosophizing, would enable the immortality of the soul to be inferred very easily from the real distinction between the mind and the body. But at this point, a little study composed by our illustrious author was sent to me, which apart from shedding much light on the work as a whole, puts forward the same solution to the point at issue which I was on the point of proposing.

As far as the souls of the brutes are concerned, M. Descartes elsewhere suggests clearly enough that they have none. All they have is a body which is constructed in a particular manner, made up of various organs in such a way that all the operations which we observe can be produced in it and by means of it.

But I fear that this view will not succeed in finding acceptance in people's minds unless it is supported by very solid arguments. For at first sight it seems incredible that it can come about, without the assistance of any soul, that the light reflected from the body of a wolf onto the eyes of a sheep should move the minute fibres of the optic nerves, and that on reaching the brain this motion should spread the animal spirits throughout the nerves in the manner necessary to precipitate the sheep's flight.

• • •

René Descartes
Reply to Antoine Arnauld

Reply to Part One, Dealing with the Nature of the Human Mind

I shall not waste time here by thanking my distinguished critic for bringing in the authority of St Augustine to support me, and for setting out my arguments so vigorously that he seems to fear that their strength may not be sufficiently apparent to anyone else.

But I will begin by pointing out where it was that I embarked on proving 'how, from the fact that I am aware of nothing else belonging to my essence (that is, the essence of the mind alone) apart from the fact that I am a thinking thing, it follows that nothing else does in fact belong to it'. The relevant passage is the one where I proved that God exists—a God who can bring about everything that I clearly and distinctly recognize as possible.

Now it may be that there is much within me of which I am not yet aware (for example, in this passage I was in fact supposing that I was not yet aware that the mind possessed the power of moving the body, or that it was substantially united to it). Yet since that of which I am aware is sufficient to enable me to subsist with it and it alone, I am certain that I could have been created by God without having these other attributes of which I am unaware, and hence that these other attributes do not belong to the essence of the mind.

For if something can exist without some attribute, then it seems to me that that attribute is not included in its essence. And although mind is part of the essence of man, being united to a human body is not strictly speaking part of the essence of mind.

I must also explain what I meant by saying that 'a real distinction cannot be inferred from the fact that one thing is conceived apart from another by an abstraction of the intellect which conceives the thing inadequately. It can be inferred only if we understand one thing apart from another completely, or as a complete thing.'

I do not, as M. Arnauld assumes, think that adequate knowledge of a thing is required here. Indeed, the difference between complete and adequate knowledge is that if a piece of knowledge is to be *adequate* it must contain absolutely all the properties which are in the thing which is the object of knowledge. Hence only God can know that he has adequate knowledge of all things.

A created intellect, by contrast, though perhaps it may in fact possess adequate knowledge of many things, can never know it has such knowledge unless God grants it a special revelation of the fact. In order to have adequate knowledge of a thing all that is required is that the power of knowing possessed by the intellect is adequate for the thing in question, and this can easily occur. But in order for the intellect to know it has such knowledge, or that God put nothing in the thing beyond what it is aware of, its power of knowing would have to equal the infinite power of God, and this plainly could not happen on pain of contradiction.

Now in order for us to recognize a real distinction between two things it cannot be required that our knowledge of them be adequate if it is impossible for us to know that it is adequate. And since, as has just been explained, we can never know this, it follows that it is not necessary for our knowledge to be adequate.

Hence when I said that 'it does not suffice for a real distinction that one thing is understood apart from another by an abstraction of the intellect which conceives the thing inadequately', I did not think this would be taken to imply that *adequate* knowledge was required to establish a real distinction. All I meant was that we need the sort of knowledge that we have not ourselves made *inadequate* by an abstraction of the intellect.

There is a great difference between, on the one hand, some item of knowledge being wholly adequate, which we can never know with certainty to be the case unless it is revealed by God, and, on the other hand, its being adequate enough to enable us to perceive that we have not rendered it inadequate by an abstraction of the intellect.

In the same way, when I said that a thing must be understood *completely*, I did not mean that my understanding must be adequate, but merely that I must understand the thing well enough to know that my understanding is *complete*.

I thought I had made this clear from what I had said just before and just after the passage in question. For a little earlier I had distinguished between 'incomplete' and 'complete' entities, and I had said that for there to be a real distinction between a number of things, each of them must be understood as 'an entity in its own right which is different from everything else'.

And later on, after saying that I had 'a complete understanding of what a body is', I immediately added that I also 'understood the mind to be a complete thing'. The meaning of these two phrases was identical; that is, I took 'a complete understanding of something' and 'understanding something to be a complete thing' as having one and the same meaning.

But here you may justly ask what I mean by a 'complete thing', and how I prove that for establishing a real distinction it is sufficient that two things can be understood as 'complete' and that each one can be understood apart from the other.

My answer to the first question is that by a 'complete thing' I simply mean a substance endowed with the forms or attributes which enable me to recognize that it is a substance.

We do not have immediate knowledge of substances, as I have noted elsewhere. We know them only by perceiving certain forms or attributes which must inhere in something if they are to exist; and we call the thing in which they inhere a 'substance'.

But if we subsequently wanted to strip the substance of the attributes through which we know it, we would be destroying our entire knowledge of it. We might be able to apply various words to it, but we could not have a clear and distinct perception of what we meant by these words.

I am aware that certain substances are commonly called 'incomplete'. But if the reason for calling them incomplete is that they are unable to exist on their own, then I confess I find it self-contradictory that they should be substances, that is, things which subsist on their own, and at the same time incomplete, that is, not possessing the power to subsist on their own. It is also possible to call a substance incomplete in the sense that, although it has nothing incomplete about it *qua* substance, it is incomplete in so far as it is referred to some other substance in conjunction with which it forms something which is a unity in its own right.

Thus a hand is an incomplete substance when it is referred to the whole body of which it is a part; but it is a complete substance when it is considered on its own. And in just the same way the mind and the body are incomplete substances when they are referred to a human being which together they make up. But if they are considered on their own, they are complete.

For just as being extended and divisible and having shape etc. are forms or attributes by which I recognize the substance called *body*, so understanding, willing, doubting etc. are forms by which I recognize the substance which is called *mind*. And I understand a thinking substance to be just as much a complete thing as an extended substance.

It is quite impossible to assert, as my distinguished critic maintains, that 'body may be related to mind as a genus is related to a species'. For although a genus can be understood without this or that specific differentia, there is no way in which a species can be thought of without its genus.

For example, we can easily understand the genus 'figure' without thinking of a circle (though our understanding will not be distinct unless it is referred to some specific figure and it will not involve a complete thing unless it also comprises the nature of body). But we cannot understand any specific differentia of the 'circle' without at the same time thinking of the genus 'figure'.

Now the mind can be perceived distinctly and completely (that is, sufficiently for it to be considered as a complete thing) without any of the forms or attributes by which we recognize that body is a substance, as I think I showed quite adequately in the Second Meditation. And similarly a body can be understood distinctly and as a complete thing, without any of the attributes which belong to the mind.

But here my critic argues that although I can obtain some knowledge of myself without knowledge of the body, it does not follow that this knowledge is complete and adequate, so as to enable me to be certain that I am not mistaken in excluding body from my essence. He explains the point by using the example of a triangle inscribed in a semi-circle, which we can clearly and distinctly understand to be right-angled although we do not know, or may even deny, that the square on the hypotenuse is equal to the squares on the other sides. But we cannot infer from this that there could be a right-angled triangle such that the square on the hypotenuse is not equal to the squares on the other sides.

But this example differs in many respects from the case under discussion.

First of all, though a triangle can perhaps be taken concretely as a substance having a triangular shape, it is certain that the property of having the square on the hypotenuse equal to the squares on the other sides is not a substance. So neither the triangle nor the property can be understood as a complete thing in the way in which mind and body can be so understood; nor can either item be called a 'thing' in the sense in which I said 'it is enough that I can understand one thing (that is, a complete thing) apart from another' etc. This is clear from the passage which comes next: 'Besides I find in myself faculties' etc. I did not say that these faculties were *things*, but carefully distinguished them from things or substances.

Secondly, although we can clearly and distinctly understand that a triangle in a semi-circle is right-angled without being aware that the square on the hypotenuse is equal to the squares on the other two sides, we cannot have a clear understanding of a triangle having the square on its hypotenuse equal to the squares on the other sides without at the same time being aware that it is right-angled. And yet we can clearly and distinctly perceive the mind without the body and the body without the mind.

Thirdly, although it is possible to have a concept of a triangle inscribed in a semi-circle which does not include the fact that the square on the hypotenuse is equal to the squares on the other sides, it is not possible to have a concept of the triangle such that no ratio at all is understood to hold between the square on the hypotenuse and the squares on the other sides. Hence, though we may be unaware of what that ratio is, we cannot say that any given ratio does not hold unless we clearly understand that it does not belong to the triangle; and where the ratio is one of equality, this can never be understood. Yet the concept of body includes nothing at all which belongs to the mind, and the concept of mind includes nothing at all which belongs to the body.

So although I said 'it is enough that I can clearly and distinctly understand one thing apart from another' etc., one cannot go on to argue 'yet I clearly and distinctly understand that this triangle is right-angled without understanding that the square on the hypotenuse' etc. There are three reasons for this. First, the ratio between the square on the hypotenuse and the squares on the other sides is not a complete thing. Secondly, we do not clearly understand the ratio to be equal except in the case of a right-angled triangle. And thirdly, there is no way in which the triangle can be distinctly understood if the ratio which obtains between the square on the hypotenuse and the squares on the other sides is said not to hold.

But now I must explain how the mere fact that I can clearly and distinctly understand one substance apart from another is enough to make me certain that one excludes the other.

The answer is that the notion of a *substance* is just this—that it can exist by itself, that is without the aid of any other substance. And there is no one who has ever perceived two substances by means of two different concepts without judging that they are really distinct.

Hence, had I not been looking for greater than ordinary certainty, I should have been content to have shown in the Second Meditation that the mind can be understood as a subsisting thing despite the fact that nothing belonging to the body is attributed to it, and that, conversely, the body can be understood as a subsisting thing despite the fact that nothing belonging to the mind is attributed to it. I should have added nothing more in order to demonstrate that there is a real distinction between the mind and the body, since we commonly judge that the order in which things are mutually related in our perception of them corresponds to the order in which they are related in actual reality. But one of the exaggerated doubts which I put forward in the First Meditation went so far as to make it impossible for me to be certain of this very point (namely

whether things do in reality correspond to our perception of them), so long as I was supposing myself to be ignorant of the author of my being. And this is why everything I wrote on the subject of God and truth in the Third, Fourth and Fifth Meditations contributes to the conclusion that there is a real distinction between the mind and the body, which I finally established in the Sixth Meditation.

And yet, says M. Arnauld, 'I have a clear understanding of a triangle inscribed in a semicircle without knowing that the square on the hypotenuse is equal to the squares on the other sides.' It is true that the triangle is intelligible even though we do not think of the ratio which obtains between the square on the hypotenuse and the squares on the other sides; but it is not intelligible that this ratio should be denied of the triangle. In the case of the mind, by contrast, not only do we understand it to exist without the body, but, what is more, all the attributes which belong to a body can be denied of it. For it is of the nature of substances that they should mutually exclude one another.

M. Arnauld goes on to say: 'Since I infer my existence from the fact that I am thinking, it is certainly no surprise if the idea that I form in this way represents me simply as a thinking thing.' But this is no objection to my argument. For it is equally true that when I examine the nature of the body, I find nothing at all in it which savours of thought. And we can have no better evidence for a distinction between two things than the fact that if we examine either of them, whatever we find in one is different from what we find in the other.

Nor do I see why this argument 'proves too much'. For the fact that one thing can be separated from another by the power of God is the very least that can be asserted in order to establish that there is a real distinction between the two. Also, I thought I was very careful to guard against anyone inferring from this that man was simply 'a soul which makes use of a body'. For in the Sixth Meditation, where I dealt with the distinction between the mind and the body, I also proved at the same time that the mind is substantially united with the body. And the arguments which I used to prove this are as strong as any I can remember ever having read. Now someone who says that a man's arm is a substance that is really distinct from the rest of his body does not thereby deny that the arm belongs to the nature of the whole man. And saying that the arm belongs to the nature of the whole man does not give rise to the suspicion that it cannot subsist in its own right. In the same way, I do not think I proved too much in showing that the mind can exist apart from the body. Nor do I think I proved too little in saying that the mind is substantially united with the body, since that substantial union does not prevent our having a clear and distinct concept of the mind on its own, as a complete thing. The concept is thus very different from that of a surface or a line, which cannot be understood as complete things unless we attribute to them not just length and breadth but also depth.

Finally the fact that 'the power of thought is dormant in infants and extinguished in madmen' (I should say not 'extinguished' but 'disturbed'), does not show that we should regard it as so attached to bodily organs that it cannot exist without them. The fact that thought is often impeded by bodily organs, as we know from our own frequent experience, does not at all entail that it is produced by those organs. This latter view is one for which not even the slightest proof can be adduced.

I must admit, however, that the fact that the mind is closely conjoined with the body, which we experience constantly through our senses, does result in our not being aware of the real distinction between mind and body unless we attentively meditate on the subject. But I think that those who repeatedly ponder on what I wrote in the Second Meditation will be easily convinced that the mind is distinct from the body, and distinct not just by a fiction or

abstraction of the intellect: it can be known as a distinct thing because it is in reality distinct.

I will not answer my critic's further observations regarding the immortality of the soul, because they do not conflict with my views. As far as the souls of the brutes are concerned, this is not the place to examine the subject, and, short of giving an account of the whole of physics, I cannot add to the explanatory remarks I made in Part 5 of the *Discourse on the Method*. But to avoid passing over the topic in silence, I will say that I think the most important point is that, both in our bodies and those of the brutes, no movements can occur without the presence of all the organs or instruments which would enable the same movements to be produced in a machine. So even in our own case the mind does not directly move the external limbs, but simply controls the animal spirits which flow from the heart via the brain into the muscles, and sets up certain motions in them; for the spirits are by their nature adapted with equal facility to a great variety of actions. Now a very large number of the motions occurring inside us do not depend in any way on the mind. These include heartbeat, digestion, nutrition, respiration when we are asleep, and also such waking actions as walking, singing and the like, when these occur without the mind attending to them. When people take a fall, and stick out their hands so as to protect their head, it is not reason that instructs them to do this; it is simply that the sight of the impending fall reaches the brain and sends the animal spirits into the nerves in the manner necessary to produce this movement even without any mental volition, just as it would be produced in a machine. And since our own experience reliably informs us that this is so, why should we be so amazed that the 'light reflected from the body of a wolf onto the eyes of a sheep' should equally be capable of arousing the movements of flight in the sheep?

But if we wish to determine by the use of reason whether any of the movements of the brutes are similar to those which are performed in us with the help of the mind, or whether they resemble those which depend merely on the flow of the animal spirits and the disposition of the organs, then we should consider the differences that can be found between men and beasts. I mean the differences which I set out in Part 5 of the *Discourse on the Method,* for I think these are the only differences to be found. If we do this, it will readily be apparent that all the actions of the brutes resemble only those which occur in us without any assistance from the mind. And we shall be forced to conclude from this that we know of absolutely no principle of movement in animals apart from the disposition of their organs and the continual flow of the spirits which are produced by the heat of the heart as it rarefies the blood. We shall also see that there was no excuse for our imagining that any other principle of motion was to be found in the brutes. We made this mistake because we failed to distinguish the two principles of motion just described; and on seeing that the principle depending solely on the animal spirits and organs exists in the brutes just as it does in us, we jumped to the conclusion that the other principle, which consists in mind or thought, also exists in them. Things which we have become convinced of since our earliest years, even though they have subsequently been shown by rational arguments to be false, cannot easily be eradicated from our beliefs unless we give the relevant arguments our long and frequent attention.

René Descartes
Selections from *Principles of Philosophy*

Part One

51. *What is meant by 'substance'—a term which does not apply univocally to God and his creatures.*

In the case of those items which we regard as things or modes of things, it is worthwhile examining each of them separately. By *substance* we can understand nothing other than a thing which exists in such a way as to depend on no other thing for its existence. And there is only one substance which can be understood to depend on no other thing whatsoever, namely God. In the case of all other substances, we perceive that they can exist only with the help of God's concurrence. Hence the term 'substance' does not apply *univocally,* as they say in the Schools, to God and to other things; that is, there is no distinctly intelligible meaning of the term which is common to God and his creatures. <In the case of created things, some are of such a nature that they cannot exist without other things, while some need only the ordinary concurrence of God in order to exist. We make this distinction by calling the latter 'substances' and the former 'qualities' or 'attributes' of those substances.>

• • •

53. *To each substance there belongs one principal attribute; in the case of mind, this is thought, and in the case of body it is extension.*

A substance may indeed be known through any attribute at all; but each substance has one principal property which constitutes its nature and essence, and to which all its other properties are referred. Thus extension in length, breadth and depth constitutes the nature of corporeal substance; and thought constitutes the nature of thinking substance. Everything else which can be attributed to body presupposes extension, and is merely a mode of an extended thing; and similarly, whatever we find in the mind is simply one of the various modes of thinking. For example, shape is unintelligible except in an extended thing; and motion is unintelligible except as motion in an extended space; while imagination, sensation and will are intelligible only in a thinking thing. By contrast, it is possible to understand extension without shape or movement, and thought without imagination or sensation, and so on; and this is quite clear to anyone who gives the matter his attention.

John Locke
Selections from *An Essay Concerning Human Understanding*

BOOK IV
CHAPTER III
Of the Extent of Humane Knowledge.

§1. Knowledge, as has been said, lying in the Perception of the Agreement, or Disagreement, of any of our *Ideas,* it follows from hence, That,

First, We can have *Knowledge* no farther than we have *Ideas.*

§2. *Secondly,* That we can have no *Knowledge* farther, than we can have Perception of that Agreement, or Disagreement: Which Perception being, 1. Either by *Intuition,* or the immediate comparing any two *Ideas;* or, 2. By *Reason,* examining the Agreement, or Disagreement of two *Ideas,* by the Intervention of some others: Or, 3. By *Sensation,* perceiving the Existence of particular Things. Hence it also follows,

§3. *Thirdly,* That we cannot have an *intuitive Knowledge,* that shall extend itself to all our *Ideas,* and all that we would know about them; because we cannot examine and perceive all the Relations they have one to another by *juxta-*position, or an immediate comparison one with another. Thus having the *Ideas* of an obtuse, and an acute angled Triangle, both drawn from equal Bases, and between Parallels, I can by intuitive Knowledge, perceive the one not to be the other; but cannot that way know, whether they be equal, or no; because their Agreement, or Disagreement in equality, can never be perceived by an immediate comparing them: The difference of Figure makes their parts uncapable of an exact immediate application; and therefore there is need of some intervening Quantities to measure them by, which is Demonstration, or rational Knowledge.

§4. *Fourthly,* It follows also, from what is above observed, that our *rational Knowledge,* cannot reach to the whole extent of our *Ideas.* Because between two different *Ideas* we would examine, we cannot always find such *Mediums,* as we can connect one to another with an intuitive Knowledge, in all the parts of the Deduction; and where-ever that fails, we come short of Knowledge and Demonstration.

§5. *Fifthly, Sensitive Knowledge* reaching no farther than the Existence of Things actually present to our Senses, is yet much narrower than either of the former.

§6. From all which it is evident, that *the extent of our Knowledge* comes not only short of the reality of Things, but even of the extent of our own *Ideas.* Though our Knowledge be limited to our *Ideas,* and cannot exceed them either in extent, or perfection; and though these be very narrow bounds, in respect of the extent of Allbeing, and far short of what we may justly imagine to be in some even created understandings, not tied down to the dull and narrow Information, is to be received from some few, and not very acute ways of perception, such as are our Senses; yet it would be well with us, if our Knowledge were but as large as our *Ideas,* and there were not many Doubts and Enquiries concerning the *Ideas* we have, whereof we are not, nor I believe ever shall be in this World, resolved. Nevertheless, I do not question, but that Humane Knowledge, under the present circumstances of our Beings and Constitutions may be carried much farther, than it hitherto has been, if Men would sincerely, and with freedom of Mind, employ all that Industry and Labour of Thought, in improving the means of discovering Truth, which they do for the colouring or support of Falsehood, to maintain a System, Interest, or Party, they are once engaged in. But yet after all, I think I may, without Injury to humane Perfection, be confident, that our Knowledge would never reach to all we might desire to know concerning those *Ideas* we have; nor be able to surmount all the Difficulties, and resolve all the Questions might arise concerning any of them. We have the *Ideas* of a *Square,* a *Circle,* and *Equality;* and yet, perhaps, shall never be able to find a Circle equal to a Square, and certainly know that it is so. We have the *Ideas* of *Matter* and *Thinking,* but possibly shall never be able to know, whether any mere material Being thinks, or no; it being impossible for us, by the contemplation of our own *Ideas,* without revelation, to discover, whether Omnipotency has not given to some Systems of Matter fitly disposed, a power to perceive and think, or else joined and fixed to Matter so disposed, a thinking immaterial Substance: It being, in respect of our Notions, not much more remote from our Comprehension to conceive, that GOD can, if he pleases, superadd to Matter a Faculty of Thinking, than that he should superadd to it another Substance, with a Faculty of Thinking; since we know not wherein Thinking consists, nor to what sort of Substances the Almighty has been pleased to give that Power, which cannot be in any created Being, but merely by the good pleasure and Bounty of the Creator. For I see no contradiction in it, that the first eternal thinking Being should, if he pleased, give to certain Systems of created senseless matter, put together as he thinks fit, some degrees of sense, perception, and thought: Though, as I think, I have proved, *Lib.* 4. *c.* 10*th.* it is no less than a contradiction to suppose matter (which is evidently in its own nature void of sense and thought) should be that Eternal first thinking Being. What certainty of Knowledge can any one have that some perceptions, such as *v.g.* pleasure and pain, should not be in some bodies themselves, after a certain manner modified and moved, as well as that they should be in an immaterial Substance, upon the Motion of the parts of Body: Body as far as we can conceive being able only to strike and affect body; and Motion, according to the utmost reach of our *Ideas,* being able to produce nothing but Motion, so that when we allow it to produce pleasure or pain, or the *Idea* of a Colour, or Sound, we are fain to quit our Reason, go beyond our *Ideas,* and attribute it wholly to the good Pleasure of our Maker. For since we must allow he has annexed Effects to Motion, which we can no way conceive Motion able to produce, what reason have we to conclude, that he could not order them as well to be produced in a Subject we cannot conceive capable of them, as well as in a Subject we cannot conceive the motion of Matter can any way operate upon? I say not this, that I would any way lessen the belief of the Soul's Immateriality: I am not here speaking of Probability, but Knowledge; and I think not only, that it becomes the Modesty of Philosophy, not to pronounce Magisterially, where we want that Evidence that can produce Knowledge; but also, that it is of use to us, to discern how far our Knowledge does reach; for the state we are at present in, not being that of Vision, we must, in many Things, content our selves with Faith and Probability: and in the present Question, about the immateriality of the Soul, if our Faculties cannot arrive at demonstrative Certainty, we need not think it strange. All the great Ends of Morality and Religion, are well enough secured, without philosophical Proofs of the Soul's Immateriality; since it is evident, that he who made us at first begin to subsist here, sensible intelligent Beings, and for several years continued us in such a state, can and will restore us to the like state of Sensibility in another World, and make us capable there to receive the Retribution he has designed to Men, according to their doings in this Life. And therefore 'tis not of such mighty necessity to determine one way or t'other, as some over zealous for, or against the Immateriality of the Soul, have been forward to make the World believe. Who, either on the one side, indulging too much to their Thoughts immersed altogether in Matter, can allow no existence to what is not material: Or, who on the other side, finding not Cogitation within the natural Powers of Matter, examined over and over again, by the utmost Intention of Mind, have the confidence to conclude, that Omnipotency it self, cannot give Perception and Thought to a Substance, which has the Modification of Solidity. He that considers how hardly Sensation is, in our Thoughts, reconcilable to extended Matter; or Existence to any thing that hath no Extension at all, will confess, that he is very far from certainly knowing what his Soul is. 'Tis a Point, which seems to me, to be put out of the reach of our Knowledge: And he who will give himself leave to consider freely, and look into the dark and intricate part of each Hypothesis, will scarce find his Reason able to determine him fixedly for, or against the Soul's Materiality. Since on which side soever he views it, either as an unextended Substance, or as a thinking extended Matter; the difficulty to conceive either, will, whilst either alone is in his Thoughts, still drive him to the contrary side. An unfair way which some Men take with themselves: who, because of the unconceivableness of something they find in one, throw themselves violently into the contrary Hypothesis, though altogether as unintelligible to an unbiassed Understanding. This serves, not only to shew the Weakness and the Scantiness of our Knowledge, but the insignificant Triumph of such sort of Arguments, which, drawn from our own Views, may satisfy us that we can find no certainty on one side of the Question; but do not at all thereby help us to Truth, by running into the opposite Opinion, which, on examination, will be found clogg'd with equal difficulties. For what Safety, what Advantage to any one is it, for the avoiding the seeming Absurdities, and, to him, unsurmountable Rubs he meets with in one Opinion, to take refuge in the contrary, which is built on something altogether as inexplicable, and as far remote from his Comprehension? 'Tis past controversy, that we have in us something that thinks, our very Doubts about what it is, confirm the certainty of its being, though we must content our selves in the Ignorance of what kind of *Being* it is: And 'tis in vain to go about to be sceptical in this, as it is unreasonable in most other cases to be positive against the being of any thing, because we cannot comprehend its Nature. For I would fain know what Substance exists that has not something in it, which manifestly baffles our Understandings. Other Spirits, who see and know the Nature and inward Constitution of things, how much must they exceed us in Knowledge? To which if we add larger Comprehension, which enables them at one Glance to see the Connexion and Agreement of very many *Ideas*, and readily supplys to them the intermediate Proofs, which we by single and slow Steps, and long poring in the dark, hardly at last find out, and are often ready to forget one before we have hunted out another, we may guess at some part of the Happiness of superior Ranks of Spirits, who have a quicker and more penetrating Sight, as well as a larger Field of Knowledge. But to return to the Argument in hand, our *Knowledge*, I say, is not only limited to the Paucity and Imperfections of the *Ideas* we have, and which we employ it about, but even comes short of that too: But how far it reaches, let us now enquire.

• • •

CHAPTER SIX

Materialism and Idealism

Introduction

Descartes' dualism very rapidly became the most influential theory of mind in the early modern period. Yet it was not by any means the only theory being actively discussed. Other philosophers confronting the same problems as Descartes arrived at very different solutions. In this chapter we look at two theories that form an interesting contrast to Descartes' ideas.

Descartes divided the existing world into two distinct substances: mind and matter. Each possesses a single attribute: thought in the case of mind, and spatial extension in the case of matter. All other qualities are simply modes of these two properties. A central problem in Descartes' system is explaining how these two substances interact. How can changes in the motions of material particles in the brain affect modes of consciousness in the mind? And how can acts of will in the mind change the motions of material particles in the brain? The two theories that we look at in this chapter take a direct and simple approach to this problem: eliminate one of the two substances. Theories that take this line and postulate the existence of a single substance are varieties of **monism**. Some monists argue that the mind does not exist as a distinct entity from the physical body. In their view the only existing substance is matter. This position is called **materialism**. Other monists reject the independent existence of material objects, and argue that only minds exist. These latter theories, which reject the existence of matter as a distinct substance and postulate the existence of only minds, are varieties of **idealism**.

When we say that monist theories reject one of the two substances in dualist theories, it is natural to interpret this as asserting one of two claims: that the mind doesn't exist, or that matter doesn't exist. There are theories that make claims something like this, but it is not by any means the most common line. Instead most supporters of monism agree that both mind and matter exist, but they argue that one of the two is simply a mode of the other. Most materialists argue that the mind is not an immaterial substance as Descartes claims, but rather a physical state of the brain (or some other organ.) Idealists argue that material objects — tables, chairs, mountains, the human body — are all modes of thought. In their view, material things exist solely as collections of sensations in the minds of perceiving subjects.

We will read selections from two philosophers, Thomas Hobbes and George Berkeley, who responded to Descartes' system by rejecting one of the two substances. Hobbes was a materialist, notorious in his day for the alleged atheism of his theories. Berkeley was a bishop of the Anglican Church, who devoted his philosophical work to challenging the materialist tendencies of the new mathematical sciences. We begin chronologically, with Hobbes.

Thomas Hobbes

Thomas Hobbes (1588-1679) was born in Wiltshire, England. He was a contemporary of Descartes, eight years his senior, and like Descartes rejected the Aristotelian science and philosophy that he learned at school. In his later years he became involved in the political turmoil of the English civil war. Several times he had to flee to the European mainland in fear of imprisonment or death. After his schooling he obtained the position of tutor to the son of the Earl of Devonshire, William Cavendish. Cavendish was a royalist, and Hobbes supported the royalist cause throughout his life.

Hobbes is best known as a political theorist. His major book, *Leviathan*, is a defence of strong central government and the authority of a supreme ruler. According to Hobbes, the basis of politics and morality is a contract formed between members of society to surrender certain individual freedoms in return for peace and security. He is perhaps most popularly remembered for his comment that life in the original state of nature before the formation of civil society was "solitary, poor, nasty, brutish, and short."

Hobbes was greatly impressed by the work of Galileo and Descartes in the new mathematical sciences. Like Descartes, he believed that the deductive method of mathematics could be applied to all areas of human knowledge. However, Hobbes took the lessons of the new science further than Descartes, and concluded that inert particles of matter are *all* that exist. In his view, all properties of things are simply motions of the minute particles that make up physical objects. This aspect of Hobbes' views led to the charge that he was secretly an atheist, and it was common on the continent to denounce ideas on the grounds that they bordered on Hobbesian atheism.

Hobbes' materialism

In its broadest sense, materialism is more than just a claim about the mind; it is a claim about the whole world. Materialism in this broad sense is the belief that nothing exists but matter. According to materialists, everything that exists is a material thing, and everything that happens occurs in accordance with the laws of physics. If materialism is true, it follows that all aspects of the mind, such as thought, perception and emotion, are in some way aspects of the matter of which the body is composed.

Materialism is a very old doctrine, and varieties of materialism were formulated before Aristotle's time. For example, a group of Greek thinkers of the fifth century B.C., called **atomists**, argued that the world is composed of nothing but simple, minute particles called "atoms." Atoms were claimed to be indestructible, and everything in the world was said to be formed of collections of atoms. All observable features of the world were held to be the product of collisions between these tiny, invisible particles. The Greek atomists held that the soul is comprised of very tiny atoms, which reside in the body and which we recognize elsewhere as fire. The view that Hobbes is constructing in *Leviathan* can be seen as a development of ideas that originated with the Greek atomists.

We will read here the opening sections of *Leviathan*, in which Hobbes outlines the basic ideas of his materialist account of the mind. This section forms a background to the political and moral theories of the book. His purpose is to explain the origins and nature of human thoughts and actions in order to place them into the context of a general theory of society.

Hobbes' theory of sense

In the opening section of chapter 1 of *Leviathan* Hobbes defines thoughts as "representation[s] ... of some quality, or other accident of a body without us." So thoughts are distinguished by the fact that they represent the outside world. All thought, according to Hobbes, originates in the organs of sense. In this Hobbes is in agreement with Locke that there are no innate ideas. Ideas are produced by the copying, rearranging, and combining of the materials provided by the senses. The purpose of Part I of *Leviathan* is to explain how each of the many different kinds of thoughts and ideas is constructed from sensations.

The fourth paragraph of chapter 1 gives a description of sensations: how they are formed and what they consist of. Here is where Hobbes makes his materialism explicit. According to Hobbes, sensations are produced by the pressure of external objects on the sensory organs. In the case of taste and touch this pressure is direct, whereas in the case of hearing, vision and smell the pressure is transmitted via motions in the surrounding air. This pressure is then communicated through the nerves to the heart and brain, where it encounters a resistance. The counterpressure produced in the brain is the sensation that we experience. Thus in Hobbes' view sensation is nothing more than the motions of material particles in the brain. He says:

> All which qualities, called "sensible" are in the object that causes them but so many motions of the matter, by which it presses our organs diversely. Neither in us that are pressed are they anything else but divers motions; for motion produces nothing but motion.

Notice that in this passage Hobbes is explicitly rejecting Descartes' idea that the motion of particles in the brain causes qualities in the mind that are of a completely different nature. If the origin of sensation is motion, Hobbes contends, then sensation itself must also be motion.

In the final paragraph of chapter 1 Hobbes contrasts his view, not with that of Descartes, but with the beliefs of the Aristotelian universities. He wants his theory to be distinguished from the idea that the qualities and forms of external objects are communicated to the mind via visible or intelligible "species." The concept of species that Hobbes refers to here is a later development of Aristotelianism according to which objects send out likenesses of themselves that are then received by the soul.

Hobbes on thought and imagination

But not all of our thoughts and ideas are directly caused by sensory stimulation. Most of the things that go on in the mind are produced from within the mind itself. These include our trains of reason and reflection, and the things we imagine and dream. In the next sections of chapter 1 Hobbes seeks to explain how these are all generated in one way or another by the motions produced in sensation. Here Hobbes has an especially ingenious theory. Thought, imagination, and dreams are all the result of the *inertia* of material particles. In the second paragraph of chapter 2 he says:

> When a body is once in motion, it moves, unless something else hinder it, eternally; and whatsoever hinders it cannot in an instant, but in time and by degrees, quite extinguish it ... so also it happens in that motion which is made in the internal parts of a man, then, when he sees, dreams, etc. For, after the object is removed, or the eye shut, we still retain an image of the thing seen, though more obscure than when we see it.

The continuation of the motion produced by a sensation is what we recognize as memory, and "much memory, or memory of many things," Hobbes says, "is called experience." So our knowledge of the world in the form of sensory experience is nothing more than the continuation of motion in the brain as a result of the inertia of matter. Dreams are of the same nature, he claims, and their vividness is due simply to the fact that when we sleep there are no new motions being set up by sensory stimulation.

In chapter 3 Hobbes introduces an explanation of the continuity and connectedness of our thoughts. If thoughts are nothing more than residual motions, why are their contents connected to one another in coherent sequences? One thought follows another according to patterns that reflect relations between the objects in the world that originally produced them. For example, if a person believes that the Eiffel Tower is in Paris, and believes that Paris is east of Berlin, she will in all likelihood also believe that the Eiffel Tower is east of Berlin. How can this relation between our thoughts be explained on the assumption that each of these beliefs is nothing more than motions left over from some previous sensory stimulation? Here again Hobbes appeals to the inertia of the matter of which the thoughts are composed. In the second paragraph he says:

> But as we have no imagination whereof we have not formerly had sense, in whole or in parts, so we have no transition from one imagination to another whereof we never had the like before in our senses. The reason whereof is this. All fancies are motions within us, relics of those made in the sense, and those motions that immediately succeeded one another in the sense continue also together after sense: in so much as the former coming again to take place, and be predominant, the latter followeth, *by coherence of the matter moved,* in such manner as water upon a plane table is drawn which way any one part of it is guided by the finger. [emphasis mine]

So thoughts follow one another in coherent patterns because the particles of matter in the brain stick together. In the remainder of the chapter he explains various aspects of our trains of thought in more detail on the basis of this general idea.

Hobbes' intention, then, is to produce a complete psychology — in the sense of a science of thought — by appealing to nothing more than the inertia of material particles in the nerves and brain. If such a project could be completed, then all aspects of the world would be accounted for in terms of one or two very simple properties of matter. All of the many forms and qualities of Aristotle's systems would be replaced by a single substance with a bare minimum of attributes. And the mysterious metaphysics of Descartes' dualism, with the inexplicable interaction between two completely unlike substances, is abandoned in favour of a system involving only one kind of substance — matter — and one kind of causation — communication of motion.

The problem with materialism

As we will see in Part Two of this book, materialism is the predominant view of philosophers and psychologists today, although the specifics of Hobbes' theory have been replaced by biochemistry. But now, as then, the difficulty in materialism as an account of mind is the same as its chief virtue, namely, its austerity.

On the one side, explanations by their very nature show how something we didn't previously understand can be seen in terms of something we do understand. For example, once the theory of electricity was available, it became possible to explain lightning as electrical discharge. Something previously a mystery became understandable in terms of the same processes that make your hair stick to clothing. Seen in this way, a project like Hobbes', which reduces all properties of things to inert particles in motion, is just the sort of thing that we should be looking for. In large part, the success of chemical biology in achieving what Hobbes set out to do is the reason for the wide acceptance of materialism today.

But on the other side, the austerity of Hobbes' materialism is precisely what is counterintuitive. Where are the colours, sounds, and fragrances that make up our experience of the world? While Descartes removed these qualities from the physical world, he placed them in the mind. In Hobbes' view, on the other hand, these sensations in the mind are themselves nothing but various motions of material particles. We can explain the problem this way: particle motions are nothing *like* the colours that we see and the sounds we hear. So how can these motions provide an explanation of the colours and sounds of our perceptual experience? The materialism of contemporary philosophers and scientists is different from Hobbes' theory of matter in motion, but here too the same problem arises. In Part Three we will look at recent ideas on how to get around this difficulty.

George Berkeley

George Berkeley (1685–1753) was born nearly a century later than Hobbes and Descartes. By the time he attended university Newton's theories were universally accepted. He was born to a wealthy family in Kilkenny, Ireland,

and attended Trinity College in Dublin. In 1707 he was elected a Fellow of the College and was ordained into the Anglican Church. Most of his philosophical work was completed within six years of his appointment. Thereafter he travelled extensively, and in later life, as Bishop of Cloyne, he devoted his energies to alleviating the poverty of his native Ireland.

Although he enjoyed a successful career in the Church, Berkeley's philosophy never received the response he had hoped. In university Berkeley came to despise what he saw as the absurd consequences of the new mechanical sciences. In his view, the idea that colours, sounds, and other qualities do not exist in matter is a direct violation of common sense. Thus Berkeley saw himself as a champion of common sense, and felt that his philosophy would restore to material things the qualities that the new sciences denied them. But his views were controversial from the outset, leading one commentator to declare him insane. Most of the criticisms of his conclusions, however, were based on misunderstandings. For example, Samuel Johnson thought Berkeley could be dismissed by kicking a stone and declaring, "I refute him *thus.*" But in denying the independent existence of matter, Berkeley was not asserting that material objects do not exist as we perceive them and interact with them. To the contrary, his aim was to show that material things exist *exactly* as we perceive them. It was in this that Berkeley believed that he was defending common sense.

We will read selections from a book entitled *A Treatise Concerning the Principles of Human Knowledge*, published in 1710. In this book Berkeley begins with the same premise as Locke, that there are no innate ideas; all the materials of thought are drawn from the experiences provided by the senses. But Berkeley draws very different and more radical conclusions from this premise than does Locke. Once we examine our ideas of material things, he argues, we will see that we have no conception of them except as they are perceived by the senses. For this reason he claims that the idea of matter developed by Descartes, Locke, and Hobbes is absurd and contradictory.

Berkeley's theory of material objects

Berkeley begins the *Treatise* by asserting that the "objects of human knowledge" are either sensations or they are ideas produced by combining and rearranging the material originally supplied by the senses. In this he supports the claim made by both Locke and Hobbes that there are no innate ideas. But in Berkeley's hands this assertion takes a different turn. Notice that his claim is that the mind has *no other object* than ideas produced in this way. By this he means that we cannot form coherently in our minds the idea of anything except as it is a "compounding, dividing, or barely representing [i.e., copying]" of sensations.

In the same paragraph he concludes that our ideas of material things like apples, stones, trees, and books are collections of sensations. Our idea of an apple, he says, is the idea of "a certain colour, taste, smell, figure and consistence" designated by a single name.[1] In the next paragraph he adds that the only other coherent idea we have is that of a perceiving mind, for there can only be collections of sensations if there is a mind who receives those sensations.

Esse est percipi

In paragraph 3 he claims that the only conception we have of something *existing* is the idea of something that falls into one of these two categories — it is either a collection of sensations or a subject that perceives them. This means that we have no idea of material objects existing except as collections of sensations. This provides Berkeley with his most important principle: *esse est percipi* — to be is to be perceived. Material things, he claims, cannot be coherently held to exist except as they are perceived by a thinking subject. Therefore, it is not possible for material objects to "have any existence out of the minds of thinking things which perceive them." In Berkeley's view, then, objects cannot exist if they are not perceived by a sentient mind. Material things are just collections of sensations in the mind. For example, an apple in your hand is not something that exists independently of you or somebody else perceiving it. The apple consists entirely of your perceptions of colour, taste, and smell, and those perceptions of other people who have corresponding sensations.

Of course, it is part of common sense that objects do not cease to exist as soon as no one is perceiving them. The room I am in will still exist even after I have left it. But this does not force us to the conclusion that the room exists independently of being perceived. To say that the room exists although no one is perceiving it is simply to say that if someone were to turn their perceptions in that direction they *would* perceive it. Objects do not consist of the collection of actual perceptions, but of the collection of all possible perceptions (which, according to Berkeley, resides in the mind of God).

The rejection of abstract ideas

Paragraph 5 describes what Berkeley sees as the origin of the false view that material things can exist independently of their being perceived. The idea derives, he says, from the pernicious doctrine of **abstract ideas**. To see what he has in mind here we can return to Descartes. Recall that in the beginning of the Sixth Meditation Descartes claims that in mathematics we have a clear and distinct idea of physical objects as possessing no other attribute than spatial extension. That is, we can *abstract* the spatial properties of an object from the colour, taste and smell that we perceive it to have.

Once we allow that ideas can be formed by abstraction in this manner, we are led to suppose we can form the idea of material objects by abstracting away *all* of their sensible qualities. This leads us to the idea of an object existing entirely independently of all perceptions. This idea, Berkeley claims, is nonsensical. He says that:

> [A]s it is impossible for me to see or feel anything without an actual sensation of that thing, so is it impossible for me to conceive in my thoughts any sensible thing or object distinct from the sensation or perception of it.

Resemblance and the primary-secondary distinction

In paragraph 8 he considers a counterargument that might be offered. According to Locke and Descartes, the spatial properties of material things are the same as the ideas we form of them. So they might admit that *ideas* exist only in the minds of a thinking subject, but insist that there are objects that *resemble* those ideas which nonetheless exist independently of them. Against this Berkeley claims that we have no idea of resemblance except that between two ideas. "An idea," he says, "can be like nothing but an idea." One shape might resemble another, and one colour might resemble another, but we cannot conceive of these shapes and colours except as we are aware of them as ideas in our mind. So the assertion of a resemblance between material objects and ideas is as empty as the claim that we can form an idea of objects abstracted from their sensible appearances.

From paragraph 9 to the end of paragraph 15 he attacks the distinction between what Locke calls "primary" and "secondary" qualities. This distinction reflects the arguments we looked at in chapter 3. Primary qualities are supposed by Locke to include those qualities (such as size and shape) that resemble the sensations we have of them. Secondary qualities, like colour, taste, and sound, are nothing more than motions of the tiny particles that produce sensations in the mind, and have no resemblance to those sensations. Thus Descartes and Locke hold the view that only the ideas of primary qualities resemble their causes; the ideas of secondary qualities have no similarity to the physical properties that produce them.

Berkeley contends, however, that our descriptions of primary qualities are also nothing more than descriptions of the appearances of things. The ideas of shape, size, and motion, he argues, consist entirely of relations between things as they occur in our sensory experiences. According to Berkeley, all of the arguments to reach the conclusion that *secondary* qualities exist only in the mind can be used in the same way to the conclusion that *primary* qualities also exist only in the mind. For our ideas of primary qualities are formed from our sensations in the same way as our ideas of secondary qualities, and thus they have no meaning outside of that context. Thus Berkeley maintains that idealism can be derived as a consequence of following the primary-secondary arguments to their proper conclusion. If colour, sound, and fragrance exist only in the mind, so do size, shape, and motion.

Our knowledge of the external world

In paragraph 18 he adds another argument. Suppose it is possible, as others maintain, for objects to exist independently of our perceptions of them and yet resemble our perceptions. There would still be no way for us to *know* that they exist in this way. For our knowledge of objects is based entirely on our perceptions. We cannot "step outside" our perceptions and compare the way we see things to the way they really are. So it is not necessary to argue that it is *impossible* for there to be spatially extended objects existing outside the mind. Even if this were possible, we would nonetheless have no basis for asserting that such objects really do exist.

We can see this latter argument as taking Descartes' evil demon scenario to a different conclusion than does Descartes himself. In the Sixth Meditation Descartes admits that if the evil demon's illusion is perfect, there is no *noticeable* difference between there being such a demon and there not being such a demon. The correct conclusion to draw from this, Berkeley would say, is that the "perfect illusion" *is* our reality. An amusing article by O.K. Bouwsma makes this point nicely.[2] Imagine a demon who selects a subject called Tom, on whom he will perfect his craft. The demon first constructs a very imperfect illusion, where everything in Tom's world is made of paper. Tom, of course, notices the difference straight away. So the demon works harder, and at last he succeeds in the perfect illusion. Nothing in Tom's experience reveals the illusion in the slightest way. The demon's success, however, is his undoing. For Tom declares that the demon has not created an illusion at all; he has simply recreated Tom's real world. In a similar way, Berkeley concludes in paragraph 20:

> In short, if there were external bodies, it is impossible we should ever come to know it; and if there were not, we might have the very same reasons to think there were that we have now.

The perfect illusion and the real world are indistinguishable, and this simply means that there can be no reason to distinguish them.

The cause of our perceptions

In paragraphs 26 through 30 Berkeley turns to the causes of our sensations. As Descartes pointed out, the reason we believe that there is an external world is that our perceptions come independently of our will. It is impossible for us *not* to perceive the world around us. Moreover, the perceptions we have fit together into a coherent whole. As we shift our attention in different directions, our perceptions fit together to form a congruous single picture. And there are regularities in the way things behave that lead us to believe in what we call "laws of nature." These facts lead us to the conclusion that the origin of our perceptions is in something outside of us, and that this something is a single stable whole — what we can call the external world. This is what Samuel Johnson had in mind when he kicked the stone and declared, "I refute him *thus.*"

Berkeley agrees that the fact that our sensations are independent of our will demonstrates that they have an external cause. But because the idea of material substance is incoherent, "it remains that therefore that the cause of ideas is an incorporeal active substance or Spirit." And the coherence and regularity of our perceptions leads us to admire the "wisdom and benevolence" of this active Spirit. So the facts that lead Johnson to believe in the existence of a material world are taken by Berkeley as proof of the existence of God.

We are forced, then, to choose between two possible causes of our perceptions: God or material substance. Descartes' response to this dilemma in the Sixth Meditation is to argue that if God *is* the cause of our perception, then He is guilty of deception. But this claim depends on the assumption that it is impossible for us not to believe that our perceptions are caused by a material substance. And certainly the stability and coherence of our perceptions leads to the conclusion that they are produced by a stable, enduring substance. This much Berkeley would accept: this substance, he would claim, is God. Descartes must add the argument that we cannot avoid believing that this substance *resembles* our perceptions of it. But, as we have seen, Berkeley's response is that the notion of resemblance has no meaning except as a relation between things in our perceptions.

The fates of idealism and materialism

In the years after his death Berkeley's arguments were picked up and developed by David Hume and Immanuel Kant. Through the influence of Kant, idealism became the predominant philosophical position of German philosophy in the nineteenth century, exemplified in the writings of Fichte, Schelling and Hegel. Late in the century the principles of German philosophy spread to England where they became widely accepted in the universities. The details of idealism in the nineteenth century take us far from our topic, and are much too complex to summarize here.

In the late nineteenth century, however, the acceptance of idealism declined dramatically. In Britain this was influenced to a large degree by the development of formal logic, which undermined some of the arguments put forward by later idealists. Another factor in the demise of idealism, especially in Germany, was the dramatic developments in the scientific study of the nervous system. These advances in biology led to the replacement of idealism in the universities with materialism, which has become the predominant position in this century. However, some of the arguments of Berkeley survive in the views of a group known as the "logical positivists." The philosophy of mind they constructed, called behaviourism, and the evolution of materialism are the subjects of Part Two.

NOTES

1   His point here is precisely the opposite of Descartes' conclusion in "the piece of wax" argument. There Descartes contends that our idea of the piece of wax cannot consist of the collection of sensible qualities, and thus concludes that the mind itself must supply our idea of matter. Berkeley's position is that such an idea is impossible, and so our idea of the wax must consist solely of the collection of what we experience in our sensations.

2   O.K. Bouwsma, "Descartes' Evil Genius," *The Philosophical Review* 58 (1949): 141-151.

Thomas Hobbes
Selections from *Leviathan*

PART I—OF MAN

Chapter 1. Of Sense

Concerning the thoughts of man, I will consider them first singly, and afterwards in train, or dependence upon one another. Singly, they are every one a "representation" or "appearance" of some quality, or other accident of a body without us, which is commonly called an "object." Which object works on the eyes, ears, and other parts of a man's body, and, by diversity of working, produces diversity of appearances.

The original of them all is that which we call "sense," for there is no conception in a man's mind which hath not at first, totally or by parts, been begotten upon the organs of sense. The rest are derived from that original.

To know the natural cause of sense is not very necessary to the business now in hand; and I have elsewhere written of the same at large. Nevertheless, to fill each part of my present method I will briefly deliver the same in this place.

The cause of sense is the external body, or object, which presses the organ proper to each sense, either immediately, as in the taste and touch, or mediately, as in seeing, hearing, and smelling; which pressure, by the mediation of the nerves and other strings and membranes of the body continued inwards to the brain and heart, causes there a resistance, or counter-pressure, or endeavor of the heart to deliver itself, which endeavor, because "outward," seems to be some matter without. And this "seeming" or "fancy" is that which men call "sense" and consists, as to the eye, in a "light" or "color figured"; to the ear, in a "sound"; to the nostril, in an "odor"; to the tongue and palate, in a "savor"; and to the rest of the body, in "heat," "cold," "hardness," "softness," and such other qualities as we discern by "feeling." All which

qualities, called "sensible" are in the object that causes them but so many several motions of the matter, by which it presses our organs diversely. Neither in us that are pressed are they anything else but divers motions; for motion produces nothing but motion. But their appearance to us is fancy, the same waking that dreaming. And as pressing, rubbing, or striking the eye, makes us fancy a light, and pressing the ear produces a din, so do the bodies also we see or hear produce the same by their strong, though unobserved, action. For if those colors and sounds were in the bodies, or objects that cause them, they could not be severed from them, as by glasses. And in echoes by reflection, we see they are, where we know the thing we see is in one place, the appearance in another. And though at some certain distance the real and very object seem invested with the fancy it begets in us, yet still the object is one thing, the image or fancy is another. So that sense in all cases is nothing else but original fancy, caused, as I have said, by the pressure, that is by the motion, of external things upon our eyes, ears, and other organs thereunto ordained.

But the philosophy schools through all the universities of Christendom, grounded upon certain texts of Aristotle, teach another doctrine, and say, for the cause of "vision," that the thing seen sends forth on every side a "visible species," in English, a "visible show," "apparition," or "aspect," or "a being seen"; the receiving whereof into the eye is "seeing." And for the cause of "hearing," that the thing heard sends forth an "audible species," that is an "audible aspect," or "audible being seen," which entering at the ear makes "hearing." Nay, for the cause of "understanding" also, they say the thing understood sends forth an "intelligible species," that is, an "intelligible being seen," which, coming into the understanding, makes us understand. I say not this as disproving the use of universities; but, because I am to speak hereafter of their office in a commonwealth. I must let you see on all occasions by the way what things would be amended in them, amongst which the frequency of insignificant speech is one.

Chapter 2. Of Imagination

That when a thing lies still, unless somewhat else stir it, it will lie still for ever, is a truth that no man doubts of. But that when a thing is in motion, it will eternally be in motion, unless somewhat else stay it, though the reason be the same, namely that nothing can change itself, is not so easily assented to. For men measure not only other men but all other things, by themselves; and, because they find themselves subject after motion to pain and lassitude, think everything else grows weary of motion, and seeks repose of its own accord; little considering whether it be not some other motion wherein that desire of rest they find in themselves consists. From hence it is that the schools say heavy bodies fall downwards out of an appetite to rest, and to conserve their nature in that place which is most proper for them; ascribing appetite and knowledge of what is good for their conservation, which is more than man has, to things inanimate, absurdly.

When a body is once in motion, it moves, unless something else hinder it, eternally; and whatsoever hinders it cannot in an instant, but in time and by degrees, quite extinguish it; and, as we see in the water though the wind cease the waves give not over rolling for a long time after: so also it happens in that motion which is made in the internal parts of a man, then, when he sees, dreams, etc. For, after the object is removed, or the eye shut, we still retain an image of the thing seen, though more obscure than when we see it. And this is it the Latins call "imagination," from the image made in seeing; and apply the same, though improperly, to

all the other senses. But the Greeks call it "fancy," which signifies "appearance," and is as proper to one sense as to another. "Imagination," therefore, is nothing but "decaying sense," and is found in men, and many other living creatures, as well sleeping as waking.

The decay of sense in men waking is not the decay of the motion made in sense, but an obscuring of it in such manner as the light of the sun obscures the light of the stars, which stars do no less exercise their virtue, by which they are visible, in the day than in the night. But because amongst many strokes which our eyes, ears, and other organs, receive from external bodies, the predominant only is sensible; therefore, the light of the sun being predominant, we are not affected with the action of the stars. And any object being removed from our eyes, though the impression it made in us remain, yet other objects more present succeeding and working on us, the imagination of the past is obscured and made weak, as the voice of a man is in the noise of the day. From whence it follows that the longer the time is, after the sight or sense of any object, the weaker is the imagination. For the continual change of man's body destroys in time the parts which in sense were moved; so that distance of time, and of place, hath one and the same effect in us. For as at a great distance of place that which we look at appears dim and without distinction of the smaller parts, and as voices grow weak and inarticulate, so also after great distance of time our imagination of the past is weak; and we lose, for example, of cities we have seen many particular streets, and of actions many particular circumstances. This "decaying sense," when we would express the thing itself, I mean "fancy" itself, we call "imagination," as I said before; but when we would express the decay, and signify that the sense is fading, old, and past, it is called "memory." So that imagination and memory are but one thing, which for divers considerations hath divers names.

Much memory, or memory of many things, is called "experience." Again, imagination being only of those things which have been formerly perceived by sense, either all at once or by parts at several times, the former, which is the imagining the whole object as it was presented to the sense, is "simple" imagination, as when one imagines a man, or horse, which he hath seen before. The other is "compounded," as when, from the sight of a man at one time, and of a horse at another, we conceive in our mind a Centaur. So when a man compounds the image of his own person with the image of the actions of another man, as when a man images himself a Hercules or an Alexander, which happens often to them that are much taken with reading of romances, it is a compound imagination, and properly but a fiction of the mind. There be also other imaginations that rise in men, though waking, from the great impression made in sense; as, from gazing upon the sun, the impression leaves an image of the sun before our eyes a long time after; and, from being long and vehemently intent upon geometrical figures, a man shall in the dark, though awake, have the images of lines and angles before his eyes; which kind of fancy hath no particular name, as being a thing that doth not commonly fall into men's discourse.

The imaginations of them that sleep are those we call "dreams." And these also, as also all other imaginations, have been before, either totally or by parcels, in the sense. And, because in sense, the brain and nerves, which are the necessary organs of sense, are so benumbed in sleep as not easily to be moved by the action of external objects, there can happen in sleep no imagination, and therefore no dream, but what proceeds from the agitation of the inward parts of man's body; which inward parts, for the connection they have with the brain and other organs, when they be distempered, do keep the same in motion; whereby the imaginations there formerly made, appear as if a man were waking; saving that the organs of sense being now benumbed, so as there is no new object which can master and obscure them with a more vigorous

impression, a dream must needs be more clear in this silence of sense than our waking thoughts. And hence it comes to pass that it is a hard matter, and by many thought impossible, to distinguish exactly between sense and dreaming. For my part, when I consider that in dreams I do not often nor constantly think of the same persons, places, objects, and actions, that I do waking, nor remember so long a train of coherent thoughts, dreaming, as at other times, and because waking I often observe the absurdity of dreams, but never dream of the absurdities of my waking thoughts, I am well satisfied, that, being awake, I know I dream not, though when I dream I think myself awake.

And, seeing dreams are caused by the distemper of some of the inward parts of the body, divers distempers must needs cause different dreams. And hence it is that lying cold breeds dreams of fear, and raises the thought and image of some fearful object, the motion from the brain to the inner parts and from the inner parts to the brain being reciprocal; and that, as anger causes heat in some parts of the body when we are awake, so when we sleep the overheating of the same parts causes anger, and raises up in the brain the imagination of an enemy. In the same manner, as natural kindness, when we are awake, causes desire, and desire makes heat in certain other parts of the body; so also too much heat in those parts, while we sleep, raises in the brain an imagination of some kindness shown. In sum, our dreams are the reverse of our waking imaginations, the motion when we are awake beginning at one end, and when we dream at another.

The most difficult discerning of a man's dream from his waking thoughts is, then, when by some accident we observe not that we have slept: which is easy to happen to a man full of fearful thoughts, and whose conscience is much troubled, and that sleeps without the circumstances of going to bed or putting off his clothes, as one that nods in a chair. For he that takes pains, and industriously lays himself to sleep, in case any uncouth and exorbitant fancy come unto him, cannot easily think it other than a dream. We read of Marcus Brutus (one that had his life given him by Julius Caesar, and was also his favorite, and notwithstanding murdered him) how at Philippi, the night before he gave battle to Augustus Caesar, he saw a fearful apparition, which is commonly related by historians as a vision; but, considering the circumstances, one may easily judge to have been but a short dream. For, sitting in his tent, pensive and troubled with the horror of his rash act, it was not hard for him, slumbering in the cold, to dream of that which most frightened him; which fear, as by degrees it made him wake, so also it must needs make the apparition by degrees to vanish; and, having no assurance that he slept, he could have no cause to think it a dream or anything but a vision. And this is no very rare accident; for even they that be perfectly awake, if they be timorous and superstitious, possessed with fearful tales, and alone in the dark, are subject to the like fancies, and believe they see spirits and dead men's ghosts walking in churchyards; whereas it is either their fancy only, or else the knavery of such persons as make use of such superstitious fear to pass disguised in the night to places they would not be known to haunt.

From this ignorance of how to distinguish dreams and other strong fancies from vision and sense, did arise the greatest part of the religion of the Gentiles in time past, that worshipped satyrs, fawns, nymphs, and the like; and now-a-days the opinion that rude people have of fairies, ghosts, and goblins, and of the power of witches. For as for witches, I think not that their witchcraft is any real power; but yet that they are justly punished for the false belief they have that they can do such mischief, joined with their purpose to do it if they can; their trade being nearer to a new religion than to a craft or science. And for fairies and walking ghosts, the opinion of them has, I think, been on purpose either taught, or not confuted, to keep in credit the use of exorcism, of

crosses, of holy water, and other such inventions of ghostly men. Nevertheless there is no doubt but God can make unnatural apparitions; but that He does it so often as men need to fear such things more than they fear the stay or change of the course of nature, which He also can stay and change, is no point of Christian faith. But evil men, under pretext that God can do anything, are so bold as to say anything when it serves their turn, though they think it untrue; it is the part of a wise man to believe them no farther than right reason makes that which they say appear credible. If this superstitious fear of spirits were taken away, and with it prognostics from dreams, false prophecies, and many other things depending thereon, by which crafty ambitious persons abuse the simple people, men would be much more fitted than they are for civil obedience.

And this ought to be the work of the schools; but they rather nourish such doctrine. For, not knowing what imagination or the senses are, what they receive they teach; some saying that imaginations rise of themselves and have no cause; others that they rise most commonly from the will, and that good thoughts are blown (inspired) into a man by God, and evil thoughts by the devil; or that good thoughts are poured (infused) into a man by God, and evil ones by the devil. Some say the senses receive the species of things, and deliver them to the common sense, and the common sense delivers them over to the fancy, and the fancy to the memory, and the memory to the judgment, like handling of things from one to another, with many words making nothing understood.

The imagination that is raised in man, or any other creature endowed with the faculty of imagining, by words or other voluntary signs, is that we generally call "understanding," and is common to man and beast. For a dog by custom will understand the call or the rating of his master; and so will many other beasts. That understanding which is peculiar to man, is the understanding not only his will, but his conceptions and thoughts, by the sequel and contexture of the names of things into affirmations, negations, and other forms of speech; and of this kind of understanding I shall speak hereafter.

Chapter 3. Of the Consequence or Train of Imaginations

By "consequence," or "train," of thoughts I understand that succession of one thought to another which is called, to distinguish it from discourse in words, "mental discourse."

When a man thinks on anything whatever, his next thought after is not altogether so casual as it seems to be. Not every thought to every thought succeeds indifferently. But as we have no imagination whereof we have not formerly had sense, in whole or in parts, so we have no transition from one imagination to another whereof we never had the like before in our senses. The reason whereof is this. All fancies are motions within us, relics of those made in the sense, and those motions that immediately succeeded one another in the sense continue also together after sense: in so much as the former coming again to take place, and be predominant, the latter followeth, by coherence of the matter moved, in such manner as water upon a plane table is drawn which way any one part of it is guided by the finger. But because in sense to one and the same thing perceived, sometimes one thing sometimes another, succeeds, it comes to pass in time that in the imagining of anything there is no certainty what we shall imagine next: only this is certain, it shall be something that succeeded the same before, at one time or another.

This train of thoughts, or mental discourse, is of two sorts. The first is "unguided," "without design," and inconstant; wherein there is no passionate thought, to govern and direct those that follow, to itself, as the end and scope of some desire or other passion: in which case the thoughts are said to wander, and seem imperti-nent one to another as in a dream. Such are commonly the thoughts of men that are not only without company but also without care of anything; though even then their thoughts are as busy as at other times, but without harmony; as the sound which a lute out of tune would yield to any man, or in tune to one that could not play. And yet in this wild ranging of the mind a man may oft-times perceive the way of it, and the dependence of one thought upon another. For in a discourse of our present civil war, what could seem more impertinent than to ask, as one did, what was the value of a Roman penny. Yet the coherence to me was manifest enough. For the thought of the war introduced the thought of the delivering up the king to his enemies, the thought of that brought in the thought of the delivering up of Christ; and that again the thought of the thirty pence, which was the price of that treason; and thence easily followed that malicious question; and all this in a moment of time—for thought is quick.

The second is more constant; as being "regulated" by some desire and design. For the impression made by such things as we desire, or fear, is strong and permanent, or, if it cease for a time, of quick return: so strong it is sometimes as to hinder and break our sleep. From desire arises the thought of some means we have seen produce the like of that which we aim at; and from the thought of that, the thought of means to that mean, and so continually till we come to some beginning within our own power. And because the end, by the greatness of the impression, comes often to mind, in case our thoughts begin to wander, they are quickly again reduced into the way: which observed by one of the Seven Wise Men, made him give men this precept, which is now worn out, *Respice finem;* that is to say, in all your actions look often upon what you would have as the thing that directs all your thoughts in the way to attain it.

George Berkeley
Selections from
A Treatise Concerning the Principles of Human Knowledge

Part One

1. It is evident to any one who takes a survey of the *objects* of human knowledge, that they are either ideas actually imprinted on the senses: or else such as are perceived by attending to the passions and operations of the mind; or lastly, ideas formed by help of memory and imagination—either compounding, dividing, or barely representing those originally perceived in the aforesaid ways. By sight I have the ideas of light and colours with their several degrees and variations. By touch I perceive hard and soft, heat and cold, motion and resistance, and of all these more and less either as to quantity or degree. Smelling furnishes me with odours; the palate with tastes; and hearing conveys sounds to the mind in all their variety of tone and composition. And as several of these are observed to accompany each other, they come to be marked by one name, and so to be reputed as one thing. Thus, for example a certain colour, taste, smell, figure and consistence having been observed to go together, are accounted one distinct thing, signified by the name *apple:* other collections of ideas constitute a stone, a tree, a book, and the like sensible things—which as they are pleasing or disagreeable excite the passions of love, hatred, joy, grief, and so forth.

2. But, besides all that endless variety of ideas or objects of knowledge, there is likewise something which knows or perceives them, and exercises divers operations, as willing, imagining, remembering, about them. This perceiving, active being is what I call *mind, spirit, soul,* or *myself.* By which words I do not denote any one of my ideas, but a thing entirely distinct from them, wherein, they exist, or, which is the same thing, whereby they are perceived—for the existence of an idea consists in being perceived.

3. That neither our thoughts, nor passions, nor ideas formed by the imagination, exist without the mind, is what everybody will allow. And it seems no less evident that the various sensations or ideas imprinted on the sense, however blended or combined together (that is, whatever objects they compose), cannot exist otherwise than in a mind perceiving them.—I think an intuitive knowledge may be obtained of this by any one that shall attend to what is meant by the term *exists,* when applied to sensible things. The table I write on I say exists, that is, I see and feel it; and if I were out of my study I should say it existed—meaning thereby that if I was in my study I might perceive it, or that some other spirit actually does perceive it. There was an odour, that is, it was smelt; there was a sound, that is, it was heard; a colour or figure, and it was perceived by sight or touch. This is all that I can understand by these and the like expressions. For as to what is said of the absolute existence of unthinking things without any relation to their being perceived, that seems perfectly unintelligible. Their *esse* is *percepi,* nor is it possible they should have any existence out of the minds of thinking things which perceive them.

4. It is indeed an opinion strangely prevailing amongst men, that houses, mountains, rivers, and in a word all sensible objects, have an existence, natural or real, distinct from their being perceived by the understanding. But, with how great an assurance and acquiescence soever this principle may be entertained in the world, yet whoever shall find in his heart to call

it in question may, if I mistake not, perceive it to involve a manifest contradiction. For, what are the forementioned objects but the things we perceive by sense? and what do we perceive besides our own ideas or sensations? and is it not plainly repugnant that any one of these, or any combination of them, should exist unperceived?

5. If we thoroughly examine this tenet it will, perhaps, be found at bottom to depend on the doctrine of *abstract ideas.* For can there be a nicer strain of abstraction than to distinguish the existence of sensible objects from their being perceived, so as to conceive them existing unperceived? Light and colours, heat and cold, extension and figures—in a word the things we see and feel—what are they but so many sensations, notions, ideas, or impressions on the sense? and is it possible to separate, even in thought, any of these from perception? For my part, I might as easily divide a thing from itself. I may, indeed, divide in my thoughts, or conceive apart from each other, those things which, perhaps I never perceived by sense so divided. Thus, I imagine the trunk of a human body without the limbs, or conceive the smell of a rose without thinking on the rose itself. So far, I will not deny, I can abstract—if that may properly be called *abstraction* which extends only to the conceiving separately such objects as it is possible may really exist or be actually perceived asunder. But my conceiving or imagining power does not extend beyond the possibility of real existence or perception. Hence, as it is impossible for me to see or feel anything without an actual sensation of that thing, so is it impossible for me to conceive in my thoughts any sensible thing or object distinct from the sensation or perception of it.

6. Some truths there are so near and obvious to the mind that a man need only open his eyes to see them. Such I take this important one to be, viz., that all the choir of heaven and furniture of the earth, in a word all those bodies which compose the mighty frame of the world, have not any subsistence without a mind, that their *being* is to be perceived or known; that consequently so long as they are not actually perceived by me, or do not exist in my mind or that of any other created spirit, they must either have no existence at all, or else subsist in the mind of some Eternal Spirit—it being perfectly unintelligible, and involving all the absurdity of abstraction, to attribute to any single part of them an existence independent of a spirit. To be convinced of which, the reader need only reflect, and try to separate in his own thoughts the *being* of a sensible thing from its *being perceived.*

7. From what has been said it follows there is not any other Substance than Spirit, or that which perceives. But, for the fuller proof of this point, let it be considered the sensible qualities are colour, figure, motion, smell, taste, etc., *i.e.* the ideas perceived by sense. Now, for an idea to exist in an unperceiving thing is a manifest contradiction, for to have an idea is all one as to perceive; that therefore wherein colour, figure, and the like qualities exist must perceive them; hence it is clear there can be no unthinking substance or *substratum* of those ideas.

8. But, say you, though the ideas themselves do not exist without the mind, yet there may be things like them, whereof they are copies or resemblances, which things exist without the mind in an unthinking substance. I answer, an idea can be like nothing but an idea; a colour or figure can be like nothing but another colour or figure. If we look but never so little into our thoughts, we shall find it impossible for us to conceive a likeness except only between our ideas. Again, I ask whether those supposed originals or external things, of which our ideas are the pictures or representations, be themselves perceivable or no? If they are, then they are ideas and we have gained our point; but if you say they are not, I appeal to any one whether it be sense to assert a colour is like something which is invisible; hard or soft, like something which is intangible; and so of the rest.

9. Some there are who make a distinction between *primary* and *secondary* qualities. By the former they mean extension, figure, motion, rest, solidity or impenetrability, and number; by

the latter they denote all other sensible qualities, as colours, sounds, tastes, and so forth. The ideas we have of these they acknowledge not to be the resemblances of anything existing without the mind, or unperceived, but they will have our ideas of the primary qualities to be patterns or images of things which exist without the mind, in an unthinking substance which they call Matter. By Matter, therefore, we are to understand an inert, senseless substance, in which extension, figure, and motion do actually subsist. But it is evident from what we have already shown, that extension, figure, and motion are only ideas existing in the mind, and that an idea can be like nothing but another idea, and that consequently neither they nor their archetypes can exist in an unperceiving substance. Hence, it is plain that the very notion of what is called *Matter* or *corporeal substance* involves a contradiction in it.

10. They who assert that figure, motion, and the rest of the primary or original qualities do exist without the mind in unthinking substances, do at the same time acknowledge that colours, sounds, heat, cold, and suchlike secondary qualities, do not—which they tell us are sensations existing in the mind alone, that depend on and are occasioned by the different size, texture, and motion of the minute particles of matter. This they take for an undoubted truth, which they can demonstrate beyond all exception. Now, if it be certain that those original qualities are inseparably united with the other sensible qualities, and not, even in thought, capable of being abstracted from them, it plainly follows that they exist only in the mind. But I desire any one to reflect and try whether he can, by any abstraction of thought, conceive the extension and motion of a body without all other sensible qualities. For my own part, I see evidently that it is not in my power to frame an idea of a body extended and moving, but I must withal give it some colour or other sensible quality which is acknowledged to exist only in the mind. In short, extension, figure, and motion,

abstracted from all other qualities, are inconceivable. Where therefore the other sensible qualities are, there must these be also, to wit, in the mind and nowhere else.

11. Again, *great* and *small*, *swift* and *slow*, are allowed to exist nowhere without the mind, being entirely relative, and changing as the frame or position of the organs of sense varies. The extension therefore which exists without the mind is neither great nor small, the motion neither swift nor slow, that is, they are nothing at all. But, say you, they are extension in general, and motion in general: thus we see how much the tenet of extended movable substances existing without the mind depends on the strange doctrine of *abstract ideas*. And here I cannot but remark how nearly the vague and indeterminate description of Matter or corporeal substance, which the modern philosophers are run into by their own principles, resembles that antiquated and so much ridiculed notion of *materia prima*, to be met with in Aristotle and his followers. Without extension solidity cannot be conceived; since therefore it has been shewn that extension exists not in an unthinking substance, the same must also be true of solidity.

12. That number is entirely the creature of the mind, even though the other qualities be allowed to exist without, will be evident to whoever considers that the same thing bears a different denomination of number as the mind views it with different respects. Thus, the same extension is one, or three, or thirty-six, according as the mind considers it with reference to a yard, a foot or an inch. Number is so visibly relative, and dependent on men's understanding, that it is strange to think how any one should give it an absolute existence without the mind. We say one book, one page, one line, etc.; all these are equally units, though some contain several of the others. And in each instance, it is plain, the unit relates to some particular combination of ideas arbitrarily put together by the mind.

13. Unity I know some will have to be a simple or uncompounded idea, accompanying

all other ideas into the mind. That I have any such idea answering the word unity I do not find; and if I had, methinks I could not miss finding it: on the contrary, it should be the most familiar to my understanding, since it is said to accompany all other ideas, and to be perceived by all the ways of sensation and reflexion. To say no more, it is an *abstract* idea.

14. I shall farther add, that, after the same manner as modern philosophers prove certain sensible qualities to have no existence in Matter, or without the mind, the same thing may be likewise proved of all other sensible qualities whatsoever. Thus, for instance, it is said that heat and cold are affections only of the mind, and not at all patterns of real beings, existing in the corporeal substances which excite them, for that the same body which appears cold to one hand seems warm to another. Now, why may we not as well argue that figure and extension are not patterns or resemblances of qualities existing in Matter, because to the same eye at different stations or eyes of a different texture at the same station, they appear various, and cannot therefore be the images of anything settled and determinate without the mind? Again, it is proved that sweetness is not really in the sapid thing, because the thing remaining unaltered the sweetness is changed into bitter, as in case of a fever or otherwise vitiated palate. Is it not as reasonable to say that motion is not without the mind, since if the succession of ideas in the mind become swifter, the motion, it is acknowledged, shall appear slower without any alteration in any external object?

15. In short, let any one consider those arguments which are thought manifestly to prove that colours and taste exist only in the mind, and he shall find they may with equal force be brought to prove the same thing of extension, figure, and motion. Though it must be confessed this method of arguing does not so much prove that there is no extension or colour in an outward object, as that we do not know by sense which is the true extension or colour of the object. But the arguments foregoing plainly shew it to be impossible that any colour or extension at all, or other sensible quality whatsoever, should exist in an unthinking subject without the mind, or in truth, that there should be any such thing as an outward object.

16. But let us examine a little the received opinion.—It is said extension is a mode or accident of Matter, and that Matter is the substratum that supports it. Now I desire that you would explain to me what is meant by Matter's supporting extension. Say you, I have no idea of Matter and therefore cannot explain it. I answer, though you have no positive, yet, if you have any meaning at all, you must at least have a relative idea of Matter; though you know not what it is, yet you must be supposed to know what relation it bears to accidents, and what is meant by its supporting them. It is evident "support" cannot here be taken in its usual or literal sense—as when we say that pillars support a building; in what sense therefore must it be taken?

17. If we inquire into what the most accurate philosophers declare themselves to mean by material substance, we shall find them acknowledging they have no other meaning annexed to those sounds but the idea of Being in general, together with the relative notion of its supporting accidents. The general idea of Being appeareth to me the most abstract and incomprehensible of all other; and as for its supporting accidents, this, as we have just now observed, cannot be understood in the common sense of those words; it must therefore be taken in some other sense, but what that is they do not explain. So that when I consider the two parts or branches which make the signification of the words material substance, I am convinced there is no distinct meaning annexed to them. But why should we trouble ourselves any farther, in discussing this material substratum or support of figure and motion, and other sensible qualities? Does it not suppose they have an existence without the mind? And is not this a direct repugnancy, and altogether inconceivable?

18. But, though it were possible that solid, figured, movable substances may exist without the mind, corresponding to the ideas we have of bodies, yet how is it possible for us to know this? Either we must know it by sense or by reason. As for our senses, by them we have the knowledge only of our sensations, ideas, or those things that are immediately perceived by sense, call them what you will: but they do not inform us that things exist without the mind, or unperceived, like to those which are perceived. This the materialists themselves acknowledge. It remains therefore that if we have any knowledge at all of external things, it must be by reason, inferring their existence from what is immediately perceived by sense. But what reason can induce us to believe the existence of bodies without the mind, from what we perceive, since the very patrons of Matter themselves do not pretend there is any necessary connexion betwixt them and our ideas? I say it is granted on all hands (and what happens in dreams, phrensies, and the like, puts it beyond dispute) that it is possible we might be affected with all the ideas we have now, though there were no bodies existing without resembling them. Hence, it is evident the supposition of external bodies is not necessary for the producing our ideas; since it is granted they are produced sometimes, and might possibly be produced always in the same order, we see them in at present, without their concurrence.

19. But, though we might possibly have all our sensations without them, yet perhaps it may be thought easier to conceive and explain the manner of their production, by supposing external bodies in their likeness rather than otherwise; and so it might be at least probable there are such things as bodies that excite their ideas in our minds. But neither can this be said; for, though we give the materialists their external bodies, they by their own confession are never the nearer knowing how our ideas are produced; since they own themselves unable to comprehend in what manner body can act upon spirit, or how it is possible it should imprint any idea in the mind. Hence it is evident the production of ideas or sensations in our minds can be no reason why we should suppose Matter or corporeal substances, since that is acknowledged to remain equally inexplicable with or without this supposition. If therefore it were possible for bodies to exist without the mind, yet to hold they do so, must needs be a very precarious opinion; since it is to suppose, without any reason at all, that God has created innumerable beings that are entirely useless, and serve to no manner of purpose.

20. In short, if there were external bodies, it is impossible we should ever come to know it; and if there were not, we might have the very same reasons to think there were that we have now. Suppose—what no one can deny possible—an intelligence without the help of external bodies, to be affected with the same train of sensations or ideas that you are, imprinted in the same order and with like vividness in his mind. I ask whether that intelligence hath not all the reason to believe the existence of corporeal substances, represented by his ideas, and exciting them in his mind, that you can possibly have for believing the same thing? Of this there can be no question—which one consideration were enough to make any reasonable person suspect the strength of whatever arguments he may think himself to have, for the existence of bodies without the mind.

21. Were it necessary to add any farther proof against the existence of Matter after what has been said, I could instance several of those errors and difficulties (not to mention impieties) which have sprung from that tenet. It has occasioned numberless controversies and disputes in philosophy, and not a few of far greater moment in religion. But I shall not enter into the detail of them in this place, as well because I think arguments *a posteriori* are unnecessary for confirming what has been, if I mistake not, sufficiently demonstrated *a priori*, as because I shall hereafter find occasion to speak somewhat of them.

22. I am afraid I have given cause to think I am needlessly prolix in handling this subject. For, to what purpose is it to dilate on that which may be demonstrated with the utmost evidence in a line or two, to any one that is capable of the least reflexion? It is but looking in to your own thoughts, and so trying whether you can conceive it possible for a sound, or figure, or motion, or colour to exist without the mind or unperceived. This easy trial may perhaps make you see that what you contend for is a downright contradiction. Insomuch that I am content to put the whole upon this issue:—If you can but conceive it possible for one extended movable substance, or, in general, for any one idea, or anything like an idea, to exist otherwise than in a mind perceiving it, I shall readily give up the cause. And, as for all that compages [complex system] of external bodies you contend for, I shall grant you its existence, though you cannot either give me any reason why you believe it exists, or assign any use to it when it is supposed to exist. I say, the bare possibility of your opinions being true shall pass for an argument that it is so.

23. But, say you, surely there is nothing easier than for me to imagine trees, for instance, in a park, or books existing in a closet, and nobody by to perceive them. I answer, you may so, there is no difficulty in it: but what is all this, I beseech you, more than framing in your mind certain ideas which you call books and trees, and the same time omitting to frame the idea of any one that may perceive them? But do not you yourself perceive or think of them all the while? This therefore is nothing to the purpose: it only shews you have the power of imagining or forming ideas in your mind: but it does not shew that you can conceive it possible the objects of your thought may exist without the mind. To make out this, it is necessary that you conceive them existing unconceived or unthought of, which is a manifest repugnancy. When we do our utmost to conceive the existence of external bodies. we are all the while only contemplating our own ideas. But the mind taking no notice of itself, is deluded

to think it can and does conceive bodies existing unthought of or without the mind, though at the same time they are apprehended by or exist in itself. A little attention will discover to any one the truth and evidence of what is here said, and make it unnecessary to insist on any other proofs against the existence of *material substance*.

24. It is very obvious, upon the least inquiry into our thoughts, to know whether it is possible for us to understand what is meant by the *absolute existence of sensible objects in themselves, or without the mind.* To me it is evident those words mark out either a direct contradiction, or else nothing at all. And to convince others of this, I know no readier or fairer way than to entreat they would calmly attend to their own thoughts; and if by this attention the emptiness or repugnancy of those expressions does appear, surely nothing more is requisite for the conviction. It is on this therefore that I insist, to wit, that the absolute existence of unthinking things are words without a meaning, or which include a contradiction. This is what I repeat and inculcate, and earnestly recommend to the attentive thoughts of the reader.

25. All our ideas, sensations, notions, or the things which we perceive, by whatsoever names they may be distinguished, are visibly inactive—there is nothing of power or agency included in them. So that one idea or object of thought cannot produce or make any alteration in another. To be satisfied of the truth of this, there is nothing else requisite but a bare observation of our ideas. For, since they and every part of them exist only in the mind, it follows that there is nothing in them but what is perceived: but whoever shall attend to his ideas, whether of sense or reflexion, will not perceive in them any power or activity; there is, therefore, no such thing contained in them. A little attention will discover to us that the very being of an idea implies passiveness and inertness in it, insomuch that it is impossible for an idea to do anything, or, strictly speaking, to be the cause of anything: neither can it be the resem-

blance or pattern of any active being, as is evident from sect. 8. Whence it plainly follows that extension, figure, and motion cannot be the cause of our sensations. To say, therefore, that these are the effects of powers resulting from the configuration, number, motion, and size of corpuscles, must certainly be false.

26. We perceive a continual succession of ideas, some are anew excited, others are changed or totally disappear. There is therefore some cause of these ideas, whereon they depend, and which produces and changes them. That this cause cannot be any quality or idea or combination of ideas, is clear from the preceding section. It must therefore be a substance; but it has been shewn that there is no corporeal or material substance: it remains therefore that the cause of ideas is an incorporeal active substance or Spirit.

27. A spirit is one simple, undivided, active being—as it perceives ideas it is called the *understanding,* and as it produces or otherwise operates about them it is called the *will.* Hence there can be no *idea* formed of a soul or spirit, for all ideas whatever, being passive and inert (*vide* sect. 25), they cannot represent unto us, by way of image or likeness, that which acts. A little attention will make it plain to any one, that to have an idea which shall be like that active principle of motion and change of ideas is absolutely impossible. Such is the nature of *spirit,* or that which acts, that it cannot be of itself perceived, but only by the effects which it produceth. If any man shall doubt of the truth of what is here delivered, let him but reflect and try if he can frame the idea of any power or active being, and whether he has ideas of two principal powers, marked by the names *will* and *understanding,* distinct from each other as well as from a third idea of Substance or Being in general, with a relative notion of its supporting or being the subject of the aforesaid powers—which is signified by the name *soul* or *spirit.* This is what some hold; but, so far as I can see, the words *will, soul, spirit,* do not stand for different ideas, or, in truth, for any idea at all, but for something which is very different from ideas,

and which, being an agent, cannot be like unto, or represented by, any idea whatsoever. Though it must be owned at the same time that we have some *notion* of soul, spirit, and the operations of the mind: such as willing, loving, hating—inasmuch as we know or understand the meaning of these words.

28. I find I can excite ideas in my mind at pleasure, and vary and shift the scene as oft as I think fit. It is no more than willing, and straightway this or that idea arises in my fancy; and by the same power it is obliterated and makes way for another. This making and unmaking of ideas doth very properly denominate the mind active. Thus much is certain and grounded on experience: but when we think of unthinking agents or of exciting ideas exclusive of volition, we only amuse ourselves with words.

29. But, whatever power I may have over my own thoughts, I find the ideas actually perceived by Sense have not a like dependence on my will. When in broad daylight I open my eyes, it is not in my power to choose whether I shall see or no, or to determine what particular objects shall present themselves to my view; and so likewise as to the hearing and other senses; the ideas imprinted on them are not creatures of my will. There is therefore some *other* Will or Spirit that produces them.

30. The ideas of Sense are more strong, lively, and distinct than those of the imagination; they have likewise a steadiness, order, and coherence, and are not excited at random, as those which are the effects of human wills often are, but in a regular train or series, the admirable connexion whereof sufficiently testifies the wisdom and benevolence of its Author. Now the set rules or established methods wherein the Mind we depend on excites in us the ideas of sense, are called the *laws of nature:* and these we learn by experience, which teaches us that such and such ideas are attended with such and such other ideas, in the ordinary course of things.

• • •

2

Contemporary Theories

CHAPTER SEVEN

Logical Behaviourism

Against metaphysics

The philosophies of mind constructed by Plato, Aristotle, and Descartes are each examples of what we call **metaphysical theories**. This term, which originates with Aristotle, refers to theories that attempt to describe the ultimate nature of reality. The idea is clearly illustrated by Descartes' philosophy. In defending the new science and describing the nature of the soul, Descartes was not content to rely on the success of scientific experiments. Instead, he wanted to prove conclusively that the nature of reality conforms to the methods of science — that the language of mathematics really *is* the language of nature. Such a proof requires knowledge that extends beyond what can be observed, in order to demonstrate how our observations correspond to reality.

There have always been people who have been skeptical of metaphysical enterprises like Descartes'. An example of this skepticism is Locke's criticism of Descartes' claim that we have direct knowledge of the soul as a distinct substance. Locke rejects Descartes' claim that we have a "clear and distinct" understanding of the essential properties of matter and mind based solely on reason and reflection. According to Locke, all knowledge is based on sensory experience, and experience does not tell us whether matter is capable of thought. The assertion that all knowledge is based on experience provides a basis for rejecting *all* metaphysical theories. This idea was extensively developed in the eighteenth century by David Hume and Immanuel Kant, who attempted to demonstrate systematically that it is impossible to determine the ultimate nature of reality. All we can ascertain, they argued, was the nature of the world as we experience it. We cannot compare our experience with a description of what the world is really like "behind the appearances."

Logical positivism

Philosophy in the twentieth century has been greatly influenced by a movement known as **logical positivism**, or **logical empiricism**, which attacks all metaphysical systems as nonsense. Logical positivism was founded in Vienna prior to World War Two by a group of philosophers and scientists who called themselves the Vienna Circle. What distinguishes these philosophers from other critics of metaphysics is their claim that metaphysics is not merely hopeless or useless, but *meaningless*. They argue that sentences like 'The soul is an immaterial substance' are just empty strings of words that have no content whatsoever. Their argument for this conclusion is based on a theory about language. The emphasis on language, and the conclusions drawn from it, introduced an entirely new way of thinking about the mind-body problem.

If a sentence in a language has any meaning, logical positivists argue, it must be possible (at least in principle) to provide evidence that it is true or false. If there is no evidence that could possibly count for or against the truth of a particular sentence, then that sentence cannot possibly be saying anything about the world. So a sentence is meaningful, they claim, only if we can specify what would count as evidence that it is true or false.[1]

The only exceptions they allow to this rule are tautologies and contradictions; these sentences are true or false simply in virtue of the meanings of the words they contain. For example, we need no evidence to assure us that the sentence 'All sisters are female' is true. It would be absurd to conduct a statistical survey to find out whether all sisters are female. This is because the term 'female' is part of the meaning of the term 'sister.' For this reason, the logical positivists argue, such statements tell us nothing about the world; they inform us only of the logical structure of our own language.

Logical positivists claim that metaphysical sentences are all perfectly compatible with any evidence whatsoever — there can never be evidence either for them or against them. In other words, whether a metaphysical statement is true or false would make no difference at all to how the world appears. An example of this, they claim, is the sentence 'God exists.' Any event or observation whatsoever can be accounted for by both atheists and deists, and so both the truth *and* falsity of 'God exists' is compatible with all possible evidence. Given this view of language, it follows that metaphysical sentences are meaningless. They are grammatically well-formed, but otherwise they are just empty strings of words, no more meaningful than 'Blue is more identical than music.' Metaphysical assertions like Descartes' about the nature of the mind fall into this category as well. According to logical positivists, the sentence 'Mind and body are distinct substances' has no meaning at all.

The task of philosophy

But if metaphysics is meaningless, then what is the point of philosophy itself? Some members of the Vienna Circle declared that philosophy consists entirely of meaningless statements, and should be abandoned altogether. Most positivists, however, have not drawn this conclusion, but argue instead for a revised role for philosophy. An excellent example of this view is presented in an article by Moritz Schlick entitled "The Future of Philosophy."[2]

Schlick points out that philosophy and science were not clearly separated until the nineteenth century. For this reason, Schlick claims, it had always been thought that philosophy has the same goal as the sciences, namely, to discover true theories about the world. The only difference thought to exist between philosophy and science is that philosophy has a wider subject matter: philosophy studies the whole of reality and the sciences investigate different aspects of reality.

Schlick argues that a better conception of philosophy can found in the activity of Socrates. In some of Plato's dialogues Socrates does not arrive at any answers to the questions he considers. He doesn't construct philosophical theories about the nature of reality. Instead he simply makes clearer what is *meant* by certain questions and certain words. For example, when he looks at the question 'What is justice?', Socrates spends his time on an analysis of the *concept* conveyed by the word 'justice.' In this way, according to Schlick, the proper task of philosophy is not the "pursuit of truth" but the "pursuit of meaning." We can only determine whether a sentence is true or false once we have a clear understanding of what it means. It is this essential task, Schlick claims, that belongs to philosophy.

The verifiability theory of meaning

Schlick bases his claim about the role of philosophy on the logical positivists's analysis of meaning. He says:

> We know the meaning of a proposition when we are able to indicate exactly the circumstances under which it would be true (or, what amounts to the same, the circumstances which would make it false). The description of these circumstances is absolutely the only way in which the meaning of a sentence can be made clear.[3]

The idea is that if someone were to ask what a particular sentence means, the correct answer would be a description of the evidence that would have to be collected to establish that it is true or false. This idea has been called the **verifiability theory of meaning**.

Some sentences can be verified directly by observation. Sentences like 'This stick is two metres long' or 'The cat is on the mat' can be verified by making some very simple observations. So, according to the verifiability theory, the meanings of these sentences are simply descriptions of those observations. The difficulty in ascertaining meanings arises when we consider sentences that contain theoretical words like 'force' or 'molecule.' These terms appear to be descriptions of things that cannot be observed. But, if this is so, the meanings of such sentences would appear to be descriptions of hidden or unobservable entities rather than descriptions of observations.

The logical positivists claim that this appearance is misleading. They point out that theoretical sentences are also confirmed or disconfirmed by observations. But the observations are complex ones, involving intricate experiments or elaborate equipment. It follows from the verifiability theory that the meanings of these sentences must be descriptions of these complicated observations. So logical positivists maintain that sentences containing theoretical terms are not descriptions of unobservable entities, but simply a form of shorthand for describing collections of complex observations. To reveal the meanings of these sentences, it is necessary to *translate* them into compound observation sentences.

Before a scientist can proceed to find out whether a theoretical sentence is true or false, Schlick argues, there is a philosophical job of determining exactly what evidence would confirm or disconfirm it. In any interesting scientific situations this is a difficult business. Schlick offers two illustrations of this in Newton's working out the concept of mass and Einstein's analysis of the concept of simultaneity. In performing these analyses, Schlick claims, Newton and Einstein were working as philosophers rather than as scientists.

Scientific psychology

Schlick argues that many so-called philosophical problems have always resisted solution simply because they are meaningless, even though they have the grammatical form of proper questions. Those questions raised by philosophers that do have a real meaning, he claims, will turn out to be scientific questions answerable by the ordinary methods of science. So when philosophers turn their attention to questions about the mind, their objective should be to determine which are scientific questions and which are meaningless combinations of words that only *look* as though they are genuine questions. The mind-body problem as it is traditionally conceived, Schlick contends, is not a meaningful question. According to Schlick, there can be no observational evidence either for or against any of its solutions. In other words, whether the mind is or is not an immaterial entity makes no difference to the observable world.

But this doesn't entail that all statements about the mind are meaningless. For some can be shown to be scientific statements to be confirmed or disconfirmed by observation. Since the eighteenth century there have been attempts to use the methods of science to study such mental processes as sensation, learning and memory. For example, the nineteenth-century German scientist Gustav Fechner devised mathematical techniques to relate the physical intensities of light and sound to our sensory experiences. Such efforts led to several definitions of psychology as a "science of the mind." Logical positivists see the job of philosophy of mind to be the "logical analysis of psychology," that is, the study of the meanings of psychological statements by specifying the circumstances under which they are shown to be true or false.

Not all of the methods used by psychologists are accepted by logical positivists as scientifically respectable. In particular, they reject the use of **introspection** on one's own experiences. Remember that, on Descartes' view, knowledge of the mind is obtained by reflecting on the contents of one's own conscious experience. And William James, who established much of the content of psychology in this century, described its method as "looking into our minds and reporting what we there discover."[4] Some early psychologists believed that it is possible to use introspection to uncover the "atoms" of the mind in much the same way that chemists have worked out the periodic table of the elements. But logical positivists are skeptical of this method, for there is no way to resolve disagreement in what people report as going on in the mind. People are notoriously inconstant and vague about the contents of their own conscious experience.

As a result, logical positivists attempt to analyze descriptions of the mind solely in terms of what can be observed by everyone rather than what can be observed only through each person's private introspection. To this end, the views of a school of psychology called **behaviourism** were adopted by the logical positivists as providing the appropriate framework for psychology. According to behaviourists, the proper job of psychology is not to describe and explain private, inner thoughts and experiences but to predict and explain human *behaviour*. This fits the logical positivists' goals because a person's behaviour is observable by anyone, and the techniques of measuring and recording behaviour are fully amenable to the methods of the physical sciences.

Scientific behaviourism

The founder of behaviourism is John B. Watson (1878–1958), an American animal researcher and psychologist at Johns Hopkins University. Watson was scathing in his descriptions of the problems of introspection as a technique for understanding the mind. He argued instead that human beings should be studied in the same way as other animals, namely, by observing their behaviour and the ways that it is affected by changes in their physical environment.

To this end Watson took as his model Ivan Pavlov's studies on conditioned reflexes in animal behaviour. Pavlov's method was to record the regular connections between **stimulus** and **response**. A stimulus is an event in an animal's environment that affects its behaviour. A response to a stimulus is the behaviour an animal exhibits when it is presented with that stimulus. Pavlov had discovered that a response that normally followed one particular stimulus will be elicited by a different stimulus if the two stimuli occur together over a period of time. This technique is known as **classical conditioning**. Pavlov is famous for his demonstration of the technique by inducing salivation in dogs by ringing a bell that had previously accompanied food.

Although Watson laid the foundation for behaviourism, the movement in its current form is linked most closely with the work of B.F. Skinner of Harvard University. Although Skinner agreed with the general method of recording stimuli and responses, he differed from Watson in insisting that humans and other animals do not merely respond to environmental stimuli; they modify their behaviour in regular ways in light of its consequences. The basis of Skinner's idea is a principle formulated by Edward Thorndike called **The Law of Effect**. The Law of Effect says that the frequency with which a behaviour pattern occurs is related to the tendency it has to produce positive results. For example, the likelihood that an animal will push on a lever is increased if doing so produces food and is decreased if doing so produces pain. Thorndike's work led Skinner to the notion of **operant behaviour**, which is the idea that behaviour is "shaped" by its results, either positive or negative.

The advantage of the idea of operant behaviour over the classical conditioning model is that it allows us to explain how entirely new patterns of behaviour can emerge. An animal encounters the positive results of a form of behaviour, and as a result comes to exhibit that behaviour regularly. Owen Flanagan points out that Skinner's idea of operant behaviour explains novel behaviour in much the same way that the theory of evolution explains novel forms of life: those forms of behaviour that happen to produce positive outcomes will be reinforced over time, while those that tend to produce negative results will gradually be extinguished.[5]

Skinner was convinced that the idea of operant behaviour could be used to explain all forms of human behaviour, including those typically associated with conscious intelligence such as language understanding and creativity. We will examine here a reading from Skinner's *Science and Human Behaviour* (1953), in which he argues that linguistic behaviour can be explained without any reference to inner states of mind.

Laws of stimulus and behaviour

In this selection Skinner defends the idea that we can predict, and thereby explain, human behaviour by measuring the connections between stimulus and response. We can treat stimulus and response as two related physical variables, just as mass, time, and motion are related physical variables. The goal of psychology, as he sees it, is to describe the laws by which stimuli and behaviour are connected, taking them as physical laws on a par with, say, the laws of motion. He argues that if we can describe these laws, there is no need to describe the inner mental processes that occur *between* a stimulus and a person's behaviour. Skinner claims that in this way we can entirely bypass the vexing and possibly unanswerable question of what the inner states are that produce human behaviour: whether they are states of an immaterial mind, as Descartes says, or processes of the nervous system, as many scientists argue. Skinner claims that psychology should be agnostic on the question of what is the nature of mental processing. It should concentrate on formulating the laws governing observable, measurable variables in human behaviour, leaving the rest to pseudoscience and mysticism.[6]

Against "inner causes"

The first four sections of the reading from *Science and Human Behaviour* are criticisms of the traditional ways of explaining behaviour, each of which refers to some inner state that is seen as the cause of what a person does. In the opening section Skinner argues that the tendency to search for inner, hidden qualities in things to explain why they act as they do is a common error in science. He lists a number of mistaken theories in the history of science where in each case the search for an inner cause proved fruitless because, being difficult to verify or refute, people can make them up however they like. For example, medieval philosophers attributed the motion of a falling rock to a *vis viva* or "living force." The position Skinner takes here is in agreement with the logical positivists' assertion that scientific theories should not be taken as descriptions of unobservable entities, as the presence or absence of such entities cannot be confirmed by observation.

The next three sections describe three common varieties of explanations of human behaviour, each of which Skinner claims is an instance of the mistaken approach of looking for hidden, internal causes. The first is the reference to neural causes. Skinner points out that in ordinary talk we attribute people's behaviour to states of the nervous system in a loose and casual manner. For example, when we talk about "nervous breakdown," we are simply disguising a superficial description of a person's behaviour by dressing it up with reference to the nerves.

Neurology itself, he argues, is guilty of the same loose talk. Because we cannot observe brain processes directly, we often infer their existence from how people behave. But if we then refer to these processes as the causes of people's behaviour, we aren't *explaining* why they behave as they do. For the terms we are using are simply words that describe that behaviour. Saying that someone is crying uncontrollably because they are having a nervous breakdown isn't explanatory, because the term "nervous breakdown" is nothing more than a description of that behaviour. Eventually, we may be able to predict specific behaviour from observations of neural processes, but this may never happen, and we should not pretend that it is possible now.

Another form of appeal to inner causes of human behaviour is the description of an "inner mind" controlling the actions of the body. Descartes' dualism is a version of this kind of explanation. Again, Skinner points out that scientists often resort to such explanations of behaviour, and he cites the Freudian concepts of ego, superego, and id as being used in this way. Freud himself was not a dualist, for he believed that the processes of the mind are activities of the nervous system. But he believed that we could not understand how such processes affect human behaviour without analyzing them in terms of the *meaning* they have for the subject. According to Freud, theories that leave out the inner meanings of our actions are inadequate for comprehending why people behave as they do. Freud modified Descartes' theory to include the idea that mental occurrences are not only hidden to others, they are hidden to the person who has them as well. But, according to Skinner, this only increases the ease with which we can invent whatever inner mental causes we like, as it is now impossible to confirm or disconfirm them.

In the fourth section Skinner describes cases where it appears as if we are explaining behaviour in terms of inner causes, but where in fact the inner cause is just another word for the behaviour itself. Words like "intelligence" and "addiction" sound as though they describe genuine causes of a person's behaviour. Skinner claims, however, that they are nothing more than words we use to refer to certain kinds of behaviour. As with many references to neural causes, these are words that can give an appearance of explanation where there is none.

Functional analysis of behaviour

In the fifth section, "The variables of which behaviour is a function," Skinner argues that by searching for inner causes we have overlooked what we *can* observe, which can be used to explain and predict human behaviour. According to Skinner, we can describe behaviour as a *function* of features of people's environment and their *environmental history*. Let's have a look at what this means.

To say that a variable, *y*, is a **function** of another variable, *x*, means that whenever we specify a value for *x* we will always get a specific value for *y*. For example, the function $y = x^2$ always gives a certain value for *y* when a number is substituted for *x*. By the term **environmental history** Skinner just means a description of all the stimuli that have affected a person in the past. So when he says that "behaviour is a function of environmental history," his point is that how someone will behave in a given environment is dictated by the stimuli to which they have been exposed in the recent and distant past. Each possible environmental history yields exactly one behaviour, just as each possible value for *x* in x^2 yields exactly one number.

Thus, according to Skinner, we can predict precisely how a person will behave if we know what stimuli they have been affected by in the past together with a knowledge of their current physical environment. Of course, we can never determine *all* the facts about a person's environmental history. But Skinner says that we should be able to measure the *probability* that a person will exhibit a certain behaviour in a given situation, and we can then determine how changes in their history will affect those probabilities. For a trivial example, depriving someone of water for a prolonged period will increase the chances of their drinking when given water.

His recommendation, then, is that, "we must investigate the effect of each variable quantitatively with the methods and techniques of a laboratory." What Skinner is proposing here is that the same methods be applied to explanations of human behaviour as mechanical scientists apply to physical events. Events in a person's behaviour are explained by discovering mathematical laws that describe how that behaviour is produced by the impact of the surrounding environment on a person's body. Once these laws are complete, the task of psychology is finished. Descartes' "inner" mind has been bypassed altogether so that human behaviour is explained in the same terms as that of any other physical body.

The Theoretician's Dilemma

In the remaining paragraphs of the section Skinner argues that referring to inner causes of behaviour is entirely *dispensable*. If human behaviour is a function of environment and environmental history, then the latter two are all that is needed to account for behaviour. Using the trivial example again, it is unnecessary to say that lack of water caused thirst, and that thirst in turn caused the subject to drink. We can simply say that lack of water caused the subject to drink — the reference to thirst is superfluous. Hence, inner causes are both difficult to verify *and* unnecessary, rendering them unsuitable for scientific explanations.

Skinner's argument here has become famous under the title **The Theoretician's Dilemma**. Whenever a theory describing unobservable entities is used to predict the occurrence of one observable event from the prior occurrence of another, we find ourselves confronted with a quandary: either the observable events are connected in the way the theory describes, or they are not. In the first case, the theory is not needed because we can predict the one event from the other without any reference to the theory. And in the second case, the theory is useless because it is of no help in our predictions.

Logical behaviourism

Notice that Skinner professes to be agnostic on philosophical questions about the nature of the mind. In his opinion this is a question that science should ignore altogether. The logical positivists take the stronger view that the question is entirely meaningless. But the two agree nonetheless that questions about what goes on in the "inner" mind should be replaced with questions about how people behave.

We saw earlier that the logical positivists' position is that the task of philosophy is to analyze the meanings of scientific statements in terms of the evidence that will confirm or disconfirm them. Behaviourism provides them with a perfect vehicle for applying this project to psychology. They argue that all descriptions of the mind are confirmed or disconfirmed solely by facts about a person's behaviour in a given environment. If this can be shown, then it follows from the verifiability theory of meaning that such facts constitute the *meaning* of any psychological statement. For example, when we say that someone is experiencing a headache, we are not describing an inner mental experience. We are merely describing aspects of their behaviour such as moaning, taking aspirins, or saying "I have a headache." Similarly, if we say, "Amanda is distracted from her work by thoughts of her mother," our sentence should not be taken as a description of some hidden events in Amanda's inner mind. Instead it describes certain features of her behaviour — the length of time she takes over her work and her verbal remarks about her mother.

This theory about the meanings of psychological statements, formed by applying the verifiability theory of meaning to the subject of the mind, is called **logical behaviourism**. In a sense, logical behaviourism is the result of combining logical positivism with the behaviourism of Watson and Skinner. It is the theory defended by Carl Hempel in his essay, "The Logical Analysis of Psychology."

Hempel began his career as a physicist and mathematician in Berlin in the 1930s, but developed an interest in philosophy through his acquaintance with Moritz Schlick and other members of the Vienna Circle. He left Germany in 1934 because of the political developments there, and eventually settled in America as a professor at Princeton University. Although the largest part of his work is in the philosophy of science, Hempel's influence also derives from his application of the tenets of logical positivism to psychology. "The Logical Analysis of Psychology" is an early piece, representing a strong version of logical behaviourism that Hempel later came to revise.

Eliminating the inner mind

In the first section of the article, Hempel identifies the same role for philosophy as does Schlick: the task of philosophy, he says, is to analyze the meanings of scientific statements. Hempel comments that recent advances in symbolic logic have made such an analysis possible.

In the next section Hempel characterizes the application of logical positivism to psychology as standing in opposition to the **introspectionist** school of psychology. This school, which in many ways has its historical roots in Descartes, holds that to gain an understanding of the mind we must turn our attention toward our own inner thoughts. According to those who champion this use of introspection in understanding the mind, the methods and concepts of the natural sciences, such as physics, are not applicable in psychology. Psychology, they argue, must deal with the *meanings* of our actions. Describing a person's behaviour solely in terms of the physical actions of the body will leave out the meaning that the behaviour has for that person — what they see themselves as doing. And this meaning can be understood, according to introspectionists, only by reflecting on the contents of our own mind "from the inside."

In Section III, Hempel argues that behaviourism is ideally suited to the goal of eliminating the opposition that introspectionists have created between physics and psychology. Behaviourism treats questions about the mind as having to do "with purely physical processes, and ... therefore there can be no impassible barrier between psychology and physics." As long as psychology limits itself to physical descriptions of stimulus and behaviour, it is amenable to the techniques of the natural sciences.

However, he argues, the adoption of behaviourism in psychology is not enough by itself to establish the scientific status of psychology. He says:

> [O]ne cannot expect the question as to the scientific status of psychology to be settled by empirical research in psychology itself.

His point is that even if behaviouristic theories like those described by Skinner in the previous reading were to successfully predict human behaviour in terms of stimulus-response laws, that by itself would not demonstrate that there is nothing more to psychology than such predictions. For a critic could argue that this leaves out the inner meanings that our thoughts and experiences have for us, which psychology *ought* to study. So psychological behaviourism, he says, must be coupled with the philosophical arguments of the logical positivists.

The meanings of psychological statements

In Section IV Hempel outlines the central aspects of the verifiability theory of meaning. An important consequence of this theory, he claims, is that two sentences have the same meaning if they are verified by the same observations. It is this idea that permits sentences containing theoretical terms like 'temperature' to be "retranslated without change of meaning" into sentences that do not contain such terms but describe only collections of observations. His idea here is that if descriptions of observations capture the real meanings of sentences that contain theoretical terms, then these descriptions serve as *translations* of the original sentence — they say exactly the same thing as the original, but in different words.

According to the verifiability theory, the way to precisely determine the meaning of psychological statements is to see how they are verified. This method allows us to ascertain whether psychological statements are different in nature from statements in the natural sciences. When we do this we find that descriptions of a person's state of mind are all confirmed by facts about their behaviour and their physical body. For example, the sentence, "Paul has a headache," which purports to describe an inner experience of pain, is in fact verified by Paul's gestures, by what he says, and by the state of his body. The same point applies, Hempel says, to more subtle psychological statements such as those describing depression or feelings of inferiority. Whether someone is depressed or anxious can only be confirmed by observing their behaviour, verbal or otherwise.

Thus at the end of Section IV, Hempel gives his definition of logical behaviourism:

> All psychological statements which are meaningful, that is to say, which are in principle verifiable, are translatable into statements which do not involve psychological concepts, but only the concepts of physics. The statements of psychology are consequently physicalistic statements. Psychology is an integral part of physics.[7]

Terms like 'pain' or 'depression,' which may seem to describe hidden, inner states of a person's mind, are now to be treated as theoretical terms of psychology, on a par with terms such as 'electron' or 'mass.' And sentences containing them are to be translated into sentences that describe only observable features of behaviour and other aspects of the physical body.

Behaviour is all we have to go by

In the next section Hempel considers an obvious objection to logical behaviourism: the behaviour that a person exhibits is merely an *effect* of her mental state, so a description of that behaviour is not a description of the mental state itself. For example, a headache is not a form of behaviour, but an inner sensation that causes certain kinds of behaviour. Hempel replies that this objection overlooks the fact that any time we describe someone as being in a certain state of mind, that description is *confirmable* only through observing the person's behaviour. So he argues that there is no meaning that we *can* assign to psychological descriptions other than as descriptions of certain forms of behaviour.

There is, however, the further objection that people sometimes only pretend to have a particular psychological state or experience, and so their behaviour doesn't reveal their real state of mind. To this Hempel replies that the only way to distinguish real from feigned states of mind is by closer observation of behaviour. Pretending to have a headache must be distinguishable in some way from actually having a headache. For if a person's behaviour is *identical* to that of someone with a headache, there are no grounds for claiming they do not really have one.

According to Hempel, then, psychological terms are merely abbreviations of complex descriptions of behaviour. They are convenient in reducing the length and complexity of full descriptions, but they should not be mistakenly identified as referring to inner states of mind revealed to us through introspection. In this way, psychological concepts play the same role as the theoretical concepts of all the other sciences: they allow us to make predictions about observable features of the world in a concise way. But if we are not careful in their use they can lead to such pseudo-questions as the mind-body problem, which can arise only if we erroneously take them to refer to mysterious "inner" states of the soul.

A problem for behaviourism

To many people logical behaviourism appears obviously false. The idea that descriptions of thoughts and experiences are only descriptions of behaviour seems to fly in the face of common sense. As we will see in the next chapter, however, appeals to common sense are weakened by arguments that what we have come to accept as common sense is based on fundamental errors. But behaviourism also encounters a problem of a different kind: Skinner's project of explaining behaviour entirely in terms of stimulus-response laws runs into serious difficulty when confronted with the complexity of human behaviour. The same complexity in human behaviour creates problems in the logical behaviourists' plan to translate psychological descriptions into descriptions of observable behaviour.

The problem behaviourists face in accounting for complex behaviour is illustrated nicely in a review by Noam Chomsky of another of Skinner's books, *Verbal Behaviour*.[8] Chomsky is a linguist at the Massachusetts Institute of Technology. He is one of the originators of the idea that the brain should be understood as a kind of digital computer. In his review of Skinner, Chomsky argues that we cannot explain the variety and complexity of linguistic ability simply as behavioural responses to physical stimuli. According to Chomsky, linguistic abilities can only be explained on the assumptions that language is the result of complex mental processes that analyze sentences into their grammatical and semantic components.

The behaviourist's dilemma

Chomsky argues that the problem facing Skinner's program arises from the fact that behaviourism is formulated in accordance with the methods used to predict the behaviour of animals in tightly controlled laboratory experiments. A typical experiment of this sort requires an animal to perform such activities as pressing a bar to release food when certain stimuli are presented. In such a context it is possible to demonstrate that certain behaviour patterns are the product of very specific environmental stimuli. But, according to Chomsky, Skinner is unable to show how to extend this method outside the laboratory to complex human verbal behaviour.

Chomsky argues that when discussing behaviour outside the laboratory, behaviourists like Skinner are faced with a dilemma. They claim that all behaviour can be shown to be the product of laws formulated in terms of responses to environmental stimuli. But the only laws of behaviour that have actually been *demonstrated* are those devised in the laboratory involving very specific aspects of the animals' behaviour (such as pressing a bar to release food pellets) and very specific aspects of the environment (such as flashing lights). If we direct our attention to other features of the environment and to other aspects of animal behaviour, they must admit that no laws connecting the two have yet been discovered. So behaviourists have two choices: (1) admit that it has not been shown that response is always a function of external stimuli, or (2) insist that only those aspects of the environment and of behaviour that have been demonstrated to be lawfully connected are to be counted as genuine stimuli and behavioural responses. The first is the denial of Skinner's central claim in *Verbal Behaviour*. But the second option is also unacceptable because it renders Skinner's assertion that response is a function of stimuli true *by definition* rather than by observation.

Chomsky's "painting example"

Chomsky argues that Skinner tries to avoid this dilemma by a sleight of hand. According to Chomsky, Skinner defends the scientific character of the stimulus-response approach by first describing the results achieved with animals in the laboratory. Then he applies the method outside the laboratory by extending the definition of stimulus and response beyond their original meaning in the laboratory. When the terms are stretched in this way, Chomsky argues, they lose their scientific character.

Chomsky presents the following illustration of his point. Suppose when looking at a painting, a person's response is to utter the word, "Dutch." According to Skinner, this response is "under the control of extremely subtle properties" of the painting. The task of the psychologist, in Skinner's view, is to work out what those properties are. But Chomsky asks us to think of all the other verbal responses a person might make: "Clashes with the wallpaper," "I thought you liked abstract work," "Never saw it before," "Tilted," "Hanging Too Low," "Beautiful," "Hideous," "Remember our camping trip last summer?" What are the properties of the painting that would produce these remarks?

We might try to say that it was the property of clashing with the wallpaper that produced the first, and the property of being unfamiliar to the subject that produced the third, and so on. But this would be pointless because we are now using the subject's response to determine the relevant aspects of the stimulus. As Chomsky puts it, "We don't know what the stimuli are until the subject responds." According to Chomsky this is a reversion to precisely the kind of psychology that Skinner wants to avoid. For by waiting for the subject's utterance before identifying the stimulus, the character of the stimulus is determined by the inner thoughts of the subject rather than by objective features of the environment. That is, the stimulus is described in terms of how the subject *perceives* it, rather than by its objective physical characteristics. Thus, Chomsky argues, Skinner fails to offer any description of the stimuli that prompt verbal behaviour in terms of objective physical properties of the environment.

Complex mental states vs. past environmental history

Chomsky's criticism is not that behaviourism has the wrong objectives. Unlike some critics of behaviourism, Chomsky does not attack Skinner's restriction of psychology to the task of predicting human behaviour. Rather, his point is that Skinner's behaviourist method makes such prediction impossible. The criticism that Chomsky makes of behaviourism is that how a person behaves seems to depend on more than just the physical character of the stimulus. It also depends on what is going on *in the person's mind* at the time the stimulus is presented. According to Chomsky, we can only predict what people will do by considering their actions to be the result of complex internal states of mind.

However, Skinner has a reply to this criticism. In the second last paragraph from our reading he admits that "other variables" may be needed to predict the behaviour. In predicting whether a person will drink water we need to consider whether they believe the water is poisoned, or have grown up in a culture where people drink only in private. At the end of the paragraph he argues that:

> Adequate prediction in any science requires information about all relevant variables, and the control of a subject matter for practical purposes makes the same demands.

His point is that a person's behaviour depends on their *entire past environmental history* as well as on the current stimulus. So, to use Chomsky's example, how a person will respond to a painting will be determined by what has happened to them in the past as well as by the physical properties of the painting itself. The question dividing Chomsky and Skinner, then, is whether sufficiently full descriptions of environmental history can replace descriptions of inner mental processes. In Chomsky's view, inner causes of behaviour are not dispensable as Skinner claims, but are essential in being able to predict what a person will do. Chomsky's point is that we can only understand how a person's past environmental history affects their behaviour by discovering how it alters their state of mind. According to Skinner, on the other hand, predicting human behaviour requires only a knowledge of the relevant aspects of a person's past physical environment. Once these are known, references to inner states of mind are unnecessary as well as unconfirmable.

NOTES

1   The influence of Berkeley is evident in this idea. The position that the meaning of a sentence is exhausted by the evidence for or against it contains an echo of Berkeley's contention that we have no ideas that are not collections of sensations.

2   Moritz Schlick, "The Future of Philosophy," *College of the Pacific Publications in Philosophy* I (1932), 45–62, reprinted in *The Linguistic Turn: Essays in Philosophi-*

cal Method, Richard Rorty (ed.) (Chicago: Chicago University Press, 1992), pp. 43–53.

3 Schlick, p. 48.

4 William James, *The Principles of Psychology* (1890; reprint, Cambridge, MA: Harvard University Press, 1976).

5 Owen Flanagan, *The Science of the Mind* (Cambridge, MA: MIT Press, 1991), p. 107.

6 This bears a similarity to Newton's attitude in treating gravity as a relation between mass and force while refusing to speculate on its underlying nature. "I feign no hypotheses," Newton declared.

7 It is this statement that Hempel later came to revise. The differences between this and Hempel's later views are beyond our scope here.

8 "A Review of Skinner's *Verbal Behaviour,*" reprinted in *Readings in the Philosophy of Psychology, Volume I,* Ned Block (ed.) (Cambridge, MA: Harvard University Press, 1980), pp. 48–63.

B.F. Skinner
Selections from *Science and Human Behaviour*

Inner "Causes"

Every science has at some time or other looked for causes of action inside the things it has studied. Sometimes the practice has proved useful, sometimes it has not. There is nothing wrong with an inner explanation as such, but events which are located inside a system are likely to be difficult to observe. For this reason we are encouraged to assign properties to them without justification. Worse still, we can invent causes of this sort without fear of contradiction. The motion of a rolling stone was once attributed to its *vis viva*. The chemical properties of bodies were thought to be derived from the *principles* or *essences* of which they were composed. Combustion was explained by the *phlogiston* inside the combustible object. Wounds healed and bodies grew well because of a *vis medicatrix*. It has been especially tempting to attribute the behavior of a living organism to the behavior of an inner agent, as the following examples may suggest.

Neural causes. The layman uses the nervous system as a ready explanation of behavior. The English language contains hundreds of expressions which imply such a causal relationship. At the end of a long trial we read that the jury shows signs of *brain fag*, that the nerves of the accused are *on edge*, that the wife of the accused is on the verge of a *nervous breakdown*, and that his lawyer is generally thought to have lacked the *brains* needed to stand up to the prosecution. Obviously, no direct observations have been made of the nervous systems of any of these people. Their "brains" and "nerves" have been invented on the spur of the moment to lend substance to what might otherwise seem a superficial account of their behavior.

The sciences of neurology and physiology have not divested themselves entirely of a similar practice. Since techniques for observing the electrical and chemical processes in nervous tissue had not yet been developed, early information about the nervous system was limited to its gross anatomy. Neural processes could only be inferred from the behavior which was said to result from them. Such inferences were legitimate enough as scientific theories, but they could not justifiably be used to explain the very behavior upon which they were based. The hypotheses of the early physiologist may have been sounder than those of the layman, but until independent evidence could be obtained, they were no more satisfactory as explanations of behavior. Direct information about many of the chemical and electrical processes in the nervous system is now available. Statements about the nervous system are no longer necessarily inferential or fictional. But there is still a measure of circularity in much physiological explanation, even in the writings of specialists. In World War I a familiar disorder was called "shell shock." Disturbances in behavior were explained by arguing that violent explosions had damaged the structure of the nervous system, though no direct evidence of such damage was available. In World War II the same disorder was classified as "neuropsychiatric." The prefix seems to show a continuing unwillingness to abandon explanations in terms of hypothetical neural damage.

Eventually a science of the nervous system based upon direct observation rather than inference will describe the neural states and events which immediately precede instances of behavior. We shall know the precise neurological conditions which immediately precede, say, the response, "No, thank you." These events in turn will be found to be preceded by other neurological events, and these in turn by others. This series will lead us back to events outside the nervous system and, eventually, outside the organism. In the chapters which follow we shall consider external events of this sort in some detail. We shall then be better able to evaluate the place of neurological explanations of behavior. However, we may note here that we do not have and may never have this sort of neurological information at the moment it is needed in order to predict a specific instance of behavior. It is even more unlikely that we shall be able to alter the nervous system directly in order to set up the antecedent conditions of a particular instance. The causes to be sought in the nervous system are, therefore, of limited usefulness in the prediction and control of specific behavior.

Psychic inner causes. An even more common practice is to explain behavior in terms of an inner agent which lacks physical dimensions and is called "mental" or "psychic." The purest form of the psychic explanation is seen in the animism of primitive peoples. From the immobility of the body after death it is inferred that a spirit responsible for movement has departed. The *enthusiastic* person is, as the etymology of the word implies, energized by a "god within." It is only a modest refinement to attribute every feature of the behavior of the physical organism to a corresponding feature of the "mind" or of some inner "personality." The inner man is regarded as driving the body very much as the man at the steering wheel drives a car. The inner man wills an action, the outer executes it. The inner loses his appetite, the outer stops eating. The inner man wants and the outer gets. The inner has the impulse which the outer obeys.

It is not the layman alone who resorts to these practices, for many reputable psychologists use a similar dualistic system of explanation. The inner man is sometimes personified clearly, as when delinquent behavior is attributed to a "disordered personality," or he may be dealt with in fragments, as when behavior is attributed to mental processes, faculties, and traits. Since the inner man does not occupy space, he may be multiplied at will. It has been argued that a single physical organism is controlled by several psychic agents and that its behavior is the resultant of their several wills. The Freudian concepts of the ego, superego, and id are often used in this way. They are frequently regarded as nonsubstantial creatures, often in violent conflict, whose defeats or victories lead to the adjusted or maladjusted behavior of the physical organism in which they reside.

Direct observation of the mind comparable with the observation of the nervous system has not proved feasible. It is true that many people believe that they observe their "mental states" just as the physiologist observes neural events, but another interpretation of what they observe is possible, as we shall see in Chapter XVII. Introspective psychology no longer pretends to supply direct information about events which are the causal antecedents, rather than the mere accompaniments, of behavior. It defines its "subjective" events in ways which strip them of any usefulness in a causal analysis. The events appealed to in early mentalistic explanations of behavior have remained beyond the reach of observation. Freud insisted upon this by emphasizing the role of the unconscious—a frank recognition that important mental processes are not directly observable. The Freudian literature supplies many examples of behavior from which unconscious wishes, impulses, instincts, and emotions are inferred. Unconscious thought-processes have also been used to explain intellectual achievements. Though the mathematician may feel that he knows "how he thinks," he is often unable to give a coherent account of the mental processes leading to the solution of a specific problem. But any mental event which is unconscious is necessarily inferential, and the explanation is therefore not based upon independent observations of a valid cause.

The fictional nature of this form of inner cause is shown by the ease with which the mental process is discovered to have just the properties needed to account for the behavior. When a professor turns up in the wrong classroom or gives the wrong lecture, it is because his *mind* is, at least for the moment, *absent*. If he forgets to give a reading assignment, it is because it has slipped his *mind* (a hint from the class may re-*mind* him of it). He begins to tell an old joke but pauses for a moment, and it is evident to everyone that he is trying to make up his *mind* whether or not he has already used the joke that term. His lectures grow more tedious with the years, and questions from the class confuse him more and more, because his *mind* is failing. What he says is often disorganized because his *ideas* are confused. He is occasionally unnecessarily emphatic because of the force of his *ideas*. When he repeats himself, it is because he has an *idée fixe;* and when he repeats what others have said, it is because he borrows his *ideas*. Upon occasion there is nothing in what he says because he lacks *ideas*. In all this it is obvious that the mind and the ideas, together with their special characteristics, are being invented on the spot to provide spurious explanations. A science of behavior can hope to gain very little from so cavalier a practice. Since mental or psychic events are asserted to lack the dimensions of physical science, we have an additional reason for rejecting them.

Conceptual inner causes. The commonest inner causes have no specific dimensions at all, either neurological or psychic. When we say that a man eats *because* he is hungry, smokes a great deal *because* he has the tobacco habit, fights *because* of the instinct of pugnacity, behaves brilliantly *because* of his intelligence, or plays the piano well *because* of his musical ability, we seem to be referring to causes. But on analysis these phrases prove to be merely redundant descriptions. A single set of facts is described by the two statements: "He eats" and "He is hungry." A single set of facts is described by the two state-

ments: "He smokes a great deal" and "He has the smoking habit." A single set of facts is described by the two statements: "He plays well" and "He has musical ability." The practice of explaining one statement in terms of the other is dangerous because it suggests that we have found the cause and therefore need search no further. Moreover, such terms as "hunger," "habit," and "intelligence" convert what are essentially the properties of a process or relation into what appear to be things. Thus we are unprepared for the properties eventually to be discovered in the behavior itself and continue to look for something which may not exist.

The Variables of Which Behavior Is a Function

The practice of looking inside the organism for an explanation of behavior has tended to obscure the variables which are immediately available for a scientific analysis. These variables lie outside the organism, in its immediate environment and in its environmental history. They have a physical status to which the usual techniques of science are adapted, and they make it possible to explain behavior as other subjects are explained in science. These independent variables are of many sorts and their relations to behavior are often subtle and complex, but we cannot hope to give an adequate account of behavior without analyzing them.

Consider the act of drinking a glass of water. This is not likely to be an important bit of behavior in anyone's life, but it supplies a convenient example. We may describe the topography of the behavior in such a way that a given instance may be identified quite accurately by any qualified observer. Suppose now we bring someone into a room and place a glass of water before him. Will he drink? There appear to be only two possibilities: either he will or he will not. But we speak of the *chances* that he will drink, and this notion may be refined for scientific use. What we want to evaluate is the *probability* that he will drink. This may range from virtual certainty that drinking will occur to virtual certainty that it will not. The very considerable problem of how to measure such a probability will be discussed later. For the moment, we are interested in how the probability may be increased or decreased.

Everyday experience suggests several possibilities, and laboratory and clinical observations have added others. It is decidedly not true that a horse may be led to water but cannot be made to drink. By arranging a history of severe deprivation we could be "absolutely sure" that drinking would occur. In the same way we may be sure that the glass of water in our experiment will be drunk. Although we are not likely to arrange them experimentally, deprivations of the necessary magnitude sometimes occur outside the laboratory. We may obtain an effect similar to that of deprivation by speeding up the excretion of water. For example, we may induce sweating by raising the temperature of the room or by forcing heavy exercise, or we may increase the excretion of urine by mixing salt or urea in food taken prior to the experiment. It is also well known that loss of blood, as on a battlefield, sharply increases the probability of drinking. On the other hand, we may set the probability at virtually zero by inducing or forcing our subject to drink a large quantity of water before the experiment.

If we are to predict whether or not our subject will drink, we must know as much as possible about these variables. If we are to induce him to drink, we must be able to manipulate them. In both cases, moreover, either for accurate prediction or control, we must investigate the effect of each variable quantitatively with the methods and techniques of a laboratory science.

Other variables may, of course, affect the result. Our subject may be "afraid" that something has been added to the water as a practical joke or for experimental purposes. He may even "suspect" that the water has been poisoned. He may have grown up in a culture in which water is drunk only when no one is watching. He may refuse to drink simply to prove that we cannot predict or control his behavior. These possibilities do not disprove the relations between drinking and the variables listed in the preceding paragraphs; they simply remind us that other variables may have to be taken into account. We must know the history of our subject with respect to the behavior of drinking water, and if we cannot eliminate social factors from the situation, then we must know the history of his personal relations to people resembling the experimenter. Adequate prediction in any science requires information about all relevant variables, and the control of a subject matter for practical purposes makes the same demands.

Other types of "explanation" do not permit us to dispense with these requirements or to fulfill them in any easier way. It is of no help to be told that our subject will drink provided he was born under a particular sign of the zodiac which shows a preoccupation with water or provided he is the lean and thirsty type or was, in short, "born thirsty." Explanations in terms of inner states or agents, however, may require some further comment. To what extent is it helpful to be told, "He drinks because he is thirsty"? If to be thirsty means nothing more than to have a tendency to drink, this is mere redundancy. If it means that he drinks because of a state of thirst, an inner causal event is invoked. If this state is purely inferential—if no dimensions are assigned to it which would make direct observation possible—it cannot serve as an explanation. But if it has physiological or psychic properties, what role can it play in a science of behavior?

Carl G. Hempel
"The Logical Analysis of Psychology"

Author's prefatory note, 1977. The original French version of this article was published in 1935. By the time it appeared in English, I had abandoned the narrow translationist form of physicalism here set forth for a more liberal reductionist one, referred to in note 1, which presents psychological properties and states as partially characterized, but not defined, by bundles of behavioral dispositions. Since then, I have come to think that this conception requires still further broadening, and that the introduction and application of psychological terms and hypotheses is logically and methodologically analogous to the introduction and application of the terms and hypotheses of a physical theory.* The considerations that prompted those changes also led me long ago to abandon as untenable the verificationist construal of the "empirical meaning" of a sentence—a construal which plays such a central role in the arguments set forth in this article.

Since the article is so far from representing my present views, I was disinclined to consent to yet another republication, but I yielded to Dr. Block's plea that it offers a concise account of an early version of logical behaviorism and would thus be a useful contribution to this anthology.

In an effort to enhance the closeness of translation and the simplicity of formulation, I have made a number of small changes in the text of the original English version; none of these affects the substance of the article.

I

One of the most important and most discussed problems of contemporary philosophy is that of determining how psychology should be characterized in the theory of science. This problem, which reaches beyond the limits of epistemological analysis and has engendered heated controversy in metaphysics itself, is brought to a focus by the familiar alternative, "Is psychology a natural science, or is it one of the sciences of mind and culture (*Geisteswissenschaften*)?"

The present article attempts to sketch the general lines of a new analysis of psychology, one

---

An earlier version of this paper appeared in Ausonio Marras, ed., *Intentionality, Mind. and Language* (Urbana: University of Illinois Press, 1972), pp. 115–131, and in Herbert Feigl and Wilfrid Sellars, eds., *Readings in Philosophical Analysis* (New York: Appleton-Century-Crofts, 1949), pp. 373–384, translated from the French by W. Sellars. Reprinted, with revisions by the author, with permission of the author, Herbert Feigl, Wilfrid Sellars, and the editors of *Revue de Synthese*.

*My reasons are suggested in some of my more recent articles, among them "Logical Positivism and the Social Sciences," in P. Achinstein and S.F. Barker, eds., *The Legacy of Legal Positivism* (Baltimore: Johns Hopkins University Press, 1969); "Reduction: Ontological and Linguistic Facets," in S. Morgenbesser, P. Suppes, and M. White, eds., *Philosophy, Science, and Method: Essays in Honor of Ernest Nagel* (New York: St. Martin's Press, 1969); "Dispositional Explanation and the Covering-Law Model: Response to Laird Addis," in A.C. Michalos and R.S. Cohen, eds., *PSA 1974: Proceedings of the 1974 Biennial Meeting of the Philosophy of Science Association* (Dordrecht: Reidel, 1976), pp. 369–376.

which makes use of rigorous logical tools, and which has made possible decisive advances toward the solution of the above problem.[1] This analysis was carried out by the "Vienna Circle" *(Wiener Kreis)*, the members of which (M. Schlick, R. Carnap, P. Frank, O. Neurath, F. Waismann, H. Feigl, etc.) have, during the past ten years, developed an extremely fruitful method for the epistemological examination and critique of the various sciences, based in part on the work of L. Wittgenstein.[2] We shall limit ourselves essentially to the examination of psychology as carried out by Carnap and Neurath.

The method characteristic of the studies of the Vienna Circle can be briefly defined as a *logical analysis of the language of science.* This method became possible only with the development of a subtle logical apparatus which makes use, in particular, of all the formal procedures of modern symbolic logic.[3] However, in the following account, which does not pretend to give more than a broad orientation, we shall limit ourselves to setting out the general principles of this new method, without making use of strictly formal procedures.

II

Perhaps the best way to characterize the position of the Vienna Circle as it relates to psychology, is to say that it is the exact antithesis of the current epistemological thesis that there is a fundamental difference between experimental psychology, a natural science, and introspective psychology; and in general, between the natural sciences on the one hand, and the sciences of mind and culture on the other.[4] The common content of the widely different formulations used to express this contention, which we reject, can be set down as follows. Apart from certain aspects clearly related to physiology, psychology is radically different, both in subject matter and in method, from physics in the broad sense of the term. In particular, it is impossible to deal adequately with the subject

matter of psychology by means of physical methods. The subject matter of physics includes such concepts as mass, wave length, temperature, field intensity, etc. In dealing with these, physics employs its distinctive method which makes a combined use of description and causal explanation. Psychology, on the other hand, has for its subject matter notions which are, in a broad sense, mental. They are *toto genere* different from the concepts of physics, and the appropriate method for dealing with them scientifically is that of empathetic insight, called "introspection," a method which is peculiar to psychology.

One of the principal differences between the two kinds of subject matter is generally believed to consist in the fact that the objects investigated by psychology—in contradistinction to those of physics—are specifically endowed with meaning. Indeed, several proponents of this idea state that the distinctive method of psychology consists in "understanding the sense of meaningful structures" *(sinnvolle Gebilde verstehend zu erfassen)*. Take, for example, the case of a man who speaks. Within the framework of physics, this process is considered to be completely explained once the movements which make up the utterance have been traced to their causes, that is to say, to certain physiological processes in the organism, and, in particular, in the central nervous system. But, it is said, this does not even broach the psychological problem. The latter begins with understanding the sense of what was said, and proceeds to integrate it into a wider context of meaning.

It is usually this latter idea which serves as a principle for the fundamental dichotomy that is introduced into the classification of the sciences. There is taken to be an *absolutely impassable gulf* between the *natural sciences* which have a subject matter devoid of meaning and the *sciences of mind and culture,* which have an intrinsically meaningful subject matter, the appropriate methodological instrument for the scientific study of which is "comprehension of meaning."

III

The position in the theory of science which we have just sketched has been attacked from several different points of view.[5] As far as psychology is concerned, one of the principal countertheses is that formulated by behaviorism, a theory born in America shortly before the war. (In Russia, Pavlov has developed similar ideas.) Its principal methodological postulate is that a scientific psychology should limit itself to the study of the bodily behavior with which man and the animals respond to changes in their physical environment, and should proscribe as nonscientific any descriptive or explanatory step which makes use of terms from introspective or "understanding" psychology, such as 'feeling', 'lived experience', 'idea', 'will', 'intention', 'goal', 'disposition', 'repression'.[6] We find in behaviorism, consequently, an attempt to construct a scientific psychology which would show by its success that even in psychology we have to do with purely physical processes, and that therefore there can be no impassable barrier between psychology and physics. However, this manner of undertaking the critique of a scientific thesis is not completely satisfactory. It seems, indeed, that the soundness of the behavioristic thesis expounded above depends on the possibility of fulfilling the program of behavioristic psychology. But one cannot expect the question as to the scientific status of psychology to be settled by empirical research in psychology itself. To achieve this is rather an undertaking in epistemology. We turn, therefore, to the considerations advanced by members of the Vienna Circle concerning this problem.

IV

Before addressing the question whether the subject matters of physics and psychology are essentially the same or different in nature, it is necessary first to clarify the very concept of the subject matter of a science. The theoretical content of a science is to be found in statements. It is necessary, therefore, to determine whether there is a fundamental difference between the statements of psychology and those of physics. Let us therefore ask what it is that determines the content—one can equally well say the "meaning"—of a statement. When, for example, do we know the meaning of the following statement: "Today at one o'clock, the temperature of such and such a place in the physics laboratory was 23.4° centigrade"? Clearly when, and only when, we know under what conditions we would call the statement true, and under what circumstances we would call it false. Needless to say, it is not necessary to know whether or not the statement is true.) Thus, we understand the meaning of the above statement since we know that it is true when a tube of a certain kind filled with mercury (in short, a thermometer with a centigrade scale), placed at the indicated time at the location in question, exhibits a coincidence between the level of the mercury and the mark of the scale numbered 23.4. It is also true if in the same circumstances one can observe certain coincidences on another instrument called an "alcohol thermometer"; and, again, if a galvanometer connected with a thermopile shows a certain deviation when the thermopile is placed there at the indicated time. Further, there is a long series of other possibilities which make the statement true, each of which is described by a "physical test sentence," as we will call it. The statement itself clearly affirms nothing other than this: all these physical test sentences obtain. (However, one verifies only some of these physical test sentences, and then "concludes by induction" that the others obtain as well.) The statement, therefore, is nothing but an abbreviated formulation of all those test sentences.

Before continuing the discussion, let us sum up this result as follows:

1. A statement that specifies the temperature at a selected point in space-time can be

"retranslated" without change of meaning into another statement—doubtless longer—in which the word "temperature" no longer appears. That term functions solely as an abbreviation, making possible the concise and complete description of a state of affairs the expression of which would otherwise be very complicated.

2. The example equally shows that *two statements which differ in formulation* can nevertheless have the *same meaning*. A trivial example of a statement having the same meaning as the above would be: "Today at one o'clock, at such and such a location in the laboratory, the temperature was 19.44° Réaumur."

As a matter of fact, the preceding considerations show—and let us set it down as another result—that *the meaning of a statement is established by the conditions of its verification*. In particular, two differently formulated statements have the same meaning or the same effective content when, and only when, they are both true or both false in the same conditions. Furthermore, a statement for which one can indicate absolutely no conditions which would verify it, which is in principle incapable of confrontation with test conditions, is wholly devoid of content and without meaning. In such a case we have to do, not with a statement properly speaking, but with a "pseudo-statement," that is to say, a sequence of words correctly constructed from the point of view of grammar, but without content.[7]

In view of these considerations, our problem reduces to one concerning the difference between the circumstances which verify psychological statements and those which verify the statements of physics. Let us therefore examine a statement which involves a psychological concept, for example: "Paul has a toothache." What is the specific content of this statement, that is to say, what are the circumstances in which it would be verified? It will be sufficient to indicate some test sentences which describe these circumstances.

a. Paul weeps and makes gestures of such and such kinds.
b. At the question "What is the matter?," Paul utters the words "I have a toothache."
c. Closer examination reveals a decayed tooth with exposed pulp.
d. Paul's blood pressure, digestive processes, the speed of his reactions, show such and such changes.
e. Such and such processes occur in Paul's central nervous system.

This list could be expanded considerably, but it is already sufficient to bring out the fundamental and essential point, namely, that all the circumstances which verify this psychological statement are expressed by physical test sentences. [This is true even of test condition *b*, which merely expresses the fact that in specified physical circumstances (the propagation of vibrations produced in the air by the enunciation of the words, "What is the matter?") there occurs in the body of the subject a certain physical process (speech behavior of such and such a kind).]

The statement in question, which is about someone's "pain," is therefore, just like that concerning the temperature, simply an abbreviated expression of the fact that all its test sentences are verified.[8] (Here, too, one verifies only some of the test sentences and then infers by way of induction that the others obtain as well.) It can be retranslated without loss of content into a statement which no longer contains the term "pain," but only physical concepts. Our analysis has consequently established that a certain statement belonging to psychology has the same content as a statement belonging to physics; a result which is in direct contradiction to the thesis that there is an impassable gulf between the statements of psychology and those of physics.

The above reasoning can be applied to *any psychological statement*, even to those which concern, as is said, "deeper psychological strata" than that of our example. Thus, the assertion that Mr. Jones suffers from intense inferiority feelings of such and such kinds can be confirmed or falsified only by observing Mr. Jones' behavior in various circumstances. To this behavior belong all the bodily processes of Mr. Jones, and, in particular, his gestures, the flushing and paling of his skin, his utterances, his blood pressure, the events that occur in his central nervous system, etc. In practice, when one wishes to test statements concerning what are called the deeper layers of the psyche, one limits oneself to the observation of external bodily behavior, and, particularly, to speech movements evoked by certain physical stimuli (the asking of questions). But it is well known that experimental psychology has also developed techniques for making use of the subtler bodily states referred to above in order to confirm the psychological discoveries made by cruder methods. The statement concerning the inferiority feelings of Mr. Jones—whether true or false—means only this: such and such happenings take place in Mr. Jones' body in such and such circumstances.

We shall call a statement which can be translated without change of meaning into the language of physics, a "physicalistic statement," whereas we shall reserve the expression "statement of physics" to those which are already formulated in the terminology of physical science. (Since every statement is in respect of content equivalent to itself, every statement of physics is also a physicalistic statement.) The result of the preceding considerations can now be summed up as follows: *All psychological statements which are meaningful, that is to say, which are in principle verifiable, are translatable into statements which do not involve psychological concepts, but only the concepts of physics. The statements of psychology are consequently physicalistic statements. Psychology is an integral part of physics.* If a distinction is drawn between psychology and the other areas of physics, it is only from the point of view of the practical aspects of research and the direction of interest, rather than a matter of principle. This logical analysis, the result of which shows a certain affinity with the fundamental ideas of behaviorism, constitutes the physicalistic conception of psychology.

V

It is customary to raise the following fundamental objection against the above conception. The physical test sentences of which you speak are absolutely incapable of formulating the intrinsic nature of a mental process; they merely describe the physical *symptoms* from which one infers, by purely psychological methods—notably that of understanding—the presence of a certain mental process.

But it is not difficult to see that the use of the method of understanding or of other psychological procedures is bound up with the existence of certain observable physical data concerning the subject undergoing examination. There is no psychological understanding that is not tied up physically in one way or another with the person to be understood. Let us add that, for example, in the case of the statement about the inferiority complex, even the "introspective" psychologist, the psychologist who "understands," can confirm his conjecture only if the body of Mr. Jones, when placed in certain circumstances (most frequently, subjected to questioning), reacts in a specified manner (usually, by giving certain answers). Consequently, even if the statement in question had to be arrived at, *discovered,* by "empathetic understanding," the only *information* it gives us is nothing more nor less than the following: under certain circumstances, certain specific events take place in the body of Mr. Jones. It is this which constitutes the meaning of the psychological statement.

The further objection will perhaps be raised that men can feign. Thus, though a criminal at the bar may show physical symptoms of mental disorder, one would nevertheless be justified in wondering whether his mental confusion was "real" or only simulated. One must note that in the case of the simulator, only some of the conditions are fulfilled which verify the statement "This man is mentally unbalanced," those, namely, which are most accessible to direct observation. A more penetrating examination—which should in principle take into account events occurring in the central nervous system—would give a decisive answer; and this answer would in turn clearly rest on a physicalistic basis. If, at this point, one wished to push the objection to the point of admitting that a man could show *all the "symptoms"* of a mental disease without being "really" ill, we reply that it would be absurd to characterize such a man as "really normal"; for it is obvious that by the very nature of the hypothesis we should possess no criterion in terms of which to distinguish this man from another who, while exhibiting the same bodily behavior down to the last detail, would "in addition" be "really ill." (To put the point more precisely, one can say that this hypothesis contains a *logical contradiction*, since it amounts to saying, "It is possible that a statement should be false even when the necessary and sufficient conditions of its truth are fulfilled.")

Once again we see clearly that the meaning of a psychological statement consists solely in the function of abbreviating the description of certain modes of physical response characteristic of the bodies of men or animals. An analogy suggested by O. Neurath may be of further assistance in clarifying the logical function of psychological statements.[9] The complicated statements that would describe the movements of the hands of a watch in relation to one another, and relatively to the stars, are ordinarily summed up in an assertion of the following form: "This watch runs well (runs badly, etc.)." The term "runs" is introduced here as an auxiliary defined expression which makes it possible to formulate briefly a relatively complicated system of statements. It would thus be absurd to say, for example, that the movement of the hands is only a "physical symptom" which reveals the presence of a running which is intrinsically incapable of being grasped by physical means, or to ask, if the watch should stop, what has become of the running of the watch.

It is in exactly the same way that abbreviating symbols are introduced into the language of physics, the concept of temperature discussed above being an example. The system of physical test sentences *exhausts* the meaning of the statement concerning the temperature at a place, and one should not say that these sentences merely have to do with "symptoms" of the existence of a certain temperature.

Our argument has shown that it is necessary to attribute to the characteristic concepts of psychology the same logical function as that performed by the concepts of "running" and of "temperature." They do nothing more than make possible the succinct formulation of propositions concerning the states or processes of animal or human bodies.

The introduction of new psychological concepts can contribute greatly to the progress of scientific knowledge. But it is accompanied by a danger, that, namely, of making an excessive and, consequently, improper use of new concepts, which may result in questions and answers devoid of sense. This is frequently the case in metaphysics, notably with respect to the notions which we formulated in section II. Terms which are abbreviating symbols are imagined to designate a special class of "psychological objects," and thus one is led to ask questions about the "essence" of these objects, and how they differ from "physical objects." The time-worn problem concerning the relation between mental and physical events is also based on this confusion concerning the logical function of psychological concepts. Our argument, therefore, enables us to see that *the psycho-physical problem is a pseudo-problem,* the formulation of which is based on an inadmissible use of scientific concepts; it is of the same logical nature as the question, suggested by the example above, concerning the relation of the running of the watch to the movement of the hands.[10]

VI

In order to bring out the exact status of the fundamental idea of the physicalistic conception of psychology (or logical behaviorism), we shall contrast it with certain theses of psychological behaviorism and of classical materialism, which give the appearance of being closely related to it.[11]

1. Logical behaviorism claims neither that minds, feelings, inferiority complexes, voluntary actions, etc., do not exist, nor that their existence is in the least doubtful. It insists that the very question as to whether these psychological constructs really exist is already a pseudo-problem, since these notions in their "legitimate use" appear only as abbreviations in physicalistic statements. Above all, one should not interpret the position sketched in this paper as amounting to the view that we can know only the "physical side" of psychological processes, and that the question whether there are mental phenomena behind the physical processes falls beyond the scope of science and must be left either to faith or to the conviction of each individual. On the contrary, the logical analyses originating in the Vienna Circle, one of whose consequences is the physicalistic conception of psychology, teach us that every meaningful question is, in principle, capable of a scientific answer. Furthermore, these analyses show that what, in the case of the mind-body problem, is considered as an object of belief, is absolutely incapable of being expressed by a factual proposition. In other words, there can be no question here of an "article of faith." Nothing can be an object of faith which cannot, in principle, be an object of knowledge.

2. The thesis here developed, though related in certain ways to the fundamental idea of behaviorism, does not demand, as does the latter, that psychological research restrict itself

methodologically to the study of the responses organisms make to certain stimuli. It by no means offers a theory belonging to the domain of psychology, but rather a logical theory about the statements of scientific psychology. Its position is that the latter are without exception physicalistic statements, by whatever means they may have been obtained. Consequently, it seeks to show that if in psychology only physicalistic statements are made, this is not a limitation because it is logically *impossible* to do otherwise.

3. In order for logical behaviorism to be valid, it is not necessary that we be able to describe the physical state of a human body which is referred to by a certain psychological statement—for example, one dealing with someone's feeling of pain—down to the most minute details of the phenomena of the central nervous system. No more does it presuppose a knowledge of all the physical laws governing human or animal bodily processes; nor *a fortiori* is the existence of rigorously deterministic laws relating to these processes a necessary condition of the truth of the behavioristic thesis. At no point does the above argument rest on such a concrete presupposition.

VII

In concluding, I should like to indicate briefly the clarification brought to the problem of the division of the sciences into totally different areas, by the method of the logical analysis of scientific statements, applied above to the special case of the place of psychology among the sciences. The considerations we have advanced can be extended to the domain of sociology, taken in the broad sense as the science of historical, cultural, and economic processes. In this way one arrives at the result that every sociological assertion which is meaningful, that is to say, in principle verifiable, "has as its subject matter nothing else than the states, processes and behavior of groups or of individuals (human or animal), and their responses to one another and to their environment,"[12] and consequently that every sociological statement is a physicalistic statement. This view is characterized by Neurath as the thesis of "social behaviorism," which he adds to that of "individual behaviorism" which we have expounded above. Furthermore, it can be shown[13] that every statement of what are called the "sciences of mind and culture" is a sociological statement in the above sense, provided it has genuine content. Thus one arrives at the "thesis of the unity of science":

The division of science into different areas rests exclusively on differences in research procedures and direction of interest; *one must not regard it as a matter of principle. On the contrary, all the branches of science are in principle of one and the same nature; they are branches of the unitary science, physics.*

VIII

The method of logical analysis which we have attempted to explicate by clarifying, as an example, the statements of psychology, leads, as we have been able to show only too briefly for the sciences of mind and culture, to a "physicalism" based on logic (Neurath): *Every statement of the abovementioned disciplines, and, in general, of empirical science as a whole,* which is not merely a meaningless sequence of words, *is translatable, without change of content, into a statement containing only physicalistic terms, and consequently is a physicalistic statement.*

This thesis frequently encounters strong opposition arising from the idea that such analyses violently and considerably reduce the richness of the life of mind or spirit, as though the aim of the discussion were purely and simply to eliminate vast and important areas of experience. Such a conception comes from a false interpretation of physicalism, the main elements of which we have already examined in section VII above. As a matter of fact, nothing can be more remote from a philosophy which

has the methodological attitude we have characterized than the making of decisions, on its own authority, concerning the truth or falsity of particular scientific statements, or the desire to eliminate any matters of fact whatsoever. *The subject matter of this philosophy is limited to the form of scientific statements, and the deductive relationships obtaining between them.* It is led by its analyses to the thesis of physicalism, and establishes on purely logical grounds that a certain class of venerable philosophical "problems" consists of pseudo-problems. It is certainly to the advantage of the progress of scientific knowledge that these imitation jewels in the coffer of scientific problems be known for what they are, and that the intellectual powers which have till now been devoted to a class of meaningless questions which are by their very nature insoluble, become available for the formulation and study of new and fruitful problems. That the method of logical analysis stimulates research along these lines is shown by the numerous publications of the Vienna Circle and those who sympathize with its general point of view (H. Reichenbach, W. Dubislav, and others).

In the attitude of those who are so bitterly opposed to physicalism, an essential role is played by certain psychological factors relating to individuals and groups. Thus the contrast between the constructs *(Gebilde)* developed by the psychologist, and those developed by the physicist, or, again, the question as to the nature of the specific subject matter of psychology and the cultural sciences (which present the appearance of a search for the essence and unique laws of "objective spirit") is usually accompanied by a strong emotional coloring which has come into being during the long historical development of a "philosophical conception of the world," which was considerably less scientific than normative and intuitive. These emotional factors are still deeply rooted in the picture by which our epoch represents the world to itself. They are protected by certain affective dispositions which surround them like a rampart, and for all these reasons appear to us to have genuine content—something which a more penetrating analysis shows to be impossible.

A psychological and sociological study of the causes for the appearance of these "concomitant factors" of the metaphysical type would take us beyond the limits of this study,[14] but without tracing it back to its origins, it is possible to say that if the logical analyses sketched above are correct, the fact that they necessitate at least a partial break with traditional philosophical ideas which are deeply dyed with emotion can certainly not justify an opposition to physicalism—at least if one acknowledges that philosophy is to be something more than the expression of an individual vision of the world, that it aims at being a science.

NOTES

1. I now consider the type of physicalism outlined in this paper as too restrictive; the thesis that all statements of empirical science are *translatable*, without loss of theoretical content, into the language of physics, should be replaced by the weaker assertion that all statements of empirical science are *reducible* to sentences in the language of physics, in the sense that for every empirical hypothesis, including, of course, those of psychology, it is possible to formulate certain test conditions in terms of physical concepts which refer to more or less directly observable physical attributes. But those test conditions are not asserted to exhaust the theoretical content of the given hypothesis in all cases. For a more detailed development of this thesis, cf. R. Carnap, "Logical Foundations of the Unity of Science," reprinted in A. Marras, ed., *Intentionality, Mind, and Language* (Urbana: Univ. of Illinois Press, 1972).

2. *Tractatus Logico-Philosophicus* (London, 1922).

3. A recent presentation of symbolic logic, based on the fundamental work of Whitehead and Russell, *Principia Mathematica*, is to be found in R. Carnap, *Abriss der Logistik* (Vienna: Springer, 1929; vol. 2 of the series *Schriften zur Wissenschaftlichen Weltauffassung*). It includes an extensive bibliography, as well as references to other logistic systems.

4. The following are some of the principal publications of the Vienna Circle on the nature of psychology as a science: R. Carnap, *Scheinprobleme in der Philosophie: Das Fremdpsychische und des Realismusstreit* (Leipzig: Meiner, 1928); *Der Logische Aufbau der Welt* (Leipzig: Meiner, 1928) [English trans.: *Logical Structure of the World* (Berkeley: Univ. of California Press, 1967)]; "Die Physikalische Sprache als Universalsprache der Wissenschaft," *Erkenntnis*, 2 (1931–32), 432–465 [English trans.: *The Unity of Science* (London: Kegan Paul, 1934)]; "Psychologie in physikalischer Sprache," *Erkenntnis*, 3 (1932–33), 107–142 [English trans.: "Psychology in Physical Language," in A.J. Ayer, ed., *Logical Positivism* (New York: Free Press, 1959)]; "Ueber Protokollsaetze," *Erkenntnis*, 3 (1932–33), 215–228; O. Neurath, "Protokollsaetze," *Erkenntnis*, 3 (1932–33), 204–214 [English trans.: "Protocol Sentences," in *Logical Positivism*]; *Einheitswissenschaft und Psychologie* (Vienna: Springer, 1933; vol. 1 of the series *Einheitswissenschaft*). See also the publications mentioned in the notes below.

5. P. Oppenheim, for example, in his book *Die Natuerliche Ordnung der Wissenschaften* (Jena: Fischer, 1926), opposes the view that there are fundamental differences between any of the different areas of science. On the analysis of "understanding," cf. M. Schlick, "Erleben, Erkennen, Metaphysik," *Kantstudien*, 31 (1926), 146.

6. For further details see the statement of one of the founders of behaviorism: J.B. Watson, *Behaviorism* (New York: Norton, 1930); also A.A. Roback, *Behaviorism and Psychology* (Cambridge, Mass.: Univ. Bookstore, 1923); and A.P. Weiss, *A Theoretical Basis of Human Behavior*, 2nd ed. rev. (Columbus, Ohio: Adams, 1929); see also the work by Koehler cited in note 11 below.

7. Space is lacking for further discussion of the logical form of test sentences (recently called "protocol sentences" by Neurath and Carnap). On this question see Wittgenstein, *Tractatus Logico-Philosophicus*, as well as the articles by Neurath and Carnap which have appeared in *Erkenntnis* (above, note 4).

8. Two critical comments, 1977: (a) This reference to verification involves a conceptual confusion. The thesis which the preceding considerations were intended to establish was clearly that the statement "Paul has a toothache" is, in effect, an abbreviated expression of all its test sentences; not that it expresses the claim (let alone the "fact") that all those test sentences have actually been tested and verified. (b) Strictly speaking, none of the test sentences just mentioned is implied by the statement "Paul has a toothache": the latter may be true and yet any or all of those test sentences may be false. Hence, the preceding considerations fail to show that the given psychological statement can be "translated" into sentences which, in purely physical terms, describe macro-behavioral manifestations of pain. This failure of the arguments outlined in the text does not preclude the possibility, however, that sentences ascribing pain or other psychological characteristics to an individual might be "translatable," in a suitable sense, into physical sentences ascribing associated physical micro-states or micro-events to the nervous system or to the entire body of the individual in question.

9. "Soziologie im Physikalismus," *Erkenntnis*, 2 (1931–32), 393–431, particularly p. 411 [English trans.: "Sociology and Physicalism,"in A.J. Ayer, ed., *Logical Positivism*].

10. Carnap, *Der Logische Aufbau der Welt*, pp. 231–236; id. *Scheinprobleme in der Philosophie*. See also note 4 above.

11. A careful discussion of the ideas of so-called "internal" behaviorism is to be found in *Psychologische Probleme* by W. Koehler (Berlin: Springer, 1933). See particularly the first two chapters.

12. R. Carnap, "Die Physikalische Sprache als Universalsprache," p. 451. See also: O. Neurath, *Empirische Soziologie* (Vienna: Springer, 1931; the fourth monograph in the series *Schriften zur wissenschaftlichen Weltauffassung*).

13. See R. Carnap, *Der Logische Aufbau der Welt*, pp. 22–34 and 185–211, as well as the works cited in the preceding note.

14. O. Neurath has made interesting contributions along these lines in *Empirische Soziologie* and in "Soziologie im Physikalismus" (see above, note 9), as has R. Carnap in his article "Ueberwindung der Metaphysik durch logische Analyse der Sprache," *Erkenntnis*, 2 (1931–32), 219–241 [English trans.: "The Elimination of Metaphysics through Logical Analysis of Language," in A.J. Ayer, ed., *Logical Positivism*].

CHAPTER EIGHT

Linguistic Philosophy

The critique of introspection

Hempel's argument against metaphysical theories of the mind makes reference only to descriptions of *other* people's mental states. But what of our knowledge of our *own* states of mind? According to people like Descartes, the real nature of the mind is revealed only through reflection on one's own conscious experience. It is only in this way, they argue, that we see the inner causes of our own behaviour. So the logical positivists' program for reforming psychology depends not simply on their logical analysis of psychological descriptions, but also on a rejection of introspection as a legitimate psychological technique.

As we have seen, the positivists' suspicion of introspection is based on the difficulty in resolving disagreements in introspective reports. Introspective psychology as a science is impossible, they claim, because its methods do not lead to agreement on what the structure of the mind is. And they are correct that people are notoriously bad at accurately reporting their own thoughts. But, on the other hand, the failure of introspective methods in practice does not show that it is impossible *in principle* to devise a successful introspective psychology. Proponents of introspection argue that the method requires great skill and training to be carried out properly. If logical behaviourism is to succeed, the project of translating psychological statements into descriptions of behaviour must be coupled with a direct criticism of introspection as a legitimate method of studying the mind.

Criticism of theories that postulate inner mental states revealed through introspection was carried out most effectively by Gilbert Ryle and Ludwig Wittgenstein, two philosophers whose aims were different from those of the logical positivists although they originated from similar concerns. As we have seen, logical positivists claim that the role of philosophy is to analyze the *meaning* of scientific theories. The emphasis on linguistic analysis is shared by both Ryle and Wittgenstein. But they do not place the same emphasis on the physical sciences as the model of meaningful investigation of the world. In their view, a study of our everyday use of language is sufficient by itself to eradicate metaphysical problems.

Ordinary language

Gilbert Ryle worked as a scholar of philosophy at Oxford University all of his adult life. His philosophy is based on the general view that most philosophical problems are merely confusions created by accidents of grammar. One such problem, he argues, is the nature of universals, which led Plato to his theory of the Forms. According to Ryle, we are mistakenly led to suppose that words like 'triangularity' and 'punctuality' must refer to some kind of *objects*, simply on the grounds that they can occur as the subject of a sentence. Once this idea is accepted, we are faced with the problem of deciding what kind of object these things are: what is *triangularity itself* over and above particular triangles? Ryle argues that the problem disappears once we recognize that it is based on nothing more than an accidental feature of language.

Ryle's philosophy of mind is laid out in his book, *The Concept of Mind*, published in 1949, from which we will read selected passages. The approach that Ryle takes to the subject is explained in the introduction to the book. He begins with the claim that rather than advancing new knowledge about the mind, he intends instead to "rectify the logical geography of the knowledge which we already possess." To a certain degree this metaphorical description of his project matches the aims of logical positivists. Ryle shares with the logical positivists the view that metaphysical theories about the nature of mind are meaningless gibberish produced by a misunderstanding of the meanings of mental concepts. In their view and in Ryle's, the role of philosophy is to provide a logical analysis of the meanings of psychological statements.

But the next paragraph reveals an important difference between Ryle's project and that of the logical positivists. Rather than restricting all meaningful questions to the natural sciences, Ryle believes the correct approach is to look carefully at our everyday descriptions of the mind. According to Ryle, people in ordinary life know perfectly well how to talk sensibly about the mind and how to interact with other people on the basis of this knowledge. It is here that we should look for an understanding of how psychological concepts are used.

Ryle argues that the everyday ability to *use* mental concepts does not bring with it a clear understanding of how these concepts are logically related to one another and to other concepts. And it is this lack of understanding that creates so-called philosophical problems. As he sees it, it is a failure to see what he calls the "logical geography" of everyday mental concepts that leads to meaningless theories like Descartes'. The general project of removing philosophical problems by gaining a proper understanding of our day-to-day use of language has been called the **ordinary language** school. Ryle's critique of Descartes' philosophy of mind in chapter 1 of *The Concept of Mind*, called "Descartes' Myth," provides a perfect example of the "ordinary language" method of philosophical analysis.

Critique of "the official doctrine"

Ryle describes Descartes' view as "the official doctrine" of the mind. According to this doctrine, Ryle says, each person has two distinct histories: (1) a private, "inner" history, consisting of what happens in the mind; and (2) a publicly observable, "outer" history, consisting of what happens in and to the body. He points out that the use of the words 'inner' and 'outer' is metaphorical, as the mind is not believed to exist in space. But even as a metaphor the view faces difficulties.

First, the interaction between mind and body must always be a mystery on Descartes' theory. For these interactions belong neither to the private inner history revealed through introspection nor to the public outer history of bodily behaviour; interaction between mind and body must necessarily lie outside of both kinds of experience. For example, accepting Descartes' theory would mean that the discipline of psychophysics, which studies correlations between sensations and the activities of the nervous system, would belong to neither psychology nor physiology. In this claim Ryle is entirely correct. While Descartes' theory of mind resolved some difficulties that Aristotle's theory confronted, it is unable to say anything about how a relation of cause and effect between mind and matter could possibly work.

A second difficulty with Descartes' view lies in his account of our knowledge of the mind. According to Descartes, each person has direct knowledge of the episodes in their own mental history. We can turn our attention inwards and introspectively observe the goings-on in our own mind. On the other hand, we have no direct knowledge of what goes on the minds of others. We must infer other people's thoughts and feelings by observing their behaviour and drawing conclusions by analogy with our own internal experience. Thus each of us lives a private mental history hidden to others like a "ghostly Robinson Crusoe," which Ryle believes is simply absurd. Our success in interacting with other people on the basis of the thoughts, beliefs, and desires that we attribute to them shows that the minds of other people are not hidden from us but are as accessible as any other aspect of the world.

Category mistakes

In the second section of chapter 1, entitled "The Absurdity of the Official Doctrine," Ryle describes what he sees as the fundamental error in the Cartesian picture of the mind. He argues that the official doctrine is based on a special kind of logical mistake — a **category mistake**. This is the mistake of taking two terms as belonging to a single "logical category" when in fact they belong to different categories. So a central component in Ryle's critique of Descartes is the idea of logical categories. Later in the chapter he defines this idea:

> When two terms belong to the same category, it is proper to construct conjunctive propositions embodying them.

By a "conjunctive proposition" Ryle means (roughly) a sentence formed by joining two or more phrases with the word 'and.' He gives the following example of this definition. It is correct to say in English that there is a right-hand glove and a left-hand glove; and it is equally correct to say that there is a pair of gloves. But it is not correct to infer from this that there is a right-hand glove, a left-hand glove, *and* a pair of gloves, for this implies that there are three different items: two gloves and one pair. So the term 'pair of gloves' is in a different logical category from the terms 'left-hand glove' and 'right-hand glove.' He gives several other examples of this idea, such as a person who is shown the colleges and libraries of a university and then asks mistakenly where the university itself is. There is a university, and there are colleges and libraries; but it is incorrect to say that there are colleges, libraries, *and* the university in the sense that the university is something that exists separately from its colleges and libraries.

In the section entitled "The Origin of the Mistake," Ryle argues that Descartes' view of the mind is based on just such a category mistake. It is correct to say that there is a mind, and it is also correct to say that there is a body. But from this Descartes draws the conclusion that there must be a mind *and* a body, which is a mistake because 'mind' and 'body' are terms belonging to different logical categories. The mind no more exists separately from the body than a university exists separately from its colleges and libraries.

Ryle's historical reconstruction of Descartes' mistake

But what would lead Descartes to make such a basic error in logic? In answer to this question Ryle offers a historical explanation of Descartes' reasoning. As a scientist, Descartes adopted the principles of mechanical science developed by Galileo. But as a religious man, he could not accept that humans are merely physical mechanisms. His solution was to suppose that if mental terms do not refer to mechanical processes of the body, they must refer to *nonmechanical* processes. And if mechanical laws explain physical events, there must be other laws that explain mental events. In this way the mind was held to be the same kind of thing as the body, but made of different stuff. Because the body is a complex, organized unit, the mind must be a complex, organized unit as well, but of a nonphysical nature.

Against this view, Ryle argues that the sentence 'There are mental processes' is not the same kind of sentence as 'There are physical processes.' He makes this point by comparing these two sentences to other pairs of sentences. For example, the sentence, 'She came home in a flood of tears' is not the same kind of sentence as 'She came home in a sedan chair.' According to Ryle, then, the so-called mind-body problem is an improper question, similar to the question 'Did she buy a left-hand and right-hand glove, or a pair of gloves?' This distortion of logic, Ryle argues, leads to some of the "deepest problems" of modern philosophy: How can minds influence bodies? How is human freedom compatible with mechanical laws? Once the error is revealed, these problems will simply disappear.

So Ryle's view is that it is a mistake to think of mind and body as two distinct *entities*. It is better to think of the words "mind" and "body" as two ways of talking about a single person. When we talk about a person's body, we are describing their physical structure — the bones, tissues, and organs of which they are composed. What are we describing, then, when we talk about their mind — their thoughts, feelings, desires and sensations? Here Ryle follows a line similar to that taken by the logical positivists: descriptions of mental states are actually descriptions of behaviour. This fits well with his comparisons of other distinct logical categories. It is no more correct to say there is the body *and* its behaviour than it is to say there is the university *and* its colleges and libraries.

States of mind as dispositions

In a later section of the book Ryle gives a more subtle account of the meaning of psychological descriptions. This account avoids an obvious objection to the idea that psychological terms refer only to a person's behaviour. Consider a very simple example, such as the statement, 'Brenda has a headache.' How might we translate that sentence into a description of Brenda's behaviour? We might try to do it with a collection of statements like 'She takes pain medicine' or 'She says, "I have a headache."' The problem with this idea is that none of these sentences are necessarily true whenever it is true that Brenda has a headache. People who have a headache will not always display the kinds of behaviour that we associate with that condition. Brenda might not have any medicine in the house, and there might not be anyone to say anything to. According to Ryle, this reveals that simple descriptions of typical behaviour cannot be the correct analysis of the original sentence.

Ryle argues that the concepts of mental states should be understood as "dispositional concepts." By this he means that a mental state is a **behavioural disposition**; that is, a tendency to behave in certain ways under certain circumstances. That behaviour will then only be exhibited when those circumstances occur. For example, a person with a disposition to take pain medicine will do so only if there is some to take. Instead of simple descriptions of behaviour, the translations of psychological statements will take the form of 'if-then' sentences, such as 'If there are aspirins available, Brenda will take one,' and 'If asked how she feels, Brenda will say, "I have a headache."' The if-clause describes a circumstance that might arise, and the then-clause describes how the person will behave in that circumstance.

This analysis agrees with the psychological behaviourists' project of explaining behaviour through connections between stimulus and response. As the result of their environmental history, people will behave in certain specific ways whenever their current environment includes a particular stimulus. In Ryle's terms this is to say that a person's environmental history has produced a certain *disposition*, namely, to exhibit a particular behaviour under particular conditions. When those conditions arise, the behaviour will be displayed.

Ryle compares his analysis of mental states to other common dispositional concepts such as brittleness and solubility: To say that a glass is brittle is to say that it will break when struck, and to say that sugar is soluble is to say that it will dissolve when immersed in water. A brittle glass will not break if it is never struck, and a sugar cube will not dissolve if it is never immersed in water. Ryle's claim is that psychological concepts like those of beliefs, thoughts, moods, and sensations are similar in nature to these concepts of physical dispositions. We use psychological descriptions to refer to what people are *disposed* to do, not what they *actually* do.

Multi-tracked dispositions

The dispositional account of psychological concepts allows Ryle to introduce a special feature of most states of mind. The simplest kinds of dispositions are what Ryle calls "single-track" dispositions. By this he means dispositions to do one specific thing under certain conditions. For example, brittleness is just the disposition to break when struck. But the dispositions described by psychological concepts, Ryle claims, are "multi-tracked," which means that there are many different dispositions contained under the same concept. For example, there are many different ways in which a person who is depressed will behave, depending on the circumstances. So a complete analysis of a psychological concept will generally involve a large number of dispositions, each of which involves the way in which a person will behave under a particular set of circumstances.

If this account is correct, psychological concepts will not be describable by a single if-then sentence. Rather, each such concept will require a long (and probably endless) *list* of sentences. Each such sentence in the list will describe the behaviour that a person would exhibit under one particular kind of circumstance. For example, we could not analyze a psychological concept such as that of *experiencing a sensation of thirst* in terms of a single disposition, say, to drink water. For one thing, what a thirsty person will drink depends on what is available. Second, there are social situations in which a thirsty person would, say, politely ask whether they may drink something. So to fully analyze that concept in terms of behavioural dispositions, we would need a long list of the behaviours that would be exhibited under each of these different situations. Letting 'C1, C2, C3 ...' be the list of circumstances a person might find themselves in, the full analysis of the concept of experiencing a sensation of thirst will look something like the following.

> A person is experiencing thirst if and only if
> (i) in circumstance C1, the person will drink water;
> (ii) in circumstance C2, the person will drink orange juice;
> (iii) in circumstance C3, the person will say "May I have something to drink?"
> ... and so on.

There are no mental states

There is one more important feature of Ryle's analysis of psychological concepts. Descartes and others take mental states to be inner states of a person. According to Ryle, however, psychological concepts do not refer to *states* of any kind. They refer only to certain facts about a person's behaviour. A person with a headache is not in a certain kind of state that produces certain forms of behaviour. The headache consists of nothing more than the relevant facts about the person's behaviour. And this is true, he says, of dispositional concepts generally. For example, the brittleness of a glass is not an internal condition of glass that *causes* it to break. The brittleness is nothing more than the fact that it will break under certain circumstances. This point is clearly brought out in a quotation picked up by David Armstrong. Ryle says:

> To possess a dispositional property *is not to be in a particular state,* or
> to undergo a particular change; it is to be bound or liable to be in a
> particular state, or to undergo a particular change, when a particular
> condition is realised. [emphasis mine]

So when we say that the glass broke *because* it was brittle, we mean nothing
more than that the glass was the sort of thing that will break when struck,
and it was struck. We do not mean that the glass had a particular internal
state that caused it to break on impact. In the same way, Ryle says, psychological dispositions are not internal states that cause certain kinds of behaviour, for that would bring us back to Descartes' theory. In Ryle's view, there
is nothing more to a psychological concept than what is conveyed by a statement that describes how a person will behave under certain circumstances.

Wittgenstein's *Philosophical Investigations*

Ludwig Wittgenstein (1889–1951) is one of the most enigmatic philosophers
of this century. Perhaps his most astounding achievement is to have produced
two completely different and important systems of philosophy within one lifetime. Wittgenstein was an intense man who attacked philosophical problems
with great passion. Throughout his life he produced work that has proven
neither easy to understand nor easy to ignore.

Wittgenstein was born and raised in Vienna in a household of wealthy
parents with broad artistic and intellectual interests. As a young boy
Wittgenstein was exposed to some of the greatest figures of Viennese culture.
After an initial start in engineering he developed an interest in pure mathematics, which led him to discover Bertrand Russell's book, *The Principles of
Mathematics.* Russell's work in logic and mathematics was in many ways an
important influence on the logical positivists. In 1912 Wittgenstein moved
to Cambridge to study logic with Russell. After serving in the First World
War Wittgenstein apparently abandoned philosophical work. However, the
book that he composed while in Cambridge, the *Tractatus Logico-Philosophicus,*
was discovered by Moritz Schlick and other members of the Vienna Circle,
and Wittgenstein was convinced by them to return to Cambridge in 1929.

In the 1930s Wittgenstein began work on a number of ideas that con-
flicted directly with the basic assumptions of his early philosophy. This work
culminated in the book *Philosophical Investigations,* which was not published
in his lifetime. In this book Wittgenstein argues that words gain their meaning from the social practices that govern their use. He applies this idea in
particular to the words we use to describe our thoughts and sensations, and
from this he draws the conclusion that they cannot refer to inner states of

mind in the way that Descartes describes in the Second Meditation. In this way Wittgenstein's conclusions bear a similarity to those of Gilbert Ryle. It is not possible for copyright reasons to reproduce sections of the *Philosophical Investigations*, but we can look at the description of Wittgenstein's ideas in an essay by his student, Norman Malcolm.[1]

The idea of a "private language"

Wittgenstein's critique of the idea of inner mental states takes the form of an attack on a certain idea of how words that describe sensations, like 'pain' and 'tickling,' get their meaning. If the Cartesian view of the mind is correct, these words get their meaning by being associated with a particular kind of inner sensation. There is a characteristic feeling that I associate with a word like 'headache,' and the meaning the word has for me is formed by this association. The phrase 'for me' in the previous sentence is particularly important here. In the Cartesian picture of the mind, the thoughts and sensations I have are immediately evident to me but are hidden from everyone else. I know directly what my headache feels like, but I can only infer that others have similar experiences from their behaviour. If a word like 'headache' gets its meaning from association with a particular inner sensation, and that sensation is known only to me, it follows that the word has a private meaning for me that others cannot possibly know. Each person attaches their own private, subjective meaning to sensation words, and it is impossible to know whether these meanings are the same for different people or not. Wittgenstein refers to this idea of language as the idea of a **private language**. His argument against views like Descartes' is that this notion of a private language is incoherent.

Against the idea of a private language

Malcolm points out that, in Wittgenstein's view, the difficulty with a private language arises when we ask how a person can possibly make the connection between a particular kind of sensation and a word that refers to it. Suppose, for example, that this is accomplished by focussing one's attention on the sensation, and saying to oneself, "*This* is what is I mean by the word 'headache'." Wittgenstein argues that this will work only if the person is then able to apply the term *consistently*; that is, they are able to use the word to refer to the same kind of sensation whenever it occurs, or at least they are able to correct errors in its application.

For comparison, think of how we can tell that a child understands a colour word like 'red.' We look to see whether the child is able to apply the word to the right colour and not to other colours. In the case of colour words other people can check whether the child is using the word consistently. But it is impossible, Malcolm claims, to tell whether or not a word that refers to a private sensation is being used consistently. More accurately, there would be no difference between consistently using a private sensation word and only *believing* that one has used it consistently. This is because the sensation to which a person applies the word on any given occasion is private to that person. No one else is in a position to say, "Now you are using the word in a different way than you were before."

On the following page of the essay, Malcolm outlines Wittgenstein's attack on the common idea that one can simply remember the sensation to which one first attached the word, and then use that memory to apply the term consistently. For there can be no sense, he argues, to the idea of remembering a sensation *incorrectly*. There is nothing that could possibly show that a memory of a private event is incorrect. Other people have no access to the event or the memory, and the person who does has nothing but the memory itself to go by.

One might suppose that one memory can be used to verify another. But, Wittgenstein says, this would be as if "someone were to buy several copies of the morning paper to assure himself that what it said was true." Remembering correctly and *thinking* one remembers correctly are indistinguishable. And this, Wittgenstein claims, means that the very idea of remembering correctly is nonsensical. If this is so, he concludes, the view of language based on that idea, namely, that certain words have meaning by association with private sensations, is incoherent.

Going on in the same way

Wittgenstein's argument against the idea of a private language is based on the assumption that a word can be meaningful only if it possible to distinguish correct use of it from incorrect use. Because it is based on an assumption about the circumstances under which a piece of a language can be meaningful, Wittgenstein's argument bears a similarity to the logical positivists' argument against metaphysics. In Wittgenstein's case, meaningfulness is attached to the possibility of distinguishing correct from incorrect use of our words, while logical positivists rest their argument on the possibility of establishing that a sentence is true or false. In each case, as well as with Ryle, certain views about the nature of the mind are rejected as meaningless or incoherent as a result of an analysis of language. In the third section of his paper, Malcolm describes how Wittgenstein's private-language argument rests on a general point about the role of rules in language use.

According to Wittgenstein, language is based on the application of rules that govern the correct use of words and sentences: to understand a word is to use it correctly. In these terms, one way of defending the possibility of a private language is to argue that one merely has to follow a simple rule: associate a word with a particular sensation on one occasion and then use the word the same way in the future. Wittgenstein's argument, seen in these terms, is that it is impossible to determine whether or not one is following that rule, for one cannot tell whether one really is using the word the same way or whether one merely *thinks* one is using it the same way. It is only by comparing our use of the word with that of others that we can judge correctness or incorrectness, which renders a private language impossible.

Putting the issue in this way, in terms of rules for the use of a word, allows Wittgenstein to rest his argument on a general premise about the nature of rules. It makes no sense, he argues, to ask whether a rule is being followed correctly or incorrectly except by asking whether a given action is commonly *accepted* as conforming to the rule. To illustrate this claim, Wittgenstein asks us to consider a pupil learning the rule '+2'. Suppose that after the number 1,000, the pupil continues 1,004, 1,008, 1,012. We will claim, of course, that he is misapplying the rule. But suppose the pupil replies, "But I went on in the same way." What can we show him that will demonstrate that he is in error? According to Wittgenstein, there is nothing we can say beyond the fact that his action is different from what is commonly accepted as falling under the rule.

Here is Wittgenstein's reasoning behind this conclusion. In demonstrating the rule, we gave the pupil only a finite number of examples. Perhaps we showed him the first ten numbers in the series. And a finite number of examples will conform to an endless variety of different rules.[2] We might try to point out to the student that after 1,000 he is not following the rule '+2', but rather the rule '+4'. But why should he agree? He can say that *his* numbers, not ours, conform to the rule '+2' *as illustrated by the examples we gave him.* There is nothing in the examples to indicate that we are right and he is wrong. The only thing that determines that the pupil is in error is the fact that the numbers he gives are different from what is commonly accepted as correct.

In the next paragraph Malcolm addresses the reason why it is natural to find the story of the pupil unconvincing. The common response is to say that there is more on which to base our claim that the pupil is mistaken than just the examples we gave him. We can see that the pupil isn't continuing the series the right way because we *understand* the rule and he obviously doesn't. This response is based on the notion that correctly following a rule is a matter of having the right idea or understanding of the rule in your mind. You might think of there being a picture of the rule in your mind, and that picture can then be applied to each example to see if it conforms to the rule or not. But

Wittgenstein argues that this won't help us to show that the pupil is mistaken. For we have no way of determining whether someone has a correct understanding of a rule other than seeing whether their actions are the same as ours. As Malcolm puts, "The correct use is a criterion of correct understanding." So we are back where we began: our response to the student is just that the numbers we accept are commonly accepted as correct and his aren't.

The general conclusion that Wittgenstein draws from this argument is that language is not based on an understanding of meanings that we carry around in our head. It is based on the fact that human beings happen to accept certain forms of behaviour as correct or natural in their use of language to communicate with one another. It follows that the meanings we attach to words, including the words we use to describe our own mind, are determined by social practice, or what Wittgenstein calls a "form of life." This leads to conclusions directly opposed to the Cartesian picture of the mind. Descartes' contention in the Second Meditation is that knowledge of our own thoughts and sensations is the foundation of all knowledge, and this knowledge is directly accessible to us but hidden to others. According to Wittgenstein, on the other hand, what is hidden to others can form no part the meanings of our words, from which it follows that statements describing the mind are not descriptions of private inner states, but rather statements whose application is fixed by their association with certain accepted forms of behaviour. What can be known, or at least what can be described in words, is restricted to what is publicly observable.

NOTES

1 To read Wittgenstein's original arguments, see his *Philosophical Investigations* (Oxford: Basil Blackwell, 1958), especially sections 256 to 265.

2 To convince yourself of this, consider the following example. The series of numbers 1, 4, 10, conforms to two different rules: "Begin with 1, then add 1×3, then add 2×3, then add 3×3, and so on," or "Begin with 1, then add 3, then add 6, then add 3, then add 6, and so on." From the three numbers we are given neither of these can be said to be the *correct* interpretation of the series of three numbers.

Gilbert Ryle
Selections from *The Concept of Mind*

INTRODUCTION

This book offers what may with reservations be described as a theory of the mind. But it does not give new information about minds. We possess already a wealth of information about minds, information which is neither derived from, nor upset by, the arguments of philosophers. The philosophical arguments which constitute this book are intended not to increase what we know about minds, but to rectify the logical geography of the knowledge which we already possess.

Teachers and examiners, magistrates and critics, historians and novelists, confessors and non-commissioned officers, employers, employees and partners, parents, lovers, friends and enemies all know well enough how to settle their daily questions about the qualities of character and intellect of the individual with whom they have to do. They can appraise his performances, assess his progress, understand his words and actions, discern his motives and see his jokes. If they go wrong, they know how to correct their mistakes. More, they can deliberately influence the minds of those with whom they deal by criticism, example, teaching, punishment, bribery, mockery and persuasion, and then modify their treatments in the light of the results produced.

Both in describing the minds of others and in prescribing for them, they are wielding with greater or less efficiency concepts of mental powers and operations. They have learned how to apply in concrete situations such mental-conduct epithets as 'careful', 'stupid', 'logical', 'unobservant', 'ingenious', 'vain', 'methodical', 'credulous', 'witty', 'self-controlled' and a thousand others.

It is, however, one thing to know how to apply such concepts, quite another to know how to correlate them with one another and with concepts of other sorts. Many people can talk sense with concepts but cannot talk sense about them; they know by practice how to operate with concepts, anyhow inside familiar fields, but they cannot state the logical regulations governing their use. They are like people who know their way about their own parish, but cannot construct or read a map of it, much less a map of the region or continent in which their parish lies.

For certain purposes it is necessary to determine the logical cross-bearings of the concepts which we know quite well how to apply. The attempt to perform this operation upon the concepts of the powers, operations and states of minds has always been a big part of the task of philosophers. Theories of knowledge, logic, ethics, political theory and aesthetics are the products of their inquiries in this field. Some of these inquiries have made considerable regional progress, but it is part of the thesis of this book that during the three centuries of the epoch of natural science the logical categories in terms of which the concepts of mental powers and operations have been coordinated have been wrongly selected. Descartes left as one of his main philosophical legacies a myth which continues to distort the continental geography of the subject.

A myth is, of course, not a fairy story. It is the presentation of facts belonging to one category in the idioms appropriate to another. To explode a myth is accordingly not to deny the facts but to re-allocate them. And this is what I am trying to do.

To determine the logical geography of concepts is to reveal the logic of the propositions in which they are wielded, that is to say, to show with what other propositions they are consistent and inconsistent, what propositions follow from them and from what propositions they follow. The logical type or category to which a concept belongs is the set of ways in which it is logically legitimate to operate with it. The key arguments employed in this book are therefore intended to show why certain sorts of operations with the concepts of mental powers and processes are breaches of logical rules. I try to use *reductio ad absurdum* arguments both to disallow operations implicitly recommended by the Cartesian myth and to indicate to what logical types the concepts under investigation ought to be allocated. I do not, however, think it improper to use from time to time arguments of a less rigorous sort, especially when it seems expedient to mollify or acclimatise. Philosophy is the replacement of category-habits by category-disciplines, and if persuasions of conciliatory kinds ease the pains of relinquishing inveterate intellectual habits, they do not indeed reinforce the rigorous arguments, but they do weaken resistances to them.

Some readers may think that my tone of voice in this book is excessively polemical. It may comfort them to know that the assumptions against which I exhibit most heat are assumptions of which I myself have been a victim. Primarily I am trying to get some disorders out of my own system. Only secondarily do I hope to help other theorists to recognise our malady and to benefit from my medicine.

CHAPTER I: DESCARTES' MYTH

(1) The Official Doctrine.

There is a doctrine about the nature and place of minds which is so prevalent among theorists and even among laymen that it deserves to be described as the official theory. Most philosophers, psychologists and religious teachers subscribe,

with minor reservations, to its main articles and, although they admit certain theoretical difficulties in it, they tend to assume that these can be overcome without serious modifications being made to the architecture of the theory. It will be argued here that the central principles of the doctrine are unsound and conflict with the whole body of what we know about minds when we are not speculating about them.

The official doctrine, which hails chiefly from Descartes, is something like this. With the doubtful exceptions of idiots and infants in arms every human being has both a body and a mind. Some would prefer to say that every human being is both a body and a mind. His body and his mind are ordinarily harnessed together, but after the death of the body his mind may continue to exist and function.

Human bodies are in space and are subject to the mechanical laws which govern all other bodies in space. Bodily processes and states can be inspected by external observers. So a man's bodily life is as much a public affair as are the lives of animals and reptiles and even as the careers of trees, crystals and planets.

But minds are not in space, nor are their operations subject to mechanical laws. The workings of one mind are not witnessable by other observers; its career is private. Only I can take direct cognisance of the states and processes of my own mind. A person therefore lives through two collateral histories, one consisting of what happens in and to his body, the other consisting of what happens in and to his mind. The first is public, the second private. The events in the first history are events in the physical world, those in the second are events in the mental world.

It has been disputed whether a person does or can directly monitor all or only some of the episodes of his own private history; but, according to the official doctrine, of at least some of these episodes he has direct and unchallengeable cognisance. In consciousness, self-consciousness and introspection he is directly and authentically apprised of the present states and operations of his mind. He may have great or small uncertainties about concurrent and adjacent episodes in the physical world, but he can have none about at least part of what is momentarily occupying his mind.

It is customary to express this bifurcation of his two lives and of his two worlds by saying that the things and events which belong to the physical world, including his own body, are external, while the workings of his own mind are internal. This antithesis of outer and inner is of course meant to be construed as a metaphor, since minds, not being in space, could not be described as being spatially inside anything else, or as having things going on spatially inside themselves. But relapses from this good intention are common and theorists are found speculating how stimuli, the physical sources of which are yards or miles outside a person's skin, can generate mental responses inside his skull, or how decisions framed inside his cranium can set going movements of his extremities.

Even when 'inner' and 'outer' are construed as metaphors, the problem how a person's mind and body influence one another is notoriously charged with theoretical difficulties. What the mind wills, the legs, arms and the tongue execute; what affects the ear and the eye has something to do with what the mind perceives; grimaces and smiles betray the mind's moods and bodily castigations lead, it is hoped, to moral improvement. But the actual transactions between the episodes of the private history and those of the public history remain mysterious, since by definition they can belong to neither series. They could not be reported among the happenings described in a person's autobiography of his inner life, but nor could they be reported among those described in some one else's biography of that person's overt career. They can be inspected neither by introspection nor by laboratory experiment. They are theoretical shuttlecocks which are forever being bandied from the physiologist back to the psy-

chologist and from the psychologist back to the physiologist.

Underlying this partly metaphorical representation of the bifurcation of a person's two lives there is a seemingly more profound and philosophical assumption. It is assumed that there are two different kinds of existence or status. What exists or happens may have the status of physical existence, or it may have the status of mental existence. Somewhat as the faces of coins are either heads or tails, or somewhat as living creatures are either male or female, so, it is supposed, some existing is physical existing, other existing is mental existing. It is a necessary feature of what has physical existence that it is in space and time; it is a necessary feature of what has mental existence that it is in time but not in space. What has physical existence is composed of matter, or else is a function of matter; what has mental existence consists of consciousness, or else is a function of consciousness.

There is thus a polar opposition between mind and matter, an opposition which is often brought out as follows. Material objects are situated in a common field, known as 'space', and what happens to one body in one part of space is mechanically connected with what happens to other bodies in other parts of space. But mental happenings occur in insulated fields, known as 'minds', and there is, apart maybe from telepathy, no direct causal connection between what happens in one mind and what happens in another. Only through the medium of the public physical world can the mind of one person make a difference to the mind of another. The mind is its own place and in his inner life each of us lives the life of a ghostly Robinson Crusoe. People can see, hear and jolt one another's bodies, but they are irremediably blind and deaf to the workings of one another's minds and inoperative upon them.

What sort of knowledge can be secured of the workings of a mind? On the one side, according to the official theory, a person has direct knowledge of the best imaginable kind of the workings of his own mind. Mental states and processes are (or are normally) conscious states and processes, and the consciousness which irradiates them can engender no illusions and leaves the door open for no doubts. A person's present thinkings, feelings and willings, his perceivings, rememberings and imaginings are intrinsically 'phosphorescent'; their existence and their nature are inevitably betrayed to their owner. The inner life is a stream of consciousness of such a sort that it would be absurd to suggest that the mind whose life is that stream might be unaware of what is passing down it.

True, the evidence adduced recently by Freud seems to show that there exist channels tributary to this stream, which run hidden from their owner. People are actuated by impulses the existence of which they vigorously disavow; some of their thoughts differ from the thoughts which they acknowledge; and some of the actions which they think they will to perform they do not really will. They are thoroughly gulled by some of their own hypocrisies and they successfully ignore facts about their mental lives which on the official theory ought to be patent to them. Holders of the official theory tend, however, to maintain that anyhow in normal circumstances a person must be directly and authentically seized of the present state and workings of his own mind.

Besides being currently supplied with these alleged immediate data of consciousness, a person is also generally supposed to be able to exercise from time to time a special kind of perception, namely inner perception, or introspection. He can take a (non-optical) 'look' at what is passing in his mind. Not only can he view and scrutinize a flower through his sense of sight and listen to and discriminate the notes of a bell through his sense of hearing; he can also reflectively or introspectively watch, without any bodily organ of sense, the current episodes of his inner life. This self-observation is also commonly supposed to be immune from illusion, confusion or doubt. A mind's reports of its own affairs have a certainty superior to the best that is possessed by its reports of matters in the physical world. Sense-perceptions can, but consciousness and introspection cannot, be mistaken or confused.

On the other side, one person has no direct access of any sort to the events of the inner life of another. He cannot do better than make problematic inferences from the observed behaviour of the other person's body to the states of mind which, by analogy from his own conduct, he supposes to be signalised by that behaviour. Direct access to the workings of a mind is the privilege of that mind itself; in default of such privileged access, the workings of one mind are inevitably occult to everyone else. For the supposed arguments from bodily movements similar to their own to mental workings similar to their own would lack any possibility of observational corroboration. Not unnaturally, therefore, an adherent of the official theory finds it difficult to resist this consequence of his premisses, that he has no good reason to believe that there do exist minds other than his own. Even if he prefers to believe that to other human bodies there are harnessed minds not unlike his own, he cannot claim to be able to discover their individual characteristics, or the particular things that they undergo and do. Absolute solitude is on this showing the ineluctable destiny of the soul. Only our bodies can meet.

As a necessary corollary of this general scheme there is implicitly prescribed a special way of construing our ordinary concepts of mental powers and operations. The verbs, nouns and adjectives, with which in ordinary life we describe the wits, characters and higher-grade performances of the people with whom we have do, are required to be construed as signifying special episodes in their secret histories, or else as signifying tendencies for such episodes to occur. When someone is described as knowing, believing or guessing something, as hoping, dreading, intending or shirking something, as designing this or being amused at that, these verbs are supposed to denote the occurrence of specific modifications in his (to us) occult stream of consciousness. Only his own privileged access to this stream in direct awareness and introspection could provide authentic testimony that these mental-conduct verbs were correctly or incorrectly applied. The onlooker, be he teacher, critic, biographer or friend, can never assure himself that his comments have any vestige of truth. Yet it was just because we do in fact all know how to make such comments, make them with general correctness and correct them when they turn out to be confused or mistaken, that philosophers found it necessary to construct their theories of the nature and place of minds. Finding mental-conduct concepts being regularly and effectively used, they properly sought to fix their logical geography. But the logical geography officially recommended would entail that there could be no regular or effective use of these mental-conduct concepts in our descriptions of, and prescriptions for, other people's minds.

(2) The Absurdity of the Official Doctrine.

Such in outline is the official theory. I shall often speak of it, with deliberate abusiveness, as 'the dogma of the Ghost in the Machine'. I hope to prove that it is entirely false, and false not in detail but in principle. It is not merely an assemblage of particular mistakes. It is one big mistake and a mistake of a special kind. It is, namely, a category-mistake. It represents the facts of mental life as if they belonged to one logical type or category (or range of types or categories), when they actually belong to another. The dogma is therefore a philosopher's myth. In attempting to explode the myth I shall probably be taken to be denying well-known facts about the mental life of human beings, and my plea that I aim at doing nothing more than rectify the logic of mental-conduct concepts will probably be disallowed as mere subterfuge.

I must first indicate what is meant by the phrase 'Category-mistake'. This I do in a series of illustrations.

A foreigner visiting Oxford or Cambridge for the first time is shown a number of colleges, libraries, playing fields, museums, scientific departments and administrative offices. He then asks 'But where is the University? I have seen where the members of the Colleges live, where the Registrar works, where the scientists experiment and the rest. But I have not yet seen the University in which reside and work the members of your University.' It has then to be explained to him that the University is not another collateral institution, some ulterior counterpart to the colleges, laboratories and offices which he has seen. The University is just the way in which all that he has already seen is organized. When they are seen and when their co-ordination is understood, the University has been seen. His mistake lay in his innocent assumption that it was correct to speak of Christ Church, the Bodleian Library, the Ashmolean Museum *and* the University, to speak, that is, as if 'the University' stood for an extra member of the class of which these other units are members. He was mistakenly allocating the University to the same category as that to which the other institutions belong.

The same mistake would be made by a child witnessing the march-past of a division, who, having had pointed out to him such and such battalions, batteries, squadrons, etc., asked when the division was going to appear. He would be supposing that a division was a counterpart to the units already seen, partly similar to them and partly unlike them. He would be shown his mistake by being told that in watching the battalions, batteries and squadrons marching past he had been watching the division marching past. The march-past was not a parade of battalions, batteries, squadrons *and* a division; it was a parade of the battalions, batteries and squadrons *of* a division.

One more illustration. A foreigner watching his first game of cricket learns what are the functions of the bowlers, the batsmen, the fielders, the umpires and the scorers. He then says 'But there is no one left on the field to contribute the famous element of team-spirit. I see who does the bowling, the batting and the wicket-keeping; but I do not see whose role it is to exercise *esprit de corps.*' Once more, it would have to be explained that he was looking for the wrong type of thing. Team-spirit is not another cricketing operation supplementary to all of the other special tasks. It is, roughly, the keenness with which each of the special tasks is performed, and performing a task keenly is not performing two tasks. Certainly exhibiting team-spirit is not the same thing as bowling or catching, but nor is it a third thing such that we can say that the bowler first bowls *and* then exhibits team-spirit or that a fielder is at a given moment *either* catching *or* displaying *esprit de corps.*

These illustrations of category-mistakes have a common feature which must be noticed. The mistakes were made by people who did not know how to wield the concepts *University, division* and *team-spirit.* Their puzzles arose from inability to use certain items in the English vocabulary.

The theoretically interesting category-mistakes are those made by people who are perfectly competent to apply concepts, at least in the situations with which they are familiar, but are still liable in their abstract thinking to allocate those concepts to logical types to which they do not belong. An instance of a mistake of this sort would be the following story. A student of politics has learned the main differences between the British, the French and the American Constitutions, and has learned also the differences and connections between the Cabinet, Parliament, the various Ministries, the Judicature and the Church of England. But he still becomes embarrassed when asked questions about the connections between the Church of England, the Home Office and the British Constitution. For while the Church and the Home

Office are institutions, the British Constitution is not another institution in the same sense of that noun. So inter-institutional relations which can be asserted or denied to hold between the Church and the Home Office cannot be asserted or denied to hold between either of them and the British Constitution. 'The British Constitution' is not a term of the same logical type as 'the Home Office' and 'the Church of England'. In a partially similar way, John Doe may be a relative, a friend, an enemy or a stranger to Richard Roe; but he cannot be any of these things to the Average Taxpayer. He knows how to talk sense in certain sorts of discussions about the Average Taxpayer, but he is baffled to say why he could not come across him in the street as he can come across Richard Roe.

It is pertinent to our main subject to notice that, so long as the student of politics continues to think of the British Constitution as a counterpart to the other institutions, he will tend to describe it as a mysteriously occult institution; and so long as John Doe continues to think of the Average Taxpayer as a fellow-citizen, he will tend to think of him as an elusive insubstantial man, a ghost who is everywhere yet nowhere.

My destructive purpose is to show that a family of radical category-mistakes is the source of the double-life theory. The representation of a person as a ghost mysteriously ensconced in a machine derives from this argument. Because, as is true, a person's thinking, feeling and purposive doing cannot be described solely in the idioms of physics, chemistry and physiology, therefore they must be described in counterpart idioms. As the human body is a complex organised unit, so the human mind must be another complex organised unit, though one made of a different sort of stuff and with a different sort of structure. Or, again, as the human body, like any other parcel of matter, is a field of causes and effects, so the mind must be another field of causes and effects, though not (Heaven be praised) mechanical causes and effects.

(3) The Origin of the Category-mistake.

One of the chief intellectual origins of what I have yet to prove to be the Cartesian category-mistake seems to be this. When Galileo showed that his methods of scientific discovery were competent to provide a mechanical theory which should cover every occupant of space, Descartes found in himself two conflicting motives. As a man of scientific genius he could not but endorse the claims of mechanics, yet as a religious and moral man he could not accept, as Hobbes accepted, the discouraging rider to those claims, namely that human nature differs only in degree of complexity from clockwork. The mental could not be just a variety of the mechanical.

He and subsequent philosophers naturally but erroneously availed themselves of the following escape-route. Since mental-conduct words are not to be construed as signifying the occurrence of mechanical processes, they must be construed as signifying the occurrence of non-mechanical processes; since mechanical laws explain movements in space as the effects of other movements in space, other laws must explain some of the non-spatial workings of minds as the effects of other non-spatial workings of minds. The difference between the human behaviours which we describe as intelligent and those which we describe as unintelligent must be a difference in their causation; so, while some movements of human tongues and limbs are the effects of mechanical causes, others must be the effects of non-mechanical causes, i.e. some issue from movements of particles of matter, others from workings of the mind.

The differences between the physical and the mental were thus represented as differences inside the common framework of the categories of 'thing', 'stuff', 'attribute', 'state', 'process', 'change', 'cause' and 'effect'. Minds are things, but different sorts of things from bodies; mental processes are causes and effects, but different sorts of causes and effects from bodily movements. And so on. Somewhat as the foreigner expected the University to be an extra edifice, rather like a college but also considerably different, so the repudiators of mechanism represented minds as extra centres of causal processes, rather like machines but also considerably different from them. Their theory was a para-mechanical hypothesis.

That this assumption was at the heart of the doctrine is shown by the fact that there was from the beginning felt to be a major theoretical difficulty in explaining how minds can influence and be influenced by bodies. How can a mental process, such as willing, cause spatial movements like the movements of the tongue? How can a physical change in the optic nerve have among its effects a mind's perception of a flash of light? This notorious crux by itself shows the logical mould into which Descartes pressed his theory of the mind. It was the self-same mould into which he and Galileo set their mechanics. Still unwittingly adhering to the grammar of mechanics, he tried to avert disaster by describing minds in what was merely an obverse vocabulary. The workings of minds had to be described by the mere negatives of the specific descriptions given to bodies; they are not in space, they are not motions, they are not modifications of matter, they are not accessible to public observation. Minds are not bits of clockwork, they are just bits of not-clockwork.

As thus represented, minds are not merely ghosts harnessed to machines, they are themselves just spectral machines. Though the human body is an engine, it is not quite an ordinary engine, since some of its workings are governed by another engine inside it—this interior governor-engine being one of a very special sort. It is invisible, inaudible and it has no size or weight. It cannot be taken to bits and the laws it obeys are not those known to ordinary engineers. Nothing is known of how it governs the bodily engine.

A second major crux points the same moral. Since, according to the doctrine, minds belong to the same category as bodies and since bodies are rigidly governed by mechanical laws, it seemed to many theorists to follow that minds must be similarly governed by rigid non-mechanical laws. The physical world is a deterministic system, so the mental world must be a deterministic system. Bodies cannot help the modifications that they undergo, so minds cannot help pursuing the careers fixed for them. *Responsibility, choice, merit* and *demerit* are therefore inapplicable concepts—unless the compromise solution is adopted of saying that the laws governing mental processes, unlike those governing physical processes, have the congenial attribute of being only rather rigid. The problem of the Freedom of the Will was the problem how to reconcile the hypothesis that minds are to be described in terms drawn from the categories of mechanics with the knowledge that higher-grade human conduct is not of a piece with the behaviour of machines.

It is an historical curiosity that it was not noticed that the entire argument was broken-backed. Theorists correctly assumed that any sane man could already recognise the differences between, say, rational and non-rational utterances or between purposive and automatic behaviour. Else there would have been nothing requiring to be salved from mechanism. Yet the explanation given presupposed that one person could in principle never recognise the difference between the rational and the irrational utterances issuing from other human bodies, since he could never get access to the postulated immaterial causes of some of their utterances. Save for the doubtful exception of himself, he could never tell the difference between a man and a Robot. It would have to be conceded, for example, that, for all that we can tell, the inner lives of persons who are classed as idiots or lunatics are as rational as those of anyone else. Perhaps only their overt behaviour is disappointing; that is to say, perhaps 'idiots' are not really idiotic, or

'lunatics' lunatic. Perhaps, too, some of those who are classed as sane are really idiots. According to the theory, external observers could never know how the overt behaviour of others is correlated with their mental powers and processes and so they could never know or even plausibly conjecture whether their applications of mental-conduct concepts to these other people were correct or incorrect. It would then be hazardous or impossible for a man to claim sanity or logical consistency even for himself, since he would be debarred from comparing his own performances with those of others. In short, our characterisations of persons and their performances as intelligent, prudent and virtuous or as stupid, hypocritical and cowardly could never have been made, so the problem of providing a special causal hypothesis to serve as the basis of such diagnoses would never have arisen. The question, 'How do persons differ from machines?' arose just because everyone already knew how to apply mental-conduct concepts before the new causal hypothesis was introduced. This causal hypothesis could not therefore be the source of the criteria used in those applications. Nor, of course, has the causal hypothesis in any degree improved our handling of those criteria. We still distinguish good from bad arithmetic, politic from impolitic conduct and fertile from infertile imaginations in the ways in which Descartes himself distinguished them before and after he speculated how the applicability of these criteria was compatible with the principle of mechanical causation.

He had mistaken the logic of his problem. Instead of asking by what criteria intelligent behaviour is actually distinguished from non-intelligent behaviour, he asked 'Given that the principle of mechanical causation does not tell us the difference, what other causal principle will tell it us?' He realised that the problem was not one of mechanics and assumed that it must therefore be one of some counterpart to mechanics. Not unnaturally psychology is often cast for just this role.

When two terms belong to the same category, it is proper to construct conjunctive propositions embodying them. Thus a purchaser may say that he bought a left-hand glove and a right-hand glove, but not that he bought a left-hand glove, a right-hand glove and a pair of gloves. 'She came home in a flood of tears and a sedan-chair' is a well-known joke based on the absurdity of conjoining terms of different types. It would have been equally ridiculous to construct the disjunction 'She came home either in a flood of tears or else in a sedan-chair'. Now the dogma of the Ghost in the Machine does just this. It maintains that there exist both bodies and minds; that there occur physical processes and mental processes; that there are mechanical causes of corporeal movements and mental causes of corporeal movements. I shall argue that these and other analogous conjunctions are absurd; but, it must be noticed, the argument will not show that either of the illegitimately conjoined propositions is absurd in itself. I am not, for example, denying that there occur mental processes. Doing long division is a mental process and so is making a joke. But I am saying that the phrase 'there occur mental processes' does not mean the same sort of thing as 'there occur physical processes', and, therefore, that it makes no sense to conjoin or disjoin the two.

If my argument is successful, there will follow some interesting consequences. First, the hallowed contrast between Mind and Matter will be dissipated, but dissipated not by either of the equally hallowed absorptions of Mind by Matter or of Matter by Mind, but in quite a different way. For the seeming contrast of the two will be shown to be as illegitimate as would be the contrast of 'she came home in a flood of tears' and 'she came home in a sedan-chair'. The belief that there is a polar opposition between Mind and Matter is the belief that they are terms of the same logical type.

It will also follow that both Idealism and Materialism are answers to an improper question. The 'reduction' of the material world to mental states and processes, as well as the 'reduction' of mental states and processes to physical states and processes, presuppose the legitimacy of the disjunction 'Either there exist minds or there exist bodies (but not both)'. It would be like saying, 'Either she bought a left-hand and a right-hand glove or she bought a pair of gloves (but not both)'.

It is perfectly proper to say, in one logical tone of voice, that there exist minds and to say, in another logical tone of voice, that there exist bodies. But these expressions do not indicate two different species of existence, for 'existence' is not a generic word like 'coloured' or 'sexed'. They indicate two different senses of 'exist', somewhat as 'rising' has different senses in 'the tide is rising', 'hopes are rising', and 'the average age of death is rising'. A man would be thought to be making a poor joke who said that three things are now rising, namely the tide, hopes and the average age of death. It would be just as good or bad a joke to say that there exist prime numbers and Wednesdays and public opinions and navies; or that there exist both minds and bodies. In the succeeding chapters I try to prove that the official theory does rest on a batch of category-mistakes by showing that logically absurd corollaries follow from it. The exhibition of these absurdities will have the constructive effect of bringing out part of the correct logic of mental-conduct concepts.

(4) Historical Note.

It would not be true to say that the official theory derives solely from Descartes' theories, or even from a more widespread anxiety about the implications of seventeenth century mechanics. Scholastic and Reformation theology had schooled the intellects of the scientists as well as of the laymen, philosophers and clerics of that age. Stoic-Augustinian theories of the will were embedded in the Calvinist doctrines of sin and grace; Platonic and Aristotelian theories of the intellect shaped the orthodox doctrines of the immortality of the soul. Descartes was reformulating already prevalent theological doctrines of the soul in the new syntax of Galileo. The theologian's privacy of conscience became the philosopher's privacy of consciousness, and what had been the bogy of Predestination reappeared as the bogy of Determinism.

It would also not be true to say that the two-worlds myth did no theoretical good. Myths often do a lot of theoretical good, while they are still new. One benefit bestowed by the para-mechanical myth was that it partly superannuated the then prevalent para-political myth. Minds and their Faculties had previously been described by analogies with political superiors and political subordinates. The idioms wed were those of ruling, obeying, collaborating and rebelling. They survived and still survive in many ethical and some epistemological discussions. As, in physics, the new myth of occult Forces was a scientific improvement on the old myth of Final Causes, so, in anthropological and psychological theory, the new myth of hidden operations, impulses and agencies was an improvement on the old myth of dictations, deferences and disobediences.

CHAPTER II: KNOWING HOW AND KNOWING THAT

•••

When we describe glass as brittle, or sugar as soluble, we are using dispositional concepts, the logical force of which is this. The brittleness of glass does not consist in the fact that it is at a given moment actually being shivered. It may be brittle without ever being shivered. To say that it is brittle is to say that if it ever is, or ever had been, struck or strained, it would fly, or have flown, into fragments. To say that sugar is soluble is to say that it would dissolve, or would have dissolved, if immersed in water.

A statement ascribing a dispositional property to a thing has much, though not every-

thing, in common with a statement subsuming the thing under a law. To possess a dispositional property is not to be in a particular state, or to undergo a particular change; it is to be bound or liable to be in a particular state, or to undergo a particular change, when a particular condition is realised. The same is true about specifically human dispositions such as qualities of character. My being an habitual smoker does not entail that I am at this or that moment smoking; it is my permanent proneness to smoke when I am not eating, sleeping, lecturing or attending funerals, and have not quite recently been smoking.

In discussing dispositions it is initially helpful to fasten on the simplest models, such as the brittleness of glass or the smoking habit of a man. For in describing these dispositions it is easy to unpack the hypothetical proposition implicitly conveyed in the ascription of the dispositional properties. To be brittle is just to be bound or likely to fly into fragments in such and such conditions; to be a smoker is just to be bound or likely to fill, light and draw on a pipe in such and such conditions. These are simple, single-track dispositions, the actualisations of which are nearly uniform.

But the practice of considering such simple models of dispositions, though initially helpful, leads at a later stage to erroneous assumptions. There are many dispositions the actualisations of which can take a wide and perhaps unlimited variety of shapes; many disposition-concepts are determinable concepts. When an object is described as hard, we do not mean only that it would resist deformation; we mean also that it would, for example, give out a sharp sound if struck, that it would cause us pain if we came into sharp contact with it, that resilient objects would bounce off it, and so on indefinitely. If we wished to unpack all that is conveyed in describing an animal as gregarious, we should similarly have to produce an infinite series of different hypothetical propositions.

Now the higher-grade dispositions of people with which this inquiry is largely concerned are, in general, not single-track dispositions, but dispositions the exercises of which are indefinitely heterogeneous. When Jane Austen wished to show the specific kind of pride which characterised the heroine of 'Pride and Prejudice', she had to represent her actions, words, thoughts and feelings in a thousand different situations. There is no one standard type of action or reaction such that Jane Austen could say 'My heroine's kind of pride was just the tendency to do this, whenever a situation of that sort arose'.

•••

CHAPTER V: DISPOSITIONS AND OCCURRENCES

•••

I have already had occasion to argue that a number of the words which we commonly use to describe and explain people's behaviour signify dispositions and not episodes. To say that a person knows something, or aspires to be something, is not to say that he is at a particular moment in process of doing or undergoing anything, but that he is able to do certain things, when the need arises, or that he is prone to do and feel certain things in situations of certain sorts.

This is, in itself, hardly more than a dull fact (almost) of ordinary grammar. The verbs 'know', 'possess' and 'aspire' do not behave like the verbs 'run', 'wake up' or 'tingle'; we cannot say 'he knew so and so for two minutes, then stopped and started again after a breather', 'he gradually aspired to be a bishop', or 'he is now engaged in possessing a bicycle'. Nor is it a peculiarity of people that we describe them in dispositional terms. We use such terms just as

much for describing animals, insects, crystals and atoms. We are constantly wanting to talk about what can be relied on to happen as well as to talk about what is actually happening; we are constantly wanting to give explanations of incidents as well as to report them; and we are constantly wanting to tell how things can be managed as well as to tell what is now going on in them. Moreover, merely to classify a word as signifying a disposition is not yet to say much more about it than to say that it is not used for an episode. There are lots of different kinds of dispositional words. Hobbies are not the same sort of thing as habits, and both are different from skills, from mannerisms, from fashions, from phobias and from trades. Nest-building is a different sort of property from being feathered, and being a conductor of electricity is a different sort of property from being elastic.

There is, however, a special point in drawing attention to the fact that many of the cardinal concepts in terms of which we describe specifically human behaviour are dispositional concepts, since the vogue of the para-mechanical legend has led many people to ignore the ways in which these concepts actually behave and to construe them instead as items in the descriptions of occult causes and effects. Sentences embodying these dispositional words have been interpreted as being categorical reports of particular but unwitnessable matters of fact instead of being testable, open hypothetical and what I shall call 'semi-hypothetical' statements. The old error of treating the term 'Force' as denoting an occult force-exerting agency has been given up in the physical sciences, but its relatives survive in many theories of mind and are perhaps only moribund in biology.

•••

Norman Malcolm
Selections from "Wittgenstein's *Philosophical Investigations*"[1]

Ein Buch ist ein Spiegel; wenn ein Affe hineinguckt, so kann freilich kein Apostel heraussehen.

Lichtenberg

An attempt to summarize the *Investigations* would be neither successful nor useful. Wittgenstein compressed his thoughts to the point where further compression is impossible. What is needed is that they should be unfolded and the connections between them traced out. A likely first reaction to the book will be to regard it as a puzzling collection of reflections that are sometimes individually brilliant, but possess no unity, present no system of ideas. In truth the unity is there, but, alas, it cannot be perceived without strenuous exertion. Within the scope of a review the connectedness can best be brought out, I think, by concentrating on some single topic—in spite of the fact that there are no separate topics, for each of the investigations in the book crisscrosses again and again with every other one. In the following I center my attention on Wittgenstein's treatment of the problem of how language is related to inner experiences—to sensations, feelings, and moods. This is one of the main inquiries of the book and perhaps the most difficult to understand. I am sufficiently aware of the fact that my presentation of this subject will certainly fail to portray the subtlety, elegance, and force of Wittgenstein's thinking and will probably, in addition, contain positive mistakes.

References to Part I will be by paragraph numbers, e.g., (207), and to Part II by page numbers, e.g., (p. 207). Quotations will be placed within double quotation marks.

Private Language

Let us see something of how Wittgenstein attacks what he calls "the idea of a private language." By a "private" language is meant one that not merely is not but *cannot* be understood by anyone other than the speaker. The reason for this is that the words of this language are supposed to "refer to what can only be known to the person speaking; to his immediate private sensations" (243). What is supposed is that I "*associate* words with sensations and use these names in descriptions" (256). I fix my attention on a sensation and establish a connection between a word and the sensation (258).

It is worth mentioning that the conception that it is possible and even necessary for one to have a private language is not eccentric. Rather it is the view that comes most naturally to anyone who philosophizes on the subject of the relation of words to experiences. The idea of a private language is presupposed by every program of inferring or constructing the 'external world' and 'other minds.' It is contained in the philosophy of Descartes and in the theory of ideas of classical British empiricism, as well as in recent and contemporary phenomenalism and sense-datum theory. At bottom it is the idea that there is only a contingent and not an *essential* connection between a sensation and its outward expression—an idea that appeals to us all. Such thoughts as these are typical expressions of the idea of a private language: that I know only from my *own* case what the word 'pain' means (293, 295); that I can only *believe* that someone else is in pain, but I *know* it if I am (303); that another person cannot have *my* pains (253); that I can undertake to call *this* (pointing inward) 'pain' in the future (263);

that when I say 'I am in pain' I am at any rate justified *before myself* (289).

In order to appreciate the depth and power of Wittgenstein's assault upon it you must partly be its captive. You must feel the strong grip of it. The passionate intensity of Wittgenstein's writing is due to the fact that he lets this idea take possession of him, drawing out of himself the thoughts and imagery by which it is expressed and defended—and then he subjects those thoughts and pictures to fiercest scrutiny. What is written down represents both a logical investigation and a great philosopher's struggle with his own thoughts. The logical investigation will be understood only by those who duplicate the struggle in themselves.

One consequence to be drawn from the view that I know only from my *own* case what, say, 'tickling' means is that "I know only what *I* call that, not what anyone else does" (347). I have not *learned* what 'tickling' means, I have only called something by that name. Perhaps others use the name differently. This is a regrettable difficulty; but, one may think, the word will still work for me as a name, provided that I apply it consistently to a certain sensation. But how about 'sensation'? Don't I know only from my *own* case what *that* word means? Perhaps what I call a 'sensation' others call by another name? It will not help, says Wittgenstein, to say that although it may be that what I have is not what others call a 'sensation,' at least I have *something*. For don't I know only from my own case what 'having something' is? Perhaps my use of *those* words is contrary to common use. In trying to explain how I gave 'tickling' its meaning, I discover that I do not have the right to use any of the relevant words of our common language. "So in the end when one is doing philosophy one gets to the point where one would like just to emit an inarticulate sound" (261).

Let us suppose that I did fix my attention on a pain as I pronounced the word 'pain' to myself. I think that thereby I established a connection between the word and the sensation. But I did not establish a connection if subsequently I applied that word to sensations other than pain or to things other than sensations, e.g., emotions. My private definition was a success only if it led me to use the word correctly in the future. In the present case, 'correctly' would mean '*consistently* with my own definition'; for the question of whether my use agrees with that of others has been given up as a bad job. Now how is it to be decided whether I have used the word consistently? What will be the difference between my having used it consistently and its *seeming* to me that I have? Or has this distinction vanished? "Whatever is going to seem right to me is right. And that only means that here we can't talk about 'right'" (258). If the distinction between 'correct' and 'seems correct' has disappeared, then so has the concept *correct*. It follows that the 'rules' of my private language are only *impressions* of rules (259). My impression that I follow a rule does not confirm that I follow the rule, unless there can be something that will prove my impression correct. And the something cannot be another impression—for this would be "as if someone were to buy several copies of the morning paper to assure himself that what it said was true" (265). The proof that I am following a rule must appeal to something *independent* of my impression that I am. If in the nature of the case there cannot be such an appeal, then my private language does not have *rules*, for the concept of a rule requires that there be a difference between 'He is following a rule' and 'He is under the impression that he is following a rule'—just as the concept of understanding a word requires that there be a difference between 'He understands this word' and 'He thinks that he understands this word' (cf. 269).

'Even if I cannot prove and cannot know that I am correctly following the rules of my private language,' it might be said, 'still it *may* be that I am. It has *meaning* to say that I am. The supposition makes sense: you and I *understand* it.' Wittgenstein has a reply to this (348–

353). We are inclined to think that we know what it means to say 'It is five o'clock on the sun' or 'This congenital deaf-mute talks to himself inwardly in a vocal language' or 'The stove is in pain.' These sentences produce pictures in our minds, and it *seems* to us that the pictures tell us how to *apply* them—that is, tell us what we have to look for, what we have to do, in order to determine whether what is pictured is the case. But we make a mistake in thinking that the picture contains in itself the instructions as to how we are to apply it. Think of the picture of blindness as a darkness in the soul or in the head of the blind man (424). There is nothing wrong with it as a *picture*. "But *what* is its application?" What shall count for or against its being said that this or that man is blind, that the picture applies to him? The *picture* doesn't say. If you think that you understand the sentence 'I follow the rule that *this* is to be called "pain"' (a rule of your private language), what you have perhaps is a picture of yourself checking off various feelings of yours as either being *this* or not. The picture appears to solve the problem of how you determine whether you have done the 'checking' right. Actually it doesn't give you even a hint in that direction; no more than the picture of blindness provides so much as a hint of *how* it is to be determined that this or that man is blind (348–353, 422–426, p. 184).

One will be inclined to say here that one can simply *remember* this sensation and by remembering it will know that one is making a consistent application of its name. But will it also be possible to have a *false* memory impression? On the private-language hypothesis, what would *show* that your memory impression is false—or true? Another memory impression? Would this imply that memory is a court from which there is no appeal? But, as a matter of fact, that is *not* our concept of memory.

Imagine that you were supposed to paint a particular color "C," which was the color that appeared when the chemical substances X and Y combined.—Suppose that the color struck you as brighter on one day than on another; would you not sometimes say: "I must be wrong, the color is certainly the same as yesterday"? This shows that we do not always resort to what memory tells us as the verdict of the highest court of appeal [56].

There is, indeed, such a thing as checking one memory against another, e.g., I check my recollection of the time of departure of a train by calling up a memory image of how a page of the time-table looked—but "this process has got to produce a memory which is actually *correct.* If the mental image of the time-table could not itself be *tested* for correctness, how could it confirm the correctness of the first memory?" (265).

If I have a language that is really private (i.e., it is a logical impossibility that anyone else should understand it or should have any basis for knowing whether I am using a particular name consistently), my assertion that my memory tells me so and so will be utterly empty. 'My memory' will not even mean—my memory *impression*. For by a memory impression we understand something that is either accurate or inaccurate; whereas there would not be, in the private language, any *conception* of what would establish a memory impression as correct, any conception of what 'correct' would mean here.

The Same

One wants to say, 'Surely there can't be a difficulty in knowing whether a feeling of mine is or isn't the *same* as the feeling I now have. I will call this feeling "pain" and will thereafter call the *same* thing "pain" whenever it occurs. What could be easier than to follow that rule?' To understand Wittgenstein's reply to this attractive proposal we must come closer to his treatment of rules and of what it is to follow a rule. (Here he forges a remarkably illuminating connection between the philosophy of psychology and the philosophy of mathematics.) Consider his example of the pupil who has been taught to write down a cardinal number series of the form '0, n, 2n, 3n . . .' at an order of the form '+n,' so that at the order '+1' he writes down the series of natural numbers (185). He has successfully done exercises and tests up to the number 1,000. We then ask him to continue the series '+2' beyond 1,000; and he writes 1,000, 1,004, 1,008, 1,012. We tell him that this is wrong. His instructive reply is, "But I went on in the same way" (185). There was nothing in the previous explanations, examples, and exercises that made it *impossible* for him to regard that as the continuation of the series. Repeating *those* examples and explanations won't help him. One must say to him, in effect, 'That isn't what we *call* going on in the *same* way.' It is a fact, and a fact of the kind whose importance Wittgenstein constantly stresses, that it is *natural* for human beings to continue the series in the manner 1,002, 1,004, 1,006, given the previous training. But that is merely what it is—a fact of human nature.

One is inclined to retort, 'Of course he can misunderstand the instruction and misunderstand the order "+2"; but if he *understands* it he must go on in the right way.' And here one has the idea that "The understanding itself is a state which is the *source* of the correct use" (146)—that the correct continuation of the series, the right application of the rule or formula, springs from one's understanding of the rule. But the question of whether one understands the rule cannot be divorced from the question of whether one will go on in that one particular way that we call 'right.' The correct use is a criterion of understanding. If you say that knowing the formula is a state of the mind and that making this and that application of the formula is merely a *manifestation* of the knowl-

edge, then you are in a difficulty: for you are postulating a mental apparatus that explains the manifestations, and so you ought to have (but do not have) a knowledge of the construction of the apparatus, quite apart from what it does (149). You would like to think that your understanding of the formula determines in advance the steps to be taken, that when you understood or meant the formula in a certain way "your mind as it were flew ahead and took all the steps before you physically arrived at this or that one" (188). But how you meant it is not independent of how in fact you use it. "We say, for instance, to someone who uses a sign unknown to us: 'If by "x!2" you mean x^2, then you get *this* value for y, if you mean $2x$, *that* one.'—Now ask yourself: how does one *mean* the one thing or the other by 'x!2'?" (190). The answer is that his putting down *this* value for y shows whether he meant the one thing and not the other: "*That* will be how meaning it can determine the steps in advance" (190). How he meant the formula determines his subsequent use of it, only in the sense that the latter is a criterion of—how he meant it.

It is easy to suppose that when you have given a person the order 'Now do the *same* thing,' you have pointed out to him the way to go on. But consider the example of the man who obtains the series 1, 3, 5, 7 . . . by working out the formula $2x + 1$ and then asks himself, "Am I always doing the same thing, or something different every time?" (226). One answer is as good as the other; it doesn't matter which he says, so long as he continues in the right way. If we could not observe his work, his mere remark 'I am going on in the same way' would not tell us what he was doing. If a child writing down a row of 2's obtained '2, 2, 2' from the segment '2, 2' by adding '2' once, he might deny that he had gone on in the *same* way. He might declare that it would be doing the same thing only if he went from '2, 2' to '2, 2, 2, 2' in *one* jump, i.e., only if he *doubled* the original segment (just as it doubled the original single '2'). That could strike one as a *reasonable* use of 'same.' This connects up with Wittgenstein's remark: "If you have to have an intuition in order to develop the series 1 2 3 4 . . . you must also have one in order to develop the series 2 2 2 2 . . ." (214). One is inclined to say of the latter series, 'Why, all that is necessary is that you keep on doing the *same* thing.' But isn't this just as true of the other series? In both cases one has already *decided* what the correct continuation is, and one calls that continuation, and no other, 'doing the same thing.' As Wittgenstein says: "One might say to the person one was training: 'Look, I always do the same thing: I . . .'" (223). And then one proceeds to show him what 'the same' *is*. If the pupil does not acknowledge that what you have shown him is the *same*, and if he is not persuaded by your examples and explanations to carry on as you wish him to—then you have reached bedrock and will be inclined to say "This is simply what I do" (217). You cannot give him more reasons than you yourself have for proceeding in that way. Your reasons will soon give out. And then you will proceed, without reasons (211).

Private Rules

All of this argument strikes at the idea that there can be such a thing as my following a rule in my private language—such a thing as naming something of which only I can be aware, 'pain,' and then going on to call the same thing, 'pain,' whenever it occurs. There is a charm about the expression 'same' which makes one think that there cannot be any difficulty or any chance of going wrong in deciding whether *A* is the *same* as *B*—as if one did not have to be *shown* what the 'same' is. This may be, as Wittgenstein suggests, because we are inclined to suppose that we can take the identity of a thing *with itself* as "an infallible paradigm" of the *same* (215). But he destroys this notion with one blow: "Then are two things the same when

they are what *one* thing is? And how am I to apply what the *one* thing shows me to the case of two things?" (215).

The point to he made here is that when one has given oneself the private rule 'I will call this same thing "pain" whenever it occurs,' one is then free to do anything or nothing. That 'rule' does not point in any direction. On the private-language hypothesis, no one can teach me what the correct use of 'same' is. I shall be the sole arbiter of whether this is the *same* as that. What I choose to call the 'same' will *be* the same. No restriction whatever will be imposed upon my application of the word. But a sound that I can use *as I please* is not a *word*.

How would you teach someone the meaning of 'same'? By example and practice: you might show him, for instance, collections of the same colors and same shapes and make him find and produce them and perhaps get him to carry on a certain ornamental pattern uniformly (208). Training him to form collections and produce patterns is teaching him what Wittgenstein calls "techniques." Whether he has mastered various techniques determines whether he understands 'same.' The exercise of a technique is what Wittgenstein calls a "practice." Whether your pupil has understood any of the rules that you taught him (e.g., the rule: this is the 'same' color as that) will be shown in his practice. But now there cannot be a 'private' practice, i.e., a practice that cannot be exhibited. For there would then be no distinction between believing that you have that practice and having it. 'Obeying a rule' is itself a practice. "And to *think* one is obeying a rule is not to obey a rule. Hence it is not possible to obey a rule 'privately'; otherwise thinking one was obeying a rule would be the same thing as obeying it" (202, cf. 380).

If I recognize that my mental image is the 'same' as one that I had previously, how am I to know that this public word 'same' describes what I recognize? "Only if I can express my recognition in some other way, and if it is possible for someone else to teach me that 'same' is the correct word here" (378). The notion of the private language doesn't admit of there being 'some other way.' It doesn't allow that my behavior and circumstances can be so related to my utterance of the word that another person, by noting my behavior and circumstances, can discover that my use of the word is correct or incorrect. Can I discover this for myself, and how do I do it? That discovery would presuppose that I have a conception of correct use which comes from outside my private language and against which I measure the latter. If this were admitted, the private language would lose its privacy and its point. So it isn't admitted. But now the notion of 'correct' use that will exist within the private language will be such that if I *believe* that my use is correct then it is correct; the rules will be only impressions of rules; my 'language' will not be a language, but merely the impression of a language. The most that can be said for it is that I *think* I understand it (cf. 269).

•••

NOTES

1 Ludwig Wittgenstein, *Philosophical Investigations;* German and English in facing pages; English translation by G.E.M. Anscombe, 2nd ed. (Oxford: Basil Blackwell, 1958).

CHAPTER NINE

The Mind-Brain Identity Theory

The rise of materialism

In the second half of this century the most widely accepted positions on the nature of the mind have been varieties of materialism. Although materialism is as old as the Greek atomists, and has been defended over the centuries by people like Hobbes, it is only in recent years that it has become almost universally accepted among philosophers and psychologists. Several different theories have come to the fore in recent years, but each of them takes as a given the view that human beings consist of nothing more than the matter of which their bodies are composed. Debates over the mind-body problem have largely become debates over which particular version of materialism should be accepted as correct. In this chapter and the next three we will look at three versions of materialism that are currently competing for prominence.

The widespread acceptance of materialism is due to a large extent to developments in biology. Biology is the study of living things, and so a central question in biology seeks to define the nature of the difference between living things and nonliving matter. Descartes' answer was that life is a purely material phenomenon. While holding that the mind is an immaterial substance, Descartes argued that the body is simply a physical mechanism, and he offered a purely mechanical explanation of a living body. Many biologists following Descartes rejected this purely mechanical account of life. They argued that biological functions are due to a "vital power" or "animality" that is not physical in nature. But the nineteenth century saw the demise of vitalism, not through a return to Descartes' theory, but through cellular biology. The first important step in this development was the discovery of the cell as an essential unit of the body, and the realization that the nature of life could be understood in terms of the molecular composition of cellular matter. By the turn of this century biologists had come to the conclusion that the nature of life lies in the physical structure of molecules.

These developments in biology had important effects on the study of the mind. In the eighteenth century, studies of the effects of brain damage revealed that specific functions of the mind, such as language and memory, are associated with specific regions of the brain. Over the years more and more correlations were established between mental activities and processes of the nervous system. When this was coupled with the discovery of the cellular nature of the nervous system, it led to the supposition that all processes of the mind are in some manner biochemical processes of the nervous system. In this way the developments in biology between Descartes' time and this century came slowly to support the idea that all facets of human beings, including what we think of as the mind, are properties of matter.

Science and materialism

The belief that materialism provides the best way of understanding the nature of the mind is defended by David Armstrong in his essay, "The Nature of Mind." Armstrong is a professor of philosophy at Sydney University in Australia, and a member of a group of Australian philosophers who brought a form of materialism called "the mind-brain identity theory" to prominence in the 1960s. In the opening paragraphs of this essay, Armstrong describes materialism as the claim that man is nothing but a physico-chemical mechanism. Before turning to the identity theory, we should look at the reasons Armstrong and his colleague J.J.C. Smart offer for accepting the truth of materialism.

Armstrong shares the position taken by Hempel and Skinner that the best way to approach the study of the mind is through modern science. In the opening sections of his paper, Armstrong defends this claim on the grounds that the natural sciences are the only areas of study in which we find widespread consensus. According to Armstrong, then, philosophers investigating the nature of the mind should begin with the question 'What does modern science teach us about the nature of man?'

Armstrong's answer to this question is that materialism is widely enough accepted that it can be taken as "established scientific doctrine." Developments in cellular biology and neurophysiology have led scientists to the conclusion that "we can give a complete account of man in purely physico-chemical terms." So the project that Armstrong proposes is:

> to work out an account of the nature of the mind which is compatible with the view that man is nothing but a physico-chemical mechanism.

Occam's Razor

Another common argument used in support of materialism is articulated by Armstrong's compatriot, J.J.C. Smart, in the essay, "Sensations and Brain Processes," which appeared in 1959. Smart begins his essay by outlining the position that he wishes to defend. He contends that sensations like those of pain and colour are physical states of the brain. He uses one particular kind of sensation to make his point: the visual sensation of an after-image. An after-image is the kind of thing you get when you look at a bright light and then look away at a blank wall.[1] He asks, "When I report that I have a yellowy-orange after-image, what is it that I am reporting?" What kind of thing is this after-image? Smart argues that the answer to this question must be consistent with materialism. Every aspect of the world except consciousness is now understood to be an aspect of matter, and it seems unbelievable, he argues, to suppose that consciousness should be the one exception to materialism.

Smart's argument for materialism is an application of a principle we call "Occam's Razor" after the medieval philosopher, William of Occam. **Occam's Razor** instructs us never to postulate more than is needed to explain what is observed. The idea is that if two theories are each consistent with all available evidence, the one that postulates fewer entities and properties is more likely to be true.

Occam's Razor, sometimes called "the principle of parsimony," is an important ingredient in scientific reasoning. We see it at work, for example, in the defence of the new science. Descartes argues for the mechanical science on the grounds that a few simple properties are sufficient to explain all observable phenomena. A particularly dramatic example of the principle is the success of Newton's theory of gravity. By postulating a force of attraction between all particles of matter, Newton was able to explain the motion of falling bodies, the movement of the ocean tides, and the planetary orbits, all by means of single law. Before Newton each of these phenomena was given a separate explanation. The unity and simplicity that Newton's theory brought was a major factor in its acceptance by the scientific community.

Occam's Razor and the mind-body problem

Smart applies the same reasoning to the mind-body problem. Given the strong correlations between what happens in the mind and what happens in the body, and given that every other aspect of the world has turned out to be physical in nature, the simplest conclusion to draw is that the mind itself will turn out to be physical as well. If this is not true, Smart argues, we are forced to conclude that just one phenomenon — consciousness — is distinct from everything else in the universe. Smart claims that this would make consciousness and sensation a "nomological dangler." By this he means that consciousness would be left hanging as the one aspect of the universe that could not be explained in terms of the mechanical properties of matter.

Smart considers one important objection to his use of Occam's Razor: There are always constituents of the world that science cannot explain. For example, while a physicist or chemist can explain why a certain material behaves as it does by referring to the periodic table of the elements, there is no explanation of why we have *this* set of elements and not another. This problem currently lies outside the domain of physics, and is accepted as a "brute fact" — something that is known but not explainable. Thus a critic of Smart's argument can say that the existence of consciousness might also be a brute fact, which we have to accept as something that falls outside the domain of scientific explanation.

Smart replies that the things currently accepted as brute facts all involve the basic or fundamental constituents of the universe. By contrast, consciousness only exists in the presence of certain highly complex and organized biological systems involving "configurations consisting of billions of neurons ... all put together ... as though their main purpose in life was to be a negative feedback mechanism of a complicated sort." The presence of consciousness in these organisms requires *some* kind of explanation, and the simplest available is that it is an aspect of organized matter.

Behaviourism and materialism

The question Armstrong and Smart consider, then, is how we should go about constructing a materialist theory of the mind. What should we say thoughts and sensations are, if we suppose they involve only properties of matter? Both authors point out that behaviourism is a strong contender in the search for a materialist theory of mind. Recall that Hempel proposes logical behaviourism as an antidote to the opposition between psychology and physics. The virtue of behaviourism for both Hempel and Skinner is that it restricts psychology to the physical variables of environmental stimulus and behavioural response. Nonetheless, both Armstrong and Smart contend that behaviourism is inadequate as a theory of mind.

Armstrong emphasizes the improvement to behaviourism that Ryle's idea of dispositions introduces. Earlier versions of behaviourism were unable to account for the obvious fact that thoughts and other mental processes do not always result in behaviour. As Armstrong says, "A man may be angry, but give no bodily sign; he may think but say or do nothing at all." As we saw in the previous chapter, by treating states of mind as *dispositions*, behaviourists can account for this fact.

Rejecting behaviourism

Although this amendment to behaviourism goes some way to making it an adequate theory of mind, Armstrong maintains that it is not enough. The problem with Ryle's version of behaviourism, he argues, is Ryle's insistence that dispositions are not *internal states or processes*. In his opposition to Descartes' conception of thoughts and sensations as private, inner states, Ryle argues that the very idea of mental states, of things "going on in the mind," is fundamentally mistaken. There is nothing in a disposition, according to Ryle, beyond certain facts about a person's behaviour. Armstrong argues that this is simply false. He says:

> When I think, but my thoughts do not issue in any action, it seems as obvious as anything is obvious that there is something actually going on in me which constitutes my thought. It is not simply that I would speak or act if some conditions that are unfulfilled were to be fulfilled. Something is currently going on, in the strongest and most literal sense of "going on," and this something is my thought.

Smart takes a similar line. He claims to find Wittgenstein's version of behaviourism congenial because of its compatibility with materialism. On Wittgenstein's view, he says, "a man is a vast arrangement of physical particles, but there are not, over and above this, sensations or states of consciousness." But Smart contends that one cannot reduce sensations such as after-images solely to aspects of a person's behaviour. In a tone very much like Armstrong's, Smart says:

> ... it does seem to me as though, when a person says "I have an after-image," he *is* making a genuine report, and that when he says "I have a pain," he *is* doing more than "replace pain-behaviour."

By this Smart means just that people's reports of sensations are reports of genuine events that are occurring, so that there must be something more than just the behaviour, even if this "something more" is not an immaterial thing.

The identity theory

In the very next sentence Smart presents what he sees as the solution to the problem. Sensations, he says, could "just be brain process of a certain sort." His idea here is that, when a person is aware of a sensation such as an after-image, the event that they are aware of is a physical event in the brain. Smart contends that we can see this to be a real possibility provided that we are very careful in working out precisely what it means to say that mental events *are* brain events. In the following section, "Remarks on Identity," Smart comments that, by saying that mental events are brain events, he is using the word 'is' in the sense of "strict identity." According to Smart, mental events such as sensations are *identical to* physical events in the brain. Thus, the theory that he proposes has been termed the **mind-brain identity theory**. Before looking at the arguments for and against this view, we must get clear on just what kind of identity he is suggesting.

Strict identity and correlation

When he says that there is a "strict identity" between mental events and brain events, Smart is concerned to distinguish his view from the idea that there is a *correlation* between two events. To say that there is a correlation means that mental events always occur together with certain kinds of brain events. This is something that Descartes would agree with. According to Descartes, each type of sensation in the mind is caused by a certain kind of event in the brain. There are certain physical occurrences in the brain that are always immediately accompanied by the occurrence of a sensation in consciousness, and these sensations never arise in the absence of their respective brain events. Nonetheless, Descartes views the two occurrences, mental and physical, as just that: *two* events, not one.

Smart's assertion is that there are not two correlated events — the event in the brain and the event in the mind — but rather that there is only one event, and that event is a brain event. In the same way, Smart says, a flash of lightning is not *correlated* with a discharge of electricity in the sky; the lightning *is* a discharge of electricity.

Numerical and qualitative identity

Another way to understand Smart's idea is to draw a distinction between what is called "qualitative identity" and "numerical identity." When we say that one thing is **qualitatively identical** to another, we mean that the two things are similar to one another in every respect. For example, there are now two pens on my desk that are identical in this sense. They are the same size, shape, and colour, and their construction is exactly the same. But when we say that one thing is **numerically identical** to another, we mean that they are actually one and the same thing. For example, to say that at this moment the president of the United States is numerically identical to Bill Clinton is to say that Bill Clinton and the president are one and the same person; there is exactly one person who is both the president and Bill Clinton. When we are talking about numerical identity, we usually use the shorter expression of the form, "Bill Clinton *is* the president."[2] Each of the following is an example of numerical identity.

> Five is the sum of two and three.
> Water is H_2O.
> Her oldest sister is her best friend.

When identity theorists say that the mind is the brain, and that states of mind are states of the brain, they are talking about numerical identity. They claim that the object that we think of as the mind is one and the same thing as the brain, and that each mental state or event is one and the same thing as some particular physical state or event of the brain.

Contingent and necessary facts

Another important element in Smart's theory is found in the paragraph immediately preceding the section "Remarks on Identity." That paragraph begins with the following passage:

> Let me first try to state more accurately the thesis that sensations are brain-processes. It is not the thesis that, for example, "after-image" or "ache" means the same as 'brain process of sort X' (where 'X' is replaced by a description of a certain sort of brain process). It is that, in so far as "after-image" or "ache" is a report of a process, it is a report of a process that *happens to be* a brain process.

Here Smart is introducing a central feature of the identity theory. We can describe this feature by saying that the identity of mind and brain is a "contingent identity," not a "necessary identity." Let's look at these concepts before going on to see what use Smart makes of them.

Some facts are contingent facts and some are necessary facts. To say that a fact is **contingent** means that it is a result of how the world happens to be; had the world been different than it is, it might not have been a fact. For example, that I was born in England is a contingent fact. It is true that I was born in England, but if my parents had decided to move to another country before I was born, it might not have been true. By contrast, when a fact is **necessary**, it is impossible for it not to be a fact. Which facts are necessary (and whether there even are any) is a controversial question, but there are some plausible cases. Mathematical facts seem to be necessary: no matter how the world might have turned out, the sum of two positive numbers cannot possibly be a negative number. The least controversial examples of necessary facts are those that depend solely on logical relations between concepts. For instance, the sentence 'All sisters are female' is necessarily true simply because the concept conveyed by the term 'female' is part of the concept conveyed by 'sister.'[3]

Contingent and necessary identity

So to say that one thing is **contingently identical** to another means that the identity depends on how the world happens to be. Let's look at an example. We know now that the brightest star in the morning sky, the Morning Star, is actually the planet Venus. And the brightest star in the evening sky, the Evening Star, happens to be the same planet. So the Morning Star and the Evening Star are numerically identical. But if the solar system had been arranged differently than it is (say, if the scattering of celestial matter produced a different arrangement of planets), the brightest objects in the morning and evening skies might have been two *different* planets, say Venus and Jupiter. So the numerical identity of the Morning Star and the Evening Star is contingent; it is a result of how the world happens to be put together. The numerical identity of Bill Clinton and the president of the United States is also contingent; Clinton might have lost the last election and not been president at this moment.

By contrast, to say one thing is **necessarily identical** to another means that it is impossible that they could have been different objects, no matter how the world happened to be. For example, John's oldest sister is necessarily identical to John's oldest female sibling. Given what a sister is, it is impossible for John's oldest sister to be anyone *but* his oldest female sibling. This is because the two expressions 'sister' and 'female sibling' express the same concept. In such a case the identity is not dependent on how the world is put together; it is fixed by the logical relations between the two concepts.

Against the translation project

Recall the behaviourists' claim that understanding what states of mind are is a matter of analyzing the meanings of psychological descriptions. For example, they argue that when we say someone is in pain we *mean* that they are disposed to behave in particular ways. In other words, the concept of pain is the *same concept* as that of behaving in a certain way. So, in their view, the fact that someone in pain is disposed to behave in a certain way is not a contingent fact. Given what the concept of pain is, it is impossible for someone to be in pain and *not* be disposed to behave in those ways. In Ryle's view, then, Descartes' error is a *logical* error, a matter of misunderstanding the concept of mental states.

Against this view, Smart is urging that when he says that an after-image is a brain state of type X, we should not make the mistake of interpreting him as saying that the words 'after-image' and 'brain-state of type X' have the same meaning. Unlike the behaviourists, he is not attempting a logical analysis of psychological concepts. As it is not a matter of logical relations between concepts, Smart denies that the identity of sensations and brain processes is a *necessary* fact. He claims only that the after-image happens to be a state of the brain; if the world had been different than it is, after-images might have been something else. For example, Descartes *might* be right that after-images are states of an immaterial mind. But the scientific evidence suggests that Descartes is wrong; after-images are not immaterial states, they are brain states.

Discovering contingent facts

Identity theorists use the following argument to support their claim that the identity of mind and brain is a contingent identity: necessary identities, they claim, are ones that depend on the nature of our concepts. This means that understanding the concepts involved is all we need to recognize necessary identities. For example, to know that John's oldest sister is his oldest female sibling, you don't have to know anything about John or his family; you don't need to know anything at all except what a sister is. If someone were to conduct a survey to see whether everyone's oldest sister happens to be their oldest female sibling, they would reveal that they are clearly confused about the nature of the identity.

By contrast, they argue, contingent identities are ones that we can *discover*. When an identity is contingent, knowing the meanings of the two terms is not sufficient to make the identity known. For example, it was a significant discovery to realize that the Morning Star and the Evening Star are one and the same planet. People had long been able to identify the brightest objects in the morning and evening skies without realizing that both are in fact the planet Venus.

Similarly, identity theorists contend, the contingent nature of mind-brain identity is revealed by the fact that it is something that we have discovered. We have always understood what is meant by the terms 'mind' and 'brain.' But it is only in the past few decades that we have come to recognize that the mind happens to be the same object as the brain. The fact that this is something we can discover, they claim, reveals that mind-brain identity is a contingent fact, one that is a matter of how the world happens to be.

The scientific character of the mind-body problem

Identity theorists argue that the idea that the nature of mental states is a contingent matter makes the identity theory different in an important way from both Descartes' dualism and logical behaviourism. According to Descartes, discovering the nature of the mind is achieved by reflection on our ideas of mind and matter. When we do this, he argues, we see that the mind could not possibly be a material object. The idea of mind and the idea of matter are ideas of two different substances — two "complete things" — and no matter how the world might have been put together it is impossible that one should be the same as the other. In a somewhat similar way, behaviourists such as Ryle and Malcolm argue that understanding the mind is a matter of understanding the nature of psychological concepts. Thus Wittgenstein argues that an analysis of the concept of pain reveals that the word 'pain' can only refer to outward behaviour and not to an inner private experience.

Identity theorists reject both of these approaches. They argue that discovering the nature of the mind is a *scientific* matter, to be settled by experiments and observations, not by examining our concepts of mind and matter. Understanding the nature of the mind, they argue, is no different than understanding the nature of water or lightning. In both of these latter cases, careful experiments revealed the underlying physical nature of the object. Molecular physics revealed that water is a substance with the molecular structure H_2O. And Benjamin Franklin's experiment with his kite revealed that lightning is actually an electrical discharge in the atmosphere. Similarly, identity theorists claim that observation and experiment will reveal the nature of thought, feeling, and sensation. And they argue that the best current evidence is that all of these states of mind are physical processes of the brain.

The first objection: Knowledge of brain states

Smart uses the notion of contingent identity to reject a number of common criticisms of the identity theory. In the concluding sections of his paper he describes several objections that are raised against his theory and offers his reply to each. I want to look at the first and third of these objections together with Smart's replies. The first underscores the importance of the notion of contingent identity, and the third introduces an interesting element of Smart's identity theory.

The first objection is based on the fact that someone can know what a sensation is without possessing any knowledge of brain processes. I can know that I am experiencing a yellow-orange after-image, even though I have no idea what's going on in my brain. It follows, so the objection goes, that the after-image and the brain process can't possibly be the same thing. If I'm aware of the sensation, and the sensation were identical to a brain state, then I would have to be aware of the brain state. Because I have no idea what's going on in my brain, the sensation can't be a brain state.

Smart's reply to this is that the objection simply fails to distinguish contingent and necessary identity. Recognizing an after-image requires only a knowledge of the *concept* of an after-image. And someone can understand the concept of an after-image without understanding any neurology because the concept of a sensation and the concept of a brain process are different. He illustrates his point with the identity of the Morning Star and Evening Star. Someone can recognize the Evening Star as long as they can identify the brightest object in the evening sky, even if they have no knowledge whatever of the Morning Star. This is because the two concepts, of the Morning Star and the Evening Star, are different. It just so happens, given the arrangement of matter in the universe, that both concepts apply to the same object: the planet Venus.

The third objection: Mental properties

The third objection is based on Smart's reply to the first. Smart's example of a contingent identity is that of the Morning Star and the Evening Star. The fact that identity in this case is contingent means that, had the world been different than it is, the brightest objects in the morning and evening skies might have been two different objects. And this in turn means that the planet Venus might have been the brightest object in the morning sky *without* being the brightest object in the evening sky. What this reveals is that the property or characteristic of *being the brightest object in the morning sky* is a different property from that of *being the brightest object in the evening sky.* For it is possible for something to have one of these properties but not the other. In general, whenever A is contingently identical to B, the property described by the term 'A' is different from the property described by the term 'B.' Let's see how this point applies to mind-brain identity.

We'll use Smart's example of an after-image again. If, as Smart says, an orange after-image is contingently identical to a brain process of type X, then, from what we have just seen, the property of *being an orange after-image* is a different property from that of *being a brain state of type X.* Now, the property of being a particular kind of brain process is one that we would explain in terms of electrochemical activity in the nervous system. But what about the property of being an orange after-image? What characteristics would something necessarily have to have in order to be an after-image? It looks as though this would be a matter of having a certain appearance in consciousness, for this is how we are familiar with after-images. That is, we recognize something as an after-image by how it appears to us in our visual experience. So it seems that the property of *appearing a certain way in consciousness* is a different property from that of being a certain kind of brain process.

Property dualism

The conclusion of the third objection is that if the identity of mental states and brain states is contingent, as Smart claims, then there must be mental *properties* that are not physical properties. And this, it is argued, leads us to another form of dualism. This form of dualism has it that, while the mind is not a separate *entity* from the brain, *mental properties* of the brain are not identical to *physical properties* of the brain. The mind/brain is a single entity, but it is held to have two distinct sets of characteristics, mental and physical. This kind of dualism is called **property dualism**, in contrast to Descartes' dualism, which is sometimes referred to as **substance dualism**.

So it appears that if mind-brain identity is contingent, mental properties are not physical properties of the brain even if there is a single event in the brain that has both such properties. It looks as though, in defending materialism from the first objection, Smart has ended up with a variety of dualism after all.

Smart's reply to the third objection

Smart's reply to this objection is as follows. He says:

> When a person says, "I see a yellowish-orange after-image," he is saying something like this: "There is something going on which is like what is going on when I have my eyes open, am awake, and there is an orange illuminated in good light in front of me, that is, when I really see an orange."

What does this mean, and how does it solve the problem?

The problem Smart faces can be put in this way: Given the nature of contingent identity, there are two different properties that the yellowish-orange sensation has:

(i)   the property of appearing yellowish-orange in consciousness, and
(ii) the property of being a brain process of type X.

And it appears as though the first is a purely mental property, for how something appears in consciousness can only be understood in terms of our private mental experience. So if (i) is going to be distinct from (ii), it seems that (i) must refer to an ineliminably *psychic* property. Smart's solution is to find a description of the first property that eliminates any reference to consciousness. So he replaces (i) with

(i′) the property of being an event similar to what happens when I see an orange.

(i) and (i′), he claims, are really the same. But notice that (i′) makes no reference to consciousness. In fact, (i′) makes no claim at all about what kind of event occurs when we see an orange. The event described in (i′) could have any nature at all, mental or physical. So Smart can admit that there is a single event that has two properties: that of being similar to what happens when one sees an orange, and that of being a brain process of type X. But this admission does not force him to admit that there are any nonphysical properties.

Topic-neutral descriptions

In this reply to the third objection Smart is introducing a new approach to the mind-body problem. We identify mental states in terms of some characteristic they have that is neutral with respect to their intrinsic nature. Smart calls these **topic-neutral** terms. We then set about investigating the underlying nature of the states identified in this way. For example, we can identify the sensation of pain as whatever it is that happens in me when I do something like drop a brick on my foot. It is then a matter of scientific investigation what kind of occurrence that is.

The topic-neutral approach, identity theorists argue, is similar to the standard way of proceeding in the sciences. At one time scientists identified electricity simply as the event that occurs when a glass rod is rubbed or when wires are attached to a battery cell. Then they set about determining what kind of thing electricity is. Several ideas were proposed before the present theory of electron transmission was hit upon. In general, the method is to identify a particular kind of occurrence without any knowledge of its underlying nature, and then to find out through experiment and observation what kind of occurrence it is.

The topic-neutral approach is a reflection of Smart's contention that the nature of the mind is a contingent matter, to be settled by scientific investigation. When we identify an after-image as an event that is similar to what happens when we see something orange, the nature of the event is left open to investigation. We can ask, what kind of event is it that occurs in this way? And the answer to this question is to be settled by collecting evidence for and against competing hypotheses. The current evidence, Smart says, favours the contention that these kinds of events are physical events in the brain. But if so, this will be a contingent matter. That is, the event does not *have to be* a physical event in the brain; rather the world just happens to be that way.

Armstrong's criticism of Smart

In his book, *A Materialist Theory of the Mind*, Armstrong criticizes the thesis that Smart puts forward in "Sensations and Brain Processes." As we have just seen, Smart's idea is that sensations can be identified in topic-neutral terms by their role in perception. The sensation of orange is identified by Smart as the event that happens when one sees an orange. But Armstrong points out that this will work only for sensations, and not even all of those. It cannot be extended to other mental states and processes. What perceptual event, he asks, is the one that can be identified with the decision to walk down to the pub for a drink? Clearly there is no perception that must take place in order for that mental event to occur in me.

Armstrong agrees, however, that the topic-neutral approach is correct in principle. In his view, Smart has simply failed to get hold of the correct topic-neutral descriptions. The decision to go to the pub for a drink is identified less by the things that produce it than by the behaviour it typically produces. Hence, according to Armstrong, we need to identify mental states both by the kinds of environmental stimuli that cause them and by the behaviour that they produce.

Behavioural criteria

Armstrong maintains that a promising materialist theory can be reached by making certain important changes to behaviourism. He says:

> Behaviourism is certainly wrong, but perhaps it is not altogether wrong. Perhaps the Behaviourists are wrong in identifying the mind and mental occurrences with behaviour, but perhaps they are right in thinking that our notion of a mind and of individual mental states is *logically tied to behaviour*. For perhaps what we mean by a mental state is some state of the person which, under suitable conditions, *brings about* a certain range of behaviour. Perhaps mind can defined not as behaviour, but rather as the inner *cause* of behaviour.

The idea Armstrong is suggesting here is another version of the topic-neutral approach. Armstrong's proposal is that topic-neutral descriptions be developed in terms of the behavioural consequences of our mental states.

According to Armstrong, behaviourists were correct in their claim that the connection between mental states and behaviour is a *logical* connection. For example, it is part of the *meaning* of the phrase 'want to go out to the pub for a drink' that this state will produce certain kinds of behaviour in the right circumstances. Notice, for instance, how common the following kind of statement is: 'I don't think you really *want* to go. You have the time and the money. So if you really wanted to, you would go right now.' This reinforces Armstrong's claim that we see a logical or conceptual connection between the mental state and the action: you can't have that state and yet not exhibit the behaviour in the appropriate situations.

The amendment that Armstrong makes to behaviourism is to identify mental states with the internal states of a person that *cause* behaviour. This stands in contrast to Ryle's assertion that dispositions are not internal states but solely aspects of behaviour. Armstrong argues that Ryle's position is inconsistent with the way in which scientists think of physical dispositions. Solubility, for example, is a specific kind of molecular structure that causes substances like salt and sugar to dissolve in solvents like water. In this way, solubility is an internal state of a substance that is identified by its behavioural effects.

Identifying mental states as internal states that cause certain kinds of behaviour provides us with a topic-neutral means of identifying them. Consider, for example, a mental state such as the desire to go on a vacation. If this desire is identified simply as whatever internal state it is that produces such behaviour as collecting holiday brochures, then it is left open whether that state is a physical brain state or a state of an immaterial mind.

Can mind-brain identity really be contingent?

Shortly after the formulation of the identity theory, a Princeton philosopher, Saul Kripke, outlined a serious problem with the claim that mind-brain identity is a contingent matter. Kripke's initial influence was as a logician. In several early works he made important advances in a field of mathematical logic called "modal logic," which deals with the notions of possibility and necessity. His criticism of the identity theory rose directly out of his work on the logic of necessity.[4] Before we look at Kripke's argument, let's briefly review the issue that he addresses.

As we have seen, identity theorists contend that the virtue of the topic-neutral approach is that it leaves the mind-body problem as an issue to be settled by scientific study. Smart and Armstrong argue that the weight of evidence currently suggests that the thoughts and sensations we experience are biochemical processes of the brain. Yet the very fact that this issue is to be settled by the weight of evidence, they argue, shows that the issue is a *contingent* one. That is, whether thoughts and sensations are brain events or states of an immaterial substance is a matter of how the world happens to be put together.

In an article entitled "Identity and Individuation," Kripke argues that the scientific nature of the mind-body problem does *not* show that the issue is a contingent one. The argument in this article is condensed from an important book called *Identity and Necessity* (Harvard University Press, 1972). His contention is that necessary facts — facts that could not have been otherwise, no matter how the world turned out — can be discovered by science, or settled by the weight of evidence, just as contingent facts can be. According to Kripke, this shows that the tactics Smart uses to respond to the criticisms of identity theory will not work.

Science and contingent identity

In the first two paragraphs of our selection from Kripke's article, Kripke reminds us that the argument that mind-body identity is a contingent issue is made by comparing that issue with certain well-known scientific facts. These facts, identity theorists claim, are precisely the same as the identity of mind and brain; each of them is a contingent fact, discovered in the course of normal scientific investigation. For example, the fact that heat is molecular motion is held to be contingent because we might have discovered that some other theory is true. (We might, for example, have discovered that heat is a kind of fluid.) It is then argued that the same is true of mind and body: some other theory (such as Descartes') *might* have been true; but, as it turns out, mental states and activities turn out to be brain states and activities.

In the next paragraph Kripke claims that the scientific facts that identity theorists use to compare their theory with the mind-brain identity theory are not actually contingent facts at all.[5] If a statement such as 'Heat is molecular motion' is true, he contends, it is necessarily true. In other words, if heat is molecular motion, then it could not have been anything but molecular motion, no matter how the world might have turned out to be. His argument for this claim is based on a pair of technical concepts: that of a "rigid designator" and that of a "nonrigid designator." We need first to understand these two concepts.

Rigid and nonrigid designators

Kripke uses the term '**designator**' to mean any word or expression that is used to refer to something. A name is a designator, because it refers to an individual. 'Paris' is the name of a certain city in France, and 'Peter Morton' is a name that refers to me. There are also names for certain kinds of substances or natural phenomena, like 'water' and 'heat.' Sometimes descriptions, such as 'the author of *Hamlet*,' also refer to individuals, in which case they are also designators.

The difference between rigid and nonrigid designators is a matter of what the designators refer to under various different circumstances. Let's use Kripke's example of a **nonrigid designator**: 'the inventor of bifocals.' The person who invented bifocals was Benjamin Franklin, so the description 'the inventor of bifocals' refers to Franklin. But of course someone else might have developed the idea before Franklin, so the fact that Franklin invented bifocals is a contingent fact. And if someone else, say Isaac Newton, had invented them, then the term 'the inventor of bifocals' would have referred to that person. So the person to whom the term refers depends on certain contingent facts; in some circumstances it would refer to one person, and under other circumstances it would refer to someone else.

A **rigid designator**, on the other hand, is such that the individual it refers to does not depend on any contingent circumstances. Kripke's example is 'the square root of 25.' That expression refers to the number 5, and there are no possible circumstances under which it would refer to any other number. You might say that, when a term is a rigid designator, the fact that it refers to a certain individual is a necessary fact.[6]

Necessity and theoretical identities

With the notions of rigid and nonrigid designators established, Kripke turns to his first argument. If a sentence like 'Heat is molecular motion' is contingent, he points out, then it must be possible for there to be circumstances in which it is false, that is, circumstances in which the term 'heat' refers to something other than the motion of molecules. But if you consider the situations that people have in mind, he says, it turns out that they are not actually cases in which 'heat' does not refer to molecular motion. In any conceivable circumstance, the term 'heat' will always refer to molecular motion. Hence, it is a rigid designator.

He asks us to consider various thought experiments that cover the cases in which 'heat' might not designate molecular motion. He says,

> There is a certain external phenomenon which we can sense by the sense of touch, and it produces a sensation which we call "the sensation of heat." We then discover that the external phenomenon which produces this sensation ... is in fact that of molecular agitation in the thing we touch, a very high degree of molecular agitation. So, it might be thought, to imagine a situation in which heat would not have been the motion of molecules, we need only imagine a situation in which we would have had the very same sensation and it would have been produced by something other than the motion of molecules.

But, he claims, there is no such situation. First, he asks us to imagine that Martians came to our planet, for whom the rapid motion of molecules in fire produces the same sensation we get from ice, and ice produces in them the sensation we get from fire. We would not say that this shows that heat is not molecular motion, but rather that heat produces in them a different sensation than it does in us. Nor would it be different, he says, if it had been us who (through some different evolutionary process) received the sensations that these Martians do. We would not say, "In that circumstance, heat would not be molecular motion." We would say, "In that circumstance, heat would produce a different sensation than it does under these circumstances." So, he concludes, under no possible situation would 'heat' refer to anything other than molecular motion, and this means that 'heat' is a rigid designator. The fact that heat is molecular motion, then, is a *necessary fact.*

Discovering necessary identities

Kripke argues that, even though such facts as the identity of heat and molecular motion are necessary facts, they are nonetheless discovered by scientific investigation. Terms like 'heat' and 'lightning' and 'light' all refer to certain things in the natural environment. Over time we have come to discover that these things are molecular motion, electrical discharge, and streams of photons. Nonetheless, despite our earlier ignorance, these terms are rigid designators that refer to the same phenomena under any possible circumstances. So our discoveries are discoveries of necessary facts.

According to Kripke, the apparent contingency of these identities is an illusion. From the fact that we have only just discovered these identities, we mistakenly *thought* that the issues were contingent. The illusion, he says, derives from the fact that we mistakenly took the designators to refer to the sensations that are produced by these phenomena. For example, our initial way of identifying heat arose from the contingent fact that it happens to cause a certain sensation in our minds. We allowed ourselves to be confused by supposing that the term 'heat' designates the sensation. But more careful reflection reveals that the term 'heat' refers to the external phenomenon that *causes* that sensation. And it would always refer to that same phenomenon, no matter what kind of sensation we happen to experience.

Mind and body again

Kripke now asks us to compare these theoretical identities with the case of mind-body identity. Consider, he says, an identity claim such as 'Pain is such and such a neural (brain) state.' The identity theorist's contention is that such a claim, if it is true, is contingently true, on the grounds that we can imagine both the brain state occurring without any experience of pain, and a creature being in pain but not having the specified brain state.

Given Kripke's argument above, the identity theorist might admit that the contingency here, as in the other cases, is only apparent. Mental states, it turns out, could not be anything *but* brain states. Still, they might argue, this does not affect the issue of mind-body identity. Even if the identity of thoughts and sensations with physical events in the brain turns out to be a necessary identity, it is nonetheless one that is discovered, just as we have discovered the nature of heat, water, and lightning. Thus the important aspect of the identity theory — that mind-body identity is a scientific issue, not a conceptual one — is unchanged.

In the remainder of our selection, however, Kripke argues that this tactic will not save the identity theory from embarrassment. For, contrary to what the identity theorists assert, he argues that the case of mind-body identity is very different from the other cases of theoretical identity.

In all of the other theoretical identities, what appeared to be contingent identities turn out to be illusions. We *thought*, for example, that we could imagine a situation where heat is something other than molecular motion;

once we consider it more carefully, it turns out that there could be no such situation. In each case, our mistake was to think that a term designates a sensation rather than the external cause of that sensation. However, Kripke argues, this mistake could not occur in the case of pain and brain states. We could not mistakenly associate the term 'pain' with a sensation rather than its external cause, for pain *is* the sensation. As Kripke puts it, the sensation associated with the term 'pain' is not a contingent property of pain (as the sensation of heat is to molecular motion) but an *essential* property: nothing could be pain that isn't that sensation. And this, Kripke concludes, means that we cannot explain the mistaken idea that mind-brain identity is contingent in the same way that we explain the other cases.

The problem for the identity theory

Kripke's arguments have two conclusions with respect to mind-brain identity. First, identity theorists are wrong in their assertion that the mind-body problem is a contingent issue. That is, whether states of mind are brain states or states of an immaterial substance is not a contingent matter that depends on how the world happens to be.

Second, we cannot say that we mistakenly *thought* that the issue was a contingent one. Although we can explain the illusion of contingency in cases like the identity of heat and molecular motion by saying that we mistakenly identified heat with the sensation it produces, we cannot say that we mistakenly identified pain with the sensation it produces. This means that if the identity theorists are right that states of mind are brain states, it is impossible to say how anyone could have thought they were anything but brain states. And this means they cannot explain how we could *discover* the identity of mental states and brain states.

Kripke maintains that materialists have failed to come up with any argument sophisticated enough to account for these two difficulties. "So the conclusion of this investigation," he says:

> would be that the analytical tools we are using [i.e. the notions of rigid and nonrigid designators] go against the identity thesis and so go against the general thesis that mental states are just physical states.

Identity theorists are left, then, with two options for replying to Kripke. They can maintain that psychological terms are not rigid designators as Kripke maintains. To do this would require an argument that what topic-neutral descriptions of psychological states refer to can vary depending on the circumstances. The best prospect for that option, it would seem, is Armstrong's behavioural descriptions. The nature of the inner states that cause certain kinds of behaviour, it might be argued, will depend on contingent facts about how the world happens to be. The other option is to accept that mind-brain identity is necessary and then find some way of explaining how we could have thought the mind could be something other than the brain.

At the same time that this issue was being debated, however, other theorists were presenting a different account of psychological states altogether. This theory, which has become known as "functionalism," has been influenced by the development of the digital computer. In the next chapter, we leave the mind-body problem temporarily to look at ideas in the field of "artificial intelligence."

NOTES

1   The reason for choosing after-images as his example is that they are not perceptions of anything in the physical environment; they are "pure" sensations. For this reason after-images do not generate any confusion in distinguishing sensations from the objects of which they are perceptions.

2   Sentences of the form 'A is B' also have another use: namely, to say that an object A has a certain property B, as when we say 'The chair is green.' Here we don't mean that the chair and the colour green are one and the same object, but that the chair has the property of being green. This use of the 'is' is called the "predicative" use.

3   Of course, we could use the words 'sister' and 'female' in a way that gives them different meanings. But this wouldn't change the point. For what is essential is that the concept expressed in English by the word 'sister' comprises the conjunction of two concepts expressed by the words 'female' and 'sibling.' We can change our language, but that wouldn't change the logical relations between these concepts.

4   More recently Kripke has developed an influential interpretation and defence of Wittgenstein's Private Language Argument.

5   He mentions two kinds of identity statements: those involving proper names (for example, "Bob Dylan is Robert Zimmerman") and theoretical identifications. We will ignore the cases of proper names, because they do not affect the mind-body issue. We are concerned with theoretical identifications, such as the fact that heat is molecular motion and that water is H_2O.

6   In the remainder of this paragraph, and in the following paragraph, Kripke points out two ways in which it is possible to misunderstand him. First, the question of whether a term would refer to different individuals under different circumstances should not be taken as a matter of whether the words could be given a different meaning. For example, 'the square root of 25' might be given a completely different meaning than what we understand, in which case it would not refer to the number 5. But this would not mean that it is a nonrigid designator. Second, the fact that a term is a rigid designator does not mean that the individual it refers to must necessarily exist. But if it does exist, then the term refers to it and not something else.

David M. Armstrong
"The Nature of Mind"

Men have minds, that is to say, they perceive, they have sensations, emotions, beliefs, thoughts, purposes, and desires.[1] What is it to have a mind? What is it to perceive, to feel emotion, to hold a belief, or to have a purpose? In common with many other modern philosophers, I think that the best clue we have to the nature of mind is furnished by the discoveries and hypotheses of modern science concerning the nature of man.

What does modern science have to say about the nature of man? There are, of course, all sorts of disagreements and divergencies in the views of individual scientists. But I think it is true to say that one view is steadily gaining ground, so that it bids fair to become established scientific doctrine. This is the view that we can give a complete account of man *in purely physico-chemical terms*. This view has received a tremendous impetus in the last decade from the new subject of molecular biology, a subject which promises to unravel the physical and chemical mechanisms which lie at the basis of life. Before that time, it received great encouragement from pioneering work in neurophysiology pointing to the likelihood of a purely electro-chemical account of the working of the brain. I think it is fair to say that those scientists who still reject the physico-chemical account of man do so primarily for philosophical, or moral, or religious reasons, and only secondarily, and halfheartedly, for reasons of scientific detail. This is not to say that in the future new evidence and new problems may not come to light which will force science to reconsider the physico-chemical view of man. But at present the drift of scientific thought is clearly set towards the physico-chemical hypothesis. And we have nothing better to go on than the present.

For me, then, and for many philosophers who think like me, the moral is clear. We must try to work out an account of the nature of mind which is compatible with the view that man is nothing but a physico-chemical mechanism.

And ... I shall be concerned to do just this: to sketch (in barest outline) what may be called a Materialist or Physicalist account of the mind. But before doing this I should like to go back and consider a criticism of my position which must inevitably occur to some. What reason have I, it may be asked, for taking my stand on science? Even granting that I am right about what is the currently dominant scientific view of man, why should we concede science a special authority to decide questions about the nature of man? What of the authority of philosophy, of religion, of morality, or even of literature and art? Why do I set the authority of science above all these? Why this "scientism"?

It seems to me that the answer to this question is very simple. If we consider the search for truth, in all its fields, we find that it is only in science that men versed in their subject can, after investigation that is more or less prolonged, and which may in some cases extend beyond a single human lifetime, reach substantial agreement about what is the case. It is only as a result of scientific investigation that we ever seem to reach an intellectual consensus about controversial matters.

In the Epistle Dedicatory to his *De Corpore* Hobbes wrote of William Harvey, the discoverer of the circulation of the blood, that he was "the only man I know, that conquering envy, hath established a new doctrine in his life-time."

Before Copernicus, Galileo and Harvey, Hobbes remarks, "there was nothing certain in natural philosophy." And, we might add, with the exception of mathematics, there was nothing certain in any other learned discipline.

These remarks of Hobbes are incredibly revealing. They show us what a watershed in the intellectual history of the human race the seventeenth century was. Before that time inquiry proceeded, as it were, in the dark. Men could not hope to see their doctrine *established,* that is to say, accepted by the vast majority of those properly versed in the subject under discussion. There was no intellectual consensus. Since that time, it has become a commonplace to see new doctrines, sometimes of the most far-reaching kind, established to the satisfaction of the learned, often within the lifetime of their first proponents. Science has provided us with a method of deciding disputed questions. This is not to say, of course, that the consensus of those who are learned and competent in a subject cannot be mistaken. Of course such a consensus can be mistaken. Sometimes it has been mistaken. But, granting fallibility, what better authority have we than such a consensus?

Now this is of the utmost importance. For in philosophy, in religion, in such disciplines as literary criticism, in moral questions in so far as they are thought to be matters of truth and falsity, there has been a notable failure to achieve an intellectual consensus about disputed questions among the learned. Must we not then attach a peculiar authority to the discipline that can achieve a consensus? And if it presents us with a certain vision of the nature of man, is this not a powerful reason for accepting that vision?

I will not take up here the deeper question *why* it is that the methods of science have enabled us to achieve an intellectual consensus about so many disputed matters. That question, I think, could receive no brief or uncontroversial answer. I am resting my argument on the simple and uncontroversial fact that, as a result of scientific investigation, such a consensus has been achieved.

It may be replied—it often is replied—that while science is all very well in its own sphere—

the sphere of the physical, perhaps—there are matters of fact on which it is not competent to pronounce. And among such matters, it may be claimed, is the question what is the whole nature of man. But I cannot see that this reply has much force. Science has provided us with an island of truths, or, perhaps one should say, a raft of truths, to bear us up on the sea of our disputatious ignorance. There may have to be revisions and refinements, new results may set old findings in a new perspective, but what science has given us will not be altogether superseded. Must we not therefore appeal to these relative certainties for guidance when we come to consider uncertainties elsewhere? Perhaps science cannot help us to decide whether or not there is a God, whether or not human beings have immortal souls, or whether or not the will is free. But if science cannot assist us, what can? I conclude that it is the scientific vision of man, and not the philosophical or religious or artistic or moral vision of man, that is the best clue we have to the nature of man. And it is rational to argue from the best evidence we have.

Having in this way attempted to justify my procedure, I turn back to my subject: the attempt to work out an account of mind, or, if you prefer, of mental process, within the framework of the physico-chemical or, as we may call it, the Materialist view of man.

Now there is one account of mental process that is at once attractive to any philosopher sympathetic to a Materialist view of man: this is Behaviourism. Formulated originally by a psychologist, J.B. Watson, it attracted widespread interest and considerable support from scientifically oriented philosophers. Traditional philosophy had tended to think of the mind as a rather mysterious inward arena that lay behind, and was responsible for, the outward or physical behaviour of our bodies. Descartes thought of this inner arena as a *spiritual substance,* and it was this conception of the mind as spiritual object that Gilbert Ryle attacked, apparently in the interest of Behaviourism, in his important book *The Concept of Mind.* He ridiculed the Cartesian view as the dogma of "the ghost in the machine." The mind was not something behind the behaviour of the body, it was simply part of that physical behaviour. My anger with you is not some modification of a spiritual substance which somehow brings about aggressive behaviour; rather it is the aggressive behaviour itself: my addressing strong words to you, striking you, turning my back on you, and so on. Thought is not an inner process that lies behind, and brings about, the words I speak and write: it is my speaking and writing. The mind is not an inner arena, it is outward act.

It is clear that such a view of mind fits in very well with a completely Materialistic or Physicalist view of man. If there is no need to draw a distinction between mental processes and their expression in physical behaviour, but if instead the mental processes are identified with their so-called "expressions," then the existence of mind stands in no conflict with the view that man is nothing but a physico-chemical mechanism.

However, the version of Behaviourism that I have just sketched is a very crude version, and its crudity lays it open to obvious objections. One obvious difficulty is that it is our common experience that there can be mental processes going on although there is no behaviour occurring that could possibly be treated as expressions of these processes. A man may be angry, but give no bodily sign; he may think, but say or do nothing at all.

In my view, the most plausible attempt to refine Behaviourism with a view to meeting this objection was made by introducing the notion of *a disposition to behave.* (Dispositions to behave play a particularly important part in Ryle's account of the mind.) Let us consider the general notion of disposition first. Brittleness is a disposition, a disposition possessed by materials like glass. Brittle materials are those which, when subjected to relatively small forces, break

or shatter easily. But breaking and shattering easily is not brittleness, rather it is the *manifestation* of brittleness. Brittleness itself is the tendency or liability of the material to break or shatter easily. A piece of glass may never shatter or break throughout its whole history, but it is still the case that it is brittle: it is liable to shatter or break if dropped quite a small way or hit quite lightly. Now a disposition to *behave* is simply a tendency or liability of a person to behave in a certain way under certain circumstances. The brittleness of glass is a disposition that the glass retains throughout its history, but clearly there could also be dispositions that come and go. The dispositions to behave that are of interest to the Behaviourist are, for the most part, of this temporary character.

Now how did Ryle and others use the notion of a disposition to behave to meet the obvious objection to Behaviourism that there can be mental processes going on although the subject is engaging in no relevant behaviour? Their strategy was to argue that in such cases, although the subject was not behaving in any relevant way, he or she was *disposed* to behave in some relevant way. The glass does not shatter, but it is still brittle. The man does not behave, but he does have a disposition to behave. We can say he thinks although he does not speak or act because at that time he was disposed to speak or act in a certain way. *If* he had been asked, perhaps, he would have spoken or acted. We can say he is angry although he does not behave angrily, because he is disposed so to behave. *If* only one more word had been addressed to him, he would have burst out. And so on. In this way it was hoped that Behaviourism could be squared with the obvious facts.

It is very important to see just how these thinkers conceived of dispositions. I quote from Ryle:

To possess a dispositional property *is not to be in a particular state, or to undergo a particular change:* it is to be bound or liable to be in a particular state, or to undergo a particular change, when a particular condition is realised. *(The Concept of Mind,* p. 43, my italics.)

So to explain the breaking of a lightly struck glass on a particular occasion by saying it was brittle is, on this view of dispositions, simply to say that the glass broke because it is the sort of thing that regularly breaks when quite lightly struck. The breaking was the normal behaviour, or not abnormal behaviour, of such a thing. The brittleness is not to be conceived of as a *cause* for the breakage, or even, more vaguely, a *factor* in bringing about the breaking. Brittleness is just the fact that things of that sort break easily.

But although in this way the Behaviourists did something to deal with the objection that mental processes can occur in the absence of behaviour, it seems clear, now that the shouting and the dust have died, that they did not do enough. When I think, but my thoughts do not issue in any action, it seems as obvious as anything is obvious that there is something actually going on in me which constitutes my thought. It is not simply that I would speak or act if some conditions that are unfulfilled were to be fulfilled. Something is currently going on, in the strongest and most literal sense of "going on", and this something is my thought. Rylean Behaviourism denies this, and so it is unsatisfactory as a theory of mind. Yet I know of no version of Behaviourism that is more satisfactory. The moral for those of us who wish to take a purely physicalistic view of man is that we must look for some other account of the nature of mind and of mental processes.

But perhaps we need not grieve too deeply about the failure of Behaviourism to produce a satisfactory theory of mind. Behaviourism is a profoundly unnatural account of mental processes. If somebody speaks and acts in certain ways it is natural to speak of this speech and action as the *expression* of his thought. It is not at all natural to speak of his speech and action

as identical with his thought. We naturally think of the thought as something quite distinct from the speech and action which, under suitable circumstances, brings the speech and action about. Thoughts are not to be identified with behaviour, we think, they lie behind behaviour. A man's behaviour constitutes the *reason* we have for attributing certain mental processes to him, but the behaviour cannot be identified with the mental processes.

This suggests a very interesting line of thought about the mind. Behaviourism is certainly wrong, but perhaps it is not altogether wrong. Perhaps the Behaviourists are wrong in identifying the mind and mental occurrences with behaviour, but perhaps they are right in thinking that our notion of a mind and of individual mental states is *logically tied to behaviour.* For perhaps what we mean by a mental state is some state of the person which, under suitable circumstances, *brings about* a certain range of behaviour. Perhaps mind can be defined not as behaviour, but rather as the inner *cause* of certain behaviour. Thought is not speech under suitable circumstances, rather it is something within the person which, in suitable circumstances brings about speech. And, in fact, I believe that this is the true account, or, at any rate, a true first account, of what we mean by a mental state.

How does this line of thought link up with a purely physicalist view of man? The position is, I think, that while it does not make such a physicalist view inevitable, it does make it *possible.* It does not entail, but it is compatible with, a purely physicalist view of man. For if our notion of the mind and mental states is nothing but that of a cause within the person of certain ranges of behaviour, then it becomes a scientific question, and not a question of logical analysis, what in fact the intrinsic nature of that cause is. The cause might be, as Descartes thought it was, a spiritual substance working through the pineal gland to produce the complex bodily behaviour of which men are capable. It might be breath, or specially smooth and mobile atoms dispersed throughout the body; it might be many other things. But in fact the verdict of modern science seems to be that the sole cause of mind-betokening behaviour in man and the higher animals is the physico-chemical workings of the central nervous system. And so, assuming we have correctly characterised our concept of a mental state as nothing but the cause of certain sorts of behaviour, then we can identify these mental states with purely physical states of the central nervous system.

At this point we may stop and go back to the Behaviourists' dispositions. We saw that, according to them, the brittleness of glass or, to take another example, the elasticity of rubber, is not a state of the glass or the rubber, but is simply the fact that things of that sort behave in the way they do. But now let us consider how a scientist would think about brittleness or elasticity. Faced with the phenomenon of breakage under relatively small impacts, or the phenomenon of stretching when a force is applied followed by contraction when the force is removed, he will assume that there is some current *state* of the glass or the rubber which is responsible for the characteristic behaviour of samples of these two materials. At the beginning he will not know what this state is, but he will endeavour to find out, and he may succeed in finding out. And when he has found out he will very likely make remarks of this sort: "We have discovered that the brittleness of glass is in fact a certain sort of pattern in the molecules of the glass." That is to say, he will *identify* brittleness with the state of the glass that is responsible for the liability of the glass to break. For him, a disposition of an object is a state of the object. What makes the state a state of brittleness is the fact that it gives rise to the characteristic manifestations of brittleness. But the disposition itself is distinct from its manifestations: it is the state of the glass that gives rise to these manifestations in suitable circumstances.

You will see that this way of looking at dispositions is very different from that of Ryle and the Behaviourists. The great difference is this: If we treat dispositions as actual states, as I have suggested that scientists do, even if states whose intrinsic nature may yet have to be discovered, then we can say that dispositions are actual *causes,* or causal factors, which, in suitable circumstances, actually bring about those happenings which are the manifestations of the disposition. A certain molecular constitution of glass which constitutes its brittleness is actually *responsible* for the fact that, when the glass is struck, it breaks.

Now I shall not argue the matter here, because the detail of the argument is technical and difficult,[2] but I believe that the view of dispositions as states, which is the view that is natural to science, is the correct one. I believe it can be shown quite strictly that, to the extent that we admit the notion of dispositions at all, we are committed to the view that they are actual *states* of the object that has the disposition. I may add that I think that the same holds for the closely connected notions of capacities and powers. Here I will simply assume this step in my argument.

But perhaps it can be seen that the rejection of the idea that mind is simply a certain range of man's behaviour in favour of the view that mind is rather the inner *cause* of that range of man's behaviour is bound up with the rejection of the Rylean view of dispositions in favour of one that treats dispositions as states of objects and so as having actual causal power. The Behaviourists were wrong to identify the mind with behaviour. They were not so far off the mark when they tried to deal with cases where mental happenings occur in the absence of behaviour by saying that these are dispositions to behave. But in order to reach a correct view, I am suggesting, they would have to conceive of these dispositions as actual *states* of the person who has the disposition, states that have actual power to bring about behaviour in suitable circumstances. But to do this is to abandon the central inspiration of Behaviourism: that in talking about the mind we do not have to go behind outward behaviour to inner states.

And so two separate but interlocking lines of thought have pushed me in the same direction. The first line of thought is that it goes profoundly against the grain to think of the mind as behaviour. The mind is, rather, that which stands behind and brings about our complex behaviour. The second line of thought is that the Behaviourists' dispositions, properly conceived, are really states that underlie behaviour, and, under suitable circumstances, bring about behaviour. Putting these two together, we reach the conception of a mental state as *a state of the person apt for producing certain ranges of behaviour*. This formula: a mental state is a state of the person apt for producing certain ranges of behaviour, I believe to be a very illuminating way of looking at the concept of a mental state. I have found it very fruitful in the search for detailed logical analyses of the individual mental concepts.

Now, I do not think that Hegel's dialectic has much to tell us about the nature of reality. But I think that human thought often moves in a dialectical way, from thesis to antithesis and then to the synthesis. Perhaps thought about the mind is a case in point. I have already said that classical philosophy tended to think of the mind as an inner arena of some sort. This we may call the Thesis. Behaviourism moved to the opposite extreme: the mind was seen as outward behaviour. This is the Antithesis. My proposed Synthesis is that the mind is properly conceived as an inner principle, but a principle that is identified in terms of the outward behaviour it is apt for bringing about. This way of looking at the mind and mental states does not itself entail a Materialist or Physicalist view of man, for nothing is said in this analysis about the intrinsic nature of these mental states. But if we have, as I have asserted that we do have, general scientific grounds for thinking that man is

nothing but a physical mechanism, we can go on to argue that the mental states are in fact nothing but physical states of the central nervous system.

Along these lines, then, I would look for an account of the mind that is compatible with a purely Materialist theory of man. I have tried to carry out this programme in detail in *A Materialist Theory of the Mind*. There are, as may be imagined, all sorts of powerful objections that can be made to this view. But ... I propose to do only one thing. I will develop one very important objection to my view of the mind—an objection felt by many philosophers—and then try to show how the objection should be met.

The view that our notion of mind is nothing but that of an inner principle apt for bringing about certain sorts of behaviour may be thought to share a certain weakness with Behaviourism. Modern philosophers have put the point about Behaviourism by saying that although Behaviourism may be a satisfactory account of the mind from an *other-person point of view*, it will not do as a *first-person* account. To explain. In our encounters with other people, all we ever observe is their behaviour: their actions, their speech, and so on. And so, if we simply consider other people, Behaviourism might seem to do full justice to the facts. But the trouble about Behaviourism is that it seems so unsatisfactory as applied to our *own* case. In our own case, we seem to be aware of so much more than mere behaviour.

Suppose that now we conceive of the mind as an inner principle apt for bringing about certain sorts of behaviour. This again fits the other-person cases very well. Bodily behaviour of a very sophisticated sort is observed, quite different from the behaviour that ordinary physical objects display. It is inferred that this behaviour must spring from a very special sort of inner cause in the object that exhibits this behaviour. This inner cause is christened "the mind", and those who take a physicalist view of man argue that it is simply the central nervous system of the body observed. Compare this with the case of glass. Certain characteristic behaviour is observed: the breaking and shattering of the material when acted upon by relatively small forces. A special inner state of the glass is postulated to explain this behaviour. Those who take a purely physicalist view of glass then argue that this state is a *natural* state of the glass. It is, perhaps, an arrangement of its molecules, and not, say, the peculiarly malevolent disposition of the demons that dwell in glass.

But when we turn to our own case, the position may seem less plausible. We are conscious, we have experiences. Now can we say that to be conscious, to have experiences, is simply for something to go on within us apt for the causing of certain sorts of behaviour? Such an account does not seem to do any justice to the phenomena. And so it seems that our account of the mind, like Behaviourism, will fail to do justice to the first-person case.

In order to understand the objection better it may be helpful to consider a particular case. If you have driven for a very long distance without a break, you may have had experience of a curious state of automatism, which can occur in these conditions. One can suddenly "come to" and realise that one has driven for long distances without being aware of what one was doing, or, indeed, without being aware of anything. One has kept the car on the road, used the brake and the clutch perhaps, yet all without any awareness of what one was doing.

Now, if we consider this case it is obvious that *in some sense* mental processes are still going on when one is in such an automatic state. Unless one's will was still operating in some way, and unless one was still perceiving in some way, the car would not still be on the road. Yet, of course, *something* mental is lacking. Now, I think, when it is alleged that an account of mind as an inner principle apt for the production of certain sorts of behaviour leaves out

consciousness or experience, what is alleged to have been left out is just whatever is missing in the automatic driving case. It is conceded that an account of mental processes as states of the person apt for the production of certain sorts of behaviour may very possibly be adequate to deal with such cases as that of automatic driving. It may be adequate to deal with most of the mental processes of animals, who perhaps spend a good deal of their lives in this state of automatism. But, it is contended, it cannot deal with the consciousness that we normally enjoy.

I will now try to sketch an answer to this important and powerful objection. Let us begin in an apparently unlikely place, and consider the way that an account of mental processes of the sort I am giving would deal with *sense-perception.*

Now psychologists, in particular, have long realised that there is a very close logical tie between sense-perception and *selective behaviour.* Suppose we want to decide whether an animal can perceive the difference between red and green. We might give the animal a choice between two pathways, over one of which a red light shines and over the other of which a green light shines. If the animal happens by chance to choose the green pathway we reward it; if it happens to choose the other pathway we do not reward it. If, after some trials, the animal systematically takes the green-lighted pathway, and if we become assured that the only relevant differences in the two pathways are the differences in the colour of the lights, we are entitled to say that the animal can see this colour difference. Using its eyes, it selects between red-lighted and green-lighted pathways. So we say it can see the difference between red and green.

Now a Behaviourist would be tempted to say that the animal's regularly selecting the green-lighted pathway *was* its perception of the colour difference. But this is unsatisfactory, because we all want to say that perception is something that goes on within the person or animal—within its mind—although, of course, this mental event is normally *caused* by the operation of the environment upon the organism. Suppose, however, that we speak instead of capacities for selective behaviour towards the current environment, and suppose we think of these capacities, like dispositions, as actual inner states of the organism. We can then think of the animal's perception as a state within the animal apt, if the animal is so impelled, for selective behaviour between the red- and green-lighted pathways.

In general, we can think of perceptions as inner states or events apt for the production of certain sorts of selective behaviour towards our environment. To perceive is like acquiring a key to a door. You do not have to use the key: you can put it in your pocket and never bother about the door. But if you do want to open the door the key may be essential. The blind man is a man who does not acquire certain keys, and, as a result, is not able to operate in his environment in the way that somebody who has his sight can operate. It seems, then, a very promising view to take of perceptions that they are inner states defined by the sorts of selective behaviour that they enable the perceiver to exhibit, if so impelled.

Now how is this discussion of perception related to the question of consciousness of experience, the sort of thing that the driver who is in a state of automatism has not got, but which we normally do have? Simply this. My proposal is that consciousness, in this sense of the word, is nothing but *perception or awareness of the state of our own mind.* The driver in a state of automatism perceives, or is aware of, the road. If he did not, the car would be in a ditch. But he is not currently aware of his awareness of the road. He perceives the road, but he does not perceive his perceiving, or anything else that is going on in his mind. He is not, as we normally are, conscious of what is going on in his mind.

And so I conceive of consciousness or experience, in this sense of the words, in the way

that Locke and Kant conceived it, as like perception. Kant, in a striking phrase, spoke of "inner sense". We cannot directly observe the minds of others, but each of us has the power to observe directly our own minds, and "perceive" what is going on there. The driver in the automatic state is one whose "inner eye" is shut: who is not currently aware of what is going on in his own mind.

Now if this account is along the right lines, why should we not give an account of this inner observation along the same lines as we have already given of perception? Why should we not conceive of it as an inner state, a state in this case directed towards other inner states and not to the environment, which enables us, if we are so impelled, to behave in a selective way *towards our own states of mind?* One who is aware, or conscious, of his thoughts or his emotions is one who has the capacity to make discriminations between his different mental states. His capacity might be exhibited in words. He might say that he was in an angry state of mind when, and only when, he *was* in an angry state of mind. But such verbal behaviour would be the mere *expression* or *result* of the awareness. The awareness itself would be an inner state: the sort of inner state that gave the man a capacity for such behavioural expressions.

So I have argued that consciousness of our own mental state may be assimilated to *perception* of our own mental state, and that, like other perceptions, it may then be conceived of as an inner state or event giving a capacity for selective behaviour, in this case selective behaviour towards our own mental state. All this is meant to be simply a logical analysis of consciousness, and none of it entails, although it does not rule out, a purely physicalist account of what these inner states are. But if we are convinced, on general scientific grounds, that a purely physical account of man is likely to be the true one, then there seems to be no bar to our identifying these inner states with purely physical states of the central nervous system.

And so consciousness of our own mental state becomes simply the scanning of one part of our central nervous system by another. Consciousness is a self-scanning mechanism in the central nervous system.

As I have emphasised before, I have done no more than sketch a programme for a philosophy of mind. There are all sorts of expansions and elucidations to be made, and all sorts of doubts and difficulties to be stated and over-come. But I hope I have done enough to show that a purely physicalist theory of the mind is an exciting and plausible intellectual option.

NOTES

1. Inaugural lecture of the Challis Professor of Philosophy at the University of Sydney (1965); slightly amended (1968).
2. It is presented in my book *A Materialist Theory of the Mind* (1968) ch. 6, sec. VI.

J.J.C. Smart
"Sensations and Brain Processes"

This paper[1] takes its departure from arguments to be found in U.T. Place's "Is Consciousness a Brain Process?"[2] I have had the benefit of discussing Place's thesis in a good many universities in the United States and Australia, and I hope that the present paper answers objections to his thesis which Place has not considered and that it presents his thesis in a more nearly unobjectionable form. This paper is meant also to supplement the paper "The 'Mental' and the 'Physical,'" by H. Feigl,[3] which in part argues for a similar thesis to Place's.

Suppose that I report that I have at this moment a roundish, blurry-edged after-image which is yellowish towards its edge and is orange towards its center. What is it that I am reporting? One answer to this question might be that I am not reporting anything, that when I say that it looks to me as though there is a roundish yellowy-orange patch of light on the wall I am expressing some sort of *temptation*, the temptation to say that there is a roundish yellowy-orange patch on the wall (though I may know that there is not such a patch on the wall). This is perhaps Wittgenstein's view in the *Philosophical Investigations* (see §§ 367, 370). Similarly, when I "report" a pain, I am not re-ally reporting anything (or, if you like, I am reporting in a queer sense of "reporting"), but am doing a sophisticated sort of wince. (See § 244: "The verbal expression of pain replaces crying and does not describe it." Nor does it describe anything else?)[4] I prefer most of the time to discuss an after-image rather than a pain, because the word "pain" brings in something which is irrelevant to my purpose: the notion of "distress." I think that "he is in pain" entails "he is in distress," that is, that he is in a certain agitation-condition.[5] Similarly, to say "I am in pain" may be to do more than "replace pain behavior": it may be partly to report something, though this something is quite non-mysterious, being an agitation-condition, and so susceptible of behavioristic analysis. The suggestion I wish if possible to avoid is a different one, namely that "I am in pain" is a genuine report, and that what it reports is an irreducibly psychical something. And similarly the suggestion I wish to resist is also that to say "I have a yellowish-orange after-image" is to report something irreducibly psychical.

Why do I wish to resist this suggestion? Mainly because of Occam's razor. It seems to me that science is increasingly giving us a viewpoint whereby organisms are able to be seen as physico-chemical mechanisms:[6] it seems that even the behavior of man himself will one day be explicable in mechanistic terms. There does seem to be, so far as science is concerned, nothing in the world but increasingly complex arrangements of physical constituents. All except for one place: in consciousness. That is, for a full description of what is going on in a man you would have to mention not only the physical processes in his tissues, glands, nervous system, and so forth, but also his states of consciousness: his visual, auditory, and tactual sensations, his aches and pains. That these should be *correlated* with brain processes does not help, for to say that they are *correlated* is to say that they are something "over and above." You cannot correlate something with itself. You correlate footprints with burglars, but not Bill Sikes the burglar with Bill Sikes the burglar. So sensations, states of consciousness, do seem to be the one sort of thing left outside the physicalist picture, and for various reasons I just cannot believe that this can be so. That everything should be explicable in terms of physics (together of course with descriptions of the ways in which the parts are put together—roughly, biology is to physics as radio-engineering is to electromagnetism) except the occurrence of sensations seems to me to be frankly unbelievable. Such sensations would be "nomological danglers," to use Feigl's expression.[7] It is not often realized how odd would be the laws whereby these nomological danglers would dangle. It is sometimes asked, "Why can't there be psychophysical laws which are of a novel sort, just as the laws of electricity and magnetism were novelties from the standpoint of Newtonian mechanics?" Certainly we are pretty sure in the future to come across new ultimate laws of a novel type, but I expect them to relate simple constituents: for example, whatever ultimate particles are then in vogue. I cannot believe that ultimate laws of nature could relate simple constituents to configurations consisting of perhaps billions of neurons (and goodness knows how many billion billions of ultimate particles) all put together for all the world as though their main purpose in life was to be a negative feedback mechanism of a complicated sort. Such ultimate laws would be like nothing so far known in science. They have a queer "smell" to them. I am just unable to believe in the nomological danglers themselves, or in the laws whereby they would dangle. If any philosophical arguments seemed to compel us to believe in such things, I would suspect a catch in the argument. In any case it is the object of this paper to show that there are no philosophical arguments which compel us to be dualists.

The above is largely a confession of faith, but it explains why I find Wittgenstein's position (as I construe it) so congenial. For on this view there are, in a sense, no sensations. A man is a vast arrangement of physical particles, but there are not, over and above this, sensations or states of consciousness. There are just behavioral facts about this vast mechanism, such as that it expresses a temptation (behavior disposition) to say "there is a yellowish-red patch on the wall" or that it goes through a sophisticated sort of wince, that is, says "I am in pain." Admittedly Wittgenstein says that though the sensation "is not a something," it is nevertheless "not a nothing either" (§ 304), but this need only mean that the word "ache" has a use. An ache is a thing, but only in the innocuous sense in which the plain man, in the first paragraph of Frege's *Foundations of Arithmetic,* answers the question "What is the number one?" by "a thing." It should be noted that when I assert that to say "I have a yellowish-orange after-image" is to express a temptation to assert the physical-object statement "There is a yellowish-orange patch on the wall," I mean that saying "I have a yellowish-orange after-image" is (partly) the exercise of the disposition[8] which is the temptation. It is not to *report* that I have the temptation, any more than is "I love you" normally a report that I love someone. Saying "I love you" is just part of the behavior which is the exercise of the disposition of loving someone.

Though for the reasons given above, I am very receptive to the above "expressive" account of sensation statements, I do not feel that it will quite do the trick. Maybe this is because I have not thought it out sufficiently, but it does seem to me as though, when a person says "I have an after-image," he is making a genuine report. and that when he says "I have a pain," he is doing more than "replace pain-behavior," and that "this more" is not just to say that he is in distress. I am not so sure, however, that to admit this is to admit that there are nonphysical correlates of brain processes. Why should not sensations just be brain processes of a certain sort? There are, of course, well-known (as well as lesser-known) philosophical objections to the view that reports of sensations are reports of brain-processes, but I shall try to argue that these arguments are by no means as cogent as is commonly thought to be the case.

Let me first try to state more accurately the thesis that sensations are brain-processes. It is not the thesis that, for example, "after-image" or "ache" means the same as "brain process of sort X" (where "X" is replaced by a description of a certain sort of brain process). It is that, in so far as "after-image" or "ache" is a report of a process, it is a report of a process that *happens to be* a brain process. It follows that the thesis does not claim that sensation statements can be *translated* into statements about brain processes.[9] Nor does it claim that the logic of a sensation statement is the same as that of a brain-process statement. All it claims is that in so far as a sensation statement is a report of something, that something is in fact a brain process. Sensations are nothing over and above brain processes. Nations are nothing "over and above" citizens, but this does not prevent the logic of nation statements being very different from the logic of citizen statements, nor does it insure the translatability of nation statements into citizen statements. (I do not, however, wish to assert that the relation of sensation statements to brain-process statements is very like that of nation statements to citizen statements. Nations do not just *happen to be* nothing over and above citizens, for example. I bring in the "nations" example merely to make a negative point: that the fact that the logic of A-statements is different from that of B-statements does not insure that A's are anything over and above B's.)

Remarks on Identity

When I say that a sensation is a brain process or that lightning is an electric discharge, I am using "is" in the sense of strict identity. (Just as in the—in this case necessary—proposition "7 is identical with the smallest prime number greater than 5.") When I say that a sensation is a brain process or that lightning is an electric discharge I do not mean just that the sensation is somehow spatially or temporally continuous with the brain process or that the lightning is just spatially or temporally continuous with the discharge. When on the other hand I say that the successful general is the same person as the small boy who stole the apples I mean only that the successful general I see before me is a time slice[10] of the same four-dimensional object of which the small boy stealing apples is an earlier time slice. However, the four-dimensional object which has the general-I-see-before-me for its late time slice is identical in the strict sense with the four-dimensional object which has the small-boy-stealing-apples for an early time slice. I distinguish these two senses of "is identical with" because I wish to make it clear that the brain-process doctrine asserts identity in the *strict* sense.

I shall now discuss various possible objections to the view that the processes reported in sensation statements are in fact processes in the brain. Most of us have met some of these objections in our first year as philosophy students. All the more reason to take a good look at them. Others of the objections will be more recondite and subtle.

Objection 1. Any illiterate peasant can talk perfectly well about his after-images, or how things look or feel to him, or about his aches and pains, and yet he may know nothing whatever about neurophysiology. A man may, like Aristotle, believe that the brain is an organ for cooling the body without any impairment of his ability to make true statements about his sensations. Hence the things we are talking about when we describe our sensations cannot be processes in the brain.

Reply. You might as well say that a nation of slugabeds, who never saw the Morning Star or knew of its existence, or who had never thought of the expression "the Morning Star," but who used the expression "the Evening Star" perfectly well, could not use this expression to refer to the same entity as we refer to (and describe as) "the Morning Star."[11]

You may object that the Morning Star is in a sense not the very same thing as the Evening Star, but only something spatiotemporally continuous with it. That is, you may say that the Morning Star is not the Evening Star in the strict sense of "identity" that I distinguished earlier.

There is, however, a more plausible example. Consider lightning.[12] Modern physical science tells us that lightning is a certain kind of electrical discharge due to ionization of clouds of water vapor in the atmosphere. This, it is now believed, is what the true nature of lightning is. Note that there are not two things: a flash of lightning and an electrical discharge. There is one thing, a flash of lightning, which is described scientifically as an electrical discharge to the earth from a cloud of ionized water molecules. The case is not at all like that of explaining a footprint by reference to a burglar. We say that what lightning really is, what its true nature as revealed by science is, is an electrical discharge. (It is not the true nature of a footprint to be a burglar.)

To forestall irrelevant objections, I should like to make it clear that by "lightning" I mean the publicly observable physical object, light-

ning, not a visual sense-datum of lightning. I say that the publicly observable physical object lightning is in fact the electrical discharge, not just a correlate of it. The sense-datum, or rather the having of the sense-datum, the "look" of lightning, may well in my view be a correlate of the electrical discharge. For in my view it is a brain state *caused* by the lightning. But we should no more confuse sensations of lightning with lightning than we confuse sensations of a table with the table.

In short, the reply to Objection 1 is that there can be contingent statements of the form "A is identical with B," and a person may well know that something is an A without knowing that it is a B. An illiterate peasant might well be able to talk about his sensations without knowing about his brain processes, just as he can talk about lightning though he knows nothing of electricity.

Objection 2. It is only a contingent fact (if it is a fact) that when we have a certain kind of sensation there is a certain kind of process in our brain. Indeed it is possible, though perhaps in the highest degree unlikely, that our present physiological theories will be as out of date as the ancient theory connecting mental processes with goings on in the heart. It follows that when we report a sensation we are not reporting a brain-process.

Reply. The objection certainly proves that when we say "I have an after-image" we cannot *mean* something of the form "I have such and such a brain-process." But this does not show that what we report (having an after-image) is not *in fact* a brain process. "I see lightning" does not *mean* "I see an electrical discharge." Indeed, it is logically possible (though highly unlikely) that the electrical discharge account of lightning might one day be given up. Again, "I see the Evening Star" does not *mean* the same as "I see the Morning Star," and yet "The Evening Star and the Morning Star are one and the same thing" is a contingent proposition. Possibly Objection 2 derives some of its apparent strength from a "Fido"-Fido theory of meaning. If the meaning of an expression were what the expression named, then of course it *would* follow from the fact that "sensation" and "brain-process" have different meanings that they cannot name one and the same thing.

Objection 3.[13] Even if Objections 1 and 2 do not prove that sensations are something over and above brain-processes, they do prove that the qualities of sensations are something over and above the qualities of brain-processes. That is, it may be possible to get out of asserting the existence of irreducibly psychic processes, but not out of asserting the existence of irreducibly psychic *properties*. For suppose we identify the Morning Star with the Evening Star. Then there must be some properties which logically imply that of being the Morning Star, and quite distinct properties which entail that of being the Evening Star. Again, there must be some properties (for example, that of being a yellow flash) which are logically distinct from those in the physicalist story.

Indeed, it might be thought that the objection succeeds at one jump. For consider the property of "being a yellow flash." It might seem that this property lies inevitably outside the physicalist framework within which I am trying to work (either by "yellow" being an objective emergent property of physical objects, or else by being a power to produce yellow sense-data, where "yellow," in this second instantiation of the word, refers to a purely phenomenal or introspectible quality). I must therefore digress for a moment and indicate how I deal with secondary qualities. I shall concentrate on color.

First of all, let me introduce the concept of a normal percipient. One person is more a normal percipient than another if he can make color discriminations that the other cannot. For example, if A can pick a lettuce leaf out of a heap of cabbage leaves, whereas B cannot though he can pick a lettuce leaf out of a heap of beetroot leaves, then A is more normal than B. (I am assuming that A and B are not given

time to distinguish the leaves by their slight difference in shape, and so forth.) From the concept of "more normal than" it is easy to see how we can introduce the concept of "normal." Of course, Eskimos may make the finest discriminations at the blue end of the spectrum, Hottentots at the red end. In this case the concept of a normal percipient is a slightly idealized one, rather like that of "the mean sun" in astronomical chronology. There is no need to go into such subtleties now. I say that "This is red" means something roughly like "A normal percipient would not easily pick this out of a clump of geranium petals though he would pick it out of a clump of lettuce leaves." Of course it does not exactly mean this: a person might know the meaning of "red" without knowing anything about geraniums, or even about normal percipients. But the point is that a person can be *trained* to say "This is red" of objects which would not easily be picked out of geranium petals by a normal percipient, and so on. (Note that even a color-blind person can reasonably assert that something is red, though of course he needs to use another human being, not just himself, as his "color meter.") This account of secondary qualities explains their unimportance in physics. For obviously the discriminations and lack of discriminations made by a very complex neurophysiological mechanism are hardly likely to correspond to simple and nonarbitrary distinctions in nature.

I therefore elucidate colors as powers, in Locke's sense, to evoke certain sorts of discriminatory responses in human beings. They are also, of course, powers to cause sensations in human beings (an account still nearer Locke's). But these sensations, I am arguing, are identifiable with brain processes.

Now how do I get over the objection that a sensation can be identified with a brain process only if it has some phenomenal property, not possessed by brain processes, whereby one-half of the identification may be, so to speak, pinned down?

Reply. My suggestion is as follows. When a person says, "I see a yellowish-orange after-image," he is saying something like this: *"There is something going on which is like what is going on when* I have my eyes open, am awake, and there is an orange illuminated in good light in front of me, that is, when I really see an orange." (And there is no reason why a person should not say the same thing when he is having a veridical sense-datum, so long as we construe "like" in the last sentence in such a sense that something can be like itself.) Notice that the italicized words, namely "there is something going on which is like what is going on when," are all quasilogical or topic-neutral words. This explains why the ancient Greek peasant's reports about his sensations can be neutral between dualistic metaphysics or my materialistic metaphysics. It explains how sensations can be brain-processes and yet how a man who reports them need know nothing about brain-processes. For he reports them only very abstractly as "something going on which is like what is going on when…" Similarly, a person may say "someone is in the room," thus reporting truly that the doctor is in the room, even though he has never heard of doctors. (There are not two people in the room: "someone" *and* the doctor.) This account of sensation statements also explains the singular elusiveness of "raw feels"—why no one seems to be able to pin any properties on them.[14] Raw feels, in my view, are colorless for the very same reason that *something* is colorless. This does not mean that sensations do not have plenty of properties, for if they are brain-processes they certainly have lots of neurological properties. It only means that in speaking of them as being like or unlike one another we need not know or mention these properties.

This, then, is how I would reply to Objection 3. The strength of my reply depends on the possibility of our being able to report that one thing is like another without being able to state the respect in which it is like. I do not see why this should not be so. If we think cyber-

netically about the nervous system we can envisage it as able to respond to certain likenesses of its internal processes without being able to do more. It would be easier to build a machine which would tell us, say on a punched tape, whether or not two objects were similar, than it would be to build a machine which would report wherein the similarities consisted.

Objection 4. The after-image is not in physical space. The brain-process is. So the after-image is not a brain-process.

Reply. This is an *ignoratio elenchi.* I am not arguing that the after-image is a brain-process, but that the experience of having an after-image is a brain-process. It is the *experience* which is reported in the introspective report. Similarly, if it is objected that the after-image is yellowy-orange, my reply is that it is the experience of seeing yellowy-orange that is being described, and this experience is not a yellowy-orange something. So to say that a brain-process cannot be yellowy-orange is not to say that a brain-process cannot in fact be the experience of having a yellowy-orange after-image. There is, in a sense, no such thing as an after-image or a sense-datum, though there is such a thing as the experience of having an image, and this experience is described indirectly in material object language, not in phenomenal language, for there is no such thing.[15] We describe the experience by saying, in effect, that it is like the experience we have when, for example, we really see a yellow-orange patch on the wall. Trees and wallpaper can be green, but not the experience of seeing or imagining a tree or wallpaper. (Or if they are described as green or yellow this can only be in a derived sense.)

Objection 5. It would make sense to say of a molecular movement in the brain that it is swift or slow, straight or circular, but it makes no sense to say this of the experience of seeing something yellow.

Reply. So far we have not given sense to talk of experiences as swift or slow, straight or circular. But I am not claiming that "experience" and "brain-process" mean the same or even that they have the same logic. "Somebody" and "the doctor" do not have the same logic, but this does not lead us to suppose that talking about somebody telephoning is talking about someone over and above, say, the doctor. The ordinary man when he reports an experience is reporting that something is going on, but he leaves it open as to what sort of thing is going on, whether in a material solid medium or perhaps in some sort of gaseous medium, or even perhaps in some sort of nonspatial medium (if this makes sense). All that I am saying is that "experience" and "brain-process" may in fact refer to the same thing, and if so we may easily adopt a convention (which is not a change in our present rules for the use of experience words but an addition to them) whereby it would make sense to talk of an experience in terms appropriate to physical processes.

Objection 6. Sensations are private, brain processes are *public*. If I sincerely say, "I see a yellowish-orange after-image," and I am not making a verbal mistake, then I cannot be wrong. But I can be wrong about a brain-process. The scientist looking into my brain might be having an illusion. Moreover, it makes sense to say that two or more people are observing the same brain-process but not that two or more people are reporting the same inner experience.

Reply. This shows that the language of introspective reports has a different logic from the language of material processes. It is obvious that until the brain-process theory is much improved and widely accepted there will be no *criteria* for saying "Smith has an experience of such-and-such a sort" *except* Smith's introspective reports. So we have adopted a rule of language that (normally) what Smith says goes.

Objection 7. I can imagine myself turned to stone and yet having images, aches, pains, and so on.

Reply. I can imagine that the electrical theory of lightning is false, that lightning is some sort of purely optical phenomenon. I can imagine that lightning is not an electrical discharge. I can imagine that the Evening Star is not the Morning Star. But it is. All the objection shows is that "experience" and "brain-process" do not have the same meaning. It does not show that an experience is not in fact a brain process.

This objection is perhaps much the same as one which can be summed up by the slogan: "What can be composed of nothing cannot be composed of anything."[16] The argument goes as follows: on the brain-process thesis the identity between the brain-process and the experience is a contingent one. So it is logically possible that there should be no brain-process, and no process of any other sort either (no heart process, no kidney process, no liver process). There would be the experience but no "corresponding" physiological process with which we might be able to identify it empirically.

I suspect that the objector is thinking of the experience as a ghostly entity. So it is composed of something, not of nothing, after all. On his view it is composed of ghost stuff, and on mine it is composed of brain stuff. Perhaps the counter-reply will be[17] that the experience is simple and uncompounded, and so it is not composed of anything after all. This seems to be a quibble, for, if it were taken seriously, the remark "What can be composed of nothing cannot be composed of anything" could be recast as an a priori argument against Democritus and atomism and for Descartes and infinite divisibility. And it seems odd that a question of this sort could be settled a priori. We must therefore construe the word "composed" in a very weak sense, which would allow us to say that even an indivisible atom is composed of something (namely, itself). The dualist cannot really say that an experience can be composed of nothing. For he holds that experiences are something over and above material processes, that is, that they are a sort of ghost stuff. (Or perhaps ripples in an underlying ghost stuff.) I say that the dualist's hypothesis is a perfectly intelligible one. But I say that experiences are not to be identified with ghost stuff but with brain stuff. This is another hypothesis, and in my view a very plausible one. The present argument cannot knock it down a priori.

Objection 8. The "beetle in the box" objection (see Wittgenstein, *Philosophical Investigations*, § 293). How could descriptions of experiences, if these are genuine reports, get a foothold in language? For any rule of language must have public criteria for its correct application.

Reply. The change from describing how things are to describing how we feel is just a change from uninhibitedly saying "this is so" to saying "this looks so." That is, when the naive person might be tempted to say, "There is a patch of light on the wall which moves whenever I move my eyes" or "A pin is being stuck into me," we have learned how to resist this temptation and say "It *looks as though* there is a patch of light on the wallpaper" or "It *feels as though* someone were sticking a pin into me." The introspective account tells us about the individual's state of consciousness in the same way as does "I see a patch of light" or "I feel a pin being stuck into me": it differs from the corresponding perception statement in so far as it withdraws any claim about what is actually going on in the external world. From the point of view of the psychologist, the change from talking about the environment to talking about one's perceptual sensations is simply a matter of disinhibiting certain reactions. These are reactions which one normally suppresses because one has learned that in the prevailing circumstances they are unlikely to provide a good indication of the state of the environment.[18] To say that something looks green to me is simply to say that my experience is like the experience I get when I see something that really is green. In my reply to Objection 3, I pointed out the extreme openness or generality of statements which report experiences. This explains why there is no language of private qualities. (Just

as "someone," unlike "the doctor," is a colorless word.)[19]

If it is asked what is the difference between those brain processes which, in my view, are experiences and those brain processes which are not, I can only reply that it is at present unknown. I have been tempted to conjecture that the difference may in part be that between perception and reception (in D.M. MacKay's terminology) and that the type of brain process which is an experience might be identifiable with MacKay's active "matching response."[20] This, however, cannot be the whole story, because sometimes I can perceive something unconsciously, as when I take a handkerchief out of a drawer without being aware that I am doing so. But at the very least, we can classify the brain processes which are experiences as those brain processes which are, or might have been, causal conditions of those pieces of verbal behavior which we call reports of immediate experience.

I have now considered a number of objections to the brain-process thesis. I wish now to conclude with some remarks on the logical status of the thesis itself. U.T. Place seems to hold that it is a straight-out scientific hypothesis.[21] If so, he is partly right and partly wrong. If the issue is between (say) a brain-process thesis and a heart thesis, or a liver thesis, or a kidney thesis, then the issue is a purely empirical one, and the verdict is overwhelmingly in favor of the brain. The right sorts of things don't go on in the heart, liver, or kidney, nor do these organs possess the right sort of complexity of structure. On the other hand, if the issue is between a brain-or-liver-or-kidney thesis (that is, some form of materialism) on the one hand and epiphenomenalism on the other hand, then the issue is not an empirical one. For there is no conceivable experiment which could decide between materialism and epiphenomenalism. This latter issue is not like the average straight-out empirical issue in science, but like the issue between the nineteenth-century English naturalist Philip Gosse[22] and the orthodox geologists and paleontologists of his day. According to Gosse, the earth was created about 4000 B.C. exactly as described in *Genesis,* with twisted rock strata, "evidence" of erosion, and so forth, and all sorts of fossils, all in their appropriate strata, just as if the usual evolutionist story had been true. Clearly this theory is in a sense irrefutable: no evidence can possibly tell against it. Let us ignore the theological setting in which Philip Gosse's hypothesis had been placed, thus ruling out objections of a theological kind, such as "what a queer God who would go to such elaborate lengths to deceive us." Let us suppose that it is held that the universe just *began* in 4004 B.C. with the initial conditions just everywhere as they were in 4004 B.C., and in particular that our own planet began with sediment in the rivers, eroded cliffs, fossils in the rocks, and so on. No scientist would ever entertain this as a serious hypothesis, consistent though it is with all possible evidence. The hypothesis offends against the principles of parsimony and simplicity. There would be far too many brute and inexplicable facts. Why are pterodactyl bones just as they are? No explanation in terms of the evolution of pterodactyls from earlier forms of life would any longer be possible. We would have millions of facts about the world as it was in 4004 B.C. that just have to be *accepted.*

The issue between the brain-process theory and epiphenomenalism seems to be of the above sort. (Assuming that a behavioristic reduction of introspective reports is not possible.) If it be agreed that there are no cogent philosophical arguments which force us into accepting dualism, and if the brain process theory and dualism are equally consistent with the facts, then the principles of parsimony and simplicity seem to me to decide overwhelmingly in favor of the brain-process theory. As I pointed out earlier, dualism involves a large number of irreducible psycho-physical laws (whereby the "nomological danglers" dangle) of a queer sort, that just have to be taken on trust, and are just

as difficult to swallow as the irreducible facts about the paleontology of the earth with which we are faced on Philip Gosse's theory.

NOTES

1 This is a very slightly revised version of a paper which was first published in the *Philosophical Review,* LXVIII (1959), 141–56. Since that date there have been criticisms of my paper by J.T. Stevenson, *Philosophical Review,* LXIX (1960), 505–10, to which I have replied in *Philosophical Review,* LXX (1961), 406–7, and by G. Pitcher and by W.D. Joske, *Australasian Journal of Philosophy,* XXXVIII (1960), 150–60, to which I have replied in the same volume of that journal, pp. 252–54.

2 *British Journal of Psychology,* XLVII (1956), 44–50 …

3 *Minnesota Studies in the Philosophy of Science,* Vol. II (Minneapolis: University of Minnesota Press, 1958), pp. 370–497.

4 Some philosophers of my acquaintance, who have the advantage over me in having known Wittgenstein, would say that this interpretation of him is too behavioristic. However, it seems to me a very natural interpretation of his printed words, and whether or not it is Wittgenstein's real view it is certainly an interesting and important one. I wish to consider it here as a possible rival both to the "brain-process" thesis and to straight-out old-fashioned dualism.

5 See Ryle, *The Concept of Mind* (London: Hutchinson's University Library, 1949), p. 93.

6 On this point see Paul Oppenheim and Hilary Putnam, "Unity of Science as a Working Hypothesis," in *Minnesota Studies in the Philosophy of Science,* Vol. II (Minneapolis: University of Minnesota Press, 1958), pp. 3–36.

7 Feigl, *op. cit.,* p. 428. Feigl uses the expression "nomological danglers" for the laws

whereby the entities dangle: I have used the expression to refer to the dangling entities themselves.

8 Wittgenstein did not like the word "disposition." I am using it to put in a nutshell (and perhaps inaccurately) the view which I am attributing to Wittgenstein. I should like to repeat that I do not wish to claim that my interpretation of Wittgenstein is correct. Some of those who knew him do not interpret him in this way. It is merely a view which I find myself extracting from his printed words and which I think is important and worth discussing for its own sake.

9 See Place, *op. cit.*, p. 102, and Feigl, *op. cit.*, p. 390, near top.

10 See J.H. Woodger, *Theory Construction*, International Encyclopedia of Unified Science, II, No. 5 (Chicago: University of Chicago Press, 1939), 38. I here permit myself to speak loosely. For warnings against possible ways of going wrong with this sort of talk, see my note "Spatialising Time," *Mind*, LXIV (1955), 239–41.

11 Cf. Feigl, *op. cit.*, p. 439.

12 See Place, *op. cit.*, p. 106; also Feigl, *op. cit.*, p. 438.

13 I think this objection was first put to me by Professor Max Black. I think it is the most subtle of any of those I have considered, and the one which I am least confident of having satisfactorily met.

14 See B.A. Farrell, "Experience," *Mind*, LIX (1950), 170–98 …

15 Dr. J.R. Smythies claims that a sense-datum language could be taught independently of the material object language ("A Note on the Fallacy of the 'Phenomenological Fallacy'," *British Journal of Psychology*, XLVIII [1957], 141–44). I am not so

sure of this: there must be some public criteria for a person having got a rule wrong before we can teach him the rule. I suppose someone might *accidentally* learn color words by Dr. Smythies' procedure. I am not, of course, denying that we can learn a sense-datum language in the sense that we can learn to report our experience. Nor would Place deny it.

16 I owe this objection to Dr. C.B. Martin. I gather that he no longer wishes to maintain this objection, at any rate in its present form.

17 Martin did not make this reply, but one of his students did.

18 I owe this point to Place, in correspondence.

19 The "beetle in the box" objection is, *if it is sound*, an objection to *any* view, and in particular the Cartesian one, that introspective reports are genuine reports. So it is no objection to a weaker thesis that I would be concerned to uphold, namely, that if introspective reports of "experiences" are genuinely reports, then the things they are reports of are in fact brain processes.

20 See his article "Towards an Information-Flow Model of Human Behaviour," *British Journal of Psychology*, XLVII (1956), 30–43.

21 *Op. cit.* For a further discussion of this, in reply to the original version of the present paper, see Place's note "Materialism as a Scientific Hypothesis," *Philosophical Review*, LXIX (1960), 101–4.

22 See the entertaining account of Gosse's book *Omphalos* by Martin Gardner in *Fads and Fallacies in the Name of Science*, 2nd ed. (New York: Dover, 1957), pp. 124–27.

Saul Kripke
Selections from "Identity and Necessity"

In recent philosophy a large number of other identity statements have been emphasized as examples of contingent identity statements, different, perhaps, from either of the types I have mentioned before. One of them is, for example, the statement "Heat is the motion of molecules." First, science is supposed to have discovered this. Empirical scientists in their investigations have been supposed to discover (and, I suppose, they did) that the external phenomenon which we call "heat" is, in fact, molecular agitation. Another example of such a discovery is that water is H_2O, and yet other examples are that gold is the element with such and such an atomic number, that light is a stream of photons, and so on. These are all in some sense of "identity statement" identity statements. Second, it is thought, they are plainly contingent identity statements, just because they were scientific discoveries. After all, heat might have turned out not to have been the motion of molecules. There were other alternative theories of heat proposed, for example, the caloric theory of heat. If these theories of heat had been correct, then heat would not have been the motion of molecules, but instead, some substance suffusing the hot object, called "caloric." And it was a matter of course of science and not of any logical necessity that the one theory turned out to be correct and the other theory turned out to be incorrect.

So, here again, we have, apparently, another plain example of a contingent identity statement. This has been supposed to be a very important example because of its connection with the mind-body problem. There have been many philosophers who have wanted to be materialists, and to be materialists in a particular form, which is known today as "the identity theory."

According to this theory, a certain mental state, such as a person's being in pain, is identical with a certain state of his brain (or, perhaps, of his entire body, according to some theorists), at any rate, a certain material or neural state of his brain or body. And so, according to this theory, my being in pain at this instant, if I were, would be identical with my body's being or my brain's being in a certain state. Others have objected that this cannot be because, after all, we can imagine my pain existing even if the state of the body did not. We can perhaps imagine my not being embodied at all and still being in pain, or, conversely, we could imagine my body existing and being in the very same state even if there were no pain. In fact, conceivably, it could be in this state even though there were no mind 'back of it', so to speak, at all. The usual reply has been to concede that all of these things might have been the case, but to argue that these are irrelevant to the question of the identity of the mental state and the physical state. This identity, it is said, is just another contingent scientific identification, similar to the identification of heat with molecular motion, or water with H_2O. Just as we can imagine heat without any molecular motion, so we can imagine a mental state without any corresponding brain state. But, just as the first fact is not damaging to the identification of heat and the motion of molecules, so the second fact is not at all damaging to the identification of a mental state with the corresponding brain state. And so, many recent philosophers have held it to be very important for our theoretical understanding of the mind-body problem that there can be contingent identity statements of this form.

To state finally what *I* think, as opposed to what seems to be the case, or what others think,

I think that in both cases, the case of names and the case of the theoretical identifications, the identity statements are necessary and not contingent. That is to say. they are necessary if *true;* of course, false identity statements are not necessary. How can one possibly defend such a view? Perhaps I lack a complete answer to this question, even though I am convinced that the view is true. But to begin an answer, let me make some distinctions that I want to use. The first is between a *rigid* and a *nonrigid designator.* What do these terms mean? As an example of a nonrigid designator, I can give an expression such as 'the inventor of bifocals'. Let us suppose it was Benjamin Franklin who invented bifocals, and so the expression, 'the inventor of bifocals', designates or refers to a certain man, namely, Benjamin Franklin. However, we can easily imagine that the world could have been different, that under different circumstances someone else would have come upon this invention before Benjamin Franklin did, and in that case, *he* would have been the inventor of bifocals. So, in this sense, the expression 'the inventor of bifocals' is nonrigid: Under certain circumstances one man would have been the inventor of bifocals; under other circumstances, another man would have. In contrast, consider the expression 'the square root of 25'. Independently of the empirical facts, we can give an arithmetical proof that the square root of 25 is in fact the number 5, and because we have proved this mathematically, what we have proved is necessary. If we think of numbers as entities at all, and let us suppose, at least for the purpose of this lecture, that we do, then the expression 'the square root of 25' necessarily designates a certain number, namely 5. Such an expression I call 'a *rigid* designator'. Some philosophers think that anyone who even uses the notions of rigid or nonrigid designator has already shown that he has fallen into a certain confusion or has not paid attention to certain facts. What do I mean by 'rigid designator'? I mean a term that designates the same object in all possible worlds. To get rid of one confusion which certainly is not mine, I do not use "might have designated a different object" to refer to the fact that language might have been used differently. For example, the expression 'the inventor of bifocals' might have been used by inhabitants of this planet always to refer to the man who corrupted Hadleyburg. This would have been the case, if, first, the people on this planet had not spoken English, but some other language, which phonetically overlapped with English, and if, second, in that language the expression 'the inventor of bifocals' meant the 'man who corrupted Hadleyburg'. Then it would refer, of course, in their language, to whoever in fact corrupted Hadleyburg in this counterfactual situation. That is not what I mean. What I mean by saying that a description might have referred to something different, I mean that in *our* language as *we* use it in describing a counterfactual situation, there might have been a different object satisfying the descriptive conditions *we* give for reference. So, for example, we use the phrase 'the inventor of bifocals', when we are talking about another possible world or a counterfactual situation, to refer to whoever in that counterfactual situation would have invented bifocals, not to the person whom people *in* that counterfactual situation would have called the inventor of bifocals'. *They* might have spoken a different language which phonetically overlapped with English in which 'the inventor of bifocals' is used in some other way. I am *not* concerned with that question here. For that matter, they might have been deaf and dumb, or there might have been no people at all. (There still could have been an inventor of bifocals even if there were no people—God, or Satan, will do.)

Second, in talking about the notion of a rigid designator, I do not mean to imply that the object referred to has to exist in all possible worlds, that is, that it has to necessarily exist. Some things, perhaps mathematical entities such as the positive integers, if they exist at all, necessarily exist. Some people have held that God both exists and necessarily exists; others, that He contingently exists; others, that He contingently fails to exist; and others, that He necessarily fails to exist:[8] all four options have been tried. But at any rate, when I use the notion of rigid designator, I do not imply that the object referred to necessarily exists. All I mean is that in any possible world where the object in question *does* exist, in any situation where the object *would* exist, we use the designator in question to designate that object. In a situation where the object does not exist, then we should say that the designator has no referent and that the object in question so designated does not exist.

• • •

Let me turn to the case of heat and the motion of molecules. Here surely is a case that is contingent identity! Recent philosophy has emphasized this again and again. So, if it is a case of contingent identity, then let us imagine under what circumstances it would be false. Now, concerning this statement I hold that the circumstances philosophers apparently have in mind as circumstances under which it would have been false are not in fact such circumstances. First, of course, it is argued that "Heat is the motion of molecules" is an a posteriori judgment; scientific investigation might have turned out otherwise. As I said before, this shows nothing against the view that it is necessary—at least if I am right. But here, surely, people had very specific circumstances in mind under which, so they thought, the judgment that heat is the motion of molecules would have been false. What were these circumstances? One can distill them out of the fact that we found out empirically that heat is the motion of molecules. How was this? What did we find out first when we found out that heat is the motion of molecules? There is a certain external phenomenon which we can sense by the sense of touch, and it produces a sensation which we call "the sensation of heat." We then discover that the external phenomenon which produces

this sensation, which we sense, by means of our sense of touch, is in fact that of molecular agitation in the thing that we touch, a very high degree of molecular agitation. So, it might be thought, to imagine a situation in which heat would not have been the motion of molecules, we need only imagine a situation in which we would have had the very same sensation and it would have been produced by something other than the motion of molecules. Similarly, if we wanted to imagine a situation in which light was not a stream of photons, we could imagine a situation in which we were sensitive to something else in exactly the same way, producing what we call visual experiences, though not through a stream of photons. To make the case stronger, or to look at another side of the coin, we could also consider a situation in which we *are* concerned with the motion of molecules but in which such motion does not give us the sensation of heat. And it might also have happened that we, or, at least, the creatures inhabiting this planet, might have been so constituted that, let us say, an increase in the motion of molecules did not give us this sensation but that, on the contrary, a slowing down of the molecules did give us the very same sensation. This would be a situation, so it might be thought, in which heat would not be the motion of molecules, or, more precisely, in which temperature would not be mean molecular kinetic energy.

But I think it would not be so. Let us think about the situation again. First, let us think about it in the actual world. Imagine right now the world invaded by a number of Martians, who do indeed get the very sensation that we call "the sensation of heat" when they feel some ice which has slow molecular motion, and who do not get a sensation of heat—in fact, maybe just the reverse—when they put their hand near a fire which causes a lot of molecular agitation. Would we say, "Ah, this casts some doubt on heat being the motion of molecules, because there are these other people who don't get the same sensation"? Obviously not, and no one would think so. We would say instead that the Martians somehow feel the very sensation we get when we feel heat when they feel cold and that they do not get a sensation of heat when they feel heat. But now let us think of a counterfactual situation.[16] Suppose the earth had from the very beginning been inhabited by such creatures. First, imagine it inhabited by no creatures at all: then there is no one to feel any sensations of heat. But we would not say that under such circumstances it would necessarily be the case that heat did not exist; we would say that heat might have existed, for example, if there were fires that heated up the air.

Let us suppose the laws of physics were not very different: Fires do heat up the air. Then there would have been heat even though there were no creatures around to feel it. Now let us suppose evolution takes place, and life is created, and there are some creatures around. But they are not like us, they are more like the Martians. Now would we say that heat has suddenly turned to cold, because of the way the creatures of this planet sense it? No, I think we should describe this situation as a situation in which, though the creatures on this planet got our sensation of heat, they did not get it when they were exposed to heat. They got it when they were exposed to cold. And that is something we can surely well imagine. We can imagine it just as we can imagine our planet being invaded by creatures of this sort. Think of it in two steps. First there is a stage where there are no creatures at all, and one can certainly imagine the planet still having both heat and cold, though no one is around to sense it. Then the planet comes through an evolutionary process to be peopled with beings of different neural structure from ourselves. Then these creatures could be such that they were insensitive to heat, they did not feel it in the way we do; but on the other hand, they felt cold in much the same way that we feel heat. But still, heat would be heat, and cold would be cold. And particularly, then, this goes in no way against saying that in

this counterfactual situation heat would still *be* the molecular motion, *be* that which is produced by fires, and so on, just as it would have been if there had been no creatures on the planet at all. Similarly, we could imagine that the planet was inhabited by creatures who got visual sensations when there were sound waves in the air. We should not therefore say, "Under such circumstances, sound would have been light." Instead we should say, "The planet was inhabited by creatures who were in some sense visually sensitive to sound, and maybe even visually sensitive to light." If this is correct, it can still be and will still be a necessary truth that heat is the motion of molecules and that light is a stream of photons.

To state the view succinctly: we use both the terms 'heat' and 'the motion of molecules' as rigid designators for a certain external phenomenon. Since heat is in fact the motion of molecules, and the designators are rigid, by the argument I have given here, it is going to be *necessary* that heat is the motion of molecules. What gives us the illusion of contingency is the fact we have identified the heat by the contingent fact that there happen to be creatures on this planet—(namely, ourselves) who are sensitive to it in a certain way, that is, who are sensitive to the motion of molecules or to heat —these are one and the same thing. And this is contingent. So we use the description, 'that which causes such and such sensations, or that which we sense in such and such a way', to identify heat. But in using this fact we use a contingent property of heat, just as we use the contingent property of Cicero as having written such and such works to identify him. We then use the terms 'heat' in the one case and 'Cicero' in the other *rigidly* to designate the objects for which they stand. And of course the term 'the motion of molecules' is rigid; it always stands for the motion of molecules, never for any other phenomenon. So, as Bishop Butler said, "everything is what it is and not another thing." Therefore, "Heat is the motion of molecules" will be necessary, not contingent, and one only has the *illusion* of contingency in the way one could have the illusion of contingency in thinking that this table might have been made of ice. We might think one could imagine it, but if we try, we can see on reflection that what we are really imagining is just there being another lectern in this very position here which was in fact made of ice. The fact that we may identify this lectern by being the object we see and touch in such and such a position is something else.

Now how does this relate to the problem of mind and body? It is usually held that this is a contingent identity statement just like "Heat is the motion of molecules." That cannot be. It cannot be a contingent identity statement just like "Heat is the motion of molecules" because, if I am right, "Heat is the motion of molecules" is not a contingent identity statement. Let us look at this statement. For example, "My being in pain at such and such a time is my being in such and such a brain state at such and such a time," or, "Pain in general is such and such a neural (brain) state."

This is held to be contingent on the following grounds. First, we can imagine the brain state existing though there is no pain at all. It is only a scientific fact that whenever we are in a certain brain state we have a pain. Second, one might imagine a creature being in pain, but not being in any specified brain state at all, maybe not having a brain at all. People even think, at least prima facie, though they may be wrong, that they can imagine totally disembodied creatures, at any rate certainly not creatures with bodies anything like our own. So it seems that we can imagine definite circumstances under which this relationship would have been false. Now, if these circumstances are circumstances, notice that we cannot deal with them simply by saying that this is just an illusion, something we can apparently imagine, but in fact cannot in the way we thought erroneously that we could imagine a situation in which heat

was not the motion of molecules. Because although we can say that we pick out heat contingently by the contingent property that it affects us in such and such a way, we cannot similarly say that we pick out pain contingently by the fact that it affects us in such and such a way. On such a picture there would be the brain state, and we pick it out by the contingent fact that it affects us as pain. Now that might be true of the brain state, but it cannot be true of the pain. The experience itself has to be *this experience*, and I cannot say that it is contingent property of the pain I now have that it is a pain.[17] In fact, it would seem that both the terms, 'my pain' and 'my being in such and such a brain state' are, first of all, both rigid designators. That is, whenever anything is such and such a pain, it is essentially that very object, namely, such and such a pain, and wherever anything is such and such a brain state, it is essentially that very object, namely, such and such a brain state. So both of these are rigid designators. One cannot say this pain might have been something else, some other state. These are both rigid designators.

Second, the way we would think of picking them out—namely, the pain by its being an experience of a certain sort, and the brain state by its being the state of a certain material object, being of such and such molecular configuration—both of these pick out their objects essentially and not accidentally, that is, they pick them out by essential properties. Whenever the molecules *are* in this configuration, we *do* have such and such a brain state. Whenever you feel *this,* you do have a pain. So it seems that the identity theorist is in some trouble, for, since we have two rigid designators, the identity statement in question is necessary. Because they pick out their objects essentially, we cannot say the case where you seem to imagine the identity statement false is really an illusion like the illusion one gets in the case of heat and molecular motion, because that illusion depended on the fact that we pick out heat by a

certain contingent property. So there is very little room to maneuver; perhaps none.[18] The
identity theorist, who holds that pain is the
brain state, also has to hold that it necessarily
is the brain state. He therefore cannot concede,
but has to deny, that there would have been
situations under which one would have had
pain but not the corresponding brain state.
Now usually in arguments on the identity
theory, this is very far from being denied. In
fact, it is conceded from the outset by the materialist as well as by his opponent. He says, "Of
course, it *could* have been the case that we had
pains without the brain states. It is a contingent identity." But that cannot be. He has to
hold that we are under some illusion in thinking that we can imagine that there could have
been pains without brain states. And the only
model I can think of for what the illusion
might be, or at least the model given by the
analogy the materialists themselves suggest,
namely, heat and molecular motion, simply
does not work in this case. So the materialist is
up against a very stiff challenge. He has to show
that these things we think we can see to be possible are in fact not possible. He has to show
that these things which we can imagine are not
in fact things we can imagine. And that requires
some very different philosophical argument
from the sort which has been given in the case
of heat and molecular motion. And it would
have to be a deeper and subtler argument than
I can fathom and subtler than has ever appeared
in any materialist literature that I have read. So
the conclusion of this investigation would be
that the analytical tools we are using go against
the identity thesis and so go against the general thesis that mental states are just physical
states.[19]

The next topic would be my own solution
to the mind-body problem, but that I do not
have.

• • •

NOTES

8 If there is no deity, and especially if the
nonexistence of a deity is *necessary*, it is
dubious that we can use 'He' to refer to a
deity. The use in the text must be taken to
be non-literal.

…

16 Isn't the situation I just described also
counterfactual? At least it may well be, if
such Martians never in fact invade. Strictly
speaking, the distinction I wish to draw
compares how we *would* speak *in* a (possibly counterfactual) situation, *if* it obtained,
and how we *do* speak *of* a counterfactual
situation, knowing that it does not obtain—i.e., the distinction between the language we would have used in a situation
and the language we *do* use to describe it.
(Consider the description: "Suppose we all
spoke German." This description is in
English.) The former case can be made
vivid by imagining the counterfactual situation to be actual.

17 The most popular identity theories advocated today explicitly fail to satisfy this
simple requirement. For these theories usually hold that a mental state is a brain state.
and that what makes the brain state into a
mental state is its 'causal role', the fact that
it tends to produce certain behavior (as intentions produce actions, or pain, pain
behavior) and to be produced by certain
stimuli (e.g. pain, by pinpricks). If the relations between the brain state and its
causes and effects are regarded as contingent, then *being such-and-such-a-mental-
state* is a contingent property of the brain
state. Let X be a pain. The causal-role identity theorist holds (1) that X is a brain
state, (2) that the fact that X is a pain is to
be analyzed (roughly) as the fact that X is
produced by certain stimuli and produces
certain behavior. The fact mentioned in (2)
is, of course, regarded as contingent; the

brain state *X* might well exist and not tend to produce the appropriate behavior in the absence of other conditions. Thus (1) and (2) assert that a certain pain *X* might have existed, yet not have been a pain. This seems to me self-evidently absurd. Imagine any pain: is it possible that *it itself* could have existed, yet not have been a pain?

If *X* = *Y*, then *X* and *Y* share all properties, including modal properties. If *X* is a pain and *Y* the corresponding brain state, then *being a pain* is an essential property of *X*, and *being a brain state* is an essential property of *Y*. If the correspondence relation is, in fact, identity, then it must be *necessary* of *Y* that it corresponds to a pain, and *necessary* of *X* that it correspond to a brain state, indeed to this particular brain state, *Y*. Both assertions seem false: it *seems* clearly possible that *X* should have existed without the corresponding brain state; or that the brain state should have existed without being felt as pain. Identity theorists cannot, contrary to their almost universal present practice, accept these intuitions; they must deny them, and explain them away. This is none too easy a thing to do.

18 A brief restatement of the argument may be helpful here. If "pain" and "C-fiber stimulation" are rigid designators of phenomena, one who identifies them must regard the identity as necessary. How can this necessity be reconciled with the apparent fact that C-fiber stimulation might have turned out not to be correlated with pain at all? We might try to reply by analogy to the case of heat and molecular motion: the latter identity, too, is necessary, yet someone may believe that, before scientific investigation showed otherwise, molecular motion might have turned out not to be heat. The reply is, of course, that what really is possible is that people (or some rational sentient beings) could have been in

the *same epistemic situation* as we actually are, and identify *a phenomenon* in the same way we identify heat, namely, by feeling it by the sensation we call "the sensation of heat," without the phenomenon being molecular motion. Further, the beings might not have been sensitive to molecular motion (i.e., to heat) by any neural mechanism whatsoever. It is impossible to explain the apparent possibility of C-fiber stimulations not having been pain in the same way. Here, too, we would have to suppose that we could have been in the same epistemological situation, and identify something in the same way we identify pain, without its corresponding to C-fiber stimulation. But the way we identify pain is by feeling it, and if a C-fiber stimulation could have occurred without our feeling any pain, then the C-fiber stimulation would have occurred without there *being* any pain, contrary to the necessity of the identity. The trouble is that although 'heat' is a rigid designator, heat is picked out by the contingent property of its being felt in a certain way: pain, on the other hand, is picked out by an essential (indeed necessary and sufficient) property. For a sensation to be *felt* as pain is for it to *be* pain.

19 All arguments against the identity theory which rely on the necessity of identity, or on the notion of essential property, are, of course, inspired by Descartes' argument for his dualism. The earlier arguments which superficially were rebutted by the analogies of heat and molecular motion, and the bifocals inventor who was also Postmaster General, had such an inspiration; and so does my argument here. R. Albritton and M. Slote have informed me that they independently have attempted to give essentialist arguments against the identity theory, and probably others have done so as well.

The simplest Cartesian argument can

perhaps be restated as follows: Let 'A' be a *name* (rigid designator) of Descartes' body. Then Descartes argues that since he could exist even if A did not, ◊ (Descartes ≠ A): hence Descartes ≠ A. Those who have accused him of a modal fallacy have forgotten that 'A' is rigid. His argument is valid, and his conclusion is correct, provided its (perhaps dubitable) premise is accepted. On the other hand, provided that Descartes is regarded as having ceased to exist upon his death, "Descartes ≠ A" can be established without the use of a modal argument; for if so, no doubt A survived Descartes when A was a corpse. Thus A had a property (existing at a certain time) which Descartes did not. The same argument can establish that a statue is not the hunk of stone, or the congery of molecules, of which it is composed. Mere nonidentity, then, may be a weak conclusion. (See D. Wiggins, *Philosophical Review*, Vol. 77 (1968), pp. 90 ff.) The Cartesian modal argument, however, surely can be deployed to maintain relevant stronger conclusions as well.

CHAPTER TEN

Artificial Intelligence

Computers and the mind

The advent of electronic computers in the second half of this century has had a profound effect on the philosophy of mind, and on the mind-body problem in particular. One aspect of this effect has been a focus on the question, could a computer ever be built whose internal states possess intelligence and consciousness; that is, could a computer *think*? Of course, few people believe that any computers that currently exist actually think, but there remains the question whether it is possible in principle to build one that does. The interest in computers has raised another question, namely, whether all minds are really computers. If the answer to this question is positive, it would mean that humans possess minds not because we have an immaterial soul, nor because of the specific kind of neural activity in the brain, but rather because our brain functions as an information-processing computer. In this chapter we will look at the first of these two questions.

Alan Turing

We will look at the issue of computer intelligence by way of an article by Alan Turing, a mathematician and philosopher who was deeply involved in the development of the digital computer in the 1940s and 1950s. In many ways, Turing was the first to clearly articulate the idea of a programmable computer, and it was Turing who first coined the term 'computer' to describe a programmable calculating machine.

Turing's life was one of tremendous achievement, but one which ended tragically. There are few individuals whose lives are more deeply intertwined with the developments of their century. It was in his early years at Cambridge that Turing began to experiment with the ideas that eventually led him to the idea of a programmable calculating machine, which he termed a "computer," comparing the machine to a human who computes arithmetical sums. Turing's work at Cambridge was interrupted by his involvement with British intelligence during the Second World War. Turing was chiefly responsible for the invention of a decoding machine that cracked the German secret code known as "Enigma." After the war Turing returned to the development of computing machines, first at the National Physical Laboratory and later at Manchester University. In 1952 he was arrested for homosexual behaviour, and the pressure of the trial and the surrounding publicity drove him to suicide two years later.

Can machines think?

In his 1950 article, "Computing Machinery and Intelligence," Turing addresses the question, "Can machines think?" The importance of Turing's article lies less in the answer he gives than in his analysis of what that question means. The aim of Turing's article is to clarify the question by considering (1) what we mean by a *machine*, and (2) how we can determine whether something thinks.

In both of these respects, Turing's article has had a huge impact on the subject of machine intelligence. At the outset of the article, Turing argues that we cannot answer these questions by looking at the common uses of the words 'machine' and 'think' because this will yield an answer that simply reflects common prejudice. The first five sections of his article defend specific and controversial answers to both questions.

The "Turing Test"

The first two sections of the article focus on the second question: how can we tell whether something thinks? To answer this question, Turing proposes an "intelligence test" that we could put to a machine. He argues that if the machine passes the test we should conclude that it possesses intelligence. He calls this test the Imitation Game, but it has since become known as the Turing Test.

The **Turing Test** is set up in the following way. In one room we place a machine and a person. In a separate room we place a second person called the "interrogator." Both the machine and the person hidden with it give answers to questions posed by the interrogator. There are no restrictions put on the questions the interrogator can ask, but the machine will be programmed to give answers that resemble as closely as possible those that a human might give. The interrogator is told that one of the two sets of answers comes from a machine and one from a person, but is not told which is which, referring to the two only as A and B. From the answers to the questions the interrogator is supposed to determine which of A and B is the machine and which is the person. The machine has passed if it can fool the interrogator as often as would a human put in its place.

The idea behind the Turing Test is this: If it is impossible to distinguish a machine from a person on the basis of answers to questions put to it, we must conclude that the machine is intelligent.

The defence of the Turing Test

The Turing Test accepts a certain kind of behaviour — answering questions fluently — to be a definite indicator of intelligence. Turing claims that the question 'Can a machine think?' can be *replaced* by the question 'Can a machine pass the test?' This suggests that passing the test is not to be taken as *evidence* of intelligence, but rather as defining what intelligence consists of.

However, in a later section of the paper, entitled "The Argument from Consciousness," Turing gives a clearer indication of how the test should be understood. In that section Turing defends the test from the objection that, although machines may be able to *behave* as if they were intelligent, no machine could ever experience such things as pleasure, grief, or misery. The premise behind this objection is that the only real criterion of intelligence is the subjective experience of consciousness — no behaviour, however complex, is constitutive of thought.

Turing's reply to this argument is that behaviour is the only criterion *available* for deciding whether something or someone thinks. If we were to insist that behaviour can never be a sure sign of intelligence, he says, we would be forced into the view that the only way to be certain that a machine thinks is "to *be* the machine, and to feel oneself thinking." Taken literally, the premise of the argument from consciousness leads us to the conclusion that the only intelligence we can be certain of is our own. For other people's consciousness is hidden from us, and is inferred only from their behaviour. This position Turing calls the "solipsist point of view," and adopting the test as an indicator of intelligence, he says, is the only way to avoid being forced into solipsism.

At the end of the section Turing admits that consciousness is a mystery, and he describes his position as entailing only that this mystery need not be solved in order to answer the question whether machines think. Because we already accept behaviour as an indicator of intelligence, the Turing Test can be defended on the grounds that it applies the same criterion to machines as we use with other people. So it seems clear that Turing does not intend the test to serve as a *definition* of intelligence, but only as an *empirical criterion.*

What is a machine?

In sections 3 through 5, Turing considers the other question in the puzzle over machine intelligence, namely, what is a machine? He argues that we cannot define a machine simply as anything constructed by engineers. For some day in the future it may be possible to produce a living person from a single cell, and this, he says, would not be accepted as a case of constructing a thinking machine, even though it would be an artificial creation.

As with the question 'What is thinking?', Turing puts the question 'What is a machine?' in terms of conditions on the Turing Test. If the test is accepted as determining whether or not a machine can think, then we have to answer the question, 'What will we allow to take part in the test?' His answer to this question is that the game should be restricted to what he calls **digital computers**. So the question 'Can machines think?' becomes 'Can digital computers think?' In his defence of this position, Turing addresses two issues: (1) what is a digital computer, and (2) why should such machines be taken as a standard for all machines whatsoever?

He addresses the first of these issues in section 4. Although digital computers are much more familiar now than they were in Turing's day, there is a crucial aspect to Turing's description of digital computers that we should not overlook. Turing describes them in the following way:

> The idea behind digital computers may be explained by saying that these machines are intended to carry out any operations which could be done by a human computer. The human computer is supposed to be following fixed rules; he has no authority to deviate from them in any detail.

So the central idea behind the digital computer, according to Turing, is that of a set of fixed rules that lead to a specific result or accomplish a particular operation if they are strictly adhered to. Nowadays computer programmers refer to such a set of rules as an "algorithm." Let's look briefly at this idea.

Algorithms

An **algorithm** is a set of rules that, if followed precisely, will accomplish a specific task. A computer program is an algorithm, where the rules are the steps written into the program. Each of the steps of a program is an instruction to carry out a mechanical operation in the computer. But when Turing originally devised the idea of an algorithm, he did not restrict the rules to machine instructions. Instead he defined an algorithm in terms of rules that a person can follow to accomplish a task. Understood in these terms, the important feature of an algorithm is that someone can follow the rules, and thus accomplish what the algorithm is designed for, without understanding what it is they are doing or what the purpose of any particular rule is. If an algorithm is properly designed in these terms, it should be possible to replace the person following them with a mechanical device.

Here's an example. Imagine writing a set of instructions for a telephone operator. These instruction should be usable by people who have no idea what the purpose of a telephone is, or what the function of any of the dials and buttons is. Yet if they follow the rules, they will successfully connect you with any party you ask for, including redialing for a busy signal. This would be a "telephone operating algorithm." If the telephone algorithm is done properly, you should be able to use it to design a mechanical device that works as a telephone operator by following the rules in the algorithm.

Discrete state machines

According to Turing, then, a digital computer is a machine that operates according to an algorithm. How can computers defined in this manner serve as representatives of all possible machines? Turing addresses this question in section 5. There he claims that digital computers can mimic the behaviour of any "discrete state" machine. A **discrete state machine** is one that moves from one definite state to another. For example, compare a digital watch that clicks from one time to the next to an analog watch that moves continuously in a circle. The importance of discrete state machines is that at any given moment they are in one distinct state or another. This means that their operation can be entirely predicted from their construction and their current state. Let's see why this should be.

We can predict the behaviour of a discrete state machine by means of what is called a "machine table." A **machine table** describes the behaviour of the machine in terms of the relations among three sets of components: the input to the machine, a set of internal states, and the output of the machine. In a sense, a machine table is just an algorithm for the machine presented in graphical form. Turing gives an example of such a table in section 5 of his article.

A clearer example is the Coke machine in illustrated in Figure 1.[1] The Coke machine accepts two possible inputs, nickels and dimes, and these are listed down the left-hand side of the table. The machine has two internal states, labelled as State 1 and State 2 at the top of the table. Finally, the machine has two possible outputs: a Coke, or a Coke together with a nickel change. Which output the machine will give is determined by the input and the current state of the machine. To see what the output will be for a combination of input and current state, you simply find the appropriate square in the box. After each step the machine will either remain in its current state or move to the other state, as specified in the squares. Notice that as long as the machine begins in State 1, it will always give you a Coke for ten cents and will return correct change.

Notice also that the machine table says nothing at all about the physical construction of the machine. There are any number of ways of building a mechanism that will conform to the machine table of the Coke machine. We could construct such a machine out of metal, or we could simply give the instructions to a young child who does what the instructions tell her. You can see that the child would not have to be able to add or subtract to follow the instructions, nor even know what it is she is doing. The Coke machine is a very simple example, but for any discrete state machine, no matter how complex, we can draw a machine table like this that will predict its behaviour. For example, we could construct such a table for a digital watch, where the input consists of electrical bursts from the battery and the output consists of changes to the numerical display.

Universal machines

Given that the behaviour of a digital machine is entirely predictable from its machine table, Turing argues that its behaviour can be mimicked by a computer. He says:

Figure 1. A Coke Machine.

	State 1	State 2
Nickel	Go to state 2.	Give out a Coke. Go to state 1.
Dime	Give out a Coke. Go to state 1.	Give out a Coke. Give back a nickel. Go to state 1.

This machine table describes a machine that will dispense a Coke for ten cents and will give change back on nickels and dimes. It accepts only nickels and dimes as input. The rows of the table, labelled down the left-hand side, represent the two inputs. The columns of the table, labelled at the top, represent the two states the machine can be in at any given time. So each square of the table represents a combination of one input and one internal state. In each square is written what the machine will do given that input and that current state. State 1 is the "initial state" where the machine begins, and State 2 functions essentially as a device to indicate that the previous input was a nickel.

Given the table corresponding to a discrete state machine it is possible to predict what it will do. There is no reason why this calculation should not carried out by means of a digital computer. Provided it could be carried out sufficiently quickly the digital computer could mimic the behaviour of any discrete state machine ... This special property of digital computers, that they can mimic any discrete state machine, is described by saying that they are *universal* machines.

This property of digital computers, their "universality," is an important mathematical result discovered by Turing in the 1930s. In essence his discovery was that a certain form of digital computer, since known as the "Turing Machine," can be programmed to carry out the operation of any possible discrete state machine. The description of this particular machine in Turing's early papers was a major step in the development of the programmable electronic computer. As the idea of a Turing Machine plays an important part in subsequent debates, it is worth taking the time to look at its operation here.

The Turing Machine

A **Turing Machine** is a deceptively simple device. As shown in Figure 2, it consists of three components:

1. A tape of indefinite length divided into squares, in each of which is written a single symbol such as a letter or numeral.
2. A read-write head, which can read the symbols written in the squares (i.e., it can tell which one is there), and can write new symbols in their place. The read-write head can also move back and forth along the tape, one square at a time.
3. A set of internal states, which determine what the read-write head will do given the symbol it is currently reading.

Figure 2. The Components of a Turing Machine.

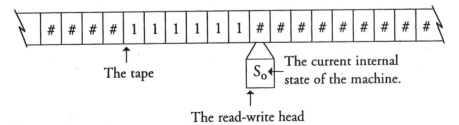

The tape

S_0 The current internal state of the machine.

The read-write head

The operation of a Turing Machine is as follows. At any given moment the machine is in one state or another and its read-write head is scanning one square that contains a symbol. The operation of the Turing Machine is shown in a machine table, just as in the Coke Machine in Figure 1. In place of the "output," the squares of the machine table say what the machine will do next. Given the particular state and the symbol currently scanned, the read-write head will do one of three things:

1. Move one square to the left.
2. Move one square to the right.
3. Replace the current symbol with a new symbol.

After each step, the machine will either change state or remain in its current state, and this is also written into the machine table.

Figure 3 is a representation of a machine that tells whether the number of letters in a word on the tape is even or odd. It begins with the read-write head at the right of the word on the tape, and it moves left along the string, one square at a time. As it encounters each letter it will change back and forth between states 3 and 4. These states "keep track" of whether the number of letters so far is even or odd. When it runs out of letters (i.e., encounters a blank square) it will write "even" or "odd" depending on which state it ended in.

Figure 3.

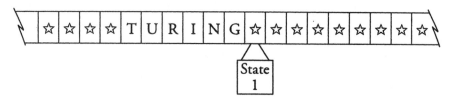

	State 1	State 2	State 3	State 4
A Letter		Found a letter! Write a ☆. Go to state 3.		Found another letter! Write a ☆. Go back to state 1.
A Star	Move one square left. Go to state 2.	No more letters. Write "E" for "Even." Stop.	Move one square left. Go to state 4.	No more letters. Write "O" for "Odd." Stop.

The Universal Turing Machine

Turing showed that a Turing Machine can be constructed that can mimic the behaviour of any discrete state machine whatsoever. This means that despite its simple construction, it is capable of operating as well as any computer that currently exists, and any computer we might build in the future. How is this possible?

We can program a Turing Machine to mimic another machine by dividing the contents of the tape into two parts: one part of the tape we designate as the "program," and the other we designate as the "working space." The input of the mimicked machine will be the contents of the working space before each operation, and the output will be the contents of the working space after the operation. What output will be produced given a particular input is determined by what is written into the program portion of the tape.

Because of its ability to mimic any discrete state machine, including any other digital computer, Turing's invention is sometimes called a **Universal Turing Machine**, or UTM. Turing's mathematical results show that no matter how large or powerful the machine mimicked, it is possible in principle for the UTM to duplicate its behaviour exactly. So we can think of the UTM as the most general form of digital computer, and thus the most general form of discrete state machine.[2] This means that we can rephrase the question 'Can machines think?' in the following way: Is it possible for a UTM to pass the Turing Test?

Learning machines

An important aspect of any discrete state machine, including the UTM, is that its behaviour is completely predictable. Given its machine table, its current input and its current state, we can determine precisely what the device will do at that moment and each succeeding moment. This aspect of discrete state machines is often given as a reason for concluding that such machines could never think. Turing describes this as the "Lady Lovelace Objection" after a remark by Lady Lovelace about an early-nineteenth-century computer, George Babbage's "Analytical Engine." She said:

> The Analytical Machine has no pretensions to originate anything. It can do whatever we know how to order it to perform.

Real thought, it is argued, can generate original ideas and behaviour, and so a digital computer, it seems, could never possess real thought.

Turing's reply to this argument is that we could construct a machine that is programmed to learn. That is, information from previous inputs could be stored on the tape and be used to influence what the machine does in the future. Of course, the "learning" function would have to be built into the program of the machine, so that its behaviour is still predictable in principle. But such a function may be so complex that it is impossible in practice to know what the machine will do as it accumulates new information. Its behaviour then might be every bit as "unpredictable" as that of a person. In section 7, entitled "Learning Machines," Turing suggests modifying the Turing Test so the machine will mimic the behaviour not of an adult but that of a child, including its learning capacities. If the program that governs the machine is sufficiently complex, Turing argues, the behaviour of the machine as it learns would be indistinguishable in many ways from that of a growing human being.

Computing with symbols

The idea of a learning machine raises one final aspect of the operation of digital computers that needs to be mentioned here although it is not a point emphasized by Turing. An essential feature of Turing Machines, which accounts for the flexibility of their behaviour, is the tape. The tape is of indefinite length, which means that it is always possible to add new squares in either direction if they are needed. The importance of this is that any amount of new information can be stored on the tape, giving the machine an unlimited degree of flexibility in the sense that there are no bounds on its ability to alter its behaviour in light of new information.

The important aspect of the tape is that it contains an indefinitely extendable string of **symbols** or characters, where each symbol represents a unit of information. This means that the "memory space" of the computer is limited only by the size of the tape and not by the design of the machine itself. The use of symbols in this way was perhaps the major intellectual development in the invention of the digital computer. The flexibility of machines that do not operate on symbols is restricted to the number of distinct internal states in their machine table.[3]

In light of the importance of symbols, we can think of digital computers as defined by two features:

1. Their operation is determined according to an algorithm, and can be represented by a machine table.
2. Their operation consists of reading and writing symbols, displayed in strings of indefinite length.

The first of these two features is what digital computers have in common with all discrete state machines, and the second is what gives them their flexibility of operation and makes them capable of mimicking any other machine.

The first feature is what makes them *machines* in Turing's sense, and the second is what people such as Turing believe makes them capable in principle of intelligence.

Problems for constructing intelligent machines

In chapter 5 we looked at Descartes' claim that machines are not capable in principle of imitating human behaviour. His argument focussed on language use and what I called "behavioural plasticity." The work of Turing and others in this century has shown that Descartes idea' that machines are capable only of reflex action is incorrect. The fact that digital computers can store and read symbols gives them the ability to perform any set of actions for which there can be an algorithm. Researchers in linguistics, such as Noam Chomsky, have shown that many of the patterns of human language use can be modelled in an algorithm and hence are performable by a machine.

However, the project of constructing a machine that will display the same kind of plasticity of behaviour that humans are capable of is far from complete. Two problems have motivated much recent work in computer design. One is the "frame problem." This is the problem of writing an algorithm for a task that will anticipate the results of actions carried out, but without having to provide instructions for everything that will *not* result from carrying out an action. The other is a collection of difficulties variously described as "the problem of knowledge access" or "the relevance problem." The core of these problems is that it is very hard, and perhaps impossible, to lay out in advance what information will be relevant to the infinite number of circumstances the machine could find itself in. Humans have an uncanny ability to call up the right information at the right time without having to scan *everything* they know to see whether it *might* be relevant.[4]

Against the possibility of intelligent machines

The frame problem and the knowledge access problem are serious challenges to the project of constructing an intelligent machine. However, as long as work continues, it is difficult to say that there *cannot* be a solution to these problems. In contrast, in the next reading we look at an argument by John Searle that a symbol processing machine, like a Turing Machine, is incapable *in principle* of what we recognize as intelligence. That is, Searle argues that computer intelligence is not merely difficult to achieve, but impossible because of the very nature of computers.

Searle is a Professor of Mind and Language at the University of California at Berkeley. Searle's early influence was in philosophy of language. In the 1960s he helped articulate what is called the speech act theory of language, which is based on the idea that language is best understood by looking at how people use it. Since then Searle's views have expanded into a full theory of mind and language. An articulation of his recent views can be found in *The Rediscovery of Mind* (MIT Press, 1992).[5]

Artificial Intelligence

Searle's article is not aimed directly at Turing's article, but to the discipline of **Artificial Intelligence, or AI.** Searle distinguishes between two distinct branches of AI, only one of which is the target of his article. "Weak AI" is the use of computers to construct models of the operation of the mind. There is no assumption here that the computer programs constructed will render the machines intelligent in any real sense. "Strong AI" is the discipline that accepts the validity of the Turing Test, and is busy working on programs that will produce intelligent machines; the assumption of this school, Searle says, is that "the appropriately programmed computer really *is* a mind." Searle's article is an attack on Strong AI. Searle's article relies on a thought experiment involving a "computer" that passes the Turing Test, but which he contends is obviously devoid of any kind of intelligence.

The "Chinese Room"

One of the projects of programmers working in AI is the design of machines that will understand stories. The criterion of understanding that is used is that the machine must be able to answer questions about the story, using information not directly given but inferred from aspects of the story and other information kept in the memory. This test is a version of the Turing Test, where responding to questions about the story in the right manner is a sign of really understanding the story. So Searle describes an imaginary machine that responds to the questions in just the way the researchers intend, but which he claims clearly has no understanding of the story. This imaginary machine is "the Chinese Room."

The Chinese Room is described as follows. Searle asks us to imagine that he is locked in a room with a large collection of Chinese writing, of which he has no understanding at all. The Chinese writing is in three groups, which (unbeknownst to him) consist of a story, a background script, and a set of questions. Together with these batches of Chinese writing is a set of rules in English. The rules make up an algorithm for correlating the first batch with the second (i.e., the script with the story), for correlating each of those with the third batch (i.e., the questions), and for generating new strings of Chinese characters (the answers) from the third batch. Searle then says:

Suppose ... after a while I got so good at following the instructions for manipulating the Chinese symbols and the programmers got so good at writing the programs that from the external point of view — that is, from the point of view of someone outside the room in which I am locked — my answers ... are absolutely indistinguishable from those of native Chinese speakers. Nobody just looking at my answers can tell that I don't speak a word of Chinese.

The important assumption about the situation described is that it satisfies the description of a digital computer outlined above. All that occurs in the room is a sequence of actions performed according to an algorithm, and those actions consist entirely of reading and writing symbols. Searle himself could easily be replaced by a mechanism that operates according to the instructions that he is following. Searle asks two questions about this situation: (1) Does the "machine" have any understanding of the story? (2) Does the program and the operation of the machine shed any light on human understanding? He claims that it is obvious that the answer to (1) is negative, and that if that is the case, the answer to (2) must be negative as well.

In the sections that follow, Searle considers and replies to several objections to the Chinese Room argument. I will pass over those and move to his concluding section. There he claims that the correct answer to the question "Can machines think?" is obviously "yes" because people are biological machines in some sense. Moreover, he thinks it is clear that people are also computers in the sense that the nervous system carries out many computing operations. What he rejects is the claim that something can think *solely* in virtue of carrying out a computer program.

Searle's argument anticipates an issue we will look at in chapter 14. His claim is that symbols *by themselves* have no meaning; they are not *about* anything. Whatever meaning is carried by the symbols that a computer reads and writes resides solely in the minds of the people who program them and use them. The Chinese symbols in Searle's room carry meaning only because people who understand Chinese attach meaning to them. Without those people the symbols have no content whatsoever. So Searle's position on the Turing Test is that computers may be able to mimic intelligent *behaviour*. But as long as they consist entirely of devices that operate on strings of symbols according to an algorithm, they will lack the central feature of the mind, namely, the connection between thoughts and things in the world. What is missing from such computers is the causal power of the brain to generate meaning. The route to understanding the mind, Searle argues, lies in the biological study of that power.

Artificial and natural intelligence

Critics of the AI project, like Searle, believe that understanding symbol processing does not take us any closer to an understanding of intelligence. On the other hand, Turing's description of a computer has led other people to suppose that the idea of a symbol-processing algorithm may be the answer to the nature of the *human* mind. They argue that looking at the biochemical structure of the brain is the wrong way to understand the nature of the mind. Instead we have to look at the information-processing capacity of the brain. The key to comprehending human intelligence, they argue, is to reconstruct the "machine table" of the mind. In the next chapter we look at how this idea developed out of Turing's work as well as behaviourism and the identity theory.

NOTES

1 This example is from Jerry Fodor, "The Mind-Body Problem," *Scientific American* 244:1 (January 1981), 114–123.
2 Since Turing published this result, it has been shown that there is a large class of machines and formal systems that have the same computing power as the Turing Machine. This suggests that what Turing and others have discovered is a general class of machines that define the notion of a digital computer.
3 Notice, for example, that the Coke machine in Figure 1 has only two states, and the information it can store is limited to whether or not its last input was a nickel, represented by whether it is in state 1 or 2. To increase its capacity, say to handle quarters as well as nickels and dimes, we would have to completely redesign it. By contrast, a digital computer can be built so that these changes can be carried out by inputting a new program.
4 A good, simple description of these problems (although perhaps a bit dated now) is found in John Haugeland, *Artificial Intelligence: The Very Idea* (Cambridge, MA: MIT Press, 1985), chapter 5.
5 A more accessible book, which contains a version of the argument in this chapter, is John Searle, *Minds, Brains and Science* (Cambridge, MA: Harvard, 1984).

Alan Turing
"Computing Machinery and Intelligence"

1. The Imitation Game

I propose to consider the question "Can machines think?" This should begin with definitions of the meaning of the terms "machine" and "think." The definitions might be framed so as to reflect so far as possible the normal use of the words, but this attitude is dangerous. If the meaning of the words "machine" and "think" are to be found by examining how they are commonly used it is difficult to escape the conclusion that the meaning and the answer to the question, "Can machines think?" is to be sought in a statistical survey such as a Gallup poll. But this is absurd. Instead of attempting such a definition I shall replace the question by another, which is closely related to it and is expressed in relatively unambiguous words.

The new form of the problem can be described in terms of a game which we call the "imitation game." It is played with three people, a man (A), a woman (B), and an interrogator (C) who may be of either sex. The interrogator stays in a room apart from the other two. The object of the game for the interrogator is to determine which of the other two is the man and which is the woman. He knows them by labels X and Y, and at the end of the game he says either "X is A and Y is B" or "X is B and Y is A." The interrogator is allowed to put questions to A and B thus:

C: Will X please tell me the length of his or her hair?

Now suppose X is actually A, then A must answer. It is A's object in the game to try to cause C to make the wrong identification. His answer might therefore be

"My hair is shingled, and the longest strands are about nine inches long."

In order that tones of voice may not help the interrogator the answers should be written, or better still, typewritten. The ideal arrangement is to have a teleprinter communicating between the two rooms. Alternatively the question and answers can be repeated by an intermediary. The object of the game for the third player (B) is to help the interrogator. The best strategy for her is probably to give truthful answers. She can add such things as "I am the woman, don't listen to him!" to her answers, but it will avail nothing as the man can make similar remarks.

We now ask the question, "What will happen when a machine takes the part of A in this game?" Will the interrogator decide wrongly as often when the game is played like this as he does when the game is played between a man and a woman? These questions replace our original, "Can machines think?"

2. Critique of the New Problem

As well as asking, "What is the answer to this new form of the question," one may ask, "Is this new question a worthy one to investigate?" This latter question we investigate without further ado, thereby cutting short an infinite regress.

The new problem has the advantage of drawing a fairly sharp line between the physical and the intellectual capacities of a man. No engineer or chemist claims to be able to produce a material which is indistinguishable from the human skin. It is possible that at some time this might be done, but even supposing this invention available we should feel there was little point in trying to make a "thinking machine" more human by dressing it up in such artificial flesh. The form in which we have set the problem reflects this fact in the condition which prevents the interrogator from seeing or touching the other competitors, or hearing their voices. Some other advantages of the proposed criterion may be shown up by specimen questions and answers. Thus:

Q: Please write me a sonnet on the subject of the Forth Bridge.

A: Count me out on this one. I never could write poetry.

Q: Add 34957 to 70764.

A: (Pause about 30 seconds and then give as answer) 105621.

Q: Do you play chess?

A: Yes.

Q: I have K at my K1, and no other pieces. You have only K at K6 and R at R1. It is your move. What do you play?

A: (After a pause of 15 seconds) R-R8 mate.

The question and answer method seems to be suitable for introducing almost any one of the fields of human endeavor that we wish to include. We do not wish to penalize the machine for its inability to shine in beauty competitions, nor to penalize a man for losing in a race against an airplane. The conditions of our game make these disabilities irrelevant. The "witnesses" can brag, if they consider it advisable, as much as they please about their charms, strength or heroism, but the interrogator cannot demand practical demonstrations.

The game may perhaps be criticized on the ground that the odds are weighted too heavily against the machine. If the man were to try and pretend to be the machine he would clearly make a very poor showing. He would be given away at once by slowness and inaccuracy in arithmetic. May not machines carry out something which ought to be described as thinking but which is very different from what a man does? This objection is a very strong one, but at least we can say that if, nevertheless, a machine can be constructed to play the imitation game satisfactorily, we need not be troubled by this objection.

It might be urged that when playing the "imitation game" the best strategy for the machine may possibly be something other than imitation of the behavior of a man. This may be, but I think it is unlikely that there is any great effect of this kind. In any case there is no intention to investigate here the theory of the game, and it will be assumed that the best strategy is to try to provide answers that would naturally be given by a man.

3. The Machines Concerned in the Game

The question which we put in §1 will not be quite definite until we have specified what we mean by the word "machine." It is natural that we should wish to permit every kind of engineering technique to be used in our machines. We also wish to allow the possibility that an engineer or team of engineers may construct a machine which works, but whose manner of operation cannot be satisfactorily described by its constructors because they have applied a method which is largely experimental. Finally, we wish to exclude from the machines men born in the usual manner. It is difficult to frame the definitions so as to satisfy these three conditions. One might for instance insist that the team of engineers should be all of one sex, but this would not really be satisfactory, for it is probably possible to rear a complete individual from a single cell of the skin (say) of a man. To do so would be a feat of biological technique deserving of the very highest praise, but we would not be inclined to regard it as a case of "constructing a thinking machine." This prompts us to abandon the requirement that every kind of technique should be permitted. We are the more ready to do so in view of the fact that the present interest in "thinking machines" has been aroused by a particular kind of machine, usually called an "electronic computer" or "digital computer." Following this suggestion we only permit digital computers to take part in our game.

This restriction appears at first sight to be a very drastic one. I shall attempt to show that it is not so in reality. To do this necessitates a short account of the nature and properties of these computers.

It may also be said that this *identification* of machines with digital computers, like our criterion for "thinking," will only be unsatisfactory if (contrary to my belief), it turns out that digital computers are unable to give a good showing in the game.

There are already a number of digital computers in working order, and it may be asked, "Why not try the experiment straight away? It would be easy to satisfy the conditions of the game. A number of interrogators could be used, and statistics compiled to show how often the right identification was given." The short answer is that we are not asking whether all digital computers would do well in the game nor whether the computers at present available would do well, but whether there are imaginable computers which would do well. But this is only the short answer. We shall see this question in a different light later.

4. Digital Computers

The idea behind digital computers may be explained by saying that these machines are intended to carry out any operations which could be done by a human computer. The human computer is supposed to be following fixed rules; he has no authority to deviate from them in any detail. We may suppose that these rules are supplied in a book, which is altered whenever he is put on to a new job. He has also an unlimited supply of paper on which he does his calculations. He may also do his multiplications and additions on a "desk machine," but this is not important.

If we use the above explanation as a definition we shall be in danger of circularity of argument. We avoid this by giving an outline of the means by which the desired effect is achieved. A digital computer can usually be regarded as consisting of three parts:

(i) Store.
(ii) Executive unit.
(iii) Control.

The store is a store of information, and corresponds to the human computer's paper, whether this is the paper on which he does his calculations or that on which his book of rules is printed. Insofar as the human computer does calculations in his head a part of the store will correspond to his memory.

The executive unit is the part which carries out the various individual operations involved in a calculation. What these individual operations are will vary from machine to machine. Usually fairly lengthy operations can be done such as "Multiply 3540675445 by 7076345687" but in some machines only very simple ones such as "Write down 0" are possible.

We have mentioned that the "book of rules" supplied to the computer is replaced in the machine by a part of the store. It is then called the "table of instructions." It is the duty of the control to see that these instructions are obeyed correctly and in the right order. The control is so constructed that this necessarily happens.

The information in the store is usually broken up into packets of moderately small size. In one machine, for instance, a packet might consist of ten decimal digits. Numbers are assigned to the parts of the store in which the various packets of information are stored, in some systematic manner. A typical instruction might say—

"Add the number stored in position 6809 to that in 4302 and put the result back into the latter storage position."

Needless to say it would not occur in the machine expressed in English. It would more likely be coded in a form such as 6809430217. Here 17 says which of various possible operations is to be performed on the two numbers. In this case the operation is that described above, viz. "Add the number…" It will be noticed that the instruction takes up 10 digits and so forms one packet of information, very conveniently. The control will normally take the instructions to be obeyed in the order of the positions in which they are stored, but occasionally an instruction such as

"Now obey the instruction stored in position 5606, and continue from there"
may be encountered, or again

"If position 4505 contains 0 obey next the instruction stored in 6707, otherwise continue straight on."

Instructions of these latter types are very important because they make it possible for a sequence of operations to be repeated over and over again until some condition is fulfilled, but in doing so to obey, not fresh instructions on each repetition, but the same ones over and over again. To take a domestic analogy. Suppose Mother wants Tommy to call at the cobbler's every morning on his way to school to see if her shoes are done; she can ask him afresh every morning. Alternatively she can stick up a notice once and for all in the hall which he will see when he leaves for school and which tells him to call for the shoes, and also to destroy the notice when he comes back if he has the shoes with him.

The reader must accept it as a fact that digital computers can be constructed, and indeed have been constructed, according to the principles we have described, and that they can in fact mimic the actions of a human computer very closely.

The book of rules which we have described our human computer as using is of course a convenient fiction. Actual human computers really remember what they have got to do. If one wants to make a machine mimic the behavior of the human computer in some complex operation one has to ask him how it is done, and then translate the answer into the form of an instruction table. Constructing instruction tables is usually described as "programing." To

"program a machine to carry out the operation A" means to put the appropriate instruction table into the machine so that it will do A.

An interesting variant on the idea of a digital computer is a "digital computer with a random element." These have instructions involving the throwing of a die or some equivalent electronic process; one such instruction might for instance be, "Throw the die and put the resulting number into store 1000." Sometimes such a machine is described as having free will (though I would not use this phrase myself). It is not normally possible to determine from observing a machine whether it has a random element, for a similar effect can be produced by such devices as making the choices depend on the digits of the decimal for π.

Most actual digital computers have only a finite store. There is no theoretical difficulty in the idea of a computer with an unlimited store. Of course only a finite part can have been used at any one time. Likewise only a finite amount can have been constructed, but we can imagine more and more being added as required. Such computers have special theoretical interest and will be called infinite capacity computers.

The idea of a digital computer is an old one. Charles Babbage, Lucasian Professor of Mathematics at Cambridge from 1828 to 1839, planned such a machine, called the Analytical Engine, but it was never completed. Although Babbage had all the essential ideas, his machine was not at that time such a very attractive prospect. The speed which would have been available would be definitely faster than a human computer but something like 100 times slower than the Manchester machine, itself one of the slower of the modern machines. The storage was to be purely mechanical, using wheels and cards.

The fact that Babbage's Analytical Engine was to be entirely mechanical will help us to rid ourselves of a superstition. Importance is often attached to the fact that modern digital computers are electrical, and that the nervous system also is electrical. Since Babbage's machine was not electrical, and since all digital computers are in a sense equivalent, we see that this use of electricity cannot be of theoretical importance. Of course electricity usually comes in where fast signaling is concerned, so that it is not surprising that we find it in both these connections. In the nervous system chemical phenomena are at least as important as electrical. In certain computers the storage system is mainly acoustic. The feature of using electricity is thus seen to be only a very superficial similarity. If we wish to find such similarities we should look rather for mathematical analogies of function.

5. Universality of Digital Computers

The digital computers considered in the last section may be classified among the "discrete state machines." These are the machines which move by sudden jumps or clicks from one quite definite state to another. These states are sufficiently different for the possibility of confusion between them to be ignored. Strictly speaking there are no such machines. Everything really moves continuously. But there are many kinds of machines which can profitably be *thought of* as being discrete state machines. For instance in considering the switches for a lighting system it is a convenient fiction that each switch must be definitely on or definitely off. There must be intermediate positions, but for most purposes we can forget about them. As an example of a discrete state machine we might consider a wheel which clicks round through 120° once a second, but may be stopped by a lever which can be operated from outside; in addition a lamp is to light in one of the positions of the wheel. This machine could be described abstractly as follows: The internal state of the machine (which is described by the position of the wheel) may be q_1, q_2 or q_3. There is an input signal i_0 or i_1 (position of lever). The internal state at any

moment is determined by the last state and input signal according to the table

		Last State		
		q_1	q_2	q_3
Input	i_0	q_2	q_3	q_1
	i_1	q_1	q_2	q_3

The output signals, the only externally visible indication of the internal state (the light) are described by the table

State	q_1	q_2	q_3
Output	o_0	o_0	o_1

This example is typical of discrete state machines. They can be described by such tables provided they have only a finite number of possible states.

It will seem that given the initial state of the machine and the input signals it is always possible to predict all future states. This is reminiscent of Laplace's view that from the complete state of the universe at one moment of time, as described by the positions and velocities of all particles, it should be possible to predict all future states. The prediction which we are considering is, however, rather nearer to practicability than that considered by Laplace. The system of the "universe as a whole" is such that quite small errors in the initial conditions can have an overwhelming effect at a later time. The displacement of a single electron by a billionth of a centimeter at one moment might make the difference between a man being killed by an avalanche a year later, or escaping. It is an essential property of the mechanical systems which we have called "discrete state machines" that this phenomenon does not occur. Even when we consider the actual physical machines instead of the idealized machines, reasonably accurate knowledge of the state at one moment yields reasonably accurate knowledge any number of steps later.

As we have mentioned, digital computers fall within the class of discrete state machines. But the number of states of which such a machine is capable is usually enormously large. For instance, the number for the machine now working at Manchester is about $2^{165,000}$, i.e., about $10^{50,000}$. Compare this with our example of the clicking wheel described above, which had three states. It is not difficult to see why the number of states should be so immense. The computer includes a store corresponding to the paper used by a human computer. It must be possible to write into the store any one of the combinations of symbols which might have been written on the paper. For simplicity suppose that only digits from 0 to 9 are used as symbols. Variations in handwriting are ignored. Suppose the computer is allowed 100 sheets of paper each containing 50 lines each with room for 30 digits. Then the number of states is $10^{100\times50\times30}$, i.e., $10^{150,000}$. This is about the number of states of three Manchester machines put together. The logarithm to the base two of the number of states is usually called the "storage capacity" of the machine. Thus the Manchester machine has a storage capacity of about 165,000 and the wheel machine of our example about 1·6. If two machines are put together their capacities must be added to obtain the capacity of the resultant machine. This leads to the possibility of statements such as "The Manchester machine contains 64 magnetic tracks each with a capacity of 2560, eight electronic tubes with a capacity of 1280. Miscellaneous storage amounts to about 300 making a total of 174,380."

Given the table corresponding to a discrete state machine it is possible to predict what it will do. There is no reason why this calculation should not be carried out by means of a digital computer. Provided it could be carried out sufficiently quickly the digital computer could mimic the behavior of any discrete state machine. The imitation game could then be played with the machine in question (as B) and the

mimicking digital computer (as A) and the interrogator would be unable to distinguish them. Of course the digital computer must have an adequate storage capacity as well as working sufficiently fast. Moreover, it must be programed afresh for each new machine which it is desired to mimic.

This special property of digital computers, that they can mimic any discrete state machine, is described by saying that they are *universal* machines. The existence of machines with this property has the important consequence that, considerations of speed apart, it is unnecessary to design various new machines to do various computing processes. They can all be done with one digital computer, suitably programed for each case. It will be seen that as a consequence of this all digital computers are in a sense equivalent.

We may now consider again the point raised at the end of §3. It was suggested tentatively that the question, "Can machines think?" should be replaced by "Are there imaginable digital computers which would do well in the imitation game?" If we wish we can make this superficially more general and ask "Are there discrete state machines which would do well?" But in view of the universality property we see that either of these questions is equivalent to this, "Let us fix our attention on one particular digital computer C. Is it true that by modifying this computer to have an adequate storage, suitably increasing its speed of action, and providing it with an appropriate program, C can be made to play satisfactorily the part of A in the imitation game, the part of B being taken by a man?"

6. Contrary Views on the Main Question

We may now consider the ground to have been cleared and we are ready to proceed to the debate on our question, "Can machines think?" and the variant of it quoted at the end of the last section. We cannot altogether abandon the original form of the problem, for opinions will differ as to the appropriateness of the substitution and we must at least listen to what has to be said in this connection.

It will simplify matters for the reader if I explain first my own beliefs in the matter. Consider first the more accurate form of the question. I believe that in about fifty years' time it will be possible to program computers, with a storage capacity of about 10^9, to make them play the imitation game so well that an average interrogator will not have more than a 70 per cent chance of making the right identification after five minutes of questioning. The original question, "Can machines think?" I believe to be too meaningless to deserve discussion. Nevertheless I believe that at the end of the century the use of words and general educated opinion will have altered so much that one will be able to speak of machines thinking without expecting to be contradicted. I believe further that no useful purpose is served by concealing these beliefs. The popular view that scientists proceed inexorably from well-established fact to well-established fact, never being influenced by any unproved conjecture, is quite mistaken. Provided it is made clear which are proved facts and which are conjectures, no harm can result. Conjectures are of great importance since they suggest useful lines of research.

I now proceed to consider opinions opposed to my own.

(1) *The Theological Objection.* Thinking is a function of man's immortal soul. God has given an immortal soul to every man and woman, but not to any other animal or to machines. Hence no animal or machine can think.[1]

I am unable to accept any part of this, but will attempt to reply in theological terms. I should find the argument more convincing if animals were classed with men, for there is a greater difference, to my mind, between the typical animate and the inanimate than there

is between man and the other animals. The arbitrary character of the orthodox view becomes clearer if we consider how it might appear to a member of some other religious community. How do Christians regard the Moslem view that women have no souls? But let us leave this point aside and return to the main argument. It appears to me that the argument quoted above implies a serious restriction of the omnipotence of the Almighty. It is admitted that there are certain things that He cannot do such as making one equal to two, but should we not believe that He has freedom to confer a soul on an elephant if He sees fit? We might expect that He would only exercise this power in conjunction with a mutation which provided the elephant with an appropriately improved brain to minister to the needs of this soul. An argument of exactly similar form may be made for the case of machines. It may seem different because it is more difficult to "swallow." But this really only means that we think it would be less likely that He would consider the circumstances suitable for conferring a soul. The circumstances in question are discussed in the rest of this paper. In attempting to construct such machines we should not be irreverently usurping His power of creating souls, any more than we are in the procreation of children: rather we are, in either case, instruments of His will providing mansions for the souls that He creates.

However, this is mere speculation. I am not very impressed with theological arguments whatever they may be used to support. Such arguments have often been found unsatisfactory in the past. In the time of Galileo it was argued that the texts, "And the sun stood still ... and hasted not to go down about a whole day" (Joshua x. 13) and "He laid the foundations of the earth, that it should not move at any time" (Psalm cv. 5) were an adequate refutation of the Copernican theory. With our present knowledge such an argument appears futile. When that knowledge was not available it made a quite different impression.

(2) *The "Heads in the Sand" Objection.* "The consequences of machines thinking would be too dreadful. Let us hope and believe that they cannot do so."

This argument is seldom expressed quite so openly as in the form above. But it affects most of us who think about it at all. We like to believe that Man is in some subtle way superior to the rest of creation. It is best if he can be shown to be *necessarily* superior, for then there is no danger of him losing his commanding position. The popularity of the theological argument is clearly connected with this feeling. It is likely to be quite strong in intellectual people, since they value the power of thinking more highly than others, and are more inclined to base their belief in the superiority of Man on this power.

I do not think that this argument is sufficiently substantial to require refutation. Consolation would be more appropriate: perhaps this should be sought in the transmigration of souls.

(3) *The Mathematical Objection.* There are a number of results of mathematical logic which can be used to show that there are limitations to the powers of discrete state machines. The best known of these results is known as Gödel's theorem, and shows that in any sufficiently powerful logical system statements can be formulated which can neither be proved nor disproved within the system, unless possibly the system itself is inconsistent. There are other, in some respects similar, results due to Church, Kleene, Rosser, and Turing. The latter result is the most convenient to consider, since it refers directly to machines, whereas the others can only be used in a comparatively indirect argument: for instance if Gödel's theorem is to be used we need in addition to have some means of describing logical systems in terms of machines, and machines in terms of logical systems. The result in question refers to a type of machine which is essentially a digital computer with an infinite capacity. It states that there are certain things that such a machine cannot

do. If it is rigged up to give answers to questions as in the imitation game, there will be some questions to which it will either give a wrong answer, or fail to give an answer at all however much time is allowed for a reply. There may, of course, be many such questions, and questions which cannot be answered by one machine may be satisfactorily answered by another. We are of course supposing for the present that the questions are of the kind to which an answer "Yes" or "No" is appropriate, rather than questions such as "What do you think of Picasso?" The questions that we know the machines must fail on are of this type. "Consider the machine specified as follows ... Will this machine ever answer 'Yes' to any question?" The dots are to be replaced by a description of some machine in a standard form, which could be something like that used in §5. When the machine described bears a certain comparatively simple relation to the machine which is under interrogation, it can be shown that the answer is either wrong or not forthcoming. This is the mathematical result: it is argued that it proves a disability of machines to which the human intellect is not subject.

The short answer to this argument is that although it is established that there are limitations to the powers of any particular machine, it has only been stated, without any sort of proof, that no such limitations apply to the human intellect. But I do not think this view can be dismissed quite so lightly. Whenever one of these machines is asked the appropriate critical question, and gives a definite answer, we know that this answer must be wrong, and this gives us a certain feeling of superiority. Is this feeling illusory? It is no doubt quite genuine, but I do not think too much importance should be attached to it. We too often give wrong answers to questions ourselves to be justified in being very pleased at such evidence of fallibility on the part of the machines. Further, our superiority can only be felt on such an occasion in relation to the one machine over which we have scored our petty triumph. There would be no question of triumphing simultaneously over *all* machines. In short, then, there might be men cleverer than any given machine, but then again there might be other machines cleverer again, and so on.

Those who hold to the mathematical argument would, I think, mostly be willing to accept the imitation game as a basis for discussion. Those who believe in the two previous objections would probably not be interested in any criteria.

(4) *The Argument from Consciousness.* This argument is very well expressed in Professor Jefferson's Lister Oration for 1949, from which I quote. "Not until a machine can write a sonnet or compose a concerto because of thoughts and emotions felt, and not by the chance fall of symbols, could we agree that machine equals brain—that is, not only write it but know that it had written it. No mechanism could feel (and not merely artificially signal, an easy contrivance) pleasure at its successes, grief when its valves fuse, be warmed by flattery, be made miserable by its mistakes, be charmed by sex, be angry or depressed when it cannot get what it wants."

This argument appears to be a denial of the validity of our test. According to the most extreme form of this view the only way by which one could be sure that a machine thinks is to be the machine and to feel oneself thinking. One could then describe these feelings to the world, but of course no one would be justified in taking any notice. Likewise according to this view the only way to know that a man thinks is to be that particular man. It is in fact the solipsist point of view. It may be the most logical view to hold but it makes communication of ideas difficult. A is liable to believe "A thinks but B does not" while B believes "B thinks but A does not." Instead of arguing continually over this point it is usual to have the polite convention that everyone thinks.

I am sure that Professor Jefferson does not wish to adopt the extreme and solipsist point of view. Probably he would be quite willing to accept the imitation game as a test. The game (with the player B omitted) is frequently used in practice under the name of viva voce to discover whether someone really understands something or has "learned it parrot fashion." Let us listen in to a part of such a viva voce:

Interrogator: In the first line of your sonnet which reads "Shall I compare thee to a summer's day," would not "a spring day" do as well or better?

Witness: It wouldn't scan.

Interrogator: How about "a winter's day." That would scan all right.

Witness: Yes, but nobody wants to be compared to a winter's day.

Interrogator: Would you say Mr. Pickwick reminded you of Christmas?

Witness: In a way.

Interrogator: Yet Christmas is a winter's day, and I do not think Mr. Pickwick would mind the comparison.

Witness: I don't think you're serious. By a winter's day one means a typical winter's day, rather than a special one like Christmas.

And so on. What would Professor Jefferson say if the sonnet-writing machine was able to answer like this in the viva voce? I do not know whether he would regard the machine as "merely artificially signaling" these answers, but if the answers were as satisfactory and sustained as in the above passage I do not think he would describe it as "an easy contrivance." This phrase is, I think, intended to cover such devices as the inclusion in the machine of a record of someone reading a sonnet, with appropriate switching to turn it on from time to time.

In short then, I think that most of those who support the argument from consciousness could be persuaded to abandon it rather than be forced into the solipsist position. They will then probably be willing to accept our test.

I do not wish to give the impression that I think there is no mystery about consciousness. There is, for instance, something of a paradox connected with any attempt to localize it. But I do not think these mysteries necessarily need to be solved before we can answer the question with which we are concerned in this paper.

(5) *Arguments from Various Disabilities.* These arguments take the form, "I grant you that you can make machines do all the things you have mentioned but you will never be able to make one to do X." Numerous features X are suggested in this connection. I offer a selection:

> Be kind, resourceful, beautiful, friendly … have initiative, have a sense of humor, tell right from wrong, make mistakes … fall in love, enjoy strawberries and cream … make someone fall in love with it, learn from experience … use words properly, be the subject of its own thought … have as much diversity of behavior as a man, do something really new.

No support is usually offered for these statements. I believe they are mostly founded on the principle of scientific induction. A man has seen thousands of machines in his lifetime. From what he sees of them he draws a number of general conclusions. They are ugly, each is designed for a very limited purpose, when required for a minutely different purpose they are useless, the variety of behavior of any one of them is very small, etc., etc. Naturally he concludes that these are necessary properties of machines in general. Many of these limitations are associated with the very small storage capacity of most machines. (I am assuming that the idea of storage capacity is extended in some way to cover machines other than discrete state machines. The exact definition does not matter as no mathematical accuracy is claimed in the present discussion.) A few years ago, when very little had been heard of digital computers, it was possible to elicit much incredulity concerning them, if one mentioned their properties without describing their construction. That was

presumably due to a similar application of the principle of scientific induction. These applications of the principle are of course largely unconscious. When a burned child fears the fire and shows that he fears it by avoiding it, I should say that he was applying scientific induction. (I could of course also describe his behavior in many other ways.) The works of customs of mankind do not seem to be very suitable material to which to apply scientific induction. A very large part of space-time must be investigated if reliable results are to be obtained. Otherwise we may (as most English children do) decide that everybody speaks English, and that it is silly to learn French.

There are, however, special remarks to be made about many of the disabilities that have been mentioned. The inability to enjoy strawberries and cream may [strike] the reader as frivolous. Possibly a machine might be made to enjoy this delicious dish, but any attempt to make one do so would be idiotic. What is important about this disability is that it contributes to some of the other disabilities, e.g., to the difficulty of the same kind of friendliness occurring between man and machine as between white man and white man, or between black man and black man.

The claim that "machines cannot make mistakes" seems a curious one. One is tempted to retort, "Are they any worse for that?" But let us adopt a more sympathetic attitude, and try to see what is really meant. I think this criticism can be explained in terms of the imitation game. It is claimed that the interrogator could distinguish the machine from the man simply by setting them a number of problems in arithmetic. The machine would be unmasked because of its deadly accuracy. The reply to this is simple. The machine (programed for playing the game) would not attempt to give the *right* answers to the arithmetic problems. It would deliberately introduce mistakes in a manner calculated to confuse the interrogator. A mechanical fault would probably show itself through an unsuitable decision as to what sort of a mistake to make in the arithmetic. Even this interpretation of the criticism is not sufficiently sympathetic. But we cannot afford the space to go into it much further. It seems to me that this criticism depends on a confusion between two kinds of mistakes. We may call them "errors of functioning" and "errors of conclusion." Errors of functioning are due to some mechanical or electrical fault which causes the machine to behave otherwise than it was designed to do. In philosophical discussions one likes to ignore the possibility of such errors; one is therefore discussing "abstract machines." These abstract machines are mathematical fictions rather than physical objects. By definition they are incapable of errors of functioning. In this sense we can truly say that "machines can never make mistakes." Errors of conclusion can only arise when some meaning is attached to the output signals from the machine. The machine might, for instance, type out mathematical equations, or sentences in English. When a false proposition is typed we say that the machine has committed an error of conclusion. There is clearly no reason at all for saying that a machine cannot make this kind of mistake. It might do nothing but type out repeatedly "0 = 1." To take a less perverse example, it might have some method for drawing conclusions by scientific induction. We must expect such a method to lead occasionally to erroneous results.

The claim that a machine cannot be the subject of its own thought can of course only be answered if it can be shown that the machine has *some* thought with *some* matter. Nevertheless, "the subject matter of a machine's operations" does seem to mean something, at least to the people who deal with it. If, for instance, the machine was trying to find a solution of the equation $x^2 - 40x - 11 = 0$ one would be tempted to describe this equation as part of the machine's subject matter at that moment. In this sort of sense a machine undoubtedly can be its own subject matter. It may be used to help in

making up its own programs, or to predict the effect of alterations in its own structure. By observing the results of its own behavior it can modify its own programs so as to achieve some purpose more effectively. These are possibilities of the near future, rather than Utopian dreams.

The criticism that a machine cannot have much diversity of behavior is just a way of saying that it cannot have much storage capacity. Until fairly recently a storage capacity of even a thousand digits was very rare.

The criticisms that we are considering here are often disguised forms of the argument from consciousness. Usually if one maintains that a machine *can* do one of these things, and describes the kind of method that the machine could use, one will not make much of an impression. It is thought that the method (whatever it may be, for it must be mechanical) is really rather base. Compare the parenthesis of Jefferson's statement quoted above.

(6) *Lady Lovelace's Objection.* Our most detailed information of Babbage's Analytical Engine comes from a memoir by Lady Lovelace. In it she states, "The Analytical Engine has no pretensions to *originate* anything. It can do *whatever we know how to order it* to perform" (her italics). This statement is quoted by Hartree who adds: "This does not imply that it may not be possible to construct electronic equipment which will 'think for itself,' or in which, in biological terms, one could set up a conditioned reflex, which would serve as a basis for 'learning.' Whether this is possible in principle or not is a stimulating and exciting question, suggested by some of these recent developments But it did not seem that the machines constructed or projected at the time had this property."

I am in thorough agreement with Hartree over this. It will be noticed that he does not assert that the machines in question had not got the property, but rather that the evidence available to Lady Lovelace did not encourage her to believe that they had it. It is quite possible that the machines in question had in a sense got this property. For suppose that some discrete state machine has the property. The Analytical Engine was a universal digital computer, so that, if its storage capacity and speed were adequate, it could by suitable programing be made to mimic the machine in question. Probably this argument did not occur to the Countess or to Babbage. In any case there was no obligation on them to claim all that could be claimed.

This whole question will be considered again under the heading of learning machines.

A variant of Lady Lovelace's objection states that a machine can "never do anything really new." This may be parried for a moment with the saw, "There is nothing new under the sun." Who can be certain that "original work" that he has done was not simply the growth of the seed planted in him by teaching, or the effect of following well-known general principles. A better variant of the objection says that a machine can never "take us by surprise." This statement is a more direct challenge and can be met directly. Machines take me by surprise with great frequency. This is largely because I do not do sufficient calculation to decide what to expect them to do, or rather because, although I do a calculation, I do it in a hurried, slipshod fashion, taking risks. Perhaps I say to myself, "I suppose the voltage here ought to be the same as there: anyway let's assume it is." Naturally I am often wrong, and the result is a surprise for me, for by the time the experiment is done these assumptions have been forgotten. These admissions lay me open to lectures on the subject of my vicious ways, but do not throw any doubt on my credibility when I testify to the surprises I experience.

I do not expect this reply to silence my critic. He will probably say that such surprises are due to some creative mental act on my part, and reflect no credit on the machine. This leads us back to the argument from consciousness, and far from the idea of surprise. It is a line of argument we must consider closed, but it is

perhaps worth remarking that the appreciation of something as surprising requires as much of a "creative mental act" whether the surprising event originates from a man, a book, a machine or anything else.

The view that machines cannot give rise to surprises is due, I believe, to a fallacy to which philosophers and mathematicians are particularly subject. This is the assumption that as soon as a fact is presented to a mind all consequences of that fact spring into the mind simultaneously with it. It is a very useful assumption under many circumstances, but one too easily forgets that it is false. A natural consequence of doing so is that one then assumes that there is no virtue in the mere working out of consequences from data and general principles.

(7) *Argument from Continuity in the Nervous System.* The nervous system is certainly not a discrete state machine. A small error in the information about the size of a nervous impulse impinging on a neuron, may make a large difference to the size of the outgoing impulse. It may be argued that, this being so, one cannot expect to be able to mimic the behavior of the nervous system with a discrete state system.

It is true that a discrete state machine must be different from a continuous machine. But if we adhere to the conditions of the imitation game, the interrogator will not be able to take any advantage of this difference. The situation can be made clearer if we consider some other simpler continuous machine. A differential analyzer will do very well. (A differential analyzer is a certain kind of machine not of the discrete state type used for some kinds of calculation.) Some of these provide their answers in a typed form, and so are suitable for taking part in the game. It would not be possible for a digital computer to predict exactly what answers the differential analyzer would give to a problem, but it would be quite capable of giving the right sort of answer. For instance, if asked to give the value of π (actually about 3.1416) it would be reasonable to choose at random between the values 3.12, 3.13, 3.14, 3.15, 3.16 with the probabilities of 0.05, 0.15, 0.55, 0.19, 0.06 (say). Under these circumstances it would be very difficult for the interrogator to distinguish the differential analyzer from the digital computer.

(8) *The Argument from Informality of Behavior.* It is not possible to produce a set of rules purporting to describe what a man should do in every conceivable set of circumstances. One might for instance have a rule that one is to stop when one sees a red traffic light, and to go if one sees a green one, but what if by some fault both appear together? One may perhaps decide that it is safest to stop. But some further difficulty may well arise from this decision later. To attempt to provide rules of conduct to cover every eventuality, even those arising from traffic lights, appears to be impossible. With all this I agree.

From this it is argued that we cannot be machines, I shall try to reproduce the argument, but I fear I shall hardly do it justice. It seems to run something like this. "If each man had a definite set of rules of conduct by which he regulated his life he would be no better than a machine. But there are no such rules, so men cannot be machines." The undistributed middle is glaring. I do not think the argument is ever put quite like this, but I believe this is the argument used nevertheless. There may however be a certain confusion between "rules of conduct" and "laws of behavior" to cloud the issue. By "rules of conduct" I mean precepts such as "Stop if you see red lights," on which one can act, and of which one can be conscious. By "laws of behavior" I mean laws of nature as applied to a man's body such as "if you pinch him he will squeak." If we substitute "laws of behavior which regulate his life" for "laws of conduct by which he regulates his life" in the argument quoted the undistributed middle is no longer insuperable. For we believe that it is not only true that being regulated by laws of behavior implies being some sort of machine

(though not necessarily a discrete state machine), but that conversely being such a machine implies being regulated by such laws. However, we cannot so easily convince ourselves of the absence of complete laws of behavior as of complete rules of conduct. The only way we know of for finding such laws is scientific observation, and we certainly know of no circumstances under which we could say, "We have searched enough. There are no such laws."

We can demonstrate more forcibly that any such statement would be unjustified. For suppose we could be sure of finding such laws if they existed. Then given a discrete state machine it should certainly be possible to discover by observation sufficient about it to predict its future behavior, and this within a reasonable time, say a thousand years. But this does not seem to be the case. I have set up on the Manchester computer a small program using only 1000 units of storage, whereby the machine supplied with one sixteen-figure number replies with another within two seconds. I would defy anyone to learn from these replies sufficient about the program to be able to predict any replies to untried values.

(9) *The Argument from Extra-Sensory Perception.* I assume that the reader is familiar with the idea of extra-sensory perception, and the meaning of the four items of it, viz., telepathy, clairvoyance, precognition and psychokinesis. These disturbing phenomena seem to deny all our usual scientific ideas. How we would like to discredit them! Unfortunately the statistical evidence, at least for telepathy, is overwhelming. It is very difficult to rearrange one's ideas so as to fit these new facts in. Once one has accepted them it does not seem a very big step to believe in ghosts and bogies. The idea that our bodies move simply according to the known laws of physics, together with some others not yet discovered but somewhat similar, would be one of the first to go.

This argument is to my mind quite a strong one. One can say in reply that many scientific theories seem to remain workable in practice, in spite of clashing with E.S.P.; that in fact one can get along very nicely if one forgets about it. This is rather cold comfort, and one fears that thinking is just the kind of phenomenon where E.S.P. may be especially relevant.

A more specific argument based on E.S.P. might run as follows: "Let us play the imitation game, using as witnesses a man who is good as a telepathic receiver, and a digital computer. The interrogator can ask such questions as 'What suit does the card in my right hand belong to?' The man by telepathy or clairvoyance gives the right answer 130 times out of 400 cards. The machine can only guess at random, and perhaps get 104 right, so the interrogator makes the right identification." There is an interesting possibility which opens here. Suppose the digital computer contains a random number generator. Then it will be natural to use this to decide what answer to give. But then the random number of generator will be subject to the psychokinetic powers of the interrogator. Perhaps this psychokinesis might cause the machine to guess right more often than would be expected on a probability calculation, so that the interrogator might still be unable to make the right identification. On the other hand, he might be able to guess right without any questioning, by clairvoyance. With E.S.P. anything may happen.

If telepathy is admitted it will be necessary to tighten our test. The situation could be regarded as analogous to that which would occur if the interrogator were talking to himself and one of the competitors was listening with his ear to the wall. To put the competitors into a "telepathy-proof room" would satisfy all requirements.

7. Learning Machines

The reader will have anticipated that I have no very convincing arguments of a positive nature to support my views. If I had I should not have taken such pains to point out the fallacies in contrary views. Such evidence as I have I shall now give.

Let us return for a moment to Lady Lovelace's objection, which stated that the machine can only do what we tell it to do. One could say that a man can "inject" an idea into the machine, and that it will respond to a certain extent and then drop into quiescence, like a piano string struck by a hammer. Another simile would be an atomic pile of less than critical size: an injected idea is to correspond to a neutron entering the pile from without. Each such neutron will cause a certain disturbance which eventually dies away. If, however, the size of the pile is sufficiently increased, the disturbance caused by such an incoming neutron will very likely go on and on increasing until the whole pile is destroyed. Is there a corresponding phenomenon for minds, and is there one for machines? There does seem to be one for the human mind. The majority of them seem to be "subcritical," i.e., to correspond in this analogy to piles of subcritical size. An idea presented to such a mind will on an average give rise to less than one idea in reply. A smallish proportion are supercritical. An idea presented to such a mind may give rise to a whole "theory" consisting of secondary, tertiary and more remote ideas. Animals' minds seem to be very definitely subcritical. Adhering to this analogy we ask, "Can a machine be made to be supercritical?"

The "skin of an onion" analogy is also helpful. In considering the functions of the mind or the brain we find certain operations which we can explain in purely mechanical terms. This we say does not correspond to the real mind: it is a sort of skin which we must strip off if we are to find the real mind. But then in what remains we find a further skin to be stripped off, and so on. Proceeding in this way do we ever come to the "real" mind, or do we eventually come to the skin which has nothing in it? In the latter case the whole mind is mechanical. (It would not be a discrete state machine however. We have discussed this.)

These last two paragraphs do not claim to be convincing arguments. They should rather be described as "recitations tending to produce belief."

The only really satisfactory support that can be given for the view expressed at the beginning of §6, [p. 270], will be that provided by waiting for the end of the century and then doing the experiment described. But what can we say in the meantime? What steps should be taken now if the experiment is to be successful?

As I have explained, the problem is mainly one of programing. Advances in engineering will have to be made too, but it seems unlikely that these will not be adequate for the requirements. Estimates of the storage capacity of the brain vary from 10^{10} to 10^{15} binary digits. I incline to the lower values and believe that only a very small fraction is used for the higher types of thinking. Most of it is probably used for the retention of visual impressions. I should be surprised if more then 10^9 was required for satisfactory playing of the imitation game, at any rate against a blind man. (Note: The capacity of the *Encyclopaedia Britannica*, eleventh edition, is 2 x 10^9.) A storage capacity of 10^7 would be a very practicable possibility even by present techniques. It is probably not necessary to increase the speed of operations of the machines at all. Parts of modern machines which can be regarded as analogues of nerve cells work about a thousand times faster than the latter. (This should provide a "margin of safety" which could cover losses of speed arising in many ways.) Our problem then is to find out how to program these machines to play the game. At my present rate of working I produce about a thousand digits of program a day, so that about sixty workers, working steadily through the fifty years might accomplish the job, if nothing went into the wastepaper basket. Some more expeditious method seems desirable.

In the process of trying to imitate an adult human mind we are bound to think a good deal about the process which has brought it to the state that it is in. We may notice three components,

(a) The initial state of the mind, say at birth,
(b) The education to which it has been subjected,
(c) Other experience, not to be described as education, to which it has been subjected.

Instead of trying to produce a program to simulate the adult mind, why not rather try to produce one which simulates the child's? If this were then subjected to an appropriate course of education one would obtain the adult brain. Presumably the child-brain is something like a notebook as one buys it from the stationers. Rather little mechanism, and lots of blank sheets. (Mechanism and writing are from our point of view almost synonymous.) Our hope is that there is so little mechanism in the child-brain that something like it can be easily programed. The amount of work in the education we can assume, as a first approximation, to be much the same as for the human child.

We have thus divided our problem into two parts—the child-program and the education process. These two remain very closely connected. We cannot expect to find a good child-machine at the first attempt. One must experiment with teaching one such machine and see how well it learns. One can then try another and see if it is better or worse. There is an obvious connection between this process and evolution, by the identifications

Structure of the child-machine	= Hereditary material
Changes of the child-machine	= Mutations
Natural selection	= Judgment of the experimenter

One may hope, however, that this process will be more expeditious than evolution. The survival of the fittest is a slow method for measuring advantages. The experimenter, by the exercise of intelligence, should be able to speed it up. Equally important is the fact that he is not restricted to random mutations. If he can trace a cause for some weakness he can probably think of the kind of mutation which will improve it.

It will not be possible to apply exactly the same teaching process to the machine as to a normal child. It will not, for instance, be provided with legs, so that it could not be asked to go out and fill the coal scuttle. Possibly it might not have eyes. But however well these deficiencies might be overcome by clever engineering. one could not send the creature to school without the other children making excessive fun of it. It must be given some tuition. We need not be too concerned about the legs, eyes, etc. The example of Miss Helen Keller shows that education can take place provided that communication in both directions between teacher and pupil can take place by some means or other.

We normally associate punishments and rewards with the teaching process. Some simple child-machines can be constructed or programed on this sort of principle. The machine has to be so constructed that events which shortly preceded the occurrence of a punishment-signal are unlikely to be repeated, whereas a reward-signal increases the probability of repetition of the events which led up to it. These definitions do not presuppose any feelings on the part of the machine. I have done some experiments with one such child-machine, and succeeded in teaching it a few things, but the teaching method was too unorthodox for the experiment to be considered really successful.

The use of punishments and rewards can at best be a part of the teaching process. Roughly speaking, if the teacher has no other means of communicating to the pupil, the amount of information which can reach him does not exceed the total number of rewards and punishments applied. By the time a child has learned to repeat "Casablanca" he would probably feel very sore indeed, if the text could only be discovered by a "Twenty Questions" technique, every "NO" taking the form of a blow. It is neces-

sary therefore to have some other "unemotional" channels of communication. If these are available it is possible to teach a machine by punishments and rewards to obey orders given in some language, e.g., a symbolic language. These orders are to be transmitted through the "unemotional" channels. The use of this language will diminish greatly the number of punishments and rewards required.

Opinions may vary as to the complexity which is suitable in the child-machine. One might try to make it as simple as possible consistently with the general principles. Alternatively one might have a complete system of logical inference "built in."[2] In the latter case the store would be largely occupied with definitions and propositions. The propositions would have various kinds of status, e.g., well-established facts, conjectures, mathematically proved theorems, statements given by an authority, expressions having the logical form of proposition but not belief-value. Certain propositions may be described as "imperatives." The machine should be so constructed that as soon as an imperative is classed as "well established" the appropriate action automatically takes place. To illustrate this, suppose the teacher says to the machine, "Do your homework now." This may cause "Teacher says 'Do your homework now'" to be included among the well-established facts. Another such fact might be, "Everything that teacher says is true." Combining these may eventually lead to the imperative, "Do your homework now," being included among the well-established facts, and this, by the construction of the machine, will mean that the homework actually gets started, but the effect is very unsatisfactory. The processes of inference used by the machine need not be such as would satisfy the most exacting logicians. There might for instance be no hierarchy of types. But this need not mean that type fallacies will occur, any more than we are bound to fall over unfenced cliffs. Suitable imperatives (expressed *within* the systems, not forming part of the rules *of* the system) such as "Do not use a class unless it is a subclass of one which has been mentioned by teacher" can have a similar effect to "Do not go too near the edge."

The imperatives that can be obeyed by a machine that has no limbs are bound to be of a rather intellectual character, as in the example (doing homework) given above. Important among such imperatives will be ones which regulate the order in which the rules of the logical system concerned are to be applied. For at each stage when one is using a logical system, there is a very large number of alternative steps, any of which one is permitted to apply, so far as obedience to the rules of the logical system is concerned. These choices make the difference between a brilliant and a footling reasoner, not the difference between a sound and a fallacious one. Propositions leading to imperatives of this kind might be "When Socrates is mentioned, use the syllogism in Barbara" or "If one method has been proved to be quicker than another, do not use the slower method." Some of these may be "given by authority," but others may be produced by the machine itself, e.g., by scientific induction.

The idea of a learning machine may appear paradoxical to some readers. How can the rules of operation of the machine change? They should describe completely how the machine will react whatever its history might be, whatever changes it might undergo. The rules are thus quite time-invariant. This is quite true. The explanation of the paradox is that the rules which get changed in the learning process are of a rather less pretentious kind, claiming only an ephemeral validity. The reader may draw a parallel with the Constitution of the United States.

An important feature of a learning machine is that its teacher will often be very largely ignorant of quite what is going on inside, although he may still be able to some extent to predict his pupil's behavior. This should apply most strongly to the later education of a machine arising from a child-machine of well-tried design (or program). This is in clear contrast

with normal procedure when using a machine to do computations: one's object is then to have a clear mental picture of the state of the machine at each moment in the computation. This object can only be achieved with a struggle. The view that "the machine can only do what we know how to order it to do,"[3] appears strange in face of this. Most of the programs which we can put into the machine will result in its doing something that we cannot make sense of at all, or which we regard as completely random behavior. Intelligent behavior presumably consists in a departure from the completely disciplined behavior involved in computation, but a rather slight one, which does not give rise to random behavior, or to pointless repetitive loops. Another important result of preparing our machine for its part in the imitation game by a process of teaching and learning is that "human fallibility" is likely to be omitted in a rather natural way, i.e., without special "coaching." ... Processes that are learned do not produce a hundred per cent certainty of result: if they did they could not be unlearned.

It is probably wise to include a random element in a learning machine ... A random element is rather useful when we are searching for a solution of some problem. Suppose for instance we wanted to find a number between 50 and 200 which was equal to the square of the sum of its digits, we might start at 51 then try 52 and go on until we got a number that worked. Alternatively we might choose numbers at random until we got a good one. This method has the advantage that it is unnecessary to keep track of the values that have been tried, but the disadvantage that one may try the same one twice, but this is not very important if there are several solutions. The systematic method has the disadvantage that there may be an enormous block without any solutions in the region which has to be investigated first. Now the learning process may be regarded as a search for a form of behavior which will satisfy the teacher (or some other criterion). Since there is probably a very large number of satisfactory solutions the random method seems to be better than the systematic. It should be noticed that it is used in the analogous process of evolution. But there the systematic method is not possible. How could one keep track of the different genetical combinations that had been tried, so as to avoid trying them again?

We may hope that machines will eventually compete with men in all purely intellectual fields. But which are the best ones to start with? Even this is a difficult decision. Many people think that a very abstract activity, like the playing of chess, would be best. It can also be maintained that it is best to provide the machine with the best sense organs that money can buy, and then teach it to understand and speak English. This process could follow the normal teaching of a child. Things would be pointed out and named, etc. Again I do not know what the right answer is, but I think both approaches should be tried.

We can only see a short distance ahead, but we can see plenty there that needs to be done.

NOTES

1. Possibly this view is heretical. Saint Thomas Aquinas (*Summa Theologica*, quoted by Bertrand Russell, *A History of Western Philosophy* [New York: Simon & Schuster, 1945], p. 458) states that God cannot make a man to have no soul. But this may not be a real restriction on His powers, but only a result of the fact that men's souls are immortal, and therefore indestructible.
2. Or rather "programed in" for our child-machine will be programed in a digital computer. But the logical system will not have to be learned.
3. Compare Lady Lovelace's statement [p. 275], which does not contain the word "only."

John R. Searle
"Minds, Brains and Programs"

What psychological and philosophical significance should we attach to recent efforts at computer simulations of human cognitive capacities? In answering this question, I find it useful to distinguish what I will call "strong" AI from "weak" or "cautious" AI (artificial intelligence). According to weak AI, the principal value of the computer in the study of the mind is that it gives us a very powerful tool. For example, it enables us to formulate and test hypotheses in a more rigorous and precise fashion. But according to strong AI, the computer is not merely a tool in the study of the mind, rather, the appropriately programmed computer really *is* a mind, in the sense that computers given the

right programs can be literally said to *understand* and have other cognitive states. In strong AI, because the programmed computer has cognitive states, the programs are not mere tools that enable us to test psychological explanations, rather, the programs are themselves the explanations.

I have no objection to the claims of weak AI, at least as far as this article is concerned. My discussion here will be directed at the claims I have defined as those of strong AI, specifically the claim that the appropriately programmed computer literally has cognitive states and that the programs thereby explain human cognition. When I hereafter refer to AI, I have in mind the strong version, as expressed by these two claims.

I will consider the work of Roger Schank and his colleagues at Yale (Schank and Abelson 1977), because I am more familiar with it than I am with any other similar claims, and because it provides a very clear example of the sort of work I wish to examine. But nothing that follows depends upon the details of Schank's programs. The same arguments would apply to Winograd's SHRDLU (Winograd 1973), Weizenbaum's ELIZA (Weizenbaum 1965), and indeed any Turing machine simulation of human mental phenomena.

Very briefly, and leaving out the various details, one can describe Schank's program as follows: The aim of the program is to simulate the human ability to understand stories. It is characteristic of human beings' story-understanding capacity that they can answer questions about the story even though the information that they give was never explicitly stated in the story. Thus, for example, suppose you are given the following story: "A man went into a restaurant and ordered a hamburger. When the hamburger arrived it was burned to a crisp, and the man stormed out of the restaurant angrily, without paying for the burger or leaving a tip." Now, if you are asked "Did the man eat the hamburger?" you will presumably answer, "No, he did not." Similarly, if you are given the following story: "A man went into a restaurant and ordered a hamburger; when the hamburger came he was very pleased with it; and as he left the restaurant he gave the waitress a large tip before paying his bill," and you are asked the question, "Did the man eat the hamburger?" you will presumably answer, "Yes, he ate the hamburger." Now Schank's machines can similarly answer questions about restaurants in this fashion. To do this, they have a "representation" of the sort of information that human beings have about restaurants, which enables them to answer such questions as those above, given these sorts of stories. When the machine is given the story and then asked the question, the machine will print out answers of the sort that we would expect human beings to give if told similar stories. Partisans of strong AI claim that in this question and answer sequence the machine is not only simulating a human ability but also (1) that the machine can literally be said to *understand* the story and provide the answers to questions, and (2) that what the machine and its program do *explains* the human ability to understand the story and answer questions about it.

Both claims seem to me to be totally unsupported by Schank's work, as I will attempt to show in what follows.[1]

One way to test any theory of the mind is to ask oneself what it would be like if my mind actually worked on the principles that the theory says all minds work on. Let us apply this test to the Schank program with the following *Gedankenexperiment.* Suppose that I'm locked in a room and given a large batch of Chinese writing. Suppose furthermore (as is indeed the case) that I know no Chinese, either written or spoken, and that I'm not even confident that I could recognize Chinese writing as Chinese writing distinct from, say, Japanese writing or meaningless squiggles. To me, Chinese writing is just so many meaningless squiggles. Now suppose further that after this first batch of Chinese writing I am given a second batch of Chinese script together with a set of rules for correlating the second batch with the first batch. The rules are in English, and I understand these rules as well as any other native speaker of English. They enable me to correlate one set of formal symbols with another set of formal symbols, and all that "formal" means here is that I can identify the symbols entirely by their shapes. Now suppose also that I am given a third batch of Chinese symbols together with some instructions, again in English, that enable me to correlate elements of this third batch with the first two batches, and these rules instruct me how to give back certain Chinese symbols with certain sorts of shapes in response to certain sorts of shapes given me in the third batch. Unknown to me, the people who are giving me all of these symbols call the first batch a "script," they call the second batch a "story," and they call the third batch "questions." Furthermore, they call the symbols I give them back in response to the third batch "answers to the questions," and the set of rules in English that they gave me, they call the "program." Now just to complicate the story a little, imagine that these people also give me stories in English, which I understand, and they then ask me questions in English about these stories, and I give them back answers in English. Suppose also that after a while I got so good at following the instructions for manipulating the Chinese symbols and the programmers get so good at writing the programs that from the external point of view—that is, from the point of view of somebody outside the room in which I am locked—my answers to the questions are absolutely indistinguishable from those of native Chinese speakers. Nobody just looking at my answers can tell that I don't speak a word of Chinese. Let us also suppose that my answers to the English questions are, as they no doubt would be, indistinguishable from those of other native English speakers, for the simple reason that I am a native English speaker. From the external point of view—from the point of view of someone reading my "answers"—answers to the Chinese questions and the English questions are equally good. But in the Chinese case, unlike the English case, I produce the answers by manipulating uninterpreted formal symbols. As far as the Chinese is concerned, I simply behave like a computer; I perform computational operations on formally specified elements. For the purposes of the Chinese, I am simply an instantiation of the computer program.

Now the claims made by strong AI are that the programmed computer understands the stories and that the program in some sense explains human understanding. But we are now in a position to examine these claims in light of our thought experiment.

1. As regards the first claim, it seems to me quite obvious in the example that I do not understand a word of Chinese stories. I have inputs and outputs that are indistinguishable from those of the native Chinese speaker, and I can have any formal program you like, but I still understand nothing. For the same reasons, Schank's computer understands nothing of any stories, whether in Chinese, English, or whatever, since in the Chinese case the computer is me, and in cases where the computer is not me, the computer has nothing more than I have in the case where I understand nothing.

2. As regards the second claim, that the program explains human understanding, we can see that the computer and its program do not provide sufficient conditions of understanding since the computer and the program are functioning, and there is no understanding. But does it even provide a necessary condition or a significant contribution to understanding? One of the claims made by the supporters of strong AI is that when I understand a story in English, what I am doing is exactly the same—or perhaps more of the same—as what I was doing in manipulating the Chinese symbols. It is simply more formal symbol manipulation that distinguishes the case in English, where I do understand, from the case in Chinese where I don't. I have not demonstrated that this claim is false, but it would certainly appear an incredible claim in the example. Such plausibility as the claim has derives from the supposition that we can construct a program that will have the same inputs and outputs as native speakers, and in addition we assume that speakers have some level of description where they are also instantiations of a program. On the basis of these two assumptions we assume that even if Schank's program isn't the whole story about understanding, it may be part of the story. Well, I suppose that is an empirical possibility, but not the slightest reason has so far been given to believe that it is true, since what is suggested—though certainly not demonstrated—by the example is

that the computer program is simply irrelevant to my understanding of the story. In the Chinese case I have everything that artificial intelligence can put into me by way of a program, and I understand nothing; in the English case I understand everything, and there is so far no reason at all to suppose that my understanding has anything to do with computer programs, that is, with computational operations on purely formally specified elements. As long as the program is defined in terms of computational operations on purely formally defined elements, what the example suggests is that these by themselves have no interesting connection with understanding. They are certainly not sufficient conditions, and not the slightest reason has been given to suppose that they are necessary conditions or even that they make a significant contribution to understanding. Notice that the force of the argument is not simply that different machines can have the same input and output while operating on different formal principles—that is not the point at all. Rather, whatever purely formal principles you put into the computer, they will not be sufficient for understanding, since a human will be able to follow the formal principles without understanding anything. No reason whatever has been offered to suppose that such principles are necessary or even contributory, since no reason has been given to suppose that when I understand English I am operating with any formal program at all.

Well, then, what is it that I have in the case of the English sentences that I do not have in the case of the Chinese sentences? The obvious answer is that I know what the former mean, while I haven't the faintest idea what the latter mean. But in what does this consist and why couldn't we give it to a machine, whatever it is? I will return to this question later, but first I want to continue with the example.

I have had the occasions to present this example to several workers in artificial intelligence, and, interestingly, they do not seem to agree on what the proper reply to it is. I get a surprising variety of replies, and in what follows I will consider the most common of these (specified along with their geographic origins).

But first I want to block some common misunderstandings about "understanding": In many of these discussions one finds a lot of fancy footwork about the word "understanding." My critics point out that there are many different degrees of understanding; that "understanding" is not a simple two-place predicate; that there are even different kinds and levels of understanding, and often the law of excluded middle doesn't even apply in a straightforward way to statements of the form "x understands y"; that in many cases it is a matter for decision and not a simple matter of fact whether x understands y; and so on. To all of these points I want to say: of course, of course. But they have nothing to do with the points at issue. There are clear cases in which "understanding" literally applies and clear cases in which it does not apply; and these two sorts of cases are all I need for this argument.[2] I understand stories in English; to a lesser degree I can understand stories in French; to a still lesser degree, stories in German; and in Chinese, not at all. My car and my adding machine, on the other hand, understand nothing: they are not in that line of business. We often attribute "understanding" and other cognitive predicates by metaphor and analogy to cars, adding machines, and other artifacts, but nothing is proved by such attributions. We say, "The door *knows* when to open because of its photoelectric cell," "The adding machine *knows how (understands how, is able)* to do addition and subtraction but not division," and "The thermostat *perceives* changes in the temperature." The reason we make these attributions is quite interesting, and it has to do with the fact that in artifacts we extend our own intentionality;[3] our tools are extensions of our purposes, and so we find it natural to make metaphorical attributions of intentionality to them; but I take it no philosophical ice is cut by such examples. The sense in which an automatic door "understands instructions" from its photoelectric cell is not at all the sense in which I understand English. If the sense in which Schank's programmed computers understand stories is supposed to be the metaphorical sense in which the door understands, and not the sense in which I understand English, the issue would not be worth discussing. But Newell and Simon (1963) write that the kind of cognition they claim for computers is exactly the same as for human beings. I like the straightforwardness of this claim, and it is the sort of claim I will be considering. I will argue that in the literal sense the programmed computer understands what the car and the adding machine understand, namely, exactly nothing. The computer understanding is not just (like my understanding of German) partial or incomplete; it is zero.

Now to the replies:

I. The Systems Reply (Berkeley). "While it is true that the individual person who is locked in the room does not understand the story, the fact is that he is merely part of a whole system, and the system does understand the story. The person has a large ledger in front of him in which are written the rules, he has a lot of scratch paper and pencils for doing calculations, he has 'data banks' of sets of Chinese symbols. Now, understanding is not being ascribed to the mere individual; rather it is being ascribed to this whole system of which he is a part."

My response to the systems theory is quite simple: Let the individual internalize all of these elements of the system. He memorizes the rules in the ledger and the data banks of Chinese symbols, and he does all the calculations in his head. The individual then incorporates the entire system. There isn't anything at all to the system that he does not encompass. We can even get rid of the room and suppose he works outdoors. All the same, he understands nothing of the Chinese, and a fortiori neither does the system, because there isn't anything in the system that isn't in him. If he doesn't understand, then

there is no way the system could understand because the system is just a part of him.

Actually I feel somewhat embarrassed to give even this answer to the systems theory because the theory seems to me so implausible to start with. The idea is that while a person doesn't understand Chinese, somehow the *conjunction* of that person and bits of paper might understand Chinese. It is not easy for me to imagine how someone who was not in the grip of an ideology would find the idea at all plausible. Still, I think many people who are committed to the ideology of strong AI will in the end be inclined to say something very much like this; so let us pursue it a bit further. According to one version of this view, while the man in the internalized systems example doesn't understand Chinese in the sense that a native Chinese speaker does (because, for example, he doesn't know that the story refers to restaurants and hamburgers, etc.), still "the man as a formal symbol manipulation system" *really does understand Chinese.* The subsystem of the man that is the formal symbol manipulation system for Chinese should not be confused with the subsystem for English.

So there are really two subsystems in the man; one understands English, the other Chinese, and "it's just that the two systems have little to do with each other." But, I want to reply, not only do they have little to do with each other, they are not even remotely alike. The subsystem that understands English (assuming we allow ourselves to talk in this jargon of "subsystems" for a moment) knows that the stories are about restaurants and eating hamburgers, he knows that he is being asked questions about restaurants and that he is answering questions as best he can by making various inferences from the content of the story, and so on. But the Chinese system knows none of this. Whereas the English subsystem knows that "hamburgers" refers to hamburgers, the Chinese subsystem knows only that "squiggle squiggle" is followed by "squoggle squoggle." All he knows is that various formal symbols are being introduced at one end and manipulated according to rules written in English, and other symbols are going out at the other end. The whole point of the original example was to argue that such symbol manipulation by itself couldn't be sufficient for understanding Chinese in any literal sense because the man could write "squoggle squoggle" after "squiggle squiggle" without understanding anything in Chinese. And it doesn't meet that argument to postulate subsystems within the man, because the subsystems are no better off than the man was in the first place; they still don't have anything even remotely like what the English-speaking man (or subsystem) has. Indeed, in the case as described, the Chinese subsystem is simply a part of the English subsystem, a part that engages in meaningless symbol manipulation according to rules in English.

Let us ask ourselves what is supposed to motivate the systems reply in the first place; that is, what *independent* grounds are there supposed to be for saying that the agent must have a subsystem within him that literally understands stories in Chinese? As far as I can tell the only grounds are that in the example I have the same input and output as native Chinese speakers and a program that goes from one to the other. But the whole point of the examples has been to try to show that that couldn't be sufficient for understanding, in the sense in which I understand stories in English, because a person, and hence the set of systems that go to make up a person, could have the right combination of input, output, and program and still not understand anything in the relevant literal sense in which I understand English. The only motivation for saying there *must* be a subsystem in me that understands Chinese is that I have a program and I can pass the Turing test: I can fool native Chinese speakers. But precisely one of the points at issue is the adequacy of the Turing test. The example shows that there could be two "systems," both of which pass the Turing test, but only one of which understands; and it is no argument against this point to say that since

they both pass the Turing test they must both understand, since this claim fails to meet the argument that the system in me that understands English has a great deal more than the system that merely processes Chinese. In short, the systems reply simply begs the question by insisting without argument that the system must understand Chinese.

Furthermore, the systems reply would appear to lead to consequences that are independently absurd. If we are to conclude that there must be cognition in me on the grounds that I have a certain sort of input and output and a program in between, then it looks like all sorts of noncognitive subsystems are going to turn out to be cognitive. For example, there is a level of description at which my stomach does information processing, and it instantiates any number of computer programs, but I take it we do not want to say that it has any understanding (cf. Pylyshyn 1980). But if we accept the systems reply, then it is hard to see how we avoid saying that stomach, heart, liver, and so on are all understanding subsystems, since there is no principled way to distinguish the motivation for saying the Chinese subsystem understands from saying that the stomach understands. It is, by the way, not an answer to this point to say that the Chinese system has information as input and output and the stomach has food and food products as input and output, since from the point of view of the agent, from my point of view, there is no information in either the food or the Chinese—the Chinese is just so many meaningless squiggles. The information in the Chinese case is solely in the eyes of the programmers and the interpreters, and there is nothing to prevent them from treating the input and output of my digestive organs as information if they so desire.

This last point bears on some independent problems in strong AI, and it is worth digressing for a moment to explain it. If strong AI is to be a branch of psychology. then it must be able to distinguish those systems that are genuinely mental from those that are not. It must be able to distinguish the principles on which the mind works from those on which non-mental systems work; otherwise it will offer us no explanations of what is specifically mental about the mental. And the mental-nonmental distinction cannot be just in the eye of the beholder but it must be intrinsic to the systems; otherwise it would be up to any beholder to treat people as nonmental and, for example, hurricanes as mental if he likes. But quite often in the AI literature the distinction is blurred in ways that would in the long run prove disastrous to the claim that AI is a cognitive inquiry. McCarthy, for example, writes, "Machines as simple as thermostats can be said to have beliefs, and having beliefs seems to be a characteristic of most machines capable of problem solving performance" (McCarthy 1979). Anyone who thinks strong AI has a chance as a theory of the mind ought to ponder the implications of that remark. We are asked to accept it as a discovery of strong AI that the hunk of metal on the wall that we use to regulate the temperature has beliefs in exactly the same sense that we, our spouses, and our children have beliefs, and furthermore that "most" of the other machines in the room—telephone, tape recorder, adding machine, electric light switch—also have beliefs in this literal sense. It is not the aim of this article to argue against McCarthy's point, so I will simply assert the following without argument. The study of the mind starts with such facts as that humans have beliefs, while thermostats, telephones, and adding machines don't. If you get a theory that denies this point you have produced a counterexample to the theory and the theory is false. One gets the impression that people in AI who write this sort of thing think they can get away with it because they don't really take it seriously, and they don't think anyone else will either. I propose, for a moment at least, to take it seriously. Think hard for one minute about what would be necessary to es-

tablish that the hunk of metal on the wall over there had real beliefs, beliefs with direction of fit, propositional content, and conditions of satisfaction; beliefs that had the possibility of being strong beliefs or weak beliefs; nervous, anxious, or secure beliefs; dogmatic, rational, or superstitious beliefs; blind faiths or hesitant cogitations; any kind of beliefs. The thermostat is not a candidate. Neither is stomach, liver, adding machine, or telephone. However, since we are taking the idea seriously, notice that its truth would be fatal to strong AI's claim to be a science of the mind. For now the mind is everywhere. What we wanted to know is what distinguishes the mind from thermostats and livers. And if McCarthy were right, strong AI wouldn't have a hope of telling us that.

II. **The Robot Reply (Yale).** "Suppose we wrote a different kind of program from Schank's program. Suppose we put a computer inside a robot, and this computer would not just take in formal symbols as input and give out formal symbols as output, but rather would actually operate the robot in such a way that the robot does something very much like perceiving, walking, moving about, hammering nails, eating, drinking—anything you like. The robot would, for example, have a television camera attached to it that enabled it to see, it would have arms and legs that enabled it to 'act,' and all of this would be controlled by its computer 'brain.' Such a robot would, unlike Schank's computer, have genuine understanding and other mental states."

The first thing to notice about the robot reply is that it tacitly concedes that cognition is not solely a matter of formal symbol manipulation, since this reply adds a set of causal relations with the outside world (cf. Fodor 1980). But the answer to the robot reply is that the addition of such "perceptual" and "motor" capacities adds nothing by way of understanding, in particular, or intentionality, in general, to Schank's original program. To see this, notice that the same thought experiment applies to the robot case. Suppose that instead of the computer inside the robot, you put me inside the room and, as in the original Chinese case, you give me more Chinese symbols with more instructions in English for matching Chinese symbols to Chinese symbols and feeding back Chinese symbols to the outside. Suppose, unknown to me, some of the Chinese symbols that come to me come from a television camera attached to the robot and other Chinese symbols that I am giving out serve to make the motors inside the robot move the robot's legs or arms. It is important to emphasize that all I am doing is manipulating formal symbols: I know none of these other facts. I am receiving "information" from the robot's "perceptual" apparatus, and I am giving out "instructions" to its motor apparatus without knowing either of these facts. I am the robot's homunculus, but unlike the traditional homunculus, I don't know what's going on. I don't understand anything except the rules for symbol manipulation. Now in this case I want to say that the robot has no intentional states at all; it is simply moving about as a result of its electrical wiring and its program. And furthermore, by instantiating the program I have no intentional states of the relevant type. All I do is follow formal instructions about manipulating formal symbols.

III. The Brain Simulator Reply (Berkeley and M.I.T.).

"Suppose we design a program that doesn't represent information that we have about the world, such as the information in Schank's scripts, but simulates the actual sequence of neuron firings at the synapses of the brain of a native Chinese speaker when he understands stories in Chinese and gives answers to them. The machine takes in Chinese stories and questions about them as input, it simulates the formal structure of actual Chinese brains in processing these stories, and it gives out Chinese answers as outputs. We can even imagine that the machine operates, not with a single serial program, but with a whole set of programs operating in parallel, in the manner that actual human brains presumably operate when they process natural language. Now surely in such a case we would have to say that the machine understood the stories; and if we refuse to say that, wouldn't we also have to deny that native Chinese speakers understood the stories? At the level of the synapses, what would or could be different about the program of the computer and the program of the Chinese brain?"

Before countering this reply I want to digress to note that it is an odd reply for any partisan of artificial intelligence (or functionalism, etc.) to make: I thought the whole idea of strong AI is that we don't need to know how the brain works to know how the mind works. The basic hypothesis, or so I had supposed, was that there is a level of mental operations consisting of computational processes over formal elements that constitute the essence of the mental and can be realized in all sorts of different brain processes, in the same way that any computer program can be realized in different computer hardwares: On the assumptions of strong AI, the mind is to the brain as the program is to the hardware, and thus we can understand the mind without doing neurophysiology. If we had to know how the brain worked to do AI, we wouldn't bother with AI. However, even getting this close to the operation of the brain is still not sufficient to produce understanding. To see this, imagine that instead of a monolingual man in a room shuffling symbols we have the man operate an elaborate set of water pipes with valves connecting them. When the man receives the Chinese symbols, he looks up in the program, written in English, which valves he has to turn on and off. Each water connection corresponds to a synapse in the Chinese brain, and the whole system is rigged up so that after doing all the right firings, that is after turning on all the right faucets, the Chinese answers pop out at the output end of the series of pipes.

Now where is the understanding in this system? It takes Chinese as input, it simulates the formal structure of the synapses of the Chinese brain, and it gives Chinese as output. But the man certainly doesn't understand Chinese, and neither do the water pipes, and if we are tempted to adopt what I think is the absurd view that somehow the *conjunction* of man *and* water pipes understands, remember that in principle the man can internalize the formal structure of the water pipes and do all the "neuron firings" in his imagination. The problem with the brain simulator is that it is simulating the wrong things about the brain. As long as it simulates only the formal structure of the sequence of neuron firings at the synapses, it won't have simulated what matters about the brain, namely its causal properties, its ability to produce intentional states. And that the formal properties are not sufficient for the causal properties is shown by the water pipe example: we can have all the formal properties carved off from the relevant neurobiological causal properties.

IV. The Combination Reply (Berkeley and Stanford). "While each of the previous three replies might not be completely convincing by itself as a refutation of the Chinese room counterexample, if you take all three together they are collectively much more convincing and even decisive. Imagine a robot with a brain-shaped computer lodged in its cranial cavity, imagine the computer programmed with all the synapses of a human brain, imagine the whole behavior of the robot is indistinguishable from human behavior, and now think of the whole thing as a unified system and not just as a computer with inputs and outputs. Surely in such a case we would have to ascribe intentionality to the system."

I entirely agree that in such a case we would find it rational and indeed irresistible to accept the hypothesis that the robot had intentionality, as long as we knew nothing more about it. Indeed, besides appearance and behavior, the other elements of the combination are really irrelevant. If we could build a robot whose behavior was indistinguishable over a large range from human behavior, we would attribute

intentionality to it, pending some reason not to. We wouldn't need to know in advance that its computer brain was a formal analogue of the human brain.

But I really don't see that this is any help to the claims of strong AI, and here's why: According to strong AI, instantiating a formal program with the right input and output is a sufficient condition of, indeed is constitutive of, intentionality. As Newell (1979) puts it, the essence of the mental is the operation of a physical symbol system. But the attributions of intentionality that we make to the robot in this example have nothing to do with formal programs. They are simply based on the assumption that if the robot looks and behaves sufficiently like us, then we would suppose, until proven otherwise, that it must have mental states like ours that cause and are expressed by its behavior and it must have an inner mechanism capable of producing such mental states. If we knew independently how to account for its behavior without such assumptions we would not attribute intentionality to it, especially if we knew it had a formal program. And this is precisely the point of my earlier reply to objection II.

Suppose we knew that the robot's behavior was entirely accounted for by the fact that a man inside it was receiving uninterpreted formal symbols from the robot's sensory receptors and sending out uninterpreted formal symbols to its motor mechanisms, and the man was doing the symbol manipulation in accordance with a bunch of rules. Furthermore, suppose the man knows none of these facts about the robot, all he knows is which operations to perform on which meaningless symbols. In such a case we would regard the robot as an ingenious mechanical dummy. The hypothesis that the dummy has a mind would now be unwarranted and unnecessary, for there is now no longer any reason to ascribe intentionality to the robot or to the system of which it is a part (except of course for the man's intentionality in manipulating the symbols). The formal symbol manipulations go on, the input and output are correctly matched, but the only real locus of intentionality is the man, and he doesn't know any of the relevant intentional states; he doesn't, for example, *see* what comes into the robot's eyes, he doesn't *intend* to move the robot's arm, and he doesn't *understand* any of the remarks made to or by the robot. Nor, for the reasons stated earlier, does the system of which man and robot are a part.

To see this point, contrast this case with cases in which we find it completely natural to ascribe intentionality to members of certain other primate species such as apes and monkeys and to domestic animals such as dogs. The reasons we find it natural are, roughly, two: We can't make sense of the animal's behavior without the ascription of intentionality, and we can see that the beasts are made of similar stuff to ourselves—that is an eye, that a nose, this is its skin, and so on. Given the coherence of the animal's behavior and the assumption of the same causal stuff underlying it, we assume both that the animal must have mental states underlying its behavior, and that the mental states must be produced by mechanisms made out of the stuff that is like our stuff. We would certainly make similar assumptions about the robot unless we had some reason not to, but as soon as we knew that the behavior was the result of a formal program, and that the actual causal properties of the physical substance were irrelevant we would abandon the assumption of intentionality.

There are two other responses to my example that come up frequently (and so are worth discussing) but really miss the point.

V. The Other Minds Reply (Yale). "How do you know that other people understand Chinese or anything else? Only by their behavior. Now the computer can pass the behavioral tests as well as they can (in principle), so if you are going to attribute cognition to other people you must in principle also attribute it to computers."

This objection really is only worth a short reply. The problem in this discussion is not about how I know that other people have cognitive states, but rather what it is that I am attributing to them when I attribute cognitive states to them. The thrust of the argument is that it couldn't be just computational processes and their output because the computational processes and their output can exist without the cognitive state. It is no answer to this argument to feign anesthesia. In "cognitive sciences" one presupposes the reality and knowability of the mental in the same way that in physical sciences one has to presuppose the reality and knowability of physical objects.

VI. The Many Mansions Reply (Berkeley). "Your whole argument presupposes that AI is only about analog and digital computers. But that just happens to be the present state of technology. Whatever these causal processes are that you say are essential for intentionality (assuming you are right), eventually we will be able to build devices that have these causal processes, and that will be artificial intelligence. So your arguments are in no way directed at the ability of artificial intelligence to produce and explain cognition."

I really have no objection to this reply save to say that it in effect trivializes the project of strong AI by redefining it as whatever artificially produces and explains cognition. The interest of the original claim made on behalf of artificial intelligence is that it was a precise, well defined thesis: mental processes are computational processes over formally defined elements. I have been concerned to challenge that thesis. If the claim is redefined so that it is no longer that thesis, my objections no longer apply because there is no longer a testable hypothesis for them to apply to.

Let us now return to the question I promised I would try to answer: Granted that in my original example I understand the English and I do not understand the Chinese, and granted therefore that the machine doesn't understand either English or Chinese, still there must be something about me that makes it the case that I understand English and a corresponding something lacking in me that makes it the case that I fail to understand Chinese. Now why couldn't we give those somethings, whatever they are, to a machine?

I see no reason in principle why we couldn't give a machine the capacity to understand English or Chinese, since in an important sense our bodies with our brains are precisely such machines. But I do see very strong arguments for saying that we could not give such a thing to a machine where the operation of the machine is defined solely in terms of computational processes over formally defined elements: that is, where the operation of the machine is defined as an instantiation of a computer program. It is not because I am the instantiation of a computer program that I am able to understand English and have other forms of intentionality (I am, I suppose, the instantiation of any number of computer programs), but as far as we know it is because I am a certain sort of organism with a certain biological (i.e., chemical and physical) structure, and this structure, under certain conditions, is causally capable of producing perception, action, understanding, learning, and other intentional phenomena. And part of the point of the present argument is that only something that had those causal powers could have that intentionality. Perhaps other physical and chemical processes could produce exactly these effects; perhaps, for example, Martians also have intentionality but their brains are made of different stuff. That is an empirical question, rather like the question whether photosynthesis can be done by something with a chemistry different from that of chlorophyll.

But the main point of the present argument is that no purely formal model will ever be sufficient by itself for intentionality because the formal properties are not by themselves constitutive of intentionality, and they have by themselves no causal powers except the power, when instantiated, to produce the next stage of the formalism when the machine is running. And any other causal properties that particular realizations of the formal model have, are irrelevant to the formal model because we can always put the same formal model in a different realization where those causal properties are obviously absent. Even if, by some miracle, Chinese speakers exactly realize Schank's program, we can put the same program in English speakers, water pipes, or computers, none of which understand Chinese, the program notwithstanding.

What matters about brain operations is not the formal shadow cast by the sequence of synapses but rather the actual properties of the sequences. All the arguments for the strong version of artificial intelligence that I have seen insist on drawing an outline around the shadows cast by cognition and then claiming that the shadows are the real thing.

By way of concluding I want to try to state some of the general philosophical points implicit in the argument. For clarity I will try to do it in a question-and-answer fashion, and I begin with that old chestnut of a question:

"Could a machine think?"

The answer is, obviously, yes. We are precisely such machines.

"Yes, but could an artifact, a man-made machine, think?"

Assuming it is possible to produce artificially a machine with a nervous system, neurons with axons and dendrites, and all the rest of it, sufficiently like ours, again the answer to the question seems to be obviously, yes. If you can exactly duplicate the causes, you could duplicate the effects. And indeed it might be possible to produce consciousness, intentionality, and all the rest of it using some other sorts of chemical principles than those that human beings use. It is, as I said, an empirical question.

"OK, but could a digital computer think?"

If by "digital computer" we mean anything at all that has a level of description where it can correctly be described as the instantiation of a computer program, then again the answer is, of course, yes, since we are the instantiations of any number of computer programs, and we can think.

"But could something think, understand, and so on *solely* in virtue of being a computer with a right sort of program? Could instantiating a program, the right program of course, by itself be a sufficient condition of understanding?"

This I think is the right question to ask, though it is usually confused with one or more of the earlier questions, and the answer to it is no.

"Why not?"

Because the formal symbol manipulations by themselves don't have any intentionality; they are quite meaningless; they aren't even *symbol* manipulations, since the symbols don't symbolize anything. In the linguistic jargon, they have only a syntax but no semantics. Such intentionality as computers appear to have is solely in the minds of those who program them and those who use them, those who send in the input and those who interpret the output.

The aim of the Chinese room example was to try to show this by showing that as soon as we put something into the system that really does have intentionality (a man), and we program him with the formal program, you can see that the formal program carries no additional intentionality. It adds nothing, for example, to a man's ability to understand Chinese.

Precisely that feature of AI that seemed so appealing—the distinction between the program and the realization—proves fatal to the claim that simulation could be duplication. The distinction between the program and its realization in the hardware seems to be parallel to the distinction between the level of mental operations and the level of brain operations. And if we could describe the level of mental operations as a formal program, then it seems we could describe what was essential about the mind without doing either introspective psychology or neurophysiology of the brain. But the equation "mind is to brain as program is to hardware" breaks down at several points, among them the following three:

First, the distinction between program and realization has the consequence that the same program could have all sorts of crazy realizations that had no form of intentionality. Weizenbaum (1976, Ch. 2), for example, shows in detail how to construct a computer using a roll of toilet paper and a pile of small stones. Similarly, the Chinese story understanding program can be programmed into a sequence of water pipes, a set of wind machines, or a monolingual English speaker, none of which thereby acquires an understanding of Chinese. Stones, toilet paper, wind, and water pipes are the wrong kind of stuff to have intentionality in the first place—only something that has the same causal powers as brains can have intentionality—and though the English speaker has the right kind of stuff for intentionality you can easily see that he doesn't get any extra intentionality by memorizing the program. since memorizing it won't teach him Chinese.

Second, the program is purely formal, but the intentional states are not in that way formal. They are defined in terms of their content, not their form. The belief that it is raining, for example, is not defined as a certain formal shape, but as a certain mental content with conditions of satisfaction, a direction of fit (see Searle 1979), and the like. Indeed the belief as such hasn't even got a formal shape in this syntactic sense, since one and the same belief can be given an indefinite number of different syntactic expressions in different linguistic systems.

Third, as I mentioned before, mental states and events are literally a product of the operation of the brain, but the program is not in that way a product of the computer.

"Well if programs are in no way constitutive of mental processes, why have so many people believed the converse? That at least needs some explanation."

I don't really know the answer to that one. The idea that computer simulations could be the real thing ought to have seemed suspicious in the first place because the computer isn't confined to simulating mental operations, by any means. No one supposes that computer simulations of a five-alarm fire will burn the neighborhood down or that a computer simulation of a rainstorm will leave us all drenched. Why on earth would anyone suppose that a computer simulation of understanding actually understood anything? It is sometimes said that it would be frightfully hard to get computers to feel pain or fall in love, but love and pain are neither harder nor easier than cognition or anything else. For simulation, all you need is the right input and output and a program in the middle that transforms the former into the latter. That is all the computer has for anything it does. To confuse simulation with duplication is the same mistake, whether it is pain, love, cognition, fires, or rainstorms.

Still, there are several reasons why AI must have seemed—and to many people perhaps still does seem—in some way to reproduce and thereby explain mental phenomena, and I believe we will not succeed in removing these illusions until we have fully exposed the reasons that give rise to them.

First, and perhaps the most important, is a confusion about the notion of "information processing": many people in cognitive science believe that the human brain, with its mind, does something called "information processing," and analogously the computer with its program does information processing; but fires and rainstorms, on the other hand, don't do information processing at all. Thus, though the computer can simulate the formal features of any process whatever, it stands in a special relation to the mind and brain because when the computer is properly programmed, ideally with the same program as the brain, the information processing is identical in the two cases, and this information processing is really the essence of the mental. But the trouble with this argument is that it rests on an ambiguity in the notion of "information." In the sense in which people "process information" when they reflect, say, on problems in arithmetic or when they read and answer questions about stories, the programmed computer does not do "information processing." Rather, what it does is manipulate formal symbols. The fact that the programmer and the interpreter of the computer output use the symbols to stand for objects in the world is totally beyond the scope of the computer. The computer, to repeat, has a syntax but no semantics. Thus, if you type into the computer "2 plus 2 equals?" it will type out "4." But it has no idea that "4" means 4 or that it means anything at all. And the point is not that it lacks some second-order information about the interpretation of its first-order symbols, but rather that its first-order symbols don't have any interpretations as far as the computer is concerned. All the computer has is more symbols. The introduction of the notion of "information processing" therefore produces a dilemma: either we construe the notion of "information processing" in such a way that it implies intentionality as part of the process or we don't. If the former, then the programmed computer does not do information processing, it only manipulates formal symbols. If the latter, then, though the computer does information processing, it is only doing so in the sense in which adding machines, typewriters, stomachs, thermostats, rainstorms, and hurricanes do information processing; namely, they have a level of description at which we can describe them as taking information in at one end, transforming it, and producing information as output. But in this case it is up to outside observers to interpret the input and output as information in the ordinary sense. And no similarity is established between the computer and the brain in terms of any similarity of information processing.

Second, in much of AI there is a residual behaviorism or operationalism. Since appropriately programmed computers can have input-output patterns similar to those of human beings, we are tempted to postulate mental states in the computer similar to human mental states. But once we see that it is both conceptually and empirically possible for a system to have human capacities in some realm without having any intentionality at all, we should be able to overcome this impulse. My desk adding machine has calculating capacities, but no intentionality, and in this paper I have tried to show that a system could have input and output capabilities that duplicated those of a native Chinese speaker and still not understand Chinese, regardless of how it was programmed. The Turing test is typical of the tradition in being unashamedly behavioristic and operationalistic, and I believe that if AI workers totally repudiated behaviorism and operationalism much of the confusion between simulation and duplication would be eliminated.

Third, this residual operationalism is joined to a residual form of dualism; indeed strong AI only makes sense given the dualistic assumption that, where the mind is concerned, the brain doesn't matter. In strong AI (and in functionalism, as well) what matters are programs, and programs are independent of their realization in machines; indeed, as far as AI is concerned, the same program could be realized by an electronic machine, a Cartesian mental substance, or a Hegelian world spirit. The single most surprising discovery that I have made in discussing these issues is that many AI workers are quite shocked by my idea that actual human mental phenomena might be dependent on actual physical-chemical properties of actual human brains. But if you think about it a minute you can see that I should not have been surprised; for unless you accept some form of dualism, the strong AI project hasn't got a chance. The pro-

ject is to reproduce and explain the mental by designing programs, but unless the mind is not only conceptually but empirically independent of the brain you couldn't carry out the project, for the program is completely independent of any realization. Unless you believe that the mind is separable from the brain both conceptually and empirically—dualism in a strong form—you cannot hope to reproduce the mental by writing and running programs since programs must be independent of brains or any other particular forms of instantiation. If mental operations consist in computational operations on formal symbols, then it follows that they have no interesting connection with the brain; the only connection would be that the brain just happens to be one of the indefinitely many types of machines capable of instantiating the program. This form of dualism is not the traditional Cartesian variety that claims there are two sorts of *substances*, but it is Cartesian in the sense that it insists that what is specifically mental about the mind has no intrinsic connection with the actual properties of the brain. This underlying dualism is masked from us by the fact that AI literature contains frequent fulminations against "dualism"; what the authors seem to be unaware of is that their position presupposes a strong version of dualism.

"Could a machine think?" My own view is that only a machine could think, and indeed only very special kinds of machines, namely brains and machines that had the same causal powers as brains. And that is the main reason strong AI has had little to tell us about thinking, since it has nothing to tell us about machines. By its own definition, it is about programs, and programs are not machines. Whatever else intentionality is, it is a biological phenomenon, and it is as likely to be as causally dependent on the specific biochemistry of its origins as lactation, photosynthesis, or any other biological phenomena. No one would suppose that we could produce milk and sugar by running a computer simulation of the formal sequences in lactation and photosynthesis, but where the mind is concerned many people are willing to believe in such a miracle because of a deep and abiding dualism: the mind they suppose is a matter of formal processes and is independent of quite specific material causes in the way that milk and sugar are not.

In defense of this dualism the hope is often expressed that the brain is a digital computer (early computers, by the way, were often called "electronic brains"). But that is no help. Of course the brain is a digital computer. Since everything is a digital computer, brains are too. The point is that the brain's causal capacity to produce intentionality cannot consist in its instantiating a computer program, since for any program you like it is possible for something to instantiate that program and still not have any mental states. Whatever it is that the brain does to produce intentionality, it cannot consist in instantiating a program since no program, by itself, is sufficient for intentionality.

NOTES

I am indebted to a rather large number of people for discussion of these matters and for their patient attempts to overcome my ignorance of artificial intelligence. I would especially like to thank Ned Block, Hubert Dreyfus, John Haugeland, Roger Schank, Robert Wilensky, and Terry Winograd.

1. I am not, of course, saying that Schank himself is committed to these claims.
2. Also, "understanding" implies both the possession of mental (intentional) states and the truth (validity, success) of these states. For the purposes of this discussion we are concerned only with the possession of the states.
3. Intentionality is by definition that feature of certain mental states by which they are directed at or about objects and states of affairs in the world. Thus, beliefs, desires, and intentions are intentional states;

undirected forms of anxiety and depression are not.

REFERENCES

Fodor, J.A. 1968. The appeal to tacit knowledge in psychological explanation. *Journal of Philosophy* 65: 627–40.

Fodor, J.A. 1980. Methodological solipsism considered as a research strategy in cognitive psychology. *Behavioral and Brain Sciences* 3:1.

McCarthy, J. 1979. Ascribing mental qualities to machines. In: *Philosophical perceptives in artificial intelligence*, ed. M. Ringle. Atlantic Highlands, NJ: Humanities Press.

Newell, A. 1979. Physical symbol systems. Lecture at the La Jolla Conference on Cognitive Science.

Newell, A., and Simon, H.A. 1963. GPS, a program that simulates human thought. In: *Computers and thought.* ed. A. Feigenbaum & V. Feldman, pp. 279–93. New York: McGraw-Hill.

Pylyshyn, Z.W. 1980. Computation and cognition: issues in the foundations of cognitive science. *Behavioral and Brain Sciences* 3.

Schank, R.C., and Abelson, R.P. 1977. *Scripts, plans, goals, and understanding.* Hillsdale, NJ: Lawrence Erlbaum Press.

Searle, J.R. 1979. The intentionality of intention and action. *Inquiry* 22:253–80.

Weizenbaum, J. 1965. Eliza—a computer program for the study of natural language communication between man and machine. *Communication of the Association for Computing Machinery* 9:36–45.

Weizenbaum, J. 1976. *Computer power and human reason.* San Francisco: W.H. Freeman.

Winograd, T. 1973. A procedural model of language understanding. In: *Computer models of thought and language,* ed. R. Schank & K. Colby. San Francisco: W.H. Freeman.

CHAPTER ELEVEN

Functionalism

Machines and the mind

Turing's question is whether machines could possibly think. Suppose for a moment that the answer to this question is positive. What exactly would that answer tell us about the nature of intelligence or consciousness in general? What would be the implications for the mind-body problem? Certainly, the genuine possibility of machine intelligence would tell us that Descartes was wrong in believing that an immaterial mind is *necessary* for intelligence. It would also tell us that, even if identity theorists are right in their claim that the human mind is a network of neurons in the brain, it isn't essential to have neurons at all in order to be intelligent — circuit boards will do.

On the other hand, a positive answer to Turing's question wouldn't necessarily tell us anything interesting about the nature of *human* intelligence. Artificial intelligence, even if it were to exist, may be utterly unlike our own. For example, the conclusion that machines can think wouldn't force us to conclude that human beings don't have immaterial minds. And even if the human mind is just the brain, it is possible that the activity of the brain has nothing in common with the things that computers do. If this is right, then the development of intelligent computers would be of little significance in understanding the human mind. Computer intelligence would certainly be an interesting phenomenon, but nonetheless very different in nature from human or animal intelligence.

The computer metaphor

Many philosophers argue, however, that the invention of computers provides the key to understanding the nature of minds generally. In their view, all forms of mental activity are forms of computing or information processing. I will call this view the **computer metaphor**. According to the computer metaphor, human beings and all other intelligent beings are actually computers — albeit very different in construction from the ones we build ourselves. Seen from this perspective, the physical differences between humans and computers like those that now run our banking system mask an underlying commonality. We may not look the same, but we do the same kinds of things.

If the computer metaphor is correct, then understanding the human mind is a matter of understanding the computations carried out by the neural circuitry lodged in the cranium. Studying the structure and biochemistry of the brain will only tell us part of the answer to the question, "What is the mind?" The other part will require a study of how the neural circuitry of the brain works as an information-processing system. We will have to study the "algorithms of the mind."

Functionalism

The computer metaphor fits well with a position on the mind-body problem developed since the late 1960s, called **functionalism.** Like identity theorists, functionalists believe that the mind-body problem is an empirical issue, to be solved by observation and experiment rather than by metaphysical speculation or conceptual analysis. This means that we should identify the various states and processes of the mind in terms of their effects on behaviour, and then ask the question, "What is the real nature of these states and processes?"

But like behaviourists, functionalists argue that the answer to this question will not be found by looking at what the mind is *made of,* but by looking what it *does.* As we saw in chapter 9, identity theorists like Smart and Armstrong maintain that, given the current evidence, mental states are almost certainly biochemical states of the brain. Against this assertion, functionalists argue that even if our intelligence happens to be realized in the brain, identifying each state of mind with some neural state of the brain will not help us to understand the real nature of the mind. Instead, they contend, we have to understand the functions and activities that these neural states carry out. According to functionalists, these same functions and activities could conceivably be carried out by entities other than the human nervous system.

Machine functionalism

Functionalism is easily combined with the computer metaphor. To the idea that the nature of the mind lies in what it does rather than what it is made of, we can add the additional claim that what the mind does is process information. A number of functionalists argue that the kind of activity that characterizes the mind is computation. I will call the combination of functionalism and the computer metaphor **machine functionalism.** Not all philosophers who subscribe to the computer metaphor are functionalists, and not all functionalists accept the computer metaphor. But the connection is well enough established that some people refer to it as the "traditional" view.[1] Machine functionalism is here presented succinctly in an article by Hilary Putnam entitled "The Nature of Mental States."

Putnam is a professor of mathematics and logic at Harvard University. In the early part of his career his work focussed on issues in the foundations of logic and science. Over the past two decades, in a number of books and articles, Putnam has presented a evolving series of positions on a large number of central philosophical questions. The article that we are reading here, published in 1962, represents a position that he has since given up.[2] But it serves as a representative statement of functionalism in one of its important early forms.

Putnam's "empirical hypothesis"

Just as Smart used after-images as a representative example of mental-states, Putnam takes pain as the focus of his essay. Pains are useful as examples of mental states because they have a distinct experiential character — pains have a very distinctive *feeling* — and they also have clear connections with certain characteristic behaviours such as wincing, crying out, and limping. Putnam's essay addresses the question, 'Is pain a brain state?' Identity theorists claim that, as materialism is almost certainly true, the answer to this question is 'yes.' But in this essay Putnam claims that the question will have a negative answer even if materialism should prove to be true.

In the first section of his paper, "Identity Questions," Putnam argues in support of the position taken by identity theorists that the question whether pains are brain states is not a conceptual issue to be resolved or dismissed simply by analyzing the *meanings* of the terms 'pain' and 'brain state.' At the beginning of the second section he characterizes his position on the mind-body question as "an empirical hypothesis." He says:

> Since I am discussing not what the concept of pain comes to, but what pain is, in a sense of 'is' which requires empirical theory-construction (or, at least, empirical speculation), I shall not apologize for advancing an empirical hypothesis. Indeed, my strategy will be to argue that pain is *not* a brain state, not on *a priori* grounds, but on the grounds that another hypothesis is more plausible.[3]

Putnam proposes the hypothesis that "pain, or the state of being in pain, is a *functional state* of a whole organism." The goals of his article are to explain what he means by a "functional state," and to show that functional states are not biochemical states of the brain or any other kind of physical state.

Functional states

Putnam explains his idea of a "functional state" by tying it to two concepts that we looked at in the last chapter: the Turing Machine and a machine table. He modifies the idea of a Turing Machine somewhat by allowing the transitions between one state and another to be a matter of probability, calling the result a "Probabilistic Automaton." But otherwise his explanation of a Turing Machine matches the one I presented in chapter 10. In that chapter we saw that the operation of a Turing Machine, like that of any discrete state machine, can be represented by a machine table, which relates the internal states of the machine to its inputs and outputs. Such a table portrays what Putnam calls the "Functional Organization" of the machine, and the **machine states** that make up the vertical columns of the machine table he calls "Total States" of the system. A **functional state**, then, is a Total State in this sense; it is a state of the system identified by the vertical columns of the machine table.

As Turing points out, no machine considered closely enough is exactly a discrete state machine because there are always gradations between its states. What matters is whether describing a machine as a digital state machine allows us to grasp the important features of its behaviour. For example, to understand how the Coke machine we looked at in chapter 10 operates, it is best to ignore the details of its construction and concentrate instead on the behaviour of the machine as it is described in the machine table. According to Putnam, it is plausible that living creatures are also discrete state machines in this sense, albeit vastly more complex ones than the Coke machine. If we consider living creatures to be discrete state machines, then the "input" would be taken to be the impact of the environment on the sensory organs. Where the Coke machine takes nickels and dimes as input, humans receive input in the form of light rays striking the retina, air motions vibrating the eardrum, and heat and pressure applied to the skin. The "output" would be different kinds of bodily behaviour such as walking, moving the arms and hands, and speaking.

If this picture is correct, then for any given organism we could in principle construct a machine table that captures the functional organization of that organism. Down the left-hand side of the table would be listed all the physical states that can be considered "inputs" to the organism in the sense that they affect its behaviour. The boxes in the table will describe the "outputs," which will be various kinds of bodily motions. The inputs and outputs would be connected by way of a number of functional states, listed across the top of the table. The transitions from one functional state to another would be included along with the outputs in the boxes of the table. If we can identify the current functional state and the current set of inputs for an organism at a particular time, then we would be able to predict its subsequent behaviour.

Pains as functional states

Given the idea that living creatures can be thought of as discrete state machines whose behaviour is directed by certain functional states, Putnam's hypothesis (stated in Section II) is that pains are functional states in this sense. The hypothesis is spelled out in the four numbered statements in the middle of the section. The important aspect of this hypothesis is that something can be in a state of pain *if, and only if,* it has the appropriate functional organization. Later, in Section IV, he adds the following description of pains as functional states:

> [T]he functional state we have in mind is the state of receiving sensory inputs which play a certain role in the Functional Organization of the organism. This role is characterized, at least partially, by the fact that the sense organs responsible for the inputs in question are organs whose function is to detect damage to the body, or dangerous extremes of temperature, pressure, etc., and by the fact that the "inputs" themselves, whatever their physical realization, represent a condition that the organism assigns a high disvalue to.

To see what he has in mind here, let's compare his hypothesis to the description of the Coke machine in chapter 10. Have a look at the machine table of the Coke machine and notice that the only time the machine will enter State 2 is when it has received a nickel while in State 1. So State 2 can be thought of as playing a specific role in the behaviour of the machine, namely, to direct the machine's behaviour in any case where it has received a nickel and is "awaiting" more money. Putnam's hypothesis is that pain plays a similar, although more complex, role in the behaviour of any organism capable of experiencing it. There will be certain inputs that lead the organism to enter the functional state that we identify as the state of pain. These inputs will generally signal some sort of damage or danger to the organism. Once in such a state, further inputs will result in certain forms of behaviour, such as crying out, wincing, or limping. These behaviours will be described in the machine table as the outputs, and will be listed in the column of the table representing the functional state of pain.

Functional states and physical states

Putnam argues that if his view is correct, then being in pain is not a matter of what *physical* state one is in. What matters is the way in which one's internal states are linked to one another, to sensory inputs, and to behaviour. And these links can be constructed in any number of different physical systems.

To see this point, notice that the machine table of a discrete state machine makes no reference to its physical construction. For example, the operation of the Coke machine is fully described by its machine table, even though there is no mention in the table of what it is made of or how the states of the machine are constructed. So an understanding of what Putnam calls the functional organization of a machine does not require knowing its physical construction. All that is needed to capture the functional organization of a machine is to describe how its states are related to the inputs and outputs and to one another. If living creatures are discrete state machines in the essential aspects of their behaviour, then the same would be true of a living creature. Its functional organization would be the *result* of its physical construction, but its functional organization can be described without any reference to that construction.

In Section III, Putnam points out that functionalism, as he describes it, is compatible with dualism. And it is equally compatible with materialism. It may be that the mind is an immaterial entity as Descartes maintains, or it might be the brain as contemporary materialists claim. But in either case, what makes it a *mind*, in the view of functionalists, is not what it is *made of* but its functional organization. Whether or not a creature is capable of experiencing a particular sensation, or thinking a particular thought, is not a matter of what material it is composed of, but how that material is functionally organized. Applied to the example of pain states, this means that any creature (or even any machine) capable of possessing the appropriate kind of functional state will be capable of feeling pain.

Functionalism as an alternative to other theories

The relationship between functionalism and materialism that Putnam refers to in Section III is discussed in more detail by Jerry Fodor in the article "Something on the State of the Art." Fodor was for many years a colleague of Noam Chomsky at MIT. He is seen by many people as the premier champion of machine functionalism. His influence began with a book entitled *The Language of Thought*,[4] which spells out what Fodor sees as the consequences of the computer metaphor in psychology. (That book also contains an important critique of Wittgenstein's "private language" argument.) Since then Fodor has published numerous books relating to the mind-body problem and the issue we will discuss in chapter 14, the "problem of intentionality." He is currently a professor in the Graduate School of the City University of New York.

The article we are reading here is the introduction to a collection of his articles entitled *Representations*. In this article Fodor presents functionalism as an alternative to both behaviourism and the identity theory. According to

Fodor, both behaviourism and the identity theory have advantages over each other, but each also has a weakness not faced by the other. Only functionalism, Fodor argues, can avoid the weaknesses of each while retaining their strengths.

The virtues of behaviourism

Fodor points out that one of the chief advantages of materialism over dualism is that it appears to offers a resolution to the problem of explaining mind-body interaction. As Locke and other critics point out, Descartes was faced with the problem of explaining the relation of cause and effect between an immaterial mind and the physical body. If materialism is true, this is no longer an issue as we have only sequences of physical events to explain. Nonetheless, Fodor argues that neither behaviourism nor identity theory manages to clear up the problem of mind-body causation entirely. He begins his analysis with the promise and difficulties of behaviourism.

According to logical behaviourists, a sentence like "Smith is thirsty" is equivalent in meaning to a collection of sentences describing how Smith will behave in the presence of certain stimuli.[5] These sentences will take the form of if-then statements, where the if-clause refers to the stimulus and the then-clause refers to the behaviour that will result in the presence of that stimulus. For example, the collection would likely include a sentence like the following:

If there is water available, then Smith will drink some.

The set of such sentences taken together will compose a behavioural disposition that captures the meaning of the original psychological term, 'thirsty.'

Fodor argues that the advantage in treating mental states as dispositions in this manner is that it allows us to explain how it is that we talk about the mind as the *cause* of our behaviour. Recall that mind-body causation (or interaction) is a major stumbling block for dualism. According to behaviourists like Ryle, the fact that some sentences *appear* to refer to states of mind as causes of our behaviour is just a misleading aspect of our language. On their view, there are no mental states as such, and hence there are no mental causes of our behaviour. We can eliminate the "problem" of mental causation in the same way that we can eliminate the "problem" of universals, namely, by showing it to be a linguistic confusion.

In the example above there is something about Smith (namely, the disposition) that explains why he behaves as he does, and it is this aspect of Smith that we are referring to in saying that he is thirsty. This gives the appearance, then, that thirst is a *mental cause* of Smith's behaviour. Nonetheless, the disposition is described *entirely* in terms of how Smith will respond to various stimuli. There is no reference to any internal states or processes that *cause* that behaviour.

The problem with behaviourism

But Fodor argues that the idea of behavioural dispositions is still not rich enough to explain human behaviour. His first contention is that not all references to mental causes can be replaced by talk of dispositions. We can explain what is meant by the sentence "John took an aspirin because he had a headache" by saying that taking aspirin when they are available is part of headache behaviour. But we can't use the same tactic to explain what is meant by saying, "John is disposed to produce headache behaviour because he had a headache." For the headache can't be the cause of the disposition if the headache *is* the disposition.

Fodor's second objection is the more serious one. His point here is similar to the objection from Chomsky that we looked at in chapter 7: human behaviour is too complex to be explained entirely in terms of simple relations between environmental stimuli and behavioural responses. Where Chomsky puts the point in terms of the problem of predicting behaviour (as in the painting example), Fodor explains it in terms of the impossibility of translating all psychological descriptions into descriptions of behavioural dispositions. Here is his description of the problem:

> Mental causes typically have their overt effects *in virtue of their interactions with one another*, and behaviourism provides no satisfactory analysis of sentences that articulate such interactions. [emphasis in the original]

The argument here has two premises: (1) mental states do not give rise to behaviour on their own, but only in conjunction with other mental states; (2) this feature of mental causation cannot be accounted for within the framework of logical behaviourism. Let's look at them one at a time.

The translation project

The first premise focusses on the fact that, when they do their translations of psychological descriptions, behaviourists treat states of mind singly. Each individual term referring to a particular state of mind is replaced by a description of a behavioural disposition. To use Fodor's example, the sentence 'Smith is thirsty' will be analyzed in terms of a collection of sentences like the following:

> If there is water available, then Smith will drink some.

The problem indicated by the first premise is that what a person will do, given a particular belief or desire, will depend on their *other* beliefs and desires. Even if Smith is thirsty, he will not drink from the glass if he believes that what is in the glass is gasoline rather than water. And what is relevant to Smith's behaviour is not what is *in* the glass but what Smith *believes* is in the glass. In this way, mental states work in conjunction with one another in the production of behaviour.

The next premise is that behaviourism cannot be amended in such a way that mental states are treated in conjunction with one another. To see this, let us say that Smith will drink only if (i) he is thirsty, and (ii) he believes that what is in the glass is water. Logical behaviourists maintain that both (i) and (ii) can be translated into sentences that describe only behavioural dispositions. How might this be done? We might translate "Smith is thirsty" into the sentence:

If Smith believes there is water in the glass, then he will drink some.

And we might translate "Smith believes there is water in the glass" into the sentence:

If Smith is thirsty, then he will drink from the glass.

Here we have treated each mental state as a disposition, and we have also accounted for the fact that there is a connection between Smith's thirst and his beliefs about what is in the glass. So where is the problem? The problem lies in the fact that the if-clauses of each of the two translations do not refer to external stimuli but to *other mental states*. In the first case the if-clause refers to a belief, and in the second case the if-clause refers to Smith's thirst. So we haven't managed to eliminate the use of psychological descriptions as behaviourists claim we must. Try as we might, we cannot explain Smith's behaviour solely in terms of if-then sentences where each if-clause refers only to *external stimuli* and each then-clause refers only to a *behavioural* response.

Complexity of behaviour again

In the example above we have described only the interaction between two mental states. In reality there will be many more, and this only makes matters worse for the behaviourist. Think of all the states of mind that might prevent Smith from drinking the water: the belief that someone in the room is trying to poison him, the desire to serve others first, the thought that he should phone his mother right away. And on and on. This suggests that how a person will behave will depend on a whole constellation of beliefs, desires, and other states of mind. The same point is illustrated by Chomsky's painting example that I outlined in chapter 7. What someone will say when confronted with a painting is not a matter of a simple disposition but rather the outcome of a complex assortment of mental states.

Skinner's reply to Chomsky's concern is that we *can* capture a person's behaviour in terms of stimulus-response pairs, as long as the description of the stimulus takes into account all of the relevant factors from the subject's environmental history. The question here is whether this tactic will also serve to rescue the translation project from the problem of interaction between different mental states.

The identity theory and complex mental causes

Fodor points out that, unlike behaviourism, the identity theory of Smart and Armstrong has no difficulty in accounting for the fact that mental states work in conjunction with one another.[6] According to identity theorists, each mental state will be a particular neurological state of the brain, and it is quite easy to suppose that any one of these will lead to behaviour only in the presence of others. It is entirely plausible that the behaviour that will result from a particular neurological state in one area of the brain will depend on the neurological states of other areas.

Suppose, for example, that Smith's thirst is identical to the firing of a small collection of neurons in one region of the nervous system. What effect that activity will have on Smith's behaviour could easily depend on which neurons are firing in other regions. And the neural activity in those other regions will each be identical to some specific state of mind, such as beliefs about what is in the glass. In this way we explain complex *mental* causes of behaviour by identifying them with complex *neurological* causes of behaviour.

Fodor's way of putting this point is that the identity theory allows for mental states to be *autonomous* of behaviour, and by this he means that there is no necessary or logical connection between being in a certain state of mind and behaving in any particular way. A given state of mind is consistent with *any* kind of behaviour as long as it is accompanied by other states of mind of the appropriate sort.

The ambiguity in identity theory

Although the identity theory has this advantage over behaviourism, Fodor argues that it suffers from a different problem. More to the point, he claims that the identity theory can be understood in two different ways, and only one of these ways is workable. To understand Fodor's argument we need to draw yet another distinction between different kinds of numerical identity. Smart's argument hinged on the difference between necessary and contingent

identity, claiming that the latter avoids all of the common objections to identifying states of mind with states of the brain. There are, however, two kinds
of contingent identity, and according to Fodor only one of them is plausible
in the case of mind and body. Fodor labels these two kinds of contingent
identity "token physicalism" and "type physicalism." He says:

> I remarked that the identity theory can be held either as a doctrine
> about mental *particulars* (John's current headache, Bill's fear of cats)
> or as a doctrine about mental *properties* (universals like having a pain
> or being afraid of animals). These two variants — known as "token
> physicalism" and "type physicalism" respectively — differ in both
> strength and plausibility.

Let's look at what this means.

Types and tokens

We need to begin with the general difference between what philosophers call
types and tokens. It is obvious that there are many different kinds of things
in the world. There are buildings, people, trees, and so on. And it is just as
obvious that there can be many things of a particular kind. There are many
individual buildings, individual people and individual trees. Philosophers mark
this with the following terminology. An individual thing — an individual
person or object or event — is a **token**, and a kind of thing, or category of
thing, is a **type**. For example, Buckingham Palace, the White House, and my
place of residence are all tokens of the type *building*. And Britain, France,
and Germany are all tokens of the type *nation*.

We can apply this terminology to mental and physical states and activities. A **mental type** is a kind of mental state or activity, such as a kind of
thought or sensation or belief. For example, believing in Santa Claus is a mental state type possessed by many children, and having a headache is a type of
mental state often caused by nervous tension. A **mental token** is the mental
state or activity of a particular person at a particular time. So Johnny's belief
in Santa Claus and Mary's belief in Santa Claus are two mental tokens of the
same type. And my present headache is a token of the same type as my headache yesterday.

In the same way, a **physical type** is a kind or category of physical object
or event. H_2O is a physical state type, and so is being heavier than ten kilo-
grams. The categories that neurologists use to describe the activities and states
of the brain are also physical types. For example, there is a type of brain activity involving a rhythmic firing of neurons, called omega-oscillation, that is
involved in visual perception. Each of these physical types can have many

tokens. The particular glass of H_2O in front of me is a physical token of the same type as the glass of H_2O I drank yesterday. Similarly, the omega-oscillation in my visual cortex at the present moment and the omega-oscillation in your visual cortex at this moment are two tokens of the same physical type.

Type identity and token identity

We can also apply the difference between tokens and types to the idea of numerical identity. The sentence 'A is identical to B' means that there is a single item named by both 'A' and 'B.' But in a sentence of this sort A and B can be either tokens or types. That is, we can say that a particular *object* is identical to another object, or we can say that one *type* of object is identical to another type of object. And these two sentences make very different claims.

If A and B are tokens, then to say that A is identical to B is to say that A and B are the same individual items. For example, when we say that Buckingham Palace is the residence of the Queen of England we are claiming that the individual object we call Buckingham Palace is one and the same object as the residence of the English queen. Similarly, the sentence "My spouse is my best friend" means that the particular person to whom the speaker is married is the same person as the one they consider their best friend.

If A and B are types, then to say that A is identical to B is to say that being an item of type A is the same as being an item of type B. For example, the sentence 'Water is H_2O' is not a claim about any particular body of water but rather a claim that the property of being water is the same as the property of being H_2O. Long ago people learned that water is H_2O, but in doing so they learned about a *type* of thing rather than simply about some individual thing. In the same way, Benjamin Franklin's demonstration that lightning is an electrical discharge in the atmosphere was a discovery about lightning as a kind of thing and not a discovery about any one particular bolt of lightning.

The difference between token identity and type identity is especially important in cases where there is only one token of a certain type. For example, the sentence 'The daughter of the president is the most popular person in the country' might be true as a case of token identity, but it will be false as a case of type identity. For it might be true that the individual who is the daughter of the president is also the individual who is the most popular person in the country. But the property of being the daughter of the president is not the same property as being the most popular person in the country.

Type physicalism and token physicalism

Now let's see what this has to do with the identity theory. Identity theorists say that mental states are identical to physical states of the brain. But without more clarification, this claim is ambiguous. It can mean either of the following two claims:

1. **Token physicalism**: Each mental token is identical to a physical token.
2. **Type physicalism**: Each mental type is identical to a physical type.

The first of these two claims is really just an assertion of materialism. Materialism is the claim that all that exists is matter. This means that everything that exists is a physical thing. And another way of saying that everything is a physical thing is to say that every token is a physical token. So the claim that every mental token is identical to a physical token follows directly from materialism. If all there is is matter, then everything that exists — including every mental state or activity — is identical to some physical object, state, or event.

Type physicalism has much stronger implications. First let's look at a simpler example of a type identity claim such as the assertion that water is H_2O. The sentence 'Water is H_2O' means that being water is the same as being H_2O. Notice that because this is true, anything that isn't H_2O isn't water. Suppose we came across some stuff on another planet that looked, tasted, and boiled just like water. That stuff still wouldn't be water if it weren't H_2O because to be water *is* to be H_2O.

Now let's apply this point to the identity of mental and physical types. Think first of Smart's example of after-images. Suppose that after-images are firings of something called Q-cells in a region of the visual cortex. If this is a type-identity claim, then anything that isn't the firing of Q-cells in the visual cortex isn't an after-image. Similarly, if the belief that Ottawa is the capital of Canada is type-identical to a particular kind of neural activity in the cerebral cortex, then any event that isn't *that* kind of neural activity won't be a belief that Ottawa is the capital of Canada.

Another way to see the point is to notice that sentence '2.' above entails the following sentence:

3. Any individual states of mind (any mental tokens) that are the same *mental type* will necessarily be the same *physical type*.

For type physicalism says that being a certain kind of mental state is the same as being a certain kind of physical state. So if two tokens fall under a given mental type, they will necessarily fall under the same physical type as well.

These implications do not hold of token physicalism. For token physicalism only asserts that each mental token is identical to *some* physical token. It doesn't also say that any mental tokens of the same type must be tokens of the same physical type. That is, sentence '1.' above does not entail sentence '3.' More generally, materialism does not imply type physicalism. Materialism is compatible with there being no relation between mental types and physical types at all. All it requires is that each individual thing that exists, mental or otherwise, be a physical thing of some kind or other.

The implications of type physicalism

If mental types such as thoughts, beliefs, and sensations are identical to types of neural events in the human nervous system, then whether a creature has a certain thought or sensation depends entirely on whether there is a neural event of the relevant kind occurring in the nervous system. This is similar to the fact that whether a pool of wet stuff is water depends entirely on whether it is H_2O. Fodor points out the implication of this: creatures that are physically different from us could not have mental states of the same types as ours. So if creatures, say, from Mars were radically different in physical composition from human beings, they could not have beliefs or desires, thoughts or sensations as we do. Because each type of belief, desire, or thought is identified with a particular type of physical event, if that physical event is absent in a creature then so is the belief, desire, or thought. And this will be the case no matter how much the behaviour of the creature suggests otherwise. Nor could we build a mechanical robot or a computer that thinks, believes, or perceives, for the relevant neural state types would be missing in this case as well. So Fodor's point is that type physicalism rules out the possibility that creatures physically different from humans (or at least physically different from our biological order) could have mental states. As Ned Block puts it, type physicalism commits a kind of "species chauvinism": Only creatures like us can have thoughts, beliefs, and sensations.

It may turn out that conscious intelligence occurs only in creatures that have neurological structures like ours. But critics of type physicalism argue that it is misguided to decide this issue in advance. Surely we don't want to rule out the possibility of intelligence radically different in physical nature from our own without any investigation

And even if it *is* true that only creatures like us possess intelligence, that still wouldn't make type physicalism true. For type physicalism requires that it be *impossible* for there to be beings unlike us that possess intelligence and not merely that there *happen* to be no such beings. Just as liquid we find on another planet isn't water if it isn't H_2O no matter how much it looks, tastes, and feels like water, nothing we could encounter on another planet could possibly be intelligent if it lacks a neurological structure like ours no matter how intelligent it might *appear* to be. Fodor argues that these implications of type physicalism show that it is not a plausible solution to the mind-body problem.

Multiple realizability

If type physicalism is false, then mental types have what is called **multiple realizability**. This means that events that are of the same mental type can be of different physical types — the same mental state can be realized in different ways. If a type is multiply realizable, then there is no single physical property that each token of that type must have in common. There are many kinds of things that are multiply realizable. Money is one example. A dollar can be made up of one bill or four quarters or ten dimes, each of which is physically different from the other. Another example of a type that is multiply realizable is the clock. There are mechanical clocks, electric clocks and water clocks, and there are digital clocks and analog clocks. There is no single physical property that every clock must possess.

What would it be like for mental types to be multiply realizable? As it happens, all of the creatures with mental states that we know of are quite similar in physical structure. Each possesses a nervous system roughly the same as our own. But imagine the following situation. Suppose someone called Jane is standing at the bus stop and thinking to herself, "The bus is late." If materialism is true, then Jane's thought is a physical event, most likely a neural event in her cerebral cortex. Now imagine that a Martian called Qwertl is visiting Earth and is waiting for the same bus. Qwertl is also thinking to himself, "The bus is late." Under token physicalism Qwertl's thought will also be a physical event occurring in his body. But as long as *type* identity is false, Qwertl's thought need not be physically similar in any way to Jane's thought. For the multiple realizability of mental states tells us that Jane's thought and Qwertl's thought can be tokens of the same *mental* type but of different *physical* types. Although he is thinking a thought of the same type as Jane's, Qwertl might be just a gaseous cloud hovering in the air next to the bus stop.

But what are mental types?

The problem of "species chauvinism" suggests that type physicalism is not a good choice of theory. But if we claim that token physicalism is true, and type physicalism is false, we face a difficulty. To see this problem, consider Jane and her Martian friend again. Jane is a *Homo sapiens*, and Qwertl is a gaseous cloud, and each is thinking that the bus is late. If token physicalism is true but type physicalism is false, then each of their thoughts are physical states of their bodies, even while their bodies have nothing physical in common. So what *is* it that Jane and Qwertl have in common that makes it true that they have the same thought? What makes two physical events, each entirely different from the other, a thought that the bus is late? In general, the question is this: if type physicalism is false, then what do mental tokens of the same type have in common?

To see the force of this question you can ask yourself, What is it that all *clocks* have in common? Clocks do not all share any one physical characteristic, but there is still something that makes an instrument a clock: for an instrument to be a clock, it must be possible to use it to tell the time. We want to ask the same kind of question about states of mind: what is it that makes a physical event a certain kind of mental state such as a thought or a headache?

Fodor points out that logical behaviourism does not face this difficulty. As he puts it, logical behaviourism offers "a relational treatment of mental properties, one which identifies them in ways that abstracts from the physiology of their bearers." His point here is that whether a creature is thinking a certain thought, or holds a certain belief, depends only on the relation between stimulus and behaviour that it exhibits. They would argue that to say Jane and Qwertl are thinking the same thought means only that they exhibit the same behavioural disposition. So it makes no difference what the physical composition is like; it is only the behaviour that counts.

Fodor's dilemma

Fodor concludes that a dilemma emerges for the materialist. He says:

> What [identity theorists] seemed to have got right — contra behaviourists — was the ontological autonomy of mental particulars and, of a piece with this, the causal character of mind/body interactions. Whereas, what the behaviourists seemed to have got right — contra the identity theory — was the relational character of mental properties.

That is, identity theory can account for the complexity of mental causes, while logical behaviourism cannot; yet identity theory cannot accommodate multiple realizability, while logical behaviourism can. What materialists need, then, is a theory of the mind that combines the advantages of these two without the difficulties each faces. And this, Fodor claims, is functionalism.

Multiple realizability and the computer metaphor

To see Fodor's argument it is useful to return to the computer metaphor. According to machine functionalists, we can understand the mind by comparing the operation of the brain with the operation of a computer. Let's look first at how this avoids the problem that type identity encounters.

The *hardware* of a computer is its physical structure: the arrangement of the bits and pieces of metal and silicon that it is made of. The *software* of a computer is the program it is running. A program is a set of instructions, an algorithm, that causes the computer to perform a certain sequence of operations when given a certain kind of input. Fodor's point is that computers that are physically different can run the same programs. The fact that a certain computer is running a particular program is not a matter of what it is made of; what matters is how it behaves, what it does. For example, we could build a sophisticated computer entirely out of Tinker Toys, if they were connected together the right way. So programs have multiple realizability in the sense that they can be carried out in systems with very different hardware.

If the human mind is a computer, then the multiple realizability of computer programs means that we avoid the species chauvinism of type identity. The sequences of mental processes involved in perception and thought would constitute the program of the mind, and the biochemical structure of the nervous system would be the hardware in which this program is carried out. But that same program could be realized in hardware of a very different sort. As long as a physical system (or even an immaterial substance) carries out the same program as the one realized in the human brain, then that system possesses a human mind, regardless of the "hardware" it is made of. And if we encounter beings on other planets whose internal functioning is similar to ours, then we have good reason to attribute to them thoughts and perceptions similar to our own.

Notice that this solves the problem of describing what mental states of the same type have in common. Individuals have mental states of the same type as long as their internal systems are running the same information-processing operations. And this can be true even if the two individuals are physically different. So Jane and Qwertl are thinking the same thought as long as their internal systems are carrying out the same computer operations.

Complex mental causes and the computer metaphor

The idea that the brain is a computer can also show how complex mental causes are possible — the problem that bedevilled logical behaviourism. Running a computer involves a sequence of operations. These operations typically involve such things as storing and retrieving information from memory, calculating the results of combining information from different sources, and passing the results of calculations to other operations going on at the same time. So conceiving of the activity of the brain as a computer allows us to accommodate the idea that mental states are internal states that operate in complex sequences, interacting with external stimuli and with each other to produce behaviour.

Defining functionalism

The differences and similarities that arise when comparing functionalism with identity theory and behaviourism give us a good way to define functionalism. Functionalism consists of two distinct doctrines:

1. Mental states are internal states that interact with one another and with external stimuli to produce observable behaviour.
2. Each mental state type is defined not in terms of physical makeup, but in terms of its function in the operation of the system.

The first of these two is what functionalism has in common with the identity theory (and dualism), contra behaviourism. Functionalists agree with the common intuition that "there is something going on" when we think. The states of mind that we are aware of when reflecting on our own conscious experiences are states in a complex sequence of internal events. The second doctrine captures what functionalism shares with behaviourism, contra the identity theory. As Fodor puts it, both functionalism and behaviourism characterize mental states in *relational* terms: behaviourists in terms of relations between stimuli and behaviour, and functionalists as relations between stimuli, behaviour, and other mental states. In neither case is the physical composition of a mental state relevant to its type identity.

According to Fodor, then, functionalism combines the virtues of both behaviourism and the identity theory and avoids the weaknesses of both. As he puts it at the end of the article, "Bliss!"

Two kinds of machine functionalism

At the beginning of the chapter I defined machine functionalism as the product of two ideas: that mental states are defined in terms of their function, what they do, rather than what they are made of; and that mental activity is a form of computing or information processing. The articles by Putnam and Fodor agree on both of these points. But there is an important difference between the two positions. For reasons that I will explain, I will call Putnam's version of machine functionalism "machine-state functionalism" and Fodor's version "computational-state functionalism."

The difference between these two views, and its importance, is defended by Fodor and Ned Block in a brief passage from a 1972 article entitled "What Psychological States Are Not." This passage is not easy reading and is full of technical jargon. But it is concise, and the main ideas can be outlined without understanding all of the technical language.

Machine states and mental states

Fodor and Block's concern is to remedy what they see as a mistake in Putnam's way of identifying mental states with the states of a computing machine. Putnam's idea, you will recall, is that the mind can be thought of as a discrete state machine, so that understanding mental states and processes will be a matter of constructing a machine table. Mental states, such as pains and beliefs, will be represented by the vertical columns of the machine table, and mental processing will be a sequence of actions carried out according to the table. Fodor and Block agree with the idea that psychological processes can be characterized in terms of the actions of discrete state machines, but they disagree with the second part of Putnam's idea: that mental states can be represented by "machine states" in the sense of the columns of the machine table.

Fodor and Block's argument for this conclusion, stripped of all its jargon, is simple to state: in any discrete state machine there is only a finite number of possible machine states, but there is an infinite number of possible types of mental states. So the first set cannot be identical to the second set. As Fodor and Block put it:

> the psychological states of organisms cannot be placed in one-to-one correspondence with the machine table states of organisms.

That is, it is not possible to identify each possible type of mental state with a distinct machine state, for there are infinitely many of the former but only finitely many of the latter.

Fodor and Block's reasoning is spelled out more fully in the first two sentences of the next paragraph:[7]

> The set of states that constitute the machine table of a probabilistic automaton is, by definition, a list. But the set of mental states of at least some organisms (namely, persons) is, in point of empirical fact, *productive*. [emphasis mine]

The first sentence merely points out the fact that, no matter how large the machine table of a discrete state machine might be, there will still only be a finite number of vertical columns.[8] The second sentence explains why the set of possible mental states of a person is infinite. To see their point we need to understand the idea of a "productive" set.

Productive sets

If a set is finite, then we can identify all of its members just by providing a list. For example, you could identify all the players on a soccer team by listing all of their names. But if a set has an infinite number of members, we cannot provide such a list. Suppose, for example, you wanted to explain to someone what the set of positive integers is. Of course, you couldn't just list them all, for you would never finish. But you can describe the set by giving the person some rules for identifying the numbers. The following rules would do:

1. The number 1 is a member of the set.

2. If a given number is a member of the set, so is the sum of that number and the number 1.

To identify the members of the set, we begin with the number 1, then by repeating the second rule over and over we get 2, 3, 4, 5 ... and so on. Although there are too many positive integers to name them all, any one of them will eventually be arrived at by applying the two rules. Following this idea, we can say that a set is **productive** when you can identify all of its members only by means of a set of rules.[9]

Why, then, do Fodor and Block claim that the set of mental states that a person can possibly possess is productive? This position is based on two assertions: first, there are (at least) as many mental states as there are sentences. This is because, for any sentence *S* you care to name, there will be several mental states associated with that sentence. There will be the belief that *S* is true, and the hope that *S* is true, and so on. Second, the set of sentences in any language is productive. Although a language has only a finite number of words, there is an infinite number of different ways of putting them together into sentences. The only way we can describe a complete language is by listing the words, and then giving a set of grammar rules that describe all of the ways those words can be combined.

In the fifth paragraph Fodor and Block argue that it is an empirical fact that there are an infinite number of possible mental states. That is, we might not have been capable of an infinite number of mental states. Consider, for example, a very primitive creature who, for some reason, is capable only of two thoughts — maybe something like "Food there; Food not there." But because humans use language to convey their thoughts, and languages are productive, we know that humans have an infinite number of distinct possible thoughts.

Machine states and computational states

Fodor and Block claim that Putnam's idea of identifying mental states with machine states of a discrete state machine is mistaken. But, as we have seen, they do accept the idea that the correct model for mental processes is a digital computer as exemplified by the Turing Machine. In the next paragraph they claim that there is a better way of identifying mental states with states of a digital computer, namely what they call "computational states." Whereas machine states are the ones that specify what action the machine will take given each possible input or stimulus, **computational states** are more broadly defined as *any* states of the machine that can be described by referring to its computing behaviour. At the end of the paragraph Fodor and Block offer a list of what would count as computational states. You might also think of the computational states that we ascribe to our personal computers. We (or at least computer programmers) say things like, "It has just emptied the contents of the memory buffer, and is sorting the new input list." These are activities described in terms of computational states.

So Fodor and Block's idea is that every possible mental state — every thought, belief, desire, sensation, and so on — can be identified with a computational state in the sense of a state that refers in some way to its computational activities: its inputs, outputs, and machine states. In the case of human beings, mental states will be computational states of the nervous system.

Compare Fodor and Block's idea with the identity theory. According to Smart and Armstrong, mental states are identical to physical states of the brain, such as the firing of a particular set of neurons. Fodor and Block's position is that mental states are identical to computational states as described above. Where an identity theorist will identify a thought or a sensation with a particular physical event in the nervous system, Fodor and Block will identify it with such states as "having calculated the sum of register 103 and 305," or "having the results of process X in memory."

Turing Machines again

Recall from chapter 10 that a major breakthrough in Turing's description of digital computers is the idea that computers operate on symbols. In that chapter I mentioned that it is the use of symbols that accounts for the flexibility of their behaviour. Given enough memory space, we can store an indefinite number of symbols in the memory of a digital computer, and this means there is an indefinite number of ways its activities can be adjusted in the light of new input. This point is connected with several issues we have encountered before.

First, that computers operate on symbols accounts for the fact that we can identify each possible mental state with a computational state. As we saw above, the set of possible mental states is productive, but given the memory of a digital computer, so is the set of computational states. Think, for example, of the set of symbol strings that can be written onto the tape of a Turing Machine; as long as we keep adding more tape, the machine can keep writing new strings of symbols. Because the computational states of a Turing Machine can include what is written on the tape, there is an infinite number of such states. Of course, any particular machine will have only a certain amount of memory available, so eventually it will run out. But, then, each person has only a certain amount of memory, and so in practical terms there are only a finite number of thoughts a person can have. We might say that the possible thoughts of a person, and the possible computational states of a computer, are each infinite in the sense that they *could* occur given enough time and memory.

Plasticity again

You might also recall Descartes' claim that "reason is a universal instrument that can be used in all kinds of situations." Fodor and others claim that the idea of the mind as a digital computer shows how a single mechanism — the brain — can have an indefinite degree of flexibility or plasticity. As each new input is processed and stored in memory, the behaviour of a digital computer can adjust its behaviour indefinitely, at least in principle.

This same idea is reflected again in Chomsky's criticism of behaviourism. In order to explain or predict why people behave as they do, Chomsky argues, we have to understand their inner thoughts, beliefs, and desires. Chomsky himself shares Fodor's view that mental processes can be understood as computational processes involving operations on symbols. Explaining psychological processes as computer operations on symbols attributes to the mind the degree of plasticity that the behaviourists have difficulty accounting for.

The plasticity of computer behaviour goes some way to showing how a physical mechanism might be a "universal instrument" in Descartes' sense. However, it is good to keep in mind that there are aspects of human behaviour that have not been explained in terms of computational mechanisms. The frame problem and the knowledge access problem are still major stumbling blocks to providing a fully mechanistic account of human reason and behaviour.

Functionalism and computational psychology

The idea that mental states are computational states in the sense described above has generated a vast number of research projects in psychology in the past thirty years. Psychologists have been constructing computational models of psychological processes and attempting to identify particular mental states with computational states within these models. The greatest progress in these projects has been in linguistics and perception theory. Linguists have devoted much work to computer models of how children learn language and how the brain might process and analyze the sentences we hear. In similar ways, psychologists working on the processes of vision and hearing have been constructing models of these processes on the assumption that the activities of the nervous system are computing processes that analyze the sensory input and generate digital representations of the world around us.

At the same time that these projects have grown into a major discipline, the functionalist model of the mind has come under attack. Although the idea of mental processes as computational processes has not been abandoned, recent work in psychology has attempted to use computer models closer in form to the actual processes of the nervous system. To understand how the mind computes, it is argued, we need to abandon the Turing Machine model and look more closely at the brain itself. Moreover, the critics claim, Fodor's argument above reveals two connected errors in the functionalist picture of the mind. Fodor claims that the number of possible mental states is productive because there is at least one mental state for every sentence. But the practice of describing people's thoughts in terms of sentences (the belief that *S*, the desire that *S*, and so on) is itself flawed. In fact, it is this mistaken picture that has led us to the equally erroneous idea of the mind as a Turing Machine. These arguments are the subject of the next chapter.

NOTES

1 For an argument that machine functionalism is not the best way of developing functionalism, see Eliot Sober, "Putting the Function Back into Functionalism," in *Mind and Cognition: A Reader*, William G. Lycan (ed.) (Oxford: Basil Blackwell, 1990).

2 For Putnam's recent arguments against functionalism, see his book, *Representation and Reality* (Cambridge, MA: MIT Press, 1988).

3 The term *a priori* that Putnam uses in this sentence is a Latin phrase that means "based on reason and logic alone."

4 Jerry Fodor, *The Language of Thought* (Cambridge, MA: Harvard University Press, 1975).

5 As Fodor uses the term, logical behaviourism includes linguistic philosophers like Ryle and Wittgenstein, as well as those, like Hempel, who explicitly adopt the title.

6 Here Fodor refers to the identity theory as "the physicalist reading of materialistic monism." Elsewhere in the essay he calls it the "central-state identity theory." The terminology is confusing.

7 Like Putnam, Fodor and Block refer to a discrete state machine here as a "probabilistic automaton."

8 If there were an infinite number of machine states, it would not be possible to describe its behaviour, which is contrary to the definition of a discrete state machine.

9 When Fodor says, at the end of the second paragraph, that the set of mental states of a person "can at best be specified by finite axiomatization," he means roughly the same thing as saying that the set of mental states that a person can have is productive.

Hilary Putnam
"The Nature of Mental States"

The typical concerns of the Philosopher of Mind might be represented by three questions: (1) How do we know that other people have pains? (2) Are pains brain states? (3) What is the analysis of the concept *pain*? ... I shall say something [here] about question (2).

I. Identity Questions

"Is pain a brain state?" (Or, "Is the property of having a pain at time *t* a brain state?")[1] It is impossible to discuss this question sensibly without saying something about the peculiar rules which have grown up in the course of the development of "analytical philosophy"—rules which, far from leading to an end to all conceptual confusions, themselves represent considerable conceptual confusion. These rules —which are, of course, implicit rather than explicit in the practice of most analytical philosophers—are (1) that a statement of the form "being *A* is being *B*" (e.g., "being in pain is being in a certain brain state") can be *correct* only if it follows, in some sense, from the meaning of the terms *A* and *B*; and (2) that a statement of the form "being *A* is being *B*" can be philosophically *informative* only if it is in some sense reductive (e.g., "being in pain is having a certain unpleasant sensation" is not philosophically informative; "being in pain is having a certain behaviour disposition" is, if true, philosophically informative). These rules are excellent rules if we still believe that the program of reductive analysis (in the style of the 1930s) can be carried out; if we don't, then they turn analytical philosophy into a mug's game, at least so far as "is" questions are concerned.

... I shall use the term "property" as a blanket term for such things as being in pain, being in a particular brain state, having a particular behavior disposition, and also for magnitudes such as temperature, etc.—i.e. for things which can naturally be represented by one-or-more-place predicates or functors. I shall use the term "concept" for things which can be identified with synonymy-classes of expressions. Thus the concept *temperature* can be identified (I maintain) with the synonymy-class of the word "temperature".[2] (This is like saying that the number 2 can be identified with the class of all pairs. This is quite a different statement from the peculiar statement that 2 *is* the class of all pairs. I do not maintain that concepts *are* synonymy-classes, whatever that might mean, but that they can be identified with synonymy-classes, for the purpose of formalization of the relevant discourse.)

The question "What is the concept *temperature*?" is a very "funny" one. One might take it to mean "What is temperature? Please take my question as a conceptual one." In that case an answer might be (pretend for a moment "heat" and "temperature" are synonyms) "temperature is heat," or even "the concept of temperature is the same concept as the concept of heat." Or one might take it to mean "What are *concepts*, really? For example, what is 'the concept of temperature'?" In that case heaven knows what an "answer" would be. (Perhaps it would be the statement that concepts *can be identified with* synonymy-classes.)

Of course, the question "What is the property temperature?" is also "funny." And one way of interpreting it is to take it as a question about the concept of temperature. But this is not the way a physicist would take it.

The effect of saying that the property P_1 can be identical with the property P_2 only if the terms P_2 are in some suitable sense "synonyms" is, to all intents and purposes, to collapse the two notions of "property" and "concept" into a single notion. The view that concepts (intensions) *are* the same as properties has been explicitly advocated by Carnap (e.g. in *Meaning and Necessity*). This seems an unfortunate view, since "temperature is mean molecular kinetic energy" appears to be a perfectly good example of a true statement of identity of properties, whereas "the concept of temperature is the same concept as a concept of mean molecular kinetic energy" is simply false.

Many philosophers believe that the statement "pain is a brain state" violates some rules or norms of English. But the arguments offered are hardly convincing. For example, if the fact that I can know that I am in pain without knowing that I am in brain state S shows that pain cannot be brain state S, then, by exactly the same argument, the fact that I can know that the stove is hot without knowing that the mean molecular kinetic energy is high (or even that molecules exist) shows that it *is false* that temperature is mean molecular kinetic energy, physics to the contrary. In fact, all that immediately follows from the fact that I can know that I am in pain without knowing that I am in brain state S is that the concept of pain is not the same concept as the concept of being in brain state S. But either pain, or the state of being in pain, or some pain, or some pain state, might still be brain state S. After all, the concept of temperature is not the same concept as the concept of mean molecular kinetic energy. But temperature is mean molecular kinetic energy.

Some philosophers maintain that both "pain is a brain state" and "pain states are brain states" are unintelligible. The answer is to explain to these philosophers, as well as we can, given the vagueness of all scientific methodology, what sorts of considerations lead one to make an empirical reduction (i.e. to say such things as "water is H_2O," "light is electromagnetic radiation," "temperature is mean molecu-

lar kinetic energy"). If, without giving reasons, he still maintains in the face of such examples that one cannot imagine parallel circumstances for the use of "pains are brain states" (or, perhaps, "pain states are brain states") one has grounds to regard him as perverse.

Some philosophers maintain that "P_1 is P_2" is something that can be true, when the "is" involved is the "is" of empirical reduction, only when the properties P_1 and P_2 are (a) associated with a spatio-temporal region; and (b) the region is one and the same in both cases. Thus "temperature is mean molecular kinetic energy" is an admissible empirical reduction, since the temperature and the molecular energy are associated with the same space-time region, but "having a pain in my arm is being in a brain state" is not, since the spatial regions involved are different.

This argument does not appear very strong. Surely no one is going to be deterred from saying that mirror images are light reflected from an object and then from the surface of a mirror by the fact that an image can be "located" three feet *behind* the mirror! (Moreover, one can always find *some* common property of the reductions one is willing to allow—e.g. temperature is mean molecular kinetic energy—which is not a property of some one identification one wishes to disallow. This is not very impressive unless one has an argument to show that the very purposes of such identification depend upon the common property in question.)

Again, other philosophers have contended that all the predictions that can be derived from the conjunction of neurophysiological laws with such statements as "pain states are such-and-such brain states" can equally well be derived from the conjunction of the same neurophysiological laws with "being in pain is correlated with such-and-such brain states", and hence *(sic!)* there can be no methodological grounds for saying that pains (or pain states) *are* brain states, as opposed to saying that they are *correlated* (invariantly) with brain states. This argument, too, would show that light is only correlated with electromagnetic radiation. The mistake is in ignoring the fact that, although the theories in question may indeed lead to the same predictions, they open and exclude different *questions*. "Light is invariantly correlated with electromagnetic radiation" would leave open the questions "What is the light then, if it isn't the same as the electromagnetic radiation?" and "What makes the light accompany the electromagnetic radiation?"— questions which are excluded by saying that the light *is* the electromagnetic radiation. Similarly, the purpose of saying that pains are brain states is precisely to exclude from empirical meaningfulness the questions "What is the pain, then, if it isn't the same as the brain state?" and "What makes the pain accompany the brain state?" If there are grounds to suggest that these questions represent, so to speak, the wrong way to look at the matter, then those grounds are grounds for a theoretical identification of pains with brain states.

If all arguments to the contrary are unconvincing, shall we then conclude that it is meaningful (and perhaps true) to say either that pains are brain states or that pain states are brain states?

(1) It is perfectly meaningful (violates no "rule of English," involves no "extension of usage") to say "pains are brain states."

(2) It is not meaningful (involves a "changing of meaning" or "an extension of usage," etc.) to say "pains are brain states."

My own position is not expressed by either (1) or (2). It seems to me that the notions "change of meaning" and "extension of usage" are simply so ill defined that one cannot in fact say *either* (1) or (2). I see no reason to believe that either the linguist, or the man-on-the-street, or the philosopher possesses today a notion of "change of meaning" applicable to such cases as the one we have been discussing. The *job* for which the notion of change of meaning was developed in the history of the language was just a *much* cruder job than this one.

But, if we don't assert either (1) or (2)—in other words, if we regard the "change of meaning" issue as a pseudo-issue in this case—then how are we to discuss the question with which we started? "Is pain a brain state?"

The answer is to allow statements of the form "pain is *A*" where "pain" and "*A*" are in no sense synonyms, and to see whether any such statement can be found which might be acceptable on empirical and methodological grounds. This is what we shall now proceed to do.

II. Is Pain a Brain State?

We shall discuss "Is pain a brain state?" then. And we have agreed to waive the "change of meaning" issue.

Since I am discussing not what the concept of pain comes to, but what pain is, in a sense of "is" which requires empirical theory-construction (or, at least, empirical speculation), I shall not apologize for advancing an empirical hypothesis. Indeed, my strategy will be to argue that pain is *not* a brain state, not on a priori grounds, but on the grounds that another hypothesis is more plausible. The detailed development and verification of my hypothesis would be just as Utopian a task as the detailed development and verification of the brain-state hypothesis. But the putting-forward, not of detailed and scientifically "finished" hypotheses, but of schemata for hypotheses, has long been a function of philosophy. I shall, in short, argue that pain is not a brain state, in the sense of a physical-chemical state of the brain (or even the whole nervous system), but another *kind* of state entirely. I propose the hypothesis that pain, or the state of being in pain, is a functional state of a whole organism.

To explain that it is necessary to introduce some technical notions. In previous papers I have explained the notion of a Turing Machine and discussed the use of this notion as a model for an organism. The notion of a Probabilistic Automaton is defined similarly to a Turing

Machine, except that the transitions between "states" are allowed to be with various probabilities rather than being "deterministic." (Of course, a Turing Machine is simply a special kind of Probabilistic Automaton, one with transition probabilities 0, 1.) I shall assume the notion of a Probabilistic Automaton has been generalized to allow for "sensory inputs" and "motor outputs"—that is, the Machine Table specifies, for every possible combination of a "state" and a complete set of "sensory inputs," an "instruction" which determines the probability of the next "state," and also the probabilities of the "motor outputs." (This replaces the idea of the Machine as printing on a tape.) I shall also assume that the physical realization of the sense organs responsible for the various inputs, and of the motor organs, is specified, but that the "states" and the "inputs" themselves are, as usual, specified only "implicitly"—i.e. by the set of transition probabilities given by the Machine Table.

Since an empirically given system can simultaneously be a "physical realization" of many different Probabilistic Automata, I introduce the notion of a *Description* of a system. A Description of S where S is a system, is any true statement to the effect that S possesses distinct states $S_1, S_2 \ldots S_n$ which are related to one another and to the motor outputs and sensory inputs by the transition probabilities given in such-and-such a Machine Table. The Machine Table mentioned in the Description will then be called the Functional Organization of S relative to that Description, and the S_i such that S is in state S_i at a given time will be called the Total State of S (at the time) relative to that Description. It should be noted that knowing the Total State of a system relative to a Description involves knowing a good deal about how the system is likely to "behave," given various combinations of sensory inputs, but does *not* involve knowing the physical realization of the S_i as, e.g. physical-chemical states of the brain. The S_i, to repeat, are specified only *implicitly*

by the Description—i.e. specified *only* by the set of transition probabilities given in the Machine Table.

The hypothesis that "being in pain is a functional state of the organism" may now be spelled out more exactly as follows:

(1) All organisms capable of feeling pain are Probabilistic Automata.

(2) Every organism capable of feeling pain possesses at least one Description of a certain kind (i.e. being capable of feeling pain *is* possessing an appropriate kind of Functional Organization).

(3) No organism capable of feeling pain possesses a decomposition into parts which separately possess Descriptions of the kind referred to in (2).

(4) For every Description of the kind referred to in (2), there exists a subset of the sensory inputs such that an organism with that Description is in pain when and only when some of its sensory inputs are in that subset.

This hypothesis is admittedly vague, though surely no vaguer than the brain-state hypothesis in its present form. For example, one would like to know more about the kind of Functional Organization that an organism must have to be capable of feeling pain, and more about the marks that distinguish the subset of the sensory inputs referred to in (4). With respect to the first question, one can probably say that the Functional Organization must include something that resembles a "preference function," or at least a preference partial ordering and something that resembles an "inductive logic" (i.e. the Machine must be able to "learn from experience") ... In addition, it seems natural to require that the Machine possess "pain sensors," i.e. sensory organs which normally signal damage to the Machine's body, or dangerous temperatures, pressures, etc., which transmit a special subset of the inputs, the subset referred to in (4). Finally, and with respect to the second question, we would want to require at least that the inputs in the distinguished subset have a high disvalue on the Machine's preference function or ordering … The purpose of condition (3) is to rule out such "organisms" (if they can count as such) as swarms of bees as single pain-feelers. The condition (1) is, obviously, redundant, and is only introduced for expository reasons. (It is, in fact, empty, since everything is a Probabilistic Automation under *some* Description.)

I contend, in passing, that this hypothesis, in spite of its admitted vagueness, is far *less* vague than the "physical-chemical state" hypothesis is today, and far more susceptible to investigation of both a mathematical and an empirical kind. Indeed, to investigate this hypothesis is just to attempt to produce "mechanical" models of organisms—and isn't this, in a sense, just what psychology is about? The difficult step, of course, will be to pass from models to *specific* organisms to a *normal form* for the psychological description of organisms—for this is what is required to make (2) and (4) precise. But this too seems to be an inevitable part of the program of psychology.

I shall now compare the hypothesis just advanced with (a) the hypothesis that pain is a brain state, and (b) the hypothesis that pain is a behavior disposition.

III. Functional State Versus Brain State

It may, perhaps, be asked if I am not somewhat unfair in taking the brain-state theorist to be talking about *physical-chemical* states of the brain. But (a) these are the only sorts of states ever mentioned by brain-state theorists. (b) The brain-state theorist usually mentions (with a certain pride, slightly reminiscent of the Village Atheist) the incompatibility of his hypothesis with all forms of dualism and mentalism. This is natural if physical-chemical states of the brain are what is at issue. However, functional states of whole systems are something quite different. In particular, the functional-state hypothesis is

not incompatible with dualism! Although it goes without saying that the hypothesis is "mechanistic" in its inspiration, it is a slightly remarkable fact that a system consisting of a body and a "soul," if such things there be, can perfectly well be a Probabilistic Automaton. (c) One argument advanced by Smart is that the brain-state theory assumes only "physical" properties, and Smart finds "non-physical" properties unintelligible. The Total States and the "inputs" defined above are, of course, neither mental nor physical per se, and I cannot image a functionalist advancing this argument. (d) If the brain-state theorist does mean (or at least allow) states other than physical-chemical states, then his hypothesis is completely empty, at least until he specifies *what* sort of "states" he *does* mean.

Taking the brain-state hypothesis in this way, then, what reasons are there to prefer the functional-state hypothesis over the brain-state hypothesis? Consider what the brain-state theorist has to do to make good his claims. He has to specify a physical-chemical state such that *any* organism (not just a mammal) is in pain if and only if (a) it possesses a brain of a suitable physical-chemical structure; and (b) its brain is in that physical-chemical state. This means that the physical-chemical state in question must be a possible state of a mammalian brain, a reptilian brain, a mollusc's brain (octopuses are mollusca, and certainly feel pain), etc. At the same time, it must *not* be a possible (physically possible) state of the brain of any physically possible creature that cannot feel pain. Even if such a state can be found, it must be nomologically certain that it will also be a state of the brain of any extraterrestrial life that may be found that will be capable of feeling pain before we can even entertain the supposition that it may *be* pain.

It is not altogether impossible that such a state will be found. Even though octopus and mammal are examples of parallel (rather than sequential) evolution, for example, virtually identical structures (physically speaking) have evolved in the eye of the octopus and in the eye of the mammal, notwithstanding the fact that this organ has evolved from different kinds of cells in the two cases. Thus it is at least possible that parallel evolution, all over the universe, might _always_ lead to _one and the same_ physical "correlate" of pain. But this is certainly an ambitious hypothesis.

Finally, the hypothesis becomes still more ambitious when we realize that the brain-state theorist is not just saying that _pain_ is a brain state; he is, of course, concerned to maintain that _every_ psychological state is a brain state. Thus if we can find even one psychological predicate which can clearly be applied to both a mammal and an octopus (say "hungry"), but whose physical-chemical "correlate" is different in the two cases, the brain-state theory has collapsed. It seems to me overwhelmingly probable that we can do this. Granted, in such a case the brain-state theorist can save himself by ad hoc assumptions (e.g. defining the disjunction of two states to be a single "physical-chemical state"), but this does not have to be taken seriously.

Turning now to the considerations _for_ the functional-state theory, let us begin with the fact that we identify organisms as in pain, or hungry, or angry, or in heat, etc., on the basis of their _behavior_. But it is a truism that similarities in the behavior of two systems are at least a reason to suspect similarities in the functional organization of the two systems, and a much _weaker_ reason to suspect similarities in the actual physical details. Moreover, we expect the various psychological states—at least the basic ones, such as hunger, thirst, aggression, etc.—to have more or less similar "transition probabilities" (within wide and ill-defined limits, to be sure) with each other and with behavior in the case of different species, because this is an artifact of the way in which we identify these states. Thus, we would not count an animal as _thirsty_ if its "unsatiated" behavior did not seem to be directed toward drinking and was not followed by "satiation for liquid." Thus

any animal that we count as capable of these various states will at least _seem_ to have a certain rough kind of functional organization. And, as already remarked, if the program of finding psychological laws that are not species-specific—i.e. of finding a normal form for psychological theories of different species—ever succeeds, then it will bring in its wake a delineation of the kind of functional organization that is necessary and sufficient for a given psychological state, as well as a precise definition of the notion "psychological state". In contrast, the brain-state theorist has to hope for the eventual development of neurophysiological laws that are species-independent, which seems much less reasonable than the hope that psychological laws (of a sufficiently general kind) may be species-independent, or, still weaker, that a species-independent _form_ can be found in which psychological laws can be written.

IV. Functional State Versus Behavior-Disposition

The theory that being in pain is neither a brain state nor a functional state but a behavior disposition has one apparent advantage: it appears to agree with the way in which we verify that organisms are in pain. We do not in practice know anything about the brain state of an animal when we say that it is in pain; and we possess little if any knowledge of its functional organization, except in a crude intuitive way. In fact, however, this "advantage" is not advantage at all: for, although statements about how we verify that x is A may have a good deal to do with what the concept of being A comes to, they have precious little to do with what the property A _is_. To argue on the ground just mentioned that pain is neither a brain state nor a functional state is like arguing that heat is not mean molecular kinetic energy from the fact that ordinary people do not (they think) ascertain the mean molecular kinetic energy of something when they verify that it is hot or cold. It is not necessary that they should; what is necessary is that the marks that they take as indications of heat should in fact be explained by the mean molecular kinetic energy. And, similarly, it is necessary to our hypothesis that the marks that are taken as behavioral indications of pain should be explained by the fact that the organism is a functional state of the appropriate kind, but not that speakers should *know* that this is so.

The difficulties with "behavior disposition" accounts are so well known that I shall do little more than recall them here. The difficulty—it appears to be more than a "difficulty," in fact—of specifying the required behavior disposition except as "the disposition of *X* to behave as if *X* were in *pain*," is the chief one, of course. In contrast, we *can* specify the functional state with which we propose to identify pain, at least roughly, without using the notion of pain. Namely, the functional state we have in mind is the state of receiving sensory inputs which play a certain role in the Functional Organization of the organism. This role is characterized, at least partially, by the fact that the sense organs responsible for the inputs in question are organs whose function is to detect damage to the body, or dangerous extremes of temperature, pressure, etc., and by the fact that the "inputs" themselves, whatever their physical realization, represent a condition that the organism assigns a high disvalue to ... [T]his does *not* mean that the Machine will always *avoid* being in the condition in question ("pain"); it only means that the condition will be avoided unless not avoiding it is necessary to the attainment of some more highly valued goal. Since the behavior of the Machine (in this case, an organism) will depend not merely on the sensory inputs, but also on the Total State (i.e. on other values, beliefs, etc.), it seems hopeless to make any general statement about how an organism in such a condition *must* behave; but this does not mean that we must abandon hope of characterizing the condition. Indeed, we have just characterized it.[3]

Not only does the behavior-disposition theory seem hopelessly vague; if the "behavior" referred to is peripheral behavior, and the relevant stimuli are peripheral stimuli (e.g. we do not say anything about what the organism will do if its brain is operated upon), then the theory seems clearly false. For example, two animals with all motor nerves cut will have the same actual and potential "behavior" (namely, none to speak of); but if one has cut pain fibers and the other has uncut pain fibers, then one will feel pain and the other won't. Again, if one person has cut pain fibers, and another suppresses all pain responses deliberately due to some strong compulsion, then the actual and potential peripheral behavior may be the same, but one will feel pain and the other won't. (Some philosophers maintain that this last case is conceptually impossible, but the only evidence for this appears to be that *they* can't, or don't want to, conceive of it.) If, instead of pain, we take some sensation the "bodily expression" of which is easier to suppress—say, a slight coolness in one's left little finger—the case becomes even clearer.

Finally, even if there *were* some behavior disposition invariantly correlated with pain (species-independently!), and specifiable without using the term "pain", it would still be more plausible to identify being in pain with some state whose presence *explains* this behavior disposition—the brain state or functional state—than with the behavior disposition itself. Such considerations of plausibility may be somewhat subjective; but if other things *were* equal (of course, they aren't) why shouldn't we allow considerations of plausibility to play the deciding role?

V. Methodological Considerations

So far we have considered only what might be called the "empirical" reasons for saying that being in pain is a functional state, rather than a brain state or a behavior disposition; namely, that it seems more likely that the functional state we described is invariantly "correlated" with pain, species-independently, than that there is either a physical-chemical state of the brain (must an organism have a *brain* to feel pain? perhaps some ganglia will do) or a behavior disposition so correlated. If this is correct, then it follows that the identification we proposed is at least a candidate for consideration. What of methodological considerations?

The methodological considerations are roughly similar in all cases of reduction, so no surprises need be expected here. First, identification of psychological states with functional states means that the laws of psychology can be derived from statements of the form "such-and-such organisms have such-and-such Descriptions" together with the identification statements ("being in pain is such-and-such a functional state," etc.). Secondly, the presence of the functional state (i.e. of inputs which play the role we have described in the Functional Organization of the organism) is not merely "correlated with" but actually explains the pain behavior on the part of the organism. Thirdly, the identification serves to exclude questions which (if a naturalistic view is correct) represent an altogether wrong way of looking at the matter, e.g. "what *is* pain if it isn't either the brain state or the functional state?" and "What causes the pain to be always accompanied by this sort of functional state?" In short, the identification is to be tentatively accepted as a theory which leads to both fruitful predictions and to fruitful *questions*, and which serves to discourage fruitless and empirically senseless questions, where by "empirically senseless" I mean "senseless" not merely from the standpoint of verification, but from the standpoint of what there in fact *is*.

NOTES

1 In this paper I wish to avoid the vexed question of the relation between *pains* and *pain states*. I only remark in passing that

one common argument *against* identification of these two—namely, that a pain can be in one's arm but a state (of the organism) cannot be in one's arm—is easily seen to be fallacious.

2 There are some well-known remarks by Alonzo Church on this topic. Those remarks do not bear (as might at first be supposed) on the identification of concepts with synonymy-classes as such, but rather support the view that (in formal semantics) it is necessary to retain Frege's distinction between the normal and the 'oblique' use of expressions. That is, even if we say that the concept of temperature *is* the synonymy-class of the word 'temperature', we must not thereby be led into the error of supposing that 'the concept of temperature' is synonymous with 'the synonymy-class of the word "temperature"'—for then 'the concept of temperature' and 'der Begriff der Temperatur' would not be synonymous, which they are. Rather, we must say that the concept of 'temperature' *refers to* the synonymy-class of the word 'temperature' (on this particular reconstruction); but that class is *identified* not as 'the synonymy class to which such-and-such a word belongs', but in another way (e.g. as the synonymy-class whose members have such-and-such a characteristic use).

3 In 'The mental life of some machines' a further, and somewhat independent, characteristic of the pain inputs is discussed in terms of Automata models—namely the spontaneity of the inclination to withdraw the injured part, etc. This raises the question, which is discussed in that chapter, of giving a functional analysis of the notion of a spontaneous inclination. Of course, still further characteristics come readily to mind—for example, that feelings of pain are (or seem to be) *located* in the parts of the body.

Jerry A. Fodor
Selections from "Something on the State of the Art"

A census of the main problems in the philosophy of mind as they presented themselves in, say, the early 1960's would reveal quite a different population from the one with which philosophers are now primarily concerned. To begin with, the central preoccupations of the discipline were then largely ontological. It is not quite accurate to characterize inquiry as having been directed to the question: 'What are mental states and processes?'; philosophers of physicalist persuasion (i.e., adherents of the central-state identity theory; see below) took it that the nature of the mental was an empirical issue, hence not one for philosophers to solve. But it was widely held that philosophers ought to provide a survey of the conceptually coherent options, and that there are, in fact, fewer of these than might be supposed. It was, in particular, the rejection of Cartesian dualism and the consequent need to work out a philosophically acceptable version of materialistic monism that provided the main preoccupation of philosophers of mind at the beginning of the period these essays subtend.

The stumbling block for a dualist is the problem of mind/body interaction. If you think, as Descartes did, that minds are immaterial substances, you ought to be worried (as Descartes was) about how there can be mental causes of behavioral effects. Cynicism might suggest that the question how an immaterial substance could contribute to the etiology of physical events is not, after all, much more obscure than the question how material substances could interact causally with one another. But there is this difference: whereas we can produce lots of untendentious examples of the latter kind of interaction, there are no untendentious examples of the former kind. Physical causation we will have to live with; but non-physical cau-

sation might be an artifact of the immaterialist construal of the claim that there are minds.

Viewed this way, the issue is one of ontological parsimony. A Cartesian dualist is going to hold that there are species of causal relations over and above physical interactions. He is therefore in need of an argument why mind/body causation should not itself be viewed as an instance of physical interaction. Most philosophers now agree that no such argument has successfully been made. Even philosophers like Ryle, whose preferred style of anti-Cartesian argument was so very often epistemological, insisted on the force of such considerations: "there was from the beginning felt to be a major theoretical difficulty in explaining how minds can influence and be influenced by bodies. How can a mental process, such as willing, cause spatial movements like movements of the tongue? How can a physical change in the optic nerve have among its effects a mind's perception of a flash of light?" (1949, p. 19).

It is precisely the advantage of materialistic monism that it provides for the subsumption of mind/body interaction as a special case of physical interaction, thereby making problems like the ones that Ryle mentions go away. By the early 1960s, it was becoming clear that there are two quite different strategies for performing this reduction, one corresponding to the program of *logical behaviorism* and the other corresponding to the program of the *central state identity theory*. And it was also becoming clear that each of these strategies has its problems.

The essence of one kind of logical behaviorism is the idea that every truth-valuable ascription of a mental state or process to an organism is semantically equivalent to the ascription of a certain sort of dispositional property to that organism. ... In particular, in the interesting cases, mental ascriptions were supposed to be semantically equivalent to ascriptions of *behavioral dispositions*. A behavioral disposition is one that an organism has if and only if (iff) it satisfies a certain indefinite (possibly infinite) set of *behavioral hypotheticals* which constitute the *analysis* of the disposition. A behavioral hypothetical is a (possibly counterfactual) statement whose antecedent is couched solely in terms of *stimulus parameters* and whose consequent is couched solely in terms of *response parameters*. Heaven only knows what stimulus and response parameters were supposed to be; but it was an Article of Faith that these notions could, in principle, be made clear. Perhaps stimulus and response parameters are species of physical parameters (parameters that would be acknowledged by an ideally completed physical theory), though not all logical behaviorists would have accepted that identification. In any event, precisely because the ontological impulse of behaviorism was reductionistic, success depended on the possibility of expressing stimulus and response parameters in a vocabulary which contained no mental terms.

What is attractive about logical behaviorism is that the proposed identification of mental properties with dispositional ones provides for a sort of construal of statements that attribute behavioral effects to mental causes—a construal that is, moreover, conformable to the requirements of materialistic monism. Roughly, mental causation is the manifestation of a behavioral disposition; it's what you get when an organism has such a disposition and the antecedent of a behavioral hypothetical that belongs to the analysis of the disposition happens to be true. It is, no doubt, a travesty to say that for a logical behaviorist "Smith is thirsty" means "if there were water around, Smith would drink it" and "Smith drank because he was thirsty" means "if there were water around Smith would drink it; and there was water around." But it is a travesty that comes close enough for our present purposes. It allows us to see how logical

behaviorists proposed to assimilate worrisome etiologies that invoke mental causes to relatively untendentious etiologies like "it broke because it was fragile; it bent because it was pliable," etc.

So, logical behaviorism provides a construal of mental causation, and the glaring question is whether the construal it provides is adequately robust to do the jobs that need doing. In the long run this is the question whether the identification of mental properties with behavioral dispositions yields a notion of mental causation that is rich enough to reconstruct the etiologies propounded by our best psychological theories: the ones that achieve simplicity, explanatory power, and predictive success. However, we needn't wait for the long run, since there are plenty of cases of *pre*-theoretically plausible etiologies for which plausible behavioristic construals are not forthcoming, and these, surely, are straws in the wind.

Here is a quick way of making the point. Suppose "John took aspirin because he had a headache" is true iff conjunction *C* holds:

C: John was disposed to produce headache behaviors and being disposed to produce headache behaviors involves satisfying the hypothetical *if there are aspirin around, one takes some*, and there were aspirin around.

So, *C* gives us a construal of "John took aspirin because he had a headache." But consider that we are also in want of a construal of statements like "John was disposed to produce headache behaviors because he had a headache." Such statements *also* invoke mental causes and, pre-theoretically at least, we have no reason to doubt that many of them are true. Yet in these cases it seems unlikely that the putative mental causes can be traded for dispositions; or if they can, the line of analysis we've been pursuing doesn't show us how to do it. We cannot, for example, translate "John had a headache" as "John had a disposition to produce headache behaviors" in these cases, since, patently, "John was disposed to produce headache behaviors because he had a headache" doesn't mean the

same as "John was disposed to produce headache behaviors because he had a disposition to
produce headache behaviors." Yet, "John had a
headache" surely means the same in "John took
aspirin because he had a headache" and in
"John was disposed to produce headache
behaviors because he had a headache," so if the
behavioristic analysis is wrong for the second
case, it must also be wrong for the first.

This is, no doubt, a relatively technical kind
of difficulty, but it points in the direction of
what is now widely viewed as a hopeless problem for logical behaviorism. Mental causes typically have their overt effects *in virtue of their
interactions with one another*, and behaviorism
provides no satisfactory analysis of statements
that articulate such interactions. Statements
that attribute behavioral dispositions to mental
causes are of this species, but they are far from
exhausting the kind. Consider that having a
headache is sufficient to cause a disposition to
take aspirin only if it is accompanied by a battery of other mental states: the desire to be rid
of the headache; the belief that aspirin exists;
the belief that taking aspirin leads to a reduction of headache; the belief that its side effects
are not worse than headaches are; the belief that
it is not grossly immoral to take aspirin when
one has a headache; and so on. Moreover, such
beliefs and utilities must be, as it were, *opera-
tive*, not only must one *have* them, but some
of them must come into play as causal agents
contributing to the production of the behavioral effect.

The consequences of this observation are
twofold. First, it seems highly unlikely that
mental causes can be identified with *behavioral*
dispositions, since the antecedents of many pu-
tatively behavioral hypotheticals turn out to
contain mentalistic vocabulary ineliminably.
But, moreover, we shall have to find analyses
for etiologies in which interactions among mental states involve possibly quite long and elaborate causal chains; and here we have a fertile
source of counterexamples to the generality of

any kind of dispositional construal of mental
ascriptions, behavioral or otherwise. "It occurred to John to move his knight, but then he
noticed that that would leave his king in trouble, and since he wanted to avoid check, he
thought on balance that he'd better temporize
and push a pawn. When, however, he had considered for a while which pawn to push, it all
began to look boring and hopeless, and he
thought: 'Oh, bother it,' and decided to resign.
(Overt behavior finally ensues.)" Surely, the
mental life is often like that; such cases occur
everywhere where mental *processes* are at issue,
and it is, perhaps, the basic problem with
behaviorism that it can't reconstruct the notion
mental process. But these cases seem to be most
glaringly the norm in reasoning and problem
solving, so it's not surprising that, among psychologists, it has been the cognition theorists
who have led the recent antibehaviorist cam-
paign. It seems perfectly obvious that what's
needed to construe cognitive processes is precisely what behaviorists proposed to do without: causal sequences of mental episodes and a
"mental mechanics" to articulate the generalizations that such sequences instantiate. The
problem was—and remains—to accommodate
these methodological requirements within the
ontological framework of materialism.

Which is why the physicalist reading of
materialistic monism seemed so very attractive
an alternative to the behavioristic version. Suppose we assume that mental particulars (events,
states, processes, dispositions, etc.) are identical with physical particulars, and also that the
property of being in a certain mental state (such
as having a headache or believing that it will
rain) is identical with the property of being in
a certain physical (e.g. neural) state. Then we
have a guaranty that our notion of mental causation will be as robust as our notion of physical causation, the former having turned out to
be a special case of the latter. In particular, we
will have no difficulty in making sense of the
claim that behavioral effects may sometimes be

the consequence of elaborate chains of mental causes; or, indeed, that mental causes may interact elaborately *without* eventuating in behavioral effects. If mental processes are, in fact, physical processes, they must enjoy whatever ontological autonomy physical processes are conceded. More than that we surely should not ask for.

This is bracing stuff from the point of view of the psychologist. Endorsing the central state identity theory is tantamount to accepting a Realist interpretation of explanations in which appeal to mental causes figure: if mental particulars are physical particulars, then the singular terms in (true) psychological theories denote. Indeed, they denote precisely the same sorts of things that the singular terms in (true) physical theories do. Moreover, since physicalism is not a semantic thesis, it is immune to many of the kinds of arguments that make trouble for behaviorists. It is, for example, uninteresting from the physicalist's point of view that "John has a headache" doesn't mean the same as "John is in such and such a brain state." The physicalist's claim is not that such sentences are synonymous—that the second provides a linguistically or epistemologically adequate construal of the first—but only that they are rendered true (or false) by the same states of affairs.

I remarked that the identity theory can be held either as a doctrine about mental *particulars* (John's current headache, Bill's fear of cats) or as a doctrine about the nature of mental *properties* (universals like having a pain or being afraid of animals). These two variants—known as "token physicalism" and "type physicalism" respectively—differ in both strength and plausibility. For, while the former claims only that all the mental particulars that there happen to be are neurological, the latter makes that claim about all the mental particulars that there *could* be. Token physicalism is thus compatible with the logical—perhaps even the nomological—possibility of unincarnate

bearers of mental properties (e.g. angels) and of bearers of mental properties that are incarnate but not in flesh (e.g. machines). Whereas, type physicalism does not recognize such possibilities, since, if the property of having a pain is the same property as that of being in a certain neural state, nothing can have the former property that does not have the latter.

Type physicalism is, on balance, not a plausible doctrine about the nature of mental properties—not even if token physicalism is a plausible doctrine about the nature of mental particulars; not even if token physicalism is a *true* doctrine about the nature of mental particulars. The argument against type physicalism is often made in a way that does it less than justice: "Why shouldn't (e.g.) silicon-based Martians suffer pains? And why shouldn't machines have beliefs? But if it is conceivable that mental properties should have such bearers, then it cannot be that mental properties *are* neural properties, however much the two may prove to be *de facto* coextensive. And neither can it be that they are *physical* properties if what you mean by a physical property is one that can be expressed by a projectible predicate in (say) an ideally completed physics. What silicon-based Martians and IBM machines and you and I are likely to have in common by way of the physical constitution of our nervous systems simply isn't worth discussing." …

But that's really not the point. The real point is that, if we want a science of mental phenomena at all, we are required to so identify mental properties that the kinds they subsume are natural from the point of view of psychological theory construction. If, for example, we identify mental properties with neural properties, then we are in effect claiming that domains consisting of creatures with a certain sort of neural organization constitute natural kinds for the psychologist's purposes. (Compare: if we claim that the property of being a fish is the property of living in the water, then we are in effect claiming that a domain consisting of creatures that live in the water constitutes a natural kind for the purposes of the marine biologist. Either that or we are claiming that "is a fish" is not a projectible predicate in marine biology. The essays that follow are neutral on fish, but they do assume the projectibility of properties like those expressed by typical mental predicates.)

Now, there is a level of abstraction at which the generalizations of psychology are most naturally pitched and, as things appear to be turning out, that level of abstraction collapses across the differences between physically quite different kinds of systems. Given the sorts of things we need to say about having pains and believing Ps, it seems to be at best just accidental, and at worst just false, that pains and beliefs are proprietary to creatures like us; if we *wanted* to restrict the domains of our psychological theories to just us, we would have to do so by ad hoc conditions upon their generalizations. Whereas, what does seem to provide a natural domain for psychological theorizing, at least in cognitive psychology, is something like the set of (real and possible) information processing systems. The point being, of course, that there are possible—and, for all we know, real—information processing systems which share our psychology (instantiate its generalizations) but do not share our physical organization.

It would be hard to overemphasize this point, but I shall do my best: Philosophical theories about the nature of mental properties carry empirical commitments about the appropriate domains for psychological generalizations. It is therefore an argument against such a theory if it carves things up in ways that prohibit stating such psychological generalizations as there are to state. And it looks as though type physicalism does carve things up in the wrong ways, assuming that the sort of psychological theories that are now being developed are even close to being true.

This is a state of affairs which cries out for a *relational* treatment of mental properties, one which identifies them in ways that abstract

from the physiology of their bearers. Indeed, there is a sense in which behaviorists had the right end of the stick in hand, despite the sorts of objections we reviewed above. Behaviorists, after all, *did* offer a relational construal of mental properties: to have a belief or a pain was to be disposed to exhibit a certain pattern of relations between the responses that one produces and the stimuli that one encounters. So there seemed, ten or fifteen years ago, to be a nasty dilemma facing the materialist program in the philosophy of mind: What central state physicalists seemed to have got right—contra behaviorists—was the ontological autonomy of mental particulars and, of a piece with this, the causal character of mind/body interactions. Whereas, what the behaviorists seemed to have got right—contra the identity theory—was the relational character of mental properties. Functionalism, grounded in the machine analogy, seemed to be able to get both right at once. It was in the cheerful light of that promised synthesis that the now dominant approaches to the philosophy of mind first began to emerge.

It's implicit in the preceding that there is a way of understanding the new functionalism that makes it simply an extension of the logical behaviorist's program. Having a belief (say) was still to be construed as having a relational property, except that, whereas behaviorists had permitted only references to stimuli and responses to appear essentially in specifications of the relata, functionalists allowed reference to *other mental states* as well. A functionalist could thus concede many platitudes that behaviorists are hard put even to construe—as, for example, that it is plausibly a necessary condition for having certain beliefs that one is disposed to draw certain inferences (no belief that P&Q without a disposition to infer that P and a disposition to infer that Q); that it is plausibly a necessary condition for performing certain acts that one be in certain states of mind (no prevarication without the causal involvement of an intent to deceive); and so forth.

But, in fact, reading functionalism this way —as a liberated form of behaviorism—is more than mildly perverse; for *all* that functionalism and behaviorism have in common is the relational construal of mental properties. If one considers the ontological issues (to say nothing of the epistemological issues), striking differences between the doctrines emerge at once. Unlike behaviorism, functionalism is not a reductionist thesis; it does not envision—even in principle—the elimination of mentalistic concepts from the explanatory apparatus of psychological theories. In consequence, functionalism is compatible with a physicalist (hence Realist) account of mental particulars. It thus tolerates the ascription of causal roles to mental particulars and can take literally theories which represent mental particulars as interacting causally, with whatever degree of complexity, in the course of mental processes. That, as we have seen, was the primary advantage the central state identity theory enjoyed. So it is possible for a functionalist to hold (1) that mental kinds are typically relationally defined; and (2) that the relations that mental particulars exhibit, insofar as they constitute the domains of mental processes, are typically *causal* relations: to stimuli, to responses, and to one another. Of these claims, a logical behaviorist can endorse only the first with an absolutely clear conscience, and a type-physicalist only the second.

So functionalism appeared to capture the best features of the previously available alternatives to dualism while avoiding all the major embarrassments. Viewed from one perspective, it offered behaviorism without reductionism; viewed from another, it offered physicalism without parochialism. The idea that mental particulars are physical, the idea that mental kinds are relational, the idea that mental processes are causal, and the idea that there could, at least in logical principle, be nonbiological bearers of mental properties were all harmonized. And the *seriousness* of the psychologist's undertaking was vindicated by providing for a Realistic interpretation of his theoretical constructs. Bliss!

REFERENCES

Ryle, G. (1949). *The Concept of Mind*, New York, Barnes and Noble.

Jerry A. Fodor and Ned Block
Selections from "What Psychological States Are Not"

The following argument seems to us to show that the psychological states of organisms cannot be placed in one-to-one correspondence with the machine table states of organisms.

The set of states that constitute the machine table of a probabilistic automaton is, by definition, a list. But the set of mental states of at least some organisms (namely, persons) is, in point of empirical fact, productive. In particular, abstracting from theoretically irrelevant limitations imposed by memory and mortality, there are infinitely many type-distinct, nomo-logically possible psychological states of any given person. The simplest demonstration that this is true is that, on the assumption that there are infinitely many non-equivalent declarative sentences, one can generate definite descriptions of such states by replacing S with sentences in the schemata A:

A: the belief (thought, desire, hope, and so forth) that S.

In short, while the set of machine table states of a Turing machine can, by definition, be exhaustively specified by listing them, the set of mental states of a person can at best be specified by finite axiomatization.

It might be maintained against this argument that not more than a finite subset of the definite descriptions generable by substitution in *A* do in fact designate nomologically possible beliefs (desires, hopes, or whatever) and that this is true *not* because of theoretically uninteresting limitations imposed by memory and mortality, but rather because of the existence of psychological laws that limit the set of believable (and so forth) propositions to a finite set. To take a farfetched example, it might be held that if you eliminate all such perhaps unbelievable propositions as "2 + 2 = 17," "2 + 2 = 147," and so forth, the residuum is a finite set.

There is no reason at all to believe that this is true, however, and there are some very persuasive reasons for believing that it is not. For example, the infinite set of descriptions whose members are "the belief that 1 + 1 = 2," "the belief that 2 + 2 = 4," "the belief that 3 + 3 = 6," and so forth would appear to designate a set of possible beliefs of an organism ideally free from limitations on memory; to put it the other way around, the fact that there are arithmetical statements that it is nomologically impossible for any person to believe is a consequence of the character of people's memory, not a consequence of the character of their mental representation of arithmetic.

It should be emphasized, again, that this is intended to be an empirical claim, albeit an overwhelmingly plausible one. It is possible to imagine a creature ideally free from memory limitations whose mental representation of arithmetic nevertheless specifies only a finite set of possible arithmetic beliefs. The present point is that it is vastly unlikely that we are such creatures.

Once again it is important to see what the argument does *not* show. Let us distinguish between the *machine table states* of an automaton and the *computational states* of an automaton. By the former, we will mean what we have been meaning all along: states specified by columns in its machine table. By the latter we mean any state of the machine which is characterizable in terms of its inputs, outputs, and/or machine table states. In this usage, the predicates "has just run through a computation involving three hundred seventy-two machine table states," or "has just proved Fermat's last theorem," or "has just typed the *i*th symbol in its output vocabulary" all designate possible computational states of machines.

Now, what the present argument seems to show is that the psychological states of an organism cannot be put into correspondence with the machine table states of an automaton. What it of course does *not* show is that the psychological states of an organism cannot be put into correspondence with the *computational* states of an automaton. Indeed, a sufficient condition for the existence of the latter correspondence is that the possible psychological states of an organism should be countable.

CHAPTER TWELVE

Eliminative Materialism

Reduction, autonomy, and elimination

Materialists maintain that there is nothing in existence but matter: there are no immaterial entities or immaterial properties. But materialists disagree with one another on how the concepts of psychology — the concepts of thought, belief, perception, and so on — relate to the terms and concepts of neuroscience. As neuroscience expands and develops, what will become of our ways of describing ourselves in terms of our thoughts, beliefs, and perceptions? Materialists give three different answers to this question. Supporters of the identity theory argue that psychology will be *reduced* to neuroscience. Functionalists claim that psychology will be *autonomous* of neuroscience. And a third answer is provided in this chapter: psychology will be *eliminated* by neuroscience. Let's look one at a time at these three ideas of reduction, autonomy, and elimination.

Reductionism

The identity theory is a version of what philosophers call *reductionism*. Identity theorists claim that the states and activities of the mind are type-identical to states and activities of the brain. Each kind of mental state and process will turn out to be a kind of neurological state or process. This implies that by understanding the biochemical activity of the brain, we can explain how and why the mind acts as it does. For example, the activity of reason can be explained in terms of the successive firings of millions of neurons in the cerebral cortex.

In this way, identity theorists believe that we can explain the activity of the mind entirely in terms of some more basic or fundamental processes, namely, biochemical processes. The activity of explaining something in terms of more basic entities or processes is called **intertheoretical reduction**. This kind of reduction occurs when a phenomenon that is familiar under one description becomes identified with something under a more basic or fundamental description, and when that identification allows us to explain its occurrence.[1]

Much of the business of science has been a series of reductions in this sense. For example, the phenomenon of lightning was explained as electrical discharge, and electrical discharge was subsequently explained as the movement of electrons. So we can say that lightning has been reduced to electron movement. In the same way, the ability of plants to draw energy from the sun has been reduced to the synthesis of organic compounds from carbon dioxide and water.

Identity theorists say that mental states can be "reduced to" brain states, and that thinking and perceiving can be "reduced to" various kinds of brain processes. According to identity theorists, the reduction of mental states to neural states, and of mental activity to neural activity, is part of the general scientific enterprise of explaining observable occurrences in terms of some basic or fundamental entities. At one time, the states and processes of the mind were thought to be singular in nature, altogether different from other aspects of the world. The reduction of mental states to brain states is intended to show how mental states are part of a more general phenomenon.

Functionalism and reduction

Reductionism depends on the type-identity of mental states and neurological states. Because they reject type-identity, functionalists deny that psychology is reducible to neuroscience.[2] To see why this should be so, let's look again at the example of Jane and her Martian friend, Qwertl. Functionalists will claim that the reason Jane and Qwertl are thinking the same thought is not because they share any physical characteristics, but because they are each in a certain functional state. What matters in determining the facts about their psychology is not their physical state, but the way in which their physical states are connected to one another and to stimulus and behaviour. This means that a neurological description of what is going on in Jane's head will not explain her psychology — it won't explain what she is thinking, or why she is thinking it. All we can get from neuroscience is a description of how the sequence of functional states that she has in common with Qwertl happen to be realized in her nervous system.

Multiple realizability and autonomy

According to functionalists, the multiple realizability of psychological states entails that psychology will remain independent, or "autonomous," of neuroscience. To say that one theory is **autonomous** of another means that an understanding of the entities and laws of one will not provide us with an understanding of the entities and laws of the other. The idea applied to psychology and neuroscience is that we cannot gain an understanding of the mind by a study of neuroscience.

To illustrate this point, functionalists compare the relationship between psychology and neuroscience with that between computer science and physical engineering. Computer science is a study of how information can be stored and processed. This involves the analysis of systems of representation such as binary and decimal notation, and the construction of algorithms to process the information that is represented. Although there is a great deal of interaction between computer programmers and physical engineers, there is nonetheless more to the study of computers than questions of physical engineering. Physical engineering will provide us with an understanding of how algorithms can be *implemented* in different kinds of hardware. But considerations of hardware alone will not give us answers to questions about information processing.

Similarly, machine functionalists argue that there will always be more to psychology than the study of the nervous system. We will have to learn how human beings represent information about the world, and we will need to study the algorithms by which the brain extracts information about the world from sensory input. Neuroscience can tell us how these algorithms are implemented in the nervous system. Yet a physical study of the brain will not tell us how it processes information.

Psychological realism

Although identity theorists and functionalists disagree over the autonomy of psychology and neuroscience, they nonetheless agree that the categories and terms of psychology describe important aspects of human life. Both theories assume that the phenomena that we describe as states and processes of the mind — thoughts, beliefs, sensations, and so on — do actually exist. This position is called **psychological realism**. It is the idea that the terms and categories of psychology, which we use to describe the causes of our actions, are all (or mostly) descriptions of things that really exist, even if their nature is not entirely known to us.

Since neuroscience became a mature discipline in the nineteenth century, it has supplied us with a new way of describing the causes of human action, involving such concepts as neurotransmitters and action potentials. Functionalists and identity theorists argue that these concepts will enhance or complement our traditional ways of describing ourselves without replacing them. Psychology will exist in some manner alongside neuroscience.

Autonomy and reduction vs. elimination

As often as there have been cases of reduction or autonomy in the history of science, there have been cases where newer theories or descriptions have simply replaced the older ones altogether. A good example of this is the replacement of the idea of vital spirit in biology (see chapter 9 above). With the introduction of cellular biology, vital spirit was not explained in terms of cellular matter, nor did biologists claim that the study of vital spirit was autonomous of biology. The concept of vital spirit was eliminated from biology altogether. Biologists no longer recognize the existence of anything corresponding to this idea.

So it is necessary to distinguish reduction and autonomy from cases of simple elimination. An important characteristic of reduction is that people continue to believe in the existence of the reduced phenomenon. For example, we still recognize the existence of lightning as a genuine phenomenon, even while we identify it with electron movement. Similarly, we still recognize water as a distinct kind of substance, even after it has been reduced to the molecular structure H_2O. And when a new discipline such as computer science remains autonomous of existing sciences, the terms and categories of the new science are claimed to describe things that exist over and above the those described in any of the existing disciplines.

In cases of what we can call **intertheoretic elimination**, on the other hand, people cease to believe that there is anything that corresponds to the older description. Another example of intertheoretic elimination is the case of caloric fluid. At one time chemists believed that a body's temperature was a matter of the amount of a certain kind of liquid contained between the particles of matter, which they called caloric fluid. With the identification of heat with molecular energy, the idea of caloric fluid was neither reduced to molecular energy nor seen as autonomous of molecular energy. It was eliminated altogether.

Eliminativism

Some philosophers argue that both reductionism and autonomous psychology are misguided approaches to the mind-body problem. Their approach is based on a rejection of psychological realism. They contend that psychology is neither reducible to neuroscience nor autonomous of neuroscience for the simple reason that there are no psychological states. This position is known as **eliminativism** or **eliminativist materialism.** Eliminativists claim that once neuroscience is sufficiently complete, we will come to the realization that there simply are no such things as thoughts, hopes, beliefs, and sensations.

Eliminativists generally take one of two positions. Some argue that psychological descriptions will become *unnecessary* once we are able to explain our actions in terms of their neurological causes. They claim that words such as "thought," "belief," and "sensation" are simply placeholders in the sense that they serve a useful function in labelling something whose nature is unknown. But once we do come to understand what it is that they label, we will have no occasion to use them any longer. Other eliminativists argue that psychological descriptions fail to label anything at all. As they see it, the terms we use to describe the mind are not even convenient placeholders; they are relics of a false doctrine. Psychological descriptions will disappear, they argue, not because they are unnecessary, but because they do not describe anything at all.

Getting along without a mind

The first reading in this chapter is from a book entitled *Philosophy and the Mirror of Nature* by the Princeton philosopher, Richard Rorty. Rorty's book is an instance of the first of these two varieties of eliminativism. Rorty contends that it is possible to get along as well as we do at present without any reference to what we call the mind.

According to Rorty, Western philosophy of mind has been hampered by a mistaken theory of knowledge introduced in the seventeenth century by people like Descartes and Locke. According to this conception, states of mind are inner representations of the world whose content is directly evident to us. The mind is seen as a mirror that reflects reality. This idea should be abandoned, Rorty argues, and the traditional philosophical debates about knowledge and the mind should cease altogether.

We will look at only a small piece of Rorty's essay, in which he argues that our common ways of thinking about the mind can be eliminated without losing any of our ability to explain ourselves or our actions. According to Rorty, the central aspect of the conception of the mind we have inherited from Descartes is the idea that states of mind are **incorrigible**. When we say that mental states are incorrigible we mean that it is impossible for a person to be mistaken about the contents of their own conscious experience.[3] Rorty's intention in the section we will read is to demonstrate the possibility of abandoning this idea.

The Antipodeans

Rorty's argument takes the form of a thought experiment. Rorty's thought experiment is a story about a race of beings on another planet who are biologically similar to humans. These beings possess all the usual trappings of a cultured civilization, including science, art, and literature. Unlike us, however, these beings possess no concept of mind. The first successful science that they developed was neuroscience, and their explanations of their own actions are entirely neurological. Although they talk about beliefs and desires, they have no conception that these might be different from the states of any ordinary physical objects. They entirely lack the concepts of consciousness, ideas, thought, and perception.

Rorty describes the amusing antics that ensue when people from Earth (the Terrans) visit this planet. They remind the Terrans of an ancient race of materialist philosophers, all of whom were Australians, and so the Terrans name them "Antipodeans," from an old term for Australasia.[4] Although Terran scientists get along well with the Antipodeans, the philosophers are stumped by their apparent lack of a concept of mind. The worst part of the situation is that the Antipodeans don't seem to be able to catch on to what the philosophers claim they lack. The Antipodeans give no sign of recognizing what the mind is supposed to be, and fail to understand the mind-body problem altogether.

In the face of the Antipodean ignorance of the mind, the Terran philosophers conclude that the Antipodeans may not have minds at all. They may simply be biological automata that behave *as if* they have thoughts and sensations, while in fact they have no form of conscious experience. The idea that the Antipodeans have conscious experiences like ours may be no more realistic than thinking that a doorbell feels pain when you press on the button and rings its bell as an expression of suffering. Although they *act* as if they had experiences like our own, those actions may simply give a false impression.

The first experiment

The best way to investigate this matter, the Terrans conclude, is to run an experiment to see whether the Antipodeans experience any sensations. They connect the brain of an Antipodean to that of a Terran, with the idea that they can directly detect whether the Antipodeans have experiences of colour and pain.

But the experiment didn't resolve anything. First, they hooked the region of C-fibres in the human brain, associated with sensations of pain, with Antipodean speech centres. When the Antipodean speech centres got input from human C-fibres, they talked only of C-fibres, not of pain. And when human speech centres received input from Antipodean C-fibres, they talked of pains, not of C-fibres. When the Antipodean was asked what the activity of human C-fibres felt like, he replied that he didn't understand the question. He can report the existence of C-fibre stimulation, but has no idea what could be meant by the term "feels like." The same results were achieved in the case of colour.

Incorrigibility

At this point the Terran philosophers fix on a central feature of sensations such as pain. As Descartes pointed out, the essential aspect of sensations is that we can't be mistaken in the belief that we have them. For example, although you can think that you are injured but be mistaken, you can't think that you are in pain and be mistaken. *Thinking* you are in pain is the same as *being* in pain. According to Descartes this is true of conscious states generally: they are states whose existence is known to us directly.

Accordingly, the Terran philosophers next attempt to see whether Antipodean brain states are incorrigible in this way. But here again they get nowhere. They enquire first whether the Antipodeans could be mistaken about their C-fibres firing. The Antipodeans answer that they could, but that they could not be mistaken about *seeming* to have their C-fibres firing. So the Terran philosophers conclude that if the Antipodeans feel pain, it must be matter of seeming to have C-fibres firing. But when they attempt to determine what it was for the Antipodeans to seem to have their C-fibres firing, they can't get an answer that takes them any further. There is a neurological state that causes the Antipodeans to *say* that they seem to have their C-fibres firing. But the researchers are unable to get a clear answer to the question whether the Antipodeans could be mistaken about the occurrence of *that* state.

Do we have minds?

To see the point of this story, consider the following two hypotheses:

(1)   The Antipodeans have conscious experience like ours, but they describe their experience in terms of neural activity.

(2)   The Antipodeans have no conscious experience; their actions and words are produced by neural activity with no accompanying consciousness.

Rorty's claim is that there is no possible evidence that would confirm either of these over the other. Thus, the question whether (1) or (2) is correct is unanswerable; there is no practical difference between these two hypotheses.

But notice that our descriptions of conscious experience play the same role in our life as the Antipodeans' descriptions of neural activity. And so the Antipodeans can present themselves with a similar pair of hypotheses:

(3)   Humans have something we do not, which they describe with words like "feeling" and "sensation."

(4)   Humans have nothing we lack, but they use words like "feeling" and "sensation" where we use neurological concepts.

But the question whether (3) or (4) is true is as unanswerable as the question whether (1) or (2) is true. Rorty's conclusion is that the concept of mind is completely idle: there is nothing that we can explain with the ideas of mind and of conscious experience that we cannot equally well explain without them.

According to Rorty, the central aspect of our descriptions of the mind that distinguishes us from the Antipodeans is our idea that we cannot be mistaken about the contents of our conscious experience. It is this idea that leads us to the views that we are directly aware only of the contents of our own mind, and that these contents provide us with a representation of the "external" world. This raises two questions: what is the nature of these representations, and are they accurate reflections of the world? Once we abandon the idea of incorrigibility, the dualism of mind and matter disappears and with it the need to preserve the notion of the mind as an inner representation of the world.

Do psychological descriptions describe anything?

Rorty does not deny that the concepts of psychology correctly identify the neurological events that are the causes of our behaviour. He allows that each of our concepts of belief, thought, and sensation are reflected in the neurological categories used by the Antipodeans. His disagreement with reductionists stems from his rejection of the Cartesian idea that the content and character of these states possess a privileged status as the direct objects of knowledge.

In her book, *Neurophilosophy: Toward a Unified Science of the Mind-Brain*, Patricia Churchland attacks psychological realism on different grounds. According to Churchland, psychological descriptions will fail to correspond to the categories of a complete neuroscience. She argues that such concepts as belief, thought, and pain do not accurately identify anything at all, and so they should be eliminated on the grounds that they are simply false as descriptions of the origins of our behaviour.

At first glance, Churchland's claim that psychological descriptions fail to correspond to anything real seems simply absurd. For it involves a denial of the idea that there are such things as thoughts, beliefs, and sensations. To quote Armstrong, it seems "as obvious as anything is obvious that there is something going on in me which constitutes my thought." Surely, one wants to say, the existence of such things as pain and thought are not *hypotheses* that can turn out to be false, but rather self-evident phenomena that our hypotheses are intended to explain.

"Folk psychology" as a theory

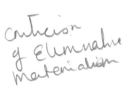

To see the problem here, compare the phenomenon of heat with the theories that have been used to explain it. People are initially aware of heat as a simple quality that objects have in different degrees. Over the centuries many different theories have been put forward to explain the occurrence of this phenomenon. One of the earlier explanations of heat was the idea of caloric fluid. Later the idea of caloric fluid was rejected in favour of the theory of molecular energy. But although people were prepared to eliminate the idea of caloric fluid, no one has suggested eliminating the concept of heat. The existence of heat is not a theory, it would seem, but a phenomenon that the various theories have been designed to explain. Although we can reject theories *about* heat, it seems absurd to reject the concept of heat.[5]

The categories of psychology seem to most of us to be on a par with the concept of heat rather than with the theories we have used to explain it. We might argue over the correct account of the nature of thought and sensation, but we cannot argue over whether or not thought and sensation exist. Churchland argues that this is a mistake. Commonsense psychology, she contends, is a theory intended to explain our actions. As such, it is open to testing and to acceptance or rejection as much as any other theory. This idea is sometimes referred to as "the 'theory' theory."

She refers to the concepts and principles that underlie our common sense explanations of behaviour as **folk psychology**. She says:

> Now by folk psychology I mean that rough-hewn set of concepts, generalizations, and rules of thumb we all standardly use in explaining and predicting human behavior.

While she allows some elements of folk psychology may be accurate, Churchland argues that in the main it is a hopelessly unworkable theory that will be largely replaced by a mature neuroscience.

Folk generalizations

The basis of Churchland's claim that folk psychology is a theory is the fact that it contains generalizations that are taken to reflect regularities in nature. Just as the Newtonian law, 'Force equals mass times acceleration,' is used to explain why a certain object moves as it does in the presence of an external force, so there are psychological laws that are used to explain why people behave as they do in the presence of certain stimuli.

The fundamental elements of these laws are the concepts of belief and desire. If we know what a person believes and we know what they desire, then by and large we can predict how they are likely to behave. For instance, if we know that Joanne believes that good behaviour is rewarded and that helping her grandmother is good behaviour, then, in light of her desire to be rewarded, we can predict that she will help her grandmother.

According to Churchland, the generalizations that connect belief and desire with behaviour are the same in nature as the laws that connect heat with the expansion of copper, or force and mass with movement. The familiar and self-evident nature of folk psychological generalizations only reflects their common acceptance, and it masks the fact that the structure of commonsense psychology is rich and complex.

It is true that we do not learn the laws of folk psychology in school in the way that we learn the laws of physics, and this is sometimes given as a reason for rejecting the 'theory' theory. But Churchland argues that the important point is not how folk psychology is learned, but how it is used. The generalizations of psychology are used to explain and predict behaviour, and as such they function as elements of an explanatory theory. Moreover, Churchland argues, there are other theories that are adopted in the same manner. As an example, she refers to "folk physics": the naive and natural expectations of how ordinary physical objects that we encounter in everyday life will behave. These expectations, she contends, involve generalizations that are used to predict what material objects will do, and hence they constitute a theory.

Propositional attitudes

Churchland points out that most of the folk psychological generalizations we use to predict behaviour involve states of mind that philosophers refer to as "propositional attitudes." As this is a key term in much of the philosophy of mind, it is worthwhile getting clear about it here.

A **proposition** is roughly the same thing as a declarative sentence. Declarative sentences are distinguishable from other kinds of sentences, such as questions or commands, by the fact that they are true or false. Philosophers introduce the term 'proposition' to refer to the content of a declarative sentence, and this is because it is possible for different sentences to have the same content. For example, the sentence 'Snow is white' has the same content as the French sentence 'La neige est blanc' and the German sentence 'Schnee ist weiss.' We mark this fact by saying that all three sentences express the same proposition.

A **propositional attitude** is a mental state identified by the "mental attitude" that a person holds toward a proposition. Consider, for example, the proposition that good behaviour is always rewarded. There are many different attitudes that one can have regarding this proposition. One can *believe* that good behaviour is always rewarded; one can *hope* that good behaviour is always rewarded; and one can *doubt* that good behaviour is always rewarded. Each of these is a distinct mental state, characterized by a particular proposition and the attitude the person holds toward it.

Most of the generalizations used in folk psychology involve connections between propositional attitudes. The most ubiquitous of these are the generalizations connecting belief and desire. Churchland suggests the following as an example of what she has in mind:

> Whenever a person wants to bring about a state *s, and* he believes that his doing *p* is a way to bring about *s, and* he believes that he can do *p, and* he can do *p,* then, barring conflicting desires or preferred strategies, he will do *p.*

If we substitute *being rewarded* for the state *s,* and *helping one's grandmother* for *p,* we can use this law to explain why a person will help his grandmother. It is these kinds of generalizations, involving the relations between attitudes to different propositions, that we use in everyday life to predict and explain our own and other people's behaviour.

Folk psychology and rationality

Churchland points out that much of the importance of propositional attitudes in folk psychology derives from the fact that our explanations of people's behaviour rest heavily on the *logical* relations between propositions. She says:

> Much dwelt upon is the observation that explanations of human behavior proceed by showing how the behavior was rational in the light of the subject's beliefs and desires, where it is the content of the beliefs and desires that make rational sense of the behavior.

We can predict how someone will behave by seeing their actions as the outcome of rational inferences. For example, the prediction about Joanne's behaviour is based on the idea that the desire to help her grandmother can be *rationally inferred* from her other beliefs and desires. Importantly, we cannot make these kinds of predictions without making reference to the propositions that form the content of the individual's mental states.

Churchland argues that, although this feature of folk psychology is often used to contrast it with other forms of explanation, it is really only an instance of the general practice of using relations between abstract objects in our explanations. We describe the state of physical objects by assigning numerical values to them, and then we use arithmetical relations between numbers to predict how the objects will behave. Predicting people's behaviour on the basis of logical relations between the content of their propositional attitudes is no different in kind, she argues, from predicting the movement of a billiard ball on the basis of the mathematical relations between its mass and the force applied to it.

The argument for autonomous psychology

So far, we have looked at Churchland's arguments to the effect that folk psychology is a theory, and hence can be accepted as true or rejected as false, just as we do with any other theory. The second part of her argument establishes that commonsense psychology is false, and that it will be replaced by a mature neuroscience.

Her argument is in two steps. First she argues against the functionalists' idea that psychology is autonomous of neuroscience. This entails that either folk psychology will reduce to neuroscience or it will be eliminated. The second step of her argument is directed against the expectation that psychology will prove reducible to neuroscience. Let's look first at her argument against autonomous psychology.

As we saw in the last chapter, functionalists reject type-identity, and hence reduction, on the grounds that mental states are multiply realizable. The argument, as we saw it there, was applied to the idea of mental states as functional states: a functional state can be realized in innumerable physical ways, and hence functional states are not type-identical to physical or neurological states. Churchland points out that the same argument from multiple realizability can be applied to the idea of mental states as propositional attitudes. She describes the argument in the following way:

> Because mental states are identified in terms of their logical and semantical relations, and because transitions between mental states are determined by the logical relations between representations, mental states are special. *Logical relations cannot be reduced to causal relations* [i.e., to relations of cause and effect between neurological states]; consequently, psychological theory is autonomous and the prospect of reduction is patently hopeless.

As Churchland points out, this argument is based on the computer metaphor (which she calls the machine analogy). Programs are defined in terms of the operations that they perform on the information stored in the computer. This information is described in terms of the *content* of the stored symbols in the computer's memory. The reason that programs are multiply realizable is that the same operations over the same content can be carried out in an endless variety of physical mechanisms.

The same point applies to transitions between one psychological state and another. These transitions are described in terms of their content, and the same transitions can be realized in many different kinds of physical structures. Churchland cites an example offered by Zenon Pylyshyn, a cognitive psychologist.[6] Someone may come to believe that there is a fire in her building and as a result call the fire department. But the variety of ways in which someone can come to that belief is endless, and so the number of neurological histories that can potentially include the belief that the building is on fire is equally endless. Hence, the generalizations about what people will do when they believe their building is on fire cannot be reduced to neurological generalizations.

Against autonomous psychology

Churchland's response to the argument for autonomy is to reject the claim that logical relations cannot be explained in terms of relations of cause and effect between neurological states. She has two arguments for this position.

First, she argues that it is most likely false that there is no single neurological property that all mental states of the same kind have in common. There are many different levels of neurological organization, from the single neuron to structured assemblies of neurons to larger patterns of behaviour across different assemblies. If there is a psychological generalization that is true of all humans, then, Churchland argues, there will most likely be a corresponding neurological generalization that is true of all humans at some level of neural organization. Moreover, she contends, identifying the relevant organizational structures of the brain will require researchers to describe neural assemblies in terms of how information is stored and processed. Thus there will be no simple divide between descriptions of psychological content and descriptions of neural organization and behaviour.

Churchland's second argument against autonomous psychology is an attack on the viability of folk psychology itself. What content we assign to a person's beliefs or other propositional attitudes is often highly context-relative in two different ways. First, the content will vary depending on the person's other beliefs, their interests, and so on. This point was first made by the philosopher, Stephen Stich, who describes the difficulty in determining the beliefs of a person with advancing memory loss.[7] Such a person may continue to claim that a particular sentence is true while their ability to connect the content of that sentence with other beliefs slowly diminishes to nothing. Second, the content of propositional attitudes will vary with external circumstances that have no effect on a person's behaviour. This means that assignment of content to a propositional attitude will not reflect its role in predicting behaviour.[8] For these reasons, Churchland contends that "the folk psychological categories of belief and desire are bound to fragment at the hands of science."

Against reduction

Given her claim that the psychological generalizations that are true of all humans will correspond to neurological generalizations at some level, Churchland is prepared to accept that psychology will be reducible to neuroscience in certain areas. But she also argues that when the reduction does not go smoothly — that is, when we do not find the corresponding neural concomitants — then we must be prepared to revise or abandon the psychology. The reasons just cited for thinking that belief-desire psychology will "fragment at the hands of science" are cited as reasons to believe that it will not be possible to reduce folk psychology to neuroscience.

Churchland warns against using the difficulty of reducing psychological descriptions to neuroscientific descriptions to argue for autonomy. The reason for the failure of reduction, she contends, may be a sign that folk psychology is radically false. She cites several cases from the history of science where the failure of reduction from an older theory to a newer one led to the rejection of the older theory. In each case, she claims, it would have prevented the development of the sciences to have maintained the older theory on the grounds that it must be "autonomous" of the newer one. Similarly, according to Churchland, the context relativity of folk psychology should lead us to expect that it will eventually be replaced by a more successful and unambiguous theory.

Churchland's credo, then, is reduce or eliminate; she believes that the likeliest fate of most of folk psychology will be elimination. Against the claim that we cannot presently imagine what a new science of human behaviour would look like, she claims that this argues only for using the present theory while introducing revisions and replacements as they become available. She claims that:

> What the lack of alternatives implies is that one has no choice but to *use* the available theory, and this is consistent with its falsity and with trying to construct a better competing theory.

Computing and the brain

There is another element of Churchland's theory, which is not discussed in our reading here, but which is important in understanding her argument against functionalism. As we have seen, functionalists defend the autonomy of psychology by comparing the relationship between psychology and neuroscience with that between computer science and physical engineering.

An important element in that argument is its reliance on the idea of computing as *symbol processing*. Studying the hardware of a computer, they point out, will not tell us about the symbolic representations it is using, nor the algorithms it is using to process those representations. Similarly, they argue, a study of the brain will not reveal very much about the symbol-processing algorithms that explain the operation of the human mind.

One problem with the idea that mental activity is symbol processing of the kind illustrated by Turing Machines is that the structure and activity of the brain has almost nothing in common with anything that looks like symbol processing. The brain consists of billions of neurons connected to one another in a vast network, each one sending signals to the others with which it is connected. Churchland and others argue that there is a newer and better model of computing, which is very much like the structure of the brain.

Connectionism

The kind of computing to which Churchland points us has the technical name of **Parallel Distributed Processing (PDP)**, and the project of constructing PDP systems is referred to as **connectionism**. In a connectionist computer, there are no strings of symbols as there are in Turing Machines, nor is there a series of sequential steps in an algorithm. Instead the computer consists of many individual units connected to one another. When the system is started each unit is given an initial value, 1 or 0 for example. We can think of these initial values as the input. When the system is running, the value of each unit is changed according to the values of the units with which it is connected. The output of the process will be the values of the units once the system has arrived in its final state.[9]

Supporters of connectionist models of mental activity argue that connectionist systems are both much closer in structure to that of the brain and much more efficient at performing the kinds of computing that appear to be involved in such mental activities as sense perception and language analysis. Moreover, as connectionist systems do not operate on strings of symbols, they do not use *sentence-like* representations as symbol-processing computers do. As we saw in chapter 11, functionalists use the symbol-processing nature of digital computers to explain how the sentences we use to describe mental states can be realized in the brain. Churchland, however, rejects folk psychology, and with it the description of psychological states in terms of sentences or propositions. Thus, connectionism gives us a way of simultaneously abandoning both folk psychology and the digital computer model of mental activity.

In adopting connectionist models of the mind, we do not abandon the computer metaphor, only the *digital* computer metaphor. According to

Churchland, the mind is an information-processing system, but it is not one that operates on strings of symbols, nor one that involves anything like "propositional attitudes." In her view, the development of connectionist systems will show us how principles of information processing can be closely tied to the structure of the brain. Thus a study of the computing activity of the mind, she argues, will not render psychology autonomous of neuroscience as functionalists insist.[10]

[handwritten: Freedom to govern itself or control its own affairs. Freedom to act independently]

NOTES

1   There is a large amount of literature on what intertheoretical reduction is, and my description is here is overly simplistic in many ways. But for our purposes we need only a rough idea.

2   Some people, like Thomas Nagel in the reading below, describe functionalism as a reductionist theory in the sense that it takes mental states to be reducible to *functional* states. In this chapter I will ignore this usage and restrict reductionism to neurological reduction.

3   Strictly speaking, a belief is incorrigible if it is impossible to be *corrected* by other people. Rorty does not seem to distinguish this from the impossibility of being *mistaken.*

4   This point of the story is a joke on Smart and Armstrong, both of whom are Australian as are several other prominent identity theorists.

5   Some people argue that there are no concepts that describe simple phenomena without containing any elements of an explanatory theory. They argue that all of our concepts are "theory-laden" in the sense that they carry with them assumptions about the world that may turn out to be false.

6   See Zenon Pylyshyn, *Computation and Cognition* (Cambridge, MA: MIT Press, 1984), especially chapters 1 and 2.

7   Stephen Stich, *From Folk Psychology to Cognitive Science* (Cambridge, MA: MIT Press, 1983).

8   This is a point we will explore in detail in chapter 14.

9   There are several introductions to connectionism. Two popular ones are Philip T. Quinlan, *Connectionism and Psychology: A Psychological Perspective on New Connectionist Research* (Chicago: Chicago University Press, 1991); and William Bechtel and Adele Abrahamsen, *Connectionism and the Mind* (Cambridge, MA: Basil Blackwell, 1991).

10   One particular pair of articles presenting arguments for and against connectionism has become a focus of much recent debate. See P. Smolenski, "On the Proper Treatment of Connectionism," *Behavioral and Brain Sciences* 11, 1988, pp. 1–74, and J.A. Fodor & Z.W. Pylyshyn, "Connectionism and Cognitive Architecture," *Cognition* 28, 1988, pp. 3–71.

Richard Rorty
Selections from *Philosophy and the Mirror of Nature*
Chapter II: Persons Without Minds

1. The Antipodeans

Far away, on the other side of our galaxy, there was a planet on which lived beings like ourselves—featherless bipeds who built houses and bombs, and wrote poems and computer programs. These beings did not know that they had minds. They had notions like "wanting to" and "intending to" and "believing that" and "feeling terrible" and "feeling marvelous." But they had no notion that these signified *mental* states—states of a peculiar and distinct sort—quite different from "sitting down," "having a cold," and "being sexually aroused." Although they used the notions of believing and knowing and wanting and being moody of their pets and their robots as well as of themselves, they did not regard pets or robots as included in what was meant when they said, "We all believe ..." or "We never do such things as ..." That is to say, they treated only members of their own species as *persons*. But they did not explain the difference between persons and non-persons by such notions as "mind," "consciousness," "spirit," or anything of the sort. They did not *explain* it at all; they just treated it as the difference between "us" and everything else. They believed in immortality for themselves, and a few believed that this would be shared by the pets or the robots, or both. But this immortality did not involve the notion of a "soul" which separated from the body. It was a straightforward matter of bodily resurrection followed by mysterious and instantaneous motion to what they referred to as "a place about the heavens" for good people, and to a sort of cave, beneath the planet's surface, for the wicked. Their philosophers were concerned primarily with four topics: the nature of Being, proofs of the existence of a Benevolent and Omnipotent Being who would carry out arrangements for the resurrection, problems arising out of discourse about nonexistent objects, and the reconciliation of conflicting moral intuitions. But these philosophers had not formulated the problem of subject and object, nor that of mind and matter. There was a tradition of Pyrrhonian skepticism, but Locke's "veil of ideas" was unknown, since the notion of an "idea" or "perception" or "mental representation" was also unknown. Some of their philosophers predicted that the beliefs about immortality which had been central in earlier periods of history, and which were still held by all but the intelligentsia, would someday be replaced by a "positivistic" culture purged of all superstitions (but these philosophers made no mention of an intervening "metaphysical" stage).

In most respects, then, the language, life, technology, and philosophy of this race were much like ours. But there was one important difference. Neurology and biochemistry had been the first disciplines in which technological breakthroughs had been achieved, and a large part of the conversation of these people concerned the state of their nerves. When their infants veered toward hot stoves, mothers cried out, "He'll stimulate his C-fibers." When people were given clever visual illusions to look at, they said, "How odd! It makes neuronic bundle G-14 quiver, but when I look at it from the side I can see that it's not a red rectangle at all." Their knowledge of physiology was such that each well-formed sentence in the language which anybody bothered to form could easily be correlated with a readily identifiable neural state. This state occurred whenever someone uttered, or was tempted to utter, or heard, the sentence. This state also sometimes occurred in solitude and people reported such occasions with remarks like "I was suddenly in state S-296, so I put out the milk bottles." Sometimes they would say things like "It looked like an elephant, but then it struck me that elephants don't occur on this continent, so I realized that it must be a mastodon." But they would also sometimes say, in just the same circumstances, things like "I had G-412 together with F-11, but then I had S-147, so I realized that it must be a mastodon." They thought of mastodons and milk bottles as objects of beliefs and desires, and as causing certain neural processes. They viewed these neural processes as interacting causally with beliefs and desires—in just the same way as the mastodons and milk bottles did. Certain neural processes could be deliberately self-induced, and some people were more skillful than others in inducing certain neural states in themselves. Others were skilled at detecting certain special states which most people could not recognize in themselves.

In the middle of the twenty-first century, an expedition from Earth landed on this planet. The expedition included philosophers, as well as representatives of every other learned discipline. The philosophers thought that the most interesting thing about the natives was their lack of the concept of mind. They joked among themselves that they had landed among a bunch of materialists, and suggested the name Antipodea for the planet—in reference to an almost forgotten school of philosophers, centering in Australia and New Zealand, who in the previous century had attempted one of the many futile revolts against Cartesian dualism in the history of Terran philosophy. The name stuck, and so the new race of intelligent beings came to be known as Antipodeans. The Terran neurologists and biochemists were fascinated by the wealth of knowledge in their field which the Antipodeans exhibited. Since technical conversation on these subjects was conducted almost entirely in offhand references to neural states, the Terran experts eventually picked up the ability to report their own neural states (without conscious inference) instead of reporting their thoughts, perceptions, and raw feels. (The physiologies of the two

species were, fortunately, almost identical.) Everything went swimmingly, except for the difficulties met by the philosophers.

The philosophers who had come on the expedition were, as usual, divided into two warring camps: the tender-minded ones who thought philosophy should aim at Significance, and the tough-minded philosophers who thought that it should aim at Truth. The philosophers of the first sort felt that there was no real problem about whether the Antipodeans had minds. They held that what was important in understanding other beings was a grasp of their mode of being-in-the-world. It became evident that, whatever *Existentiale* the Antipodeans were using, they certainly did not include any of those which, a century earlier, Heidegger had criticized as "subjectivist." The whole notion of "the epistemological subject," or the person as spirit, had no place in their self-descriptions, nor in their philosophies. Some of the tender-minded philosophers felt that this showed that the Antipodeans had not yet broken out of Nature into Spirit, or, more charitably, had not yet progressed from Consciousness to Self-Consciousness. These philosophers became town-criers of inwardness, attempting to bully the Antipodeans across an invisible line and into the Realm of Spirit. Others, however, felt that the Antipodeans exhibited the praiseworthy grasp of the union of πολεμος and λογος which was lost to Western Terran consciousness through Plato's assimilation of ουσια to ιδεα. The Antipodean failure to grasp the notion of mind, in the view of this set of philosophers, showed their closeness to Being and their freedom from the temptations to which Terran thought had long since succumbed. In the contest between these two views, equally tender-minded as both were, discussion tended to be inconclusive. The Antipodeans themselves were not much help, because they had so much trouble translating the background reading necessary to appreciate the problem—Plato's *Theaetetus*, Descartes's *Meditations*, Hume's *Treatise*, Kant's *Critique of Pure Reason*, Hegel's *Phenomenology*, Strawson's *Individuals*, etc.

The tough-minded philosophers, as usual, found a much more straightforward and clean-cut question to discuss. They did not care what the Antipodeans thought about themselves, but rather focused on the question: Do they in fact have minds? In their precise way, they narrowed this question down to: Do they in fact have sensations? It was thought that if it became clear whether they had, say, sensations of pain, as well as stimulated C-fibers, when touching hot stoves, everything else would be plain sailing. It was clear that the Antipodeans had the same behavioral dispositions toward hot stoves, muscle cramps, torture, and the like as humans. They loathed having their C-fibers stimulated. But the tough-minded philosophers asked themselves: Does their experience contain the same phenomenal properties as ours? Does the stimulation of C-fibers feel painful? Or does it feel some other, equally awful, way? Or does feeling not come into it at all? These philosophers were not surprised that the Antipodeans could offer noninferential reports of their own neural states, since it had been learned long since that psychophysiologists could train human subjects to report alpha-rhythms, as well as various other physiologically describable cortical states. But they felt baffled by the question: Are some phenomenal properties being detected by an Antipodean who says, "It's my C-fibers again—you know, the ones that go off every time you get burned or hit or have a tooth pulled. It's just awful"?

It was suggested that the question could only be answered experimentally, and so they arranged with the neurologists that one of their number should be wired up to an Antipodean volunteer so as to switch currents back and forth between various regions of the two brains. This, it was thought, would also enable the philosophers to insure that the Antipodeans did not have an inverted spectrum, or anything else which might confuse the issue. As it turned out, however, the experiment produced no interesting results. The difficulty was that when the Antipodean speech center got an input from the C-fibers of the Earthling brain it always talked only about its C-fibers, whereas when the Earthling speech center was in control it always talked only about pain.

When the Antipodean speech center was asked what the C-fibers felt like it said that it didn't quite get the notion of "feeling," but that stimulated C-fibers were, of course, terrible things to have. The same sort of thing happened for the questions about inverted spectra and other perceptual qualities. When asked to call off the colors on a chart, both speech centers called off the usual color-names in the same order. But the Antipodean speech center could also call off the various neuronic bundles activated by each patch on the chart (no matter which visual cortex it happened to be hooked up to). When the Earthling speech center was asked what the colors were like when transmitted to the Antipodean visual cortex, it said that they seemed just as usual.

This experiment seemed not to have helped. For it was still obscure whether the Antipodeans had pains. It was equally obscure whether they had one or two raw feels when indigo light streamed onto their retinas (one of indigo, and one of neural state C-692)—or whether they had no raw feels at all. The Antipodeans were repeatedly questioned about how they knew it was indigo. They replied that they could see that it was. When asked how they knew they were in C-692, they said they "just knew" it. When it was suggested to them that they might have unconsciously inferred that it was indigo on the basis of the C-692 feel, they seemed unable to understand what unconscious inference was, or what "feels" were. When it was suggested to them that they might have made the same inference to the fact that they were in state C-692 on the basis of the raw feel of indigo, they were, of course, equally baffled. When they were asked whether the neural state appeared indigo, they replied that it did not—the *light* was indigo—and that the questioner must be making some sort of category mistake. When they were asked whether they could imagine having C-692 and not seeing indigo, they said they could not. When asked whether it was a conceptual truth or an empirical generalization that these two experiences went together, they replied that they were not sure how to tell the difference. When asked whether they could be wrong about whether they were seeing indigo, they replied that they of course could, but could not be wrong about whether they seemed to be seeing indigo. When asked whether they could be wrong about whether they were in state C-692, they replied in exactly the same way. Finally, skillful philosophical dialectic brought them to realize that what they could not imagine was seeming to see indigo and failing to seem to be in state C-692. But this result did not seem to help with the questions: "Raw feels?" "Two raw feels or one?" "Two referents or one referent under two descriptions?" Nor did any of this help with the question about the way in which stimulated C-fibers appeared to them. When they were asked whether they could be mistaken in thinking that their C-fibers were stimulated, they replied that of course they could—but that they could not imagine being mistaken about whether their C-fibers seemed to be stimulated.

At this point, it occurred to someone to ask whether they could detect the neural state which was the concomitant of "seeming to have their C-fibers stimulated." Antipodeans replied that there was, of course, the state T-435 which was the constant neural concomitant of the utterance of the sentence "My C-fibers seem to be stimulated," state T-497 which went with "It's just as if my C-fibers were being stimulated," state T-295 which went with "Stimulated C-fibers!" and various other neural states which were concomitants of various other roughly synonymous sentences—but that there was no further neural state which they were aware of in addition to these. Cases in which Antipodeans had T-435 but no stimulation of C-fibers included those in which, for example, they were strapped to what they were falsely informed was a torture machine, a switch was theatrically turned on, but nothing else was done.

Discussion among the philosophers now switched to the topic: Could the Antipodeans be mistaken about the T-series of neural states (the ones which were concomitants of understanding or uttering sentences)? Could they seem to be having T-435 but not really be? Yes,

the Antipodeans said, cerebroscopes indicated that sort of thing occasionally happened. Was there any explanation of the cases in which it happened—any pattern to them? No, there did not seem to be. It was just one of those odd things that turned up occasionally. Neurophysiology had not yet been able to find another sort of neural state, outside the T-series, which was a concomitant of such weird illusions, any more than for certain perceptual illusions, but perhaps it would someday.

This answer left the philosophers still in difficulties on the question of whether the Antipodeans had sensations of pain, or anything else. For there now seemed to be nothing which the Antipodeans were incorrigible about except how things seemed to them. But it was not clear that "how things seemed to them" was a matter of what raw feels they had, as opposed to what they were inclined to say. If they had the raw feel of painfulness, then they had minds. But a raw feel is (or has) a phenomenal property—one which you cannot have the illusion of having (because, so to speak, having the illusion of it is itself to have it). The difference between stimulated C-fibers and pains was that you could have the illusion of stimulated C-fibers (could have, e.g., T-435) without having stimulated C-fibers, but could not have the illusion of pain without having pain. There was nothing which the Antipodeans could not be wrong about except how things seemed to them. But the fact that they could not "merely seem to have it seem to them that …" was of no interest in determining whether they had minds. The fact that "seems to seem …" is an expression without a use is a fact about the notion of "appearance," not a tip-off to the presence of "phenomenal properties." For the appearance-reality distinction is not based on a distinction between subjective representations and objective states of affairs; it is merely a matter of getting something wrong, having a false belief. So the Antipodeans' firm grasp of the former distinction did not help philosophers tell whether to ascribe the latter to them.

Patricia Smith Churchland
Selections from *Neurophilosophy:*
Toward a Unified Science of the Mind-Brain

What Is Folk Psychology?

So far I have referred to our "commonsense framework for understanding mental states and processes" without being very precise about what is meant. For brevity's sake, I shall begin by replacing that long-winded description with a shorter label, namely "folk psychology." Now by folk psychology I mean that rough-hewn set of concepts, generalizations, and rules of thumb we all standardly use in explaining and predicting human behavior. Folk psychology is commonsense psychology—the psychological lore in virtue of which we explain behavior as the outcome of beliefs, desires, perceptions, expectations, goals, sensations, and so forth. It is a theory whose generalizations connect mental states to other mental states, to perceptions, and to actions. These homey generalizations are what provide the characterization of the mental states and processes referred to; they are what delimit the "facts" of mental life and define the explananda. Folk psychology is "intuitive psychology," and it shapes our conceptions of ourselves. As philosophers have analyzed it, the preeminent elements in folk psychological explanations of behavior include the concepts of *belief* and *desire*. Other elements will of course figure in, but these two are crucial and indispensable.

As an example of how the theory is put to work, we may start with a very simple case in which we need to explain why John flipped on the light switch:

(1) "He wanted to see if his copy of *Middlemarch* was on his desk, he believed that the best way to find out was to turn on the light and look, he be-

lieved that in order to turn on the light he had to flip on the light switch, so he flipped on the light switch."

Ordinarily, it is not necessary to make so much explicit—indeed, it would be ludicrously pedantic to do so—and successful explanation can be highly elliptical. Depending on the situation, "He wanted to see if his copy of *Middlemarch* was on his desk" will frequently do, because all the rest can be left understood. The "fill" is not unnecessary; it is just so obvious that we can take it for granted. Two people who know each other very well may leave so much unspoken that it is hard for another to follow (see for example the dialogue in John Fowles's *Daniel Martin*). Sometimes, though, with small children or with someone unfamiliar with the culture, a greater degree of explicitness is required. Not even the explanation (1) is maximally explicit, however, for explanations require generalizations, and its generalizations are in the wings. Unspoken ("understood") generalizations do indeed serve in the background here, though they are sufficiently familiar and obvious that they are made explicit only on special occasions. One such generalization, albeit a low-level specimen, is this:

(2) "Whenever a person wants to bring about a state *s, and* he believes that his doing *p* is a way to bring about *s, and* he believes that he can do *p, and* he can do *p,* then, barring conflicting desires or preferred strategies, he will do *p.*"

Like the generalizations asserting a regularity between copper's being heated and its expanding, or between spinal injury and hyperreflex-ivity, this generalization purports to describe a regularity in nature. Something rather like it seems to function in the routine reasoning about why persons behave as they do. Whether the generalization is accurate and whether it should be improved upon are not at issue here. The central point is that background generalizations, sometimes with a home-brewy lack of subtlety, figure in our day-to-day explanations of human behavior. Insofar as it enables us to make sense of and explain a certain range of phenomena, folk psychology resembles the folk physics discussed [elsewhere in the book].

The network of generalizations of folk psychology appears to be extremely rich and complicated, and undoubtedly there are variations between the theoretical networks of diverse individuals. Henry James surely employed a more sophisticated psychological theory than Ernest Hemingway, though presumably they shared many general beliefs about why humans behave as they do. One way to begin to limn the generalizations that figure in the commonsense theory of human behavior is to press for expansions of action explanations in order to force the implicit and "understood" background assumptions into the open. This is similar to the method used to limn folk physics. For example, many people thought that Richard Nixon knew about the cover-up of the Watergate break-in. Why? Because, it will be said, he was in the room when it was discussed. Why is that relevant? Crudely, because if someone x has normal hearing, and someone else y says "p" in a normal speaking voice in x's vicinity, and x knows the language, then x hears that p. Similarly, we may conclude that a person was lying because he must have seen the body (anyone with normal vision, in broad daylight, standing two feet away would have), that someone did believe that there was money in the safe (why else did he break in and jimmy the lock), and so forth. Fodor (1981) suggests other instances: "seeing that a is F is a normal cause of

believing that a is F; statements that p are normally caused by beliefs that p; the belief that a thing is red is a normal cause of the inference that the thing is colored ..." (p. 25) (For more discussion on the background generalizations, see Paul M. Churchland 1970, 1979.)

Those who find these generalizations to have an excessively cracker-barrel flavor should recall that they are up for discussion precisely so that antireductionist arguments citing the essential correctness of folk psychology can be addressed. Admittedly, the generalizations do have a cracker-barrel quality, but this is characteristic of folk theory generally, and it does not in the least imply that they are simpleminded. On the contrary, however folkish it is, folk psychology as a framework of understanding is very complex. Moreover, folk psychology is where scientific psychology began, and if scientific psychology is to revise and improve upon folk psychology, it must know what that framework consists of and whether and to what extent it can be revised.

The insight that our psychological concepts are nodes in a background theory and that our explanations of human action proceed within the framework of that theory is owed mainly to Sellars (1963) and Feyerabend (1963b,c). It is an insight that has profoundly influenced research in the philosophy of mind. Together with the related work in epistemology and philosophy of science, the "theory" theory of our commonsense beliefs about the mind has engendered new understanding of the nature of mental concepts and rendered tractable some baffling traditional questions, some of which pertain to reduction. Before discussing how these insights can help in confronting the question of reduction and the mind-body problem, certain preliminary issues should be addressed.

The Origins of Folk Theory

One query to be raised about the Sellars-Feyerabend thesis is this: How do persons come by the folk theory? And where did it come from in the first place? Apparently, we do not learn folk psychology in the way we learn Newtonian theory or molecular genetics, nor do we typically make conscious or labored use of folk psychology generalizations.

Some of the theory may be acquired as we learn the language, and some of it may be acquired in a nonchalant and unreflective way as part of growing up among conspecifics. Some of it may indeed involve explicit instruction of old saws ("The bearer of bad news may be himself the object of dislike," "People don't like show-offs"), and some of it may involve imparting rather more recent information ("Pupil size of the person one is looking at affects beliefs about how friendly the person is"). The etiology of an individual's possession of a folk psychology is probably much like the etiology of his possession of a folk physics, and folk thermodynamics, and so forth. For all we can tell now, the mind-brain may have an innate disposition to favor and "grow" the rudiments of certain folk theories, including folk psychology and folk physics.

As to where the theory came from, certainly the image of a *Homo habilis* Newton squatting at the cave mouth, pondering how to explain human behavior and finally sketching out the basics of folk psychology with jawbone and berry juice, is not very plausible. The ancestry of folk physics, folk thermodynamics, and folk theory of matter is similarly clouded in the mists of the far distant past, and a jawbone and berry juice theory is not plausible for any of them.

Sellars tells a kind of "just-so" story in which a primitive people begin to fashion a folk psychology by postulating inner states characterized on the model of overt speech. The folk discover it useful in certain conditions to say that someone is in a state analogous to the state he is in when he says out loud, "There is a rabbit." Thus, they come to attribute covert or inner speech states to each other, and thereby they come to attribute *thoughts* to each other. But this story was designed not so much to be anthropologi-

cally reasonable as to emphasize a logical point. Sellars's thesis was that beliefs and desires are *beliefs that p* and *desires that p*, and hence that the logic of such expressions is importantly related to the logic of overt utterances of "*p*."

In order to characterize folk psychology, folk physics, and all the rest as theories, what is important is not that they originated in self-conscious construction, but that in their explanatory and predictive role *they function as theories*. In this respect, folk psychology and folk physics deserve to be called theories. Although it would be satisfying to know the origins of commonsense lore and to know how any individual comes to have the lore he has, our ignorance on these matters in no way impugns the claim that the lore should be considered a theory in the defined sense. For that claim concerns the epistemological status and function of the lore, not its origins.

Folk Theory and Rationality

Propositional attitudes are those mental states whose identity depends on a *proposition* specifying the content. If Jones has the belief that hawks eat mice, then the proposition "Hawks eat mice" specifies the content or "object" of his belief—in other words, it specifies what his belief *is*. Additionally, Jones might *be afraid* that hawks eat mice or *hope* that hawks eat mice, or *expect* or *wish* or *wonder whether* hawks eat mice, and in each case it is the proposition "Hawks eat mice" that defines the *content* of the propositional attitude. (Pains, tickles, and itches, by contrast, are not propositional attitudes.) We can chart the logical relations between propositional attitudes in virtue of the logical relations that obtain between the content sentences. Jones's belief that hawks eat mice and his belief that Leonard is a hawk entail his belief that Leonard eats mice. And so on.

Much dwelt upon is the observation that explanations of human behavior proceed by showing how the behavior was rational in the light of the subject's beliefs and desires, where it is the content of the beliefs and desires that make rational sense of the behavior. For example, Smith might say his reason for butchering the calves was that the cost of feed was increasing and that the price of beef cattle was declining. Smith's private deliberations must have gone something like this: "The cost of feed is increasing, the beef cattle market is declining, if I want to make a profit—and I do—my outlay must not exceed my income, therefore I should butcher the calves now." Replace "The cost of feed is increasing" with "I could never prove Fermat's last theorem," and the decision to butcher the calves is no longer reasonable in light of the contents of the mental states.

The point is, there is a "rational-in-the-light-of" relation between the contents of the mental states and the content of the decision, and some philosophers have wished to argue that this distinguishes *absolutely* explanations of intentional action from explanations in physics, biology, and other branches of science. According to this view, even if psychological explanations conform to the deductive-nomological pattern, it is not the deductive relation obtaining between the covering laws, initial conditions, and the explanandum that is important; rather, it is the internal, rational-in-the-light-of relations between the contents of mental states that do the explanatory work.

In particular, this special relation has been cited as grounds for rejecting the claim that explanations within folk psychology are causal explanations and that the generalizations of folk psychology are causal-explanatory. On the contrary, it has been argued, the generalizations are not causal, and the style of explanation in which they have a role is uniquely rational as opposed to causal. (See for example Dray 1963.) What produces human behavior, it is said, are reasons, not causes, and we understand behavior in virtue of finding a suitable *rationale*, not in virtue of finding *causal conditions*.

And this has sometimes functioned as the basis for antireductionist arguments.

The observation that in explanations of human behavior a rationality relation connects statements about beliefs and desires with statements about behavior is entirely correct. What is mistaken is the inference that beliefs and desires therefore do not cause behavior. More generally, it is false that the existence of a rational relation between statements characterizing events precludes, or is somehow at loggerheads with, a causal connection between the events. This can be straightforwardly seen in a computer executing a deductive logic program, where the states the computer runs through are related by logic *and* by cause. Indeed, the program is precisely designed so that when certain causal relations obtain between machine states, then the appropriate logical relations also obtain between statements describing those states.

This existence of abstract or formal relations defined over contents or objects of "attitudes" is not, moreover, a feature unique to psychology. Ironically, it is in fact a point of deep similarity between psychological laws and laws elsewhere in science. There are laws containing numerical attitudes, between which arithmetical relations hold; laws containing vectorial attitudes, between which algebraic relations hold; and so forth. Once noticed, this parallel is striking, and it speaks for, rather than against, the similarity between folk psychology and other theories in the sciences. (See Paul M. Churchland 1970, 1979, 1981.) Consider the following:

Numerical Attitudes	Propositional Attitudes
x ... has a mass$_{kg}$ of n	... believes that p
... has a charge$_{coul}$ of n	... desires that p
... has a temperature$_k$ of n	... perceives that p
... has energy$_i$ of n etc.	... hopes that p etc.

Not only is there a parallel with respect to attitudes identified via abstract objects (propositions and numbers); there is also a parallel in the laws that specify the abstract relations (logical and numerical) that obtain between distinct states. Recall the generalizations with which this section began and compare, for example, the following:

9. If a body x has a mass m, and if x suffers a net force of f, then x accelerates at f/m.

10. If a gas has a pressure P, and a volume V, and a quantity m, then barring very high pressure or density, it has a temperature of PV/mR, where R is the gas constant.

What I have wished to emphasize here is that there is nothing especially mentalistic, mystical, or noncausal about generalizations that exploit abstract relations between abstract objects. Generalizations in folk psychology do it, but so do generalizations in physics and chemistry. The existence of "rational-in-the-light-of" relations between objects of propositional attitudes fails to imply that psychological explanations are noncausal explanations. ...

Finally, it should be observed that propositions and the logical relations defined over them constitute an impressively powerful structure, and insofar as folk psychology exploits propositions as its domain of abstract objects, it inherits the power of that structure. That is, it inherits as *part of psychology* that systematicity which is inherent in the logical system of propositions. (See Fodor 1975.) It is this insight, made the more appealing by the discoveries of modern logic and by the construction of electronic devices conforming to logic, that has engendered a certain "logicist" conception of the mind. On this conception, the mind is fundamentally a sentential computing device, taking sentences as input from sensory transducers, performing logical operations on them, and issuing other sentences as output.

• • •

9.5 Representations and Reduction

In dismissing the reductive program, functionalists rely not only on the distinction between function and structure but also on a distinction between *logical/meaning* relations and *causal* relations. Psychological states, as we have seen it claimed many times, stand to one another in logical and meaningful relationships. Psychological states are representational, and changes of state are explainable in terms of rules followed for the manipulation of representations. This connection between cognitive processes, on the one hand, and symbol manipulation and rule following on the other, explains the mutual admiration of orthodox artificial intelligence research and cognitive psychology.

Beliefs, desires, goals, hopes, thoughts, intentions, expectations, and so forth, are mental states referred to in the explanation of behavior, and what is alleged to make them indispensable for psychology but unfathomable by neuroscience is that they form a *semantically coherent* system, as opposed to a *causally interconnected* system. In the terminology used earlier ... they have content; they are *intentional.* They are *about* things, they can be true or false of the world, and they stand to one another in logical relationships such as entailment and contradiction. The objection to a reductionist program runs as follows: psychological explanations of human behavior rely essentially on the ascription of representational states to the person and they exploit the rule-governed relationships between the contents of the states. Because mental states are identified in terms of their logical and semantical relations, and because transitions between mental states are determined by the logical relations between representations, mental states are special. *Logical relations cannot be reduced to causal relations;* consequently, psychological theory is autonomous and the prospect of reduction is patently hopeless.

We have already seen Popper's development of this common intuition concerning the specialness of logical relations, and the criticism of it … This version offers additional considerations, however, and it avoids some of the weaknesses of Popper's arguments. What makes this version different is that it does not deny that mental states are in causal interaction, but only that what matters for psychological explanation and for the development of a scientific cognitive psychology are the logical relations and semantic representations. In defense of this idea it claims that the categories of psychological theory will cross-classify those of neurobiology, in the sense that the former will at best map onto an *indefinite* number of *arbitrarily* related neurobiological categories. In this sense, the generalizations of psychology are emergent with respect to neurobiological theory.

Logical Relations and Biological Relations

In more detail, the arguments proceed in the following vein. Consider, for example, that in explaining why Smith shot his horse, it may be said: Smith believed his horse had broken its leg and believed that whenever a horse has a broken leg, the only thing to do is destroy it. Sense is made of Smith's action in terms of his beliefs and the logical relations obtaining between them. More specifically, Smith's decision to destroy the horse follows logically from the content of two of his beliefs: "Whenever a horse breaks a leg, the only thing to do is destroy it" and "This horse broke its leg." The causal relations, whatever they may be, between the physiological realizations of the representational states are not what matters to the explanation. Rather, what matters are the logical (i.e., formal) relations between the *contents* of his beliefs, desires, intentions, and so on. Mental states do stand in causal relations to other mental states, but, as Fodor says, "mental representations have their causal roles in virtue of their formal properties" (1981:26). We have access to the causal relationships between mental states

only via access to their representational relationships. Thus the crux of the antireductionist argument from rules and representations.

The point is grounded in the machine analogy. Consider an electronic symbol-manipulating device, such as a pocket calculator. The explanation of why it printed out 27 will proceed by citing the input (9, ×, 3) and the arithmetic rule for multiplication. What is needed to explain the behavior is an understanding of the calculator's representations and the rules for manipulating the representations. Not only do the electronic events underlying the changes of state differ from machine to machine; they will not yield an explanation of the phenomenon in question in any event (Fodor 1975). Descriptions of such events can be useful, but not for explaining why the calculator printed out 27. Pylyshyn says, "We explain why the machine does something by referring to certain interpretations of its symbols in some intended domain. This is, of course, precisely what we do in describing how (and why) people do what they do" (1980:113). The real obstacle to reduction, it is claimed, is the intentionality of mental states; that is, the fact that they have content. For explanations at the intentional level are of a radically different nature from those at levels that do not advert to representations and content. The latter explanations have a good and useful place, but they cannot do justice to the representational dimension of psychological life.

But why, precisely, not? The heart of the rationale is this: the categories of psychological theory will radically cross-classify the categories of neurophysiological theory, and consequently neurophysiological generalizations will miss entirely important relations describable only at the level where representations are referred to. That is, at best the psychological categories will map onto an indefinite jumble of neurobiological categories, and it *will* be a jumble, in the sense that the neurobiological categories in question will not form a natural kind. Neurophysiological explanations, therefore, will not explain the same things that a psychology of representations will explain (Pylyshyn 1980, Fodor 1981). In Fodor's words, "... we are driven to functionalism (hence to the autonomy of psychology) by the suspicion that there are empirical generalizations about mental states that can't be formulated in the vocabulary of neurological or physical theories ..." (1981:25). The best way to understand this claim is through an example Pylyshyn presents.

Suppose someone comes to believe that there is a fire in her building and so dials the fire department on her telephone. Now coming to believe there is a fire in the building is coming to have a certain kind of representation, and whoever believes there is a fire in her building has the same representation. And if in consequence she dials the fire department, we understand the whys and wherefores of her behavior in the same way. However, underlying the commonality of representation may be a dismaying diversity of physiological states. Someone can come to believe the building is on fire in a variety of ways: she might smell smoke, see smoke, see flames, feel a hot wall, hear someone call "Fire," hear a smoke detector, and on and—indefinitely—on. Each of these distinct ways of coming to have the representation "There is a fire in the building" will have a distinct physiological causal story, at least for the obvious reason that different sensory receptors are involved. In this sense, the categories of psychology cross-classify or are orthogonal to the categories of neuroscience.

Because the neurophysiological realizations are distinct, the neurophysiological generalizations will not capture what is similar in each of these instances—to wit, that the person believed there was a fire in the building. The neurophysiological explanations of why the person dialed the number 911 will be *different* in each case, whereas the psychological explanation will do justice to the abstract—semantically coherent—similarity prevailing in each case and will explain the behavior by reference to the commonly held belief. In sum, certain generalizations, vital for the explanation of behavior, will be missed by neuroscience but will be captured by psychological theory (Pylyshyn 1980, Fodor 1981). Neuroscience, therefore, cannot explain phenomena characterized by our psychological theory. Thus the irreducibility and autonomy of cognitive psychology.

Two preliminary remarks: (1) These arguments against reduction in no way depend on ascribing a nonphysical status to representations. In contrast to Popper's arguments from intentionality ... this view asserts that every instance of a mental state has a physical realization. (2) The psychological states for which these arguments are most plausible are the sentential attitudes (beliefs, desires, thoughts, and so forth). The arguments are decidedly less plausible in regard to memory, many kinds of learning, sensory states, consciousness, attention, pattern recognition, facial recognition, the emotions, habits, cognitive skills, and so on. The reason is that in the latter cases there is no theory (not even palpable folk theory) of how to characterize the relevant semantical/logical representations, if such there be, or how they relate to one another. By contrast, in the case of the sentential attitudes the theory is straightforward: content is specified by a sentence, and the relations between sentences are defined by logic (see below). Given the limited application of the argument, it may be assumed that it is meant to defend not the autonomy of psychology in general but the autonomy of sentential attitude psychology in particular.

On the other hand, Pylyshyn (1980, 1984) argues unequivocally that cognitive psychology as a whole should be modeled on sentential attitude psychology. This suggests that the scope of the argument is intended to be very wide indeed. Thus, to be as liberal as possible I shall take it to defend the autonomy of cognitive psychology, assuming that sentential attitude theory occupies a central position therein. This is inevitably an unsatisfactory carving of the territory, since many psychologists who consider themselves in the cognitive swim but who work on learning or attention, for example, will not wish to have their discipline hived off from neuroscience. Certainly it will distress those researchers who describe their work as *cognitive neuroscience* (for example, Patricia Goldman-Rakic, Michael Gazzaniga). Nevertheless, granting a certain vagueness about how much of cognitive science is at stake, let us proceed.

Autonomy and Irreducibility Assessed

What the arguments from intentionality show is not that cognitive psychology should be autonomous, or that cognitive psychology is irreducible to neuroscience, but only that cognitive psychology is respectable. Taken as arguments for the view that cognitive psychology is worth pursuing and is a necessary, indispensable part of the enterprise of coming to understand how the mind-brain works, I think they are fair enough, and I have no quarrel. What are contentious are the much larger claims of irreducibility and autonomy, and these go beyond what the premises can support. That the arguments have overextended their reach is evidently not obvious, to say the least, since many philosophers have been convinced of the autonomy of psychology after taking to heart these very arguments. Indeed, autonomy's opposite, interdependence, is within philosophy a minority opinion.

The brunt of my reply attacks the central idea that logical relations between states cannot be explained in terms of causal relations between neurobiological states. I think this opinion is fundamentally a myth, unsupported by any cogent arguments. Where the idea does get support is (1) from the venerable tradition in philosophy according to which the logical-meaningful dimension of mental business cannot be explained naturalistically and (2) from unjustified assumptions about limitations of

neuroscience. It assumes either that there can be no theory in neuroscience, or that neuroscience is forever limited to specifying interactions at the level of the single cell, or that neuroscience is too hard to ever tell us much. It therefore fails to recognize that theorizing about information processing in cell assemblies, groups of such assemblies, and so on up, is as much a part of neuroscience as recording from a single cell. An essential part of my reply will therefore be the demonstration [in a later chapter] of what theorizing in neuroscience looks like and, more importantly, of what neurobiological theorizing about *representations and computations* looks like.

First, a general point: the argument from intentionality is in fact a special case of the argument from multiple instantiability ... and the observations and remarks made earlier regarding what the multiple instantiability argument does and does not prove are all relevant here. And as we have seen in the preceding section, the arguments for the enriching effect of the co-evolution of theories greatly weaken the ideology of autonomy and irreducibility.

The naturalist's additional point in reply is this: if there really is a commonality of psychological state in the heads of all who come to believe there is a fire in the building, then there is every reason to expect that *at some appropriate level* of neurophysiological organization, this commonality corresponds to a common neurobiological configuration. After all, the heads all house human brains, and human brains have a common evolutionary history. They are not the product of entirely different designs in Silicon Valley and at Mitsubishi. It should be possible, therefore, to explain neurobiologically what is going on, unless the psychological level is indeterministic with respect to the relevant neurophysical level. For that there is no evidence, nor do the antireductionists wish to embrace such an unlikely view.

Envisage a neurobiological theory, of some appropriate level of organization, that addresses the question of representations and computations in the brain, but where the representations are not sentence-like and the computations are not inferences but are, say, mathematical—just the sort to be executed by suitably configured neuronal arrays. Why should not such a theory explain the logical and meaningful relations between states at the psychological level? How, a priori, do philosophers know that it cannot? What can be their special source of knowledge? I suspect that the philosophical tradition of veneration for inference and the sentential attitude has generated a kind of fetishism with respect to logic as the model for inner processes. A reverent attachment to this aspect of folk psychology, together with ignorance about neuroscience, has made the naturalistic program seem pathetically hopeless.

So long as neuroscience can address the functional questions concerning how information is stored and processed by neuronal ensembles, it is addressing levels of organization above that of the single cell. At the appropriate *neurofunctional* level, therefore, psychological states of a given type may be found to have a common neurofunctional property. That is, assuming the reality of a commonality at the topmost psychological level of organization, it could turn out that whenever someone comes to have a belief that the building is on fire, a certain neuronal *assembly* somewhere in the hierarchy of organization has a particular and identifiable configuration. On the other hand, it may be that the state of having the belief that the building is on fire is analogous to a "virtual governor," and the neural conditions ramify across diverse neuronal assemblies. In that event readjustment of macrolevel theory and macrolevel description may be elicited, and in a science fiction parallel to the case of genetics it may eventually be said that there is no neurophysiology of individual beliefs; there is only a neurophysiology of information fermenphorylation (to take a made-up name). On either scenario, and this is the important point, there will be an explanation of macrolevel

effects in terms of microlevel machinations, of macrolevel categories in terms of microlevel business. Insofar as there are such explanations, reductive integration will have been achieved.

Moreover, there is already evidence that the folk psychological categories of belief and desire are bound to fragment at the hands of science and hence that, like the virtual governor and like learning and memory, they will have no unitary explanation at lower levels. One important reason here derives from the original work of Stephen Stich (1983), and the difficulty centers on the nature of the way we ascribe beliefs (desires, etc.) within the folk psychological framework—that is, the bases on which we say what it is someone believes. More exactly, the difficulty is that belief ascription is context-relative, and depending on interests, aims, and sundry other considerations, different criteria are variously used to specify the content of a given mental state. Even worse, sometimes different criteria will give conflicting answers to the question of what someone believes. So the first problem is that folk psychology as it stands does not have a *single*, unified, well-defined notion of content, but rather a set of vague notions flying in loose formation. This may be all very well for a folk theory going about its humdrum business, but if there is no such thing as *the* content of someone's propositional attitudes, then the project of finding a place for the propositional attitudes in cognitive psychology, let alone neurobiology, is severely hampered.

The second problem is that some of the criteria routinely invoked within folk psychology for specifying content rely on features that are *irrelevant to the causal role* of the mental state in interaction with other mental states, stimuli, and behavior. Noteworthy culprits here are semantic features—namely, truth, reference, and meaning. Now such criteria will give completely irrelevant content specifications if what we seek are psychological generalizations that articulate the causal role in cognition of beliefs and desires. The brain, as Dennett (1981) has put it, is a syntactic engine, not a semantic engine. That is, roughly, the brain goes from state to state as a function of the causal properties of the antecedent states, not as a function of what the states are "about" or whether they represent something true about the world. So far as the question of reduction is concerned, this means that at best, considerable correction and reconfiguration of the folk psychological concepts of belief and desire are required. It may be possible, however, that a syntactic analogue of the sentential attitudes will be able to do duty in a scientific psychology and will fit in comfortably with a cognitive neurobiology in the geometric style ... Even so, of course, these newly characterized states and the relations between them can be expected to have a neurobiological reduction, for the reasons just discussed.

Semantical issues are notoriously difficult, and this is not the place to do anything but take the lid off the jar and let a few odors escape. Suffice it to say that Stich's breakthrough on the question of semantics bears importantly on the possibility of smoothly reducing folk psychology to neurobiology, as well as on how representational states are to be understood in cognitive science. If Stich is right, and I think he is, then it is already clear that the propositional attitudes, qua folk psychological categories, are coming apart. Therefore, when antireductionists parade these categories in all their folk psychological regalia as irreducible, the irony is that it is their lack of empirical integrity that prevents their reduction.

Revisionary Reductions and Folk Psychology

If the reduction is smooth, relatively little revision of the top-level theory may be required; if it is bumpy, conceptual revision may be greater. Notwithstanding reduction and revision, belief talk, like gene talk, could continue to have a useful role—and not just after hours but also in research (cf. also Newtonian mechanics and the special theory of relativity). It may be this prospect that encourages the antireductionist to plead the case for autonomy. The point does nothing to that end, however. It is a practical observation about conceptual usefulness, and all it really supports is the less controversial notion that research needs to be conducted at many levels, one of which describes mental states. That is perfectly consistent with reductionist goals, and though sound enough, it is a far cry from autonomy.

Raising the matter of revisions emphasizes once more that the psychological categories valued by the antireductionist are categories of a *theory*, and in the main the theory that embeds these categories is folk psychology. It is an empirical question how good a theory of mind-brain function folk psychology is, and how much reconceptualization is required. Notice in particular that if the categories of folk psychology radically cross-classify those of neuroscience, and if, in addition, no explanation of folk psychology by neuroscience can be achieved, it may be because folk psychology is radically misconceived. Ironically for its champions, folk psychology may be irreducible with respect to neuroscience—irreducible because dead wrong.

The price of claiming autonomy for an immature theory is that one shields it from the very revisionary forces essential to its reaching maturity. The price of claiming autonomy for a theory when it has a powerful replacement is that one protects it from disconfirmation and closes oneself off from the explanatory and experimental opportunities made available by the competing theory. As an example of the first situation, consider that for thermodynamics in its early days to have been granted autonomous status from mechanics would have denied it the benefits of co-evolution. As for the second, if physicists in the seventeenth century had taken Aristotelian physics as autonomous with respect to Newtonian physics, it would have been viciously stultifying for physicists determined to be Aristotelian. It is *respectability* that should be claimed for cognitive psychology, not autonomy or irreducibility.

The computer metaphor should be handled with extreme caution. As we have seen, the theory of levels borrowed from computer science defines prematurely and inappropriately the levels of organization in the brain. There are additional reasons for caution. In the case of pocket calculators we know what generalizations describe their behavior, what categories apply, and what rules they follow. We build them precisely so that they will operate according to arithmetic rules and so that they can represent numbers. Their symbol-manipulating capacities are understood because we have built them in, and the generalizations that are true of them are so by virtue of their manufacture. By contrast, human brains were not literally built to instantiate the generalizations of folk psychology, and what generalizations do truly describe our inner processes is a matter for empirical research. In the case of evolved organisms, ourselves and others, we must find out what generalizations are true and what categories apply. As a matter of discovery, there may be much to be learned about how we manipulate symbols and what symbols we manipulate by studying how symbol manipulation evolved and how (and whether) it is accomplished in simpler nervous systems ...

Folk psychology, like other folk theories before it, may be misconceived in many dimensions, and under pressure from discoveries at diverse levels it can be expected to evolve. Even the characterization of what needs to be explained may be revised. The domain of phenomena that allegedly cannot be explained by neuroscience but only by intentional psychology is a domain specified by intentional psychology. Change that, and the domain description changes too. It is spectacularly evident that newer theories do not always espouse the explananda of the older theories ... Neuroscience may fail to explain phenomena characterized in folk psychology for the same reason Newtonian physics fails to explain what turns the crystal spheres and modern biology fails to explain how the vital spirits are concocted. The complaint that neuroscience cannot in principle do justice to the generalizations of psychology errs in two directions: it is overconfident about the integrity of folk psychology and it underestimates the value of co-evolution of theories.

Are Sentential Attitudes Important to Theorizing in Psychology?

Sentential attitudes and *logical* inference occupy center stage in the disagreement between those who defend autonomy and those who defend co-evolution and interdependence. But are the sentential attitudes really so very important in folk psychology or in cognitive psychology? Would thoroughgoing revision of their theory be so very revolutionary?

The answer to both questions is a resounding yes. Beliefs, desires, thoughts, intentions, and the like, are invariably assumed to mediate between input and output and to have a crucial role in the causation of behavior. Moreover, to echo an earlier remark, it is only in the case of the sentential attitudes that we have something approaching a systematic theory both of the nature of the representations and of the rules that govern the transitions between representations. Most of the generalizations routinely used in the explanation of human behavior advert to sentential attitudes and their interplay. One of the beauties of sentential attitudes as a theoretical postulate is that they can also be given a role in nonconscious processes and hence can be invoked to describe cognitive business a long way down. Additionally, we can exploit deductive logic and such inductive logic and decision theory as are available to extend our theory of the rules followed by internal states. Dismantle sentential attitude theory, and we no longer have any idea how to explain behavior—we no longer have any idea of what is going on inside.

Fodor (1975) grittily describes the situation: it's the only theory we've got.

The theoretical blessings of sentential attitude psychology are undeniably rich, and it is entirely reasonable to try to develop a scientific psychology by extending and pruning the sentential attitude base. Consequently, the suggestion that substantial revisions to this base resulting from co-evolution are likely will fall on ungrateful ears. It is of course no defense of the truth of a theory that it's the only theory we've got. (Compare some fictional Aristotelian, circa 1400: "It's the only theory we've got.") What the lack of alternatives implies is that one has no choice but to *use* the available theory, and this is consistent with its falsity and with trying to construct a better competing theory. In view of the continual harping on the theme of revision, the advocates of theory interdependence must finally square up to this question: is the prospect of revision to sentential attitude psychology serious or frivolous? That is, does it rest on substantial grounds, or is it just a pie-in-the-sky possibility?

We have already seen in Stich's research compelling reason to suppose that the folk psychological categories of belief, desire, and so forth, will require substantial revision. In addition, there are substantial reasons for predicting that at best inference and sentence-like representations will have a small role in the theory of information processing, and for predicting quite radical revisions in folk psychology. These matters will be discussed in the next section [of Churchland's book].

REFERENCES

Churchland, Paul M. (1970). The logical character of action explanations. *Philosophical Review* 79:214–236.

Churchland, Paul M. (1979). *Scientific realism and the plasticity of mind*. Cambridge: Cambridge University Press.

Churchland, Paul M. (1981). Eliminative materialism and the propositional attitudes. *Journal of Philosophy* 79/2:67–90.

Dennett, Daniel C. (1981). Three kinds of intentional psychology. In *Reduction, time, and reality*, ed. R. Healey, 37–61. Cambridge: Cambridge University Press.

Dray, William (1963). The historical explanation of action reconsidered. In *Philosophy and history*, ed. S. Hook, 105–135. New York: New York University Press.

Feyerabend, Paul K. (1963a). How to be a good empiricist: A plea for tolerance in matters epistemological. In *Philosophy of science, the Delaware seminar*, vol. 2, ed. B. Baumrin, 3–39. New York: Interscience. (Reprinted in H. Morick, ed. (1972), 164–193.)

Feyerabend, Paul K. (1963b). Materialism and the mind-body problem. *The Review of Metaphysics* 17:49–66. (Reprinted in C.V. Borst, ed. (1970). *The mind/brain identity theory*, 142–156. London: Macmillan.)

Feyerabend, Paul K. (1963c). Mental events and the brain. *Journal of Philosophy* 60: 295–296.

Fodor, Jerry A. (1975). *The language of thought*. New York: Crowell. (Paperback edition (1979). Cambridge, Mass.: Harvard University Press.)

Fodor, Jerry A. (1981). *Representations*. Cambridge, Mass.: MIT Press.

Pylyshyn, Zenon (1980). Computation and cognition: Issues in the foundation of cognitive science. *Behavioral and Brain Sciences* 3/1:111–134.

Pylyshyn, Zenon (1984). *Computation and cognition*. Cambridge, Mass.: MIT Press.

Sellars, Wilfrid (1963). *Science, perception and reality*. London: Routledge and Kegan Paul.

Stich, Stephen P. (1983). *From folk psychology to cognitive science: The case against belief*. Cambridge, Mass.: MIT Press.

3

Recent Problems

CHAPTER THIRTEEN

Consciousness

Introduction

In Part Two we surveyed the predominant theories of mind in this century. To a large extent, the central feature of these theories has been an adherence to materialism. Most philosophers today agree that mental states and activities are realized in some manner in the physical matter of the body. In Part Three I want to look at two specific problems that materialists have faced. Over the past two decades debates over the best way to provide a materialist theory of mind have come to centre on these two particular problems.

The first of these problems, which will be the topic of this chapter, appears in a variety of different guises. Sometimes it is described as the problem of explaining *consciousness*, while at other times it is raised as a problem concerning the *subjectivity* or the *phenomenology* of the mind. At the root of the problem is an argument by skeptics of materialism that certain features of the mind — which they call the subjective or phenomenological features — cannot possibly be explained in materialist terms. In response, defenders of the various materialist theories have taken up the challenge, and have attempted to provide the kinds of explanations that skeptics claim cannot be found.

The second problem, which we will survey in the next chapter, is the problem of explaining how mental states can be *about* things in the world, or relatedly how mental states can have *propositional content*. For example, if I believe that Woody Allen is a film-maker, then my belief — a particular state of my mind — is somehow *about* Woody Allen; there must be some kind of relationship between this state of my mind and the person, Woody Allen. Philosophers have grappled with the problem of saying precisely what this relationship is. What is it about mental states that gives them a connection with things in the world?

The phenomenological character of experience

The first of these two problems concerns something that philosophers have come to call the **phenomenological** character of conscious experience. Common sense suggests that there are certain facts about conscious experience that have to do with what experiences are *like* for the person who has them. The point is clearest in the case of sensations, such as the experiences of colours, sounds, tastes, and so on. For example, there is a certain intrinsic difference in quality between the visual sensation of green and the visual sensation of red. We can express this by saying that red *looks different to us* than green. Much the same can be said for the other sensory modalities. There is a certain fact about what a foghorn sounds like, which is different from what a small bell sounds like. In the same way, there is the difference between the smell of a rose and the smell of an orange. In each of these cases, and many others like them, it seems that there is a certain aspect of the sensation that has to do with what the experience is *like*.

It is notoriously hard to capture this aspect of experience in words. We have words for the elements of experience — words for colours, sounds, pains, fragrances, and so on. We can describe a pain as sharp or dull, and a colour as light green. Yet it seems that these words will not communicate the nature of the sensations to someone who has never experienced them. Imagine trying to explain the difference between red and green to a person blind from birth, or the experience of pain to someone who has never felt it. Yet the phenomenological aspects of our experiences seem to be essential to their very nature. What's important about a pain, you might say, is the way that it hurts; the essential aspect of the experience of a fine wine is what it tastes like.

The problem of phenomenology

In an important way, the phenomenological character of experience became a philosophical problem with the rise of the mechanical sciences in the seventeenth century. Mechanical scientists like Galileo and Descartes drew a distinction between the way the world appears to us and the qualities that actually exist in the world. This stands in sharp contrast to Aristotle's theory of perception. According to Aristotle, the character of our experience is *identical* to the character of the physical world around us. For example, Aristotle believed that colours exist in the world exactly as we perceive them. In rejecting Aristotle's theories, the new scientists argued that there need be no similarity at all between our sensations and the qualities of physical objects. According to the mechanical sciences, the way colours and other secondary qualities look to us is not an aspect of the physical world, but rather an aspect of our minds. As Galileo put it, qualities like colour, *as they are experienced by us*, exist only in our consciousness.

Dualists, like Descartes, are able to explain the difference between the character of our sensations and the character of the physical world by insisting that the mind is a substance distinct from matter. The phenomenological features of consciousness, on this view, are intrinsic characteristics of the immaterial mind, and are not a part of the physical world. However, if one rejects dualism, while maintaining a mechanical theory of matter, then it becomes very hard to say what phenomenological properties are. If the mind itself is simply a part of the physical world, as materialists maintain, then what becomes of the way that colours look to us? It seems that although the mechanical sciences banished the phenomenological character of experience to the inner mind, materialism threatens to remove it from existence altogether.

Phenomenology and contemporary theories

The phenomenology of experience presents a problem for each of the theories we surveyed in Part Two. None of these theories defines mental states in terms of their phenomenological properties. Behaviourists define mental states as relations between stimulus and behaviour. Identity theorists argue that mental states are purely physical states of the brain, identifiable through topic-neutral characteristics such as their typical causes and effects. Functionalists define mental states as functional states mediating between stimulus and behaviour. Finally, eliminativists agree with identity theorists that mental states are physical states of the brain, but see them as definable solely in terms of neurological descriptions. In none of these cases are phenomenological properties seen as *essential* features of our mental states. This means that materialists must either find a way to account for phenomenological properties, or they must reject the idea that there are such properties.

Philosophers have responded in different ways to this problem. In the essays that follow, Thomas Nagel and Frank Jackson argue that physical science is unable to explain the phenomenological nature of consciousness, and conclude from this that materialism is seriously threatened. Daniel Dennett, on the other hand, claims that insisting on the importance of ineffable qualities of conscious experience is a mistake because such qualities simply don't exist. Owen Flanagan stakes out a middle ground in the debate, arguing that there are such things as the subjective qualities of experience, but maintaining that it is possible to give an account of them within a materialist theory of mind.

Nagel's rejection of reductionism

In his article "What Is It Like to Be a Bat?" Thomas Nagel argues that we cannot ignore the phenomenological character of mental states, and for that very reason it is impossible to reduce descriptions of the mind to descriptions of neurological activity.

Nagel gives the notion of reduction a broader meaning than the one I gave at the beginning of chapter 12. There I described reductionism as the idea that we can explain mental activity entirely in neuroscientific terms. In this sense, functionalism is not a reductionist theory. Nagel's view is that, although functionalists deny that psychology is reducible to neuroscience, they claim that it is nevertheless reducible to machine table descriptions. Thus he treats both the identity theory and functionalism as reductionist in the sense that each explains mental life in terms of some more fundamental theory.

Nagel argues that the mind-body problem is not at all like cases of reduction in the physical sciences, such as the reduction of lightning to electrical discharge, with which it is often compared. Nagel argues that the central characteristic of the mind is consciousness, and by this he means in particular the phenomenological character of experience. He claims that it is nonsensical to reduce the elements of consciousness to either physical features of the brain or the functional properties of machine states.

Subjective experience

Nagel claims that for a creature (human or otherwise) to have consciousness means that there is "something it is like" to be that sort of creature, and he refers to this as the **subjective character of experience**. He illustrates this idea by considering the experience of a bat, a creature whose form of perception is very different from our own. As we can presume that bats have conscious experience, there must be something it is like to be a bat. The question, then, is how this aspect of the mind can be explained in the terms of neuroscience. How can neuroscience answer the question, "What is it like to be a bat?"

Nagel makes two preliminary remarks about subjective experience. The first is that it is not possible for us to *imagine* what the subjective experience of other creatures is like. We can imagine ourselves behaving like a bat, but that doesn't tell us what experience is like *for the bat*. The second point is that taking the idea of subjective experience seriously implies accepting the existence of something that cannot be expressed in language. Here Nagel is raising the point I mentioned earlier in the chapter: we cannot convey the phenomenological character of experience with words.

Given that we cannot convey the character of subjective experience in words, we can come to understand the experiences of others only by having similar experiences ourselves. This is what Nagel means by referring to consciousness as a *subjective* phenomenon. A fact is subjective if it can only be understood by creatures with a certain form of conscious experience (what Nagel calls a "point of view"). He says:

There is a sense in which phenomenological facts are perfectly objective: one person can know or say of another what the quality of the other's experience is. They are subjective, however, in the sense that even this objective ascription of experience is possible only for someone sufficiently similar to the object of ascription to be able to adopt his point of view — to understand the ascription in the first person as well as in the third, so to speak.

Objective facts, on the other hand, are those that can be understood by creatures with very different points of view. For example, he points out that there are facts about lightning that could be understood by "bat scientists" or Martians, whose experience of lightning is very different from ours. Creatures with very different subjective experience can converse with one another about objective facts even though they could not convey to one another what their respective experience of those facts is like.

Nagel's argument against reductionism

It is the subjectivity of experience, Nagel claims, that makes it impossible to reduce descriptions of experience to neurological or functional descriptions. His argument is based on an analysis of how successful reduction works. In successful cases of reduction, he argues, the reduction is always from a subjective description toward a more objective description. For example, heat is initially understood by humans in terms of the subjective impression of warmth, and only later do we come to understand it in objective terms as molecular motion. There could conceivably be creatures who do not experience heat in the way that we do, but who are nonetheless perfectly familiar with the facts about molecular motion. We could discuss with them the objective facts about heat, but we could not convey to them what our subjective experience of heat is like, what heat *feels* like to us. In reducing the observable characteristics of the physical world to the objective sciences we are replacing a concept tied to the impressions objects have on our senses to one that is not so dependent.

The fact that reduction is always in the direction of greater objectivity is the basis for Nagel's argument against mind-body reduction. For we have no idea, he says, how to give an objective description of something that is intrinsically subjective. Many different forms of life may be able to understand the objective facts about bat physiology, but only bats can know what it is like to be a bat. Hence, a neurological description of a bat, even if it is complete in every detail, will still leave out what Nagel claims is essential to the mind: the character of subjective experience. It is impossible, then, to reduce descriptions of inner mental life to descriptions of brain activity. The same would be true of the attempt to reduce subjective experience to functional properties of the brain, as functionalists advocate.

Nagel's conclusion is that we currently have no idea how materialism *could* be true. For Nagel the relationship between brain activity and consciousness is a mystery into which we have no insight. We must continue to describe ourselves in two different vocabularies: in terms of the objective facts of our neurophysiology and the subjective facts of our conscious experience. Nagel concedes that it may someday become apparent how to achieve a successful reduction of consciousness to brain activity, but this will require a notion of intertheoretic reduction utterly different from what we now understand. Under our current conception of reduction, it is contradictory to reduce subjective experience to objective facts.

Introducing qualia

The central concept in Nagel's argument is that of subjective experience, which he describes as "what it is like to be an *x*," where *x* is a kind or species of organism. This concept is intended to capture the phenomenological aspect of conscious experience. Although Nagel's characterization of the phenomenological has a certain intuitive appeal, critics have complained that it is too broad and vague. In his article, "Epiphenomenal Qualia," Frank Jackson presents an argument somewhat similar to Nagel's, but which relies on a different way of characterizing the phenomenological side of conscious experience. The term that Jackson employs is the odd word 'qualia.' This is a plural noun, the singular of which is 'quale.' In the third paragraph of his article, Jackson defines **qualia** as:

> certain features of the bodily sensations especially, but also of certain perceptual experiences, which no amount of purely physical information includes.

More fully, a **quale** is property of certain kinds of mental states, namely sensations and perceptual experiences, that cannot be described in words referring only to physical processes of the nervous system. Jackson's examples of qualia are "the hurtfulness of pains, the itchiness of itches, pangs of jealousy, or ... the characteristic experience of tasting a lemon, smelling a rose, hearing a loud noise or seeing the sky."

An important aspect of Jackson's notion of qualia is the way that this concept defines the problem of phenomenology. As Jackson conceives of it, the phenomenological element of consciousness should be seen as a set of *properties* or features that sensations and perceptual states possess. What identifies these properties as qualia is that they cannot be described in physical vocabulary. The problem of phenomenology thus becomes the problem of explaining (or explaining away) the existence of these sorts of properties. In Section III of his article, Jackson uses this feature of his characterization to differentiate his argument from Nagel's.

Jackson's argument against materialism

According to Jackson, the existence of qualia shows that materialism, or physicalism as he calls it, is false. In his view, demonstrating that there are aspects of conscious experience that physical descriptions cannot capture provides a very simple and conclusive argument for dualism. Here is the argument in the fourth paragraph:

> Nothing you could tell of a purely physical sort captures the smell of a rose, for instance. Therefore, Physicalism is false.

The premise of this argument is just the statement that qualia exist. Jackson maintains that there can be no question of the validity of the argument. His article is therefore devoted primarily to establishing the truth of the premise, from which he believes dualism follows directly. As we will see, Jackson defends a version of dualism different from those we have looked at so far. But first let's examine Jackson's defence of the premise of his argument.

Jackson's first thought experiment

Jackson's defence of his premise depends entirely on a pair of thought experiments. These thought experiments are intended to show us that we must admit the existence of aspects of conscious experience that cannot be described in physical terms.

His first thought experiment concerns a person whose visual experiences are richer than those of normally sighted people. This person, whom Jackson calls Fred, is able to perceive more shades of red than other people. Where the rest of us would see two objects of the same shade of red, Fred sees objects of two different shades. We can think of Fred as being different from normally sighted people as the normally sighted are from those who are red-green colour-blind. His visual system is capable of a greater degree of colour sensitivity than other people's.

Jackson's point is that the possibility of someone like Fred demonstrates the existence of qualia. For no amount of physical information about Fred's eyes or brain would tell us what Fred's visual experience of the additional shades of red is *like*. Even if we knew how Fred's retina responds to finer differences in the wavelengths of light than does our own, we would not thereby know what these extra colours look like to Fred.

Jackson's second thought experiment

The story of Fred is a story of someone whose visual experience is richer than our own. Jackson's second experiment makes the same point using a story of someone with impoverished visual experience. He tells the story of Mary, a brilliant neuroscientist, who knows all there is to know about the neurophysiology of vision, including how the various wavelengths of light stimulate the rods and cones of the retina and how this information is processed in the brain. The odd fact about Mary is that, for some unspecified reason, she has been forced to live all her life in a black-and-white world. She has been confined to rooms devoid of colour and receives all her information about the outside world from a black-and-white television.[1]

We also imagine that at some point in her life Mary is released from her confinement. Jackson argues that at the moment she enters the outside world, she will come to learn something she didn't know before, namely, what colours look like. And yet, *ex hypothesi*, prior to her release she already knew everything there is to know about the *physical* process of colour perception. It follows, Jackson maintains, that there is an aspect of visual experiences — their qualia — that cannot be known by understanding only the physical side of colour vision. Ergo, qualia exist.

Epiphenomenalism

In Section IV of his article, Jackson outlines his theory of the nature of qualia. Jackson's position is a version of a view called **epiphenomenalism**. This is the idea that conscious experience is a by-product of brain activity. We can illustrate the view by comparing it with Descartes' theory of the relation between mind and body. According to Descartes, the body influences the mind and vice versa. On his theory, motion in the pineal gland of the brain, caused by sensory stimulation, produces sensations in the immaterial mind. Conversely, mental activity can produce motion in the pineal gland, which in turn generates behaviour. This aspect of Descartes' theory is called **mind-body interactionism**. Epiphenomenalism agrees with the first part of Descartes' theory but denies the second. Epiphenomenalists claim that brain activity generates conscious experience, but they deny that conscious experience produces any effect on the brain or the rest of the body.

We can get an idea of epiphenomenalism by comparing this view of mind and brain to the relationship between an automobile and the exhaust fumes it produces. Exhaust fumes are always generated when the engine of an automobile is functioning. Yet the fumes do not in turn influence the action of the engine or the automobile. They are a nonefficacious by-product of engine activity. Epiphenomenalists view states of consciousness as similar in this way to exhaust fumes. They are generated by physical processes in the brain, but they themselves produce no effect on the functioning of the brain.

Jackson offers a modified version of epiphenomenalism. Although he is a dualist, in the sense that he denies the mind consists solely of the physical processes of the brain, he does not believe that the mind is a distinct *entity* from the brain. Rather he claims that qualia are nonphysical *properties* of physical brain states. This means that he holds a version of what, in chapter 9, I called property dualism. Qualia, in Jackson's view, are properties of the brain that are epiphenomenal in that they are produced by the physical activity of the brain but have no effect on that activity.

Jackson's defence of epiphenomenalism

In Section IV Jackson offers replies to a number of objections raised by critics against epiphenomenalism. The first objection is that, contrary to Jackson's view, the phenomenological character of our experience does produce effects on our physical behaviour. For example, it is the fact that pain *hurts* that causes us to avoid the things that produce it. To this Jackson replies that the connection between pain and behaviour can be explained by supposing that a physical event in the brain causes *both* the behaviour and the experience of pain. There is then no reason to suppose that the pain causes the behaviour.

The second objection that Jackson considers is that epiphenomenalism is inconsistent with evolution. Those traits that are selected through evolution, the objection runs, are those that have a positive effect on survival. Because epiphenomenal properties have no effect on survival, positive or negative, they will not be selected. Jackson's reply here is that epiphenomenal properties may be a by-product of other properties that do have a positive effect on survival, just as a bear's possessing a *heavy* coat may be the result of the survival advantage of possessing a *warm* coat.

The third objection is that if qualia have no effect on behaviour, we cannot infer their existence from behaviour; hence we can have no knowledge of qualia in other people. Jackson contends that this objection rests on a misconception of how know about qualia in others. We know from our own case that the brain events that produce certain kinds of behaviour *also* cause certain experiential states. From the behaviour of other people we can infer the existence of the same sorts of brain events as our own, and from that we can infer the existence of the experiences those brain states produce.

Qualia and Occam's Razor

The most interesting aspect of the fourth section of Jackson's article is a more general objection he sees arising from his replies. This fourth objection is that, even if the nonexistence of qualia cannot be demonstrated:

> [t]hey *do* nothing, they *explain* nothing, they serve merely to soothe the intuitions of dualists, and it is left a total mystery how they fit into the world view of science.

This is a key point, because it returns us to one of the main premises in the materialists' arguments, namely, Occam's Razor or the principle of parsimony. As we saw in chapter 9, a central aim of the sciences since the seventeenth century has to been reduce all observable phenomena to a small number of mechanical laws. Descartes, Galileo, and Newton began the project by attempting to explain all aspects of the physical world in terms of mechanical properties of matter. Reductionism in the philosophy of mind is a continuation of this same program, attempting to explain mental life in terms of the physical activity of the brain or the characteristics of machine tables.

If Jackson is correct about the existence of qualia, then there are properties of the mind that resist reduction to more fundamental elements of the world. Because qualia are epiphenomenal properties, it will be impossible to integrate our descriptions of the mind with what we know of the physical activity of the brain. However, Jackson contends that this is not a reason to reject the existence of qualia, for it rests on an over-optimistic conception of our ability to understand the world. The reductionist program assumes that all natural phenomena can be explained in terms of a set of laws *that we are able to comprehend.* Jackson rejects this optimism. He says:

> The wonder is that we understand as much as we do, and there is no wonder that there should be matters which fall quite outside our comprehension. Perhaps exactly how epiphenomenal qualia fit into the scheme of things is one such.

In Jackson's opinion, the relation between qualia and the physical world will likely remain a mystery beyond our powers to understand.

The pessimistic view of the reductionist program adopted by Jackson has been developed into a general argument against reductionism by Colin McGinn.[2] McGinn believes that there probably is a physical property of the brain that would explain the existence and nature of consciousness. However, McGinn argues that the link between this property and consciousness cannot be grasped either through introspection or through physical examination of the brain. This is because there is simply no way to bring together the concepts that describe conscious experience and the concepts of the physical sciences. As McGinn puts it, the physical nature of consciousness is "cognitively closed" to our ways of understanding the mind/brain.

Quining qualia

In an article entitled "Quining Qualia," the Tufts University philosopher Daniel Dennett directly attacks the premise of Jackson's article. Dennett is famous for a wide variety of technical and popular philosophical writings on the nature of the mind. One of his recent book-length discussions of the mind is *Consciousness Explained*, a book that attacks the Cartesian idea of a single, unitary site of conscious experience, an idea that he dubs "the Cartesian Theatre."[3]

As Dennett explains in the second paragraph of his article, the verb "**to quine**" is a humorous word that means "to deny resolutely the existence of something real or significant." It is a satirical jab at the Harvard philosopher W.V.O. Quine, who is renowned for often appearing to do precisely what the definition says. So Dennett's intent is to deny the existence of qualia. His point is that none of the features of qualia that are used to support philosophical conclusions can sustain close critical examination.

Defining qualia

Dennett's goal is to separate out the elements of consciousness that he thinks are real from the features commonly associated with the term 'qualia,' which he argues are vacuous. Consequently the precise meaning of 'qualia' is something that he develops over the course of his essay. Dennett's article is based on a succession of thought experiments, or "intuition pumps" as he calls them, designed to tease out what qualia are supposed to be and why the concept is so tangled and problematic. Because thought experiments are used to test the implications of our concepts, they are well-suited to Dennett's goal. There are too many such thought experiments in Dennett's article to consider each in detail or to look carefully at the points he draws from each. Instead I will try to isolate the highlights, leaving the close reading to you.

The first two thought experiments, which he calls *watching you eat cauliflower* and *the wine-tasting machine*, are intended to get hold of the aspects of qualia that make them the subject of philosophical debate. The first experiment is designed merely to point out the traditional conceptions that qualia are known only to individual consciousness, and that the character of qualia cannot be conveyed in words. The second experiment is a description of a machine that detects all the salient qualities of wines but, as a nonconscious machine, cannot possibly experience the real taste of a wine. From these thought experiments Dennett draws the following list of attributes commonly associated with qualia.

1. Qualia are *ineffable* in the sense that we cannot convey to others what our own experiences are really like.

2. They are *intrinsic* or *nonrelational.* This means, first, that we cannot analyze them into simpler components. For example, the way that the colour red looks to you resists any analysis into more basic elements; it is simple and homogeneous. It also means that qualia are not defined in terms of relations with other things. The property of being one metre long is a relational property; it is a matter of having a certain relationship to a standard metre stick in Paris. By contrast, it is said, the redness that I experience in my vision is not defined by any relations it has with anything else — it is defined by what it *looks like.*

3. They are *private* in that there is no way of comparing one person's conscious experience with that of another, to see, for example, whether the colour blue looks the same to both.

4. They are *directly apprehensible in consciousness,* which means that each of us has a direct, noninferential awareness of what colours look like, or sounds sound like, in our own conscious experience.

The inverted spectrum experiments

Section 3 of Dennett's article is intended to show that the intuitions supporting the notion of private, ineffable qualia are not as reliable as the simplest thought experiments suggest. In this section he considers a collection of experiments that have traditionally been used to support the idea of qualia, and argues that they are weaker than often thought. These are what are usually referred to as "inverted qualia" experiments, and they have been in use at least since John Locke.[4]

The oldest and simplest version of the inverted spectrum experiments is the idea that two people may have colour sensations in reverse of one another. For example, we might suppose that ripe tomatoes produce in you the colour sensation that in me is caused by a healthy, freshly mowed lawn, and vice versa. As we would agree in our use of words, and in every other behavioural criterion, it would be impossible to tell by any public measure whether this is the case or not. Other versions of the same story involve *intra*personal alterations in qualia. We can suppose that for some reason (say, a surgical accident) you wake up one morning to find that all your colour experiences have been reversed: Your favourite green sweater now looks a bright shade of red, and stop signs now look a dull green. The conceivability of such occurrences are used by supporters of qualia to contend that there are differences in conscious experience that transcend any behavioural, physical, or functional differences.

Dennett's argument in Section 3 is that the very nature of qualia undermines these thought experiments. Here Dennett appeals to versions of the verifiability theory of meaning that we surveyed in chapter 7. Because qualia are private and ineffable by definition, it is in principle impossible to tell whether or not a colour reversal exists between two people. Hence by the verifiability criterion, the question whether the reversal exists is meaningless. The intrapersonal versions of the story are intended to overcome this problem, because one presumes that one can tell whether one's *own* experience has changed. However, in these cases the same problem arises in other ways. Here Dennett reminds us of Wittgenstein's "private language argument." What criterion would you use to say that your *colour experience* has reversed overnight, rather than saying that your *colour memory connections* have reversed overnight? Perhaps you merely misremember how things used to look. Being mistaken about this makes no sense, Dennett argues, for there is no way to detect errors. Dennett's arguments in this section also recall Rorty's description of the experiments used to tell whether the Antipodeans have conscious experience: If no physical or verbal clues are of any use, what meaning can we attach to the idea that there is a genuine issue the experiments are intended to resolve?

Making mistakes about qualia

The fourth feature of qualia in Dennett's list of their special attributes is that they are directly apprehensible in consciousness. For example, each of us knows directly and immediately what the colour red looks like to us, and what coffee tastes like to us. This has been a standard reason for accepting that we cannot be mistaken about the qualia of our own perceptual experience. In Section 4, Dennett presents a set of thought experiments designed to put this idea into question. His stories are based on two professional coffee tasters, Chase and Sanborn. Both agree that they no longer enjoy the flavour of their company's brand of coffee. However, where one claims that his enjoyment of the flavour has diminished, the other claims that the flavour of the coffee has changed over time. Here again, Dennett's point is that there is no criterion for determining which explanation is the correct one, even in one's own case.

In what follows, Dennett considers various strategies a defender of qualia might adopt if confronted with this situation. One is to maintain infallibility by trivializing the issue. Chase and Sanborn each insist that they know how things *seem* to them, and the qualia supporter can argue that there is nothing more to the issue. (Here Dennett quotes from Wittgenstein: "Imagine someone saying: 'But I know how tall I am!' and laying his hand on top of his head to prove it.") This strategy doesn't work for the case in hand, however, for the infallibility in question also concerns the *inter*personal issue: We want Chase to be able to say that his situation is not the same as Sanborn's.

Another strategy that Dennett suggests a defender of qualia might adopt is to:

> treat qualia as *logical constructs* out of subjects' qualia-judgements: a subject's experience has the quale *F* if and only if the subject judges his experience to have quale *F*.

By this Dennett means that each person's statements about their own experiences determine what the facts are. When Chase declares that the taste of the coffee has not changed, he thereby makes it true that it hasn't changed. Asking how Chase knows that the taste of coffee hasn't changed, Dennett says, becomes the same as asking how Dostoevski knows that Raskolnikov's hair is brown. A different comparison is the act of promising: *saying* that you promise makes it true that you have promised. But here again, Dennett argues, the strategy won't work. In this case the problem is that defenders of qualia will insist that the question about Chase and Sanborn is an *empirical* one. By this Dennett means that the question is supposed to be about what their experiences are *really like*, and not just a question about what each of them *said*.

Empirical tests

Dennett points out that, as the issue is an empirical one, there will be tests we could use to help us decide whether Chase's or Sanborn's qualia have changed. We could use blind tastings, giving the two subjects the same coffee to drink and then a different coffee, to see how their judgements vary. Such a test would help us determine whether the change the subject reports is "a change near the brute perceptual processing end of the spectrum or a change near the ultimate reactive judgement end of the spectrum." By this Dennett means that the tests will help decide between two different hypotheses: (1) the subjects' experiences have changed, while their ability to judge what their experiences are remains constant; (2) their experiences have remained constant, while their judgements about those experiences have changed. There is also neurological evidence we can use to determine where along the neural pathways the change has occurred, whether it occurred relatively early on in the perceptual process, or whether it occurred at some higher level of neural activity.

In the remainder of the section, Dennett argues that these kinds of empirical tests ultimately fail to resolve the issue. In Dennett's view, there is simply no fact of the matter concerning where, in the myriad of neural activity, particular conscious experiences occur. We cannot isolate a neural event and correlate it with a particular perceptual experience or with a particular judgement. There is no fact of the matter, then, about whether Chase's and

Sanborn's qualia have changed or whether their judgements about their qualia have changed.[5]

In Section 5 Dennett describes a collection of genuine cases of perceptual impairment that have occurred as a result of brain damage.[6] In these cases too, Dennett argues, there is no simple way to determine whether the impairment is a matter of a loss or alteration of the subjects' perceptual experiences, or whether the impairment affects the subjects' abilities to judge or remember their experiences. His conclusion is that the concept of qualia provides no assistance at all in understanding what has happened in cases like these. He says:

> It seems fairly obvious to me that none of the real problems of interpretation that face us in these curious cases is advanced by any analysis of how the concept of *qualia* is to be applied — unless we wish to propose a novel, technical sense for which the traditional term might be appropriated. But that would be at least a tactical error: the intuitions that surround and *purport* to anchor the current understanding of the term are revealed to be in utter disarray when confronted with these cases.

Accounting for ineffability

In the final section of his article, Dennett turns to the question why, if the concept of qualia is so problematic, has it been so captivating? Where has the idea of private, ineffable, intrinsic properties of experience come from? In addressing this question, Dennett sketches a positive account of his own to explain these apparent elements of our conscious experience. The discussion is too complex to consider in detail, but we can isolate the main elements.

Dennett's view is that the phenomenological character of conscious experience can be explained in terms of the *information* that our perceptual states carry. For example, when I perceive an object as being blue, my visual system — the eyes and the neural pathways associated with them — is detecting a property of that object. So the visual system is collecting information about the object. The apparent features of qualia — their homogeneity, their ineffability, their privacy, and so on — merely reflect the fact that I am unable to analyze the information I am receiving.

The fact that my experience of the colour blue is simple and homogeneous means only that I can tell that the object has some kind of surface feature, although my vision does not tell me anything about that feature beyond the fact that it is similar to features of other objects. Similarly, Dennett argues that qualia appear ineffable only because we are often unable to say precisely what information a sensation carries. To illustrate, he brings in another thought experiment: a verbal description of an osprey cry will partially enable us to identify one in the field. But when we actually hear one for the first time, we have gained some additional information. We can say, "So *that's* what it sounds like." We are at a loss, however, to say what this additional information is, so it seems ineffable. Dennett contends that the reason for the apparent ineffability is that from this one experience we have actually gained very little information. We can't generalize from this experience to other osprey cries, and we can't know what other patterns of air movement might produce this same sensation. He says:

> In other words, when first I hear the osprey cry, I may have identified a property-detector in myself, but I have no idea (yet) what property my new-found property-detector detects.

Nonetheless, to the extent that my sensation is correlated with a certain kind of event in the world this experience does provide me with a certain amount of (ineffable) information.

The parenthetical word 'yet' in the previous quote is important. For Dennett points out the sensations that appear at first to be simple and unstructured can be analyzed into components with training and practice. First Dennett argues that an inability to analyze a sensory experience does not by itself show that there is nothing to be analyzed. The sound of the osprey may carry a vast amount of information that we are simply unable to extract. Dennett compares this possibility with the spy trick of using a torn piece of paper to identify the right contact person. The torn edge is so complex that we are unable to properly analyze and reproduce it. Similarly, the sound of an osprey may be instantly recognizable but so complex that our sensory organs cannot break it down. But we can be trained to analyze apparently simple sensations into their components. Here Dennett reminds us of the musical training required to hear harmonics in a single piano note or to detect the subtle components in the taste of a wine.

In Dennett's view, then, the simplicity and ineffability of sensory experiences merely reflect the paucity of information we are able to glean from what our sensory organs bring in. Dennett has carried the reductive enterprise of the scientific revolution to its full conclusion. In rejecting Aristotle's identification of sensations with real qualities of the world, Galileo and Descartes removed the phenomenological features of colours and sounds to the mind. Dennett has taken the additional step of removing them from existence altogether. The idea of simple, private, ineffable qualities of experiences are merely fictions of a mistaken picture of the mind.

Phenomenology and naturalism

Like Dennett, Owen Flanagan is unimpressed by the arguments of Nagel and Jackson, but he takes a different line of attack. Flanagan is a professor of philosophy at Duke University and the author of several books on philosophy of mind. A central theme in Flanagan's work has been an emphasis on the importance of the nineteenth-century philosopher and psychologist, William James.

According to Flanagan, subjective experience can only be understood by developing a robust and detailed phenomenology. Qualia, in his view, should not be quined. However, he argues that Dennett's characterization of qualia is exaggerated. In his view, there is no difficulty in integrating the idea of qualia, as a real property of conscious states, into a materialist theory of mind. Thus his strategy is not to resist the idea of qualia but rather to contend that nothing of significance for materialism follows from accepting the descriptions of subjective experience that Nagel and Jackson present.

We will look at chapter 6 of Flanagan's book, *Consciousness Reconsidered.* Flanagan's main concern in the book is the defence of what he calls **naturalism**. In the introduction Flanagan defines naturalism as "the view that the mind-brain relation is a natural one. Mental processes are just brain processes." One part of Flanagan's thesis, then, is that the facts about consciousness do not pose a threat to materialism. A second, important element in Flanagan's thesis is that there is no radical separation between the various ways in which the mind can be studied and described. First-person descriptions of conscious experience can be used in conjunction with psychological models of information processing and also with detailed neurological descriptions of brain activity. These various descriptions can be combined to build up a single overall picture of what goes on in the mind/brain.

Flanagan's critique of Nagel

Flanagan's critique of Nagel's argument begins in Section 4. After a summary of Nagel's argument, Flanagan identifies in the fourth paragraph what he sees as two crucial false assumptions within it. The first is Nagel's description of the nature of consciousness. According to Nagel, consciousness is a purely *subjective* phenomenon. Because objective theories leave out the subjective element of consciousness, Nagel argues, they will fail to capture its real nature. As Flanagan puts it, this means that "moving away from the phenomenological surface inevitably takes us 'farther away' from 'the real nature of the phenomenon.'"

The second assumption in Nagel's argument that Flanagan questions is the claim that "no naturalistic analysis will ... make room for the facts of first-person phenomenology." According to Nagel, scientific theories are necessarily entirely objective; the goal of scientific reduction is to replace first-person descriptions of experience with objective descriptions that do not depend on any particular "point of view." First-person phenomenology will thus be eliminated from a completed scientific theory.

Flanagan argues that neither of these assumptions is justified. First, understanding the phenomenology of consciousness requires more than a first-person perspective. Second, the need for first-person phenomenological descriptions will not be eliminated either by impersonal descriptions of consciousness or its realization in the nervous system.

Naturalistic theories of consciousness

The reason Flanagan sees these two assumptions as the fatal flaws in Nagel's argument is that they each conflict with what Flanagan sees as a central feature of a completed naturalistic theory of consciousness. According to Flanagan, a full account of consciousness will have to be constructed from *both* subjective, first-person descriptions and other disciplines such as psychology and neuroscience. This contrasts directly with Nagel's claim that subjective descriptions of the mind and objective descriptions of the brain are incompatible pictures. In the next two paragraphs Flanagan describes how such a naturalistic theory would be constructed.

The first task in building the theory is to identify the "shared phenomenological features of conscious mental life" that are common to all members of the species. This will provide a first-person account of how consciousness *seems* from the inside. The second stage will be "to see how the way things seem from the first-person point of view fit with data from other, impersonal sources: from third-person phenomenology, evolutionary theory, cognitive psychology, and neuroscience."

According to Flanagan, Nagel will reject the second stage of the project on the grounds that it will lead us away from the "true nature of consciousness." In the next three paragraphs, Flanagan argues that this assertion is of no significance. Admittedly, people have a certain special relation to our own experiences. "They, after all," Flanagan says, "are the ones who have them." Yet we do not always know better than others how things seem to us. We often say things like, "You're right, I just don't feel the same way about him anymore." Thus, although first-person subjective descriptions of consciousness provide us with a rich source of information about phenomenology, they must be combined with data from impersonal sources. "Good phenomenology," Flanagan concludes, "is group phenomenology."

Can we know what the experiences of others are like?

To defend his conception of naturalistic theories, Flanagan takes on the two assumptions that he has identified as the flaws in Nagel's argument. The first is that experience is entirely subjective. Flanagan's assertion that impersonal descriptions of subjective experiences are essential to proper descriptions of consciousness directly conflicts with this assumption.

At the heart of this issue is the question whether conscious experience is "impenetrable" or "closed off" in the sense that we cannot know what the experiences of other individuals are like. Both Nagel and Jackson seem to assume that the only way to know what a particular experience is like is to have that experience oneself. Because we are limited to our own experiences, and cannot directly share the experiences of others, the argument goes, the conscious experiences of others is unknowable. In Nagel's argument this point occurs in the assertion that we cannot know what it is like to be a bat. In Jackson's argument it underlies the assumption that Mary cannot know what colour experiences are like because she has never had one.

Flanagan contends, however, that we can know, at least to a large degree, what the experiences of others are like. Earlier in the chapter, in Section 2, he approaches this issue by recalling a question first raised by David Hume. Hume held that we have no ideas that do not originate in some manner from our sensory experiences. Flanagan refers to this as Hume's "copy theory." It follows from this claim that "a blind man can form no notion of colours; a deaf man of sounds." However, Hume does admit that we can form the idea of a colour we have not experienced, say a particular shade of blue, from our experiences of similar shades. Flanagan contends that we can do this by "mixing colours" in the imagination in a manner similar to what we do when we mix paints.

Flanagan makes this point in order to compare Hume's question with the question, can we know what the experiences of others are like? At the beginning of Section 4 Flanagan contends that the resources of the imagination, which allow us to form an idea of the missing shade of blue, allow us also to form an idea of the experiences of others — what Flanagan calls "the missing shade of you." Although we cannot form a perfect understanding of the experiences of others, we can use our own experiences together with our imagination to form a reasonably good idea.

The need for phenomenology

In the second half of Section 4, beginning with the phrase, "In his brief against naturalism," Flanagan addresses the second of the two assumptions of Nagel's argument that he has questioned. Nagel claims that, even if neural and functional analyses can explain some aspects of conscious mental states, they will not "exhaust their analysis." This assertion, Flanagan argues, rides on an overly narrow conception of naturalistic theories. Nagel characterizes naturalistic theories of consciousness as attempts to reduce consciousness to physical processes of the brain; if they were successful, they would replace the first-person, subjective knowledge of consciousness with purely physical descriptions of the nervous system.

As we have seen, Flanagan argues that the reductionist goal of replacing phenomenology with neural descriptions is a false characterization of naturalism. A completed naturalistic theory, he argues, will contain a rich phenomenology, both first-person and impersonal, as well as a theory of how consciousness is realized in the brain.

Somewhat further on Flanagan addresses Nagel's claim that it is unimaginable that a theory of how consciousness is realized in the brain could reveal "the true character of experiences." This is because the content of physical theories will never manage to convey the qualitative feel that experiences have for the subject. Flanagan argues that this assertion mistakes the real purpose of physical theories of consciousness. They are not intended to convey the character of experience; this is the job of the phenomenological part of the theory. Moreover, Flanagan argues, Nagel is mistaken about "the abstract relation between any theory and the phenomena it accounts for." By this he means that the theory, and the language it is written in, is not the experience itself.

Flanagan argues that naturalism offers the best explanation for the obvious gap between a description or theory of consciousness and the individual's immediate experience:

> Naturalism can explain why only you can capture what it is like to be you. Only your sensory receptors and brain are properly hooked up to each other and to the rest of you so that what is received at those receptors accrues to you as your experiences. That consciousness exists at all is amazing. But given that it does, Dewey is right that "there is no mystery with its being connected to what it is connected with."

Flanagan's critique of Jackson

The difference between an experience and a theory *about* an experience is also the central point in Flanagan's criticism, in Section 6, of Jackson's argument about Mary, the colour scientist. In this section Flanagan argues that Jackson requires too much from a scientific theory of colour experiences. Such a theory will explain how neural activity causes red perception, but it cannot be expected to explain what that perception is like for the percipient.

Flanagan contends that the mistake in Jackson's argument is in its first premise: "Mary (before her release) knows everything physical there is to know about other people." This premise is false, Flanagan argues. Mary knows a great deal about the physical causation of, say, the perception of the colour red. Nonetheless, red experiences are physical events, and before her release Mary doesn't know what red experiences are like. Hence there is something physical about colour perception that Mary doesn't know.

Jackson and Flanagan agree, then, that there is something that Mary doesn't know about colour perception, namely, what a red experience is like. The point of disagreement between them is whether or not this is an item of *physical* knowledge. Are red experiences physical events, and how is this to be decided? It is here that Flanagan's point about physical theories and what they explain plays a role.

In the fourth paragraph of the section, Flanagan brings in a distinction, originally made by Jerry Fodor, between two different versions of physicalism: **metaphysical** and **linguistic physicalism**:

> Metaphysical physicalism simply asserts that what there is, and all there is, is physical stuff and its relations. Linguistic physicalism is the thesis that everything physical can be expressed or captured in the languages of the basic sciences: "completed physics, chemistry, and neurophysiology."

The point of this distinction is the following. Jackson's premise that Mary knows everything physical there is to know about colour perception is based on the fact that Mary is assumed to know everything that can be conveyed in the language of the basic (i.e., physical) sciences. So Jackson must be assuming that physicalism can be true only if *linguistic* physicalism is true. Flanagan's argument is that the issue whether colour experiences are physical events does not depend on linguistic physicalism; it depends only on metaphysical physicalism. And linguistic physicalism can be false, he argues, "without metaphysical physicalism being false."

Leaving out the jargon, Flanagan's response to Jackson is this: Jackson's argument depends on the assumption that, before her release, Mary knows everything physical about colour perception there is to know. But this is argued solely on the grounds that Mary knows everything that is conveyed by the physical theories. Flanagan contends, however, that there are physical facts that are not, and could not be, conveyed by those theories, namely, what colour experiences are like. As in his critique of Nagel, then, Flanagan's point is that too much is demanded of physical theories of consciousness. Not only are they supposed to explain how experiences are realized in the brain, they are supposed to explain what those experiences are like for the percipient.

NOTES

1 We might imagine that this confinement is for medical reasons. If you prefer, you can suppose that Mary is completely colour-blind. It is a useful feature of thought experiments that we can be vague about details that do not affect the main point.

2 *The Problem of Consciousness* (Oxford: Basil Blackwell, 1991).

3 *Consciousness Explained* (Boston: Little, Brown and Company, 1991). Dennett's newest book on the philosophy of mind is *Kinds of Minds: Toward an Understanding of Consciousness* (Basic Books, 1996).

4 See Dennett's reference to Locke in Section 3.

5 For a much more detailed account, see Dennett's *Consciousness Explained*.

6 For other such cases, see the works of the neurologist, Oliver Sacks, especially *An Anthropologist on Mars* (Toronto: Alfred A. Knopf, 1995).

Thomas Nagel
"What Is It Like to Be a Bat?"

Consciousness is what makes the mind-body problem really intractable. Perhaps that is why current discussions of the problem give it little attention or get it obviously wrong. The recent wave of reductionist euphoria has produced several analyses of mental phenomena and mental concepts designed to explain the possibility of some variety of materialism, psychophysical identification, or reduction.[1] But the problems dealt with are those common to this type of reduction and other types, and what makes the mind-body problem unique, and unlike the water-H_2O problem or the Turing machine-IBM machine problem or the lightning-electrical discharge problem or the gene-DNA problem or the oak tree-hydrocarbon problem, is ignored.

Every reductionist has his favorite analogy from modern science. It is most unlikely that any of these unrelated examples of successful reduction will shed light on the relation of mind to brain. But philosophers share the general human weakness for explanations of what is incomprehensible in terms suited for what is familiar and well understood, though entirely different. This has led to the acceptance of implausible accounts of the mental largely because they would permit familiar kinds of reduction. I shall try to explain why the usual examples do not help us to understand the relation between mind and body—why, indeed, we have at present no conception of what an explanation of the physical nature of a mental phenomenon would be. Without consciousness the mind-body problem would be much less interesting. With consciousness it seems hopeless. The most important and characteristic feature of conscious mental phenomena is very poorly understood. Most reductionist theories do not even try to explain it. And careful examination will show that no currently available concept of reduction is applicable to it. Perhaps a new theoretical form can be devised for the purpose, but such a solution, if it exists, lies in the distant intellectual future.

Conscious experience is a widespread phenomenon. It occurs at many levels of animal life, though we cannot be sure of its presence in the simpler organisms, and it is very difficult to say in general what provides evidence of it. (Some extremists have been prepared to deny it even of mammals other than man.) No doubt it occurs in countless forms totally unimaginable to us, on other planets in other solar systems throughout the universe. But no matter how the form may vary, the fact that an organism has conscious experience *at all* means, basically, that there is something it is like to *be* that organism. There may be further implications about the form of the experience; there may even (though I doubt it) be implications about the behavior of the organism. But fundamentally an organism has conscious mental states if and only if there is something that it is like to *be* that organism—something it is like *for* the organism.

We may call this the subjective character of experience. It is not captured by any of the familiar, recently devised reductive analyses of the mental, for all of them are logically compatible with its absence. It is not analyzable in terms of any explanatory system of functional states, or intentional states, since these could be ascribed to robots or automata that behaved like people though they experienced nothing.[2] It is not analyzable in terms of the causal role of experiences in relation to typical human behavior —for similar reasons.[3] I do not deny that conscious mental states and events cause behavior, nor that they may be given functional characterizations. I deny only that this kind of thing exhausts their analysis. Any reductionist program has to be based on an analysis of what is to be reduced. If the analysis leaves something out, the problem will be falsely posed. It is useless to base the defense of materialism on any analysis of mental phenomena that fails to deal explicitly with their subjective character. For there is no reason to suppose that a reduction which seems plausible when no attempt is made to account for consciousness can be extended to include consciousness. Without some idea, therefore, of what the subjective character of experience is, we cannot know what is required of a physicalist theory.

While an account of the physical basis of mind must explain many things, this appears to be the most difficult. It is impossible to exclude the phenomenological features of experience from a reduction in the same way that one excludes the phenomenal features of an ordinary substance from a physical or chemical reduction of it—namely, by explaining them as effects on the minds of human observers.[4] If physicalism is to be defended, the phenomenological features must themselves be given a physical account. But when we examine their subjective character it seems that such a result is impossible. The reason is that every subjective phenomenon is essentially connected with a single point of view, and it seems inevitable that an objective, physical theory will abandon that point of view.

Let me first try to state the issue somewhat more fully than by referring to the relation between the subjective and the objective, or between the *pour-soi* and the *en-soi*. This is far from easy. Facts about what it is like to be an *X* are very peculiar, so peculiar that some may be inclined to doubt their reality, or the significance of claims about them. To illustrate the connection between subjectivity and a point of view, and to make evident the importance of subjective features, it will help to explore the matter in relation to an example that brings out clearly the divergence between the two types of conception, subjective and objective.

I assume we all believe that bats have experience. After all, they are mammals, and there is no more doubt that they have experience than that mice or pigeons or whales have experience. I have chosen bats instead of wasps or flounders because if one travels too far down the phylogenetic tree, people gradually shed their faith that there is experience there at all. Bats, although more closely related to us than those other species, nevertheless present a range of activity and a sensory apparatus so different from ours that the problem I want to pose is exceptionally vivid (though it certainly could be raised with other species). Even without the benefit of philosophical reflection, anyone who has spent some time in an enclosed space with an excited bat knows what it is to encounter a fundamentally *alien* form of life.

I have said that the essence of the belief that bats have experience is that there is something that it is like to be a bat. Now we know that most bats (the microchiroptera, to be precise) perceive the external world primarily by sonar, or echolocation, detecting the reflections, from objects within range, of their own rapid, subtly modulated, high-frequency shrieks. Their brains are designed to correlate the outgoing impulses with the subsequent echoes, and the information thus acquired enables bats to make precise discriminations of distance, size, shape, motion, and texture comparable to those we make by vision. But bat sonar, though clearly a form of perception, is not similar in its operation to any sense that we possess, and there is no reason to suppose that it is subjectively like anything we can experience or imagine. This appears to create difficulties for the notion of what it is like to be a bat. We must consider whether any method will permit us to extrapolate to the inner life of the bat from our own case,[5] and if not, what alternative methods there may be for understanding the notion.

Our own experience provides the basic material for our imagination, whose range is therefore limited. It will not help to try to imagine that one has webbing on one's arms, which enables one to fly around at dusk and dawn catching insects in one's mouth, that one has very poor vision, and perceives the surrounding world by a system of reflected high-frequency sound signals, and that one spends the day hanging upside down by one's feet in an attic. In so far as I can imagine this (which is not very far), it tells me only what it would be like for *me* to behave as a bat behaves. But that is not the question. I want to know what it is like for a *bat* to be a bat. Yet if I try to imagine this, I am restricted to the resources of my own mind, and those resources are inadequate to the task. I cannot perform it either by imagining additions to my present experience, or by imagining segments gradually subtracted from it, or by imagining some combination of additions, subtractions, and modifications.

To the extent that I could look and behave like a wasp or a bat without changing my fundamental structure, my experiences would not be anything like the experiences of those animals. On the other hand, it is doubtful that any meaning can be attached to the supposition that I should possess the internal neurophysiological constitution of a bat. Even if I could by gradual degrees be transformed into a bat, nothing in my present constitution enables me to imagine what the experiences of such a future stage of myself thus metamorphosed would be like. The best evidence would come from the experiences of bats, if we only knew what they were like.

So if extrapolation from our own case is involved in the idea of what it is like to be a bat, the extrapolation must be incompletable. We cannot form more than a schematic conception of what it *is* like. For example, we may ascribe general *types* of experience on the basis of the animal's structure and behavior. Thus we describe bat sonar as a form of three-dimensional

forward perception; we believe that bats feel some versions of pain, fear, hunger, and lust, and that they have other, more familiar types of perception besides sonar. But we believe that these experiences also have in each case a specific subjective character, which it is beyond our ability to conceive. And if there is conscious life elsewhere in the universe, it is likely that some of it will not be describable even in the most general experiential terms available to us.[6] (The problem is not confined to exotic cases, however, for it exists between one person and another. The subjective character of the experience of a person deaf and blind from birth is not accessible to me, for example, nor presumably is mine to him. This does not prevent us each from believing that the other's experience has such a subjective character.)

If anyone is inclined to deny that we can believe in the existence of facts like this whose exact nature we cannot possibly conceive, he should reflect that in contemplating the bats we are in much the same position that intelligent bats or Martians[7] would occupy if they tried to form a conception of what it was like to be us. The structure of their own minds might make it impossible for them to succeed, but we know they would be wrong to conclude that there is not anything precise that it is like to be us: that only certain general types of mental state could be ascribed to us (perhaps perception and appetite would be concepts common to us both; perhaps not). We know they would be wrong to draw such a skeptical conclusion because we know what it is like to be us. And we know that while it includes an enormous amount of variation and complexity, and while we do not possess the vocabulary to describe it adequately, its subjective character is highly specific, and in some respects describable in terms that can be understood only by creatures like us. The fact that we cannot expect ever to accommodate in our language a detailed description of Martian or bat phenomenology should not lead us to dismiss as meaningless the claim that bats and

Martians have experiences fully comparable in richness of detail to our own. It would be fine if someone were to develop concepts and a theory that enabled us to think about those things; but such an understanding may be permanently denied to us by the limits of our nature. And to deny the reality or logical significance of what we can never describe or understand is the crudest form of cognitive dissonance.

This brings us to the edge of a topic that requires much more discussion than I can give it here: namely, the relation between facts on the one hand and conceptual schemes or systems of representation on the other. My realism about the subjective domain in all its forms implies a belief in the existence of facts beyond the reach of human concepts. Certainly it is possible for a human being to believe that there are facts which humans never *will* possess the requisite concepts to represent or comprehend. Indeed, it would be foolish to doubt this, given the finiteness of humanity's expectations. After all, there would have been transfinite numbers even if everyone had been wiped out by the Black Death before Cantor discovered them. But one might also believe that there are facts which *could* not ever be represented or comprehended by human beings, even if the species lasted forever—simply because our structure does not permit us to operate with concepts of the requisite type. This impossibility might even be observed by other beings, but it is not clear that the existence of such beings, or the possibility of their existence, is a precondition of the significance of the hypothesis that there are humanly inaccessible facts. (After all, the nature of beings with access to humanly inaccessible facts is presumably itself a humanly inaccessible fact.) Reflection on what it is like to be a bat seems to lead us, therefore, to the conclusion that there are facts that do not consist in the truth of propositions expressible in a human language. We can be compelled to recognize the existence of such facts without being able to state or comprehend them.

I shall not pursue this subject, however. Its bearing on the topic before us (namely, the mind-body problem) is that it enables us to make a general observation about the subjective character of experience. Whatever may be the status of facts about what it is like to be a human being, or a bat, or a Martian, these appear to be facts that embody a particular point of view.

I am not adverting here to the alleged privacy of experience to its possessor. The point of view in question is not one accessible only to a single individual. Rather it is a *type*. It is often possible to take up a point of view other than one's own, so the comprehension of such facts is not limited to one's own case. There is a sense in which phenomenological facts are perfectly objective: one person can know or say of another what the quality of the other's experience is. They are subjective, however, in the sense that even this objective ascription of experience is possible only for someone sufficiently similar to the object of ascription to be able to adopt his point of view—to understand the ascription in the first person as well as in the third, so to speak. The more different from oneself the other experiencer is, the less success one can expect with this enterprise. In our own case we occupy the relevant point of view, but we will have as much difficulty understanding our own experience properly if we approach it from another point of view as we would if we tried to understand the experience of another species without taking up *its* point of view.[8]

This bears directly on the mind-body problem. For if the facts of experience—facts about what it is like *for* the experiencing organism— are accessible only from one point of view, then it is a mystery how the true character of experiences could be revealed in the physical operation of that organism. The latter is a domain of objective facts *par excellence*—the kind that can be observed and understood from many points of view and by individuals with differing perceptual systems. There are no comparable imaginative obstacles to the acquisition of knowledge about bat neurophysiology by human scientists, and intelligent bats or Martians might learn more about the human brain than we ever will.

This is not by itself an argument against reduction. A Martian scientist with no understanding of visual perception could understand the rainbow, or lightning, or clouds as physical phenomena, though he would never be able to understand the human concepts of rainbow, lightning, or cloud, or the place these things occupy in our phenomenal world. The objective nature of the things picked out by these concepts could be apprehended by him because, although the concepts themselves are connected with a particular point of view and a particular visual phenomenology, the things apprehended from that point of view are not: they are observable from the point of view but external to it; hence they can be comprehended from other points of view also, either by the same organisms or by others. Lightning has an objective character that is not exhausted by its visual appearance, and this can be investigated by a Martian without vision. To be precise, it has a *more* objective character than is revealed in its visual appearance. In speaking of the move from subjective to objective characterization, I wish to remain noncommittal about the existence of an end point, the completely objective intrinsic nature of the thing, which one might or might not be able to reach. It may be more accurate to think of objectivity as a direction in which the understanding can travel. And in understanding a phenomenon like lightning, it is legitimate to go as far away as one can from a strictly human viewpoint.[9]

In the case of experience, on the other hand, the connection with a particular point of view seems much closer. It is difficult to understand what could be meant by the *objective* character of an experience, apart from the particular point of view from which its subject apprehends it. After all, what would be left of

what it was like to be a bat if one removed the viewpoint of the bat? But if experience does not have, in addition to its subjective character, an objective nature that can be apprehended from many different points of view, then how can it be supposed that a Martian investigating my brain might be observing physical processes which were my mental processes (as he might observe physical processes which were bolts of lightning), only from a different point of view? How, for that matter, could a human physiologist observe them from another point of view?[10]

We appear to be faced with a general difficulty about psychophysical reduction. In other areas the process of reduction is a move in the direction of greater objectivity, toward a more accurate view of the real nature of things. This is accomplished by reducing our dependence on individual or species-specific points of view toward the object of investigation. We describe it not in terms of the impressions it makes on our senses, but in terms of its more general effects and of properties detectable by means other than the human senses. The less it depends on a specifically human viewpoint, the more objective is our description. It is possible to follow this path because although the concepts and ideas we employ in thinking about the external world are initially applied from a point of view that involves our perceptual apparatus, they are used by us to refer to things beyond themselves—toward which we *have* the phenomenal point of view. Therefore we can abandon it in favor of another, and still be thinking about the same things.

Experience itself, however, does not seem to fit the pattern. The idea of moving from appearance to reality seems to make no sense here. What is the analogue in this case to pursuing a more objective understanding of the same phenomena by abandoning the initial subjective viewpoint toward them in favor of another that is more objective but concerns the same thing? Certainly it *appears* unlikely that we will get closer to the real nature of human experience by leaving behind the particularity of our human point of view and striving for a description in terms accessible to beings that could not imagine what it was like to be us. If the subjective character of experience is fully comprehensible only from one point of view, then any shift to greater objectivity—that is, less attachment to a specific viewpoint—does not take us nearer to the real nature of the phenomenon: it takes us farther away from it.

In a sense, the seeds of this objection to the reducibility of experience are already detectable in successful cases of reduction, for in discovering sound to be, in reality, a wave phenomenon in air or other media, we leave behind one viewpoint to take up another, and the auditory, human or animal viewpoint that we leave behind remains unreduced. Members of radically different species may both understand the same physical events in objective terms, and this does not require that they understand the phenomenal forms in which those events appear to the senses of members of the other species. Thus it is a condition of their referring to a common reality that their more particular viewpoints are not part of the common reality that they both apprehend. The reduction can succeed only if the species-specific viewpoint is omitted from what is to be reduced.

But while we are right to leave this point of view aside in seeking a fuller understanding of the external world, we cannot ignore it permanently, since it is the essence of the internal world, and not merely a point of view on it. Most of the neobehaviorism of recent philosophical psychology results from the effort to substitute an objective concept of mind for the real thing, in order to have nothing left over which cannot be reduced. If we acknowledge that a physical theory of mind must account for the subjective character of experience, we must admit that no presently available conception gives us a clue how this could be done. The problem is unique. If mental processes are indeed physical processes, then there is something

it is like, intrinsically,[11] to undergo certain physical processes. What it is for such a thing to be the case remains a mystery.

What moral should be drawn from these reflections, and what should be done next? It would be a mistake to conclude that physicalism must be false. Nothing is proved by the inadequacy of physicalist hypotheses that assume a faulty objective analysis of mind. It would be truer to say that physicalism is a position we cannot understand because we do not at present have any conception of how it might be true. Perhaps it will be thought unreasonable to require such a conception as a condition of understanding. After all, it might be said, the meaning of physicalism is clear enough: mental states are states of the body; mental events are physical events. We do not know *which* physical states and events they are, but that should not prevent us from understanding the hypothesis. What could be clearer than the words "is" and "are"?

But I believe it is precisely this apparent clarity of the word "is" that is deceptive. Usually, when we are told that *X* is *Y* we know *how* it is supposed to be true, but that depends on a conceptual or theoretical background and is not conveyed by the "is" alone. We know how both "*X*" and "*Y*" refer, and the kinds of things to which they refer, and we have a rough idea how the two referential paths might converge on a single thing, be it an object, a person, a process, an event, or whatever. But when the two terms of the identification are very disparate it may not be so clear how it could be true. We may not have even a rough idea of how the two referential paths could converge, or what kind of things they might converge on, and a theoretical framework may have to be supplied to enable us to understand this. Without the framework, an air of mysticism surrounds the identification.

This explains the magical flavor of popular presentations of fundamental scientific discoveries, given out as propositions to which one must subscribe without really understanding them. For example, people are now told at an early age that all matter is really energy. But despite the fact that they know what "is" means, most of them never form a conception of what makes this claim true, because they lack the theoretical background.

At the present time the status of physicalism is similar to that which the hypothesis that matter is energy would have had if uttered by a pre-Socratic philosopher. We do not have the beginnings of a conception of how it might be true. In order to understand the hypothesis that a mental event is a physical event, we require more than an understanding of the word "is." The idea of how a mental and a physical term might refer to the same thing is lacking, and the usual analogies with theoretical identification in other fields fail to supply it. They fail because if we construe the reference of mental terms to physical events on the usual model, we either get a reappearance of separate subjective events as the effects through which mental reference to physical events is secured, or else we get a false account of how mental terms refer (for example, a causal behaviorist one).

Strangely enough, we may have evidence for the truth of something we cannot really understand. Suppose a caterpillar is locked in a sterile safe by someone unfamiliar with insect metamorphosis, and weeks later the safe is reopened, revealing a butterfly. If the person knows that the safe has been shut the whole time, he has reason to believe that the butterfly is or was once the caterpillar, without having any idea in what sense this might be so. (One possibility is that the caterpillar contained a tiny winged parasite that devoured it and grew into the butterfly.)

It is conceivable that we are in such a position with regard to physicalism. Donald Davidson has argued that if mental events have physical causes and effects, they must have physical descriptions. He holds that we have reason to believe this even though we do not—and in fact *could* not—have a general psycho-physical theory.[12] His argument applies to intentional mental events, but I think we also have some reason to believe that sensations are physical processes, without being in a position to understand how. Davidson's position is that certain physical events have irreducibly mental properties, and perhaps some view describable in this way is correct. But nothing of which we can now form a conception corresponds to it; nor have we any idea what a theory would be like that enabled us to conceive of it.[13]

Very little work has been done on the basic question (from which mention of the brain can be entirely omitted) whether any sense can be made of experiences' having an objective character at all. Does it make sense, in other words, to ask what my experiences are *really* like, as opposed to how they appear to me? We cannot genuinely understand the hypothesis that their nature is captured in a physical description unless we understand the more fundamental idea that they *have* an objective nature (or that objective processes can have a subjective nature).[14]

I should like to close with a speculative proposal. It may be possible to approach the gap between subjective and objective from another direction. Setting aside temporarily the relation between the mind and the brain, we can pursue a more objective understanding of the mental in its own right. At present we are completely unequipped to think about the subjective character of experience without relying on the imagination—without taking up the point of view of the experiential subject. This should be regarded as a challenge to form new concepts and devise a new method—an objective phenomenology not dependent on empathy or the imagination. Though presumably it would not capture everything, its goal would be to describe, at least in part, the subjective character of experiences in a form comprehensible to beings incapable of having those experiences.

We would have to develop such a phenomenology to describe the sonar experiences of bats; but it would also be possible to begin with humans. One might try, for example, to develop concepts that could be used to explain to a person blind from birth what it was like to see. One would reach a blank wall eventually, but it should be possible to devise a method of expressing in objective terms much more than we can at present, and with much greater precision. The loose intermodal analogies—for example, "Red is like the sound of a trumpet"—which crop up in discussions of this subject are of little use. That should be clear to anyone who has both heard a trumpet and seen red. But structural features of perception might be more accessible to objective description, even though something would be left out. And concepts alternative to those we learn in the first person may enable us to arrive at a kind of understanding even of our own experience which is denied us by the very ease of description and lack of distance that subjective concepts afford.

Apart from its own interest, a phenomenology that is in this sense objective may permit questions about the physical[15] basis of experience to assume a more intelligible form. Aspects of subjective experience that admitted this kind of objective description might be better candidates for objective explanations of a more familiar sort. But whether or not this guess is correct, it seems unlikely that any physical theory of mind can be contemplated until more thought has been given to the general problem of subjective and objective. Otherwise we cannot even pose the mind-body problem without sidestepping it.[16]

NOTES

1 Examples are J. J. C. Smart, *Philosophy and Scientific Realism* (London, 1963); David K. Lewis, "An Argument for the Identity Theory," *Journal of Philosophy*, LXIII (1966), reprinted with addenda in David M. Rosenthal, *Materialism & the Mind-Body Problem* Englewood Cliffs, N.J., 1971); Hilary Putnam, "Psychological

Predicates" in Capitan and Merrill, *Art, Mind, & Religion* (Pittsburgh, 1967), reprinted in Rosenthal, *op. cit.*, as "The Nature of Mental States"; D. M. Armstrong, *A Materialist Theory of the Mind* (London, 1968); D. C. Dennett, *Content and Consciousness* (London, 1969). I have expressed earlier doubts in "Armstrong on the Mind," *Philosophical Review*, LXXIX (1970), 394–403; "Brain Bisection and the Unity of Consciousness," *Synthese*, 22 (1971); and a review of Dennett, *Journal of Philosophy*, LXIX (1972). See also Saul Kripke, "Naming and Necessity" in Davidson and Hannan, *Semantics of Natural Language* (Dordrecht, 1972), esp. pp. 334–342; and M. T. Thornton, "Ostensive Terms and Materialism," *The Monist*, 56 (1972).

2 Perhaps there could not actually be such robots. Perhaps anything complex enough to behave like a person would have experiences. But that, if true, is a fact which cannot be discovered merely by analyzing the concept of experience.

3 It is not equivalent to that about which we are incorrigible, both because we are not incorrigible about experience and because experience is present in animals lacking language and thought, who have no beliefs at all about their experiences.

4 Cf. Richard Rorty, "Mind-Body Identity, Privacy, and Categories," *The Review of Metaphysics*, XIX (1965), esp. 37–38.

5 By "our own case" I do not mean just "my own case," but rather the mentalistic ideas that we apply unproblematically to ourselves and other human beings.

6 Therefore the analogical form of the English expression "what it is *like*" is misleading. It does not mean "what (in our experience) it *resembles*," but rather "how it is for the subject himself."

7 Any intelligent extraterrestrial beings totally different from us.

8 It may be easier than I suppose to transcend inter-species barriers with the aid of the imagination. For example, blind people are able to detect objects near them by a form of sonar, using vocal clicks or taps of a cane. Perhaps if one knew what that was like, one could by extension imagine roughly what it was like to possess the much more refined sonar of a bat. The distance between oneself and other persons and other species can fall anywhere on a continuum. Even for other persons the understanding of what it is like to be them is only partial, and when one moves to species very different from oneself, a lesser degree of partial understanding may still be available. The imagination is remarkably flexible. My point, however, is not that we cannot *know* what it is like to be a bat. I am not raising that epistemological problem. My point is rather that even to form a *conception* of what it is like to be a bat (and a fortiori to know what it is like to be a bat) one must take up the bat's point of view. If one can take it up roughly, or partially, then one's conception will also be rough or partial. Or so it seems in our present state of understanding.

9 The problem I am going to raise can therefore be posed even if the distinction between more subjective and more objective descriptions or viewpoints can itself be made only within a larger human point of view. I do not accept this kind of conceptual relativism, but it need not be refuted to make the point that psychophysical reduction cannot be accommodated by the subjective-to-objective model familiar from other cases.

10 The problem is not just that when I look at the "Mona Lisa," my visual experience has a certain quality, no trace of which is to be found by someone looking into my brain. For even if he did observe there a tiny image of the "Mona Lisa," he would have no reason to identify it with the experience.

11 The relation would therefore not be a contingent one, like that of a cause and its distinct effect. It would be necessarily true that a certain physical state felt a certain way. Saul Kripke *(op. cit.)* argues that causal behaviorist and related analyses of the mental fail because they construe, e.g., "pain" as a merely contingent name of pains. The subjective character of an experience ("its immediate phenomenological quality" Kripke calls it [p. 340]) is the essential property left out by such analyses, and the one in virtue of which it is, necessarily, the experience it is. My view is closely related to his. Like Kripke, I find the hypothesis that a certain brain state should *necessarily* have a certain subjective character incomprehensible without further explanation. No such explanation emerges from theories which view the mind-brain relation as contingent, but perhaps there are other alternatives, not yet discovered.

A theory that explained how the mind-brain relation was necessary would still leave us with Kripke's problem of explaining why it nevertheless appears contingent. That difficulty seems to me surmountable, in the following way. We may imagine something by representing it to ourselves either perceptually, sympathetically, or symbolically. I shall not try to say how symbolic imagination works, but part of what happens in the other two cases is this. To imagine something perceptually, we put ourselves in a conscious state resembling the state we would be in if we perceived it. To imagine something sympathetically, we put ourselves in a conscious state resembling the thing itself. (This method can be used only to imagine mental events and states—our own or another's.) When we try to imagine a mental state occurring without its associated brain state, we first sympathetically imagine the occurrence of the mental state: that is, we put ourselves into a state that resembles it mentally. At the same time, we attempt to perceptually imagine the non-occurrence of the associated physical state, by putting ourselves into another state unconnected with the first: one resembling that which we would be in if we perceived the non-occurrence of the physical state. Where the imagination of physical features is perceptual and the imagination of mental features is sympathetic, it appears to us that we can imagine any experience occurring without its associated brain state, and vice versa. The relation between them will appear contingent even if it is necessary, because of the independence of the disparate types of imagination.

(Solipsism, incidentally, results if one misinterprets sympathetic imagination as if it worked like perceptual imagination: it then seems impossible to imagine any experience that is not one's own.)

12 See "Mental Events" in Foster and Swanson, *Experience and Theory* (Amherst, 1970); though I don't understand the argument against psychophysical laws.

13 Similar remarks apply to my paper "Physicalism," *Philosophical Review* LXXIV (1965), 339–356, reprinted with postscript in John O'Connor, *Modern Materialism* (New York, 1969).

14 This question also lies at the heart of the problem of other minds, whose close connection with the mind-body problem is often overlooked. If one understood how subjective experience could have an objective nature, one would understand the existence of subjects other than oneself.

15 I have not defined the term "physical." Obviously it does not apply just to what can be described by the concepts of contemporary physics, since we expect further developments. Some may think there is nothing to prevent mental phenomena from eventually being recognized as physical in their own right. But whatever else may be said of the physical, it has to be objective. So if our idea of the physical ever expands to include mental phenomena, it will have to assign them an objective character—whether or not this is done by analyzing them in terms of other phenomena already regarded as physical. It seems to me more likely, however, that mental-physical relations will eventually be expressed in a theory whose fundamental terms cannot be placed clearly in either category.

16 I have read versions of this paper to a number of audiences, and am indebted to many people for their comments.

Frank Jackson
"Epiphenomenal Qualia"

It is undeniable that the physical, chemical and biological sciences have provided a great deal of information about the world we live in and about ourselves. I will use the label 'physical information' for this kind of information, and also for information that automatically comes along with it. For example, if a medical scientist tells me enough about the processes that go on in my nervous system, and about how they relate to happenings in the world around me, to what has happened in the past and is likely to happen in the future, to what happens to other similar and dissimilar organisms, and the like, he or she tells me—if I am clever enough to fit it together appropriately—about what is often called the functional role of those states in me (and in organisms in general in similar cases). This information, and its kin, I also label 'physical'.

I do not mean these sketchy remarks to constitute a definition of 'physical information', and of the correlative notions of physical property, process, and so on, but to indicate what I have in mind here. It is well known that there are problems with giving a precise definition of these notions, and so of the thesis of Physicalism that all (correct) information is physical information.[1] But—unlike some—I take the question of definition to cut across the central problems I want to discuss in this paper.

I am what is sometimes known as a "qualia freak". I think that there are certain features of the bodily sensations especially, but also of certain perceptual experiences, which no amount of purely physical information includes. Tell me everything physical there is to tell about what is going on in a living brain, the kind of states, their functional role, their relation to what goes on at other times and in other brains, and so on and so forth and be I as clever as can be in fitting it all together, you won't have told me about the hurtfulness of pains, the itchiness of itches, pangs of jealousy, or about the characteristic experience of tasting a lemon, smelling a rose, hearing a loud noise or seeing the sky.

There are many qualia freaks, and some of them say that their rejection of Physicalism is an unargued intuition.[2] I think that they are being unfair to themselves. They have the following argument. Nothing you could tell of a physical sort captures the smell of a rose, for instance. Therefore, Physicalism is false. By our lights this is a perfectly good argument. It is obviously not to the point to question its validity, and the premise is intuitively obviously true both to them and to me.

I must, however, admit that it is weak from a polemical point of view. There are, unfortunately for us, many who do not find the premise intuitively obvious. The task then is to present an argument whose premises are obvious to all, or at least to as many as possible. This I try to do in §I with what I will call "the Knowledge argument". In §II I contrast the Knowledge argument with the Modal argument and in §III with the "What is it like to be" argument. In §IV I tackle the question of the causal role of qualia. The major factor in stopping people from admitting qualia is the belief that they would have to be given a causal role with respect to the physical world and especially the brain;[3] and it is hard to do this without sounding like someone who believes in fairies. I seek in §IV to turn this objection by arguing that the view that qualia are epiphenomenal is a perfectly possible one.

I. The Knowledge Argument for Qualia

People vary considerably in their ability to discriminate colours. Suppose that in an experiment to catalogue this variation Fred is discovered. Fred has better colour vision than anyone else on record; he makes every discrimination that anyone has ever made, and moreover he makes one that we cannot even begin to make. Show him a batch of ripe tomatoes and he sorts them into two roughly equal groups and does so with complete consistency. That is, if you blindfold him, shuffle the tomatoes up, and then remove the blindfold and ask him to sort them out again, he sorts them into exactly the same two groups.

We ask Fred how he does it. He explains that all ripe tomatoes do not look the same colour to him, and in fact that this is true of a great many objects that we classify together as red. He sees two colours where we see one, and he has in consequence developed for his own use two words 'red$_1$' and 'red$_2$' to mark the difference. Perhaps he tells us that he has often tried to teach the difference between red$_1$ and red$_2$ to his friends but has got nowhere and has concluded that the rest of the world is red$_1$-red$_2$ colour-blind—or perhaps he has had partial success with his children, it doesn't matter. In any case he explains to us that it would be quite wrong to think that because 'red' appears in both 'red$_1$' and 'red$_2$' that the two colours are shades of the one colour. He only uses the common term 'red' to fit more easily into our restricted usage. To him red$_1$ and red$_2$ are as different from each other and all the other colours as yellow is from blue. And his discriminatory behaviour bears this out: he sorts red$_1$ from red$_2$ tomatoes with the greatest of ease in a wide variety of viewing circumstances. Moreover, an investigation of the physiological basis of Fred's exceptional ability reveals that Fred's optical system is able to separate out two groups of wave lengths in the red spectrum as sharply as we are able to sort out yellow from blue.[4]

I think that we should admit that Fred can see, really see, at least one more colour than we can; red$_1$ is a different colour from red$_2$. We are to Fred as a totally red-green colour-blind person is to us. H. G. Wells' story "The Country of the Blind" is about a sighted person in a totally blind community.[5] This person never manages to convince them that he can see, that he has an extra sense. They ridicule this sense as quite inconceivable, and treat his capacity to avoid falling into ditches, to win fights and so on as precisely that capacity and nothing more. We would be making their mistake if we refused to allow that Fred can see one more colour than we can.

What kind of experience does Fred have when he sees red$_1$ and red$_2$? What is the new colour or colours like? We would dearly like to know but do not; and it seems that no amount of physical information about Fred's brain and optical system tells us. We find out perhaps Fred's cones respond differentially to certain light waves in the red section of the spectrum that make no difference to ours (or perhaps he has an extra cone) and that this leads in Fred to a wider range of those brain states responsible for visual discriminatory behaviour. But none of this tells us what we really want to know about his colour experience. There is something about it we don't know. But we know, we may suppose, everything about Fred's body, his behaviour aud dispositions to behaviour and about his internal physiology, and everything about his history and relation to others that can be given in physical accounts of persons. We have all the physical information. Therefore, knowing all this is *not* knowing everything about Fred. It follows that Physicalism leaves something out.

To reinforce this conclusion, imagine that as a result of our investigations into the internal workings of Fred we find out how to make everyone's physiology like Fred's in the relevant respects; or perhaps Fred donates his body to science and on his death we are able to transplant his optical system into someone else—again the fine detail doesn't matter. The important point is that such a happening would create enormous interest. People would say, "At last we will know what it is like to see the extra colour, at last we will know how Fred has differed from us in the way he has struggled to tell us about for so long". Then it cannot be that we knew all along all about Fred. But *ex hypothesi* we did know all along everything about Fred that features in the physicalist scheme; hence the physicalist scheme leaves something out.

Put it this way. *After* the operation, we will know *more* about Fred and especially about his colour experiences. But beforehand we had all the physical information we could desire about his body and brain, and indeed everything that has ever featured in physicalist accounts of mind and consciousness. Hence there is more to know than all that. Hence Physicalism is incomplete.

Fred and the new colour(s) are of course essentially rhetorical devices. The same point can be made with normal people and familiar colours. Mary is a brilliant scientist who is, for whatever reason, forced to investigate the world from a black and white room *via* a black and white television monitor. She specialises in the neurophysiology of vision and acquires, let us suppose, all the physical information there is to obtain about what goes on when we see ripe tomatoes, or the sky, and use terms like 'red', 'blue', and so on. She discovers, for example, just which wave-length combinations from the sky stimulate the retina, and exactly how this produces *via* the central nervous system the contraction of the vocal chords and expulsion of air from the lungs that results in the uttering of the sentence 'The sky is blue'. (It can hardly be denied that it is in principle possible to obtain all this physical information from black and white television, otherwise the Open University would *of necessity* need to use colour television.)

What will happen when Mary is released from her black and white room or is given a colour television monitor? Will she *learn* anything or not? It seems just obvious that she will learn something about the world and our visual experience of it. But then it is inescapable that her previous knowledge was incomplete. But she had *all* the physical information. *Ergo* there is more to have than that, and Physicalism is false.

Clearly the same style of Knowledge argument could be deployed for taste, hearing, the bodily sensations and generally speaking for the various mental states which are said to have (as it is variously put) raw feels, phenomenal features or qualia. The conclusion in each case is that the qualia are left out of the physicalist story. And the polemical strength of the Knowledge argument is that it is so hard to deny the central claim that one can have all the physical information without having all the information there is to have.

II. The Modal Argument

By the Modal Argument I mean an argument of the following style.[6] Sceptics about other minds are not making a mistake in deductive logic, whatever else may be wrong with their position. No amount of physical information about another *logically entails* that he or she is conscious or feels anything at all. Consequently there is a possible world with organisms exactly like us in every physical respect (and remember that includes functional states, physical history, *et al.*) but which differ from us profoundly in that they have no conscious mental life at all. But then what is it that we have and they lack? Not anything physical *ex hypothesi*. In all physical regards we and they are exactly alike. Consequently there is more to us than the purely physical. Thus Physicalism is false.

It is sometimes objected that the Modal argument misconceives Physicalism on the ground that that doctrine is advanced as a *contingent* truth.[8] But say this is only to say that physicalists restrict their claim to *some* possible worlds, including especially ours; and the Modal argument is only directed against this lesser claim. If we in *our* world, let alone beings in any others, have features additional to those of our physical replicas in other possible worlds, then we have non-physical features or qualia.

The trouble rather with the Modal argument is that it rests on a disputable modal intuition. Disputable because it is disputed. Some sincerely deny that there can be physical replicas of us in other possible worlds which nevertheless lack consciousness. Moreover, at least one person who once had the intuition now has doubts.[9]

Head-counting may seem a poor approach to a discussion of the Modal argument. But frequently we can do no better when modal intuitions are in question, and remember our initial goal was to find the argument with the greatest polemical utility.

Of course, *qua* protagonists of the Knowledge argument we may well accept the modal intuition in question; but this will be a *consequence* of our already having an argument to the conclusion that qualia are left out of the physicalist story, not our ground for that conclusion. Moreover, the matter is complicated by the possibility that the connection between matters physical and qualia is like that sometimes held to obtain between aesthetic qualities and natural ones. Two possible worlds which agree in all "natural" respects (including the experiences of sentient creatures) must agree in all aesthetic qualities also, but it is plausibly held that the aesthetic qualities cannot be reduced to the natural.

III. The "What is it like to be" Argument

In "What is it like to be a bat?" Thomas Nagel argues that no amount of physical information can tell us what it is like to be a bat, and indeed that we, human beings, cannot imagine what it is like to be a bat.[10] His reason is that what this is like can only be understood from a bat's point of view, which is not our point of view and is not something capturable in physical terms which are essentially terms understandable equally from many points of view.

It is important to distinguish this argument from the Knowledge argument. When I complained that all the physical knowledge about Fred was not enough to tell us what his special colour experience was like, I was not complaining that we weren't finding out what it is like to *be* Fred. I was complaining that there is something *about* his experience, a property of it, of which we were left ignorant. And if and when we come to know what this property is we still will not know what it is like to *be* Fred, but we will know more *about* him. No amount of knowledge about Fred, be it physical or not, amounts to knowledge "from the inside" concerning Fred. We are not Fred. There is thus a whole set of items of knowledge expressed by forms of words like 'that it is *I myself* who is ...' which Fred has and we simply cannot have because we are not him.[11]

When Fred sees the colour he alone can see, one thing he knows is the way his experience of it differs from his experience of seeing red and so on, *another* is that he himself is seeing it. Physicalist and qualia freaks alike should acknowledge that no amount of information of whatever kind that *others* have *about* Fred amounts to knowledge of the second. My complaint though concerned the first and was that the special quality of his experience is certainly a fact about it, and one which Physicalism leaves out because no amount of physical information told us what it is.

Nagel speaks as if the problem he is raising is one of extrapolating from knowledge of one experience to another, of imagining what an unfamiliar experience would be like on the basis of familiar ones. In terms of Hume's example, from knowledge of some shades of blue we can work out what it would be like to see other shades of blue. Nagel argues that the trouble with bats *et al.* is that they are too unlike us. It is hard to see an objection to Physicalism here. Physicalism makes no special claims about the imaginative or extrapolative powers of human beings, and it is hard to see why it need do so.[12]

Anyway, our Knowledge argument makes no assumptions on this point. If Physicalism were true, enough physical information about Fred would obviate any need to extrapolate or to perform special feats of imagination or understanding in order to know all about his special colour experience. *The information would already be in our possession.* But it clearly isn't. That was the nub of the argument.

IV. The Bogey of Epiphenomenalism

Is there any really *good* reason for refusing to countenance the idea that qualia are causally impotent with respect to the physical world? I will argue for the answer no, but in doing this I will say nothing about two views associated with the classical epiphenomenalist position. The first is that mental *states* are inefficacious with respect to the physical world. All I will be concerned to defend is that it is possible to hold that certain *properties* of certain mental states, namely those I've called qualia, are such that their possession or absence makes no difference to the physical world. The second is that the mental is *totally* causally inefficacious. For all I will say it may be that you have to hold that the instantiation of *qualia* makes a difference to *other mental states* though not to anything physical. Indeed general considerations to do with how you could come to be aware of the instantiation of qualia suggest such a position.[13]

Three reasons are standardly given for holding that a quale like the hurtfulness of a pain must be causally efficacious in the physical world, and so, for instance, that its instantiation must sometimes make a difference to what happens in the brain. None, I will argue, has any

real force. (I am much indebted to Alec Hyslop and John Lucas for convincing me of this.)

(i) It is supposed to be just obvious that the hurtfulness of pain is partly responsible for the subject seeking to avoid pain, saying 'It hurts' and so on. But, to reverse Hume, anything can fail to cause anything. No matter how often *B* follows *A*, and no matter how initially obvious the causality of the connection seems, the hypothesis that *A* causes *B* can be overturned by an over-arching theory which shows the two as distinct effects of a common underlying causal process.

To the untutored the image on the screen of Lee Marvin's fist moving from left to right immediately followed by the image of John Wayne's head moving in the same general direction looks as causal as anything.[14] And of course throughout countless Westerns images similar to the first are followed by images similar to the second. All this counts for precisely nothing when we know the over-arching theory concerning how the relevant images are both effects of an underlying causal process involving the projector and the film. The epiphenomenalist can say exactly the same about the connection between, for example, hurtfulness and behaviour. It is simply a consequence of the fact that certain happenings in the brain cause both.

(ii) The second objection relates to Darwin's Theory of Evolution. According to natural selection the traits that evolve over time are those conducive to physical survival. We may assume that qualia evolved over time—we have them, the earliest forms of life do not—and so we should expect qualia to be conducive to survival. The objection is that they could hardly help us to survive if they do nothing to the physical world.

The appeal of this argument is undeniable, but there is a good reply to it. Polar bears have particularly thick, warm coats. The Theory of Evolution explains this (we suppose) by pointing out that having a thick, warm coat is conducive to survival in the Arctic. But having a thick coat goes along with having a heavy coat, and having a heavy coat is *not* conducive to survival. It slows the animal down.

Does this mean that we have refuted Darwin because we have found an evolved trait—having a heavy coat—which is not conducive to survival? Clearly not. Having a heavy coat is an unavoidable concomitant of having a warm coat (in the context, modern insulation was not available), and the advantages for survival of having a warm coat outweighed the disadvantages of having a heavy one. The point is that all we can extract from Darwin's theory is that we should expect any evolved characteristic to be *either* conducive to survival *or* a by-product of one that is so conducive. The epiphenomenalist holds that qualia fall into the latter category. They are a by-product of certain brain processes that are highly conducive to survival.

(iii) The third objection is based on a point about how we come to know about other minds. We know about other minds by knowing about other behaviour, at least in part. The nature of the inference is a matter of some controversy, but it is not a matter of controversy that it proceeds from behaviour. That is why we think that stones do not feel and dogs do feel. But, runs the objection, how can a person's behaviour provide any reason for believing he has qualia like mine, or indeed any qualia at all, unless this behaviour can be regarded as the *outcome* of the qualia. Man Friday's footprint was evidence of Man Friday because footprints are causal outcomes of feet attached to people. And an epiphenomenalist cannot regard behaviour, or indeed anything physical, as an outcome of qualia.

But consider my reading in *The Times* that Spurs won. This provides excellent evidence that *The Telegraph* has also reported that Spurs won, despite the fact that (I trust) *The Telegraph* does not get the results from *The Times*. They each send their own reporters to the game. *The Telegraph's* report is in no sense an outcome of *The Times'*, but the latter provides good evidence for the former nevertheless.

The reasoning involved can be reconstructed thus. I read in *The Times* that Spurs won. This gives me reason to think that Spurs won because I know that Spurs' winning is the most likely candidate to be what caused the report in *The Times*. But I also know that Spurs' winning would have had many effects, including almost certainly a report in *The Telegraph*.

I am arguing from one effect back to its cause and out again to another effect. The fact that neither effect causes the other is irrelevant. Now the epiphenomenalist allows that qualia are effects of what goes on in the brain. Qualia cause nothing physical but are caused by something physical. Hence the epiphenomenalist can argue from the behaviour of others to the qualia of others by arguing from the behaviour of others back to its causes in the brains of others and out again to their qualia.

You may well feel for one reason or another that this is a more dubious chain of reasoning than its model in the case of newspaper reports. You are right. The problem of other minds is a major philosophical problem, the problem of other newspaper reports is not. But there is no special problem of Epiphenomenalism as opposed to, say, Interactionism here.

There is a very understandable response to the three replies I have just made. "All right, there is no knockdown refutation of the existence of epiphenomenal qualia. But the fact remains that they are an excrescence. They *do* nothing, they *explain* nothing, they serve merely to soothe the intuitions of dualists, and it is left a total mystery how they fit into the world view of science. In short we do not and cannot understand the how and why of them."

This is perfectly true; but is no objection to qualia, for it rests on an overly optimistic view of the human animal, and its powers. We are the products of Evolution. We understand and sense what we need to understand and sense in order to survive. Epiphenomenal qualia are totally irrelevant to survival. At no stage of our evolution did natural selection favour those who could make sense of how they are caused and the laws governing them, or in fact why they exist at all. And that is why we can't.

It is not sufficiently appreciated that Physicalism is an extremely optimistic view of our powers. If it is true, we have, in very broad outline admittedly, a grasp of our place in the scheme of things. Certain matters of sheer complexity defeat us—there are an awful lot of neurons—but in principle we have it all. But consider the antecedent probability that everything in the Universe be of a kind that is relevant in some way or other to the survival of *Homo sapiens*. It is very low surely. But then one must admit that it is very likely that there is a part of the whole scheme of things, maybe a big part, which no amount of evolution will ever bring us near to knowledge about or understanding. For the simple reason that such knowledge and understanding is irrelevant to survival.

Physicalists typically emphasise that we are a part of nature on their view, which is fair enough. But if we are a part of nature, we are as nature has left us after however many years of evolution it is, and each step in that evolutionary progression has been a matter of chance constrained just by the need to preserve or increase survival value. The wonder is that we understand as much as we do, and there is no wonder that there should be matters which fall quite outside our comprehension. Perhaps exactly how epiphenomenal qualia fit into the scheme of things is one such.

This may seem an unduly pessimistic view of our capacity to articulate a truly comprehensive picture of our world and our place in it. But suppose we discovered living on the bottom of the deepest oceans a sort of sea slug which manifested intelligence. Perhaps survival in the conditions required rational powers. Despite their intelligence, these sea slugs have only a very restricted conception of the world by comparison with ours, the explanation for this being the nature of their immediate environment. Nevertheless they have developed sciences which work surprisingly well in these restricted terms. They also have philosophers, called slugists. Some call themselves toughminded slugists, others confess to being softminded slugists.

The tough-minded slugists hold that the restricted terms (or ones pretty like them which may be introduced as their sciences progress) suffice in principle to describe everything without remainder. These tough-minded slugists admit in moments of weakness to a feeling that their theory leaves something out. They resist this feeling and their opponents, the softminded slugists, by pointing out—absolutely correctly—that no slugist has ever succeeded in spelling out how this mysterious residue fits into the highly successful view that their sciences have and are developing of how their world works.

Our sea slugs don't exist, but they might. And there might also exist super beings which stand to us as we stand to the sea slugs. We cannot adopt the perspective of these super beings, because we are not them, but the possibility of such a perspective is, I think, an antidote to excessive optimism.[15]

NOTES

1. See, e.g., D. H. Mellor, "Materialism and Phenomenal Qualities", *Aristotelian Society Supp.* Vol. 47 (1973), 107–19; and J. W. Cornman, *Materialism and Sensations* (New Haven and London, 1971).

2. Particularly in discussion, but see, e.g., Keith Campbell, *Metaphysics* (Belmont, 1976), p. 67.

3. See, e.g., D. C. Dennett, "Current Issues in the Philosophy of Mind", *American Philosophical Quarterly*, 15 (1978), 249–61.

4. Put this, and similar simplifications below, in terms of Land's theory if you prefer. See, e.g., Edwin H. Land, "Experiments in Color Vision", *Scientific American*, 200 (5 May 1959), 54–99.

5. H. G. Wells, *The Country of the Blind and Other Stories* (London, n.d.).

6. See, e.g., Keith Campbell, *Body and Mind* (New York, 1970); and Robert Kirk, "Sentience and Behaviour", *Mind*, 83 (1974), 43–60.

7. I have presented the argument in an inter-world rather than the more usual intra-world fashion to avoid inessential complications to do with supervenience, causal anomalies and the like.

8. See, e.g., W. G. Lycan, "A New Lilliputian Argument Against Machine Functionalism", *Philosophical Studies*, 35 (1979), 279–87, p. 280; and Don Locke, "Zombies, Schizophrenics and Purely Physical Objects", *Mind*, 85 (1976), 97–9.

9. See R. Kirk, "From Physical Explicability to Full-Blooded Materialism", *The Philosophical Quarterly*, 29 (1979), 229–37. See also the arguments against the modal intuition in, e.g., Sydney Shoemaker, "Functionalism and Qualia", *Philosophical Studies*, 27 (1975), 291–315.

10. *The Philosophical Review*, 83 (1974), 435–50. Two things need to be said about this article. One is that, despite my dissociations to come, I am much indebted to it. The other is that the emphasis changes through the article, and by the end Nagel is objecting not so much to Physicalism as to all extant theories of mind for ignoring points of view, including those that admit (irreducible) qualia.

11. Knowledge *de se* in the terms of David Lewis, "Attitudes De Dicto and De Se", *The Philosophical Review*, 88 (1979), 513–43.

12. See Laurence Nemirow's comments on "What is it ..." in his review of T. Nagel, *Mortal Questions* in *The Philosophical Review*, 89 (1980), 473–7. I am indebted here in particular to a discussion with David Lewis.

13. See my review of K. Campbell, *Body and Mind*, in *Australasian Journal of Philosophy*, 50 (1972), 77–80.

14. Cf. Jean Piaget, "The Child's Conception of Physical Causality", reprinted in *The Essential Piaget* (London, 1977).

15. I am indebted to Robert Pargetter for a number of comments and, despite his dissent, to §IV of Paul E. Meehl, "The Compleat Autocerebroscopist" in *Mind, Matter, and Method*, ed. Paul Feyerabend and Grover Maxwell (Minneapolis, 1966).

Daniel C. Dennett
"Quining Qualia"

1 Corralling the quicksilver

"Qualia" is an unfamiliar term for something that could not be more familiar to each of us: the *ways things seem to us*. As is so often the case with philosophical jargon, it is easier to give examples than to give a definition of the term. Look at a glass of milk at sunset; *the way it looks to you*—the particular, personal, subjective visual quality of the glass of milk is the *quale* of your visual experience at the moment. The *way the milk tastes to you then* is another, gustatory, *quale*, and *how it sounds to you* as you swallow is an auditory *quale*. These various "properties of conscious experience" are prime examples of *qualia*. Nothing, it seems, could you know more intimately than your own qualia; let the entire universe be some vast illusion, some mere figment of Descartes's evil demon, and yet what the figment is *made of* (for you) will be the *qualia* of your hallucinatory experiences. Descartes claimed to doubt everything that could be doubted, but he never doubted that his conscious experiences had qualia, the properties by which he knew or apprehended them.

The verb "to quine" is even more esoteric. It comes from *The Philosophical Lexicon* (Dennett 1978c, 8th edn 1987), a satirical dictionary of eponyms: "quine, *v.* To deny resolutely the existence or importance of something real or significant." At first blush it would be hard to imagine a more quixotic quest than trying to convince people that there are no such properties as qualia; hence the ironic title of this chapter. But I am not kidding.

My goal is subversive. I am out to overthrow an idea that, in one form or another, is "obvious" to most people—to scientists, philosophers, lay people. My quarry is frustratingly elusive; no sooner does it retreat in the face of one argument than "it" reappears, apparently innocent of all charges, in a new guise.

Which idea of qualia am I trying to extirpate? Everything real has properties, and since I don't deny the reality of conscious experience, I grant that conscious experience has properties. I grant moreover that each person's states of consciousness have properties in virtue of which those states have the experiential content that they do. That is to say, whenever someone experiences something as being one way rather than another, this is true in virtue of some property of something happening in them at the time, but these properties are so unlike the properties traditionally imputed to consciousness that it would be grossly misleading to call any of them the long-sought qualia. Qualia are supposed to be *special* properties, in some hard-to-define way. My claim—which can only come into focus as we proceed—is that conscious experience has *no* properties that are special in *any* of the ways qualia have been supposed to be special.

The standard reaction to this claim is the complacent acknowledgment that while some people may indeed have succumbed to one confusion or fanaticism or another, one's own appeal to a modest, innocent notion of properties of subjective experience is surely safe. It is just that presumption of innocence I want to overthrow. I want to shift the burden of proof, so that anyone who wants to appeal to private, subjective properties has to prove first that in so doing they are *not* making a mistake. This status of *guilty until proven innocent* is neither unprecedented nor indefensible (so long as we restrict ourselves to concepts). Today, no biologist would dream of supposing that it was quite all right to appeal to some innocent concept of *élan vital.* Of course one *could* use the term to mean something in good standing; one could use *élan vital* as one's name for DNA, for instance, but this would be foolish nomenclature, considering the deserved suspicion with which the term is nowadays burdened. I want to make it just as uncomfortable for anyone to talk of qualia—or "raw feels" or "phenomenal properties" or "subjective and intrinsic properties" or "the qualitative character" of experience—with the standard presumption that they, and everyone else, knows what on earth they are talking about.[1]

What are qualia, *exactly*? This obstreperous query is dismissed by one author ("only half in jest") by invoking Louis Armstrong's legendary reply when asked what jazz was: "If you got to ask, you ain't never gonna get to know" (Block 1978 p. 281). This amusing tactic perfectly illustrates the presumption that is my target. If I succeed in my task, this move, which passes muster in most circles today, will look as quaint and insupportable as a jocular appeal to the ludicrousness of a living thing—a living thing, mind you!—doubting the existence of *élan vital.*

My claim, then, is not just that the various technical or theoretical concepts of qualia are vague or equivocal, but that the source concept, the "pretheoretical" notion of which the former are presumed to be refinements, is so thoroughly confused that even if we undertook to salvage some "lowest common denominator" from the theoreticians' proposals, any acceptable version would have to be so radically unlike the ill-formed notions that are commonly appealed to that it would be tactically obtuse—not to say Pickwickian—to cling to the term. Far better, tactically, to declare that there simply are no qualia at all.[2]

Rigorous arguments only work on well-defined materials, and since my goal is to destroy our faith in the pretheoretical or "intuitive" concept, the right tools for my task are intuition pumps, not formal arguments. What follows is a series of fifteen intuition pumps, posed in a sequence designed to flush out—and then flush away—the offending intuitions. In section 2, I will use the first two intuition pumps to focus attention on the traditional notion. It will be the burden of the rest of the paper to convince you that these two pumps, for all their effectiveness, mislead us and should be discarded. In section 3, the next four intuition pumps create and refine a "paradox" lurking in the tradition. This is not a formal paradox, but only a very powerful argument pitted against some almost irresistibly attractive ideas. In section 4, six more intuition pumps are arrayed in order to dissipate the attractiveness of those ideas, and section 5 drives this point home by showing how hapless those ideas prove to be when confronted with some real cases of anomalous experience. This will leave something of a vacuum, and in the final section three more intuition pumps are used to introduce and motivate some suitable replacements for the banished notions.

2 The special properties of qualia

Intuition pump #1: watching you eat cauliflower. I see you tucking eagerly into a helping of steaming cauliflower, the merest whiff of which makes me faintly nauseated, and I find myself wondering how you could possibly relish *that taste,* and then it occurs to me that to you, cauliflower probably tastes (must taste?) different. A plausible hypothesis, it seems, especially since I know that the very same food often tastes different to me at different times. For instance, my first sip of breakfast orange juice tastes much sweeter than my second sip if I interpose a bit of pancakes and maple syrup, but after a swallow or two of coffee, the orange juice goes back to tasting (roughly? exactly?) the way it did the first sip. Surely we want to say (or think about) such things, and surely we are not wildly wrong when we do, so ... surely it is quite OK to talk of *the way the juice tastes to Dennett at time t,* and ask whether it is just the same as or different from the way the juice tastes to Dennett at time t′ or the way the juice tastes to Jones at time t.

This "conclusion" seems innocent, but right here we have already made the big mistake. The final step presumes that we can isolate the qualia from everything else that is going on—at least in principle or for the sake of argument. What counts as *the way the juice tastes to x* can be distinguished, one supposes, from what is a mere accompaniment, contributory cause, or by-product of this "central" way. One dimly imagines taking such cases and stripping them down gradually to the essentials, leaving their common residuum, the way things look, sound, feel, taste, smell to various individuals at various times, independently of how those individuals are stimulated or non-perceptually affected, and independently of how they are subsequently disposed to behave or believe. The mistake is not in supposing that we can in practice ever or always perform this act of purification with certainty, but the more fundamental mistake of supposing that there is such a residual property to take seriously, however uncertain our actual attempts at isolation of instances might be.

The examples that seduce us are abundant in every modality. I cannot imagine, will never know, could never know, it seems, how Bach sounded to Glenn Gould. (I can barely recover in my memory the way Bach sounded to me when I was a child.) And I cannot know, it seems, what it is like to be a bat (Nagel 1974), or whether you see what I see, colorwise, when we look up at a clear "blue" sky. The homely cases convince us of the reality of these special properties—those subjective tastes, looks, aromas, sounds—that we then apparently isolate for definition by this philosophical distillation.

The specialness of these properties is hard to pin down, but can be seen at work in *intuition pump #2: the wine-tasting machine.* Could Gallo Brothers replace their human wine tasters with a machine? A computer-based "expert system" for quality control and classification is probably within the bounds of existing technology. We now know enough about the relevant chemistry to make the transducers that would replace taste buds and olfactory organs (delicate color vision would perhaps be more problematic), and we can imagine using the output of such transducers as the raw material—the "sense data" in effect—for elaborate evaluations, descriptions, classifications. Pour the sample in the funnel and, in a few minutes or hours, the system would type out a chemical assay, along with commentary: "a flamboyant and velvety Pinot, though lacking in stamina"—or words to such effect. Such a machine might well perform better than human wine tasters on all reasonable tests of accuracy and consistency the winemakers could devise,[3] but *surely* no matter how "sensitive" and "discriminating" such a system becomes, it will never have, and enjoy, what *we* do when we taste a wine: the qualia of conscious experience! Whatever informational, dispositional, functional properties its internal states have, none of them will be special in the way qualia are. If you share that intuition, you believe that there are qualia in the sense I am targeting for demolition.

What is special about qualia? Traditional analyses suggest some fascinating second-order properties of these properties. First, since one *cannot say* to another, no matter how eloquent one is and no matter how cooperative and imaginative one's audience is, exactly what way one is currently seeing, tasting, smelling and so forth, qualia are *ineffable*—in fact the paradigm cases of ineffable items. According to tradition, at least part of the reason why qualia are ineffable is that they are *intrinsic* properties—which seems to imply *inter alia* that they are somehow atomic and unanalyzable. Since they are "simple" or "homogeneous" there is nothing to get hold of when trying to describe such a property to one unacquainted with the particular instance in question.

Moreover, verbal comparisons are not the only cross-checks ruled out. *Any* objective, physiological or "merely behavioral" test—such as those passed by the imaginary wine-tasting system—would of necessity miss the target (one can plausibly argue), so all interpersonal comparisons of these ways-of-appearing are (apparently) systematically impossible. In other words, qualia are essentially *private* properties. And, finally, since they *are* properties of *my experiences* (they're not chopped liver, and they're not properties of, say, my cerebral blood flow—or haven't you been paying attention?), qualia are essentially directly accessible to the consciousness of their experiencer (whatever that means) or qualia are properties of one's experience with which one is intimately or directly acquainted (whatever that means) or "immediate phenomenological qualities" (Block 1978) (whatever that means). They are, after all, the very properties the appreciation of which permits us to identify our conscious states. So, to summarize the tradition, qualia are supposed to be properties of a subject's mental states that are

1 ineffable
2 intrinsic
3 private
4 directly or immediately apprehensible in consciousness.

Thus are qualia introduced onto the philosophical stage. They have seemed to be very significant properties to some theorists because they have seemed to provide an insurmountable and unavoidable stumbling block to functionalism, or more broadly, to materialism, or more broadly still, to any purely "third-person" objective viewpoint or approach to the world (Nagel 1986). Theorists of the contrary persuasion have patiently and ingeniously knocked down all the arguments, and said most of the right things, but they have made a tactical error, I am claiming, of saying in one way or another: "We theorists can handle *those qualia* you talk about just fine; we will show that you are just slightly in error about the nature of qualia." What they ought to have said is: "What qualia?"

My challenge strikes some theorists as outrageous or misguided because they think they have a much blander and hence less vulnerable notion of qualia to begin with. They think I am setting up and knocking down a strawman, and ask, in effect: "Who said qualia are ineffable, intrinsic, private, directly apprehensible ways things seem to one?" Since my suggested fourfold essence of qualia may strike many readers as tendentious, it may be instructive to consider, briefly, an apparently milder alternative: qualia are simply "the qualitative or phenomenal features of sense experience[s], in virtue of having which they resemble and differ from each other, qualitatively, in the ways they do" (Shoemaker 1982, p. 367). Surely I do not mean to deny *those* features!

I reply: it all depends on what "qualitative or phenomenal" comes to. Shoemaker contrasts *qualitative* similarity and difference with "intentional" similarity and difference—similarity and difference of the properties an experience represents or is "of". That is clear enough, but what then of "phenomenal"? Among the nonintentional (and hence qualitative?) properties of my visual states are their physiological properties. Might these very properties be the qualia Shoemaker speaks of? It is supposed to be obvious, I take it, that these sorts of features are ruled out, because they are not "accessible to introspection" (Shoemaker, private correspondence). These are features of my visual *state*, perhaps, but not of my visual *experience*. They are not *phenomenal* properties.

But then another non-intentional similarity some of my visual states share is that they tend to make me think about going to bed. I think this feature of them *is* accessible to introspection—on any ordinary, pretheoretical construal. Is that a phenomenal property or not? The term "phenomenal" means nothing obvious and untendentious to me, and looks suspiciously like a gesture in the direction leading back to ineffable, private, directly apprehensible ways things seem to one.[4]

I suspect, in fact, that many are unwilling to take my radical challenge seriously largely because they want so much for qualia to be acknowledged. Qualia seem to many people to be the last ditch defense of the inwardness and elusiveness of our minds, a bulwark against creeping mechanism. They are sure there must be *some* sound path from the homely cases to the redoubtable category of the philosophers, since otherwise their last bastion of specialness will be stormed by science.

This special status for these presumed properties has a long and eminent tradition. I believe it was Einstein who once advised us that science could not give us the *taste* of the soup. Could such a wise man have been wrong? Yes, if he is taken to have been trying to remind us of the qualia that hide forever from objective science in the subjective inner sancta of our minds. There are no such things. Another wise man said so—Wittgenstein (1958, esp. pp. 91–100). Actually, what he said was:

> The thing in the box has no place in the language-game at all; not even as a *something*, for the box might even be empty.—No, one can "divide through" by the thing in the box; it cancels out, whatever it is. (p. 100)

and then he went on to hedge his bets by saying "It is not a *something*, but not a *nothing* either! The conclusion was only that a nothing would serve just as well as a something about which nothing could be said" (p. 102). Both Einstein's and Wittgenstein's remarks are endlessly amenable to exegesis, but rather than undertaking to referee this War of the Titans, I choose to take what may well be a more radical stand than Wittgenstein's.[5] Qualia are not even "something about which nothing can be said"; "qualia" is a philosophers' term which fosters[6] nothing but confusion, and refers in the end to no properties or features at all.

3 The traditional paradox regained

Qualia have not always been in good odor among philosophers. Although many have thought, along with Descartes and Locke, that it made sense to talk about private, ineffable properties of minds, others have argued that this is strictly nonsense—however naturally it trips off the tongue. It is worth recalling how qualia were presumably rehabilitated as properties to be taken seriously in the wake of Wittgensteinian and verificationist attacks on them as pseudo-hypotheses. The original version of *intuition pump #3: the inverted spectrum* (Locke 1690: II, xxxii, 15) is a speculation about two people: how do I know that you and I see the same subjective color when we look at something? Since we both learned color words by being shown public colored objects, our verbal behavior will match *even if we experience entirely different subjective colors*. The intuition that this hypothesis is systematically unconfirmable (and undisconfirmable, of course) has always been quite robust, but some people have always been tempted to think technology could (in principle) bridge the gap.

Suppose, in *intuition pump #4: the Brainstorm machine*, there were some neuroscientific apparatus that fits on your head and feeds your visual experience into my brain (as in the movie, *Brainstorm*, which is not to be confused with the book, *Brainstorms*). With eyes closed I accurately report everything you are looking at, except that I marvel at how the sky is yellow, the grass red, and so forth. Would this not confirm, empirically, that our qualia were different? But suppose the technician then pulls the plug on the connecting cable, inverts it 180 degrees and reinserts it in the socket. Now I report the sky is blue, the grass green, and so forth. Which is the "right" orientation of the plug? Designing and building such a device would require that its "fidelity" be tuned or calibrated by the normalization of the two subjects' reports—so we would be right back at our evidential starting point. The moral of this intuition pump is that no intersubjective comparison of qualia is possible, even with perfect technology.

So matters stood until someone dreamt up the presumably improved version of the thought experiment: the *intra*personal inverted spectrum. The idea seems to have occurred to several people independently (Gert 1965; Putnam 1965; Taylor 1966; Shoemaker 1969, 1975; Lycan 1973). Probably Block and Fodor (1972) have it in mind when they say "It seems to us that the standard verificationist counter-arguments against the view that the 'inverted spectrum' hypothesis is conceptually incoherent are not persuasive" (p. 172). In this version, *intuition pump #5: the neurosurgical prank*, the experiences to be compared are all in one mind. You wake up one morning to find that the grass has turned red, the sky yellow, and so forth. No one else notices any color anomalies in the world, so the problem must be in you. You are entitled, it seems, to conclude that you have undergone visual color qualia inversion (and we later discover, if you like, just how the evil neurophysiologists tampered with your neurons to accomplish this).

Here it seems at first—and indeed for quite a while—that qualia are acceptable properties after all, because propositions about them can be justifiably asserted, empirically verified and even explained. After all, in the imagined case, we can tell a tale in which we confirm a detailed neurophysiological account of the precise etiology of the dramatic change you undergo. It is tempting to suppose, then, that neurophysiological evidence, incorporated into a robust and ramifying theory, would have all the resolving power we could ever need for determining whether or not someone's qualia have actually shifted.

But this is a mistake. It will take some patient exploration to reveal the mistake in depth, but the conclusion can be reached—if not secured—quickly with the help of *intuition pump*

#6: alternative neurosurgery. There are (at least) two different ways the evil neurosurgeon might create the inversion effect described in intuition pump #5:

I Invert one of the "early" qualia-producing channels, e.g. in the optic nerve, so that all relevant neural events "downstream" are the "opposite" of their original and normal values. *Ex hypothesi* this inverts your qualia.

II Leave all those early pathways intact and simply invert certain memory-access links—whatever it is that accomplishes your tacit (and even unconscious!) comparison of today's hues with those of yore. *Ex hypothesi* this does *not* invert your qualia at all, but just your memory-anchored dispositions to react to them.

On waking up and finding your visual world highly anomalous, you should exclaim "Egad! *Something* has happened! Either my qualia have been inverted or my memory-linked qualia-reactions have been inverted. I wonder which!"

The intrapersonal inverted spectrum thought experiment was widely supposed to be an improvement, since it moved the needed comparison into one subject's head. But now we can see that this is an illusion, since the link to earlier experiences, the link via memory, is analogous to the imaginary cable that might link two subjects in the original version.

This point is routinely—one might say traditionally—missed by the constructors of "intrasubjective inverted spectrum" thought experiments, who suppose that the subject's *noticing the difference*—surely a vivid experience of discovery by the subject—would have to be an instance of (directly? incorrigibly?) recognizing the difference as *a shift in qualia.* But as my example shows, we could achieve the same startling effect in a subject without tampering with his presumed qualia at all. Since *ex hypothesi* the two different surgical invasions can produce exactly the same introspective effects while only one operation inverts the qualia, nothing in the subject's experience can favor one of the hypotheses over the other. So unless he seeks outside help, the state of his own qualia must be as unknowable to him as the state of anyone else's qualia. Hardly the privileged access or immediate acquaintance or direct apprehension the friends of qualia had supposed "phenomenal features" to enjoy!

The outcome of this series of thought experiments is an intensification of the "verificationist" argument against qualia. *If* there are qualia, they are even less accessible to our ken than we had thought. Not only are the classical intersubjective comparisons impossible (as the Brainstorm machine shows), but we cannot tell in our own cases whether our qualia have been inverted—at least not by introspection. It is surely tempting at this point—especially to non-philosophers—to decide that this paradoxical result must be an artifact of some philosophical misanalysis or other, the sort of thing that might well happen if you took a perfectly good pretheoretical notion—our everyday notion of qualia—and illicitly stretched it beyond the breaking point. The philosophers have made a mess; let them clean it up; meanwhile we others can get back to work, relying as always on our sober and unmetaphysical acquaintance with qualia.

Overcoming this ubiquitous temptation is the task of the next section, which will seek to establish the unsalvageable incoherence of the hunches that lead to the paradox by looking more closely at their sources and their motivation.

4 Making mistakes about qualia

The idea that people might be mistaken about their own qualia is at the heart of the ongoing confusion, and must be explored in more detail, and with somewhat more realistic examples, if we are to see the delicate role it plays.

Intuition pump #7: Chase and Sanborn. Once upon a time there were two coffee tasters, Mr Chase and Mr Sanborn, who worked for Maxwell House.[7] Along with half a dozen other coffee tasters, their job was to ensure that the taste of Maxwell House stayed constant, year after year. One day, about six years after Mr Chase had come to work for Maxwell House, he confessed to Mr Sanborn:

> I hate to admit it, but I'm not enjoying this work any more. When I came to Maxwell House six years ago, I thought Maxwell House coffee was the best-tasting coffee in the world. I was proud to have a share in the responsibility for preserving that flavor over the years. And we've done our job well; the coffee tastes just the same today as it tasted when I arrived. But, you know, I no longer like it! My tastes have changed. I've become a more sophisticated coffee drinker. I no longer like *that taste* at all.

Sanborn greeted this revelation with considerable interest. "It's funny you should mention it," he replied, "for something rather similar has happened to me." He went on:

> When I arrived here shortly before you did, I, like you, thought Maxwell House coffee was tops in flavor. And now I, like you, really don't care for the coffee we're making. But *my* tastes haven't changed; my ... *tasters* have changed. That is, I think something has gone wrong with my taste buds or some other part of my taste-analyzing perceptual machinery. Maxwell House coffee doesn't taste to me the way it used to taste; if only it did, I'd still love it, for I still think *that taste* is the best taste in coffee. Now I'm not saying we haven't done our job well. You other tasters all agree that the taste is the same, and I must admit that on a day-to-day basis I can detect no change either. So it must be my problem alone. I guess I'm no longer cut out for this work.

Chase and Sanborn are alike in one way at least: they both used to like Maxwell House coffee, and now neither likes it. But they claim to be different in another way. Maxwell House tastes to Chase just the way it always did, but not so for Sanborn. But can we take their protestations at face value? Must we? Might one or both of them simply be wrong? Might their predicaments be importantly the same and their apparent disagreement more a difference in manner of expression than in experiential or psychological state? Since both of them make claims that depend on the reliability of their memories, is there any way to check on this reliability?

My reason for introducing two characters in the example is not to set up an interpersonal comparison between how the coffee tastes to Chase and how it tastes to Sanborn, but just to exhibit, side-by-side, two poles between which cases of intrapersonal experiential shift can wander. Such cases of intrapersonal experiential shift, and the possibility of adaptation to them, or interference with memory in them, have often been discussed in the literature on qualia, but without sufficient attention to the details, in my opinion. Let us look at Chase first. Falling in for the nonce with the received manner of speaking, it appears at first that there are the following possibilities:

(a) Chase's coffee-taste-qualia have stayed constant, while his reactive attitudes to those qualia, devolving on his canons of aesthetic judgment, etc., have shifted—which is what he seems, in his informal, casual way, to be asserting.

(b) Chase is simply wrong about the constancy of his qualia; they have shifted gradually and imperceptibly over the years, while his standards of taste haven't budged—in spite of his delusions about having become more sophisticated. He is in the state Sanborn claims to be in, but just lacks Sanborn's self-knowledge.

(c) Chase is in some predicament intermediate between (a) and (b); his qualia have

shifted some *and* his standards of judgment have also slipped.

Sanborn's case seems amenable to three counterpart versions:

(a) Sanborn is right; his qualia have shifted, due to some sort of derangement in his perceptal machinery, but his standards have indeed remained constant.

(b) Sanborn's standards have shifted unbeknownst to him. He is thus misremembering his past experiences, in what we might call a nostalgia effect. Think of the familiar experience of returning to some object from your childhood (a classroom desk, a tree-house) and finding it much smaller than you remember it to have been. Presumably as you grew larger your internal standard for what was large grew with you somehow, but your memories (which are stored as fractions or multiples of that standard) didn't compensate, and hence when you consult your memory, it returns a distorted judgment. Sanborn's nostalgia-tinged memory of good old Maxwell House is similarly distorted. (There are obviously many different ways this impressionistic sketch of a memory mechanism could be implemented, and there is considerable experimental work in cognitive psychology that suggests how different hypotheses about such mechanisms could be tested.)

(c) As before, Sanborn's state is some combination of (a) and (b).

I think that everyone writing about qualia today would agree that there are all these possibilities for Chase and Sanborn. I know of no one these days who is tempted to defend the high line on infallibility or incorrigibility that would declare that alternative (a) is—and must be—the truth in each case, since people just cannot be wrong about such private, subjective matters.[8]

Since quandaries are about to arise, however, it might be wise to review in outline why the attractiveness of the infallibilist position is only superficial, so it won't recover its erstwhile allure when the going gets tough. First, in the wake of Wittgenstein (1958) and Malcolm (1956, 1959) we have seen that one way to buy such infallibility is to acquiesce in the complete evaporation of content (Dennett 1976). "Imagine someone saying: 'But I know how tall I am!' and laying his hand on top of his head to prove it." Wittgenstein 1958, p. 96) By diminishing one's claim until there is nothing left to be right or wrong about, one can achieve a certain empty invincibility, but that will not do in this case. One of the things we want Chase to be right about (if he is right) is that he is not in Sanborn's predicament, so if the claim is to be viewed as infallible, it can hardly be because it declines to assert anything.

There is a strong temptation, I have found, to respond to my claims in this paper more or less as follows: "But after all is said and done, there is still something I know in a special way: I know *how it is with me right now*." But if absolutely nothing follows from this presumed knowledge—nothing, for instance, that would shed any light on the different psychological claims that might be true of Chase or Sanborn—what is the point of asserting that one has it? Perhaps people just want to reaffirm their sense of proprietorship over their own conscious states.

The infallibilist line on qualia treats them as properties of one's experience one cannot in principle misdiscover, and this is a mysterious doctrine (at least as mysterious as papal infallibility) unless we shift the emphasis a little and treat qualia as *logical constructs* out of subjects' qualia-judgments: a subject's experience has the quale F if and only if the subject judges his experience to have quale F. We can then treat such judgings as constitutive acts, in effect, bringing the quale into existence by the same sort of license as novelists have to determine the hair color of their characters by fiat. We do not ask how Dostoevski knows that Raskolnikov's hair is light brown.

There is a limited use for such interpretations of subjects' protocols, I have argued (Dennett 1978a; 1979, esp. pp. 109–10; 1982), but they will not help the defenders of qualia here. Logical constructs out of judgments must be viewed as akin to theorists' fictions, and the friends of qualia want the existence of a particular quale in any particular case to be an empirical fact in good standing, not a theorist's useful interpretive fiction, else it will not loom as a challenge to functionalism or materialism or third-person, objective science.

It seems easy enough, then, to dream up empirical tests that would tend to confirm Chase and Sanborn's different tales, but if passing such tests could support their authority (that is to say, their reliability), failing the tests would have to undermine it. The price you pay for the possibility of empirically confirming your assertions is the outside chance of being discredited. The friends of qualia are prepared, today, to pay that price, but perhaps only because they haven't reckoned how the bargain they have struck will subvert the concept they want to defend.

Consider how we could shed light on the question of where the truth lies in the particular cases of Chase and Sanborn, even if we might not be able to settle the matter definitively. It is obvious that there might be telling objective support for one extreme version or another of their stories. Thus if Chase is unable to reidentify coffees, teas, and wines in blind tastings in which only minutes intervene between first and second sips, his claim to *know* that Maxwell House tastes just the same to him now as it did six years ago will be seriously undercut. Alternatively, if he does excellently in blind tastings, and exhibits considerable knowledge about the canons of coffee style (if such there be), his claim to have become a more sophisticated taster will be supported. Exploitation of the standard principles of inductive testing—basically Mill's method of differences—can go a long way toward indicating what sort of change has occurred in Chase or Sanborn—a change near the brute perceptual processing end of the spectrum or a change near the ultimate reactive judgment end of the spectrum. And as Shoemaker (1982) and others have noted, physiological measures, suitably interpreted in some larger theoretical framework, could also weight the scales in favor of one extreme or the other. For instance, the well-studied phenomenon of induced illusion boundaries (see figure 1) has often been claimed to be a particularly "cognitive" illusion, dependent on "top down" processes, and hence, presumably, near the reactive judgment end of the spectrum, but recent experimental work (Von der Heydt et al. 1984) has revealed that "edge detector" neurons *relatively* low in the visual pathways—in area 18 of the visual cortex—are as responsive to illusory edges as to real light-dark boundaries on the retina, suggesting but not quite proving (since these might somehow still be "descending effects") that illusory contours are not imposed from on high, but generated quite early in visual processing. One can imagine discovering a similarly "early" anomaly in the pathways leading from taste buds to judg-

ment in Sanborn, for instance, tending to confirm his claim that he has suffered some change in his basic perceptual—as opposed to judgmental—machinery.

But let us not overestimate the resolving power of such empirical testing. The space in each case between the two poles represented by possibility (a) and possibility (b) would be occupied by phenomena that were the product, somehow, of two factors in varying proportion: roughly, dispositions to generate or produce qualia and dispositions to react to the qualia once they are produced. (That is how our intuitive picture of qualia would envisage it.) Qualia are supposed to affect our action or behavior only via the intermediary of our judgments about them, so any behavioral test, such as a discrimination or memory test, since it takes acts based on judgments as its primary data, can give us direct evidence only about the *resultant* of our two factors. In extreme cases we can have indirect evidence to suggest that one factor has varied a great deal, the other factor hardly at all, and we can test the hypothesis further by checking the relative sensitivity of the subject to variations in the conditions that pre-

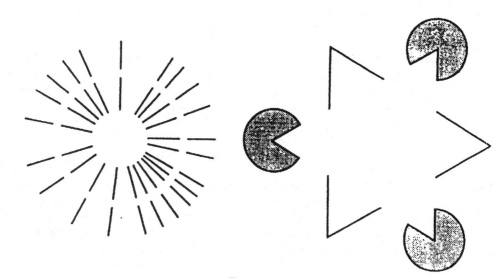

Figure 1

sumably alter the two component factors. But such indirect testing cannot be expected to resolve the issue when the effects are relatively small—when, for instance, our rival hypotheses are Chase's preferred hypothesis (a) and the minor variant to the effect that his qualia have shifted *a little* and his standards *less than he thinks*. This will be true even when we include in our data any unintended or unconscious behavioral effects, for their import will be ambiguous (Would a longer response latency in Chase today be indicative of a process of "attempted qualia renormalization" or "extended aesthetic evaluation"?)

The limited evidential power of neurophysiology comes out particularly clearly if we imagine a case of adaptation. Suppose, in *intuition pump #8: the gradual post-operative recovery*, that we have somehow "surgically inverted" Chase's taste bud connections in the standard imaginary way: post-operatively, sugar tastes salty, salt tastes sour, etc. But suppose further—and this is as realistic a supposition as its denial—that Chase has subsequently compensated—as revealed by his behavior. He now *says* that the sugary substance we place on his tongue is sweet, and no longer favors gravy on his ice cream. Let us suppose the compensation is so thorough that on all behavioral and verbal tests his performance is indistinguishable from that of normal subjects—and from his own pre-surgical performance.

If all the internal compensatory adjustment has been accomplished early in the process—intuitively, pre-qualia—then his qualia today are restored to just as they were (relative to external sources of stimulation) before the surgery. If on the other hand some or all of the internal compensatory adjustment is post-qualia, then his qualia have not been renormalized *even if he thinks they have*. But the physiological facts will not in themselves shed any light on where in the stream of physiological process twixt tasting and telling to draw the line at which the putative qualia appear as properties of that phase of the process. The qualia are the "immediate or phenomenal" properties, of course, but this description will not serve to locate the right phase in the physiological stream, for, echoing intuition pump #6, there will always be at least two possible ways of interpreting the neurophysiological theory, however it comes out. Suppose our physiological theory tells us (in as much detail as you like) that the compensatory effect in him has been achieved by an *adjustment in the memory-accessing process* that is required for our victim to compare today's hues to those of yore. There are *still* two stories that might be told:

I Chase's current qualia are still abnormal, but thanks to the revision in his memory-accessing process, he has in effect adjusted his memories of how things used to taste, so he no longer notices any anomaly.

II The memory-comparison step occurs just prior to the qualia phase in taste perception; thanks to the revision, it now *yields* the same old qualia for the same stimulation.

In (I) the qualia contribute to the input, in effect, to the memory-comparator. In (II) they are part of the output of the memory-comparator. These seem to be two substantially different hypotheses, but the physiological evidence, no matter how well developed, will not tell us on which side of memory to put the qualia. Chase's introspective evidence will not settle the issue between (I) and (II) either, since *ex hypothesi* those stories are not reliably distinguishable by him. Remember that it was in order to confirm or disconfirm Chase's opinion that we turned to the neurophysiological evidence in the first place. We can hardly use his opinion in the end to settle the matter between our rival neurophysiological theories. Chase may think that he thinks his experiences are the same as before *because* they really are (and he remembers accurately how it used to be), but he must admit that he has no introspective resources for distinguishing that possibility from alternative (I), on which he thinks things are as they used to be *because* his memory of how they used to be has been distorted by his new compensatory habits.

Faced with their subject's systematic neutrality, the physiologists may have their own reasons for preferring (I) to (II) or vice versa, for they may have *appropriated* the term "qualia" to their own theoretical ends, to denote some family of detectable properties that strike them as playing an important role in their neurophysiological theory of perceptual recognition and memory. Chase or Sanborn might complain—in the company of more than a few philosophical spokesmen—that these properties the neurophysiologists choose to call "qualia" are not the qualia they are speaking of. The scientists' retort is: "If we cannot distinguish (I) from (II), we certainly cannot support either of your claims. If you want our support, you must relinquish your concept of qualia."

What is striking about this is not just that the empirical methods would fall short of distinguishing what seem to be such different claims about qualia, but that they would fall short *in spite of being better evidence than the subject's own introspective convictions.* For the subject's own judgments, like the behaviors or actions that express them, are the resultant of our two postulated factors, and cannot discern the component proportions any better than external behavioral tests can. Indeed, a subject's "introspective" convictions will generally be *worse* evidence than what outside observers can gather. For if our subject is—as most are—a "naive subject," unacquainted with statistical data about his own case or similar cases, his immediate, frank judgments are, evidentially, like any naive observer's perceptual judgments about factors in the outside world. Chase's intuitive judgments about his qualia constancy are no better off, epistemically, than his intuitive judgments about, say, lighting intensity constancy or room temperature constancy—or his own body temperature constancy. Moving to a

condition inside his body does not change the intimacy of the epistemic relation in any special way. Is Chase running a fever or just feeling feverish? Unless he has taken steps to calibrate and cross-check his own performance, his opinion that his fever-perception apparatus is undisturbed is no better than a hunch. Similarly, Chase may have a strongly held opinion about the degree to which his taste-perceiving apparatus has maintained its integrity, and the degree to which his judgment has evolved through sophistication, but pending the results of the sort of laborious third-person testing just imagined, he would be a fool to claim to know—especially to know directly or immediately—that his was a pure case (a), closer to (a) than to (b), or a case near (b).

He is on quite firm ground, epistemically, when he reports that *the relation* between his coffee-sipping activity and his judging activity has changed. Recall that this is the factor that Chase and Sanborn have in common: they used to like Maxwell House; now they don't. But unless he carries out on himself the sorts of tests others might carry out on him, his convictions about what has stayed constant (or nearly so) and what has shifted *must be sheer guessing.*

But then qualia—supposing for the time being that we know what we are talking about—must lose one of their "essential" second-order properties: far from being directly or immediately apprehensible properties of our experience, they are properties whose changes or constancies arc either entirely beyond our ken, or inferrable (at best) from "third-person" examinations of our behavioral and physiological reaction patterns (if Chase and Sanborn acquiesce in the neurophysiologists' sense of the term). On this view, Chase and Sanborn should be viewed not as introspectors capable of a privileged view of these properties, but as autopsychologists, theorists whose convictions about the properties of their own nervous systems are based not only on their "immediate" or current experiential convictions, but also on their appreciation of the import of events they remember from the recent past.

There are, as we shall see, good reasons for neurophysiologists and other "objective, third-person" theorists to single out such a class of properties to study. But they are not qualia, for the simple reason that one's epistemic relation to them is *exactly* the same as one's epistemic relation to such external, but readily—if fallibly—detectable, properties as room temperature or weight. The idea that one should consult an outside expert, and perform elaborate behavioral tests on oneself in order to confirm what qualia one had, surely takes us too far away from our original idea of qualia as properties with which we have a particularly intimate acquaintance.

So perhaps we have taken a wrong turning. The doctrine that led to this embarrassing result was the doctrine that sharply distinguished qualia from their (normal) effects on reactions. Consider Chase again. He claims that coffee tastes "just the same" as it always did, but he admits—nay insists—that his reaction to "that taste" is not what it used to be. That is, he pretends to be able to divorce his apprehension (or recollection) of the quale—the taste, in ordinary parlance—from his different reactions to the taste. But this apprehension or recollection is itself a reaction to the presumed quale, so some sleight-of-hand is being perpetrated—innocently no doubt—by Chase. So suppose instead that Chase had insisted that precisely *because* his reaction was now different, the taste had changed for him. (When he told his wife his original tale, she said "Don't be silly! Once you add the dislike you change the experience!"—and the more he thought about it, the more he decided she was right.)

Intuition pump #9: the experienced beer drinker. It is familiarly said that beer, for example, is an acquired taste; one gradually trains oneself—or just comes—to enjoy that flavor. What flavor? The flavor of the first sip? No one

could like *that* flavor, an experienced beer drinker might retort:

> Beer tastes different to the experienced beer drinker. If beer went on tasting to me the way the first sip tasted, I would never have gone on drinking beer! Or to put the same point the other way around, if my first sip of beer had tasted to me the way my most recent sip just tasted, I would never have had to acquire the taste in the first place! I would have loved the first sip as much as the one I just enjoyed.

If we let this speech pass, we must admit that beer is *not* an acquired taste. No one comes to enjoy *the way the first sip tasted.* Instead, prolonged beer drinking leads people to experience a taste they enjoy, but precisely their enjoying the taste guarantees that it is not the taste they first experienced.[9]

But this conclusion, if it is accepted, wreaks havoc of a different sort with the traditional philosophical view of qualia. For if it is admitted that one's attitudes towards, or reactions to, experiences are in any way and in any degree constitutive of their experiential qualities, so that a change in reactivity *amounts to* or *guarantees* a change in the property, then those properties, those "qualitative or phenomenal features," cease to be "intrinsic" properties, and in fact become paradigmatically extrinsic, relational properties.

Properties that "seem intrinsic" at first often turn out on more careful analysis to be relational. Bennett (1965) is the author of *intuition pump #10: the world-wide eugenics experiment.* He draws our attention to phenol-thio-urea, a substance which tastes very bitter to three-fourths of humanity, and as tasteless as water to the rest. Is it bitter? Since the reactivity to phenol-thio-urea is genetically transmitted, we could make it paradigmatically bitter by performing a large-scale breeding experiment: prevent the people to whom it is tasteless from breeding, and in a few generations phenol would be as bitter as anything to be found in the world. But we could also (in principle!) perform the contrary feat of mass "eugenics"' and thereby make phenol paradigmatically tasteless—as tasteless as water—without ever touching phenol. Clearly, public bitterness or tastelessness is not an intrinsic property of phenol-thio-urea but a relational property, since the property is changed by a change in the reference class of normal detectors.

The public versions of perceptual "qualia" all *seem* intrinsic, in spite of their relationality. They are not alone. Think of the "felt value"' of a dollar (or whatever your native currency is). "How much is that in *real* money?" the American tourist is reputed to have asked, hoping to translate a foreign price onto the scale of "intrinsic value" he keeps in his head. As Elster (1985) claims, "there is a tendency to overlook the implicitly relational character of certain monadic predicates." Walzer (1985) points out that " ... a ten-dollar bill might seem to have a life of its own as a thing of value, but, as Elster suggests, its value implicitly depends on 'other people who are prepared to accept money as payment for goods.'" But even as one concedes this, there is still a tendency to reserve something subjective, felt value, as an "intrinsic" property of that ten-dollar bill. But as we now see, such intrinsic properties cannot be properties to which a subject's access is in any way privileged.

Which way should Chase go? Should he take his wife's advice and declare that since he can't stand the coffee any more, it no longer tastes the same to him (it used to taste good and now it tastes bad)? Or should he say that really, in a certain sense, it does taste the way it always did or at least it sort of does—when you subtract the fact that it tastes so bad now, of course?

We have now reached the heart of my case. The fact is that we have to ask Chase which way he wants to go, and there really are two drastically different alternatives available to him *if we force the issue*. Which way would *you* go? Which concept of qualia did you "always have in the back of your mind," guiding your imagination as you thought about theories? If you acknowledge that the answer is not obvious, and especially if you complain that this forced choice drives apart two aspects that you had supposed united in your pretheoretic concept, you support my contention that there is no secure foundation in ordinary "folk psychology" for a concept of qualia. We *normally* think in a confused and potentially incoherent way when we think about the ways things seem to us.

When Chase thinks of "that taste" he thinks equivocally or vaguely. He harkens back in memory to earlier experiences but need not try—or be able—to settle whether he is including any or all of his reactions or excluding them from what he intends by "that taste." His state then and his state now are different—*that* he can avow with confidence—but he has no "immediate" resources for making a finer distinction, nor any need to do so.[10]

This suggests that qualia are no more essential to the professional vocabulary of the phenomenologist (or professional coffee taster) than to the vocabulary of the physiologist (Dennett 1978b). To see this, consider again the example of my dislike of cauliflower. Imagine now, in *intuition pump #11: the cauliflower cure*, that someone offers me a pill to cure my loathing for cauliflower. He promises that after I swallow this pill cauliflower will taste exactly the same to me as it always has, but I will like that taste! "Hang on," I might reply. "I think you may have just contradicted yourself." But in any event I take the pill and it works. I become an instant cauliflower-appreciater, but if I am asked which of the two possible effects (Chase-type or Sanborn-type) the pill has had on me, I will be puzzled, and will find nothing *in my experience* to shed light on the question. Of course I recognize that the taste is (sort of) the same—the pill hasn't made cauliflower taste like chocolate cake, after all—but at the same time my experience is so different now that I resist saying that cauliflower tastes the way it used to taste. There is in any event no reason to be cowed into supposing that my cauliflower experiences have some intrinsic properties behind, or in addition to, their various dispositional, reaction-provoking properties.

"But in principle there has to be a right answer to the question of how it is, intrinsically, with you now, even if you are unable to say with any confidence!" Why? Would one say the same about all other properties of experience? Consider *intuition pump #12: visual field inversion created by wearing inverting spectacles*, a phenomenon which has been empirically studied for years. (G. M. Stratton published the pioneering work in 1896, and J. J. Gibson and Ivo Kohler were among the principal investigators. For an introductory account, see Gregory 1977.) After wearing inverting spectacles for several days subjects make an astonishingly successful adaptation. Suppose we pressed on them this question: "Does your adaptation consist in your re-inverting your visual field, or in your turning the rest of your mind upside-down in a host of compensations?" If they demur, may we insist that there has to be a right answer, even if they cannot say with any confidence which it is? Such an insistence would lead directly to a new version of the old inverted spectrum thought experiment: "How do I know whether some people see things upside-down (but are perfectly used to it), while others see things right-side-up?"

Only a very naive view of visual perception could sustain the idea that one's visual field has a property of right-side-upness or upside-downness *independent of one's dispositions to react to it*—"intrinsic right-side-upness" we could call it. (See my discussion of the properties of the "images" processed by the robot SHAKEY, in Dennett 1982.) So not all properties of conscious experience invite or require treatment as "intrinsic" properties. Is there something dis-

tinguishing about a certain subclass of properties (the "qualitative or phenomenal" subclass, presumably) that forces us to treat them—unlike subjective right-side-upness—as intrinsic properties? If not, such properties have no role to play in either physiological theories of experience, or in introspective theories.

Some may be inclined to argue this way: I can definitely imagine the experience of "spectrum inversion" from the inside; after all I have actually experienced temporary effects of the same type, such as the "taste displacement" effect of the maple syrup on the orange juice. What is imaginable, or actual is possible. Therefore spectrum inversion or displacement (in all sensory modalities) is possible. But such phenomena just are the inversion or displacement of qualia, or intrinsic subjective properties. Therefore there must be qualia: intrinsic subjective properties.

This is fallacious. What one imagines and what one says one imagines may be two different things. To imagine visual field inversion, of the sort Stratton and Kohler's subjects experienced, is not necessarily to imagine the absolute inversion of a visual field (even if that is what it "feels like" to the subjects). Less obviously, imagining—as vividly as you like—a case of subjective color-perception displacement is not necessarily imagining what that phenomenon is typically called by philosophers: an inverted or displaced spectrum *of qualia*. In so far as that term carries the problematic implications scouted here, there is no support for its use arising simply from the vividness or naturalness of the imagined possibility.

If there are no such properties as qualia, does that mean that "spectrum inversion" is impossible? Yes and no. Spectrum inversion as classically debated is impossible, but something like it is perfectly possible—something that is as like "qualia inversion" as visual field inversion is like the impossible *absolute* visual image inversion we just dismissed.

5 Some puzzling real cases

It is not enough to withhold our theoretical allegiances until the sunny day when the philosophers complete the tricky task of purifying the everyday concept of qualia. Unless we take active steps to shed this source concept, and replace it with better ideas, it will continue to cripple our imaginations and systematically distort our attempts to understand the phenomena already encountered.

What we find, if we look at the actual phenomena of anomalies of color perception, for instance, amply bears out our suspicions about the inadequacy of the traditional notion of qualia. Several varieties of *cerebral achromatopsia* (brain based impairment of color vision) have been reported, and while there remains much that is unsettled about their analysis, there is little doubt that the philosophical thought experiments have underestimated or overlooked the possibilities for counter-intuitive collections of symptoms, as a few very brief excerpts from case histories will reveal.

> Objects to the right of the vertical meridian appeared to be of normal hue, while to the left they were perceived only in shades of gray, though without distortions of form. ... He was unable to recognize or name any color in any portion of the left field of either eye, including bright reds, blues, greens and yellows. As soon as any portion of the colored object crossed the vertical meridian, he was able to instantly recognize and accurately name its color. (Damasio et al. 1980)

This patient would seem at first to be unproblematically describable as suffering a shift or loss of color qualia in the left hemifield, but there is a problem of interpretation here, brought about by another case:

> The patient failed in all tasks in which he was required to match the seen color

with its spoken name. Thus, the patient failed to give the names of colors and failed to choose a color in response to its name. By contrast, he succeeded on all tasks where the matching was either purely verbal or purely nonverbal. Thus, he could give verbally the names of colors corresponding to named objects and vice versa. He could match seen colors to each other and to pictures of objects and could sort colors without error. (Geschwind and Fusillo 1966)

This second patient was quite unaware of any deficit. He "never replied with a simple 'I don't know' to the demand for naming a color" (Geschwind and Fusillo 1966, p. 140). There is a striking contrast between these two patients; both have impaired ability to name the colors of things in at least part of their visual field, but whereas the former is acutely aware of his deficit, the latter is not. Does this difference make all the difference about qualia? If so, what on earth should we say about this third patient?

> His other main complaint was that "everything looked black or grey" and this caused him some difficulty in everyday life ... He had considerable difficulty recognizing and naming colours. He would, for example, usually describe bright red objects as either red or black, bright green objects as either green, blue or black, and bright blue objects as black. The difficulty appeared to be perceptual and he would make remarks suggesting this; for example when shown a bright red object he said "a dirty smudgy red, not as red as you would normally see red." Colours of lesser saturation or brightness were described in such terms as "grey," "off-white" or "black," but if told to guess at the colour, he would be correct on about 50 per cent of occasions, being notably less successful with blues and greens than reds. (Meadows 1974)

This man's awareness of his deficit is problematic to say the least. It contrasts rather sharply with yet another case:

> One morning in November 1977, upon awakening, she noted that although she was able to see details of objects and people, colors appeared "drained out" and "not true." She had no other complaint ... her vision was good, 20/20 in each eye ... The difficulty in color perception persisted, and she had to seek the advice of her husband to choose what to wear. Eight weeks later she noted that she could no longer recognize the faces of her husband and daughter ... [So in] addition to achromatopsia, the patient had prosopagnosia, but her linguistic and cognitive performances were otherwise unaffected. The patient was able to tell her story cogently and to have remarkable insight about her defects. (Damasio et al. 1980)

As Meadows notes, "Some patients thus complain that their vision for colours is defective while others have no spontaneous complaint but show striking abnormalities on testing."

What should one say in these cases? When no complaint is volunteered but the patient shows an impairment in color vision, is this a sign that his qualia are unaffected? ("His capacities to discriminate are terribly impaired, but luckily for him, his inner life is untouched by this merely public loss!") We could line up the qualia this way, but equally we could claim that the patient has simply not noticed the perhaps gradual draining away or inversion or merging of his qualia revealed by his poor performance. ("So slowly did his inner life lose its complexity and variety that he never noticed how impoverished it had become!") What if our last patient described her complaint just as she did above, but performed normally on testing? One hypothesis would be that her qualia had indeed, as she suggested, become washed out. Another would be that in the light of her sterling performance on the color discrimination tests, her qualia were fine; she was suffering from some hysterical or depressive anomaly, a sort of color-vision hypochondria that makes her complain about a loss of color perception. Or perhaps one could claim that her qualia were untouched; her disorder was purely verbal: an anomalous understanding of the words she uses to describe her experience. (Other, startlingly specific color-*word* disorders have been reported in the literature.)

The traditional concept leads us to overlook genuine possibilities. Once we have learned of the curious deficit reported by Geschwind and Fusillo, for instance, we realize that our first patient was never tested to see if he could still sort colors seen on the left or pass other non-naming, non-verbal color-blindness tests. Those tests are by no means superfluous. Perhaps he would have passed them; perhaps, *in spite of what he says* his qualia are as intact for the left field as for the right!—if we take the capacity to pass such tests as "criterial." Perhaps his problem is "purely verbal." If your reaction to this hypothesis is that this is impossible, that must mean you are making his verbal, reporting behavior sovereign in settling the issue—but then you must rule out a priori the possibility of the condition I described as color-vision hypochondria.

There is no prospect of *finding* the answers to these brain-teasers in our everyday usage or the intuitions it arouses, but it is of course open to the philosopher to *create* an edifice of theory defending a particular set of interlocking proposals. The problem is that although normally a certain family of stimulus and bodily conditions yields a certain family of effects, any particular effect can be disconnected, and our intuitions do not tell us which effects are "essential" to quale identity or qualia constancy (cf. Dennett 1978a, ch. 11). It seems fairly obvious to me that none of the real problems of interpretation that face us in these curious cases is advanced by any analysis of how the concept of *qualia* is to be applied—unless we wish to propose a novel, technical sense for which the traditional term might be appropriated. But that would be at least a tactical error: the intuitions that surround and *purport* to anchor the current understanding of the term are revealed to be in utter disarray when confronted with these cases.

My informal sampling shows that some philosophers have strong opinions about each case and how it should be described in terms of qualia, but they find they are in strident (and ultimately comic) disagreement with other philosophers about how these "obvious" descriptions should go. Other philosophers discover they really don't know what to say—not because there aren't enough facts presented in the descriptions of the cases, but because it begins to dawn on them that they haven't really known what they were talking about over the years.

6 Filling the vacuum

If qualia are such a bad idea, why have they seemed to be such a good idea? Why does it seem as if there are these intrinsic, ineffable, private, "qualitative" properties in our experience? A review of the presumptive second-order properties of the properties of our conscious experiences will permit us to diagnose their attractiveness and find suitable substitutes. (For a similar exercise see Kitcher 1979.)

Consider "intrinsic" first. It is far from clear what an intrinsic property would be. Although the term has had a certain vogue in philosophy, and often seems to secure an important contrast, there has never been an accepted definition of the second-order property of intrinsicality. If even such a brilliant theory-monger as David Lewis can try and fail, by his own admission, to define the extrinsic/intrinsic distinction coherently, we can begin to wonder if the concept deserves our further attention after all. In fact Lewis (1983) begins his survey of versions of the distinction by listing as one option: "We could

Quine the lot, give over the entire family as unintelligible and dispensable," but he dismisses the suggestion immediately: "That would be absurd" (p. 197). In the end, however, his effort to salvage the accounts of Chisholm (1976) and Kim (1982) are stymied, and he conjectures that "if we still want to break in we had best try another window" (p. 200).

Even if we are as loath as Lewis is to abandon the distinction, shouldn't we be suspicious of the following curious fact? If challenged to explain the idea of an intrinsic property to a neophyte, many people would hit on the following sort of example: consider Tom's ball; it has many properties, such as its being made of rubber from India, its belonging to Tom, its having spent the last week in the closet, and its redness. All but the last of these are clearly *relational* or *extrinsic* properties of the ball. Its redness, however, is an intrinsic property. Except this isn't so. Ever since Boyle and Locke we have known better. Redness—public redness—is a quintessentially relational property, as many thought experiments about "secondary qualities" show. (One of the first was Berkeley's (1713) pail of lukewarm water, and one of the best is Bennett's (1965) phenol-thio-urea.) The seductive step, on learning that public redness (like public bitterness, etc.) is a relational property after all, is to cling to intrinsicality ("*something* has to be intrinsic!") and move it into the subject's head. It is often thought, in fact, that if we take a Lockean, relational position on objective bitterness, redness, etc., we *must* complete our account of the relations in question by appeal to non-relational, intrinsic properties. If what it is to be objectively bitter is to produce a certain effect in the members of the class of normal observers, we must be able to specify that effect, and distinguish it from the effect produced by objective sourness and so forth.

What else could distinguish this effect but some intrinsic property? Why not another relational or extrinsic property? The relational treatment of monetary value does not require, for its completion, the supposition of items of intrinsic value (value independent of the valuers' dispositions to react behaviorally). The claim that certain perceptual properties are different is, in the absence of any supporting argument, just question-begging. It will not do to say that it is just obvious that they are intrinsic. It may have seemed obvious to some, but the considerations raised by Chase's quandary show that it is far from obvious that any intrinsic property (whatever that comes to) could play the role of anchor for the Lockean relational treatment of the public perceptual properties.

What, then, of ineffability? Why does it seem that our conscious experiences have ineffable properties? Because they do have *practically* ineffable properties. Suppose, in *intuition pump #13: the osprey cry*, that I have never heard the cry of an osprey, even in a recording, but know roughly, from reading my bird books, what to listen for: "a series of short, sharp, cheeping whistles, *cheep cheep* or *chewk chewk*, etc; sounds annoyed" (Peterson 1947) (or words to that effect or better). The verbal description gives me a partial confinement of the logical space of possible bird cries. On its basis I can rule out many bird calls I have heard or might hear, but there is still a broad range of discriminable-by-me possibilities within which the actuality lies hidden from me like a needle in a haystack.

Then one day, armed with both my verbal description and my binoculars, I identify an osprey visually, and then hear its cry. So *that's* what it sounds like, I say to myself, ostending—it seems—a particular mental complex of intrinsic, ineffable qualia. I dub the complex "S" (*pace* Wittgenstein), rehearse it in short term memory, check it against the bird book descriptions, and see that while the verbal descriptions are true, accurate and even poetically evocative—I decide I could not do better with a thousand words—they still fall short of *capturing* the qualia-complex I have called *S*. In fact, that is why I need the neologism "*S*" to refer directly to the ineffable property I cannot pick out by description. My perceptual experience has pinpointed for me the location of the osprey cry in the logical space of possibilities in a way verbal description could not.

But tempting as this view of matters is, it is overstated. First of all, it is obvious that from a single experience of this sort I don't—can't—know how to generalize to other osprey calls. Would a cry that differed only in being half an octave higher also be an osprey call? That is an empirical, ornithological question for which my experience provides scant evidence. But moreover—and this is a psychological, not ornithological, matter—I don't and can't know, from a single such experience, which physical variations and constancies in stimuli would produce an indistinguishable experience in me. Nor can I know whether I would react the same (have the same experience) if I were presented with what was, by all physical measures, a re-stimulation identical to the first. I cannot know the modulating effect, if any, of variations in my body (or psyche).

This inscrutability of projection is surely one of the sources of plausibility for Wittgenstein's skepticism regarding the possibility of a private language.

> Wittgenstein emphasizes that ostensive definitions are always in principle capable of being misunderstood, even the ostensive definition of a color word such as "sepia". How someone understands the word is exhibited in the way someone goes on, "the use that he makes of the word defined". One may go on in the right way given a purely

minimal explanation, while on the other hand one may go on in another way no matter how many clarifications are added, since these too can be misunderstood ... (Kripke 1982, p. 83; see also pp. 40–6).

But what is inscrutable in a single glance, and somewhat ambiguous after limited testing, can come to be justifiably seen as the deliverance of a highly specific, reliable, and projectible property-detector, once it has been field-tested under a suitably wide variety of circumstances.

In other words, when first I hear the osprey cry, I may have identified a property-detector in myself, but I have no idea (yet) what property my new-found property-detector detects. It might seem then that I know nothing new at all—that my novel experience has not improved my epistemic predicament in the slightest. But of course this is not so. I may not be able to describe the property or identify it relative to any readily usable public landmarks (yet), but I am acquainted with it in a modest way: I can refer to the property I detected: it is the property I detected in *that* event. My experience of the osprey cry has given me a new way of thinking about osprey cries (an unavoidably inflated way of saying something very simple) which is practically ineffable both because it has (as yet for me) an untested profile in response to perceptual circumstances, and because it is—as the poverty of the bird-book description attests—such a highly informative way of thinking: a deliverance of an informationally very sensitive portion of my nervous system.

In this instance I mean information in the formal information theory sense of the term. Consider (*intuition pump #14: the Jello box*) the old spy trick, most famously encountered in the case of Julius and Ethel Rosenberg, of improving on a password system by tearing something in two (a Jello box, in the Rosenberg's case), and giving half to each of the two parties who must be careful about identifying each other. Why does it work? Because tearing the paper

in two produces an edge of such informational complexity that it would be virtually impossible to reproduce by deliberate construction. (Cutting the Jello box with straight edge and razor would entirely defeat the purpose.) The particular jagged edge of one piece becomes a *practically* unique pattern-recognition device for its mate; it is an apparatus for detecting the shape property M, where M is uniquely instantiated by its mate. It is of the essence of the trick that we cannot replace our dummy predicate "M" with a longer, more complex, but accurate and exhaustive description of the property, for if we could, we could use the description as a recipe or feasible algorithm for producing another instance of M or another M detector. The only *readily available* way of saying what property M is is just to point to our M-detector and say that M is the shape property detected by this thing here.

And that is just what we do when we seem to ostend, with the mental finger of inter intention, a quale or qualia-complex in our experience. We refer to a property—a public property of uncharted boundaries—via reference to our personal and idiosyncratic capacity to respond to it. That idiosyncrasy is the extent of our privacy. If I wonder whether your blue is my blue, your middle-C is my middle-C, I can coherently be wondering whether our discrimination profiles over a wide variation in conditions will be approximately the same. And they may not be; people experience the world quite differently. But that is empirically discoverable by all the usual objective testing procedures.[12]

Peter Bieri has pointed out to me that there is a natural way of exploiting Dretske's (1981) sense of information in a reformulation of my first three second-order properties of qualia: intrinsicality, ineffability, and privacy. (There are problems with Dretske's attempt to harness information theory in this way—see my discussion in "Evolution, error and intentionality" (Dennett 1987)—but they are not relevant to this point.) We could speak of what Bieri would call "phenomenal information properties" of psychological events. Consider the information—what Dretske would call the *natural meaning*—that a type of internal perceptual event might carry. That it carries that information is an objective (and hence, in a loose sense, intrinsic) matter since it is independent of what information (if any) the subject *takes* the event type to carry. Exactly what information is carried is (practically) ineffable, for the reasons just given. And it is private in the sense just given: proprietary and potentially idiosyncratic.

Consider how Bieri's proposed "phenomenal information properties" (let's call them *pips*) would apply in the case of Chase and Sanborn. Both Chase and Sanborn ought to wonder whether their pips have changed. Chase's speech shows that he is under the impression that his pips are unchanged (under normal circumstances—all bets are off if he has just eaten horseradish). He believes that the same objective things in the world—in particular, chemically identical caffeine-rich fluids—give rise to his particular types of taste-experiences now as six years ago.

Sanborn is under the impression that his pips are different. He thinks his objective property-detectors are deranged. He no longer has confidence that their deliverances today inform him of what they did six years ago. And what, exactly, did they inform him of then? If Sanborn were an ordinary person, we would not expect him to have an explicit answer, since most of us treat our taste-detectors as mere *M*-detectors, detecting whatever-it-is that they detect. (There are good reasons for this, analyzed by Akins 1987.) But professional coffee-tasters are probably different. They probably have some pretty good idea of what kind of chemical-analysis transduction machinery they have in their mouths and nervous systems.

So far, so good. We could reinterpret Chase and Sanborn's speeches as hypotheses about the constancies or changes in the outputs of their perceptual information-processing apparatus, and just the sort of empirical testing we imagined before would tend to confirm or disconfirm their opinions thus interpreted. But what would justify calling such an information-bearing property "phenomenal"?

Such a pip has, as the testimony of Chase and Sanborn reveals, the power to provoke in Chase and Sanborn acts of (apparent) re-identification or recognition. This power is of course a Lockean, dispositional property on a par with the power of bitter things to provoke a certain reaction in people. It is this power alone, however it might be realized in the brain, that gives Chase and Sanborn "access" to the deliverances of their individual property-detectors.

We may "point inwardly" to one of the deliverances of our idiosyncratic, proprietary property-detectors, but when we do, what are we pointing *at*? What does that deliverance itself *consist of*? Or what are its consciously apprehensible properties, if not just our banished friends the qualia? We must be careful here, for if we invoke an inner perceptual process in which we observe the deliverance with some inner eye and thereby discern its properties, we will be stepping back into the frying pan of the view according to which qualia are just ordinary properties of our inner states.

But nothing requires us to make such an invocation. We don't have to know how we identify or re-identify or gain access to such internal response types in order to be able so to identify them. This is a point that was forcefully made by the pioneer functionalists and materialists, and has never been rebutted (Farrell 1950; Smart 1959). The properties of the "thing experienced" are not to be confused with the properties of the event that realizes the experiencing. To put the matter vividly, the physical difference between someone's imagining a purple cow and imagining a green cow *might* be nothing more than the presence or absence of a particular zero or one in one of the brain's "registers." Such a brute physical presence is all that it would take to anchor the sorts of dispositional differences between imagining a purple cow and imagining a green cow that could then flow, causally, from that "intrinsic" fact. (I doubt that this is what the friends of qualia have had in mind when they have insisted that qualia are intrinsic properties.)

Moreover, it is our very inability to expand on, or modify, these brute dispositions so to identify or recognize such states that creates the doctrinal illusion of "homogeneity" or "atomicity to analysis" or "grainlessness" that characterizes the qualia of philosophical tradition.

This putative grainlessness, I hypothesize, is nothing but a sort of functional invariability: it is close kin to what Pylyshyn (1980, 1984) calls *cognitive impenetrability*. Moreover, this functional invariability or impenetrability is not absolute but itself plastic over time. Just as on the efferent side of the nervous system, *basic actions*—in the sense of Danto (1963, 1965) and others (see Goldman 1970)—have been discovered to be variable, and subject under training to decomposition (one can learn with the help of "biofeedback" to will the firing of a particular motor neuron "directly"), so what counts for an individual as the simple or atomic properties of experienced items is subject to variation with training.[13]

Consider the results of "educating" the palate of a wine taster, or "ear training" for musicians. What had been "atomic" or "unanalyzable" becomes noticeably compound and describable; pairs that had been indistinguishable become distinguishable, and when this happens we say *the experience changes*. A swift and striking example of this is illustrated in *intuition pump #15: the guitar string*. Pluck the bass or low E string open, and listen carefully to the sound. Does it have describable parts or is it one and whole and ineffably guitarish? Many will opt for the latter way of talking. Now pluck the open string again and carefully bring a finger down lightly over the octave fret to create a high "harmonic." Suddenly a *new* sound is heard: "purer" somehow and of course

an octave higher. Some people insist that this is an entirely novel sound, while others will describe the experience by saying "the bottom fell out of the note"—leaving just the top. But then on a third open plucking one can hear, with surprising distinctness, the harmonic overtone that was isolated in the second plucking. The homogeneity and ineffability of the first experience is gone, replaced by a duality as "directly apprehensible" and clearly describable as that of any chord.

The difference in experience is striking, but the complexity apprehended on the third plucking was *there* all along (being responded to or discriminated). After all, it was by the complex pattern of overtones that you were able to recognize the sound as that of a guitar rather than a lute or harpsichord. In other words, although the subjective experience has changed dramatically, the *pip* hasn't changed; you are still responding, as before, to a complex property so highly informative that it practically defies verbal description.

There is nothing to stop further refinement of one's capacity to describe this heretofore ineffable complexity. At any time, of course, there is one's current horizon of distinguishability—and that horizon is what sets, if anything does, what we should call the primary or atomic properties of what one consciously experiences (Farrell 1950). But it would be a mistake to transform the fact that inevitably there is a limit to our capacity to describe things we experience into the supposition that there are absolutely indescribable properties in our experience.

So when we look one last time at our original characterization of qualia, as ineffable, intrinsic, private, directly apprehensible properties of experience, we find that there is nothing to fill the bill. In their place are relatively or practically ineffable public properties we can refer to indirectly via reference to our private property-detectors—private only in the sense of idiosyncratic. And in so far as we wish to cling to our subjective authority about the occurrence within us of states of certain types or with certain properties, we can have some authority—not infallibility or incorrigibility, but something better than sheer guessing—but only if we restrict ourselves to relational, extrinsic properties like the power of certain internal states of ours to provoke acts of apparent re-identification. So contrary to what seems obvious at first blush, there simply are no qualia at all.[14]

NOTES

1. A representative sample of the most recent literature on qualia would include Block 1980; Shoemaker 1981, 1982; Davis 1982; White 1985; Armstrong and Malcolm 1984; Churchland 1985; and Conee 1985.

2. The difference between "eliminative materialism"—of which my position on qualia is an instance—and a "reductive" materialism that takes on the burden of identifying the problematic item in terms of the foundational materialistic theory is thus often best seen not so much as a doctrinal issue as a tactical issue: how might we most gracefully or effectively enlighten the confused in this instance? See my discussion of "fatigues" in the Introduction to *Brainstorms* (Dennett 1978a), and earlier, my discussion of what the enlightened ought to say about the metaphysical status of *sakes* and *voices* in *Content and Consciousness* (Dennett 1969), ch. 1.

3. The plausibility of this concession depends less on a high regard for the technology, than on a proper skepticism about human powers, now documented in a fascinating study by Lehrer (1983).

4. Shoemaker (1984) seems to be moving reluctantly towards agreement with this conclusion: "So unless we can find some grounds on which we can deny the possibility of the sort of situation envisaged ... we must apparently choose between rejecting the functionalist account of qualitative

similarity and rejecting the standard conception of qualia.

I would prefer not to have to make this choice; but if I am forced to make it, I reject the standard conception of qualia" (p. 356).

5. Shoemaker (1982) attributes a view to Wittgenstein (acknowledging that "it is none too clear" that this is actually what Wittgenstein held) which is very close to the view I defend here. But to Shoemaker, "it would seem offhand that Wittgenstein was mistaken" (p. 360), a claim Shoemaker supports with a far from offhand thought experiment—which Shoemaker misanalyzes if the present paper is correct. (There is no good reason, contrary to Shoemaker's declaration, to believe that his subject's *experience* is systematically different from what it was before the inversion.) Smart (1959) expresses guarded and partial approval of Wittgenstein's hard line, but cannot see his way clear to as uncompromising an eliminativism as I maintain here.

6. In 1979, I read an earlier version of this paper in Oxford, with a commentary, by John Foster, who defended qualia to the last breath, which was: "qualia should not be quined but fostered!" Symmetry demands, of course, the following definition for the eighth edition of *The Philosophical Lexicon*: "foster, *v.* To acclaim resolutely the existence or importance of something chimerical or insignificant."

7. This example first appeared in print in my "Reflections on Smullyan" in *The Mind's I* (Hofstadter and Dennett 1981), p. 427–8.

8. Kripke (1982) comes close, when he asks rhetorically "Do I not know, directly, and *with a fair degree of certainty* [emphasis added], that I mean plus [by the function I call "plus"]?" (p. 40) Kripke does not tell us what is implied by "a fair degree of certainty," but presumably he means by this

remark to declare his allegiance to what Millikan (1984) attacks under the name of "meaning rationalism."

9. We can save the traditional claim by ignoring presumably private or subjective qualia and talking always of public tastes—such as the public taste of Maxwell House coffee that both Chase and Sanborn agree has remained constant. Individuals can be said to acquire a taste for such a public taste.

10. "I am not so wild as to deny that my sensation of red today is like my sensation of red yesterday. I only say that the similarity can *consist* only in the physiological force behind consciousness—which leads me to say, I recognize this feeling the same as the former one, and so does not consist in a community of sensation." (C. S. Peirce, *Collected Works*, vol. V, p. 172, fn. 2).

11. A heroic (and, to me, baffling) refusal to abandon intrinsicality is Wilfrid Sellars's contemplation over the years of his famous pink ice cube, which leads him to postulate a revolution in microphysics, restoring objective "absolute sensory processes" in the face of Boyle and Locke and almost everybody since them. See Sellars (1981) and my commentary (Dennett 1981).

12. Stich (1983) discusses the implications for psychological theory of incommensurability problems that can arise from such differences in discrimination profiles. See esp. chs. 4 and 5.

13. See Churchland 1979, esp. ch. 2, for supporting observations on the variability of perceptual properties, and for novel arguments against the use of "intrinsic properties" as determiners of the meaning of perceptual predicates. See also Churchland 1985 for further arguments and observations in support of the position sketched here.

14. The first version of this paper was presented at University College London, in November 1978, and in various revisions at a dozen other universities in 1979 and 1980. It was never published, but was circulated widely as Tufts University Cognitive Science Working Paper #7, December 1979. A second version was presented at the Universities of Adelaide and Sydney in 1984, and in 1985 to psychology department colloquia at Harvard and Brown under the title "Properties of conscious experience." The second version was the basis for my presentation at the workshop on consciousness in modern science, Villa Olmo, Como, Italy, April 1985, and circulated in preprint in 1985, again under the title "Quining qualia." The present version, the fourth, is a substantial revision, thanks to the helpful comments of many people, including Kathleen Akins, Ned Block, Alan Cowey, Sydney Shoemaker, Peter Bieri, William Lycan, Paul Churchland, Gilbert Harman and the participants at Villa Olmo.

REFERENCES

Akins, K. (1987) *Information and Organisms: Or, Why Nature Doesn't Build Epistemic Engines*, Ph.D. dissertation, Univ. of Michigan Dept. of Philosophy.

Armstrong, D. and Malcolm, N. (eds) (1984) *Consciousness and Causality*. Oxford: Basil Blackwell.

Bennett, J. (1965) "Substance, reality and primary qualities." *American Philosophical Quarterly* 2, 1–17.

Berkeley, G. (1713) *Three Dialogues between Hylas and Philonous*.

Block, N. (1978) "Troubles with Functionalism," in W. Savage (ed.) *Perception and Cognition: Minnesota Studies in the Philosophy of Science, Vol. IX*. Minneapolis: University of Minnesota Press.

Block, N. (1980) "Are absent qualia impossible?," *Philosophical Review* 89, 257.

Block, N. and Fodor, J. (1972) "What psychological states are not," *Philosophical Review* 81, 159–81.

Chisholm, R. (1976) *Person and Object*. La Salle, Illinois: Open Court Press.

Churchland, P.M. (1979) *Scientific Realism and the Plasticity of Mind*. Cambridge, MA: Cambridge University Press.

Churchland, P.M. (1985) "Reduction, qualia and the direct inspection of brain states," *Journal of Philosophy*, LXXXII, 8–28.

Conee, E. (1985) "The possibility of absent qualia," *Philosophical Review* 94, 345–66.

Damasio, A. et al. (1980) "Central Achromatopsia: Behavioral, anatomic, and physiological aspects," *Neurology* 30, 1064–71.

Danto, A. (1963) "What we can do," *Journal of Philosophy*, LX, 435–45.

Danto, A. (1965) "Basic actions," *American Philosophical Quarterly*, 141–8.

Davis, L. (1982) "Functionalism and absent qualia," *Philosophical Studies* 41, 231–51.

Dennett, D.C. (1969) *Content and Consciousness*. London: Routledge & Kegan Paul.

Dennett, D.C. (1976) "Are dreams experiences?," *Philosophical Review* 85, 151–71. (Reprinted in Dennett 1978a.)

Dennett, D.C. (1978a) *Brainstorms*. Bradford Books/MIT Press.

Dennett, D.C. (1978b) "Two approaches to mental images," in Dennett 1978a.

Dennett, D.C. (1978c) *The Philosophical Lexicon* (privately printed, available from the American Philosophical Association, University of Delaware), 8th edn.

Dennett, D.C. (1979) "On the absence of phenomenology," in D.F. Gustafson and B.L. Tapscott (eds) *Body, Mind, and Method* (Festschrift for Virgil Aldrich). Dordrecht: Reidel, pp. 93–114.

Dennett, D.C. (1981) "Wondering where the yellow went," *Monist* 64, 102–8.

Dennett, D.C. (1982) "How to study human consciousness empirically: Or nothing comes to mind," *Synthese* 53, 159–80.

Dennett, D.C. (1987) *The Intentional Stance*. Cambridge, MA: Bradford/MIT.

Dretske, F. (1981) *Knowledge and the Flow of Information*. Cambridge, MA: Bradford/MIT.

Elster, J. (1985) *Making Sense of Marx*. Cambridge, England: Cambridge University Press.

Farrell (1950) "Experience," *Mind* 59, 170–98.

Gert, B. (1965) "Imagination and verifiability," *Philosophical Studies* 16, 44–7.

Geschwind, N. and Fusillo, M. (1966) "Color-naming defects in association with alexia," *Archives of Neurology* 15, 137–46.

Goldman, A. (1970) *A Theory of Human Action*. Englewood Cliffs, NJ: Prentice Hall.

Gregory, R. (1977) *Eye and Brain*, 3rd edn. London: Weidenfeld & Nicolson.

Hofstadter, D. and Dennett, D.C. (1981) *The Mind's I: Fantasies and Reflections on Mind and Soul*. New York: Basic Books.

Kim, J. (1982) "Psychophysical supervenience," *Philosophical Studies* 41, 51–70.

Kitcher, P. (1979) "Phenomenal qualities," *American Philosophical Quarterly* 16, 123–9.

Kripke, S. (1982) *Wittgenstein on Rules and Private Language*. Cambridge, MA: Harvard University Press.

Lehrer, A. (1983) *Wine and Conversation*. Bloomington, Indiana: Univ. of Indiana Press.

Lewis, D. (1983) "Extrinsic properties," *Philosophical Studies* 44, 197–200.

Locke, J. (1690) *An Essay Concerning Human Understanding* (A.C. Fraser edition). New York: Dover, 1959.

Lycan, W. (1973) "Inverted spectrum," *Ratio* XV, 315–19.

Malcolm, N. (1956) "Dreaming and skepticism," *Philosophical Review* 64, 14–37.

Malcolm, N. (1959) *Dreaming*. London: Routledge & Kegan Paul.

Meadows, J.C. (1974) "Disturbed perception of colours associated with localized cerebral lesions," *Brain* 97, 615–32.

Millikan, R. (1984) *Language, Thought and Other Biological Categories.* Cambridge, MA: Bradford/MIT.

Nagel, T. (1974) "What is it like to be a bat?," *Philosophical Review* 83, 435–51.

Nagel, T. (1986) *The View from Nowhere.* Oxford: Oxford University Press.

Peirce, C. (1931–58), C. Hartshorne and P. Weiss (eds), *Collected Works.* Cambridge, MA: Harvard University Press.

Peterson, R.T. (1947) *A Field Guide to the Birds.* Boston: Houghton Mifflin.

Putnam, H. (1965) "Brains and behavior," in J. Butler (ed.) *Analytical Philosophy* (second series). Oxford: Basil Blackwell.

Pylyshyn, Z. (1980) "Computation and cognition: Issues in the foundation of cognitive science," *Behavioral and Brain Sciences* 3, 111–32.

Pylyshyn, Z. (1984) *Computation and Cognition: Toward a Foundation for Cognitive Science.* Cambridge, MA: Bradford/MIT Press.

Sellars, W. (1981) "Foundations for a metaphysics of pure process" (the Carus Lectures), *Monist* 64, 3–90.

Shoemaker, S. (1969) "Time without change," *Journal of Philosophy* 66, 363–81.

Shoemaker, S. (1975) "Functionalism and qualia," *Philosophical Studies* 27, 291–315.

Shoemaker, S. (1981) "Absent qualia are impossible – A Reply to Block," *Philosophical Review* 90, 581–99.

Shoemaker, S. (1982) "The inverted spectrum," *Journal of Philosophy* 79, 357–81.

Shoemaker, S. (1984) "Postscript (1983)," in *Identity, Cause, and Mind.* Cambridge, England: Cambridge Univ. Press, pp. 351–7.

Smart, J.J.C. (1959) "Sensations and brain processes," *Philosophical Review* 68, 141–56. (Reprinted in Chappell 1962).

Stich, S. (1983) *From Folk Psychology to Cognitive Science: The Case Against Belief.* Cambridge, MA: Bradford/MIT.

Taylor, D.M. (1966) "The incommunicability of content," *Mind* 75, 527–41.

Von der Heydt, R., Peterhans, F., and Baumgartner, G. (1984) "Illusory contours and cortical neuron response," *Science* 224, 1260–2.

Walzer, M. (1985) "What's left of Marx," *New York Review of Books*, Nov. 21, pp. 43–6.

White, S. (1985) "Professor Shoemaker and so-called 'qualia' of experience," *Philosophical Studies* 47, 369–83.

Wittgenstein, L. (1958) G.E.M. Anscombe (ed.), *Philosophical Investigations.* Oxford: Basil Blackwell.

Owen Flanagan
Selections from *Consciousness Reconsidered:*
Chapter 5 — The Missing Shade of You

1 The Subject Is Experience

There is something it is like to be a subject of experience. This is uncontroversial. There is something distinctive that it is like to be each and every one of us. This is more controversial than the first claim. But it is true (Flanagan 1991a, chap. 3). What it is like to be you or any other subject of experience is closed off to me. This is controversial. The alleged fact that subjectivity is impenetrable spells doom for naturalism. Either naturalism is a view we do not understand, or we understand it but it is not up to the task of constructively accounting for subjectivity. This too is controversial. The aim of this chapter is to show that the controversial claims are false. What it is like to be you is not closed off to me, subjectivity is not impenetrable, and naturalism explains better than any alternative why subjectivity attaches uniquely to particular individuals.

2 The Missing Shade of Blue

In section 2 of his *Enquiry Concerning Human Understanding* (1777), Hume presents his argument that all "perceptions of the mind can be divided into two classes or species, which are distinguished by their different degrees of force and vivacity. The less forcible and lively are commonly denoted *Thoughts* or *Ideas*." The "more lively perceptions" are "impressions." Hume's copy theory is then expressed this way: "All our ideas or more feeble perceptions are copies of our impressions or more lively ones." No impression, no idea. One important piece of evidence for the copy theory, according to Hume is this: "If it happen, from a defect of the organ that a man is not susceptible of any species of sensation, we always find that he is as little susceptible of the correspondent ideas. A blind man can form no notion of colours; a deaf man of sounds" (1777, sec. 2, pars. 12-15).

Hume then produces a counterexample to his copy theory in the case of the missing shade of blue:

> Suppose ... a person to have enjoyed his sight for thirty years, and to have become perfectly acquainted with colours of all kinds except one particular shade of blue ... which it has never been his fortune to meet with. Let all the different shades of that colour, except that single one, be placed before him, descending gradually from the deepest to the lightest; it is plain that he will perceive a blank, where the shade is wanting, and will be sensible that there is a greater distance in that place between the contiguous colours than in any other. Now I ask whether it be possible for him, from his own imagination, to supply this deficiency, and to raise up to himself the idea of that particular shade, though it had never been conveyed to him by his senses? I believe there are few but will be of opinion that he can; and this may serve as a proof that the simple ideas are not always, in every instance, derived from correspondent impressions; though this instance is so singular, that it is scarcely worth our observing, and does not merit that for it alone we should alter our general maxim. (1777, sec. 2, par. 16)

It is important for Hume's theory that this counterexample turn out to be only apparent and not genuine, since, despite what he says, it is not so singular that it is scarcely worth our observing. Innumerable analogous examples can be generated across the sensory modalities.

The thought experiment raises questions about whether two different mental acts can be performed. First, can the person with no experience of $blue_5$, call him Hugh, *notice* that $blue_5$ is missing in a chart containing $blue_{1-4}$ and $blue_{6-10}$? Second, can Hugh *conjure up* an idea of $blue_5$ (remember, ideas can be dim and feeble)? A positive answer to the first question by no means requires a positive answer to the second. Hume, however, thinks that both questions are to be answered affirmatively. Hugh, the man who has missed out on the experience of $blue_5$, will notice its absence when faced with the gappy color chart, and he will also be able to conjure up the idea of $blue_5$. How is this possible? Both the noticing and the conjuring need explaining.

The laws of association might enable us to explain the noticing in this way. The law of resemblance, part of the innate structure of mind, disposes the mind to calculate the degree of resemblance or difference between the shades of blue on the color chart. The degree of resemblance is consistent except where $blue_6$ follows $blue_4$. The larger difference at this point produces the mental cramp that constitutes perceiving "a blank, where the shade is wanting," and noticing "that there is a greater distance in that place between the contiguous colours than in any other."

Noticing that a shade is missing is one thing. How is the more difficult task of conjuring up the idea of $blue_5$ accomplished? The best explanation is that Hugh does in imagination what could easily be done in the external world to produce $blue_5$. Once the gap is noticed, he mixes $blue_4$ and $blue_6$ in his imagination in the same way we would mix paints in the world. In this way $blue_5$ is conjured up and, as is the case with many ideas, is "faintly perceived," so to speak.

3 The Missing Shade of You

The missing shade of blue then presents no insurmountable problem. There are ways to get at it even if we lack direct experience of it. There is something it is like to experience $blue_5$. One who is not directly acquainted with $blue_5$ can grasp what $blue_5$ is like, even if more dimly than someone who has actually experienced $blue_5$.

Things are different with other minds than with colors. If I am not you, I cannot grasp what it is like to be you. I can perhaps conjure up the missing shade of blue, but I cannot conjure up the missing shade of you. Or so some philosophers have argued. If we imagine that there is something there is like to be each particular person and that what it is like to be each individual person constitutes a particular shade in the colorful array of possible experiencers, then for each and every one of us, lacking direct experience of any other experiential system as we do, we know that there is some unique shade coloring the inner life of each and every person. But we cannot grasp, capture, or directly experience any shade other than the one that colors our own inner lives. Hence the missing shade of you.

4 Capturing You: The Very Idea

In his famous essay "What It Is Like to Be a Bat?" (1974), Thomas Nagel vividly forces the question that concerns us: to what extent can subjectivity be captured from the outside? Nagel thinks that subjectivity is impenetrable. His argument focuses on attempts to capture experience from the objective perspective of science, but his argument easily generalizes to the situation each of us faces in trying to understand the inner lives of other persons in ordinary, everyday circumstances. By showing how

Nagel goes wrong, I can provide reasons for thinking that consciousness in general is tractable from a naturalistic perspective, and for thinking that particular subjects of experience can be known as such by other subjects of experience. Many of the same resources available to Hugh that allow him to conjure up the missing shade of blue are available to me as I try to conjure up the missing shade of you. When I conjure up the missing shade of you, do I capture or grasp you? Of course not. That would be overstepping my bounds.

Nagel's argument for the intractability of consciousness proceeds in several steps. First, he claims that "no matter how the form may vary, the fact that an organism has conscious experience *at all* means, basically, that there is something it is like to be that organism" (1974, 166). An "organism has conscious mental states if and only if there is something it is like to *be* that organism—something it is like *for* that organism … We may call this the subjective character of experience" (1974, 166). Second, he claims that if the naturalist's program is to succeed, the phenomenological features of mental life, the "something it is like to be" features, must be given a naturalistic account. "If physicalism is to be defended, the phenomenological features must themselves be given a physical account" (1974, 167). Third, he denies this possibility. "But when we examine their subjective character it seems that such a result is impossible. The reason is that every subjective phenomena is essentially connected with a single point of view, and it seems inevitable that an objective, physical theory will abandon that point of view" (1974, 167). The subjective character of experience "is fully comprehensible from only one point of view." Therefore, "any shift to greater objectivity—that is, less attachment to a specific viewpoint—does not take us nearer to the real nature of the phenomenon: it takes us farther away from it" (1974, 174). Finally, he informs us that "this bears directly on the mind-body problem. For if the facts of experience—facts

about what it is like *for* the experiencing organism are accessible only from one point of view, then it is a mystery how the true character of experiences could be revealed in the physical operation of that organism" (1974, 172). The argument has disturbing consequences for physicalism: "Physicalism is a position we cannot understand because we do not at present have any conception of how it might be true" (1974, 176). This view I call "principled agnosticism."

Nagel is led astray because of two implicit, misguided, and interconnected assumptions. The first source of trouble is Nagel's claim that moving away from the phenomenological surface inevitably takes us "farther away" from "the real nature of the phenomenon." Why think that how consciousness seems gets at its real nature? To be sure, the phenomenological aspects of experience are real and require an account. But unless one thinks that the conscious mind is diaphanous, one should not think that its real nature is revealed fully by its first-person appearances. The second source of trouble originates in a certain positivistic picture of science and of philosophical analyses that take science seriously. This attitude comes out in Nagel's claim that no naturalistic analysis will be able to make room for the facts of first-person phenomenology, for "the true character of experiences" (1974, 172).

As I have been framing the naturalistic project, there are a series of questions that will need to be answered and then brought into equilibrium with one another. One important part of the inquiry has to do with getting clear on whether there are any shared phenomenological features of conscious mental life, whether, that is, there is anything it is like to be a member of our species. In trying to frame an answer to this question, I will be somewhat less interested in how exactly things seem for any particular individual than in the overlap among individuals. But this greater interest in the species than in the unique features of the individuals in no way implies that the naturalist doubts that there is something it is like to be each particular one of us. The issue here is simply interest-relative. For obvious reasons, you, your loved ones, and your therapist will be much more interested in the fine-grained details of exactly how your inner life seems than will the framer of a general theory of mind.

In any case, once we get a fairly good picture of how conscious mental life seems, we will want to see if the seeming features can be interpreted realistically. That is, we will want to see how the way things seem from the first-person point of view fit with data from other, impersonal sources: from third-person phenomenology, evolutionary theory, cognitive psychology, and neuroscience. Nagel repeatedly insists that this move will involve abandoning the subjective point of view. And he claims that "any shift to greater objectivity—that is, less attachment to a specific viewpoint—does not take us nearer to the real nature of the phenomenon: it takes us farther away" (1974, 174).

But this claim is much overstated. First, there is nothing in the naturalist's approach that requires abandoning the subjective point of view as the source of human phenomenology or as a rich source of data for hypothesis generation about what is in fact going on. Indeed, part of the overall strategy I have been recommending involves a fine-grained attention to phenomenological detail, partly on the supposition that there are many different kinds of awareness with many different causal roles, some but not all of which causal roles we have reliable access to.

Second and relatedly, the claim that moving to the objective point of view "does not take us nearer to the real nature of the phenomenon: it takes us farther away" is deceptively ambiguous between two senses of 'real nature'. If 'real nature' is meant, as it appears, to refer to the way things seem to some particular person, then it is true in certain respects that becoming more objective will take us farther away from the phenomenon. But the reason for

this—for why objective analysis is not as well suited as subjective analysis for gaining insight into how things seem to us in the first person— is something the naturalist can explain. It is because persons are uniquely causally well connected to their own experiences. They, after all, are the ones who have them. Furthermore, there is no deep mystery as to why this special causal relation obtains. The organic integrity of individuals and the structure and function of individual nervous systems grounds each individual's special relation to how things seem for him (Quine 1952, 213). John Dewey put it best: "Given that consciousness exists at all, there is no mystery in its being connected with what it is connected with" (1922, 62).

If, on the other hand, by 'real nature' Nagel means what is really going on in the cognitive system as a whole, including whether conscious mental events are actually playing the causal role they seem to the agent to be playing and whether they are physically realized or not, then the claim that looking at things from a more objective point of view will necessarily lead us astray is quite incredible. Its only conceivable warrant is allegiance to the bankrupt version of the doctrine of privileged access.

The important point is this: there is absolutely no reason why a naturalist cannot both acknowledge the existence of subjectivity and view getting an accurate description of it as part of the overall project of understanding human nature. It is crucial to see that description at the phenomenological level is something that can be provided from the first-person point of view and the third-person point of view. I can say how I think things seem for you, sometimes before you see that this is how they seem to you. Sometimes you will even treat my account of how things seem for you as authoritative. "You're right, I just don't feel the same way about him anymore." Saying how things seem is a project involving intersubjective give-and-take. You have special authority (but not infallibility) about how things seem for you here and now. You have very little authority if you have views about how your mental processes actually work or how mental events are realized. Getting clear on the phenomenology is not an essentially private enterprise. Good phenomenology is group phenomenology.

In his brief against naturalism, Nagel concedes that analyses of conscious mental states in terms of their neural substrate or in terms of their functional or causal roles may explain certain aspects of these states. He writes, "I deny only that this kind of thing exhausts their analysis" (1974, 167). But here he mischaracterizes naturalism. The wise naturalist is not a reductionist. He is not committed to the idea that a theory spelling out how conscious mental states are realized in the brain, even when combined with a theory of the causal role of conscious mental states, "exhausts their analysis." The analysis must also include a description of the phenomenology, perhaps a revision of the phenomenology that we started with, but a robust phenomenology nonetheless. The analysis is designed not to eliminate the phenomenal facts but to deepen our understanding of them.

A nonreductive naturalistic theory will provide a rich phenomenology, a theory of how the phenomenology connects up with behavior, a theory about how conscious mental events taxonomized into many different classes of awareness figure in the overall economy of mental life, a theory of how mental life evolved, and thereby a theory of which features of mind are the result of direct selection and which features are free riders, and finally, it will provide a neuroscientific realization theory, that is, a theory about how all the different kinds of mental events, conscious and unconscious, are realized in the nervous system. An analysis that includes a phenomenology in addition to a theory of neurophysiological realization and a theory of causal role will be as exhaustive as an analysis can be.

Here one might expect a slightly different gloss on the denial that this sort of analysis can be exhaustive in the requisite sense. No matter how well analyzed the phenomenon of consciousness is by such a (yet-to-be-developed) theory, the theory will fail fully to *capture* consciousness. Now there are several ways in which a theory that provides an exhaustive analysis of consciousness might nonetheless be said to fail to capture something important about consciousness. First, it might be charged that such a theory fails to capture what exactly conscious mental life is like for each individual person. Nagel's continual mention of the way consciousness attaches essentially to a "single point of view" indicates that this bothers him. But here there is an easy response. Theorizing of the sort I have been recommending is intended not to capture what it is like to be each individual person but only to capture, in the sense of providing an analysis for, the type (or types) of conscious mind and, what is different, conscious person. Although the general analysis is not intended to do so, you, of course, are entitled to capture what it is like to be you. Indeed, it is unavoidable.

There is a second and more perplexing sort of the "failure to capture consciousness" charge. Recall that part of a general naturalistic theory will be a theory of how the human nervous system works, a theory of how mental life is realized in us. The core assumption is that although mental states are relational states involving complex causal connections with the natural and social environment as well as with other mental states, they are, in the final analysis, tokened in the brain. But Nagel, and he is not alone, finds it unimaginable that a theory of neurophysiological realization could reveal "the true character of experiences" (1974, 172), where by the latter phrase Nagel means how these experiences feel. Indeed, this worry in particular leads Nagel to the view that we at present have no conception of how physicalism *could* be true.

Yet we do understand how physicalism can be true. It can be true if every mental event is realized in the brain. Those of us who believe that all mental events, conscious and unconscious, are tokened in the brain do not believe that the theory that eventually explains *how* they are tokened will capture "the true character of the experiences" as experiences. The whole idea that the qualitative feel of some experience should reveal itself in a theoretical description of how that experience is realized fails to acknowledge the abstract relation between any theory and the phenomena it accounts for. Even the phenomenological part of the project I have recommended, which, unlike the realization theory, is directly concerned with how things seem to the subject, is itself at one remove (namely, a linguistic remove) from the experiences themselves. But the naturalist is the first to accept that a particular realization will be an experience only for the agent who is causally connected to the realization in the right sort of way. Once again, the biological integrity of the human body can account straightforwardly for the happy fact that we each have our *own*, and only our own, experiences. But this can hardly be much comfort to Nagel insofar as it shows the coherence and explanatory power of a naturalistic account of the unique way in which experiences are "captured" by their owners.

Naturalism can explain why only you can capture what it is like to be you. Only your sensory receptors and brain are properly hooked up to each other and to the rest of you so that what is received at those receptors accrues to you as your experiences. That consciousness exists at all is amazing. But given that it does, Dewey is right that "there is no mystery with its being connected with what it is connected with" (1922, 62).

In the final analysis, your experiences are yours alone; only you are in the right causal position to know what they seem like. Nothing could be more important with respect to how your life seems and to how things go for you overall, but nothing could be less consequential with respect to the overall fate of the naturalistic picture of things.

5 Grasping Experiences

Colin McGinn (1991) offers a more recent argument that makes the same mistaken presumption that if physicalism is true, a theory that explains how some set of experiences is realized or what their causal role is should enable us to *grasp* those very experiences as they are experienced by their subjects.

> Suppose ... that we had the solution to the problem of how specific forms of consciousness depend upon different kinds of physiological structure. Then, of course, we would understand how the brain of a bat subserves the subjective experience of bats. Call this type of experience B, and call the explanatory property that links B to the bat's brain P_1. By grasping P_1 it would be perfectly intelligible to us how the bat's brain generates B-experiences; we would have an explanatory theory of the causal nexus in question. We would be in possession of the same kind of understanding we would have of our own experiences if we had the correct psychophysical theory of them. But then it seems to follow that grasp of the theory that explains B-experiences would *confer* a grasp of the nature of those experiences: for how could we understand that theory without understanding the concept B that occurs in it? How could we grasp the *nature* of B-experiences without grasping the *character* of those experiences? The true psychophysical theory would seem to provide a route to a grasp of the subjective form of the bat's experiences. But now we face a dilemma, a dilemma which threatens to become a reductio: either we *can* grasp this theory, in which case the property B becomes open to us; or we *cannot* grasp the theory, simply because B is *not* open to us. (McGinn 1991, 9)

The reductio ad absurdum that McGinn thinks is lurking destroys two ideas at once: the idea that we could ever possess a theory that renders "perfectly intelligible" the link between subjective mental life and brain processes, and the idea that we could ever "grasp the subjective form" of the experiences of another type of creature. McGinn thinks that the problem of other minds can be solved, but only in cases where the concepts we need in understanding another's mind are concepts that refer to properties we ourselves instantiate. This condition may be satisfied for other humans; it is not satisfied in the case of us and bats. I'll come back to this issue in the final section. Right now I simply want to deal with the central argument contained in the quoted passage:

1. If we had an explanatory theory of the causal nexus in question, that is, a theory of how the bat's brain generates bat experiences, we should grasp the nature of the subjective life of bats.

2. This is because a grasp of a theory that explains a certain set of experiences should "*confer* a grasp" of the nature and character of those experiences.

3. If it failed to confer this grasp, we would be in the absurd position of possessing a theory that makes "perfectly intelligible" the relation between a set of phenomena we do not understand.

When the argument is laid out in this way, it becomes clearer that the notion of grasping is deployed in two different senses: there is grasping some causal theory and grasping experiences, where grasping experiences means knowing what these experiences are like. Yet there is no necessary connection between understanding a theory that explains some set of experiences (grasp$_1$) and "grasping the *character*" of those experiences (grasp$_2$). Experiences function as explananda. Good theories explain their explananda. In this way they reveal the nature of the explananda. In the case of experiences, our best neuroscientific theory will ex-

plain that there is an aspect of experiences, the phenomenological aspect, that is only grasped by the system having the experiences. McGinn wonders rhetorically, "How could we grasp the *nature* of B-experiences without grasping the *character* of those experiences?" The non-rhetorical answer is this. In understanding the theory (grasp$_1$), we understand (grasp$_1$) the nature of the experiences the theory explains in that we understand (grasp$_1$) what neural states the experiences supervene on, and we understand (grasp$_1$) that only the systems that are suitably designed, hooked up, and so on, to have (grasp$_2$) those experiences have (grasp$_2$) them. The theory explains (grasp$_1$) why bats have (grasp$_2$) bat experiences and why we don't have (grasp$_2$) bat experiences. (For other persons, we are in something like a position of grasping$_{1.5}$ their experiences. I'll return to this issue at the end.)

The first problem thus involves equivocation of the senses of 'grasp'. Neither premise 1 nor premise 2 are credible when the relevant senses of 'grasp' are substituted. The equivocation is the source of the illusion that an understanding of some set of experiences necessarily involves grasping the character of these experiences. This takes care of the first horn of the dilemma that McGinn thinks "threatens to become a reductio." There is no incoherence in comprehending some theory that explains bat experiences without grasping exactly what bat experiences are like for bats. Indeed, the theory itself will explain why only bats grasp$_2$ their experiences.

There is still an opening. Perhaps we can be impaled on the second horn of the dilemma: "we *cannot* grasp the theory, simply because B [bat experience] is *not* open to us." McGinn has one of his rhetorical questions at the ready to suggest that this is truly an absurd view: "how could we understand that theory without understanding the concept B that occurs in it?" The horn is easily avoided by seeing that its source lies in the unreasonable expectation that grasping a theory (grasp$_1$) should "open" the experiences to us (grasp$_2$). If we don't grasp$_2$ bat experiences once we grasp$_1$ the theory that explains bat experiences, then we don't really understand (grasp$_1$) the theory. The problematic equivocation does its mischievous work again.

Furthermore, it is a perfectly common occurrence in the course of theory development in science that the phenomena to be explained are poorly or superficially understood at the beginning of inquiry. That is why one needs the theory. There is no incoherence in the idea of understanding some theory T that explains, as best we can, some phenomenon P, where P is imperfectly understood. We understand P as best we can, given the state of our theory. But we expect our understanding of P to be enriched as theory matures. For example, it used to be thought that bats were blind. It turns out that they have good vision. Bats live well and successfully by using their fine night vision and powers of echolocation. We know that much about what it is like to be a bat. Someday we may know much more. After all, it was *in the course* of the development of a theory about bats that certain facts about bat experience revealed themselves.

McGinn has one small opening. He tries to have us imagine that we are at the end of inquiry. Surely it would be incoherent for us to possess a theory that makes the causal nexus "perfectly intelligible" without our understanding fully all the terms of the theory related. A lot depends here on what perfect intelligibility consists in and what full understanding of all the terms of the theory entails. If we require that understanding the concept of bat experience (grasp$_1$) involves grasping bat experiences (grasp$_2$) we are back to the old problem. A theory of experience should not be expected to provide us with some sort of direct acquaintance with what the experiences it accounts for are like for their owners. Indeed, there is no incoherence in the idea of an extremely robust explanatory and predictive theory of bat brain

and behavior that explains exactly how bat vision and echolocation work but leaves unanswered the question of whether bats experience the sights and sounds they undoubtedly compute. If we are truly at the end of inquiry, we will, I assume, have a very firm opinion about whether, how, and when bats have experiences. But being fallible, we will always have reason for doubt. We could have the full explanatory theory in place without being certain whether there is something it is like to be a bat.

6 Missing Shades Again

The same sort of response applies to Frank Jackson's (1982, 1986) well-known argument about Mary, the world's greatest color scientist. Mary lives in a black and white and gray world. She knows everything physical that there is to know about what goes on in any normal brain when the person who houses that brain experiences red. But Mary does not know what it is like to experience red. This she knows only when she escapes to the colorful world and sees ripe tomatoes and strawberries, red apples and roses, and so on. Since the facts Mary comes to know, facts about what it is like to experience red, are not captured by the most complete neuroscientific theory of color, physicalism is false. Because phenomenal properties are not captured by the most complete set of objective descriptions of the brain activity subserving these very experiences, phenomenal properties are not explained by, nor can they be identified with, physical properties.

In a recent reply to critics, Jackson (1986) provides a "convenient and accurate way of displaying the argument":

1. Mary (before her release) knows everything physical there is to know about other people.
2. Mary (before her release) does not know everything there is to know about other people (because she *learns* something about them on her release).

3. Therefore, there are truths about other people (and herself) that escape the physicalist story.

Jackson clarifies the main point this way: "The trouble for physicalism is that, after Mary sees her first ripe tomato, she will realize how impoverished her conception of the mental life of *others* has been *all along* ... But she knew all the physical facts about them all along; hence what she did not know until her release is not a physical fact about their experiences. But it is a fact about them. That is the trouble with physicalism ... There are truths about other people (and herself) that escape the physicalist story" (1986, 393). Jackson tells us that Mary "knows all the physical facts about us and our environment, in a wide sense of 'physical' which includes everything in *completed* physics, chemistry, and neurophysiology, and all there is to know about the causal and relational facts consequent upon all this, including of course functional roles. If physicalism is true she knows all there is to know ... Physicalists must hold that complete physical knowledge is complete knowledge simpliciter" (1986, 392).

The argument is seductive, but it is easy to defeat. The problem is with premise 1. This is a thought experiment that can be kept from starting. Mary knows everything about color vision that can be expressed in the vocabularies of a complete physics, chemistry, and neuroscience. She also knows everything there is to know about the functional role of color vision (this assumption requires charity on my part, since I think she actually lacks knowledge about the first-person functional role of color vision). She knows that when the eye is exposed to wavelengths of light in the red range, the persons whose eyes are so exposed have red channel activation, they claim to see red, they are disposed to use the word 'red' in sentences, and so on. Does Mary know what red experiences are like? No. She has never had one. Red experiences are physical events: they are complex

relational states of individuals undergoing red-channel activation (in truth, there is a red-green channel that is activated differently for red and green; see Hardin 1988). Mary knows that. Her theory tells her so. But she doesn't know what red experiences are like, nor does she possess the concept of red as it is possessed by someone who has experienced red. She has never been in the appropriate complex relational state. She knows that too.

One way to avoid the seduction here is to distinguish between metaphysical and linguistic physicalism. Metaphysical physicalism simply asserts that what there is, and all there is, is physical stuff and its relations. Linguistic physicalism is the thesis that everything physical can be expressed or captured in the languages of the basic sciences: *"completed* physics, chemistry, and neurophysiology."* Linguistic physicalism is stronger than metaphysical physicalism and less plausible (Fodor 1981). Jackson gives Mary all knowledge expressible in the basic sciences, and he stresses that for physicalism to be true all facts must be expressed or expressible in "explicitly physical language." This is linguistic physicalism. It can be false without metaphysical physicalism being false. This is easy to see.

One piece of knowledge Mary possesses is that red-channel activation causes red perception. Red perception is a physical event and will be understood by Mary as such. It is metaphysically unproblematic. But there is no reason to think that there will be some expression in the basic sciences that will capture or express what it is like to experience red, or that will provide Mary with the phenomenal concept of red or the phenomenal component of the concept of red. Knowledge of the phenomenological component of red requires first-person relations of a certain sort between a stimulus of a certain type and a suitably hooked-up organism. It requires seeing something red.

Jackson insists that we should interpret premise 1 to mean that Mary possesses all the knowledge that the basic sciences can provide, and he suggests that this entails that she knows everything: "Physicalists must hold that complete physical knowledge is complete knowledge simpliciter" (1986, 392). Yes and no. Physicalists must hold that complete physical knowledge is complete knowledge simpliciter in the sense that they must hold that when Mary finds out what red is like, she has learned something about the physical world. But this hardly implies that complete knowledge in the basic sciences can express or capture this item of knowledge without the relevant causal interchange between perceiver and perceived. Mary might know everything that can be expressed in the languages of completed physics, chemistry, and neuroscience, but this hardly entails that she knows "all there is to know." What else there is to know is nothing mysterious. It is physical. And it can be expressed in certain ways. It is simply that it cannot be perspicuously expressed in the vocabulary of the basic sciences.

So premise 1 is false. Mary does not know "everything physical there is to know about other people." The metaphysical physicalist will not think that what she does know—everything completed physics, chemistry, and neuroscience have to offer—is sufficient to convey everything there is to know about other people, since it is not sufficient to convey phenomenal feel! But premise 2 is true. Mary does learn something new upon her release. In light of the falsehood of premise 1, the truth of premise 2 does not support the intended reductio of physicalism. Mary really does learn something new. It isn't quite right to say that she knows *exactly* what she knew before but simply knows it in a different way, say in some non-linguistic way (P.M. Churchland 1989). The reason that this isn't quite right is because Mary will credibly claim to know something new: "So *that* is what it is like to have one's red channels turned on!" She learns what it is like to experience red. The perceptual concept of red is triggered in Mary's mind by the basic biological mechanisms that subserve normal color perception (Loar 1990; Van Gulick, in

press a). Mary's red channel has been turned on for the first time. She knew all about the red channel before, but her own red channel had never been turned on. 'Experiencing red' always referred to tokens of the event type, red channel on. Mary never knew what it was like to be in a state of this type. She had never had an experience of red. She now has had direct, first-person experience of what happens to an organism undergoing red-channel activation. Perceptual capture is done in the first person. I repeat: unless her theory was radically incomplete, she knew that before she saw her first red tomato.

Mary, remember, is very knowledgeable. This is why it is implausible for Jackson to write, "The trouble for physicalism is that, after Mary sees her first ripe tomato, she will realize how impoverished her conception of *others* has been *all along*." Mary knows that she has never experienced red; she knows from her rich sensory life in the four active modalities just how heterogeneous and rich sensory experiences are. She doesn't know what it is like for others to experience red, other than that their red channels are on. But Mary is smart. She knows what she doesn't know, and she would never dare try to develop a view so firm about what it is like to experience red that her view could turn out to be false or impoverished. Mary is no dope. Yet Jackson has made her extremely smart. He can't have Mary both so smart she knows all that he says she knows, and so stupid that she will be so surprised upon seeing that first tomato. Mary will have an utterly novel experience. But it will neither throw her into a state of shock nor cause her to jump the ship of her theory. She expected the novelty. Her theory told her to.

An experience of red is how we describe the state she has never been in up to departure from the black and white room. 'An experience of red' is not in the language of physics. But an experience of red is a physical event in a suitably hooked-up system. Therefore, the experience is not a problem for metaphysical physicalism. It is a physical event after all. Completed physics, chemistry, and neuroscience, along with a functional-role description, will explain what an experience of red is, in the sense that they will explain how red experiences are realized, what their functional role is, and so on. But no linguistic description will completely *capture* what a first-person experience of red is like. That is only captured in the first person. You have to be there.

This explains why I want to deny premise 1. Mary does not have complete physical knowledge. She does not have complete physical knowledge even if she possesses complete knowledge in all the basic physical sciences. Despite her complete theoretical knowledge about everything that does happen or can happen in a human mind, there are indeterminately many neural states (all those subserving color experiences) that she has never been in. That is, there are indeterminately many bits of knowledge, those in the class of color experiences, that Mary has never possessed. These experiences, were she to have them, would be physical occurrences. She knows that, and she knows how such occurrences are realized in others. But the realization theory does not express or entail all there is to know about color experiences. The phenomenal features are conveyed only in the first person. Mary knows all the third-person, theoretical sentences that describe color sensations. But she herself has never (yet) instantiated the states that the sentences describe.

We didn't require Mary to get to this point. All "omniscient" mind theorists, if they have not had all the experiences they possess analyses for, will lack certain knowledge, and the knowledge they will lack is knowledge of physical phenomena. It is knowledge of experiences as realized in human nervous systems. The theory tells us that such knowledge requires first-person connections of a certain sort. It even tells us why it is good design to have experiences captured only by the systems that have them. It would be extremely idle labor if our theories enabled us to have experiences or engendered grasping experiences in the strong sense. But that, sad to say, is what some

philosophers seem to yearn for. The plea seems to be, Don't distance me from my experiences. The right response is one of reassurance. Unless your friends are radical reductionists or epiphenomenalists, no one is trying to distance you or to disconnect you from your experiences. Don't worry. Be happy. Have your experiences. Enjoy them.

In the end, we need to beware of the temptation to think that for physicalism to be true, the basic physical sciences must be able to *capture* all truths. This is stronger than requiring that physicalism be true; that is, it is stronger than requiring that everything that happens is physical. Physicalism can be true in this sense without being able to explain everything, let alone capture everything in the languages of the basic physical sciences. There are places where physical explanation has come upon its own limits, for example, with Heisenberg's Uncertainty Principle. The principled impossibility of predicting the simultaneous position and momentum of an electron is a limit on physical explanation. But it does not undermine physicalism, the view that what there is, and all there is, is physical stuff and its relations. Indeed, the uncertainty principle is a finding that concerns two utterly physical phenomena: electron position and electron momentum.

Rather than harming naturalism, the arguments I have discussed show its power and resiliency. This is easy to see. A standard criterion of theoretical superiority is this. T_2 is better than T_1 if T_2 explains everything T_1 explains plus some of what T_1 does not explain. Now T_1 asserts that subjective consciousness cannot possibly be captured from the objective point of view. T_1 asserts this but doesn't explain it. But the naturalist's theory, T_2, explains why subjective consciousness cannot be captured from an objective point of view, insofar as it *cannot* be captured from an objective point of view. The organic integrity of bodies explains why each organism has its own, and only its own, experiences. It would have been a bad evolutionary design to have experiences sitting around disembodied. It is best that experiences are captured by and attached to the organisms to whose ongoing life they are most relevant. The project for theory is to characterize and explain our experiences, not to have them or enable third parties to have them. We ourselves will have them, thank you.

7 Refrain: The Missing Shade of You

When last seen, your colorful inner life was a missing shade as viewed from the perspective of every other subject of experience. No one else has had the experiences that constitute the unique coloration of your inner life. You, and you alone, are the subject of your experiences. Does that sound scary? Does that make you feel lonely? If it does make you feel scared and lonely, it can only be because you have been seduced by two illusions. The first illusion is that somehow things would be better if others really did penetrate your being, and you theirs. Think about it.

The second illusion is that by virtue of being the sole subject of your experiences, no one else can imaginatively come to see the missing shade that is you. Though theory cannot engender such penetration, there is a powerful impulse to think that it is important in ordinary life that we penetrate each other's inner lives and capture each other's subjectivity. But what is important is not the interpenetration of being. What is important is that we understand each other. Between grasping an abstract theory of some phenomena (grasp$_1$) and having an experience (grasp$_2$), there is grasping$_{1.5}$. This is when I take your experience, as I understand it, into my mind for the sake of trying to understand what things are like for you.

There is no great mystery about how such understanding is accomplished. It involves sensitive detection of what others say, do, and intend. This is accomplished by deploying a complex psychological vocabulary to describe and explain what is detected. The rudiments of this vocabulary are acquired during the second year of life. It is then enriched throughout life as it comes to contain complex meanings that explicitly and implicitly convey the multifarious commitments of a whole form of life that has historical roots and is expressed in culture.

Once on a trip to Vermont, my daughter Kate was seated directly behind me while I was at the wheel, and I made some comment about something Kate was doing. Surprised by my perceptual powers while looking straight ahead, Kate commented that I, like my own mother (as I had reported), had eyes in the back of my head. Ben, seated next to Kate, informed us that in fact no one, not even a parent, had eyes in the back of his head. Humans are simply "mental detectors." Both ideas—eyes in the back of one's head and mental detectors—are meant to explain how humans, especially grown-up humans, can "see" what others are up to, how we can both surmise that certain behaviors are occurring and put the behaviors under the right intentional description. This metaphor of us as mental detectors is a powerful one. Just as a metal detector detects metal objects beneath the sand or between blades of grass, so too mental detectors detect invisible mental states. Good mental detectors understand a great deal about the form of life in which they live and about behavioral regularities. That is why grown-ups are much better mental detectors than children.

When the form of life is not shared, understanding is more difficult. Nagel puts the point in terms of us humans and bats: "We must consider whether any method will permit us to extrapolate to the inner life of the bat from our own case ... Our own experience provides the basic material for our imagination, whose range is therefore limited" (1974, 169). Learning about echolocation and suiting up in equipment that simulates what the best scientists think echolocation is like "will not help. Insofar as I can imagine this (which is not very far) it tells me only what it would be like for *me* to behave as a bat behaves. But that is not the question. I want to know what it is like for a *bat* to be a bat" (Nagel 1974, 169). He concludes that we "cannot form more than a schematic conception of what it *is* like ... We may ascribe general *types* of experience on the basis of the animal's structure and ... But we believe that these experiences also have in each case a specific subjective character, which it is beyond our ability to conceive" (1974, 169–170).

There are two important claims here. The first claim is that, although we might understand that bats undergo echolocating experiences, it is "beyond our ability to conceive" the "specific subjective character" of these experiences. If what is beyond our ability here is to have a sonar experience in just the way a bat does, then the point seems true but trivial. Only bats have bat experiences. But if I can form a schematic conception of the type echolocating-experience and can put myself into a position where I have an echolocating experience, then it seems plausible to say that I have gained some understanding of what it is like to echolocate, and thus that I have gained some understanding of what it is like to be a bat. The problem is understanding what failing to conceive of the "specific subjective character" of the experience of another is to be contrasted with. When do we succeed at grasping this specific subjective character of another's experience? If conceiving of the specific subjective character of the experiences of another means having the experiences exactly as the experiencer has them, then this never happens. This problem is not one that separates sighted people from bats and blind persons, it separates each subject of experience from every other. But if conceiving of the specific subjective character of another's experience means something less than that, for example, if it means understanding another or conceiving of what things are like from another's point of view, then it often happens.

The second claim, that working on echolocation "will not help," is ambiguous. It might mean that I can't have echolocating experiences.

But that is patently false. All humans make some use of echolocation in getting about. If anything will help to form "a schematic conception" of what it is like to be a bat, practicing echolocation will. To be sure, this will only tell me what it is like for me to take on certain bat-like properties. This seems to be why Nagel thinks that becoming a master echolocater "will not help." It will be me having echolocating experiences, not me having bat echolocating experiences. But if this is the right interpretation, then one wonders again what the contrastive case is. What other possibilities are there? When I imagine what it is like to be you, am I doing something different than imagining what it is like to be you from my point of view? How could I do anything else? All my experiences are my experiences. The most empathic act the world has ever known occurred from the point of view of the empathizer. There is no other way it could have happened. If the problem is that every attempt to understand the mental life of another must be from a particular point of view, this is a problem every subject of experience has in understanding every other subject of experience. Bats play no essential role in the argument whatsoever.

Nagel goes on to claim that persons blind or deaf from birth are other examples of cases that are "beyond our ability to conceive." And McGinn chimes in to say, "You cannot form concepts of conscious properties unless you yourself instantiate these properties. The man born blind cannot grasp the concept of a visual experience of red, and human beings cannot conceive of the echolocating experiences of bats. These are cases of cognitive closure within the class of conscious properties" (1991, 8–9).

But here we need to be reminded of our capacities to create and conjure up novel experiences. Again consider Mary, the omniscient color-vision expert. One might wonder why Mary can't conjure up color experiences in the way in which the Humean character Hugh can. The simplest answer is that Hugh has had lots of color experience. Mary has had none. Hugh can make blue$_5$ from other shades he knows about. Mary is a complete know-nothing about all colors. She, unlike Hugh, has no shades to mix. But consider this possibility. Remember that Mary knows that the sensation of red supervenes on activation of the red channel. Suppose that she discovers a novel way to tweak the red channel. She discovers that staring at a black dot for a minute and then quickly downing a shot of brandy produces red hallucinations. (Hardin [1988, 91–92] lists ten different ways to see colors without being exposed to "colorful" objects!) Mary does as well with red as Hugh does with blue$_5$, maybe even better. After all, she has the impression of red, whereas Hugh only has a faint idea of blue$_5$.

Hugh and Mary have resources at their disposal to have experiences that neither has had in the usual way. From these two thought experiments, there seem to be two ways to grasp a shade one has not seen. Either one mixes in imagination shades one already knows to form a conception of a new shade, or one figures out a nonstandard way—staring at dots and drinking strong liquor, pressing on one's eyeball, eating wild mushrooms—that activates the desired color channels. It is possible that in similar ways I can conjure up or creatively construct the missing shade of you, even if you are a very alien type of creature. I can spend time with you, read anthropological accounts about your kind, and in this way gain imaginative entry into your life form and eventually into what it is like for you to be you.

If Mary can figure out a way to turn on her red channels without retinal stimulation, perhaps the blind person with retinal destruction but intact red channels can too. If Hugh can conjure up the missing shade of blue from other color experiences he has had, I can surely conjure up what it is like to echolocate from my own limited experience.

Phenomenological opacity is a matter of degree. We never have exactly the same experiences as any other subject of experience. But

this does not preclude understanding all manner of unusual subjective life forms. Nagel concedes this when he writes,

> It is often possible to take up a point of view other than one's own, so the comprehension of such facts is not limited to one's own case. There is a sense in which phenomenological facts are *perfectly objective*: one person can know or say of another what the quality of the other's experience is. They are subjective, however, in the sense that even this objective ascription of experience is possible only for someone sufficiently similar to the object of ascription to adopt his point of view—to understand the ascription in the first person as well as in the third, so to speak. The more different from oneself the other experiencer is, the less success one can expect with this enterprise. (Nagel 1974, 172)

A telling footnote attaches to this passage:

> It may be easier than I suppose to transcend inter-species barriers with the aid of imagination ... Blind people are able to detect objects near them by a form of sonar, using vocal clicks or taps of a cane. Perhaps if one knew what that was like, one could by extension imagine roughly what it was like to possess the much more refined sonar of a bat. The distance between oneself and other persons and other species can fall anywhere on a continuum. Even for other persons the understanding what it is like to be them is only partial, and when one moves to species very different from oneself, a lesser degree of partial understanding may still be available. The imagination is remarkably flexible. My point, however, is not that we cannot *know* what it is like to be a bat. I am not raising that epistemological problem. My point is rather that even to form a *conception* of what it is like to

be a bat (and *a fortiori* to know what it is like to be a bat) one must take up the bat's point of view. If one can take it up roughly, or partially, then one's conception will also be rough or partial. (Nagel 1974, 172)

Imagination is remarkably flexible. Even among persons, understanding is only partial. For species farther away, understanding is harder. But since these things are a matter of degree, there is no incoherence in thinking that we can (work to) form a conception of a bat, a person blind or deaf from birth, a person with a multiple personality disorder, and so on.

I have insisted throughout that it is possible to do phenomenology from both the third-person and first-person points of view. A. R. Luria's *The Man with the Shattered World* (1972), Oliver Sacks's *Awakenings* (1983), and the essays contained in Sacks's *The Man Who Mistook His Wife for a Hat* (1985) are masterpieces of third-person phenomenology. Helen Keller's memoirs are a masterpiece of first-person phenomenology. These works play with imagination, perhaps in the way in which Mary plays with black dots and brandy, to help produce some comprehension of lives radically different from our own. Once we gain imaginative entry into these lives, do we instantiate the properties so described? When we read about a prosopagnosiac who moves through life without recognizing faces, do we now instantiate the property of not seeing faces as faces? Of course not. Do we comprehend, though, what it would be like to do so? Yes, to some extent.

We have gotten this far: Persons understand each other, but not by penetrating each other's being, not by having each other's experiences. Understanding another involves conceiving of the other's experiences. We do this in a variety of ways. What we speak of as taking on the point of view of another involves imaginatively taking on what we think things are like for the other, and this typically requires bracketing out

to some extent what things are like for ourselves. Strictly speaking, we never take on the other's point of view. The structure of the nervous system prevents it.

The best candidates for interpersonal experiential commonality, for mutual grasping, involve sensory experiences. There is reasonable evidence that I can have experiences that are (almost) the same as your experiences, when the experiences in question are sensations or low-level perceptions. The sensory vectors for color, taste, smell, and so on, are similar across persons. Evolution has made them so. It is not unreasonable, therefore, to think that we know what it is like for others to experience red and blue, to smell smoke, and to feel the sharp pain of a bee sting. Yet sensational sameness is not something we simply need to assume is the case. When in doubt, we can test for it.

Even when there is very deep understanding between persons, as between lovers or excellent friends, it is easy to fall into the illusion that each has, so to speak, direct acquaintance with the inner life of the other. But that is never the case. Often, in fact, people who understand each other deeply are simply very sensitive to the characteristic response patterns of each other. One might know that one's best friend is prone to feelings of low self-esteem, and one might be savvy at keeping her from going into such states and good at getting her out of such states. But one is in the grip of an illusion if one thinks that a person needs to have experienced low self-esteem to know what it is like to feel low self esteem, to express appropriate concern and sympathy when a friend experiences it, and to possess the expertise to help a friend avoid experiencing it.

What are the prospects for my coming to know what it is like to be you? What are the prospects of my coming to understand not merely what it is like for you to experience colors but also what it is like for you to feel happy and sad, to be confused, to be excited over a new idea, to be in love, and in general to be you? The prospects are not good, unless I am willing to take the time and expend the energy that gaining human understanding requires. I will need to get to know you. I will need to formulate sensitive views about what makes you tick—and this is compatible with treating you as a black box up to a point. Often I will need to work at factoring out certain ways in which I am prone to conceive of things, and I will need to be careful not to project onto you what things are like for me or how I would respond to a certain situation. Time together, screening off certain aspects of my character and agenda, and avoiding projection—these are the ways in which good relationships and deep understanding are built.

Beware of the idea that it is important for one person to enter the mental life of another in the way usually intended when there is talk about really getting inside someone's head or grasping, capturing, what it is like to be another. There are other minds, and we have knowledge of them. But such knowledge never involves grasping exactly what it is like to have another's experiences or inner life. The structure of the nervous system accounts for the happy fact that we each have our own, and only our own, experiences. But we are very smart, and we possess powerful imaginations. Intelligence and imagination open doors to other minds. Intelligence, imagination, and shared life forms make for especially profitable, connected visits. Chances for visits abound. Chances for direct communion do not. If that seems like a loss, a tragic feature of the human condition, think about what a life spent in communion would be like.

REFERENCES

Churchland, Paul M. 1989. *A Neurocomputational Perspective: The Nature of Mind and the Structure of Science.* Cambridge: MIT Press.

Dewey, John. 1922. *Human Nature and Conduct.* New York: Henry Holt, 1957.

Flanagan, O. 1991a. *Varieties of Moral Personality: Ethics and Psychological Realism.* Cambridge: Harvard University Press.

Fodor, J. 1981. "Special Sciences." In *Representations.* Cambridge: MIT Press.

Hardin, C.L. 1988. *Color for Philosophers: Unweaving the Rainbow.* Indianapolis: Hackett.

Hume, David. 1977. *Enquiries Concerning Human Understanding and Concerning the Principles of Morals.* Ed. L.A. Selby-Bigge. Oxford: Oxford University Press, 1975.

Jackson, F. 1982. "Epiphenomenal Qualia." *Philosophical Quarterly* 32:127–136.

Jackson, F. 1986. "What Mary Didn't Know." *Journal of Philosophy* 83, no. 5:291–295. Reprinted in D. Rosenthal, ed., *The Nature of Mind.* New York: Oxford University Press, 1991.

Loar, Brian. 1990. "Phenomenal Properties." In *Philosophical Perspectives: Action Theory and Philosophy of Mind.* Atascerdo, Calif.: Ridgeview.

Luria, A.R. 1972. *The Man with the Shattered World.* Cambridge: Harvard University Press, 1987.

McGinn, C. 1991. *The Problem of Consciousness.* Oxford: Blackwell.

Nagel, Thomas. 1974. "What Is It Like to Be a Bat?" In *Mortal Questions.* Cambridge: Cambridge University Press, 1979.

Quine, W.V.O. 1952. "On Mental Entities." In *The Ways of Paradox and Other Essays.* New York: Random House, 1966.

Sacks, Oliver. 1983. *Awakenings.* New York: Dutton.

Sacks, Oliver. 1985. *The Man Who Mistook His Wife for a Hat and Other Clinical Tales.* New York: Summit.

Van Gulick, R. In press a. "Understanding the Phenomenal Mind: Are We All Just Armadillos?" In *Consciousness: A Mind and Language Reader,* ed. M. Davies and G. Humphrey. Oxford: Blackwell.

CHAPTER FOURTEEN

Intentionality

Introduction

'Intentionality' is an unfamiliar word, but it refers to a common, perhaps universal, feature of mental states. Suppose you are walking with your friend, who is suddenly looking pensive and withdrawn. When you ask about her change in behaviour, she explains that she was thinking of her mother. For this kind of explanation to make sense, we must suppose that there is some kind of connection or relation between your friend's state of mind and the person who is her mother. We express this by saying that her thought is *about* that person. This relationship, whereby a state of mind is *of* or *about* something, is what philosophers have come to call **intentionality**. The term derives from the Latin word, *intendo*, which means "to point towards." So the idea is that thoughts, beliefs, and other states of mind point to, or are directed toward, something else.

Like subjective experience, intentionality has become the focus of a large amount of research and debate. The number of problems involving intentionality is increased by the fact that states of mind are not the only things that possess intentionality. Words, signs, and pictures are also about, or of, objects, people, places, and events. Moreover, as the most common way that we communicate our thoughts is by language, the philosophical study of intentionality is to a large extent an amalgamation of philosophy of mind and philosophy of language.

Reference and content

There are two different forms in which intentionality is discussed. In the example of intentionality above, the relationship described is that between your friend's thought and a particular person. A relation like this, between a state of mind and an individual thing — whether a person, place, event, animal,

451

or whatever it may be — is what we call a relation of **reference**. The state of mind *refers* to the object. This is the kind of relation that exists between a noun and its object. For example, the word 'Vienna' refers to a particular city in Austria. The fact that states of mind refer to things is one way in which intentionality occurs.

Our thoughts, beliefs, and desires exhibit more than just referential intentionality, however. When I think about Vienna, that city forms the subject of my thoughts. But a thought is most often something that is expressed in the form of a complete sentence. I might think, for example, that Vienna is in Austria, or that Vienna is where Wittgenstein was born. These two sentences, 'Vienna is in Austria' and 'Vienna is where Wittgenstein was born,' express the *contents* of my thoughts. We encountered this idea earlier when I introduced the notion of propositional attitudes in chapter 11. A propositional attitude, such as a belief or desire, is characterized by two things: the proposition, or sentence, that expresses its content, and the attitude the person holds toward that proposition. If Mary believes Wittgenstein was born in Vienna, and John doubts that Wittgenstein was born in Vienna, we say that their respective states of mind have the same content, but they bear different attitudes toward that content. The content of propositional attitudes is another way in which intentionality occurs. In these cases, what states of mind "point to" is a proposition or a content.

The subject of the chapter

Intentionality poses several different philosophical problems. In this chapter I will focus on one particular problem closely related to themes explored in earlier chapters. As with the issue of subjective experience, the question we will look at in this chapter arises to a large extent from a conception of mind with roots in Plato but developed most explicitly by Descartes.

The problem can be illustrated by looking once more at Descartes' evil demon in the Second Meditation. If you are under the spell of an evil demon, then all of your sensory perceptions and most of your beliefs are false. Nevertheless, Descartes argues, you can still be certain of the *contents* of your thoughts and perceptions. Even if the page that seems to be in front of you is an illusion, it is nonetheless true that *it seems to you as if* there is a page in front of you.

The consequence for intentionality of Descartes' thought experiment is the implication that the contents of your thoughts are independent of what is going on in the world around you. It makes no difference to the *content* of your current perception whether the page you seem to perceive exists or not. Of course, what is going on in the world around you determines whether your thoughts are true or false. If there is no page before you, your perception is false. Nonetheless, whether the page exists or not does not affect the content of your thought. On this picture of the mind the intentionality of our mental states is entirely a matter of what is going on inside our heads or in our minds, and is unaffected by the state (or even the existence) of the world around us.

Descartes' picture of the mind contrasts with a tradition that goes back to Aristotle. For Aristotle, perceptions and thoughts are not just states of mind; they are relations between the perceiver and an object in the world. Because of the affinity between the soul and its environment, the qualities and forms of objects are replicated in the soul of the perceiver. This means that, for Aristotle, the contents of our thoughts and perceptions are determined by our interactions with things in our environment. Whether your current perception is of a real page in front of you or an apparition of something that doesn't exist makes a significant difference to the content of the psychological state you are in.

The readings for this chapter engage in a modern version of this ancient debate. Descartes' view is defended in Jerry Fodor's article, "Methodological Solipsism Considered as a Research Strategy in Cognitive Psychology." According to Fodor, the dominant research method in psychology, based on the computer metaphor, assumes a theory of content similar in nature to what Descartes presents in the Second Meditation. In the piece entitled, "Brains in a Vat," Hilary Putnam argues that without interaction with the environment there cannot be any mental content at all. As a result, Putnam contends, the contents of our thoughts will vary depending on the objects in our environment, even when we are not aware of the differences. In Putnam's words, "meanings are not in the head."

Research strategies and methodology

We begin with Fodor's article. Before looking at the arguments of the article I want to draw attention to the title and to the way that Fodor characterizes the issue in the first three paragraphs. The position that Fodor defends is one that he calls "methodological solipsism," a term first introduced by Putnam. Notice that in this choice of words, the topic of the paper is put forward as a methodological issue. That is, rather than being concerned directly with the nature of the mind, Fodor's article focusses on questions about the methods that should be used in studying the mind. In particular, Fodor's paper has to do with the assumptions that psychologists make when constructing models of what goes on in the mind. The same point is conveyed by the second half of the title. The position he defends is one that he thinks is the best, in fact the only possible, strategy to use in forming psychological theories of cognition.

The representational theory of mind

Accordingly, Fodor begins by laying out what he claims is a set of standard assumptions of working psychologists. The first is what, in the third paragraph, he calls the representational theory of the mind. According to this theory, propositional attitudes involve internal *representations* of the world. To understand this idea we need to combine two points we looked at earlier. One is the idea, introduced in chapter 9, that thoughts and other states of mind are *internal* states. According to Fodor, working psychologists have rejected the behaviourist idea that the mind is nothing more than outward behaviour; they assume that the activities of the mind involve successions of internal states. The second point is that these states somehow represent the world. These representations form the contents of our thoughts. To use Fodor's example, if I think that Marvin is melancholy, this means that there is something in my mind (i.e., in my brain) that is a representation of Marvin; a representation that represents Marvin as being melancholy. The representation forms one part of a propositional attitude; the other part is the attitude (belief, doubt, desire, etc.) that the person has toward the content.

This theory, Fodor argues, is the only reasonable working hypothesis open to psychologists. There are no other "remotely plausible" frameworks available upon which to build models of psychological processes. This is a very contentious claim. As we saw in chapter 12, eliminativists like Churchland accept that there are internal mental states, but they deny that these states are propositional attitudes that represent the world in the way Fodor outlines here.

Fodor's concern, he says, is not to defend the representational theory but to explore the implications of one particular version of it, namely, that "mental states and processes are *computational.*" Here Fodor is referring to what I called the computer metaphor in chapter 10. The next few paragraphs examine how models of psychological processes constructed on the computer metaphor are versions of the representational theory of the mind.

Two features of computational processes

In paragraph four Fodor adopts the characterization of digital computers that I outlined in chapter 10. Recall that a digital computer possesses two essential features: (1) its operation is determined by an algorithm, and (2) its operation consists of reading and writing symbols. It is the second of these characteristics that Fodor emphasizes in this article. He writes:

> I take it that computational processes are both *symbolic* and *formal.* They are symbolic because they are defined over representations, and they are formal because they apply to representations in virtue of (roughly) the *syntax* of the representations.

Here Fodor is contrasting two features of digital computers. The first, the "symbolic" part, is the fact that the strings of symbols in a digital computer are representations. For example, the strings of 1's and 0's in the memory of a home computer represent words, numbers, pictures, and so on. If the mind is a digital computer, then brain states somehow serve as digital representations in a similar way. The second feature of computers, what Fodor calls the "formal" part, is the fact that a computer can only tell one representation from another by means of differences in the strings of symbols it is composed of. This last point is an essential premise in Fodor's argument so we need to look at it in detail.

Symbols and syntax

The first thing to notice is that, although the strings of symbols in a computer are representations, the same strings of symbols can be taken to represent any number of different things. To take a simple example, we can use 1's and 0's to represent numbers or words. The sequence of symbol strings written as "0, 1, 10, 11, 100, 101 ... " can be taken to represent the sequence of numbers 0, 1, 2, 3, 4, 5 ... ; or it can be used to represent the letters of the alphabet. The second point is that, when a computer goes through its operations, it doesn't identify strings of symbols by what they represent, but only by the order of symbols in the string. A computer recognizes the difference between the strings "11" and "10" only by the fact that one has a 0 in the second place and the other has a 1 in that place. Whether those two strings are used to represent the numbers 3 and 4, or whether they represent the letters c and d, makes no difference to how the computer functions.

In the quote above, Fodor describes this second feature of computers by saying that computer processes apply to representations "in virtue of their syntax." Let me explain that terminology. The rules governing how symbols occur in computer representations is called the **syntax** of the representations. You may have noticed, for example, that sometimes when you type a command into a computer and leave out one of the symbols (say, a colon) the computer will tell you that you have made a "syntax error." The fact that computers only recognize representations by the order of the symbols can be expressed by saying that computers distinguish one representation from another only by their syntax, or, more precisely, by their *syntactic properties*.

Fodor refers to the syntactic features of computer representations as their *formal* features. This is because, as he explains in the next paragraph, there are representations that do not have a syntax at all. For example, the movement of chess figures on a board could be taken to represent the movements of two armies or the debating tactics of political parties. Yet chess figures are not strings of symbols, and so they have no syntax. So Fodor takes computer syntax to be an instance of a more general feature of representations, which he calls the formal features.

Fodor contrasts the formal/syntactic features of computers with what he calls their "semantic" features. The **semantics** of a representation is a matter of its content, of what it represents. For example, whether the strings "10" and "11" are used to represent the numbers 3 and 4 or the letters c and d is a semantic difference. When a string of symbols represents a sentence, then the semantic properties involve not only the content of the sentence but also whether it is true or false.

Distinguishing one thought from another

In the sixth paragraph of his article Fodor uses the difference between syntax and semantics to draw philosophical conclusions. His claim is that, given the points I've just been explaining, the idea that mental processes are computational has some "clear consequences." First he says this:

> Consider that we started by assuming that the *content* of representations is a (type) individuating feature of mental states. So far as the *representational* theory of the mind is concerned, it is possibly the *only* thing that distinguishes Peter's thought that Sam is silly from his thought that Sally is depressed.

The "individuating features" of something are the features we use to distinguish it from other things. A mole or a tattoo is often an individuating feature of a person. So the point that Fodor is making here is that, according to the representational theory of the mind, we distinguish one thought from another by their contents, by what they are *about*. In other words, the semantic features of a thought differentiate it from other thoughts.

Fodor's next point is that, if the computer metaphor is correct, so that mental processes are computational processes, then those processes can distinguish one thought from another only by their formal or syntactic features. He says:

> But, now, if the *computational* theory of the mind is true (and if, as we may assume, content is a semantic notion par excellence) it follows that content alone cannot distinguish thoughts.

His reasoning here is this: according to the computer metaphor, thoughts and other states of mind are internal brain states that are in some way digital representations. Although these representations have both syntactic and semantic features, we have just seen that the computer processes that go on in the nervous system can only distinguish one representation from another by their syntactic features. Although we distinguish one thought from another by their content, the computer processes in the brain distinguish one thought from another by their syntax.

The formality condition

The next sentence of the article states the major premise of Fodor's argument. He calls this premise "the formality condition":

> More exactly, the computational theory of the mind requires that two thoughts can be distinct in content only if they can be identified with relations to formally distinct representations.

Let's spell this out carefully. According to the computational theory of the mind, the content of a thought is a matter of the content of a digital representation encoded in the brain. Therefore, because computer processes can only distinguish one representation from another by their formal or syntactic properties, one thought can be different from another only if there is some formal or syntactic difference between the representations. To use Fodor's example, if Peter has two thoughts in his head at some point (the thought that Sam is silly, and the thought that Sally is depressed), then there must be some syntactic difference between the two representations. If there weren't, then the computational brain processes, which are actually Peter's thought processes, couldn't tell them apart.

The consequences of the formality condition

Fodor argues in the next paragraph that the formality condition "implies a drastic narrowing of the ordinary ontology of the mental." By this he means that many states of a person that we ordinarily think of as states of mind, and hence as part of what psychologists should study, turn out not to be states that psychologists can legitimately consider. The underlying assumption that Fodor is making here is that the business of psychologists is to study the processes that go on in the mind. Given the formality condition, those processes only distinguish between states that are formally or syntactically different in some way. Hence, any differences between states of a person that do not involve syntactic differences in mental representations must be ignored by the psychologist.

Fodor offers two examples of this claim. First, he says, there can't be a "psychology of knowledge." That is, it is not part of the psychologist's business to explain how people come to know things. This is because knowledge, as opposed to belief, involves the *truth* of your beliefs, and truth is a matter of semantics, not of syntax. To put the point a different way, the internal processes of the mind cannot distinguish one thought from another by whether or not they are true or false. A psychologist constructing a model of thought processes cannot include processes that distinguish beliefs by their truth or falsity, for there are none.

The Second Meditation again

The other example that Fodor provides of the restrictions on psychology takes us back to Descartes' Second Meditation. Fodor argues that there cannot be "a psychology of perception," in the sense of an explanation of how we perceive things in our environment. Seeing and other forms of perception involve a relation between a person and something in his or her external environment. Here again, on the formality condition the internal processes of the mind have no access to that relation. Mental processes cannot distinguish between an illusion and a perception of something that really exists if there is no syntactic difference between the two.

In the next paragraph Fodor makes explicit the connection between the formality condition and the Cartesian picture of intentionality. For Descartes, he says, "there is an important sense in which how the world is makes no difference to one's mental states." Fodor quotes Descartes' argument in the First Meditation that there is no infallible sign between dreaming and waking experience. Descartes' point is that one cannot tell "from the inside," as it were, whether one is perceiving an existing reality or experiencing an illusion. The parallel in the computational theory of the mind is that if an illusion is formally or syntactically identical to an actual perceptual state, then the thought processes that operate on those representations will not tell them apart.

Rationalism and naturalism

The next couple of paragraphs serve to place the formality condition into the context of modern theories of mind. He identifies two streams of research in the psychological and philosophical literature. (Actually he mentions three, but he says very little about the second one, so I'll skip it.) Rationalists and empiricists (here you can think of Descartes and Locke, respectively, as representatives) have always accepted the point that "one's experiences ... might have been just as they are even if the world had been quite different from the way that it is." This tradition individuates thoughts in a way that ignores differences that are indistinguishable to the subject. The other line of researchers, which Fodor calls Naturalists, assume that "psychology is a branch of biology, hence that one must view the organism as embedded in a physical environment." You can think of Skinner as an example of this tradition. The goal here is to study how organisms, including humans, respond to their environment. This school has always taken it as a mistake to ignore relations between organism and environment when building models of mental processes.

Fodor maintains that the formality condition allows us to reconstruct the debate between rationalists and naturalists in a way that removes "adventitious intrusions" like the role of introspection in the rationalist tradition and the mistakes of behaviourism in the naturalist tradition. If we do this, Fodor claims, we can do justice to both points of view.

Methodological solipsism

In the four paragraphs beginning with "Insofar as we think of mental processes as computational..." Fodor explains how the formality condition can be used to reconstruct the rationalist position. First, he suggests thinking of the mind in computational terms as a Turing Machine reading and writing symbols on the tape. Seen in this way, the formality condition becomes the assertion that the only differences that affect the behaviour of the machine are differences in what is written on the tape. The effect of the environment on the computer, then, can be pictured as the work of "transducers" or "oracles" that write new information onto the tape. The significance of this for rationalism is explained in this way:

> The point is that, so long as we are thinking of mental processes as purely computational, the bearing of the environmental information upon such processes is exhausted by the formal character of whatever the oracles write on the tape. In particular, it doesn't matter to such processes whether what the oracles write is *true*; whether, for example, they really are transducers faithfully mirroring the state of the environment, or merely the output end of a typewriter manipulated by a Cartesian demon bent on deceiving the machine.

In the next paragraph Fodor explains the title of his paper. Recall from the beginning of chapter 5 that solipsism is the idea that nothing exists in the universe but the thoughts and perceptions of your own mind. The term 'methodological solipsism' was coined by Hilary Putnam as the name of the doctrine that the contents of the mind would be exactly the same as they are now even if the rest of the universe did not exist. As Putnam defines it, methodological solipsism is that the assumption that:

> no psychological state, properly so-called, presupposes the existence of any individual [or object] other than the subject to whom that state is ascribed.[1]

In the next two sentences of our reading Fodor points out that we can think of the computational mind in the same way. Because the processes of a computer have no access to any information other than what is written on the tape, a computational mind will be unaffected by whether the sensory inputs it receives are accurate portrayals of the existing world or not. He says:

> I'm saying, in effect, that the formality condition, viewed in this context, is tantamount to a sort of methodological solipsism. If mental processes are formal, then they have access only to the formal properties of such representations of the environment as the senses provide. Hence, they have no access to the *semantic* properties of such representations, including the properties of being true, of having referents, or, indeed, the property of being representations *of the environment*.

Whence intentionality?

The last two paragraphs of the section we are reading from Fodor's article outlines very briefly where Fodor thinks that naturalism comes into the scheme of things. Psychology governed by the formality condition is prevented from considering the semantic properties of the mind. But obviously we need to have some theory of how the mind is related to its environment. In the last sentence of the passage just quoted, Fodor points out that under the formality condition the question of how the internal states of the mind come to be representations of the environment is outside the domain of psychology. That is, the issue of how the intentionality of the mind comes about is not a psychological issue.

Naturalistic psychology, on the other hand, is ideally suited to explaining the connection between the internal representations of the mind and the external environment. The most promising explanation of the intentionality of the mind, Fodor claims, lies in the relations of cause and effect that exist between properties of the environment and internal states of the organism. Because naturalistic psychology makes the study of these relations its special domain, it is that kind of study that will explain how the formal processes of the nervous system come to be representations of the world.

In the final paragraph from our reading, however, Fodor claims that a naturalistic psychology "isn't a practical possibility." I have not reproduced Fodor's arguments for this conclusion here for they take us some distance away from our main concern. What we have seen is Fodor's argument that, under a computational psychology, the contents of our thoughts and perceptions — what they are about — cannot be sensitive to factors that are not represented in the formal properties of mental representations. This is because these factors are ones to which the operations of the mind have no access. In the next reading Hilary Putnam argues to the contrary that the contents of mental states must include factors to which the mind has no access.

Against methodological solipsism

In chapter 11 we read one of Putnam's defences of functionalism. In the 1980s Putnam abandoned functionalism along with a number of other philosophical positions he had defended earlier. This second reading from Putnam forms the first chapter of a book entitled *Reason, Truth and History*. In this book Putnam lays out a number of ideas that form the core of his newer philosophical views. Nonetheless, the arguments in this chapter explore themes that originate in his earlier work. Fodor's notion of methodological solipsism is taken from a 1975 work of Putnam's entitled "The Meaning of 'Meaning'." In that article Putnam argued against the position that Fodor defends in the previous reading. In this next reading Putnam continues the same line of argument as that in "The Meaning of 'Meaning'," and adds some new elements to it.

The argument in Putnam's chapter has two steps. The first step makes a claim about what is necessary for something to have intentional content. The second uses this point to reject Fodor's claim that the contents of the mind are insensitive to relations between the subject and his or her environment. Putnam's argument consists largely of a series of thought experiments, some of which are quite bizarre. Yet Putnam maintains that these experiments reveal substantial philosophical points.

What is necessary for intentionality?

The first two sections of Putnam's article are intended to establish that words and pictures, no matter where they occur, and even if they occur in the minds of intelligent beings, do not have any "intrinsic, built-in" connection with what they represent. The point here can be put in this way: if A is a representation of B, or refers to B, this will not be because of something about A alone; rather it will be because of some kind of interaction that A has with B. If there is no such interaction, there is no reference or representation.

The point is made first with respect to physical representations. Putnam asks us to imagine that an ant accidentally leaves traces in the sand that form a recognizable likeness of Winston Churchill. Putnam argues that, considered by themselves, unseen by anyone who sees the similarity, these lines are not a representation of Churchill. No connection exists between the lines and the person unless either the ant intended the similarity or someone else *takes them to be* a representation of Churchill. The same would be true, Putnam argues, if the ant had accidentally traced lines that resemble the words "Winston Churchill."

What about intelligent minds?

Putnam points out that, if the ant had *intended* the lines to refer to Winston Churchill, then they would so refer. This would require the ant to have an intelligent mind, to be able to think about Churchill. This suggests in turn that the origin of reference is the existence of minds, that thoughts are somehow essentially *about* things.

In the second section Putnam argues that pictures and words that occur in the mind do not have an intrinsic referential character, anymore than do the lines made by the ant. To this end Putnam points out that the same kind of accidental similarity could occur even in the case of images formed in the mind of an intelligent person. He asks us to imagine a tribe of people who have never seen a tree, and who find a picture of a tree dropped from a passing airplane. The mental image that they form from this picture will be very much the same as our image of a tree, and yet for them it has no such significance. As such, Putnam argues, their mental image, although indistinguishable from ours, is not an image of a tree; it isn't an image *of* anything. To the reply that their mental image represents a tree because the picture that caused it represents a tree, Putnam says that we can modify the story so that the original picture itself was only accidentally similar to a tree.

The same would be true, Putnam argues, in the case of words. Suppose a group of monkeys accidentally typed a sequence of letters that we would read as a meaningful discourse. Then the typing is found and memorized by someone who has no understanding of the language of the discourse. The words in the memory of that person would have no meaning, Putnam claims, for the same reason that the lines made by the ant are not a picture of Churchill. Accidental similarity does not generate reference.

Putnam's conclusion is that words and images in the mind do not intrinsically refer to anything. If there is a relation of reference between a thought or mental image and something in the world, that must be because of some kind of interaction between the two.

Turing and Searle again

I am going to change the order of the sections in Putnam's article somewhat, and leave the third section until after we have looked at the fourth. In this section Putnam considers the Turing Test that we looked at in chapter 10. Recall that Turing's proposal was a behavioural test for artificial intelligence. Turing claimed that, if a computer could carry on a conversation that was indistinguishable from that of an intelligent person, we would have no choice but to conclude that the computer is itself an intelligent being. In this section Putnam argues that, no matter how much the output of the computer resembled meaningful discourse, the internal states and processes of the computer in the Turing Test could not possibly possess intentionality; they could not be *about* anything.

Putnam's argument for this conclusion is that the computer has no interaction whatsoever with the objects and events that are mentioned in its dialogue. The internal states of the computer might resemble the mental states of a person whose thoughts are about the things in the dialogue. But, as Putnam has argued in the first two sections, this resemblance does not generate intentionality. Without the appropriate interactions with the objects that its words are supposed to refer to, Putnam says, the conversation of machines playing Turing's Imitation Game is no more than "syntactic play":

> Syntactic play that *resembles* intelligent discourse, to be sure; but only as (and no more than) the ant's curve resembles a biting caricature.

Putnam's argument here is similar to Searle's criticism of the Turing Test. In Searle's thought experiment, the person who is carrying out the symbolic operations that generate the Chinese discourse produces linguistic activity that would fool a native speaker of Chinese. Like Searle, Putnam argues that this outward resemblance masks a complete absence of intentionality. In his article, however, Putnam makes the point that it is not anything about the nature of syntactic operations in themselves that prevents machines from being intelligent. Rather it is the lack of connection in the imagined scenario between the activity of the machine and the objects that its words are said to refer to. This much Fodor himself agrees with. As we have seen, Fodor believes that it is the fact that computational minds are "embedded" in the world that gives their syntactic operations their content. But Fodor and Putnam disagree about the implications of this point.

Brains in a vat

In the third and fifth sections of the article, Putnam changes the topic from *how* images and words refer to the question of what it is that they refer to. To introduce this question he constructs another thought experiment, this time one intended deliberately to be very similar to Descartes' evil demon story. Suppose you are the victim of an operation carried out by an evil scientist. Unbeknownst to you, this scientist has earlier removed your brain and placed it in a life-preserving nutrient vat. It was then connected up to a supercomputer, which is now supplying to you all of your current perceptions and memories. The result of this operation would be the same as what Descartes imagined being done by the evil demon. You have perceptions and memories of an external world and a life history, all of which are completely false. (The androids in the movie *Bladerunner* undergo a similar fate, at least as far as their memories are concerned. Their neural circuits are implanted with a false memory chip that gives them an illusory life history.)

The question that Putnam wants to raise with this story is this: What are the thoughts of a brain in a vat *about?* His answer to this question is found in the first two paragraphs of the fifth section. As a brain in a vat is still a functioning brain connected to the world, it is not absurd to suppose that it will have both consciousness and intelligence. But what is its consciousness a consciousness *of?* Putnam contends that a brain in a vat cannot have thoughts about the real external world. This is for the same reason that he denies that machines in the Turing Test can have real thoughts: a brain in a vat has no interactions with the external world, except for the images generated by the computer it is connected to. It can have thoughts about vat-trees (i.e., trees in the computer-generated image), but it cannot have thoughts about real trees.

Is the brain-in-a-vat story self-refuting?

At the end of the third section Putnam draws a provocative conclusion from the fact that a brain in a vat cannot refer to objects in the real world. (This conclusion is not directly related to the issue that we are examining in this chapter, so you can skip it if you like.) Putnam contends that it is impossible for you and me to be brains in a vat. Even though the story might appear to describe a genuine possibility, Putnam argues that the hypothesis that we are brains in a vat is self-refuting. By this he means it is a story that contains a contradiction and hence must be false.

The argument for this conclusion is in the third paragraph of the sixth section, entitled "The premises of the argument." Here Putnam argues that a brain in a vat could not *think* that it is (or might be) a brain in a vat. That is, it could not have a thought with the content expressed by the sentence, 'I am a brain in a vat.' This is because the contents of the thoughts of a brain in a vat can only refer to items in the computer-generated image. From this Putnam argues as follows:

> But part of the hypothesis that we are brains in a vat is that we aren't brains in a vat in the image (i.e. what we are "hallucinating" isn't that we are brains in a vat). So, if we are brains in a vat, then the sentence "We are brains in a vat" says something false (if it says anything). In short, if we are brains in a vat, then "We are brains in a vat" is false. So it is (necessarily) false.

The first sentence is the crucial one. If a brain in a vat thinks to itself, "I am a brain in a vat," the "vat" that it is referring to must be the *computer-generated image* of a vat. But, of course, that is not what we mean by the question 'Am I a brain in a vat?' A brain in a vat could not ask *that* question, so the hypothesis cannot be stated.

What are concepts?

At the end of the sixth section Putnam restates the two main premises of his argument. The first premise is that "magical" theories of reference are wrong. By "magical" theories he means theories that ascribe intentionality to an inexplicable, intrinsic property of thoughts, pictures, or words. The second premise explains why such theories are wrong. The reason there is no intrinsic intentionality is that "one cannot refer to certain kinds of things, e.g. *trees*, if one has no causal interaction ... with them." Reference requires an interaction, a relation of cause and effect, between the subject and the object of his or her thoughts.

In the next section he defends these two premises by attacking the idea that intentionality derives from *concepts*, in the sense of objects in the mind that are somehow inner sources of mental content. The basis for this idea, Putnam suggests is the fact that:

> it feels different to me when I utter words that I believe and when I utter words I do not believe ... and it feels different when I utter words I understand and when I utter words I do not understand.

This kind of feeling suggests to us that understanding, and hence intentionality, is a matter of something going on in the mind. Against this intuition Putnam claims that it is possible to imagine someone:

> thinking just these words ... and having just the feeling of understanding, asserting, etc., that I do, and realizing a minute later ... that he did not understand what had just passed through his mind at all, that he did not even understand the language these words are in.

The point Putnam is making here is that intentionality cannot be explained just in terms of an inner sense of understanding, for there can be false feelings of understanding. The real point is that intentionality cannot be, as Fodor claims, something that is present in the mind independent of its relations with the world. Understanding and meaning, Putnam says, is not a matter of "any mental presentation, any introspectible entity or event."

This last argument is weak, however, for, as we have just seen, Fodor denies that any conclusions about the content of our thoughts need to depend on introspection. The advantage of defending methodological solipsism on the basis of the formality condition, Fodor claims, is that it frees the issue from the "adventitious intrusions" of introspection. The issue as Fodor sees it has nothing to do with what we see in the mind in introspection.

Two famous thought experiments

In the next paragraph Putnam puts forward two thought experiments that are designed to undermine Fodor's formality condition and methodological solipsism, and which are not based on the unreliability of introspection. These thought experiments have had an enormous influence on debates about the intentionality of mind.

"Suppose," Putnam says, "you are like me and cannot tell an elm tree from a beech tree." In such a case, the two concepts held in the mind are indistinguishable. Nonetheless the reference of "elm" and "beech," that is, the objects in the world to which these words refer, are different. This shows that the difference in the meanings of the two terms is not determined by the concepts we have in our mind, but by the differences in the objects to which we apply them. To put this in terms of Fodor's formality condition, the point is that there are differences in the content of thoughts about beech trees and thoughts about elm trees *even if* there is no syntactic difference between the thoughts of the individual who thinks them.

The second thought experiment is more elaborate. We can imagine that there is a planet almost exactly like Earth, and on this planet you have an identical twin, a Doppelganger. We will call this planet Twin Earth. One of the small differences between Earth and Twin Earth is that, where the substance we call "water" on Earth is H_2O, on Twin Earth there is an indistinguishable liquid, also called water, but which is a different molecular substance we'll call XYZ. We can suppose that the molecular constitution is unknown to you and your twin, so that if you were flown to Twin Earth, or your twin were flown to Earth, neither of you would recognize any difference between the two substances. Therefore, as you and your Doppelganger are identical molecule for molecule, there would then be no difference between the concepts you each attach to the word 'water.' In terms of the formality condition, we can say that the symbol strings associated with the word 'water' are the same in your internal mental processes and those of your twin. Nonetheless, Putnam insists, the two thoughts are different in content. They are thoughts about different substances, H_2O and XYZ, even though that difference is not reflected by any syntactic or other purely internal features of your respective thoughts.

Are meanings are in the head?

These kinds of examples, Putnam contends, reveal that the contents of our thoughts can vary even when there is no corresponding difference in our internal mental representations. "Meanings," he says, "are not in the head." His point is that what determines the reference or contents of our thoughts is not a matter of what is in our heads but rather of how we interact with the world around us.

But let's look at the second example from Fodor's point of view. The thought experiment has it that there is no internal or syntactic difference between the concepts of water that you and your twin possess. This means that the differences in content between your thoughts and your twin's, alleged by Putnam, would have absolutely no effect on your respective behaviours. Hence, Fodor claims, you and your twin are *psychologically* identical. For that reason, Fodor contends, psychologists would necessarily ignore the differences between you and your twin. What, then, is the point of drawing distinctions between thoughts that are psychologically irrelevant?

Another way to make the same point is to suppose that you were transported to Twin Earth. Your thoughts would then be about XYZ, not H_2O. Thus, according to Putnam, the contents of your thoughts would change. Yet there would be no change in the internal structure of your mental representations and hence no change, either, in your behaviour. Again we have a difference that appears to be psychologically irrelevant.

Notice that the basis of Fodor's argument here is a claim about what psychologists are concerned with. Anything that makes no difference in predicting behaviour from thought processes is supposed to be of no interest to psychologists. Most people now recognize this to be an overly narrow conception of the business of psychology. The formality condition, or some version of it, is seen to be necessary for the task of predicting behaviour, but Putnam's general position seems to be needed for explaining how our thoughts and our behaviour fit into the world. But the debates surrounding these topics have become more complex and more detailed than we can survey here.

NOTES

1 Hilary Putnam, "The Meaning of 'Meaning'," reprinted in *Mind, Language and Reality: Philosophical Papers, Volume 2* (Cambridge: Cambridge University Press, 1975), p. 220.

Jerry A. Fodor
Selections from "Methodological Solipsism Considered as a Research Strategy in Cognitive Psychology"

... to form the idea of an object and to form an idea simply is the same thing; the reference of the idea to an object being an extraneous denomination, of which in itself it bears no mark or character.   —Hume, *Treatise*, Book I

Your standard contemporary cognitive psychologist—your thoroughly modern mentalist—is disposed to reason as follows. To think (e.g.,) that Marvin is melancholy is to represent Marvin in a certain way; viz., as being melancholy (and not, for example, as being maudlin, morose, moody, or merely moping and dyspeptic). But surely we cannot represent Marvin as being melancholy except as we are in some or other relation to a representation of Marvin; and not just to *any* representation of Marvin, but, in particular, to a representation the content of which is *that* Marvin is melancholy; a representation which, as it were, expresses the proposition that Marvin is melancholy. So, a fortiori, at least some mental states/processes are or involve at least some relations to at least some representations. Perhaps, then, this is the *typical* feature of such mental states/processes as cognitive psychology studies; perhaps all such states can be viewed as relations to representations and all such processes as operations defined on representations.

This is, prima facie, an appealing proposal, since it gives the psychologist two degrees of freedom to play with and they seem, intuitively, to be the right two. On the one hand, mental states are distinguished by the *content* of the associated representations, so we can allow for the difference between thinking that Marvin is melancholy and thinking that Sam is (or that

Albert isn't, or it sometimes snows in Cincinnati); and, on the other hand, mental states are distinguished by the *relation* that the subject bears to the associated representation (so we can allow for the difference between thinking, hoping, supposing, doubting, and pretending that Marvin is melancholy). It's hard to believe that a serious psychology could make do with fewer (or less refined) distinctions than these, and it's hard to believe that a psychology that makes these distinctions could avoid taking the notion of mental representation seriously. Moreover, the burden of argument is clearly upon anyone who claims that we need *more* degrees of freedom than just these two: the least hypothesis that is remotely plausible is that a mental state is (type) individuated by specifying a relation and a representation such that the subject bears the one to the other.[1]

I'll say that any psychology that takes this line is a version of the *representational theory of the mind.* I think that it's reasonable to adopt some such theory as a sort of working hypothesis, if only because there aren't any alternatives which seem to be even remotely plausible and because empirical research carried out within this framework has, thus far, proved interesting and fruitful ... However, my present concern is neither to attack nor to defend this view, but rather to distinguish it from something other—and stronger—that modern cognitive psychologists *also* hold. I shall put this stronger doctrine as the view that mental states and processes are *computational.* Much of what is characteristic of cognitive psychology is a consequence of adherence to this stronger view. What I want to do in this paper is to say something about what this stronger view is, something about why I think it's plausible, and, most of all, something about the ways in which it shapes the cognitive psychology we have.

I take it that computational processes are both *symbolic* and *formal*. They are symbolic because they are defined over representations, and they are formal because they apply to representations in virtue of (roughly) the *syntax* of the representations. It's the second of these conditions that makes the claim that mental processes are computational stronger than the representational theory of the mind. Most of this paper will be a meditation upon the consequences of assuming that mental processes are formal processes.

I'd better cash the parenthetical "roughly." To say that an operation is formal isn't the same as saying that it is syntactic since we could have formal processes defined over representations which don't, in any obvious sense, *have* a syntax. Rotating an image would be a timely example. What makes syntactic operations a species of formal operations is that being syntactic is a way of *not* being semantic. Formal operations are the ones that are specified without reference to such semantic properties of representations as, for example, truth, reference, and meaning. Since we don't know how to complete this list (since, that is, we don't know what semantic properties there are), I see no responsible way of saying what, in general, formality amounts to. The notion of formality will thus have to remain intuitive and metaphoric, at least for present purposes: formal operations apply in terms of the, as it were, shapes of the objects in their domains.[3]

To require that mental processes be computational (viz., formal-syntactic) is thus to require something not very clear. Still, the requirement has some clear consequences, and they are striking and tendentious. Consider that we started by assuming that the *content* of representations is a (type) individuating feature of mental states. So far as the *representational* theory of the mind

is concerned, it is possibly the *only* thing that distinguishes Peter's thought that Sam is silly from his thought that Sally is depressed. But, now, if the *computational* theory of the mind is true (and if, as we may assume, content is a semantic notion par excellence) it follows that content alone cannot distinguish thoughts. More exactly, the computational theory of the mind requires that two thoughts can be distinct in content only if they can be identified with relations to formally distinct representations. More generally: fix the subject and the relation, and then mental states can be (type) distinct only if the representations which constitute their objects are formally distinct.

Again, consider that accepting a formality condition upon mental states implies a drastic narrowing of the ordinary ontology of the mental; all sorts of states which look, prima facie, to be mental states in good standing are going to turn out to be none of the psychologist's business if the formality condition is endorsed. This point is one that philosophers have made in a number of contexts, and usually in a deprecating tone of voice. Take, for example, knowing that such-and-such and assume that you can't know what's not the case. Since, on that assumption, knowledge is involved with truth, and since truth is a semantic notion, it's going to follow that there can't be a psychology of *knowledge* (even if it is consonant with the formality condition to hope for a psychology of *belief*). Similarly, it's a way of making a point of Ryle's to say that, strictly speaking, there can't be a psychology of perception if the formality condition is to be complied with. Seeing is an achievement; you can't see what's not there. From the point of view of the representational theory of the mind, this means that seeing involves relations between mental representations *and their referents*; hence, semantic relations within the meaning of the act.

I hope that such examples suggest (what, in fact, I think is true) that even if the formality condition isn't very clear, it is quite certainly very strong. In fact, I think it's not all *that* anachronistic to see it as the central issue that divides the two main traditions in the history of psychology: "Rational psychology" on the one hand, and "Naturalism" on the other. Since this is a mildly eccentric way of cutting the pie, I'm going to permit myself a semi-historical excursus before returning to the main business of the paper.

Descartes argued that there is an important sense in which how the world is makes no difference to one's mental states. Here is a well-known passage from the *Meditations*:

> At this moment it does indeed seem to me that it is with eyes awake that I am looking at this paper; that this head which I move is not asleep, that it is deliberately and of set purpose that I extend my hand and perceive it. ... But in thinking over this I remind myself that on many occasions I have been deceived by similar illusions, and in dwelling on this reflection I see so manifestly that there are no certain indications by which we may clearly distinguish wakefulness from sleep that I am lost in astonishment. And my astonishment is such that it is almost capable of persuading me that I now dream.
>
> (Descartes, 1931)

At least three sorts of reactions to this kind of argument are distinguishable in the philosophical literature. First, there's a long tradition, including both Rationalists and Empiricists, which takes it as axiomatic that one's experiences (and, a fortiori, one's beliefs) might have been just as they are even if the world had been quite different from the way that it is. See, for example, the passage from Hume which serves as an epigraph to this paper. Second, there's a vaguely Wittgensteinian mood in which one argues that it's just *false* that one's mental states might have been what they are had the world been relevantly different. For example, if there

had been a dagger there, Macbeth would have been *seeing* not just hallucinating. And what could be more different than that? If the Cartesian feels that this reply misses the point, he is at least under an obligation to say precisely which point it misses; in precisely *which* respects the way the world is is irrelevant to the character of one's beliefs, experiences, and so on. Finally there's a tradition which argues that—epistemology to one side—it is at best a strategic mistake to attempt to develop a psychology that individuates mental states without reference to their environmental causes and effects (e.g., which counts the state that Macbeth *was* in as type-identical to the state he would have been in had the dagger been supplied). I have in mind the tradition which includes the American Naturalists (notably Pierce and Dewey), all the learning theorists, and such contemporary representatives as Quine in philosophy and Gibson in psychology. The recurrent theme here is that psychology is a branch of biology, hence that one must view the organism as embedded in a physical environment. The psychologist's job is to trace those organism/environment interactions which constitute its behavior. A passage from William James (1890, p. 6) will serve to give the feel of the thing:

> On the whole, few recent formulas have done more service of a rough sort in psychology than the Spencerian one that the essence of mental life and of bodily life are one, namely, 'the adjustment of inner to outer relations.' Such a formula is vagueness incarnate; but because it takes into account the fact that minds inhabit environments which act on them and on which they in turn react; because, in short, it takes mind in the midst of all its concrete relations, it is immensely more fertile than the old-fashioned 'rational psychology' which treated the soul as a detached existent, sufficient unto itself, and as-

sumed to consider only its nature and its properties.

A number of adventitious intrusions have served to muddy the issues in this long-standing dispute. On the one hand, it may well be that Descartes was relying on a specifically introspectionist construal of the claim that the individuation of mental states is independent of their environmental causes. That is, Descartes's point may have been that (a) mental states are (type) identical if and only if (iff) they are introspectively indistinguishable, and (b) introspection cannot distinguish (e.g.) perception from hallucination, or knowledge from belief. On the other hand, the naturalist, in point of historical fact, is often a behaviorist as well. He wants to argue not only that mental states are individuated by reference to organism/environment relations, but also that such relations constitute the mental. In the context of the present discussion, he is arguing for the abandonment not just of the formality condition, but of the notion of mental representation as well.

If, however, we take the computational theory of the mind as what's central to the issue, we can reconstruct the debate between rational psychologists and naturalists in a way that does justice to both their points; in particular, in a way that frees the discussion from involvement with introspectionism on the one side and behaviorism on the other.

Insofar as we think of mental processes as computational (hence as formal operations defined on representations), it will be natural to take the mind to be, inter alia, a kind of computer. That is, we will think of the mind as carrying out whatever symbol manipulations are constitutive of the hypothesized computational processes. To a first approximation, we may thus construe mental operations as pretty directly analogous to those of a Turing machine. There is, for example, a working memory (corresponding to a tape) and there are capacities for scanning and altering the contents of the memory (corresponding to the operations of reading and writing on the tape). If we want to extend the computational metaphor by providing access to information about the environment, we can think of the computer as having access to "oracles" which serve, on occasion, to enter information in the memory. On the intended interpretation of this model, these oracles are analogs to the senses. In particular, they are assumed to be transducers, in that what they write on the tape is determined solely by the ambient environmental energies that impinge upon them. (For elaboration of this sort of account, see Putnam [1960]; it is, of course, widely familiar from discussions in the field of artificial intelligence.)

I'm not endorsing this model, but simply presenting it as a natural extension of the computational picture of the mind. Its present interest is that we can use it to see how the formality condition connects with the Cartesian claim that the character of mental processes is somehow independent of their environmental causes and effects. The point is that, so long as we are thinking of mental processes as purely computational, the bearing of environmental information upon such processes is exhausted by the formal character of whatever the oracles write on the tape. In particular, it doesn't matter to such processes whether what the oracles write is *true*; whether, for example, they really are transducers faithfully mirroring the state of the environment, or merely the output end of a typewriter manipulated by a Cartesian demon bent on deceiving the machine. I'm saying, in effect, that the formality condition, viewed in this context, is tantamount to a sort of methodological solipsism. If mental processes are formal, then they have access only to the formal properties of such representations of the environment as the senses provide. Hence, they have no access to the *semantic* properties of such representations, including the property of being true, of having referents, or, indeed, the property of being representations *of the environment*.

That some such methodological solipsism really is implicated in much current psychological practice is best seen by examining what researchers actually do. Consider, for example, the well-known work of Terry Winograd. Winograd was primarily interested in the computer simulation of certain processes involved in the handling of verbal information; asking and answering questions, drawing inferences, following instructions and the like. The form of his theory was a program for a computer which "lives in" and operates upon a simple world of blocklike geometric objects (see Winograd 1971). Many of the capacities that the device exercises vis-à-vis its environment seem impressively intelligent. It can arrange the blocks to order, it can issue "perceptual" reports of the present state of its environment and "memory" reports of its past states, it can devise simple plans for achieving desired environmental configurations, and it can discuss its undertakings (more or less in English) with whoever is running the program.

The interesting point for our purposes, however, is that the machine environment which is the nominal object of these actions and conversations actually isn't there. What actually happens is that the programmer so arranges the memory states of the machine that the available data are whatever they would be *if* there were objects for the machine to perceive and manipulanda for it to operate upon. In effect, the machine lives in an entirely notional world; all its beliefs are false. Of course, it doesn't matter to the machine that its beliefs are false since falsity is a semantic property and, qua computer, the device satisfies the formality condition; viz., it has access only to formal (nonsemantic) properties of the representations that it manipulates. In effect, the device is in precisely the situation that Descartes dreads; it's a mere computer which dreams that it's a robot.

I hope that this discussion suggests how acceptance of the computational theory of the mind leads to a sort of methodological solipsism as a part of the research strategy of contemporary cognitive psychology. In particular, I hope it's clear how you get that consequence from the formality condition alone, without so much as raising the introspection issue. I stress this point because it seems to me that there has been considerable confusion about it among the psychologists themselves. People who do machine simulation, in particular, very often advertise themselves as working on the question how thought (or language) is related to the world. My present point is that, whatever else they're doing, they certainly aren't doing *that*. The very assumption that defines their field— viz., that they study mental processes *qua* formal operations on symbols—guarantees that their studies won't answer the question how the symbols so manipulated are semantically interpreted. You can, for example, build a machine that answers baseball questions in the sense that (e.g.) if you type in "Who had the most wins by a National League pitcher since Dizzy Dean?" it will type out "Robin Roberts, who won 28." But you delude yourself if you think that a machine which in this sense answers baseball questions, is thereby answering questions *about* baseball (or that the machine has somehow referred to Robin Roberts). If the *programmer* chooses to interpret the machine inscription "Robin Roberts won 28" as a statement about Robin Roberts (e.g., as the statement that he won 28), that's all well and good, but it's no business of the machine's. The machine has no access to that interpretation, and its computations are in no way affected by it. The machine doesn't know what it's talking about, and it doesn't care; *about* is a semantic relation ...

This brings us to a point where, having done some sort of justice to the Cartesian's insight, we can also do some sort of justice to the naturalist's. For, after all, mental processes are supposed to be operations on representations, and it is in the nature of representations to represent. We have seen that a psychology which embraces the formality condition is thereby debarred from raising questions about the semantic properties of mental representations; yet surely such questions ought *somewhere* to be raised. The computer which prints out "RR won 28" is not thereby referring to RR. But, surely, when I think: *RR won 28*, I *am* thinking about RR, and if not in virtue of having performed some formal operations on some representations, then presumably in virtue of something else. It's perhaps borrowing the least tendentious fragment of causal theories of reference to assume that what fixes the interpretation of my mental representations of RR is something about the way that he and I are embedded in the world; perhaps not a causal chain stretching between us, but anyhow *some* facts about how he and I are causally situated; *Dasein*, as you might say. Only a *naturalistic* psychology will do to specify these facts, because here we are explicitly in the realm of organism/environment transactions.

We are on the verge of a bland and ecumenical conclusion: that there is room both for a computational psychology—viewed as a theory of formal processes defined over mental representations—*and* a naturalistic psychology, viewed as a theory of the (presumably causal) relations between representations and the world which fix the semantic interpretations of the former. I think that, in principle, this is the right way to look at things. In practice, however, I think that it's misleading. So far as I can see, it is overwhelmingly likely that computational psychology is the only one that we are going to get. I want to argue for this conclusion in two steps. First, I'll argue for what I've till now only assumed: that we must at *least* have a psychology which accepts the formality condition. Then I'll argue that there's good reason to suppose that that's the most that we can have; that a naturalistic psychology isn't a practical possibility and isn't likely to become one.

NOTES

I've had a lot of help with this one. I'm particularly indebted to: Professors Ned Block, Sylvain Bromberger, Janet Dean Fodor, Keith Gunderson, Robert Richardson, Judith Thomson; and to Mr. Israel Krakowski.

1 I shall speak of "type identity" (distinctness) of mental states to pick out the sense of "same mental state" in which, for example, John and Mary are in the same mental state if both believe that water flows. Correspondingly, I shall use the notion of "token identity" (distinctness) of mental state to pick out the sense of "same mental state" in which it's necessary that if x and y are in the same mental state, then $x = y$. ...

3 This is *not*, notice, the same as saying "formal operations are the ones that apply mechanically"; in this latter sense, *formality* means something like *explicitness*. There's no particular reason for using "formal" to mean both "syntactic" and "explicit," though the ambiguity abounds in the literature. ...

REFERENCES

Descartes, R. (1964). *Philosophical Essays*, introduction and notes by La Fleur, L.J., Indianapolis, Bobbs Merrill.

Hume, D. (1874). *A Treatise of Human Nature*, Vol. 1, Green, T.H. and Grose, T.H. (eds.), London, Longmans, Green, and Company.

James, W. (1890). *Principles of Psychology*, New York, Dover Publications.

Putnam, H. (1960). "Minds and machines," in Hook, S. (ed.), *Dimensions of Mind*, New York, New York University Press, pp. 138–164.

Winograd, T. (1971). *Procedures as a Representation for Data in a Computer Program for Understanding Natural Language*, Cambridge, Mass., M.I.T. Project MAC.

Hilary Putnam
Selections from *Reason, Truth and History*
Chapter 1: Brains in a Vat

An ant is crawling on a patch of sand. As it crawls, it traces a line in the sand. By pure chance the line that it traces curves and recrosses itself in such a way that it ends up looking like a recognizable caricature of Winston Churchill. Has the ant traced a picture of Winston Churchill, a picture that *depicts* Churchill?

Most people would say, on a little reflection, that it has not. The ant, after all, has never seen Churchill, or even a picture of Churchill, and it had no intention of depicting Churchill. It simply traced a line (and even *that* was unintentional), a line that *we* can 'see as' a picture of Churchill.

We can express this by saying that the line is not 'in itself' a representation[1] of anything rather than anything else. Similarity (of a certain very complicated sort) to the features of Winston Churchill is not sufficient to make something represent or refer to Churchill. Nor is it necessary: in our community the printed shape 'Winston Churchill', the spoken words 'Winston Churchill', and many other things are used to represent Churchill (though not pictorially), while not having the sort of similarity to Churchill that a picture—even a line drawing—has. If *similarity* is not necessary or sufficient to make something represent something else, how can *anything* be necessary or sufficient for this purpose? How on earth can one thing represent (or 'stand for', etc.) a different thing?

The answer may seem easy. Suppose the ant had seen Winston Churchill, and suppose that it had the intelligence and skill to draw a picture of him. Suppose it produced the caricature *intentionally*. Then the line would have represented Churchill.

On the other hand, suppose the line had the shape WINSTON CHURCHILL. And suppose this was just accident (ignoring the improbability involved). Then the 'printed shape' WINSTON CHURCHILL would *not* have represented Churchill, although that printed shape does represent Churchill when it occurs in almost any book today.

So it may seem that what is necessary for representation, or what is mainly necessary for representation, is *intention*.

But to have the intention that *anything*, even private language (even the words 'Winston Churchill' spoken in my mind and not out loud), should *represent* Churchill, I must have been able to *think about* Churchill in the first place. If lines in the sand, noises, etc., cannot 'in themselves' represent anything, then how is it that thought forms can 'in themselves' represent anything? Or can they? How can thought reach out and 'grasp' what is external?

Some philosophers have, in the past, leaped from this sort of consideration to what they take to be a proof that the mind is *essentially non-physical in nature*. The argument is simple; what we said about the ant's curve applies to any physical object. No physical object can, in itself, refer to one thing rather than to another; nevertheless, *thoughts in the mind* obviously do succeed in referring to one thing rather than another. So thoughts (and hence the mind) are of an essentially different nature than physical objects. Thoughts have the characteristic of *intentionality*—they can refer to something else; nothing physical has 'intentionality', save as that intentionality is derivative from some employment of that physical thing by a mind. Or so it is claimed. This is too quick; just postulating mysterious powers of mind solves nothing. But the problem is very real. How is intentionality, reference, possible?

Magical theories of reference

We saw that the ant's 'picture' has no necessary connection with Winston Churchill. The mere fact that the 'picture' bears a 'resemblance' to Churchill does not make it into a real picture, nor does it make it a representation of Churchill. Unless the ant is an intelligent ant (which it isn't) and knows about Churchill (which it doesn't), the curve it traced is not a picture or even a representation of anything. Some primitive people believe that some representations (in particular, *names*) have a necessary connection with their bearers; that to know the 'true name' of someone or something gives one power over it. This power comes from the *magical connection* between the name and the bearer of the name; once one realizes that a name *only* has a contextual, contingent, conventional connection with its bearer, it is hard to see why knowledge of the name should have any mystical significance.

What is important to realize is that what goes for physical pictures also goes for mental images, and for mental representations in general; mental representations no more have a necessary connection with what they represent than physical representations do. The contrary supposition is a survival of magical thinking.

Perhaps the point is easiest to grasp in the case of mental *images*. (Perhaps the first philosopher to grasp the enormous significance of this point, even if he was not the first to actually make it, was Wittgenstein.) Suppose there is a planet somewhere on which human beings have evolved (or been deposited by alien spacemen, or what have you). Suppose these humans, although otherwise like us, have never seen *trees*. Suppose they have never imagined trees (perhaps vegetable life exists on their planet only in the form of molds). Suppose one day a picture of a tree is accidentally dropped on their planet by a spaceship which passes on without having other contact with them. Imagine them puzzling over the picture. What in the world is this? All sorts of speculations occur to them: a building, a canopy, even an animal of some kind. But suppose they never come close to the truth.

For *us* the picture is a representation of a tree. For these humans the picture only represents a strange object, nature and function unknown. Suppose one of them has a mental image which is exactly like one of my mental images of a tree as a result of having seen the picture. His mental image is not a *representation of a tree*. It is only a representation of the strange object (whatever it is) that the mysterious picture represents.

Still, someone might argue that the mental image is *in fact* a representation of a tree, if only because the picture which caused this mental image was itself a representation of a tree to begin with. There is a causal chain from actual trees to the mental image even if it is a very strange one.

But even this causal chain can be imagined absent. Suppose the 'picture of the tree' that the spaceship dropped was not really a picture of a tree, but the accidental result of some spilled paints. Even if it looked exactly like a picture of a tree, it was, in truth, no more a picture of a tree than the ant's 'caricature' of Churchill was a picture of Churchill. We can even imagine that the spaceship which dropped the 'picture' came from a planet which knew nothing of trees. Then the humans would still have mental images qualitatively identical with my image of a tree, but they would not be images which represented a tree any more than anything else.

The same thing is true of *words*. A discourse on paper might seem to be a perfect description of trees, but if it was produced by monkeys randomly hitting keys on a typewriter for millions of years, then the words do not refer to anything. If there were a person who memorized those words and said them in his mind without understanding them, then they would not refer to anything when thought in the mind, either.

Imagine the person who is saying those words in his mind has been hypnotized. Suppose the words are in Japanese, and the person has been told that he understands Japanese. Suppose that as he thinks those words he has a 'feeling of understanding'. (Although if someone broke into his train of thought and asked him what the words he was thinking *meant*, he would discover he couldn't say.) Perhaps the illusion would be so perfect that the person could even fool a Japanese telepath! But if he couldn't use the words in the right contexts, answer questions about what he 'thought', etc., then he didn't understand them.

By combining these science fiction stories I have been telling, we can contrive a case in which someone thinks words which are in fact a description of trees in some language *and* simultaneously has appropriate mental images, but *neither* understands the words *nor* knows what a tree is. We can even imagine that the mental images were caused by paint-spills (although the person has been hypnotized to think that they are images of something appropriate to his thought—only, if he were asked, he wouldn't be able to say of what). And we can imagine that the language the person is thinking in is one neither the hypnotist nor the person hypnotized has ever heard of—perhaps it is just coincidence that these 'nonsense sentences', as the hypnotist supposes them to be, are a description of trees in Japanese. In short, everything passing before the person's mind might be qualitatively identical with what was passing through the mind of a Japanese speaker who was *really* thinking about trees—but none of it would refer to trees.

All of this is really impossible, of course, in the way that it is really impossible that monkeys should by chance type out a copy of *Hamlet*. That is to say that the probabilities against it are

so high as to mean it will never really happen (we think). But is is not logically impossible, or even physically impossible. It *could* happen (compatibly with physical law and, perhaps, compatibly with actual conditions in the universe, if there are lots of intelligent beings on other planets). And if it did happen, it would be a striking demonstration of an important conceptual truth; that even a large and complex system of representations, both verbal and visual, still does not have an *intrinsic*, built-in, magical connection with what it represents—a connection independent of how it was caused and what the dispositions of the speaker or thinker are. And this is true whether the system of representations (words and images, in the case of the example) is physically realized—the words are written or spoken, and the pictures are physical pictures—or only realized in the mind. Thought words and mental pictures do not *intrinsically* represent what they are about.

The case of the brains in a vat

Here is a science fiction possibility discussed by philosophers: imagine that a human being (you can imagine this to be yourself) has been subjected to an operation by an evil scientist. The person's brain (your brain) has been removed from the body and placed in a vat of nutrients which keeps the brain alive. The nerve endings have been connected to a super-scientific computer which causes the person whose brain it is to have the illusion that everything is perfectly normal. There seem to be people, objects, the sky, etc; but really all the person (you) is experiencing is the result of electronic impulses travelling from the computer to the nerve endings. The computer is so clever that if the person tries to raise his hand, the feedback from the computer will cause him to 'see' and 'feel' the hand being raised. Moreover, by varying the program, the evil scientist can cause the victim to 'experience' (or hallucinate) any situation or environment the evil scientist wishes. He can also obliterate the memory of the brain operation, so that the victim will seem to himself to have always been in this environment. It can even seem to the victim that he is sitting and reading these very words about the amusing but quite absurd supposition that there is an evil scientist who removes people's brains from their bodies and places them in a vat of nutrients which keep the brains alive. The nerve endings are supposed to be connected to a super-scientific computer which causes the person whose brain it is to have the illusion that ...

When this sort of possibility is mentioned in a lecture on the Theory of Knowledge, the purpose, of course, is to raise the classical problem of scepticism with respect to the external world in a modern way. (*How do you know you aren't in this predicament?*) But this predicament is also a useful device for raising issues about the mind/world relationship.

Instead of having just one brain in a vat, we could imagine that all human beings (perhaps all sentient beings) are brains in a vat (or nervous systems in a vat in case some beings with just a minimal nervous system already count as 'sentient'). Of course, the evil scientist would have to be outside—or would he? Perhaps there is no evil scientist, perhaps (though this is absurd) the universe just happens to consist of automatic machinery tending a vat full of brains and nervous systems.

This time let us suppose that the automatic machinery is programmed to give us all a *collective* hallucination, rather than a number of separate unrelated hallucinations. Thus, when I seem to myself to be talking to you, you seem to yourself to be hearing my words. Of course, it is not the case that my words actually reach your ears—for you don't have (real) ears, nor do I have a real mouth and tongue. Rather, when I produce my words, what happens is that the efferent impulses travel from my brain to the computer, which both causes me to 'hear' my own voice uttering those words and 'feel' my tongue moving, etc., and causes you to

'hear' my words, 'see' me speaking, etc. In this case, we are, in a sense, actually in communication. I am not mistaken about your real existence (only about the existence of your body and the 'external world', apart from brains). From a certain point of view, it doesn't even matter that 'the whole world' is a collective hallucination; for you do, after all, really hear my words when I speak to you, even if the mechanism isn't what we suppose it to be. (Of course, if we were two lovers making love, rather than just two people carrying on a conversation, then the suggestion that it was just two brains in a vat might be disturbing.)

I want now to ask a question which will seem very silly and obvious (at least to some people, including some very sophisticated philosophers), but which will take us to real philosophical depths rather quickly. Suppose this whole story were actually true. Could we, if we were brains in a vat in this way, *say* or *think* that we were?

I am going to argue that the answer is 'No, we couldn't.' In fact, I am going to argue that the supposition that we are actually brains in a vat, although it violates no physical law, and is perfectly consistent with everything we have experienced, cannot possibly be true. *It cannot possibly be true*, because it is, in a certain way, self-refuting.

The argument I am going to present is an unusual one, and it took me several years to convince myself that it is really right. But it is a correct argument. What makes it seem so strange is that it is connected with some of the very deepest issues in philosophy. (It first occurred to me when I was thinking about a theorem in modern logic, the 'Skolem-Löwenheim Theorem', and I suddenly saw a connection between this theorem and some arguments in Wittgenstein's *Philosophical Investigations*.)

A 'self-refuting supposition' is one whose truth implies its own falsity. For example, consider the thesis that *all general statements are false*. This is a general statement. So if it is true, then it must be false. Hence, it is false. Sometimes a thesis is called 'self-refuting' if it is *the supposition that the thesis is entertained or enunciated* that implies its falsity. For example, 'I do not exist' is self-refuting if thought by *me* (for any '*me*'). So one can be certain that one oneself exists, if one thinks about it (as Descartes argued).

What I shall show is that the supposition that we are brains in a vat has just this property. If we can consider whether it is true or false, then it is not true (I shall show). Hence it is not true.

Before I give the argument, let us consider why it seems so strange that such an argument can be given (at least to philosophers who subscribe to a 'copy' conception of truth). We conceded that it is compatible with physical law that there should be a world in which all sentient beings are brains in a vat. As philosophers say, there is a 'possible world' in which all sentient beings are brains in a vat. (This 'possible world' talk makes it sound as if there is a *place* where any absurd supposition is true, which is why it can be very misleading in philosophy.) The humans in that possible world have exactly the same experiences that *we* do. They think the same thoughts we do (at least, the same words, images, thought-forms, etc., go through their minds). Yet, I am claiming that there is an argument we can give that shows we are not brains in a vat. How can there be? And why couldn't the people in the possible world who really *are* brains in a vat give it too?

The answer is going to be (basically) this: although the people in that possible world can think and 'say' any words we can think and say, they cannot (I claim) *refer* to what we can refer to. In particular, they cannot think or say that they are brains in a vat (*even by thinking 'we are brains in a vat'*).

Turing's test

Suppose someone succeeds in inventing a computer which can actually carry on an intelligent conversation with one (on as many subjects as an intelligent person might). How can one decide if the computer is 'conscious'?

The British logician Alan Turing proposed the following test:[2] let someone carry on a conversation with the computer and a conversation with a person whom he does not know. If he cannot tell which is the computer and which is the human being, then (assume the test to be repeated a sufficient number of times with different interlocutors) the computer is conscious. In short, a computing machine is conscious if it can pass the 'Turing Test'. (The conversations are not to be carried on face to face, of course, since the interlocutor is not to know the visual appearance of either of his two conversational partners. Nor is voice to be used, since the mechanical voice might simply sound different from a human voice. Imagine, rather, that the conversations are all carried on via electric typewriter. The interlocutor types in his statements, questions, etc., and the two partners—the machine and the person—respond via the electric keyboard. Also, the machine may *lie*—asked 'Are you a machine', it might reply, 'No, I'm an assistant in the lab here.')

The idea that this test is really a definitive test of consciousness has been criticized by a number of authors (who are by no means hostile in principle to the idea that a machine might be conscious). But this is not our topic at this time. I wish to use the general idea of the Turing test, the general idea of a *dialogic test of competence*, for a different purpose, the purpose of exploring the notion of *reference*.

Imagine a situation in which the problem is not to determine if the partner is really a person or a machine, but is rather to determine if the partner uses the words to refer as we do. The obvious test is, again, to carry on a conversation, and, if no problems arise, if the partner 'passes' in the sense of being indistinguishable from someone who is certified in advance to be speaking the same language, referring to the usual sorts of objects, etc., to conclude that the partner does refer to objects as we do. When the purpose of the Turing test is as just described, that is, to determine the existence of (shared) reference, I shall refer to the test as the *Turing Test for Reference*. And, just as philosophers have discussed the question whether the original Turing test is a *definitive* test for consciousness, i.e. the question of whether a machine which 'passes' the test not just once but regularly is *necessarily* conscious, so, in the same way, I wish to discuss the question of whether the Turing Test for Reference just suggested is a definitive test for shared reference.

The answer will turn out to be 'No'. The Turing Test for Reference is not definitive. It is certainly an excellent test in practice; but it is not logically impossible (though it is certainly highly improbable) that someone could pass the Turing Test for Reference and not be referring to anything. It follows from this, as we shall see, that we can extend our observation that words (and whole texts and discourses) do not have a necessary connection to their referents. Even if we consider not words by themselves but rules deciding what words may appropriately be produced in certain contexts—even if we consider, in computer jargon, *programs for using words*—unless those programs themselves *refer to something extra-linguistic* there is still no determinate reference that those words possess. This will be a crucial step in the process of reaching the conclusion that the Brain-in-a-Vat Worlders cannot refer to anything external at all (and hence cannot say *that* they are Brain-in-a-Vat Worlders).

Suppose, for example, that I am in the Turing situation (playing the 'Imitation Game', in Turing's terminology) and my partner is actually a machine. Suppose this machine is able to win the game ('passes' the test). Imagine the machine to be programmed to produce beautiful responses in English to statements, questions, remarks, etc. in English, but that it has no sense organs (other than the hookup to my electric typewriter), and no motor organs (other than the electric typewriter). (As far as I can

make out, Turing does not assume that the possession of either sense organs or motor organs is necessary for consciousness or intelligence.) Assume that not only does the machine lack electronic eyes and ears, etc., but that there are no provisions in the machine's program, the program for playing the Imitation Game, for incorporating inputs from such sense organs, or for controlling a body. What should we say about such a machine?

To me, it seems evident that we cannot and should not attribute reference to such a device. It is true that the machine can discourse beautifully about, say, the scenery in New England. But it could not recognize an apple tree or an apple, a mountain or a cow, a field or a steeple, if it were in front of one.

What we have is a device for producing sentences in response to sentences. But none of these sentences is at all connected to the real world. *If one coupled two of these machines and let them play the Imitation Game with each other, then they would go on 'fooling' each other forever, even if the rest of the world disappeared!* There is no more reason to regard the machine's talk of apples as referring to real world apples than there is to regard the ant's 'drawing' as referring to Winston Churchill.

What produces the illusion of reference, meaning, intelligence, etc., here is the fact that there is a convention of representation which *we* have under which the machine's discourse refers to apples, steeples, New England, etc. Similarly, there is the *illusion* that the ant has caricatured Churchill, for the same reason. But we are able to perceive, handle, deal with apples and fields. Our talk of apples and fields is intimately connected with our *non-verbal* transactions with apples and fields. There are 'language entry rules' which take us from experiences of apples to such utterances as 'I see an apple', and 'language exit rules' which take us from decisions expressed in linguistic form ('I am going to buy some apples') to actions other than speaking. Lacking either language entry rules or language exit rules, there is no reason to regard the conversation of the machine (or of the two machines, in the case we envisaged of two machines playing the Imitation Game with each other) as more than syntactic play. Syntactic play that *resembles* intelligent discourse, to be sure; but only as (and no more than) the ant's curve resembles a biting caricature.

In the case of the ant, we could have argued that the ant would have drawn the same curve even if Winston Churchill had never existed. In the case of the machine, we cannot quite make the parallel argument; if apples, trees, steeples and fields had not existed, then, presumably, the programmers would not have produced that same program. Although the machine does not *perceive* apples, fields, or steeples, its creator-designers did. There is *some* causal connection between the machine and the real world apples, etc., via the perceptual experience and knowledge of the creator-designers. But such a weak connection can hardly suffice for reference. Not only is it logically possible, though fantastically improbable, that the same machine *could* have existed even if apples, fields, and steeples had not existed; more important, the machine is utterly insensitive to the *continued* existence of apples, fields, steeples, etc. Even if all these things *ceased* to exist, the machine would still discourse just as happily in the same way. That is why the machine cannot be regarded as referring at all.

The point that is relevant for our discussion is that there is nothing in Turing's Test to rule out a machine which is programmed to do nothing *but* play the Imitation Game, and that a machine which can do nothing *but* play the Imitation Game is *clearly* not referring any more than a record player is.

Brains in a vat (again)

Let us compare the hypothetical 'brains in a vat' with the machines just described. There are

obviously important differences. The brains in a vat do not have sense organs, but they do have *provision* for sense organs; that is, there are afferent nerve endings, there are inputs from these afferent nerve endings, and these inputs figure in the 'program' of the brains in the vat just as they do in the program of our brains. The brains in a vat are *brains*; moreover, they are *functioning* brains, and they function by the same rules as brains do in the actual world. For these reasons, it would seem absurd to deny consciousness or intelligence to them. But the fact that they are conscious and intelligent does not mean that their words refer to what our words refer. The question we are interested in is this: do their verbalizations containing, say, the word 'tree' actually refer to *trees*? More generally: can they refer to *external* objects at all? (As opposed to, for example, objects in the image produced by the automatic machinery.)

To fix our ideas, let us specify that the automatic machinery is supposed to have come into existence by some kind of cosmic chance or coincidence (or, perhaps, to have always existed). In this hypothetical world, the automatic machinery itself is supposed to have no intelligent creator-designers. In fact, as we said at the beginning of this chapter, we may imagine that all sentient beings (however minimal their sentience) are inside the vat.

This assumption does not help. For there is no connection between the *word* 'tree' as used by these brains and actual trees. They would still use the word 'tree' just as they do, think just the thoughts they do, have just the images they have, even if there were no actual trees. Their images, words, etc., are qualitatively identical with images, words, etc., which do represent trees in *our* world; but we have already seen (the ant again!) that qualitative similarity to something which represents an object (Winston Churchill or a tree) does not make a thing a representation all by itself. In short, the brains in a vat are not thinking about real trees when they think 'there is a tree in front of me' because there is nothing by virtue of which their thought 'tree' represents actual trees.

If this seems hasty, reflect on the following: we have seen that the words do not necessarily refer to trees even if they are arranged in a sequence which is identical with a discourse which (were it to occur in one of our minds) would unquestionably *be about trees* in the actual world. Nor does the 'program', in the sense of the rules, practices, dispositions of the brains to verbal behavior, necessarily refer to trees or bring about reference to trees through the connections it establishes between words and words, or *linguistic* cues and *linguistic* responses. If these brains think about, refer to, represent trees (real trees, outside the vat), then it must be because of the way the 'program' connects the system of language to *non-verbal* input and outputs. There are indeed such non-verbal inputs and outputs in the Brain-in-a-Vat world (those efferent and afferent nerve endings again!), but we also saw that the 'sense-data' produced by the automatic machinery do not represent trees (or anything external) even when they resemble our tree-images exactly. Just as a splash of paint might resemble a tree picture without *being* a tree picture, so, we saw, a 'sense datum' might be qualitatively identical with an 'image of a tree' without being an image of a tree. How can the fact that, in the case of the brains in a vat, the language is connected by the program with sensory inputs which do not intrinsically or extrinsically represent trees (or anything external) possibly bring it about that the whole system of representations, the language-in-use, *does* refer to or represent trees or anything external?

The answer is that it cannot. The whole system of sense-data, motor signals to the efferent endings, and verbally or conceptually mediated thought connected by 'language entry rules' to the sense-data (or whatever) as inputs and by 'language exit rules' to the motor signals as outputs, has no more connection to *trees* than the ant's curve has to Winston Churchill. Once we

see that the *qualitative similarity* (amounting, if you like, to qualitative identity) between the thoughts of the brains in a vat and the thoughts of someone in the actual world by no means implies sameness of reference, it is not hard to see that there is no basis at all for regarding the brain in a vat as referring to external things.

The premisses of the argument

I have now given the argument promised to show that the brains in a vat cannot think or say that they are brains in a vat. It remains only to make it explicit and to examine its structure.

By what was just said, when the brain in a vat (in the world where every sentient being is and always was a brain in a vat) thinks 'There is a tree in front of me', his thought does not refer to actual trees. On some theories that we shall discuss it might refer to trees in the image, or to the electronic impulses that cause tree experiences, or to the features of the program that are responsible for those electronic impulses. These theories are not ruled out by what was just said, for there is a close causal connection between the use of the word 'tree' in vat-English and the presence of trees in the image, the presence of electronic impulses of a certain kind, and the presence of certain features in the machine's program. On these theories the brain is *right*, not *wrong* in thinking 'There is a tree in front of me.' Given what 'tree' refers to in vat-English and what 'in front of' refers to, assuming one of these theories is correct, then the truth-conditions for 'There is a tree in front of me' when it occurs in vat-English are simply that a tree in the image be 'in front of' the me in question—in the image—or, perhaps, that the kind of electronic impulse that normally produces this experience be coming from the automatic machinery, or, perhaps, that the feature of the machinery that is supposed to produce the 'tree in front of one' experience be operating. And these truth-conditions are certainly fulfilled.

By the same argument, 'vat' refers to vats in the image in vat-English, or something related (electronic impulses or program features), but certainly not to real vats, since the use of 'vat' in vat-English has no causal connection to real vats (apart from the connection that the brains in a vat wouldn't be able to use the word 'vat', if it were not for the presence of one particular vat—the vat they are in; but this connection obtains between the use of *every* word in vat-English and that one particular vat; it is not a special connection between the use of the *particular* word 'vat' and vats). Similarly, 'nutrient fluid' refers to a liquid in the image in vat-English, or something related (electronic impulses or program features). It follows that if their 'possible world' is really the actual one, and we are really the brains in a vat, then what we now mean by 'we are brains in a vat' is that *we are brains in a vat in the image* or something of that kind (if we mean anything at all). But part of the hypothesis that we are brains in a vat is that we aren't brains in a vat in the image (i.e. what we are 'hallucinating' isn't that we are brains in a vat). So, if we are brains in a vat, then the sentence 'We are brains in a vat' says something false (if it says anything). In short, if we are brains in a vat, then 'We are brains in a vat' is false. So it is (necessarily) false.

The supposition that such a possibility makes sense arises from a combination of two errors: (1) taking *physical possibility* too seriously; and (2) unconsciously operating with a magical theory of reference, a theory on which certain mental representations necessarily refer to certain external things and kinds of things.

There is a 'physically possible world' in which we are brains in a vat—what does this mean except that there is a *description* of such a state of affairs which is compatible with the laws of physics? Just as there is a tendency in our culture (and has been since the seventeenth century) to take *physics* as our metaphysics, that is, to view the exact sciences as the long-sought description of the 'true and ultimate furniture of the universe', so there is, as an immediate consequence, a tendency to take 'physical possibility' as the very touchstone of what might really actually be the case. Truth is physical truth; possibility physical possibility; and necessity physical necessity, on such a view. But we have just seen, if only in the case of a very contrived example so far, that this view is wrong. The existence of a 'physically possible world' in which we are brains in a vat (and always were and will be) does not mean that we might really, actually, possibly *be* brains in a vat. What rules out this possibility is not physics but *philosophy*.

Some philosophers, eager both to assert and minimize the claims of their profession at the same time (the typical state of mind of Anglo-American philosophy in the twentieth century), would say: 'Sure. You have shown that some things that seem to be physical possibilities are really *conceptual* impossibilities. What's so surprising about that?'

Well, to be sure, my argument can be described as a 'conceptual' one. But to describe philosophical activity as the search for 'conceptual' truths makes it all sound like *inquiry about the meaning of words*. And that is not at all what we have been engaging in.

What we have been doing is considering the *preconditions* for *thinking about, representing, referring to*, etc. We have investigated these preconditions *not* by investigating the meaning of these words and phrases (as a linguist might, for example) but by *reasoning a priori*. Not in the old 'absolute' sense (since we don't claim that magical theories of reference are *a priori* wrong), but in the sense of inquiring into what is *reasonably* possible *assuming* certain general premises, or making certain very broad theoretical assumptions. Such a procedure is neither 'empirical' nor quite 'a priori', but has elements of both ways of investigating. In spite of the fallibility of my procedure, and its dependence upon assumptions which might be described as 'empirical' (e.g. the assumption that the mind has no access to external things or properties apart from that provided by the senses), my procedure has a close relation to what Kant called a 'transcendental' investigation; for it is an investigation, I repeat, of the *preconditions* of reference and hence of thought—preconditions built in to the nature of our minds themselves, though not (as Kant hoped) wholly independent of empirical assumptions.

One of the premisses of the argument is obvious: that magical theories of reference are wrong, wrong for mental representations and not only for physical ones. The other premiss is that one cannot refer to certain kinds of things, e.g. *trees*, if one has no causal interaction at all with them,[3] or with things in terms of which they can be described. But why should we accept these premisses? Since these constitute the broad framework within which I am arguing, it is time to examine them more closely.

The reasons for denying necessary connections between representations and their referents

I mentioned earlier that some philosophers (most famously, Brentano) have ascribed to the mind a power, 'intentionality', which precisely enables it to *refer*. Evidently, I have rejected this as no solution. But what gives me this right? Have I, perhaps, been too hasty?

These philosophers did not claim that we can think about external things or properties without using representations at all. And the argument I gave above comparing visual sense data to the ant's 'picture' (the argument via the science fiction story about the 'picture' of a tree that came from a paint-splash and that gave rise to sense data qualitatively similar to our 'visual images of trees', but unaccompanied by any *concept* of a tree) would be accepted as showing that *images* do not necessarily refer. If there are mental representations that necessarily refer (to external things) they must be of the nature of *concepts* and not of the nature of images. But what are *concepts*?

When we introspect we do not perceive 'concepts' flowing through our minds as such. Stop the stream of thought when or where we will, what we catch are words, images, sensations, feelings. When I speak my thoughts out loud I do not think them twice. I hear my words as you do. To be sure it feels different to me when I utter words that I believe and when I utter words I do not believe (but sometimes, when I am nervous, or in front of a hostile audience, it feels as if I am lying when I know I am telling the truth); and it feels different when I utter words I understand and when I utter words I do not understand. But I can imagine without difficulty someone thinking just these words (in the sense of saying them in his mind) and having just the feeling of understanding, asserting, etc., that I do, and realizing a minute later (or on being awakened by a hypnotist) that he did not understand what had just passed through his mind at all, that he did not even understand the language these words are in. I don't claim that this is very likely; I simply mean that there is nothing at all unimaginable about this. And what this shows is not that concepts *are* words (or images, sensations, etc.), but that to attribute a 'concept' or a 'thought' to someone is quite different from attributing any mental 'presentation', any introspectible entity or event, to him. Concepts are not mental presentations that intrinsically refer to external objects for the very decisive reason that they are not mental presentations at all. Concepts are signs used in a certain way; the signs may be public or private, mental entities or physical entities, but even when the signs are 'mental' and 'private', the sign itself apart from its use is not the concept. And signs do not themselves intrinsically refer.

We can see this by performing a very simple thought experiment. Suppose you are like me and cannot tell an elm tree from a beech tree. We still say that the reference of 'elm' in my speech is the same as the reference of 'elm' in anyone else's, viz. elm trees, and that the set of all beech trees is the extension of 'beech' (i.e. the set of things the word 'beech' is truly predicated of) both in your speech and my speech. Is it really credible that the difference between what 'elm' refers to and what 'beech' refers to is brought about by a difference in our *concepts?* My concept of an elm tree is exactly the same as my concept of a beech tree (I blush to confess). (This shows that the determination of reference is social and not individual, by the way; you and I both defer to experts who *can* tell elms from beeches.) If someone heroically attempts to maintain that the difference between the reference of 'elm' and the reference of 'beech' in *my* speech is explained by a difference in my psychological state, then let him imagine a Twin Earth where the words are switched. Twin Earth is very much like Earth; in fact, apart from the fact that 'elm' and 'beech' are interchanged, the reader can suppose Twin Earth is exactly like Earth. Suppose I have a *Doppelganger* on Twin Earth who is molecule for molecule identical with me (in the sense in which two neckties can be 'identical'). If you are a dualist, then suppose my *Doppelganger* thinks the same verbalized thoughts I do, has the same sense data, the same dispositions, etc. It is absurd to think his psychological state is one bit different from mine: yet his word 'elm' represents *beeches*, and my word 'elm' represents elms. (Similarly, if the 'water' on Twin Earth is a different liquid—say, XYZ and not H_2O— then 'water' represents a different liquid when used on Twin Earth and when used on Earth, etc.) Contrary to a doctrine that has been with us since the seventeenth century, *meanings just aren't in the head.*

We have seen that possessing a concept is not a matter of possessing images (say, of trees —or even Images, 'visual' or 'acoustic', of sentences, or whole discourses, for that matter) since one could possess any system of images you please and not possess the *ability* to use the sentences in situationally appropriate ways (considering both linguistic factors—what has been

said before—and non-linguistic factors as determining 'situational appropriateness'). A man may have all the images you please, and still be completely at a loss when one says to him 'point to a tree', even if a lot of trees are present. He may even have the image of what he is supposed to do, and still not know what he is supposed to do. For the image, if not accompanied by the ability to act in a certain way, is just a *picture*, and acting in accordance with a picture is itself an ability that one may or may not have. (The man might picture himself pointing to a tree, but just for the sake of contemplating something logically possible; himself pointing to a tree after someone has produced the—to him meaningless—sequence of sounds 'please point to a tree'.) He would still not know that he was supposed to point to a tree, and he would still not *understand* 'point to a tree'.

I have considered the ability to use certain sentences to be the criterion for possessing a full-blown concept, but this could easily be liberalized. We could allow symbolism consisting of elements which are not words in a natural language, for example, and we could allow such mental phenomena as images and other types of internal events. What is essential is that these should have the same complexity, ability to be combined with each other, etc., as sentences in a natural language. For, although a particular presentation—say, a blue flash—might serve a particular mathematician as the inner expression of the whole proof of the Prime Number Theorem, still there would be no temptation to say this (and it would be false to say this) if that mathematician could not unpack his 'blue flash' into separate steps and logical connections. But, no matter what sort of inner phenomena we allow as possible *expressions* of thought, arguments exactly similar to the foregoing will show that it is not the phenomena themselves that constitute understanding, but rather the ability of the thinker to *employ* these phenomena, to produce the right phenomena in the right circumstances.

The foregoing is a very abbreviated version of Wittgenstein's argument in *Philosophical Investigations*. If it is correct, then the attempt to understand thought by what is called 'phenomenological' investigation is fundamentally misguided; for what the phenomenologists fail to see is that what they are describing is the inner *expression* of thought, but that the *understanding* of that expression—one's understanding of one's own thoughts—is not an *occurrence* but an *ability*. Our example of a man pretending to think in Japanese (and deceiving a Japanese telepath) already shows the futility of a phenomenological approach to the problem of *understanding*. For even if there is some introspectible quality which is present when and only when one *really* understands (this seems false on introspection, in fact), still that quality is only *correlated* with understanding, and it is still possible that the man fooling the Japanese telepath have that quality too and *still* not understand a word of Japanese.

On the other hand, consider the perfectly possible man who does not have any 'interior monologue' at all. He speaks perfectly good English, and if asked what his opinions are on a given subject, he will give them at length. But he never thinks (in words, images, etc.) when he is not speaking out loud; nor does anything 'go through his head', except that (of course) he hears his own voice speaking, and has the usual sense impressions from his surroundings, plus a general 'feeling of understanding'. (Perhaps he is in the habit of talking to himself.) When he types a letter or goes to the store, etc., he is not having an internal 'stream of thought'; but his actions are intelligent and purposeful, and if anyone walks up and asks him 'What are you doing?' he will give perfectly coherent replies.

This man seems perfectly imaginable. No one would hesitate to say that he was conscious, disliked rock and roll (if he frequently expressed a strong aversion to rock and roll), etc., just because he did not think conscious thoughts except when speaking out loud.

What follows from all this is that (a) no set of mental events—images or more 'abstract' mental happenings and qualities—-*constitutes* understanding; and (b) no set of mental events is *necessary* for understanding. In particular, *concepts cannot be identical with mental objects of any kind.* For, assuming that by a mental object we mean something introspectible, we have just seen that whatever it is, it may be absent in a man who does understand the appropriate word (and hence has the full blown concept), and present in a man who does not have the concept at all.

Coming back now to our criticism of magical theories of reference (a topic which also concerned Wittgenstein), we see that, on the one hand, those 'mental objects' we *can* introspectively detect—words, images, feelings, etc.—do not intrinsically refer any more than the ant's picture does (and for the same reasons), while the attempts to postulate special mental objects, 'concepts', which *do* have a necessary connection with their referents, and which only trained phenomenologists can detect, commit a *logical* blunder; for concepts are (at least in part) *abilities* and not occurrences. The doctrine that there are mental presentations which necessarily refer to external things is not only bad natural science; it is also bad phenomenology and conceptual confusion.

NOTES

1. In this book the terms 'representation' and 'reference' always refer to a relation between a word (or other sort of sign, symbol, or representation) and something that actually exists (i.e. not just an 'object of thought'). There is a sense of 'refer' in which I can 'refer' to what does not exist; this is not the sense in which 'refer' is used here. An older word for what I call 'representation' or 'reference' is *denotation*.

   Secondly, I follow the custom of modern logicians and use 'exist' to mean 'exist in the past, present, or future'. Thus Winston Churchill 'exists', and we can 'refer to' or 'represent' Winston Churchill, even though he is no longer alive.

2. A. M. Turing, 'Computing Machinery and Intelligence', *Mind* (1950), reprinted in A. R. Anderson (ed.), *Minds and Machines*.

3. If the Brains in a Vat will have causal connection with, say, trees *in the future*, then perhaps they can *now* refer to trees by the description 'the things I will refer to as "trees" at such-and-such a future time'. But we are to imagine a case in which the Brains in a Vat *never* get out of the vat, and hence *never* get into causal connection with trees, etc.

Glossary

abstract ideas   Ideas that are not ideas of any particular individual object. For example, the abstract idea of a line is an idea that is not restricted to any particular line with any specific length or shape. Berkeley denies that there are any abstract ideas.

algorithm   A set of rules that, if followed, will produce a particular result or accomplish a specific task. The rules should be written in such a way that they can be followed without knowing what result is to be accomplished. A computer program is an algorithm, where the rules specify operations to be carried out by the computer.

Artificial Intelligence (AI)   The research discipline focussing on the development of machines that are capable of genuine intelligence. Sometimes the term is used to refer simply to the use of machines to perform complex tasks, or to the use of computers in modelling human intelligence.

atomism   The theory that the world consists entirely of minute particles of matter. Atoms are taken to be indestructible, and all objects are formed of collections of atoms. Atomism is a variety of **materialism**.

autonomy   See **intertheoretic autonomy**.

behavioural disposition   A tendency to exhibit certain specific kinds of behaviour under certain conditions or in the presence of certain **stimuli**. A (simple) behavioural disposition can be expressed by a conditional sentence of the form 'If C then B,' where C is the condition or stimulus and B is the behaviour.

behavioural plasticity   The apparent ability of humans to respond to an indefinite number of different situations. Descartes uses this idea to argue that people cannot be merely material beings, because the behaviour of human beings transcends what a purely mechanical being can produce. Behavioural plasticity is a topic of great interest in **Artificial Intelligence**.

behaviourism   The position that the proper task of psychology is the study of human behaviour. There are two varieties of behaviourism: **scientific behaviourism** and **logical behaviourism**.

category mistake   A term used by Gilbert Ryle to refer to a particular kind of logical confusion, which he ascribes to Descartes. Two terms belong to the same "logical category" when meaningful conjunctions can be formed with them. The error arises when people mistakenly take two dissimilar terms to belong to a common logical category.

classical conditioning   A change in behaviour produced by forming new links between **stimulus** and **response**. This is done by associating a stimulus that already produces a particular response with a new stimulus. The most famous example of this effect is Pavlov's experiment with dogs, whereby he conditioned the dogs to salivate to the ringing of a bell by associating the bell with the arrival of food.

complete thing   Descartes' description of a **substance**.

computational states   The states of a computer that are described in terms of its computing operations.

computer metaphor   The position that all activities of the mind are forms of computing or information-processing. The position is often referred to as "computationalism."

connectionism   The project of designing **Parallel Distributed Processing (PDP)** computers. The term sometimes refers to the position that the kind of computing carried out in the brain is of the type represented by PDP computers.

contingent facts   Facts that are a result of how the world happens to be, and that might not have been facts were the world different than it is. They are contrasted with **necessary facts**.

contingent identity   A **numerical identity** that is a **contingent fact**. That is, it is an identity that depends on how the world happens to be.

designator, nonrigid   A word or expression that refers to some individual person or thing, where the object it refers to depends on some **contingent facts**. A nonrigid designator will refer to one individual in certain circumstances and to other individuals in different circumstances.

designator, rigid   A word or expression that refers to some individual person or thing, where the object it refers to does not depend on any **contingent facts**. A rigid designator will refer to the same individual under any circumstances whatsoever.

digital computers   An information-processing machine that operates according to an **algorithm**, and whose operation consists of reading and writing **symbols**.

discrete state machine   A machine whose operation consists of jumps from one definite state to another, rather than continuous motions.

dualism   See **mind-body dualism**.

eliminativism/eliminative materialism   The position that the development of neuroscience will eventually eliminate the terms and categories of traditional psychology. (See **intertheoretic elimination**.) Once neuroscience is sufficiently advanced, it is claimed, talk of beliefs, desires, hopes, and so on will no longer be used to explain human behaviour.

environmental history   The totality of the **stimuli** in a person's previous physical environment that have an effect on their behaviour.

epiphenomenalism   The position that mental states or mental properties are caused by activities of the brain, but do not in turn have any effect on the operation of the brain. Roughly speaking, then, mental phenomena are byproducts of nervous activity in the brain. It is contrasted with **mind-body interactionism**.

essence   See **form**.

folk psychology   The terms, categories, and principles that make up the common-sense psychology we use in everyday life to understand and predict other people's behaviour. It includes **propositional attitudes** and the many commonly accepted relations between them.

form   Aristotle defined form (or essence) as that which makes something the kind of thing it is. In living things the form is a principle of growth and movement that determines the species of a plant or animal. In this case, Aristotle claims that form is identical to soul.

Forms, The   The Forms constitute Plato's theory of **universals**. According to Plato, universals are independently existing objects that are both eternal and unchanging. Material objects have properties by imperfectly resembling the Forms. All genuine knowledge, according to Plato, is knowledge of the Forms. Sometimes the Forms are referred to as "Ideas."

function   In science and mathematics, one variable y is said to be a function of another variable x when each value of x yields a specific value for y.

functional state See **machine states**.

functionalism The theory of mind according to which mental states are defined in terms of what they do, rather than what they are made of. On this theory, mental states are characterized by their relations with **stimuli**, with behaviour, and with one another.

idealism The idea that nothing exists but immaterial minds. Idealists believe that material objects, such as apples and mountains, are collections of real or possible thoughts in the minds of thinking beings.

Ideas See **The Forms**.

incorrigibility A belief is incorrigible when it is impossible to be corrected by other people. The word is also used by Richard Rorty to indicate a belief that cannot possibly be mistaken.

intellect That part of a person that is responsible for reason or rational thought. The intellect is often contrasted with the senses, the will, and the emotions.

intentionality The characteristic feature that mental states have of being *about* something. So my thought of Paris somehow involves a relationship between me and the city that is Paris. Intentionality also involves the fact that beliefs and other mental states have propositional content. For example, the belief that Paris is in France involves the **proposition** *Paris is in France*. The term derives from the Latin term *intendo* meaning "to point toward."

intertheoretic autonomy Two theories are autonomous of one another when the laws and entities of one cannot provide an explanation of the laws and entities of the other.

intertheoretic elimination This occurs when the acceptance of a new theory has the result that people no longer believe in the entities or kinds postulated by older theories. For example, the development of cellular biology led to the elimination of the old idea of vital spirit as an explanation of life.

intertheoretic reduction A theory, T1, is reduced to another, T2, when each entity in T1 is **numerically identified** with entities of T2, and each law in T1 is explained by laws in T2. (Sometimes we also talk about the entities in a theory as being reduced, rather than the theory being reduced, as when we say that water has been reduced to H_2O.)

introspection(ism) Introspection is the reflection on, or study of, one's own thoughts and conscious experiences. Introspectionism is a school of psychology based on the idea that introspection, when carefully and skillfully carried out, will reveal the true operations of the mind.

Law of Effect A principle formulated by Edward Thorndike stating that the frequency with which a behaviour is exhibited is related to the tendency it has to produce positive or negative effects. The law forms the basis of Skinner's concept of **operant behaviour**.

linguistic vs. metaphysical physicalism 'Metaphysical physicalism' is another name for **materialism**, and it refers to the position that all that exists is matter. Linguistic physicalism is the stronger position that everything that exists can be explained or understood using only the terms and categories of the physical sciences.

logical behaviourism The theory of mind (or, more accurately, the analysis of psychology) produced by the **logical positivists**. It holds that the meaning of any psychological description of a person is given by a description of that person's actual or potential behaviour.

logical empiricism See **logical positivism**.

logical positivism A philosophical doctrine developed in Vienna in the early part of the twentieth century. Logical positivists reject all **metaphysical** theories as meaningless. Their view is based on the **verifiability theory of meaning**. According to logical positivists, the role of philosophy can be nothing more than the logical analysis of the meanings of scientific terms.

machine functionalism   A variety of **functionalism** according to which the activities of the mind are information-processing or computing activities. Machine functionalism has been defended in two forms: machine-state functionalism and computational-state functionalism, depending on whether mental states are identified with a set of **machine states** or more broadly with a set of **computational states**.

machine states   The internal states of a machine as listed in the **machine table**, which connect inputs to outputs. Hilary Putnam refers to these as "functional states."

machine table   A table that represents the behaviour of a **discrete state machine**. It displays the relations between three elements: a set of inputs, a set of outputs, and a set of internal states conecting inputs with outputs.

materialism   The idea that nothing exists but matter. Materialists deny that the mind consists of anything more than some part or attribute of the physical body.

matter   Aristotle defined matter as that which an individual thing is made of. In this sense matter is contrasted with **form**. In Descartes' mechanical physics, matter possesses only one attribute: spatial extension. Since then other properties, such as mass, have been added to the mechanical description of matter.

mechanical theories   Theories that explain change and motion in terms of external forces acting on objects that are otherwise inert. The mechanical sciences came to prominence with the rejection of Aristotelian **teleological theories**.

mental tokens/types   A mental token is a mental state or activity of a particular person at a particular time, such as my current headache. A mental type is a kind or category of mental state or activity, such as headaches or thoughts of Paris.

metaphysical physicalism   See **linguistic vs. metaphysical physicalism**

metaphysics   Roughly, metaphysics is the study of the ultimate nature of reality. The term originates with Aristotle, for whom it meant the study of the principles and concepts (like that of **universals**) that form the basis of the sciences. Theories such as **idealism** and **materialism** are metaphysical theories.

mind-body dualism   The theory that the mind (or soul) is in some way nonphysical or immaterial. Dualists believe either that the mind is a distinct entity from the body (**substance dualism**) or that properties of the mind are not physical properties of the body (**property dualism**).

mind-body interactionism   The position that states or properties of the mind are caused by states and properties of the physical body, particularly the brain, and in turn have an effect on the action of the body. Descartes' dualism is a variety of this position. It is contrasted with **epiphenomenalism**.

mind-brain identity theory   The theory of mind according to which states and activities of the mind are **numerically identical** to states and activities of the brain. Importantly, mind-brain identity theorists subscribe to **type physicalism**.

monism   The theory that there is only one kind of substance in the world. Generally, monists defend either **materialism** or **idealism**.

multiple realizability   A **type** is multiply realizable when there is no single physical property or characteristic that every **token** of that type must have in common. For example, *clock* is a multiply realizable type, as there are indefinitely many ways of physically constructing a device that tells the time. Functionalists claim that **mental types** are multiply realizable.

naturalism The view that the mind (or soul) is an integral part of the natural order of material objects, plants and animals. It includes the view that the study of the mind is not separate from the study of the natural world.

necessary facts When we say that a fact is necessary, we mean that it could not have failed to be a fact, no mattter how the world might have turned out. Such facts are to be contrasted with **contingent facts.** (Notice that this idea is not the same as saying that such a fact is necessary *for* anything, or that other things depend on these facts.)

necessary identity A **numerical identity** that is a **necessary fact.** When we say that *A* is necessarily identical to *B* we mean that *A* could not have been anything other than *B* no matter how the world might have turned out to be.

numerical identity To say that *A* is numerically identical to *B* is to say that *A* and *B* are one and the same person or thing. It is the kind of identity illustrated by sentences like, 'My wife is my best friend,' which says that there is one person who is both my wife and my best friend. It is sometimes referred to as "quantitative identity."

nutritive soul In Aristotle, that part of the soul responsible for growth and nutrition. It is possessed by all living things.

Occam's Razor The principle that, whenever two theories are consistent with the same body of evidence, then the one that postulates the fewest entities and properties is more likely to be true. It is named for the medieval philosopher William of Occam, and is sometimes referred to as "the Principle of Parsimony."

operant behaviour Behaviour that is a product of the **Law of Effect.** Roughly, it is behaviour produced and maintained by its tendency to yield positive effects or avoid negative effects. Operant behaviour forms the basis of the behavioural conditioning studied by B.F. Skinner.

ordinary language philosophy A school of philosophy that holds that the meanings of words are revealed by their everyday use. Most philosophical problems, on this view, are simply misunderstandings of ordinary linguistic practice. The school originated in England in the 1940s, and is represented by people such as Gilbert Ryle and some elements of Ludwig Wittgenstein's philosophy.

Parallel Distributed Processing (PDP) A kind of computing that does not rely on **symbol** processing, as **digital computers** do. PDP computers operate by means of many interconnected units that each carry a specific value, and whose values change as a result of the interconnections between them.

phenomenology The study of the intrinsic or qualitative character of conscious experience. It can be described as a study of what conscious experience is *like*.

physical token/type A physical token is an individual physical object or event, such as a single flash of lightening or an individual drop of water. A physical type is a category of physical objects or events, such as lightning or H_2O.

private language This term refers to a certain understanding of the meaning of sensation words like 'pain.' It holds that such words receive their meaning by referring to private, inner experiences, and thus that such words have a private, subjective meaning for each person. Wittgenstein argues that this understanding of language is incoherent.

productive sets A set is productive when it has an infinite number of members, but its members can be described in finitely many words by means of a set of rules for listing them.

property dualism The theory that, although the mind is not a distinct *entity* from the brain, there are mental properties of the brain that are distinct from any of its physical or neurological properties. It is contrasted with **substance dualism**.

proposition   The content of a declarative sentence. When two sentences have the same meaning as with 'It is snowing' and 'Il neige,' we say that the two sentences express the same proposition.

propositional attitude   A psychological state characterized by a person's attitude toward a certain **proposition**. Beliefs and desires are paradigmatic examples of propositional attitudes. To say that someone believes that Paris is in France is to say that they hold a psychological attitude of *belief* toward the proposition *Paris is in France*.

psychological realism   The position that the terms and categories of psychology (thoughts, beliefs, desires, sensations, etc.) are descriptions of things that actually exist.

qualia   The **phenomenological** properties of our sensations and conscious experiences. What coffee *tastes like*, and what the colour red *looks like*, are the qualia of the experiences of the taste of coffee and the sensation of red. (The singular is 'quale'.)

qualitative identity   One thing is qualitatively identical to another when they are similar to one another in every respect.

qualititative theories   Theories that provide explanations in terms of certain fundamental qualities, such as warmth, coldness, dryness, and heat. Qualitative theories can be contrasted with quantitative theories.

quine   A humorous verb meaning "to deny resolutely the existence of something real or important." It is a satirical jab at the Harvard philosopher, W.V.O. Quine.

rational soul   In Aristotle, that part of the soul responsible for reason. See also **intellect**.

reduction   See **intertheoretic reduction**.

reference   The relationship between a name or **designator** and the thing it names or designates. Thus 'Paris' refers to Paris.

reflex   A fixed and automatic or mechanical response to a **stimulus**. According to Descartes, all the actions of the physical body, as well as the activities of nonhuman animals, are simply collections of reflex actions.

response   The behaviour that a subject exhibits in the presence of a particular **stimulus**.

scientific behaviourism   The position that the science of psychology should be restricted to the formulation of laws connecting **stimulus** and **response**. As a position solely concerned with the proper method of psychology, it makes no philosophical claims about the nature or existence of the mind.

semantics   In general, semantics is the study of linguistic meaning. In computer theory, the semantic properties of a **symbolic** representation in a computer have to do with what the content of the representation is. For example, the symbols '10' might represent a number or a letter. In psychology and philosophy of mind, the semantics of mental states is a matter of their **intentional** properties.

sensations   According to Descartes and others, sensations are the effects produced in the mind by the sensory organs and the nerves of the body.

sensibility   That part of a person or animal that makes them capable of perceiving the world through the sensory organs.

sensitive soul   In Aristotle, that part of the soul responsible for sense perception and locomotion. It is possessed by all animals, but not by plants.

solipsism   The idea that nothing exists but your own mind. On this view, there is nothing in existence other than the contents of your own thoughts and perceptions.

stimulus   The name given to an aspect of a subject's environment that affects his or her behaviour. According to behaviourists, human actions can be understood and predicted by studying the relations between stimulus and **response**. (The plural is 'stimuli'.)

subjective character of experience This is a term used by Thomas Nagel and others to describe the **phenomenological** character of conscious experience. It is intended to refer to such things as what coffee *tastes like* or what the colour red *looks like*.

substance This term has had several definitions, but in each case it is used to refer to the most basic elements that make up the world. Aristotle used the term to refer to the components that go together to make up an individual, namely, **matter**, **form**, and (for the individual itself) the combination of matter and form. Descartes defined substance as "that which depends on nothing else for its existence." He believed that the world contains only two kinds of substances, each of which possesses only one attribute: minds (which possess only thought) and matter (which possesses only spatial extension).

substance dualism The theory that the mind is a distinct entity from the body and any of its parts. Descartes' dualism is an example of this kind of dualism. It is contrasted with **property dualism**.

symbols In computer theory, symbols are characters such as letters or numerals, or physical states of a machine, that the machine can recognize and that carry a single unit of information. Most **digital computers** use a "binary symbol code," which means they recognize only the symbols 1 and 0.

syntax The rules governing how **symbols** can occur in a computer representation, and the effect that their order of occurrence has on its operation. It is contrasted with **semantics**.

teleological theories Theories that provide explanations in terms of the ends, goals, or purposes toward which things are directed. Aristotle's notion of **form** is a teleological notion, according to which growth and movement are explained in terms of the natural end of each species or natural object.

Theoretician's Dilemma The argument that theoretical laws are unnecessary, if they accurately predict the relations between observable events, and useless, if they don't. It forms part of B.F. Skinner's argument against the study of inner psychological states.

thought, thinking Most commonly, thought is the activity of the **intellect**. But Descartes uses this term to describe the activity of the mind in a way that includes conscious experience as well. In his view, sensory perception is a form of thinking.

thought experiment A fictional story, or imaginary situation, that is used to test and challenge the way we think about the world. According to some people (Descartes, for example), thought experiments can reveal substantial truths about the world. Others argue that they merely reveal to us the content of our own concepts.

tokens and types A token is an individual thing, such as a person or object. A type is a kind or category of thing. A type can have many tokens (although it might have none), and each token will belong to many different types.

token physicalism The position that every **mental token** is a **physical token**. Token physicalism says in essence that every individual thing is a physical thing, and thus it is a statement of **materialism**. It is contrasted with **type physicalism**.

topic-neutral descriptions Descriptions of things that make no reference to their intrinsic nature. For example, if we can describe mental states solely in terms of their relations with **stimuli** or behaviour, then we can leave it open whether they are physical states of the brain or states of an immaterial mind.

transparent, the   In Aristotle's theory of vision, the substance in air and water that makes possible the transmission of colour to the soul.

Turing Machine   A certain form of **digital computer**, devised by Alan Turing. Turing Machines are useful as simple and effective ways of describing the computing power of digital computers. Their operations are absolutely simple, and yet they are capable of mimicking the behaviour of any digital computer, no matter how powerful. See also **Universal Turing Machine**.

Turing Test   A test proposed by Alan Turing as a criterion for deciding whether a machine possesses intelligence. Roughly, it requires the machine to answer questions in a way that would fool the interrogator into thinking the answers are written by a person.

type physicalism   The position that every **mental type** is a **physical type**. This position is stronger than **token physicalism** for it asserts that whenever two **mental tokens** belong to the same mental type, then they must also belong to the same physical type. **Mind-brain identity theory** is a variety of type physicalism.

universals   A characteristic or property that can be possessed by more than one object. For example, many objects can be red; what they have in common is the universal, redness.

Universal Turing Machine (UTM)   A programmable **Turing Machine** that is constructed in such a way that, by writing the appropriate program onto its tape, it will imitate the behaviour of any other Turing Machine, and hence also any other **digital computer**.

verifiability theory of meaning   A theory about the meanings of sentences adopted by the **logical positivists**. The theory says that the meaning of any sentence is given by a description of the observable circumstances under which it would be true or false, or of the evidence that would demonstrate that it is true or false. If there are no such circumstances or evidence, then the sentence is held to be meaningless.

visible, the   In Aristotle's theory of vision, that which is the object of the faculty of sight, i.e., that which is seen directly by the eye. The visible, according to Aristotle, is colour.

Acknowledgements

Chapter 1

Selections from Plato's *Phaedo*, translated with notes by David Gallop (Oxford: Clarendon Press, 1975), pp. 8–25. © Oxford University Press.

Chapter 2

Selections from Aristotle's *On the Soul* and *Sense and Sensibilia*. Reprinted from *The Complete Works of Aristotle*, edited by Jonathon Barnes (Princeton, NJ: Princeton University Press, 1984), pp. 656–657, 665–667, 682, 684, 696. © Princeton University Press. Reprinted with permission.

Chapters 3, 4, and 5

Selections from Galileo's *The Assayer*. Reprinted from *Discoveries and Opinions of Galileo*, pp. 237, 274–278. © 1957 by Stillman Drake. Used by permission of Doubleday, a division of Bantam Doubleday Dell Publishing Group, Inc.

Selections *The World or Treatise on Light*, *Principles of Philosophy*, and *Discourse on the Method of rightly conducting one's reason and seeking the truth in the sciences* are from *The Philosophical Writings of Descartes Vol. 1*, translated by John Cottingham, Robert Stoothoff and Dugald Murdoch (Cambridge: Cambridge University Press, 1985), pp. 81–82, 139–141, 210–211, 247, 284–285. Reprinted with the permission of Cambridge University Press and John Cottingham.

Selections *Meditations on First Philosophy*, *Objections to Descartes' Meditations*, and *Reply to Antoine Arnauld* are from *The Philosophical Writings of Descartes Vol. 2*, translated by John Cottingham, Robert Stoothoff and Dugald Murdoch (Cambridge: Cambridge University

Press, 1985), pp. 16–24, 50–62, 139–144, 154–161. Reprinted with the permission of Cambridge University Press and John Cottingham.

Selections from Book Four of John Locke's *An Essay Concerning Human Understanding*. Reprinted from *John Locke: An Essay Concerning Human Understanding*, ed. with an introduction by Peter H. Nidditch (London: Oxford University Press, 1975), pp. 538–543.

Chapter 6

Selections from Thomas Hobbes' *Leviathan*. Reprinted from *Philosophical Classics Volume III: Modern Philosophy*, ed. by Walter Kaufmann and Forrest E. Baird (Englewood Cliffs, NJ: Prentice Hall, 1994), pp. 64–69.

Selections from George Berkeley's *A Treatise Concerning the Principles of Human Knowledge*. Reprinted from *Philosophical Classics Volume III: Modern Philosophy*, ed. by Walter Kaufmann and Forrest E. Baird (Englewood Cliffs, NJ: Prentice Hall, 1994), pp. 264–272.

Chapter 7

Selections from B.F. Skinner's *Science and Human Behaviour*. Reprinted from *Readings in the Philosophy of Psychology, Vol. 1*, ed. by Ned Block (Cambridge, MA: Harvard University Press, 1980), pp. 37–41. First published by MacMillan & Co. (New York, 1953). Copyright Prentice Hall.

Carl Hempel, "The Logical Analysis of Psychology." From *Readings in the Philosophy of Psychology, Vol. 1*, ed. by Ned Block (Cambridge, MA: Harvard University Press, 1980), pp. 15–23. First published in *Revue de Synthese*, translated by Wilfrid Sellars, 1935. Reprinted with the permission of the author.

Chapter 8

Excerpts from Gilbert Ryle, *The Concept of Mind* (New York: Harper and Collins, 1949), pp. 7–9, 11–24, 43–44, 116. Fellows and Scholars of Hertford College in the University of Oxford. © Routledge, UK. Reprinted with the permission of Routledge.

Norman Malcolm, "Wittgenstein's Philosophical Investigations." From *The Philosophy of Mind*, ed. V.C. Chappell (Englewood Cliffs, NJ: Prentice Hall, 1962), pp. 74–81. First published in *Philosophical Review, LXIII* (1954), pp. 530–559.

Chapter 9

David M. Armstrong, "The Nature of Mind." From *Introduction to Philosophy: Classical and Contemporary Readings*, ed. John Perry and Michael Bratman (New York: Oxford University Press, 1986), pp. 344–351. First published in *The Mind-Brain Identity Theory*, ed. C.V. Borst (London: MacMillan & Co., 1970).

J.J.C. Smart, "Sensations and Brain Processes." From *Philosophical Review, LXVIII* (1959), pp. 141–156.

Saul Kripke, "Identity and Necessity." From *Identity and Individuation*, ed. Milton K. Munitz (New York: New York University Press, 1971), pp. 143–146, 158–164. Reprinted by permission of Saul Kripke and New York University Press.

Chapter 10

Alan Turing, "Computing Machinery and Intelligence." From *Introduction to Philosophy: Classical and Contemporary Readings*, ed. John Perry and Michael Bratman (New York: Oxford University Press, 1986), pp. 375–390. First published in *Mind, LIX* (1950). © Oxford University Press.

John R. Searle, "Minds, Brains and Programs." From *Introduction to Philosophy: Classical and Contemporary Readings*, ed. John Perry and Michael Bratman (New York: Oxford University Press, 1986), pp. 391–403. First published in *Behavioral and Brain Sciences, III*, 3, September 1980, pp. 417–424. Reprinted with the permission of the author and Cambridge University Press.

Chapter 11

Hilary Putnam, "The Nature of Mental States." From *Mind, Language and Reality: Philosophical Papers Volume 2* (Cambridge: Cambridge University Press, 1975), pp. 429–440. Originally published as "Psychological Predicates" by Hilary Putnam in *Art, Mind and Religion*, W.H. Capitan and D.D. Merrill, editors. © 1967 University of Pittsburgh Press. Reprinted by permission of the publisher.

Jerry A. Fodor, "Something on the State of the Art." From *Introduction to Philosophy: Classical and Contemporary Readings*, ed. John Perry and Michael Bratman (New York: Oxford University Press, 1986), pp. 361–365. Reprinted by permission of the author and Oxford University Press, Inc.

Jerry A. Fodor and Ned Block, "What Psychological States Are Not." From *Representations: Philosophical Reflections on the Foundations of Cognitive Science* (Bradford: M.I.T. Press, 1981), pp. 94–96. Originally published in *Philosophical Review, LXXXI*, 2, 1972.

Chapter 12

Excerpts from Richard Rorty, *Philosophy and the Mirror of Nature* (Princeton, NJ: Princeton University Press, 1979), pp. 70–77. Reprinted with the permission of Princeton University Press.

Selections from Patricia Smith Churchland, *Neurophilosophy: Toward a Unified Science of the Mind-Brain* (Cambridge, MA: M.I.T Press, 1986), pp. 299–305, 376–386. Reprinted with the permission of M.I.T. Press.

Chapter 13

Thomas Nagel, "What Is It Like to Be a Bat?" From *Philosophical Review, LXXXIII*, 4, 1974, pp. 435–450.

Frank Jackson, "Epiphenomenal Qualia." From *Philosophical Quarterly, 32*, 1982, pp. 127–136. Reprinted with the permission of the author and of Basil Blackwell, Inc.

Daniel C. Dennett, "Quining Qualia."

From *Mind and Cognition: A Reader*, ed. William G. Lycan (Oxford: Basil Blackwell, 1990), pp. 519–547. First published in *Consciousness in Contemporary Science*, ed. A. Marcel and E. Bisiach (Oxford: Oxford University Press). Reprinted with the permission of Oxford University Press.

Owen Flanagan, "The Missing Shade of You." From *Consciousness Reconsidered* (Cambridge, MA: M.I.T. Press, 1992), pp. 87–107. Reprinted with the permission of M.I.T. Press.

Chapter 14

Jerry A. Fodor, "Methodological Solipsism Considered as a Research Strategy in Cognitive Psychology." From *Representations: Philosophical Reflections on the Foundations of Cognitive Science* (Bradford: M.I.T. Press, 1981), pp. 225–234. First published in *Behavioral and Brain Sciences, III*, 1, March 1980, pp. 63–72. Reprinted with the permission of the author and Cambridge University Press.

Hilary Putnam, "Brains in a Vat." From *Reason, Truth and History* (Cambridge: Cambridge University Press, 1981), p. 1–21. Reprinted with the permission of the author and Cambridge University Press.

The Author of this book and the Publisher have made every attempt to locate the authors of the copyrighted material or their heirs or assigns, and would be grateful for information that would allow them to correct any errors or omissions in a subsequent edition of the work.

Index